Conceptual Structures: Information Processing in Mind and Machine

JOHN F. SOWA
IBM Systems Research Institute

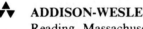

ADDISON-WESLEY PUBLISHING COMPANY
Reading, Massachusetts • Menlo Park, California
London • Amsterdam • Don Mills, Ontario • Sydney

To the memory of my father,
my first and most exacting teacher
of science and language

The text of this book was composed at the
IBM T. J. Watson Research Center, Yorktown Heights, NY.
The typesetting algorithm was developed by Linda D. Misek-Falkoff.

Library of Congress Cataloging in Publication Data

Sowa, John F.
Conceptual structures.

(System programming series)
Bibliography: p.

Includes index.
1. Artificial intelligence. 2. Cognition.
3. Human information processing. I. Title. II. Series.
Q335.S68 1983 001.53'5 82-20720
ISBN 0-201-14472-7

Reproduced by Addison-Wesley from camera-ready copy supplied by the author.

ISBN 0-201-14472-7
BCDEFGHIJ-HA-89876543

THE SYSTEMS PROGRAMMING SERIES

The Program Development Process Part I — The Individual Programmer — Joel D. Aron

The Program Development Process Part II — The Programming Team — Joel D. Aron

Mathematical Foundations of Programming — Frank Beckman

An Introduction to Operating Systems — Harvey M. Deitel

Structured Programming: Theory and Practice — Richard C. Linger, Harlan D. Mills, Bernard I. Witt

Coded Character Sets: History and Development — Charles E. Mackenzie

The Structure and Design of Programming Languages — John E. Nicholls

The Environment for Systems Programs — Frederic G. Withington

Communications Architecture for Distributed Systems — R.J. Cypser

An Introduction to Database Systems, Third Edition — C. J. Date

An Intoduction to Database Systems: Vol. II — C. J. Date

Database Security and Integrity — Eduardo B. Fernandez, R. C. Summers, C. Wood

Fundamentals of Interactive Computer Graphics — James Foley, Andries Van Dam

Compiler Design Theory — Philip M. Lewis II, Daniel J. Rosenkrantz, Richard E. Stearns

Sorting and Sort Systems — Harold Lorin

Operating Systems — Harold Lorin, Harvey M. Deitel

Recursive Programming Techniques — William Burge

Modeling and Analysis: An Introduction to System Performance Evaluation Methodology — Hisashi Kobayashi

Conceptual Structures: Information Processing in Mind and Machine — John F. Sowa

Foreword

The field of systems programming primarily grew out of the efforts of many programmers and managers whose creative energy went into producing practical, utilitarian systems programs needed by the rapidly growing computer industry. Programming was practiced as an art where each programmer invented unique solutions to problems with little guidance beyond that provided by immediate associates. In 1968, the late Ascher Opler, then at IBM, recognized that it was necessary to bring programming knowledge together in a form that would be accessible to all systems programmers. Surveying the state of the art, he decided that enough useful material existed to justify a significant codification effort. On his recommendation, IBM decided to sponsor The Systems Programming Series as a long-term project to collect, organize, and publish those principles and techniques that would have lasting value throughout the industry.

The Series consists of an open-ended collection of text-reference books. The contents of each book represent the individual author's view of the subject area and do not necessarily reflect the views of the IBM Corporation. Each is organized for course use but is detailed enough for reference. Further, the Series is organized in three levels: broad introductory material in the foundation volumes, more specialized material in the software volumes, and very specialized theory in the computer science volumes. As such, the Series meets the needs of the novice, the experienced programmer, and the computer scientist.

Taken together, the Series is a record of the state of the art in systems programming that can form the technological base for the systems programming discipline.

The Editorial Board

Preface

Knowledge-based systems emphasize meaning. Instead of processing data as a string of bits, they represent the meaning of data in terms of the real world. They carry on conversations with people in ordinary language, they find important facts before they are requested, and they solve complex problems at expert levels of performance. This book introduces the theory and practice of knowledge-based systems.

Two fields devoted to knowledge-based systems are cognitive science and artificial intelligence. Cognitive science is a merger of philosophy, linguistics, and psychology with a strong influence from computer science. Artificial intelligence (AI) is the engineering counterpart; it pays more attention to programming tools and techniques than to philosophical issues. This book combines the AI and cognitive science approaches: Chapter 1 surveys the philosophical issues, Chapter 2 is an overview of cognitive psychology, Chapters 3 and 4 develop the theory of conceptual graphs from an AI point of view, Chapter 5 applies the theory to linguistics, and Chapter 6 applies it to knowledge engineering. In combining insights from each of the separate fields, the book gives a unified view of knowledge representation.

Aristotle and Leibniz are the heroes of the first six chapters of this book. Aristotle was the founder of cognitive science: all the work on representing knowledge for the past 2300 years can be viewed as an application, refinement, extension, or re-invention of something that Aristotle either developed in detail or mentioned in passing. Leibniz was the first proponent of artificial intelligence. With his Characteristica Universalis, he attempted to quantify all knowledge and reasoning. In the future, he predicted, if a dispute arose between two philosophers, they would reach for pencil and paper and say *calculemus* (let us calculate). Even his invention of the first calculator with multiplication and division was motivated by his dream of automating his philosophy. Modern knowledge-based systems are the culmination of that dream.

Although current AI systems have some claim to being intelligent, the human mind has mysteries that do not fit the neat Aristotelian categories. As Alfred North

Whitehead (1954) observed, all the great truths of Aristotle are only half truths. To show the limitations, Chapter 7 surveys the areas where current approaches are inadequate. Within the next two decades, techniques based on the first six chapters may lead to highly intelligent, useful systems. But intuition and creative insight are processes that are not understood, even in human beings. During the next century, such processes might be simulated on digital computers. As yet, we don't know how.

Since cognitive science is an interdisciplinary field, this book is designed to be read at different levels by readers with different backgrounds. Each chapter presents introductory material in its first section, and each section presents introductory material in its first page or two. A reader who wants a quick overview without mathematical detail can start with the first section of each chapter and read only the first page of the other sections. When the material in any section becomes more advanced, the reader may skip to the beginning of the next section without losing continuity. An introduction to knowledge-based systems could be based on Sections 1.1 through 1.7, 2.1, 3.1 through 3.3, 4.1, 4.2, 5.1 through 5.3, and 6.1 through 6.7. Instructors who want to survey applications before discussing theoretical topics could assign Sections 6.1 and 6.2 immediately after Section 1.1. For emphasis on cognitive science, the instructor could assign further reading from Chapters 2, 5, and 7; and for emphasis on AI, further reading from Chapters 3, 4, and 5.

Most AI textbooks emphasize algorithms and programming techniques. This book emphasizes knowledge representation. Both aspects are important, and either one could be taught first. For a mixed class that includes students in philosophy, psychology, and linguistics, this book could be used as the primary introduction to AI. For systems analysts and database designers, conceptual graphs could be taught as a notation for analyzing system specifications. For AI specialists, this book could be taught after a course on AI programming techniques. Those students could pursue Chapters 3 through 6 in more depth and implement sample programs in a language like LISP or PROLOG.

At the end of each chapter are exercises and suggested readings. The exercises for Chapter 1 would make good topics for classroom discussion at the beginning of a course. After the formalism is introduced in Chapter 3, the exercises become more detailed. Some of them are routine applications of the notation, and others are theoretical points that require mathematical training. The exercises at the end of Chapter 7 are suggested topics for a term paper or research article; they address global issues that range over topics from the entire book. References in the text cite supporting material in journals and reports, some of which may be difficult to find; suggested readings at the ends of the chapters cite books that should be available in a library for AI or cognitive science. To make this book self-contained, Appendix A surveys the mathematical background that is assumed in the more advanced sections. Appendix B presents a sample lexicon and a list of the concept and relation types that are used in exercises and examples.

This book evolved over many years while dozens of students, colleagues, and friends looked at, studied, and commented upon early versions of the manuscript.

Discovering the passages that kept them awake and put them to sleep was the most valuable writing guide I have ever had. Besides the readers who made short comments, I must thank many for more extended contributions: Charlie Bontempo for six years of discussions about philosophy, semantics, and databases; Ted Codd for discussions of database semantics and fruitful collaboration on knowledge-based systems; Norman Foo for detailed discussions of logic, conceptual graphs, and their relationships to model theory; Jon Handel for writing an English parsing program and doing a preliminary implementation of conceptual graphs; Chuck Haspel for detailed suggestions for revising the content and presentation of several sections; George Heidorn for eight years of comments, criticism, and collaboration that have had a major impact on this book and the papers that preceded it; Tony Hwang for his studies on implementing conceptual graphs and his work with the dictionary programs; Karen Jensen for advice on linguistic issues, collaboration on conceptual analysis, and detailed comments on Chapter 5; Laurie Kuslansky for suggestions that improved the presentation of Chapter 2; Larry Margolis for revising and extending the ILIS parsing system and participating in discussions on conceptual graphs; Lance Miller for discussions of cognitive science and support in maintaining good interactions with the EPISTLE group; Allen Morton for supporting the Knowledge-Based Systems Project and helping me to get assistance for related implementation work; Eva Maria Mückstein for discussions of linguistic issues at many seminars and workshops; S. Jack Odell for discussions (often heated) of Wittgenstein and for important insights during a course we jointly taught on Language and Knowledge in Man and Machine; Freeman Rawson for his analysis of type hierarchies and the efficiency of algorithms for processing conceptual graphs; Sharon Salveter for comments and discussions during the six months we were jointly teaching a course on AI; Dennis Shasha for developing the use of conceptual graphs for database design; Doug Skuce for a careful reading of the entire book with numerous suggestions for clarifying the analysis and presentation; Cora Angier Sowa for introducing me to the formulaic analysis of literature and the interpretation of science as a mythology and for helping me translate the quotes from Latin and Greek. Besides these individuals, the workshops in which I participated have given me a broader and deeper perspective on the issues. Especially important were the ones that met weekly or monthly for several years: the Vassar Seminar on the Nature of Consciousness, the Study Group on Language and Perception at IBM Yorktown, and the Workshops on Semantics and Representation of Knowledge at the IBM Systems Research Institute.

After successfully using a photocomposer to typeset some reports and articles, I innocently volunteered to typeset this book. Although straight text is easy to format, I soon discovered that formulas, diagrams, examples, and special symbols make the problem much more challenging. In doing the typesetting, I owe the greatest debt to Linda Misek-Falkoff. She defined the GML macros and symbols to make an experimental version of SCRIPT match the Addison-Wesley specifications. Taking the defaults that come with GML would have been easy, but thanks to Linda's heroic efforts and the flexibility of SCRIPT, we were able to match the formats for the Systems Programming Series. I also want to thank Geoff Bartlett for his help with the fine points of SCRIPT and for contributing a macro to overlay accents on Greek characters. As this book evolved, I used many versions of the editors, terminals, printers, formatters, and spelling checkers supported by VM/370. I must thank all the people who produced those systems and my managers at IBM for providing the facilities to use them. Finally, I thank the people at Addison-Wesley for advising, organizing, and editing—and most especially for their patience.

J. F. S.

New York City
July 1983

Contents

ABOUT THE AUTHOR

John F. Sowa is a senior staff member at the IBM Systems Research Institute. After graduating from MIT in 1962, he joined an applied mathematics group at IBM. Four years later, he went to graduate school at Harvard under the IBM Resident Graduate Study Program.

At IBM, his early work was in programming languages and machine architecture. Since 1972, he has concentrated on artificial intelligence and natural languages: teaching, writing, implementing a parsing system, and directing a project on knowledge-based systems. His current research is on the design of a knowledge acquisition facility for expert systems. This book is the product of his professional experience with a long-term fascination with language and philosophy.

1
Philosophical Basis

Any representation of knowledge and meaning inside a computer must embody some philosophical assumptions. Yet philosophers have been debating such issues for centuries without reaching final agreement. To avoid the controversy, many people working with computers try to ignore it. But to write a program without analyzing the issues is to make a blind choice instead of a reasoned commitment. This chapter poses the philosophical questions, surveys various approaches to them, and sets the stage for the developments in later chapters.

1.1 KNOWLEDGE AND MODELS

"All men by nature desire to know." With these words, Aristotle began his *Metaphysics*. But what is knowledge? What do people have inside their heads when they know something? Is knowledge expressed in words? If so, how could one know things that are easier to do than to say, like tying a shoestring or hitting a baseball? If knowledge is not expressed in words, how can it be transmitted in language? How is knowledge related to the world? And what are the relationships between the external world, knowledge in the head, and the language used to express knowledge about the world?

Those are traditional questions that have been analyzed by philosophers, psychologists, and linguists. With the advent of computers, an entirely new series of questions arises: Can knowledge be programmed in a digital computer? Can computers encode and decode that knowledge in ordinary language? Can they use it to interact with people and with other computer systems in a more flexible or helpful way? These are the questions addressed by the field of artificial intelligence (AI). In one sense, they are new, but in another sense, they raise the same issues about knowledge and its relationship to language and to the world that have been addressed by philosophers for the past two and a half millennia.

Knowledge is more than a static encoding of facts; it also includes the ability to use those facts in interacting with the world. A basic premise of AI is that knowledge of something is the ability to form a mental model that accurately represents the thing as well as the actions that can be performed by it and on it. Then by testing actions on the model, a person (or robot) can predict what is likely to happen in the real world.

To test possible actions, AI systems construct *microworlds* that simulate electrical circuits, robot manipulators, or fairy tales with talking bees and bears. Heidorn (1972), for example, developed his Natural Language Processor for Queuing problems (NLPQ), which could carry on a dialog in English, build a model of a miniature world (Fig. 1.1), and translate that model into a computer program. In the first stage of using NLPQ, the user describes a queuing problem to the system:

```
Vehicles arrive at a station.
The station has just one pump.
A vehicle will leave the station immediately after
arriving if the length of the line at the pump is not
less than two.
```

As the user types this input, NLPQ analyzes it and builds an abstract model consisting of blocks of storage that represent *concepts* linked by pointers that represent *conceptual relations*. If the model is incomplete, the system can prompt the user for additional information (computer output in upper case):

```
WHERE DO THE TRUCKS UNLOAD CARGO?
at a dock.
HOW LONG DO THE TRUCKS UNLOAD CARGO AT THE DOCK?
10 minutes.
```

If the system detects an inconsistency, it issues a warning:

```
THE FOLLOWING PERCENTAGES DO NOT TOTAL 100:  AFTER
UNLOADING CARGO AT THE DOCK FOR 10 MINUTES, 50 PERCENT
OF THE TRUCKS LEAVE THE STATION, AND 33 PERCENT WAIT
IN THE DEPOT UNTIL THE PIER IS AVAILABLE.
```

After NLPQ builds the internal model, the user can change the model or ask questions about it:

```
Where do trucks unload cargo?
TRUCKS UNLOAD CARGO AT THE DOCK IN THE STATION FOR 10 MINUTES.
It should take from 6 to 12 minutes to unload at a dock.
```

When the complete model has been constructed, the system translates it into a program for the General Purpose Simulation System (GPSS). For this example, NLPQ translates each action in the model into a section of GPSS code:

Fig. 1.1 Microworld for queuing problems

```
*       THE VEHICLES ARE SERVICED AT THE PUMP.
ACT3    QUEUE       PUMP2
        SEIZE       PUMP2
        DEPART      PUMP2
        ADVANCE     FN3,FN1
        RELEASE     PUMP2
        TRANSFER    ,FN5
```

Note that NLPQ generates instructions in GPSS interspersed with comments in English. This system illustrates several common themes in AI: an English dialog using terminology appropriate to the problem, a mixed initiative where either the user or the system can state a fact or ask a question at any time, an internal network of concepts and relations, and final output in a conventional programming form. The example also raises some important issues that this book addresses: How does such a system interpret and generate English? What information must it have before a dialog begins? How does it add new information to its internal model? How can it tell when the model is incomplete or inconsistent? And what are the system's strengths and limitations?

Models of reality are just as important for database systems as they are for artificial intelligence. According to Abrial (1974), a database is a "*model* of an evolving physical world. The state of this model, at a given instant, represents the *knowledge* it has acquired from this world." Yet models are abstractions from reality. The systems analyst or database administrator must play the role of philosopher-king in determining what knowledge to represent, how to organize and express it, and what constraints to impose to keep it a consistent, faithful model of the outside world. To do a good job in analyzing reality, a systems analyst must be sensitive to semantic issues and have a working knowledge of conceptual structures.

The hypothesis that people understand the world by building mental models raises fundamental issues for all the fields of cognitive science:

- *Psychology.* How are models represented in the brain, how do they interact with the mechanisms of perception, memory, and learning, and how do they affect or control behavior?

- *Linguistics.* What is the relationship between a word, the object it names, and a mental model? What are the rules of syntax and semantics that relate models to sentences?

- *Philosophy.* What is the relationship between knowledge, meaning, and mental models? How are the models used in reasoning, and how is such reasoning related to formal logic?

- *Computer science.* How can a person's model of the world be reflected in a computer system? What languages and tools are needed to describe such models and relate them to outside systems? Can the models support a computer interface that people would find easy to use?

Since the subject is growing rapidly, no final answers are possible. This book develops the theory of conceptual graphs as a method of representing mental models, shows how it explains results in several different fields, and applies it to the design of more intelligent, more usable computer systems.

1.2 PSYCHOLOGICAL ISSUES

The oldest theory of psychology is *associationism*: a *sensation* is associated with an *idea*, and that idea leads to another idea, which leads to still other ideas. The theory started with Aristotle and was pursued in detail by British philosophers such as Hobbes and Locke. The following example by James Mill (1829) illustrates the principle:

> I see a horse: that is a sensation. Immediately, I think of his master: that is an idea. The idea of his master makes me think of his office; he is a minister of state: that is another idea. The idea of a minister of state makes me think of public affairs; and I am led into a train of political ideas; when I am summoned to dinner. This is a new sensation, followed by the idea of dinner, and of the company with whom I am to partake it. The sight of the company and of the food are other sensations; these suggest ideas without end; other sensations perpetually intervene, suggesting other ideas: and so the process goes on.

Mill's example illustrates a common form of thinking. But such a vague description cannot support a precise, testable theory. Without more detailed measurements, associationism could say little more than the obvious point that people do have associations between ideas.

To make their theories more precise, the *behaviorists* emphasized rigorous experiment. They eliminated all talk about ideas, mental states, and thinking. Instead, they maintained that a theory should relate external *stimulus* to observable *response* without any assumptions about mental states and processes. As experimental techniques, they developed *conditioning* and *reinforcement* for building and strengthening stimulus-response chains. To train a pigeon to play ping-pong, for example, they would reward any random peck at a ping-pong ball with a grain of corn. Once the pigeon began to peck at the ball consistently, the experimenters would only reward those pecks that knocked the ball in the right direction. With appropriate reinforcements, they could eventually get two pigeons to play a complete game.

Conditioning and reinforcement work just as well with people as with rats and pigeons. Marvin Minsky, one of the founders of AI who was highly critical of behaviorism, tells how his students conspired to condition him. As he strolled in front of the class, they gave positive reinforcement to moves to the right: they would appear alert, attentively taking notes. When he moved left, they gave negative reinforcement: they would cough, shuffle their feet, and look out the window. By the end of the hour, Minsky was lecturing from the far right-hand corner of the room. When the students finally confessed their experiment, he immediately walked to the center of the room.

Conditioning is a powerful means of establishing unconscious habits. Yet it cannot explain the students' novel behavior in analyzing the situation, predicting Minsky's responses, and planning a strategy for conditioning him. Language is also beyond the scope of behaviorism—one sentence reversed the effect of an hour of conditioning. Besides explaining habitual behavior, a theory must explain how language can exert a powerful effect with a single sentence or even just one word. But behaviorism narrowed the scope of psychology to such an extent that the most interesting questions could not even be asked. Hull (1951), for example, gave formulas for computing responses to five decimal places but ignored language, thought, planning, logic, and problem solving.

Today, behaviorism has been supplanted by *cognitive psychology*. Although their experiments are just as rigorous, cognitive psychologists willingly talk about mind, intelligence, thought, and knowledge. Tolman (1932), one of the pioneers of the cognitive approach, conducted a series of experiments with the behaviorists' favorite animal, the Norwegian white rat. According to a behaviorist, when a rat learns to run a maze, the passageways are stimuli that trigger running motions in the learned directions. Yet when the maze is flooded, the rat will swim the maze correctly even though it has never associated swimming motions with the stimuli. Tolman maintained that a rat does not respond blindly to the immediate stimulus. Instead, it has a *cognitive map* that relates the local surroundings to the eventual goal. When the rat is still learning the maze, it is more likely to make wrong turns heading in the approximate direction of the reward than ones heading away—even its mistakes show that it knows where the goal is.

As an illustration of the competing theories, suppose that a person named Connie happens to be hungry when she sees a street vendor selling ice cream. She may then walk up to the vendor, take out some money, buy some ice cream, and eat it. Somehow, the possibility of eating ice cream in the future "causes" her to carry out a sequence of actions in the present. Yet the laws of physics say that future events cannot affect the present. How can a merely possible event have a causal effect?

A behaviorist would say that the stimulus of seeing the vendor, enhanced by Connie's hunger, triggers a conditioned response that leads to eating ice cream. For habitual reactions, the behaviorist may be right. But people can override habits and deal with novel situations for which they have no ready-made responses. If Connie intended to have dinner at a fine restaurant, she would be less likely to buy the ice cream. The more remote event has a greater effect than the present stimulus. Conversely, if she did not expect to eat for several hours, she might still buy some ice cream. Intentions and expectations have at least as great an influence on behavior as immediate stimuli.

A cognitive psychologist would say that when Connie sees the vendor, she forms a model of the situation. But she also forms models of future states where she may be eating ice cream, dining at a restaurant, or going hungry. Which course of action she chooses depends on her options for transforming a model of the current state into each of the possible models. Her actions, therefore, are not caused by future events, but by operations on models that exist in her brain at the present. As Craik (1943) suggested, reasoning is a system of *artificial causation* that transforms models in the head.

To explain the reasoning process, Otto Selz (1913, 1922) developed his theory of *schematic anticipation*: the solution to a problem is not found by undirected association, but by finding the concepts to fill in the gaps of a partially completed *schema*. In psychological terms, Selz described mechanisms that were later developed for AI: backtracking, pattern-directed invocation, and networks of concepts and relations. His work was not appreciated during his lifetime, partly because of its novelty and partly because it ran counter to the dominant trend of behaviorism. Yet Selz had an indirect influence on AI through de Groot's analyses of chess playing (1965) and Newell and Simon's work on problem solving (1972).

One of Newell and Simon's students, Ross Quillian (1966), implemented networks similar to Selz's in a computer program. Given two types of concepts, such as CRY and COMFORT, Quillian's program would search a network of concepts to find the shortest path of associations linking them. For this example, paths starting at CRY and COMFORT intersected at SAD. The program then converted the two paths into the sentences, "Cry is among other things to make a sad sound. To comfort can be to make something less sad." Although Quillian's program found associations that are similar to human associations, he needed further evidence that the results were more than a lucky coincidence. To gather evidence for the networks of concepts, Collins and Quillian (1969, 1972) measured human reaction times for various kinds of associations. The responses that were fastest for the computer were also fastest for human memory.

Since behaviorism is now on the wane, mental phenomena have again become the object of scientific study. But one phenomenon, *imagery*, has remained controversial. Pylyshyn (1973), for example, ridiculed the notion of a mind's eye that observes images in the brain: presumably the mind's eye would transmit stimulation to a mind's brain, which would have its own mental images observed by another mind's eye and so on in an infinite regress. Despite such ridicule, psychologists developed experiments that show the importance of both image-based reasoning and conceptual reasoning (Kosslyn 1980):

- Mental images are projected on a *visual buffer*. They can be scanned, rotated, enlarged, or reduced.
- Novel images can be constructed from a verbal suggestion: *Imagine George Washington slapping Mr. Peanut on the back.*
- Reasoning about sizes, shapes, and actions is faster and more accurate in terms of images.
- Abstract thought and logical deduction are faster and more accurate in terms of concepts.
- A complete theory of human thinking must show how images are interpreted in concepts and how concepts can give rise to images.

1.3 LINGUISTIC ISSUES

Language is a means of communication. But far more than other means, such as gestures, a knowing glance, or a baby's screaming and crying, language is organized in a system with complex levels of rules. Each level handles one aspect of the communication process. *Semantics* is the study of meaning itself. *Pragmatics* studies how the basic meaning is related to the current context and the listener's expectations. *Syntax* studies the grammar rules for expressing meaning in a string of words.

Of all three levels, syntax is the best understood. *Traditional grammar* consists of the informal rules that are taught in schools. *Transformational grammar* is a more detailed, formal theory whose most notable proponent is Noam Chomsky. Although transformational grammar has evolved as an elaborate theory of syntax, it largely neglects semantics and pragmatics. Because of that neglect, it has been criticized as an unlikely model of how people use language. To answer the criticism, Chomsky (1965) distinguished *competence* from *performance*: competence is an idealized knowledge of language; performance is the actual use of language in speaking and understanding. Chomsky maintained that transformational grammar is an abstract theory of competence and should not be judged as a theory of performance.

For AI, programmers needed a theory of performance that could support communication between people and machines. In AI systems, *conceptual graphs* are widely used for representing meaning. Figure 1.2 is an example of a conceptual graph: the boxes are called *concepts*, and the circles are called *conceptual relations*. Concepts represent any entity, action, or state that can be described in language, and conceptual relations show the *roles* that each entity plays. In this example, the concept [MAN] represents a person who is playing the role of agent (AGNT) of the act [BITE], and the concept [DOG] represents an entity that is playing the role of object (OBJ) of [BITE].

Conceptual graphs emphasize semantics. The earliest forms, called *existential graphs*, were invented by the philosopher Charles Sanders Peirce (1897) as a graphical notation for symbolic logic. Peirce was impressed by the diagrams of molecules in organic chemistry and believed that graphs could simplify the rules of logic. In linguistics, Lucien Tesnière (1959) used similar graphs for his *dependency grammar*. The earliest forms implemented on a computer were the *correlational nets* by Silvio Ceccato (1961), who used them as an intermediate language for machine translation.

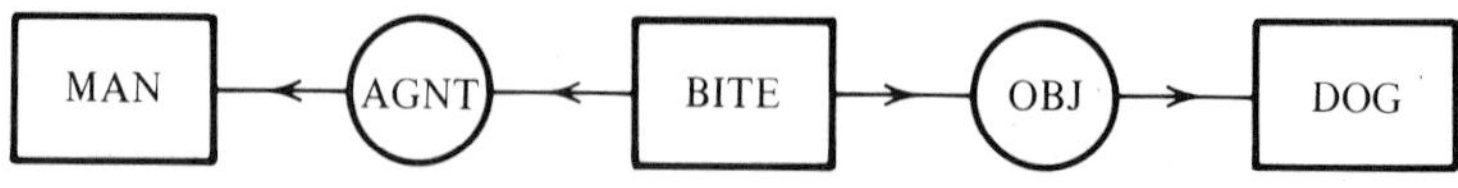

Fig. 1.2 Conceptual graph for the phrase "man biting dog"

Under various names, such as *semantic nets*, *conceptual dependency graphs*, *partitioned nets*, and *structured inheritance nets*, the graphs have been implemented in many AI systems.

Linguists were not quick to adopt conceptual graphs because most of them were already committed to transformational grammar. Yet disputes arose among linguists as Chomsky's students began to diverge from the master's path. Points of disagreement arose over several issues:

- Roles of syntax and semantics in generating sentences,
- Nature of the underlying *base structures*,
- Logic, quantifiers, and methods of binding pronouns to their antecedents,
- Constraints that limit transformations to just those patterns that actually occur in natural languages.

Contrary to Chomsky's generative syntax, Sgall (1964) proposed *generative semantics*: semantic rules generate the *base structure*, syntactic rules map the base into the *surface structure* of a sentence, and phonological rules map the surface structure into actual speech (Fig. 1.3). Generative semantics developed as a rival form of transformational grammar that was also called *semantic syntax* (Seuren 1974).

Generative semantics packaged all the meaning of a sentence in a single base structure. Figure 1.3 implies that each stage in generating a sentence unfolds a layer of meaning already present in the base. Jackendoff (1972), however, maintained that different aspects of meaning are contained in separate semantic structures. As a sentence is generated, transformations combine the separate aspects into a single utterance. Similar issues arise with conceptual graphs. Woods (1975) had a debate with Quillian over the representation of meaning in graphs. Like the generative semanticists, Woods believed that the graph should contain all the information present in the sentence. Like Jackendoff, Quillian maintained that the basic meaning is separate from the "stage directions" that determine how the meaning is expressed.

Keeping stage directions out of the base seems correct. The semantic base depends on what the speaker knows about the topic. The way the speaker presents the topic depends on pragmatics—context, external circumstances, and the listener's

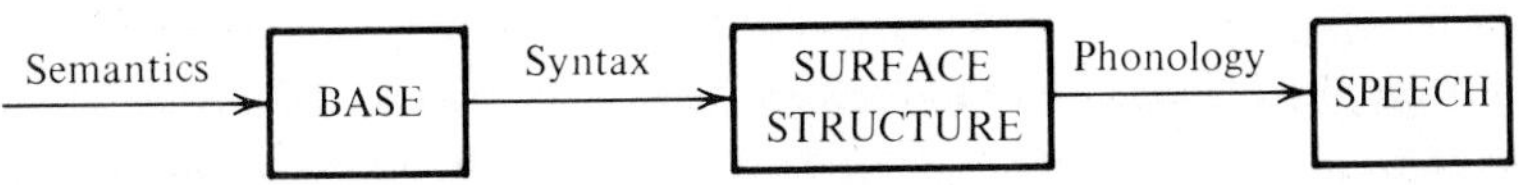

Fig. 1.3 Basic version of generative semantics

expectations. There is no reason to believe that all these aspects of meaning originate in a single base structure. Instead, a sentence is derived from six different kinds of information:

- *Conceptual graphs* are the logical forms that state relationships between persons, things, attributes, and events.
- *Tense* and *modality* describe how conceptual graphs relate to the real world. They state whether something has happened, can happen, will happen, or should happen.
- *Presupposition* is the background information that the speaker and listener tacitly assume.
- *Focus* is the new point that the speaker is trying to make.
- *Coreference links* show which concepts refer to the same entities. In a sentence, these links are expressed as pronouns and other *anaphoric references.*
- *Emotional connotations* are determined by associations in the minds of the speaker and listener.

As an example, consider the sentence *The man bit a dog*. The conceptual graph in Fig. 1.2 represents the basic meaning of this sentence. The past tense and indicative mood imply that the event actually occurred at some time in the past. The presupposition is that the phrase *the man* is an anaphoric reference to a specific individual in the context—either he was just mentioned, or he is present at the scene. The focus is the new information about biting a dog. Since *the man* refers to someone previously mentioned, a coreference link connects the concept [MAN] in Fig. 1.2 to a previous occurrence of [MAN]. These first five structures constitute the literal or conceptual meaning of a sentence. The sixth, emotional connotation, is not expressed directly by words in a sentence nor by concepts in a graph. Instead, it is determined by associations to prior experience that may differ widely for different people. The sentence *My cat gave birth to kittens* would evoke different emotional responses from an apprehensive landlord and a child who wants a pet.

1.4 INTENSIONS AND EXTENSIONS

People remember particular facts and general principles. Tulving (1972) classified the memories in two categories: *episodic* and *semantic*. Episodic memory stores detailed facts about individual things and events. It includes such facts as *Morris is an orange tomcat* and *Charlie lost his wallet on the train*. Semantic memory stores universal principles. It includes such general information as *All cats are animals* and *Wallets are designed for carrying money*. Semantic memory corresponds to dictionary definitions, and episodic memory corresponds to history and biography.

The two categories of memory reflect two aspects of word meaning. The *intension* of a word is that part of meaning that follows from general principles in seman-

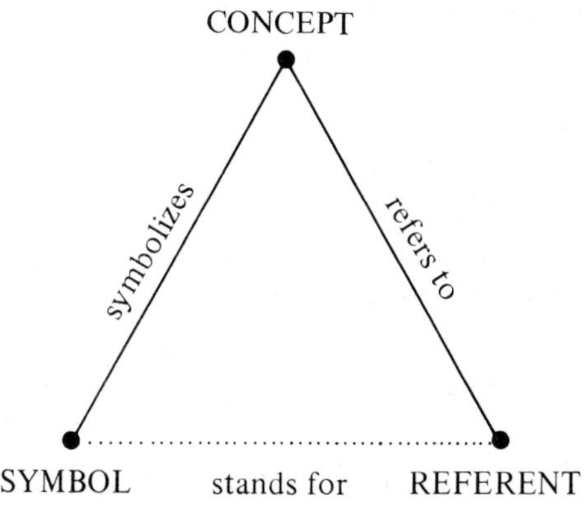

Fig. 1.4 The meaning triangle

tic memory. The *extension* of a word is the set of all existing things to which the word applies. The intension of *mammal*, for example, is a definition, such as "warm-blooded animal, vertebrate, having hair and secreting milk for nourishing its young"; the extension is the set of all mammals in the world. Extensions are usually unwieldy sets that cannot be observed in their entirety and cannot serve as practical definitions. But a zoologist can identify a new type of mammal from the intensional definition, even though the species may not be listed in any catalog of mammals.

Perception maps extensional objects to intensional concepts, and speech maps concepts to words. But the relationship between word and object is an indirect mapping, derived from the two direct mappings of perception and speech. Aristotle first made that observation:

> Spoken words are symbols of experiences (παθήματα) in the *psyche;* written words are symbols of the spoken. As writing, so is speech not the same for all peoples. But the experiences themselves, of which these words are primarily signs, are the same for everyone, and so are the objects of which those experiences are likenesses. (*On Interpretation* 16a4)

Aristotle's distinction has been recognized and restated many times throughout the history of philosophy. Ogden and Richards (1923) codified it as the *meaning triangle* (Fig. 1.4). The left corner is the *symbol* or *word*; the peak is the *concept*, *intension*, *thought*, *idea*, or *sense*; and the right corner is the *referent*, *object*, or *extension*. For some concepts, one corner of the triangle may be absent: a person may have a concept of an object for which he knows no word, or he may have a word for a concept that has no extension. The word *unicorn* is mapped to the concept [UNICORN] in the same way that *horse* is mapped to [HORSE], even though there are millions of horses in the world, but no unicorns.

Reasoning about intensions depends on logic, not observation. Aristotle used the term *logos* (λόγος) for intensional meaning, and he developed the *syllogism* (συλλογισμός) as a means of analyzing *logos*. Syllogism, he said, "is not concerned with external *logos*, but with *logos* in the *psyche*" (*Posterior Analytics* 76b24). Following is one of Aristotle's examples of a syllogism (*Posterior Analytics* 98b5):

```
If all broad-leafed plants are deciduous,
and all vines are broad-leafed plants,
then all vines are deciduous.
```

Syllogisms show how the intension of a general concept is inherited by its subtypes. In this example, VINE inherits the property DECIDUOUS from the more general type BROAD-LEAFED-PLANT.

Two words or phrases that have the same intension must always have the same extension. Since *grandfather* and *father of parent* have the same intension, they must apply to exactly the same people. Intensions are true by definition: no observation could make *grandfather* have a different intension from *father of parent.* Two expressions with the same extension, however, may have very different intensions. The phrases *featherless biped* and *animal with speech* have the same extension, the set of human beings; but they have different intensions. Extensions are matters of fact that can be falsified by changing events: Diogenes demonstrated a featherless biped that couldn't speak simply by plucking a chicken.

To state relationships between intensions, Carnap (1956) introduced *meaning postulates*, which are general principles stored in semantic memory. Following are some meaning postulates:

If x is crimson, then x is red.
If x buys y, then x pays money in order to own y.
If x kills y, then x causes y to become not alive.

Meaning postulates imply a set of *analytic statements* whose truth follows from intensions. A *synthetic statement*, by contrast, is verified by observing extensions. The statement *All dogs are animals* is analytic because the intension of *dog* implies *animal.* No observation can falsify an analytic statement: if some dog-like thing turned out not to be an animal, then it wouldn't be a dog. Mathematical statements are all analytic: the statement $2+2=4$ is true by the axioms and definitions of arithmetic. An example of a synthetic statement is *Bette Davis starred in "Gone with the Wind."* That statement can be proven false by watching the movie.

With his preference for an extensional point of view, Quine (1960) had a behaviorist aversion to intensions. He objected to *ad hoc* collections of meaning postulates and seemingly arbitrary distinctions between analytic and synthetic statements. He gave the example *Everything green is extended*, where it is not obvious that a concept of type GREEN implies one of type EXTENDED. Although Quine could not refute Carnap, his objections show the need for careful distinctions. A statement is only analytic with respect to a specific system of meaning postulates. Since no two persons have the same conceptual systems, they are likely to have different sets of analytic statements. McNeill (1970) observed that a child might say *Lassie's not an animal—Lassie's a dog* .

Quine tried to avoid intensions by defining meaning as a *disposition to behavior.* But his notion of disposition remained vague: "some subtle neural condition, induced by language-learning, that disposes the subject to assent or dissent from a certain sentence in response to certain supporting stimulations" (1960, p. 223). Quine merely related the noun *disposition* to the verb *dispose* and surrounded it with a cloud of words that have a behaviorist flavor. As a basis for meaning, Quine's subtle neural conditions are hardly better than Aristotle's experiences of the *psyche.* The vagueness of Quine's statement shows the problem of erasing the peak of the meaning triangle. A complete theory of knowledge must include a theory of the knower.

The distinction between intensions and extensions applies to all representations. Mealy (1967) applied it to the symbols in a database. Files of data that describe things in the real world represent extensions, and constraints in data dictionaries are meaning postulates that define intensions. The statement *Every employee has a serial number* is analytic if it follows from constraints in the data dictionary. The statement *John Smith's serial number is 85301* is synthetic because it must be verified by looking at the data. A given statement may be analytic for one database, but synthetic for another. The statement *Every employee whose last name begins with S has a serial number that begins with 8* may be a coincidence that happens to be true for the current state of the data. It would then be a synthetic statement that might be falsified with the next person hired. On the other hand, the personnel department may have allocated a range of serial numbers for every letter of the alphabet. If that statement follows from those constraints, it would be analytic. Systems analysis is the task of analyzing some aspect of the world to determine meaning postulates. In AI, systems analysis is explicitly called *knowledge engineering.*

1.5 PRIMITIVES AND PROTOTYPES

The intension of a complex concept may be defined in terms of more primitive concepts. Aristotle defined the concept type MAN in terms of RATIONAL and ANIMAL. The type ANIMAL is the *genus* or general type, and RATIONAL is the *differentia* that distinguishes MAN from other types of ANIMAL. The concept types RATIONAL and ANIMAL could themselves be defined in terms of still more primitive genera with appropriate differentiae until, perhaps, everything would be defined in terms of indivisible primitives. Aristotle's primitives, which he called *categories*, include Substance, Quantity, Quality, Relation, Time, Position, State, Activity, and Passivity. These are ultimate primitives to which all other concepts are supposed to be reducible.

The AI goal of mechanically reducing concepts to primitives was first proposed by Ramon Lull in the thirteenth century. His *Ars Magna* was a system of disks inscribed with primitive concepts, which could be combined in various ways by rotating the disks. Under the influence of Lull's system, Leibniz (1679) developed his *Universal Characteristic*. He represented primitive concepts by prime numbers and compound concepts by products of primes. Then statements of the form *All A is B* are verified by checking whether the number for *A* is divisible by the number for *B*. If PLANT is represented by 17 and DECIDUOUS by 29, their product 493 would represent DECIDUOUS-PLANT. If BROAD-LEAFED-PLANT is represented by 20,213 and VINE by 1,192,567, the statement *All vines are broad-leafed plants* is judged to be true because 1,192,567 is divisible by 20,213. Leibniz envisioned a universal dictionary for mapping concepts to numbers and a calculus of reasoning that would automate the syllogism. To simplify the computations, he invented the first calculating machine that could do multiplication and division.

With the advent of electronic computers, computational linguists set out to implement Leibniz's universal dictionary. Masterman's *semantic nets* (1961) were based on 100 primitives, such as FOLK, STUFF, CHANGE, GO, TALK. Her program represented the sentence *This man is greedy, but pusillanimous* as,

```
(THIS: MAN:) (HE: (CAN/ DO/ (MUCH: EAT:)))
(BUT: NOT:) (HE: (CAN/ DO/ (MUCH: FIGHT:))).
```

Masterman and her colleagues created a dictionary of 15,000 words defined in terms of the 100 primitives. For *conceptual dependency graphs*, Schank (1975) reduced the number of primitive acts to 11. The phrase *x bought y*, for example, could be represented as *x obtained possession of y in exchange for money*.

Transforming high-level concepts into primitives can show that two different phrases are synonymous. But many deductions are shorter and simpler in terms of a single concept like LIAR than a graph for *one who mentally transfers information that is not true*. In general, a system should allow high-level concepts to be expanded in terms of lower ones, but such expansions should be optional, not obligatory. In recent versions, Schank and his colleagues have relied on high-level concept types, like AUTHORIZE and KISS, instead of expanding everything into primitives.

Definitions in terms of primitives ultimately derive from Aristotle's mode of definition by genus and differentiae. Yet Aristotle himself listed different categories in different writings and never gave a final, definitive set of primitives. Modern dictionaries analyze thousands of words into more primitive ones, but they are not limited to a fixed set of categories. They also allow circular definitions: word *A* is defined in terms of *B*, which is directly or indirectly defined in terms of *A*. In linguistics, Katz and Fodor (1963) introduced primitives called *semantic markers* with combining operations called *projection rules*. Like other theories based on primitives, it had some serious weaknesses:

- No linguistic or psychological evidence has uncovered a truly universal set of primitives.
- Most languages contain families of synonyms like *glad, happy, cheerful, lighthearted, joyful*, each with a slightly different shade of meaning. But semantic markers only support either-or dichotomies.
- Semantic markers, like Leibniz's prime numbers, only represent conjunctions of primitives. More complex structures are needed for representing all logical relationships.

In his early philosophy, Wittgenstein (1921) presented an extreme statement of the classical Aristotelian view: compound propositions are made up of elementary propositions, which in turn are related to atomic facts about elementary objects in the world. Yet Wittgenstein never found a single example of a truly unanalyzable atomic fact or an elementary object that had no components. A chair, for example, is a simple object to someone who wants to sit down; but for a cabinet maker, it has many parts that must be carefully fit together. For a chemist developing a new paint or glue, even the wood is a complex mixture of chemical compounds, and those compounds are made up of *atoms*, which are not really atomic after all.

In his later philosophy, Wittgenstein (1953) repudiated his earlier position. He showed that ordinary words like *game* have no common properties that characterize all their uses. Competition is present in ball games, but absent in solitaire or ring around the rosy. Organized sport follows strict rules, but not spontaneous play. And serious games of life or war lack the aspects of leisure and enjoyment. The concept GAME has no differentiae that distinguish games from all other activities. Instead, games share a sort of *family resemblance*: baseball is a game because it resembles the family of activities that people call games. Except for technical terms in mathematics, Wittgenstein maintained that most words are defined by family resemblances. He considered the meaning of a word to be its use within the language. A word is like a chess piece, which is not defined by its shape or physical composition, but by the rules for using the piece in the game of chess. Ryle (1949) codified that principle: "The logical type or category to which a concept belongs is the set of ways in which it is logically legitimate to operate with it" (p. 8).

Biological classification, another science founded by Aristotle, developed a form of definition that does not depend on primitives. Each species is defined by describing a typical member, and each genus by describing a typical species. Coope et al. (1970) cited a nineteenth century debate between Whewell and J. S. Mill over types or primitives as a basis for definition. Whewell (1858) maintained that the two methods were incompatible:

> Natural groups are given by Type, not by Definition. And this consideration accounts for that indefiniteness and indecision which we frequently find in the descriptions of such groups, and which must appear so strange and inconsistent to anyone who does not suppose these descriptions to assume any deeper ground of

> connection than an arbitrary choice of the botanist. Thus in the family of the rose tree, we are told that the *ovules* are *very rarely* erect, the *stigmata usually* simple. Of what use, it might be asked, can such loose accounts be? To which the answer is, that they are not inserted to distinguish the species, but in order to describe the family, and the total relations of the ovules and the stigmata of the family are better known by this general statement....
>
> Though in a Natural group of objects a definition can no longer be of any use as a regulative principle, classes are not therefore left quite loose, without any certain standard or guide. The class is steadily fixed, though not precisely limited; it is given, though not circumscribed; it is determined, not by a boundary line without, but by a central point within; not by what it strictly excludes, but by what it eminently includes; by an example, not by a precept; in short, instead of a Definition we have a Type for our director. (vol. 2, pp. 120-122)

Mill (1865) dropped the assumption of necessary and sufficient conditions, but he still assumed that types were defined by primitives. He leaned towards a probabilistic view that required a preponderance of defining characteristics, though not necessarily all of them:

> Whatever resembles the genus Rose more than it resembles any other genus, does so because it possesses a greater number of the characters of that genus, than of the characters of any other genus. Nor can there be the smallest difficulty in representing, by an enumeration of characters, the nature and degree of the resemblance which is strictly sufficient to include any object in the class. There are always some properties common to all things which are included. Others there often are, to which some things, which are nevertheless included, are exceptions. But the objects which are exceptions to one character are not exceptions to another: the resemblance which fails in some particulars must be made up for in others. The class, therefore, is constituted by the possession of *all* the characters which are universal, and *most* of those which admit of exceptions. (p. 277)

For most of the concepts of everyday life, meaning is determined not by definition, but by family resemblances or a characteristic ***prototype***. In a study of concepts, Smith and Medin (1981) summarized three views on definitions:

- *Classical.* A concept is defined by a genus or supertype and a set of necessary and sufficient conditions that differentiate it from other species of the same genus. This approach was first stated by Aristotle and is still used in formal treatments of mathematics and logic. It is the approach that Wittgenstein presented most vigorously in his early philosophy, but rejected in his later writings.

- *Probabilistic.* A concept is defined by a collection of features and everything that has a preponderance of those features is an instance of that concept. This is the position taken by J. S. Mill. It is also the basis for modern techniques of *cluster analysis.*

- *Prototype*. A concept is defined by an example or prototype. An object is an instance of a concept *c* if it resembles the characteristic prototype of *c* more closely than the prototypes of concepts other than *c*. This is the position taken by Whewell and is closely related to Wittgenstein's notion of family resemblances.

In *fuzzy set theory*, Zadeh (1974) tried to formalize the probabilistic point of view. His related theory of *fuzzy logic* extends uncertainty to every step of reasoning. In prototype theory, however, judgments are made in a state of uncertainty, but once a plant is classified as a member of the rose family, further reasoning about it is done with discrete logic. Fuzzy set theory has important applications to pattern recognition, but fuzzy logic is problematical.

Although classical definitions are not possible for all concepts, some concepts are more general than others. All games are activities even if one cannot say exactly what differentiates them from other activities. Yet children learn concrete types like DOLL or HOPSCOTCH long before they learn general ones like ENTITY or ACTIVITY. The statement *All dogs are animals* remains true whether or not a person fills in the type hierarchy with mammals and carnivores. A realistic theory must support a type hierarchy, but it must not require that every concept be reduced to primitives. This book supports a compromise between Aristotle and Wittgenstein: Section 3.6 introduces definitions by genus and differentiae, and Section 4.1 allows open-ended families of schemata and prototypes that can grow and change with experience.

1.6 SYMBOLIC LOGIC AND COMMON SENSE

From the time of Aristotle to the nineteenth century, the traditional purpose of logic was to characterize the forms of reasoning in ordinary thought and language. In the first major work on symbolic logic, Boole (1854) called his rules the *laws of thought*. Even Frege (1879), who invented the first complete theory of first-order logic, called his notation *Begriffsschrift* (concept writing). In the *Principia Mathematica*, however, Whitehead and Russell (1910) codified symbolic logic in its present form as a system for reducing mathematics to logic. Since then, mathematicians have developed logic into forms that are far removed from ordinary language.

Shortly after the *Principia* was published, Lewis (1912) objected to interpreting the operators $\vee$ and $\supset$ as the equivalent of English conjunctions *or* and *if-then*. The English conditional *If it rains, you'll get wet* is normal because there is a causal connection between the clauses. In standard logic, however, the truth of a compound proposition depends only on the truth of its parts, not on their meaning. With such an interpretation, all the following statements are considered true:

```
Either Caesar died or the moon is made of green cheese.
If Socrates is a monkey, then Socrates is human.
If elephants have wings, then 2+2=5.
```

The two clauses *Caesar died* and *the moon is made of green cheese* have nothing to do with each other. The condition *Socrates is a monkey* is inconsistent with the conclusion *Socrates is human.* And no property of elephants could have any effect on a statement about numbers. Such combinations of unrelated clauses sound exceedingly odd. Calling them true is even odder.

A second weakness of symbolic logic as an approximation to natural language is its *extensionality.* The English statement *Every unicorn is a cow* is obviously false by the intensions of UNICORN and COW. But in symbolic logic, that statement is represented by the formula,

$$\forall x(\text{UNICORN}(x) \supset \text{COW}(x)),$$

which may be read, *For all x, if x is a unicorn, then x is a cow.* By the rules of logic (see Appendix A.5), that formula is equivalent to the following:

$$\sim\exists x(\text{UNICORN}(x) \wedge \sim\text{COW}(x)),$$

which may be read, *It is false that there exists an x that is a unicorn and not a cow.* Since no unicorns exist, the statement is considered true. In English, the intensions of UNICORN and COW make the statement false; but in symbolic logic, the empty extension of UNICORN makes it true.

Deductive reasoning is a third area where symbolic logic diverges from the way people think. In logic, a *proof* is a sequence of formulas that starts with axioms and generates each formula from preceding ones by manipulating symbols. When people follow an argument, however, they get at its "meaning" without generating a formal proof. An intelligent person who has not studied logic may be precise in speech and quick at detecting contradiction, yet be utterly incapable of constructing a formal proof. Somehow, people have a way of reasoning that is different from the proof procedures of logic.

A fourth area where symbolic logic differs from natural language is in the syntax of formulas and the use of variables. Keenan (1972) cited the following English sentence and its translation into logic:

Some girl screamed.
$\exists x(\text{GIRL}(x) \wedge \text{SCREAMED}(x)).$

The most obvious difference between the two forms is in the use of the variable x. A variable is a kind of pronoun that is not, in itself, unnatural. What is unnatural is the translation of a sentence with no pronouns into one with three. Another awkward feature is the need for a conjunction to represent a simple sentence. These objections about syntax are not as serious as the semantic objections in the preceding paragraphs. In fact, some versions of logic treat variables differently or eliminate them altogether. Nevertheless, logical form should be tailored to linguistic form to avoid needless complication in the grammar.

Because the forms of symbolic logic are so different from natural language, many people in AI have rejected logic in favor of informal methods for *common sense reasoning*. To implement such a method, Schank et al. (1975) built a system that would take the sentence *John gave Mary an aspirin*, translate it into conceptual dependency graphs, and generate the following plausible inferences:

```
John believes that Mary wants an aspirin.
Mary is sick.
Mary wants to feel better.
Mary will ingest the aspirin.
```

These inferences all have a high probability of being true, but they are not necessarily true. Mary might want an aspirin to put in a vase of water to keep her flowers fresh. The rules of plausible inference are not rigorously valid; they actually correspond to forms of *fallacy* identified by Aristotle and the medieval Scholastics. Since people sometimes commit fallacies, a program that simulated human thinking might also commit an occasional fallacy. Yet people are capable of detecting fallacies and correcting them. A theory of common sense must be general enough to incorporate both plausible inference and exact deduction.

Instead of proving theorems, people assimilate separate facts into a coherent image. In psychological tests, Bransford and Franks (1971) gave subjects a list of separate sentences like the following:

```
The rock rolled down the mountain.
The rock crushed the hut.
The hut was tiny.
The hut was at the edge of the woods.
```

After hearing these sentences, the subjects could not remember whether they heard the facts in a series of simple sentences or in a single sentence, *The rock that rolled down the mountain crushed the tiny hut at the edge of the woods.* When a new sentence, *The hut was at the top of the mountain*, is added to the list, people immediately "see" the contradiction: the hut had to be where the rock was rolling, at or near the bottom of the mountain. Although people differ widely in how graphically they imagine the situation, they normally detect the contradiction as if they were looking at a model or picture.

To explain common sense reasoning, Craik (1943) viewed the brain as a system for making models: "If the organism carries a *small-scale model* of external reality and of its own possible actions within its head, it is able to carry out various alternatives, conclude which is the best of them, react to future situations before they arise, utilize the knowledge of past events in dealing with the present and the future, and in every way react in a fuller, safer, and more competent manner to the emergencies which face it" (p. 61). To simulate such a system, Minsky (1975) proposed the notion of *frames*, which are prefabricated patterns, assembled to form mental models.

For the story about the rock crushing the hut, people have frames for mountains, for things that roll, for huts made of flimsy materials, and for massive rocks. In response to a story, a person assembles frames to form a model. If the frames do not fit together, the story is self-contradictory; if no frames are available, the story is incomprehensible; if more than one frame can be applied, the story is ambiguous.

The word *model* has multiple meanings in engineering, logic, and common speech. Petri (1977) noted three different meanings in the phrases *model of an airplane*, *model of an axiom system*, and *model farm*:

- *Simulation.* A model airplane is a simplified system that simulates some significant characteristics of some other system in the real world or a possible world.
- *Realization.* A model for a set of axioms is a data structure for which those axioms are true. Consistent axioms may have many different models, but inconsistent axioms have no model.
- *Prototype.* A model farm is an ideal or standard for evaluating other less perfect farms or for designing new ones.

Petri maintained that a common basis should be found for these three different ways of modeling. Conceptual graphs, indeed, form models in all three senses of the term: the graphs simulate significant structures and events in a possible world; a set of axioms, called *laws of the world*, must at all times be true of the graphs; and certain graphs, called *schemata* and *prototypes*, serve as patterns or frames that are joined to form the models.

Besides serving as realizations for axioms, mental models must be related to the real world if people are to act effectively in it. In Fig. 1.5, a policeman is communicating his model of the world to another man by means of language. Yet the relationship between language and the world is indirect: a sentence must be interpreted in terms of a conceptual model, and rules of perception must relate that model to a situation. Errors may arise either in mapping language to the model (as in the cartoon) or in mapping the model to the world. Whether a sentence is true or false depends on the criteria for interpreting the sentence in terms of a model and for applying the model to the real world. The sentence *This steak weighs 12 ounces* may be true in terms of a model where the standard of weight is a butcher scale, but it is probably false in terms of a precision balance.

To meet the objections to standard logic, conceptual graphs have been designed as a more natural notation for logic. They form the semantic basis of natural language and represent models of the real world or other possible worlds.

- Rules of syntax map the graphs to and from sentences in natural languages.
- Arcs of the graphs correspond to the *function words* and *case relations* of natural language.

Fig. 1.5 Using language to express a mental model

- Nodes of the graphs are intensional concepts of individuals that may exist in the real world or some hypothetical world.
- Exact reasoning is based on Peirce's existential graphs, which eliminate the extraneous variables that Keenan objected to. The graphs are a complete notation for first-order logic with direct extensions to modal and higher-order logic.
- Plausible reasoning is based on schemata and prototypes, which codify the defaults and family resemblances that accommodate the variability of the real world.
- Model theory uses the same kinds of graph structures for both formal models and propositions about the models.

Chapter 3 of this book presents the basic notation of conceptual graphs, Chapter 4 develops them as a form of logic, and Chapter 5 shows how they are mapped to and from natural language.

1.7 ARTIFICIAL INTELLIGENCE

Encoding knowledge in a digital computer presents a challenge and an opportunity. The challenge is to describe the forms of knowledge so precisely that they can be processed by computer. The opportunity arises from the results of such processing:

- Computer systems that are easier to use and to learn to use,
- More flexible systems that can adapt to changing conditions without having to be reprogrammed,
- An exploration of the limits of computer processing and a better appreciation of human intelligence and creativity.

Artificial intelligence is the study of knowledge representations and their use in language, reasoning, learning, and problem solving. AI programs gain flexibility over conventional systems by using a changing *knowledge base* rather than a fixed, preprogrammed algorithm.

A basic issue is how closely AI should try to simulate human ways of knowing and thinking. Cognitive science attempts to understand human intelligence by developing better and better simulations of it. But since the human brain is so different from ordinary digital computers, the ultimate goals of cognitive science conflict with an engineering approach, whose only criterion for judging a system is how well it works. Advocates of the engineering approach to AI argue that a psychological theory would not be suitable for computer implementation:

- People excel at tasks that require small amounts of computation, but large amounts of loosely organized knowledge.
- Computers excel at repetitive tasks that perform large amounts of computation on highly regular data.
- Instead of simulating the knowledge-based processes that people use, intelligent computers should use fast, precise algorithms.

This argument holds up to a point: for mathematical tasks like multiplication and division, no one would suggest that computers should simulate a child learning multiplication tables. Yet for many tasks, such as the traveling salesman problem, the exact algorithms take exponential amounts of time, but *heuristic* approaches that "guess" the answer can give a good approximation in linear time. For the most interesting problems of AI, the known algorithms are all exponential. The fact that people can find adequate solutions in a reasonable amount of time gives hope of finding practical heuristics by studying human performance.

Most scientific fields are polarized between theory and practice: theoretical physicists vs. experimentalists, pure mathematicians vs. applied mathematicians, and research psychologists vs. clinicians. Both sides grudgingly accept the need for the other, but they almost always disagree on the most promising research directions and the proper methodologies. In some fields, the theoreticians and the practitioners even attend different conferences. Large AI conferences, however, usually attract both types of people. Bundy (1981) summarized the arguments at one such conference:

> The debate was between the *scruffies*, led by Roger Schank and Ed Feigenbaum, and the *neats*, led by Nils Nilsson. The neats argued that no education in AI was complete without a strong theoretical component, containing, for instance, courses on predicate logic and automata theory. The scruffies maintained that such a theoretical component was not only unnecessary, but harmful.... The end product of the scruffy researcher is a working computer program, whereas the neat researcher is not satisfied until he has abstracted a theory from the program.

The neat view of AI assumes that a few elegant principles underlie all the manifestations of human intelligence. Discovery of those principles would provide the magic key to the workings of the mind. The scruffy view is that intelligence is a *kludge*: people have so many *ad hoc* approaches to so many different activities that no universal principles can be found. A chess-playing machine, for example, requires dozens of routines that would be useless for understanding English or French. A system for automatic programming and a system for composing Baroque fugues would also have little in common. Every application requires a large amount of *domain-specific knowledge* that cannot be shared with any other application.

Both sides in the controversy can claim some victories, but neither side has fully established its case. Some general theories have been found for deduction, problem solving, and game playing. Yet some of these elegant techniques run too slow for practical problems. Scruffy programmers, on the other hand, can point to running systems that guide robots and carry on conversations. Yet most of those programs are "toys" that are not commercially profitable. Recently, however, the toys have moved from research to development: robots now build cars and typewriters on assembly lines; natural-language query systems are offered for sale; expert systems are used to diagnose diseases and find oil deposits; and public libraries have reading machines for the blind that can scan a book printed in any standard font and read it aloud.

A separate issue in AI is the *procedural-declarative* controversy, which revolves around the question of knowledge as *knowing how* or *knowing that*. The procedural approach assumes that a person's knowledge of the world is embodied in procedures that actively interpret the environment and operate on it. The declarative approach assumes that knowledge is a collection of facts that can be stated in logical propositions, conceptual graphs, or other symbols. As an example, Simon (1969) cited the following two specifications for a circle (p. 111):

- A circle is the locus of all points equidistant from a given point.
- To construct a circle, rotate a compass with one arm fixed until the other arm has returned to its starting point.

The first sentence is a declarative definition that does not say how to draw a circle. The second is a procedure for drawing one that does not say how to recognize one. A different procedure, such as rolling a piece of clay and cutting a cross section, has little similarity to the compass procedure. Without a declarative definition of circle, it may be difficult or impossible to show how the two procedures are related.

Procedures have an advantage in controlling actions that are easier to do than to define in concepts. Winograd's SHRDLU (1972), which converses in English about stacks of blocks, is an example of the procedural approach. Its grammar for English is embodied in LISP programs, and its knowledge for dealing with blocks and moving them around is embodied in a set of PLANNER programs. SHRDLU demonstrated the power of procedures as a paradigm for AI, yet it was so specialized for the blocks world that it could not be applied to other problems without a complete redesign. Winograd (1975) summarized the arguments in the controversy:

- *Economy.* Procedures specify knowledge by saying how it is used, and every use requires a different procedure. A declarative approach requires only a single copy for all uses.
- *Modularity.* Procedures bind knowledge and control in a single package. By keeping them separate, a declarative approach makes it easier to update and generalize the knowledge base.
- *Exception handling.* Procedures can do anything, and problems that are not covered by the formal theory can often be handled by an *ad hoc* piece of code. A declarative approach may find difficulty with exceptions that were not anticipated by the theory.

Issues in the procedural-declarative controversy appear throughout this book: the representation of schemata in human memory; semantics defined by model theory or computation; parsing techniques for natural languages; and the form of inference rules for expert systems. In all these areas, procedures allow a "quick and dirty" solution when theoretical issues are still unsolved. As theory progresses, more of the knowledge can be removed from procedures and put in declarative form.

To resolve the controversies, Bundy proposed a "rational reconstruction" of AI—an analysis of all the scruffy programs with the goal of extracting a central core of neat structures and techniques. This book presents such a reconstruction. Instead of discussing the classic AI programs in their original notations and terminology, it presents the underlying principles in a unified framework. Economical systems cannot be built from scratch for every application. Instead, commercial systems have to start with general facilities that can be quickly tailored for each domain. If the common core is truly general, it will also have to be abstract and will thus represent a unified theory of intelligence. This argument does not refute the claim that human intelligence may be a kludge, but it makes the counterclaim that human beings cannot cope with highly complex systems without an adequate theory. Perhaps God can build a kludge that works, but mere mortals need a theory to guide them.

Partly because of its name, artificial intelligence excites emotional responses that have not affected (or plagued) computational linguistics or cognitive science. Some people feel threatened by it, others are passionately devoted to it, and still others are simply confused by it. The purpose of this book is to reduce the confusion and to show the relationships to linguistics, philosophy, and psychology. For those who feel threatened by AI (and even more for those who make unwarranted claims about it), Chapter 7 discusses the limits of conceptual thinking and the unsolved problems of creativity and intuition. Intelligent machines may answer questions, generate programs, and untangle the intricacies of tax forms, travel arrangements, and even their own arcane command languages. Yet even as the theory helps us to understand the mysteries of intelligence, it leads us to still more complex mysteries of the mind. Intelligent machines are being designed, but a machine that would make the human mind obsolete is not going to be built for a long, long time.

EXERCISES

As preparation for the rest of this book, ask yourself the following questions. These are profound issues for which no final answers are possible, but thinking about them sets a framework for the following chapters. First try to formulate an answer based on your own background and experience. Then compare your answer with a definition in a dictionary or encyclopedia and extend it or modify it if necessary.

1.1 Define *thinking*, *knowledge*, and *understanding*. Do each of these terms refer to a single, unified thing or process or to some complex collection of related things?

1.2 The flow of conversation is determined by the speaker's intentions and the listener's expectations. Could intention and expectation be simulated on a computer? How?

1.3 What is the difference between knowledge and data? What features distinguish a knowledge-based system from a database system?

1.4 How do people acquire knowledge from experience? Could that process be simulated on a digital computer? How?

1.5 What is the relation between language and thought? Is thinking possible without words? Without images?

1.6 Do present-day computer systems think or understand? If not now, do you believe that they ever will? On what grounds?

1.7 Suppose you were sitting at a terminal connected to a machine that someone claimed was thinking or understanding. How would you test that claim? What questions would you ask? What answers would discriminate between thinking and nonthinking?

1.8 Even if a computer does not "really" think, it may be able to process English in some interesting and practical ways. Suggest some.

SUGGESTED READING

For an introduction to philosophical analysis, see Alston's *Philosophy of Language*. Klemke (1983) has a good selection of original sources. For more background on the philosophers and issues, see *From Descartes to Wittgenstein* by Scruton. The *Dictionary of Philosophy*, edited by Flew, defines the philosophical and logical terms used in this book. Three major works in philosophy of language are Carnap's *Meaning and Necessity*, Wittgenstein's *Philosophical Investigations*, and Quine's *Word and Object*. The analysis of AI has become an important topic of philosophy; see Boden (1977, 1981), Dennet (1978), Sloman (1978), and the collections of papers edited by Haugeland (1981), Ringle (1979), and Dreyfus (1982).

George Miller's *Language and Speech* is a short, readable study of language from a psychological point of view. For collections of articles on cognitive science, see *Perspectives on Cognitive Science* edited by Norman and *Thinking* edited by Johnson-Laird and Wason. An introductory psychology book based on the cognitive approach is Lindsay and Norman's *Human Information Processing*. The review article by Hilgard (1980) documents the ascendancy of cognitive psychology over behaviorism.

For Chomsky's view of the linguistic issues, see his books *Reflections on Language* and *Language and Responsibility*. Leiber (1975) analyzes the philosophical and psychological issues raised by Chomsky's work. Newmeyer (1980) surveys the development of transformational grammar, the issues involved, and the polemical disputes. For a survey of semantic issues from a linguistic point of view, see Lyons (1977), Fodor (1977), and Kempson (1977). For computational linguistics, Tennant (1981) surveys a variety of systems that have been implemented over the past twenty years with a short explanation of each one.

For a survey of the major topics in logic and their application to linguistics see *Logic in Linguistics* by Allwood et al. and *Everything that Linguists have Always Wanted to Know about Logic* by McCawley. Hofstadter (1979) gives an entertaining, intuitive presentation of various points in logic and computing theory. For comprehensive histories of logic, see Bocheński (1970) and Kneale and Kneale (1962).

The three volume *Handbook of Artificial Intelligence*, edited by Barr and Feigenbaum, gives an introduction to everything in AI, interspersed with copious references. For textbooks on AI, see Jackson (1974), Raphael (1976), Winston (1977), Bundy et al. (1978), Nilsson (1980), and Rich (1983). AI is well documented in collections of classic papers edited by Feigenbaum and Feldman (1962), Minsky (1968), Schank and Colby (1973), Winston (1975), Winston and Brown (1979), Webber and Nilsson (1982), and Pao and Ernst (1982). *Machines Who Think* by McCorduck is a history of AI with emphasis on the people and issues. For dissenting views, see Dreyfus (1979) and Weizenbaum (1976).

2
Psychological Evidence

This chapter surveys cognitive psychology and its relationships to linguistics and artificial intelligence. It begins with perception because the mental models used in thinking are an outgrowth of perceptual mechanisms: the brain interprets input from the sense organs by assembling a model of the environment. Thinking, talking, and problem solving are then based on that model.

2.1 PERCEPTS

The simplest patterns for people to recognize are the hardest for a computer to detect. Recognizing faces is almost instantaneous and error free for people, but it is a difficult problem for computers. Conversely, the easiest patterns for a computer are time consuming and error prone for human beings. Counting letters, matching character strings, and doing arithmetic are simple for computers. For humans, however, they require a lengthy series of perceptions and memory searches. Whatever the mechanisms of perception may be, they are very different from the primitives built into digital computers.

During perception, the brain keeps a temporary record of the sensory input. Neisser (1967) called that record an *icon*. For visual input, it lasts about 250 milliseconds. An icon is not the same as an after-image: after a bright flash, the image on the retina lasts for seconds or minutes; but a visual icon is stored in the brain for just a fraction of a second. When a person is watching a movie, an icon bridges the interval between each frame that is flashed on the screen. In reading, an icon holds a few words from one eye fixation to the next.

Since the eyes are constantly flitting from one point to another, each icon presents just a partial view. For a person to "see" a complete figure or scene, perception must construct a complete model out of many incomplete views. To explain how perceptual mechanisms can correctly assemble partial views, Bartlett (1932) proposed the notion of a *schema*, which acts as a blueprint for a mental model. With the right schema, separate icons are integrated into a stable image. With the wrong schema, only confusing, erratic flashes are seen. Errors and optical illusions result from ambiguous input that could fit equally well in two or more conflicting schemata.

A schema is a pattern for assembling units called *percepts*. The percepts are like prefabricated building blocks derived from previous experience and used to build models for interpreting new experience. To study the units, Pritchard et al. (1960) used a special projector that would stabilize an image in a fixed position on the subject's retina. Although the image was projected continuously, the subject could not see it continuously: parts of it would alternately fade and reappear. Sometimes the image appeared as a whole, but often it vanished and reappeared in fragments. Invariably, the fragments were meaningful units, such as the front of a face, the top of a head, an eye, or an ear. In an image of a triangle, an entire line would vanish as a unit. The meaningful units included larger ones like words and smaller ones like single letters. When parts of the word *BEER* faded, the remaining fragments tended to be familiar words like *PEER, PEEP, BEE*, and *BE* (Pritchard 1961). These familiar units are prime candidates for percepts because they act at an early stage of perception and have the unity and stability expected of prefabricated structures.

How people interpret sensory input depends on their stock of percepts. People with different experiences not only react differently to what they see, they may not even "see" the same things:

- Boring (1953) compared published drawings of cell nuclei before and after the discovery of chromosomes: "Chromosomes kept showing up in the later drawings, not in the former. In other words, microscopes do not reveal concepts until the concepts have been invented" (p. 176).

- In a drawing of an aircraft carrier by a child from a Mexican village, "The mast was a totem pole, the aircraft were eagles, and the portholes were decorated with Aztec frescoes. The child, transplanted to a completely unfamiliar environment, tried unsuccessfully to bridge the gap by using the only concepts available to him" (Lenihan 1974, p. 204).

- Many optical illusions depend on experience with straight lines and angles. Segall et al. (1966) found that African villagers who live in circular houses were much less susceptible to the illusions than urban Europeans, who live in precisely constructed rectangular houses. For illusions that depend on perspective, Zulus who live in dense forests are less susceptible than Zulus who live in open country.

- In studying peasants in Uzbekistan, Luria (1976) found that for optical illusions that depend on the physiology of the eye, all groups were equally susceptible. But for illusions that depend on experience, susceptibility was directly correlated with level of education. Paradoxically, the illiterate peasants see the images more objectively because their perceptions have not been distorted by experience.

Hearing and touch also rely on percepts and icons. Keele (1973) found that an auditory icon may last about 8 seconds, considerably longer than the visual icon. For touch, a *kinesthetic icon* may last as long as 20 seconds. Hearing, touch, and vision have dedicated *projection areas* in the cerebral cortex where images are formed. The sense of smell, however, has no representation in the cortex. As a result, olfactory icons and percepts do not exist. As Altman (1978) noted, "We have no difficulty in distinguishing the fragrance of a lemon from the fragrance of a rose, but only in terms of a unitary Gestaltless impression—not the way we distinguish visually a lemon tree from a rose bush. Smells do not provide us with structural information about objects; only data about their presence, their intensity, and our subjective-affective reactions to them" (p. 98).

Sounds of language are interpreted in percepts called *phonemes*, which correspond to vowels and consonants. When a person hears a foreign language with unfamiliar phonemes, it may sound like meaningless babble. Even English loan words sound very different in a French context: *Les boy-scouts font du camping pendant le weekend.* One of the most difficult tasks in mastering a new language is to overcome the old patterns. While trying to teach an American class to pronounce the German phoneme /ö/, a native German speaker told the students, "I don't see vhy you haf so much trouble vis zis sound becauss you haf zee same sound in your English vord *önion.*"

Phonemes form syllables, syllables form words, and words form phrases and sentences. An important question is whether perception is a *bottom-up process* that first matches smaller units and combines them into larger ones or whether it is a *top-down process* that first matches large units and then fills in smaller details. *Gestalt psychology* is the classic example of a top-down theory. Figure 2.1 is a schematic face that illustrates the Gestalt phenomena. When reading the characters *V* and *O* in a line of text, a person normally interprets them as letters. But in the context of a face, they are interpreted as a nose and eyes. Even caricatures with just a few obvious features are easily recognized. When *New York* magazine printed a picture of an eggplant with pendulous jowls and an extra lobe jutting out for a nose, it was instantly recognized as Richard Nixon. Perceptual mechanisms find a schema that fits the overall stimulus before they analyze finer details.

In the context of a word, a reader does not normally see letters as separate units. Especially in speed reading, letters pass before the eyes at a faster rate than people can recognize them. Konorski (1967) found some patients with brain lesions who could read words, but they could not analyze words into letters. One patient "was able to read known words fairly well. However, when he was asked to spell them, he

Fig. 2.1 Example of top-down perception

failed completely. He was also totally unable to read nonsensical words. When a word was presented to him in which one letter was changed, he usually did not notice the difference and read the word as if it were written correctly. For example, seeing the word *okilary* he read it as *okulary* (in Polish, *spectacles*) not being able to discover that one letter was changed. When more letters were changed, he failed completely to read the word" (p. 121). Konorski concluded that these patients saw the words as unitary percepts, not as composite structures.

Studies of the speed of perception also support top-down theories. When a picture of a man is briefly flashed on a screen, a person first identifies the general form and later notices the details of face, hands, shirt, and tie. Bever (1970) found that people could recognize spoken syllables faster than they could recognize single phonemes: when subjects were told to listen for a word starting with the syllable *bo-*, they responded 70 milliseconds faster than when they were listening for a word beginning with the phoneme /b/. Furthermore, people can recognize sentences faster than single words: subjects responded consistently faster when they were listening for the sentence *Boys like girls* than when they were listening for the first sentence beginning with the word *boys*. For recognizing large vocabularies by computer, White (1978) proposed a top-down method of matching templates for complete words instead of first trying to recognize individual phonemes. He estimated that the processing time would be reduced by a factor of 10 to 100.

Multiple levels of percepts can help a person deal with novelty. A common phrase like *United States* may be matched by a single percept, but a less common phrase like *United Fruit* may require two separate percepts. For an unfamiliar word like *antidisestablishmentarianism*, perception may carry the analysis down to single syllables or groups of syllables like *anti-*. And for a rare syllable like *Omsk*, it may go down to the level of individual phonemes. The mechanisms for handling percepts are innate, but the particular stock of percepts must be learned. Some percepts are learned by rote memory, but the most productive source is the construction of compound percepts from smaller ones. Even though adults read an complete word or phrase as one unit, children learn to build up words from combinations of letters.

Some evidence favors a top-down approach, and other evidence favors a bottom-up approach. In their work on stabilized images, Pritchard et al. (1960) found evidence both for the stability of the whole, as Gestalt theory maintains, and for the existence of parts for building the whole. They concluded that both approaches "are valid and complement one another." This psychological conclusion has also emerged as a basic principle of AI: top-down reasoning is a goal-directed process that imposes a tightly controlled organization; bottom-up reasoning is a data-directed or stimulus-directed process that leads to more diffuse chains of associations. The two approaches may be combined in *bidirectional reasoning*, which is originally triggered by some stimulus in the data, but which then invokes a high-level goal that controls the rest of the process. Some problems are more naturally handled by one approach or the other, but the combination of the two is especially powerful.

2.2 MECHANISMS OF PERCEPTION

When the brain receives a new sensory icon, it must search its stock of percepts to find ones that match parts of the icon. The cerebral cortex stores the percepts, but other parts of the brain may control the actual searching and comparing. The searching mechanism, called the *associative comparator*, must have the following characteristics:

- *Associative retrieval.* An ordinary computer retrieves data by an address in storage. The brain has an *associative* mechanism, which retrieves the pattern that matches best.

- *Top-down match.* Perception finds percepts that match the overall pattern of an icon before it fills in percepts for the details.

- *Stimulus constancy.* Stimuli from the same external object are recognized as equivalent despite varying size, brightness, and retinal position.

- *Distributed storage.* A particular memory is not located at a specific point in the brain. Lashley (1950) showed that any area of the cortex can be destroyed without erasing the memory. As larger amounts of brain tissue are destroyed, learning and recall may be degraded, but particular memories will remain after the greater part of the cortex has been removed.

Lashley (1942) suggested that images are stored as wave-like interference patterns. In a review of visual mechanisms, De Valois and De Valois (1980) found strong evidence for Lashley's hypothesis. The *hologram*, which is based on a frequency analysis of wave patterns, has many of the characteristics required for the associative comparator:

- *Associative retrieval.* A hologram can either recreate an image when a laser beam is projected on it or bring light to a focus when the original image is projected on it. This focusing property can be used for associative retrieval by simultaneously projecting an image on a large number of holograms—the one that matches best is the one that brings the light to the sharpest focus.

- *Top-down match.* When an image is projected on a hologram that does not match exactly, the light is brought to a fuzzy focus. The lower frequencies, corresponding to the larger structures, are the most critical in determining the match: a mismatch in higher frequencies, corresponding to fine detail, will not blur the focus as much as a mismatch of low frequencies.

- *Stimulus constancy.* Frequency analysis can handle changes in size, brightness, and position with three simple scale factors: an increase in size corresponds to a factor that lowers all frequencies, an increase in brightness to a factor that increases the amplitudes, and a change of position to an added phase constant.

- *Distributed storage.* Whereas an ordinary photograph preserves spatial continuity by mapping local parts of a scene onto local parts of the picture, a hologram is a distributed form of storage where every part of the hologram stores some information about every part of the scene. If any part of a hologram is destroyed, the complete scene can be reconstructed from any part that remains, although fine details are not reproduced with as sharp a resolution. This shows a striking parallel to the neural case where any part of the cortex may be removed without completely erasing a particular memory.

Perception requires other mechanisms besides the associative comparator. Holograms cannot explain why an elliptical form is seen as a circle when the subject "knows" that it is viewed from an angle. Something must rotate or project an image to get it in a standard form. Kosslyn (1980) found evidence for a *visual buffer* on which images are rotated, projected, and combined with other images. In a long series of experiments, Shepard and Cooper (1982) showed that mental images are transformed as though people had a miniature model in the head. To determine the stages in perception, Weisstein (1973) varied the amount of time that a subject could spend in viewing a scene. By analyzing what people recognize at different time intervals, she distinguished three stages: at the first stage, stimulation is registered as a sensory icon; at the next stage, isolated parts are recognized; and at the final stage, the parts are assembled as the "picture in the head."

The second mechanism of perception is called the *assembler*. It assembles and transforms percepts, each of which matches part of a sensory icon. Hebb (1949) noted that motor mechanisms, especially eye movements, play an important role in organizing parts of an image into a complete form. His basic points can be restated in the terms of this book:

- Familiar forms are matched by ready-made percepts that are found by the associative comparator.
- Unfamiliar forms are reconstructed from percepts for their parts. The assembler combines the parts into a distinctive figure.
- The assembler is intimately linked with motor mechanisms that guide the eye movements. Visual fixations first distinguish parts of an object clearly. During assembly, eye movements are required for maximal clarity.
- Previous assemblies, stored in long-term memory, need not be reconstructed from low-level percepts. Familiar forms can be recognized at a glance, but unfamiliar ones require repeated eye movements.

The assembler and the associative comparator are independent mechanisms. When a monkey's visual cortex is surgically removed, it can still find objects by visual clues. When the monkey is offered a nut, it makes no response; but when the nut is moved, the monkey reaches in the right direction. In experiments on hamsters, the visual cortex was not disturbed, but the superior colliculus was removed. These animals could still recognize patterns, but they were unable to localize objects. The hamster was placed in a box having two doors marked with different patterns; one of the patterns indicated a reward on the other side. Without the superior colliculus, the animal was unable to orient itself towards the correct door. It could still find the door, however, by shuffling along the walls of the box until it was directly in front it. Such experiments show that pattern recognition and spatial reconstructions are supported by independent neural mechanisms (Schneider 1969).

In human beings as well, brain lesions can disrupt the assembler without affecting the associative comparator. Konorski's patient who could read words but could not assemble them from separate letters had that problem. Konorski found that he was "completely unable to grasp any spatial relations between objects seen. On the contour map of Poland he failed to show the location of any well-known cities or the neighboring countries. Nor could he draw a clock or tell whether a cow's horns are nearer the head or the tail. In spite of these most dramatic disturbances of evaluating spatial relations, he had not the slightest difficulty in recognizing and naming human faces, objects, and letters of the alphabet" (1967, p. 115).

Not all percepts are equally available for matching icons. *Attention* increases sensitivity to certain stimuli and ignores others. It blocks out unimportant or unwanted detail in order to emphasize the significant information. The effects of attention can even be detected in brain waves: Horn (1960) found that when a cat is sitting quietly, a sharp click causes a sudden jump in its pattern of brain waves. When the cat is intently watching a mouse, the same click hardly affects them. Similar effects occur in human beings (Spong et al. 1965).

Attention can increase sensitivity either to stimuli from a particular location or to particular kinds of stimuli, no matter where they occur. When many people are talking in a crowded room, a person can listen to one conversation while ignoring others. The listener can discriminate either by direction or by voice quality: one can discriminate between a male voice and a female voice coming from the same direction, between two similar voices from different directions, but not between two similar voices from the same direction. This phenomenon is known as the *cocktail party effect* (Cherry 1962).

Internal images rely on the same mechanisms used for perceiving external images. According to Hebb, "If the image is a reinstatement of the perceptual process, it should include the eye movements (and in fact usually does).... It is easy to form a clear image of a triangle when eye movement is made freely (not necessarily following the contours of the imagined figure), harder to do with fixation of gaze while imagining the eye movement, but impossible if one attempts to imagine the figure as being seen with fixation on one point"(1968, p. 470).

The connection between images and motor mechanisms runs both ways: motor mechanisms help to assemble images, and images help to control motor mechanisms. For precise movements, the brain creates an image of the goal and monitors the sensory feedback to determine when it has been attained. A person's signature has the same shape when he signs it on paper using finger and wrist motions and when he signs it on a blackboard using sweeping motions of arm and shoulder. The signals to the muscles are totally different, but the mental image is the same. Pribram (1971) coined the term *image of achievement* for the mental image that controls behavior. He compared it to a thermostat: the dial of a thermostat does not have a schedule for turning the furnace on and off; it only marks the high and low points to be achieved. An image of achievement is also used in controlling robots. When a robot builds a stack of blocks, its computer calculates an image of the desired goal. It then instructs the robot's arm to move a block to the approximate location. Next it compares the image from the television camera with the image of achievement and instructs the arm to make fine adjustments.

In perception, the assembler generates a *working model* that matches incoming sensory icons. Previous expectations may raise the level of attention for certain percepts, but if those percepts do not match the input, the working model is refined with a better selection. As Fig. 2.2 shows, sensory icons come from external sources, and the working model is generated by internal processes.

- The associative comparator searches for available percepts that match all or part of an incoming sensory icon. Attention determines which parts of a sensory icon are matched first or which classes of percepts are searched.

- The assembler combines percepts from long-term memory under the guidance of schemata. The result is a working model that matches the sensory icons. Larger percepts assembled from smaller ones are added to the stock of percepts and become available for future matching by the associative comparator.

- Motor mechanisms help the assembler to construct a working model, and they, in turn, are directed by a working model that represents the goal to be achieved.

Dreams, hallucinations, and the *phantom limbs* experienced by amputees are internal images that use the perceptual mechanisms. A noise from the outside may intrude into a dream, but internal mechanisms weave it into the story. In normal perception, the working model must match a sensory icon, at least approximately. For dreams, it is under no constraint, and an object that is not at the center of attention may disappear or be transformed. Dreams still bear some resemblance to reality, however, because the percepts and schemata for assembling them were originally derived from sensory icons. The working model that guides motor mechanisms does not match current sensations, but those desired future sensations that the motor mechanisms are to achieve. A person who is learning a new skill, must direct each step with a separate command. Upon attaining mastery, the person has a ready-made image for a complete sequence of actions.

Reconstructed images are so similar to sensory icons that people are sometimes unaware of what is external and what is internal. Perky (1910) told her subjects to "imagine a banana." While they were describing the images, a faint, vertical yellow form was projected before their eyes. Although most subjects originally imagined a banana lying horizontal, they lined up their internal images with the external form without being aware of it. Segal (1972) told subjects to "imagine a glass of iced tea" and then projected a barely perceptible image in front of them. When the external

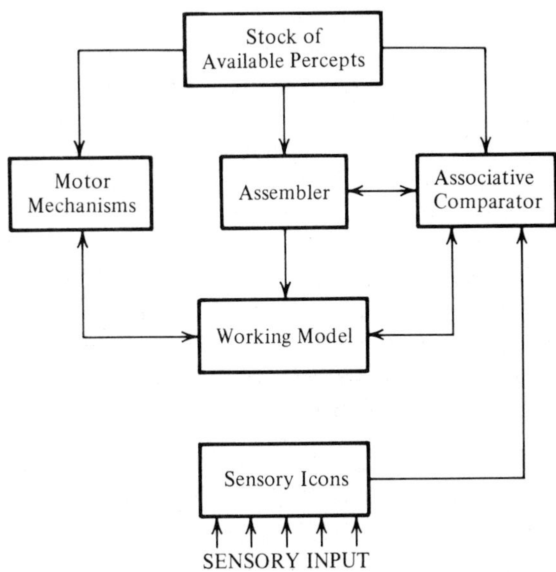

Fig. 2.2 Mechanisms of perception

image was iced tea, the subjects reported ordinary mental images of iced tea. But when the external image was an elephant, the subjects reported unusual distortions and combinations such as a caterpillar drinking iced tea. In general, the subjects assimilated the external stimulus to the internal image without being aware of the stimulus.

Internal images can produce the same patterns of brain waves as the sensory stimuli they are mimicking. Since brain waves are hard to decipher, John (1964) chose a flickering light as the stimulus because its rhythmic pattern could easily be detected. He conditioned cats to obtain milk by pressing a lever in response to the light. When the stimulus was first presented, its rhythmic pattern was found in the visual projection area of the cat's cortex. As the conditioned reflex became established, more widely scattered parts of the brain began to show the rhythm. Not only did the pattern appear when the stimulus was present, it occasionally appeared in the brain when the external stimulus was absent. The spontaneously generated pattern did not cause the cat to turn towards the lever, but the more often it appeared, the more quickly the reflex was established. When the reflex became completely automatic, the spontaneous pattern tended to disappear and only reappeared when the animal made a mistake.

In terms that would give a behaviorist apoplexy, one could say that the cat was "thinking" about the light. The more it pondered the situation, the sooner it noticed the connection between the flickering light and milk, and the more quickly the reflex was established. The pattern disappeared when the reflex was fully established because, as the introspectionists said, behavior becomes less conscious as it becomes more automatic. One should not hazard too many guesses about a cat's mental imagery on the basis of this experiment, but the least it shows is that processes in the brain can regenerate patterns that resemble sensory input. It also shows that learning involves more than strengthening stimulus-response chains.

2.3 CONCEPTUAL ENCODING

Elephants are smarter than mice, and they also have bigger brains. Yet brain size alone is not a good measure of intelligence. A better measure is the ratio of brain weight to body weight: larger animals tend to have larger brains, and this ratio adjusts for the increase devoted to supporting the nerves for a large body. Even that measure depends on extraneous elements such as bone and fat. What Hebb (1949) considered significant was the ratio of total *association cortex* to total *sensory cortex*, which he called the *A/S ratio*. The sensory cortex consists of projection areas for the various sense organs; the association cortex is the remaining area, devoted to associations between sensory input and behavior. A high A/S ratio suggests a high potential for sophisticated, intelligent behavior.

Hebb maintained that the A/S ratio should be strongly correlated with the length of learning required for an animal to reach intellectual maturity. The rat, with a low A/S ratio, fills up its association area much more quickly than a chimpanzee or human being with a high A/S ratio. "Training in pattern vision is slower for the rat reared in darkness than for normal rats, but the difference is not nearly as great as for chimpanzee or man. The rat reared in darkness is capable of a selective visual discrimination, definitely learned, after a total visual experience of less than 15 minutes... the corresponding time for primates is a matter of weeks or months" (Hebb 1949, p. 113). Since connections in the association area develop from sensory input, animals with a high A/S ratio require a great deal of input to reach their full potential.

For an animal with a low A/S ratio, such as a rat, the associations are relatively simple compared to those of a chimpanzee. For a human being, the association cortex is so big that internal processes exercise greater control over behavior than immediate stimuli—a quantitative increase in the A/S ratio can lead to a qualitative difference in the complexity of behavior. Four mechanisms have been considered for encoding information in the association cortex:

- *Synesthesia.* Input to one primary zone, such as hearing, may directly stimulate an image in another primary zone, such as vision. Some people "see" patches of color or flashes of light when they hear particular words or musical chords. Yet synesthesia is a rare condition that most people never experience.

- *Mental images.* People differ widely in how vividly they experience images. Nikolai Tesla, the inventor of the alternating current motor, would imagine the details of motors in his mind, assemble them, watch them run, take them apart, and examine the pieces for wear—all in vivid mental imagery (Hoffman 1980).

- *Language.* The most detailed encoding for external communication is language. Because it is so versatile, some psychologists have identified thinking with *inner speech* and have virtually ignored other possible encodings.

- *Concepts.* More abstract than language are concepts and conceptual relations. In the early twentieth century, the Würzburg psychologists argued that ordinary thinking is often free from sensory content. Images may be helpful in some contexts, but a hindrance in others. In analyzing introspective reports, they found sophisticated thinking that did not depend on either words or images (Külpe 1912).

Since concepts are so abstract, evidence for them must be obtained indirectly. In studying how mathematicians think, Hadamard (1945) found that only a few of them regularly used language to develop mathematical ideas. He quoted a comment by Einstein that is typical of many mathematicians: "Conventional words or other signs have to be sought for laboriously only in a secondary stage, when the mentioned associative play is sufficiently established and can be reproduced at will." Alexander Willwoll (1926), who worked in the tradition of Otto Selz and the Würzburgers, analyzed protocols from subjects who were given a pair of words and asked to find an appropriate relation between them. When given the words *Baugerüst* [scaffolding] and *Krücke* [crutch], one subject, after a 20 second delay, said, "I immediately saw the similarity, but I didn't know any word for it." From such protocols, Willwoll concluded that the subject may have a completely clear thought in consciousness, yet lack the words for expressing it. Although thoughts without words are possible, such thoughts are elusive and easy to forget. Willwoll quoted a saying by Paul Keller: "Symbols are necessary; thoughts without symbols fly away in the wind" (p. 134).

Studies of the deaf give direct evidence that language is not essential for complex thought. Piaget (1970) found that the development of logic in children depends more on experience than on language. Deaf-mute children develop logical operations despite their lack of language although their progress is slower than normal. Blind children, who do have language, lag much further behind normal children than deaf-mutes. Since deafness is a handicap in schoolwork, the abilities of deaf-mutes should be tested on problems that require no use of language. Cohors-Fresenborg and Strüber (1980) devised a test where children were supposed to build automata out of bricks and movable objects like levers, flip-flops, and counters. They tested a group of 9 and 10-year old deaf children together with a control group of normal children who were at the same level of achievement in mathematics and were matched on a cognitive test (Raven APM). Contrary to expectations, the deaf children outperformed the normal children. Out of a possible 35 points, the deaf children scored 24, and the control group scored only 13. The experimenters were surprised to find that the deaf were much better in dealing with abstraction:

> After the construction of a machine which could separate two kinds of bottles the children were asked to build a two-coin selling automaton. These machines would be very different in reality, but mathematically they are seen as isomorphic automata. None of the normal children noted the isomorphism, but four of the deaf saw it immediately.

One reason the deaf children scored better was that matching them with hearing children who had reached the same level in the curriculum paired them with children who were about a year younger. The ability to think abstractly can develop independently of language skill and scholastic achievement.

Language and logic are independent skills. Brain lesions that leave language intact can still disturb logical operations. Luria (1973) found a group of patients with deep lesions of the right hemisphere who "firmly believed that at one and the same time they were in Moscow and also in another town. They suggested that they had left Moscow and gone to the other town, but having done so, they were still in Moscow where an operation had been performed on their brain. Yet they found nothing contradictory about these conclusions" (p. 168). These patients masked their defects with excessive verbosity. They could use the forms of logic implicit in language, but they could not deal with spatial relations.

To deal with language and imagery, concepts must be associated with both words and percepts. David Waltz (1981), who has done research on both computer vision and natural language processing, has been seeking a uniform underlying representation. He cited the following examples:

```
My dog bit the mailman's leg.
My dachshund bit the mailman's ear.
My doberman bit the mailman's ear.
```

To understand the first sentence, no images are necessary. For the second one, people wonder how the dachshund could reach so high. But the third sentence is reasonable because a doberman is a much larger dog. Waltz argued that the brain must use visual and spatial mechanisms for interpreting such sentences. Although people may not have conscious images of the dachshund and doberman, they must use some sort of spatial processing. The close connection between sensory percepts and abstract concepts is also reflected in common metaphors: *see the point of an argument*, *overthrow the government*, *raise a stink*, and *run for office*.

Concepts may be associated with images, but they are more abstract than images. Figure 2.3 shows the mechanisms implicit in the meaning triangle (Fig. 1.4). When a person sees a cat sitting on a mat, perception maps the image into a conceptual graph. A person who is bilingual in French and English may say, in speaking French, *Je vois un chat assis sur une natte*. In describing the same perception in English, the person may say *I see a cat sitting on a mat*. The same conceptual graph, which originates in a perceptual process, may be mapped to either language. Conceptual graphs are a universal, language-independent deep structure.

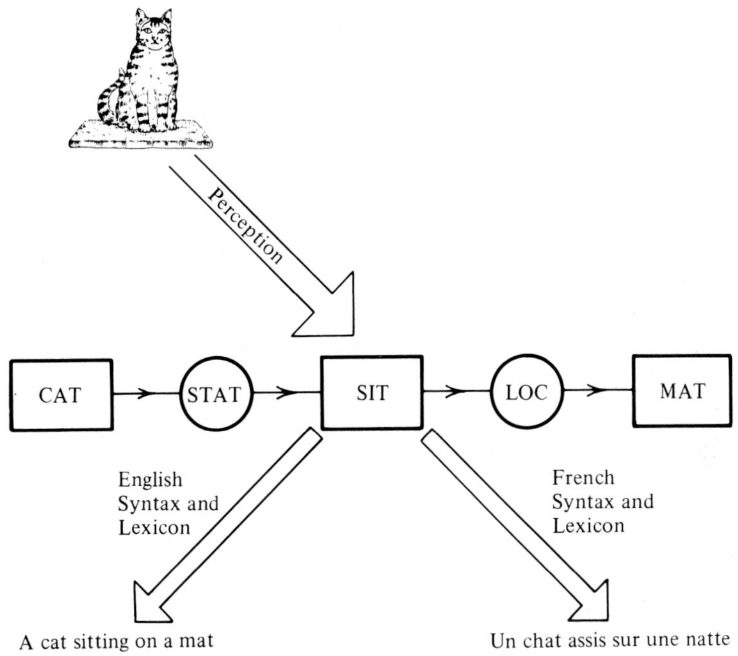

Fig. 2.3 Perception, concepts, and language

In AI, the term *concept* is used for the nodes that encode information in networks or graphs: a concept is a basic unit for representing knowledge. Defining a concept as a *unit* presupposes that concepts are discrete. This assumption is supported by the fact that discrete relationships are remembered more accurately than continuous quantities. When people are asked to describe or draw a scene from memory, what they remember are discrete properties: *The tree is to the left of the car*, *The dot is above the circle*, or *There are three red houses and a yellow one*. Sizes, times, and temperatures are remembered by discrete comparisons: *The corn is knee high*, *I waited until the parking lot emptied out*, or *The water is scalding hot*. All human languages name only a discrete set of colors out of the continuous spectrum. Most people can remember the discrete steps of a melody; but perfect pitch, the ability to remember an exact frequency, is rare even among musicians.

Even if people cannot remember continuous quantities, they can still detect them. They cannot, however, encode them in long-term memory. When comparing two objects directly, people readily notice small differences in color, weight, temperature, and size; but they cannot remember those quantities for more than a few seconds. Temperature, emotional state, and distance are continuous; but languages represent them by discrete words like *cold, cool, tepid, lukewarm, warm, hot; happy, sad; far, near.* Instruments like clocks and thermometers aid the memory by converting a continuous time or temperature into a string of discrete digits that can be remembered indefinitely.

To adapt the discrete words to a continuous world, natural languages have "fuzzy" words like *somewhat, very, almost, rather, more or less, approximately, just about,* and *not quite.* Such words cannot provide a continuous range of variability: *very hot* is just one more discrete state beyond hot, and *very very hot* is another one beyond that. Zadeh (1974) developed a theory of *fuzzy logic* to assign precise values to such terms, but his calculus of fuzzy values makes distinctions that no natural language ever represents. People use hedges like *more or less warm* when their standard for *warm* is not quite attained, but the world has a continuous range of temperatures that discrete words can never describe. The reason language has fuzzy terms is not that human thought is fuzzy, but that the world is fuzzy.

Since people are part of nature, the human body partakes of the continuous variability or fuzziness of the natural world. For classifying both continuity and discreteness in human behavior, Pike (1967) coined the terms *etic* and *emic* by extracting the endings from the words *phonetic* and *phonemic.* The science of phonetics studies the continuous range of acoustic phenomena, which the listener interprets as a discrete set of phonemes. The etic (continuous) aspects of behavior arise from the movements of the human body, which rarely have the rigidity of a military drill and tend towards graceful shifts or glides from one position to the next:

- Motions of tongue, lips, and other parts of the body must be continuous according to the laws of physics. Hence, minor variations are inevitable.
- Sensory channels for receiving input are either continuous or discretized with such a fine mesh that distinct units are not perceptible.
- Emotions are internal states that depend on the continuous variability of hormones and other substances in the blood.

Since the brain is part of the body, continuity in sensory input or bodily movement is likely to be represented in it. Yet the brain also has emic (discrete) units for classifying continuous information. Normal behavior results from the interactions of discrete and continuous forms:

- *Vocalization.* Human speech has two distinct components: a continuous range of dynamics for expressing emotions and discrete words or *morphemes* for expressing concepts. Other primates, including the great apes, have a fixed number of calls which are not combined to form new ones, but which are varied continuously in volume, pitch, and rate of repetition (McNeill 1970). Like other primates, people use the continuous system when they scream in fright or growl in anger. But only humans have a vocal system that combines discrete sounds to form an arbitrary number of messages. Even physiology shows the difference between the two systems:

Magoun et al. (1960) noted that emotional vocalization in both humans and lower animals is controlled by the middle brain stem, but symbolic speech is controlled by the associational cortex of the human brain.

- *Durability of word forms.* The word forms of natural languages keep their identity over centuries. Even though the Indo-European languages have been separated for at least 5,000 years, hundreds of clearly recognizable cognates remain: English *three*, Latin *tres*, Russian *tri*, and Sanskrit *tri*; English *mother*, Latin *mater*, Russian *materi*, and Sanskrit *matar*. The durability of word forms and meanings shows that the underlying concepts must be discrete units: if the mental processes that dealt with concepts were continuous, they would be likely to blur the distinctions between so many words over such a long period of time.

- *Variability of emotional terms.* Watkins (1969) observed that words for value judgments are not as stable as most other words in the Indo-European languages. Even closely related languages use words from different roots for common emotive terms: English *good*, Latin *bonus*, Greek *ἀγαθός*, Russian *khoroshy*, and Polish *dobry* are completely unrelated. Words meaning happy, sad, and beautiful or pretty also have a rapid turnover: the German equivalents *froh, traurig*, and *schön* or *hübsch* are unrelated to the English forms; the classical Latin *pulcher* was replaced by derivatives of the colloquial *bellus* in French and Italian, and the classical Greek *καλός* was replaced by *ὄμορφος* in modern Greek. Slang terms like *bus* and *mob* that express discrete concepts often become part of the standard language, but emotional terms like *groovy* or *far out* become obsolete within a decade. The instability of emotional words is not caused by their abstract character, because abstract legal and sacred terms are highly stable. The words *legal* and *sacred* themselves come from Indo-European roots with the same basic meaning. Variability of emotional terms supports the point that stable terms express discrete concepts.

- *Difficulty of expressing emotions in words.* Words do not express emotions in the same way they express concepts. If two people meet face to face, one of them could say "It was a really great party!" and convey the feeling of the party by tone of voice, facial expression, and general animation of the whole body. But if a novelist wrote that same sentence in a book, even with a dozen exclamation points, it would fail to communicate the emotion. Good writing does not express emotion. Instead, it describes scenes and events in a way that leads the reader to experience the emotion for himself.

- *Music.* Discrete and continuous processes also appear in music. Dynamics, tempo, and tonic pitch have a continuous range of variation; but scales, rhythms, and melodies are made up of discrete units. Lerdahl and Jackendoff (1983) developed a grammar of music that describes the way those units are put together. By means of the grammar, they distinguished cognitive principles that determine the way people perceive music. Modern atonal music typically sounds formless and boring because its forms are not compatible with human perceptual processes.

- *Behavioremes.* Pike coined the term *behavioreme* for the discrete units that appear in all forms of behavior. They vary from the informal gestures of *body language* to the stylized patterns of rituals, dances, and games. For baseball, the rule books list emic units such as innings, home runs, and foul balls as well as syntactic rules for combining innings into a game or turns at bat into an inning. As in language, the emic units of physical movements have a continuous infinity of etic forms. A foul ball could be a mighty blast that misses being a home run by inches, or it could be a foul tip that barely touches the ball. The umpire is an impartial judge who classifies the continuous etic forms into discrete emic units.

Advocates of AI, who concentrate on the discrete aspects, are optimistic about the prospects for simulating intelligence on a digital computer. Critics who concentrate on the continuous forms maintain that simulation of intelligence by digital means is impossible. Since the human brain uses both kinds of processes, a complete simulation may require some combination of digital and analog means. Analog processes can be approximated on a digital computer by overlaying the field of interest with a fine grid—a technique that is commonly used in numerical analysis. Some pattern recognition programs combine continuous transformations with a discrete analysis. To recognize a visual scene, the programs first move, rotate, and enlarge or reduce the image to get it in a standard orientation. Then they carry out a discrete analysis to determine what objects and structures are present. But whether all continuous processes can be simulated effectively is an open question. In particular, holograms for the associative comparator may require analog devices.

2.4 SCHEMATA

Concepts and percepts are building blocks for constructing mental models. But rules or patterns are needed to organize the building blocks into larger structures. Immanuel Kant (1781) introduced the term *schema* for a rule that organizes perceptions into a unitary whole:

> The fact is that our pure sensuous concepts do not depend on images of objects, but on schemata. No image of a triangle in general could ever be adequate to its concept. It would never attain to that generality of the concept, which makes it applicable to all triangles, whether right-angled, or acute-angled, or anything else, but would always be restricted to one portion only of the sphere of the concept.... The concept of dog means a rule according to which my imagination can always draw a general outline of the figure of a four-footed animal, without being restricted to any particular figure supplied by experience or to any possible image which I may draw in the concrete. (A:141, B:180)

The psychologist Otto Selz, who published articles on Kant's philosophy, chose the schema as a basis for his theory of *schematic anticipation* (1913, 1922). Unlike the diffuse links of associationism, Selz's schema is a network of concepts and relations that guides the thinking process.

For Selz, a schema is a network of concepts. Bartlett (1932), whose work is better known among contemporary psychologists, gave an operational definition of *schema*:

> ...an active organization of past reactions, or of past experiences, which must always be supposed to be operating in any well-adapted organic response. That is, whenever there is any order or regularity of behavior, a particular response is possible only because it is related to other similar responses which have been serially organized, yet which operate, not simply as individual members coming one after another, but as a unitary mass. (p. 201)

That definition is obscure, partly because Bartlett was groping to express an intuition that he could not yet relate to established theory. But it makes two important points: a schema is an active organization, and a schema must be operating in all orderly behavior.

Despite the vagueness of his definition, Bartlett showed that the patterns stored in the brain impose an organization on the material that is recalled. In some of his experiments, he presented pictures to various subjects and asked them to draw what they remembered. After analyzing the distortions in the way subjects reproduced the pictures, he formulated the following principles (p. 185):

- Reproduced material tends to assume the form of the conventional designs that occur in the culture.
- When material cannot be identified, the subjects tend to elaborate it until a recognizable form is produced.
- If the subjects cannot find any other purpose for some detail, they may replicate it to form a decorative pattern.
- When a recognizable form is presented, it tends to undergo simplification into a conventional representation.
- Naming, of the whole or of the parts, strongly affects reproduction. Counting tends to preserve order and number although the form may be altered.
- Apparently trivial or disconnected detail that cannot otherwise be interpreted tends to be preserved.

Yet Bartlett only described the effects of schemata, not their internal structure. He did not say anything more about their form than Kant, who simply said that it "is an art hidden in the depth of the human soul" (A:142, B:181).

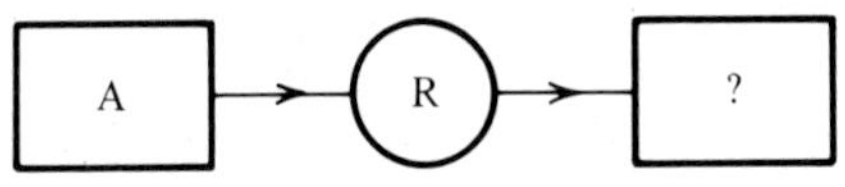

Fig. 2.4 Anticipatory schema

Selz, who followed the traditions of the Würzburg school, was free from behaviorist inhibitions against discussing mental structures. His schemata were networks like Fig. 2.4, which shows a concept A linked by the relation R to an unknown concept represented by a question mark. An *anticipatory schema* presents an outline of the anticipated solution, whose complete solution is found by replacing the question mark with the correct concept. Selz's diagrams are networks of concepts and relations that resemble the notations used in artificial intelligence. Like Minsky's frames (1975), they contain general slots to be filled with specific values. The unfilled slots set up *expectations* that initiate a train of thought and guide it in the most promising directions.

All complex behavior shows the need for schemata that organize elementary units into larger patterns. Games of strategy, such as bridge or chess, are especially good for illustrating such patterns. In using Selz's methods to analyze thinking in chess, de Groot (1965) found no significant difference between masters and experts in the number of moves considered, depth of analysis, or time spent. Yet out of dozens of legal moves, a master would only consider one or two moves at each turn as worth playing. Former world champion Emanuel Lasker said that chess is a highly stereotyped game. Instead of exhaustively analyzing all options, the master simply looks at the board and "sees" which moves are worth considering.

Figure 2.5 shows one of the positions for which de Groot collected protocols from 20 subjects (1965, p. 89). He had them study the position and select White's next move while saying whatever came to mind, what moves or lines of play they were considering. The only significant difference was that the masters usually found the winning move (Bishop captures Knight at Q5), while the nonmasters consistently overlooked it: 4 out of 5 grandmasters and 3 out of 4 masters chose the correct move, but all 11 nonmasters, including 5 experts, chose moves that dissipated White's advantage. This position is a tactical one on which computers excel. One such machine, Sargon 2.5, did find the correct move after an exhaustive search for 6 levels deep that took over an hour of computing time. During that time, the computer examined over a million positions, yet former world champion Alexander Alekhine picked that move as the first one to consider and never analyzed any variations further than 5 levels deep. De Groot concluded that the chess master has a stock of patterns that enable him to analyze and classify a position and immediately select the one or two most promising moves.

To determine the schemata for chess, Chase and Simon (1973) studied three chess players: a master, a class A player, and a beginner. They asked the subjects to reconstruct a chess position, sometimes from memory and sometimes with the original position in plain view. In the memory task, the experimenters assumed that a pause would occur each time a new schema (which they called a *chunk*) was retrieved. When subjects reconstructed a position with the original in plain view, they noted the player's head movements. They assumed that each glance back at the position encodes a single schema. The schemata included logical configurations of

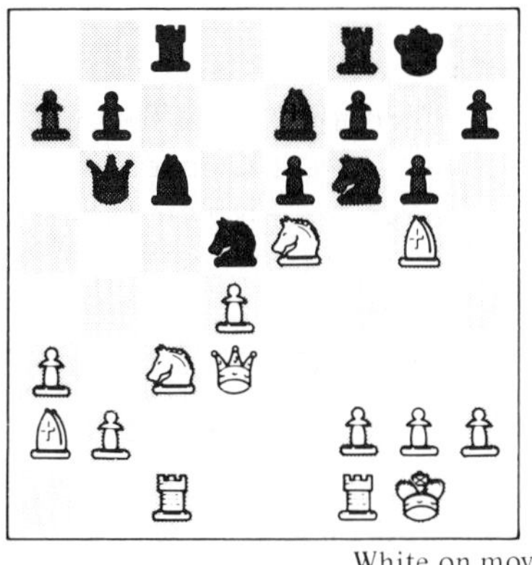

Fig. 2.5 Chess position for de Groot's protocols

pieces, such as pawn chains with blockading and defending pieces, castled king positions, and clusters of pieces of the same color. Both the number of pieces in a schema and the number of schemata recalled were greater for the master than for the class A player, who in turn scored better than the beginner. Simon (1974) estimated that a class A player has a repertoire of about 1,000 schemata while a master has between 25,000 and 100,000—the same range as an educated person's vocabulary.

Following the approach used for studying chess, Thomas Wolf (1976) found that musicians who are gifted in sight reading also perceive a musical score in well-defined schemata. He quoted the pianist Andrew Wolf, who is a good sight reader:

> No one could sight read note-by-note. You don't have that much time. Everybody to a certain extent sight-reads in patterns and when you see a chord of three notes, you don't just read the three notes and then put your fingers on one and then the other and then the other. You see the pattern of that chord and then you play it.

Talent for sight reading is independent of performing skill. Some mediocre musicians can play at sight anything they can perform, while some excellent performers must laboriously work through a piece before they can play it. Good musicians who are poor sight readers are overly conscientious about reading every note. They never learn to see entire chords and melodic patterns. Good sight readers know all the patterns of melodies, harmonies, and ornamentation of a period, such as Baroque, or a composer, such as Mozart. When they see the start of a familiar schema, they anticipate the rest of the pattern. Modern atonal music is difficult to sight read because it does not divide into standard chunks.

Not everyone plays chess or reads music, but everyone speaks some language. The similarity in the structures of human language and games like chess was recognized by Saussure (1916), who said, "A game is like an artificial realization of what language offers in a natural form" (p. 88). Just as a chess position appears to be a jumble of pieces to the beginner, a human language sounds like confused babble to someone who does not understand it. Schemata operate on various levels to give structure to speech—at the phonemic level of individual sounds, at the morphemic level of words, and at the phrase, sentence, paragraph, and higher levels. The patterns are especially noticeable in stylized reports about a particular subject, such as sports or weather. Following is a typical pattern for a stock market report:

```
{Because of | Despite} current newspaper headline,
the market {staged a broad advance | dropped sharply
| rallied | rebounded | crept upward | drifted lower}
in {heavy | active | moderate | light} trading
with {advances | declines} leading {declines | advances}
by a margin of —— to ——.
```

Wandering bards in many different cultures use traditional patterns in *oral composition*: Homer and Hesiod in ancient Greece, medieval *jongleurs* with their *chansons de geste*, *guslari* in the coffee houses of Yugoslavia, and tribal historians in African villages. All these bards compose epic poems by stringing together standard patterns. What is especially fascinating is their ability to improvise hundreds or thousands of lines in strict verse form before a live audience. Peabody (1975) estimated that Homer could compose Greek hexameter at the rate of 7 to 14 lines per minute. By contrast, Vergil, who composed Latin hexameter in imitation of Homer, first wrote a prose sketch for the *Aeneid* and then spent nearly ten years in converting it to verse—an average rate of 3 to 5 lines per day. The difference in speed of composition is so great that it demands an explanation. As Peabody said, "The notion that some illiterate bard could toss off a work of comparable magnitude and complexity at the rate of one or two books an hour seems manifestly unacceptable. That such a product could become the model for so consummate a craftsman as Vergil transcends the possibility of belief" (p. 7). The disparity in speed indicates a fundamental difference between oral and written techniques.

Oral composition is best compared to a jazz performance: a jazz group may use traditional melodies, but each performance is a new creation. During rehearsals or informal jam sessions, the players build up their stock of ornamentation, harmonic patterns, and transitional phrases. Even more importantly, they develop a strong sense of rhythm that controls the flow of the music while individual players explore their own variations. The oral poet also works out variations by rehearsing passages in solitary practice sessions. In an actual performance, the bard does not recite a memorized text, but like the jazz musician, combines thematic elements from previous performances to create a new composition. Each time the bard tells the same story, it has the same overall structure, but the amount of detail varies according to the occasion and the mood of the audience.

Oral epic is characterized by repetitious lines and phrases, such as *Then when rosy-fingered dawn appeared*. Achilles is called *swift-footed* in some instances and *god-like* or *son of Peleus* in others. The epithet is chosen partly for its meaning and partly for the number of syllables needed to fill the hexameter line. Parry (1930) showed that not only epithets, but essentially every phrase of every line of verse belongs to a stock of standard patterns of well-defined syntactic and metrical shape. He defined a *formula* as "a group of words which is regularly employed under the same metrical conditions to express a given essential idea." Like the chess master with a vocabulary of 25,000 positions, the master bard has thousands of formulas that fit together to generate a line of verse, a description of a battle, or the complete plot of a story.

In the Serbocroatian epics, each line has ten syllables, with a first half line of exactly four syllables and a second half of exactly six syllables. The following examples from Lord (1960) show standard formulas for expressing an idea in the first half line, second half line, or full line:

```
First:    Marko kaže                 Marko said
Second:   govorio Marko              said Marko
Full:     Govorio Kraljeviću Marko   Said Prince Marko
```

These formulas accommodate any two-syllable name. Other formulas are used with names of other lengths. In the following formulas, the word *kuli* for *tower* could be replaced by two-syllable words for other structures:

```
First:    A na kuli                    In the tower
Second:   na bijeloj kuli              in the white tower
Full:     Na bijeloj od kamena kuli    In the white stone tower
```

To fill out a line of verse, the poet either selects a ready-made formula or adapts a more general formula by substituting words of the same metrical and syntactic form.

Even occasional lapses of meter show the power of formulas. Most patterns for sending messages in the Serbocroatian epics accommodate two-syllable and four-syllable missives. But *teligraf* has three syllables. In trying to fit *teligraf* into the old patterns, one of the poets created several awkward lines before inventing a new formula to fit the word. This example shows that a particular line of verse is determined both by the concepts to be expressed and by the available formulas. If there is no ready-made formula to express a given idea, the poet must invent one before expressing the idea in well-formed verse.

Although the Serbocroatian bards work in a highly constrained form, in a language with complex inflections, and in verse with strict meter, they do not perceive the constraints as problems to be solved by conscious decisions. Native speakers of inflected languages simply say the right form because it "sounds right." Instead of counting syllables, the poets make the verse fit their traditional melodies. Certain formulas always occur at the same positions in the melody, just as certain case endings always go with the same verbs or prepositions. The melody is not a decorative accompaniment, but a blueprint for the creation of verse. Without music, the metrical constraints are relaxed, but the guidelines are also gone. Lord found that many of the poets could not recite a poem without musical accompaniment. In

Joey is a sissy.
Sally has a boy friend.
Nya-nya nya nya nyaah nyah.

Fig. 2.6 A formulaic incantation

the Homeric *Hymn to Hermes*, C. A. Sowa (1983) observed that Hermes speaks of consulting the lyre as though it were an oracle—as though the melody were the source of the verse rather than an auxiliary decoration. Peabody noted that constraints of melody and form are not obstacles to be overcome. They actually aid composition by reducing the number of choices the poet has to make.

The effect of formulas in modern speech is illustrated by a series of television commercials in 1972 that established a particular formula as a fad:

```
I can't believe I ate the who-o-ole thing.
```

In this formula, *ate* may be replaced by another verb, *thing* may be replaced by another noun, and the second *I* may be replaced by another pronoun. After an inept baseball game in which the Mets gave up a large lead, a sports announcer said:

```
I can't believe they blew the who-o-ole game.
```

After winning three primary elections in one night, Senator McGovern told his supporters:

```
I can't believe we won the who-o-ole thing.
```

This formula illustrates the dominance of strict metrical and syntactic shape: the lengthening of the word *whole* occurs in every variation, a pronoun is always replaced by another pronoun, and the one-syllable verb *ate* is always replaced by another one-syllable verb. The baseball announcer and Senator McGovern were probably as unconscious of the metrical rules as the oral poets, yet they applied them as precisely as a computer. Other formulas are used in greetings, rituals, and games. Figure 2.6 shows a formulaic incantation that children use for teasing other children. As in oral poetry, this formula is set to a melody that determines the number of syllables and the points of stress. The mocking form is so effective that even with meaningless syllables it can send a child home crying.

Oral composition is an extension of normal linguistic mechanisms. The rules of oral poetry are like a second grammar that operates with the primary grammar of a language. Yet formulaic composition is incompatible with transformational grammar. According to Chomsky (1965), the grammar of a language contains two com-

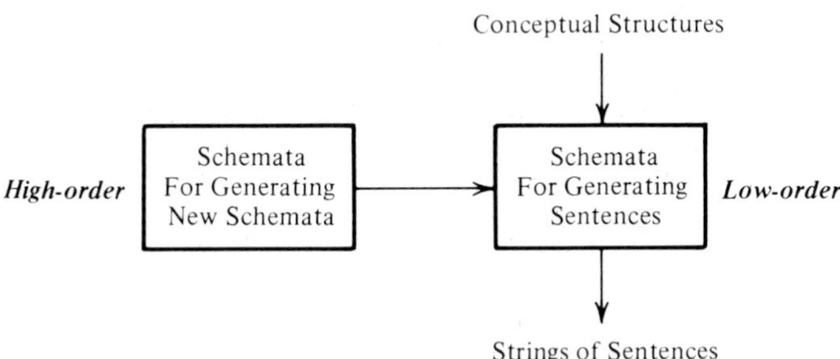

Fig. 2.7 High-order and low-order schemata for language

ponents: the *base component* generates strings of words with associated structural descriptions; then the *transformational component* converts the base strings into the *surface structures* of spoken sentences. Oral poets, however, assemble their verses directly from formulas, which are units of surface structure. The generation of a line of verse depends on two factors: the meaning the poet wants to express and the stock of formulas available for various surface structures.

The difference between mastery of a grammar and mastery of formulas corresponds to the difference between theory and practice. A student can study Latin grammar for four years without learning to speak a single coherent sentence in the language. But a conversational training course can drill students in the formulas of a difficult language like Japanese and have them speaking fluent sentences after a few days. Fluent speech on a few topics, however, is quite different from total mastery. The students learn enough vocabulary to order food or ask directions, but they cannot carry on a conversation about business or politics. Torrey (1969) did experiments in teaching Russian that showed the importance of both oral drill and conventional study of grammar. The drill develops fluency, but the study of grammar can generalize the skills to a wider range of topics.

Fries's (1952) emphasized *sentence frames*, which are surface patterns similar to formulas. Chomsky emphasized *production rules* for generating patterns as they are needed. Both theories capture an important aspect of the psychological processes. Rapid speech is generated directly from pre-existing sentence frames. A speaker who is struggling with a complex idea, however, can generate new sentence frames by applying the general production rules. Fries's theory and Chomsky's theory can be reconciled by assuming that a speaker has a repertoire of *low-order schemata* that resemble formulas, and *high-order schemata* that can generate new low-order schemata for all possible formulas. Figure 2.7 shows the relationship between the high-order schemata that generate new sentence frames and the low-order schemata that generate fluent speech. The left box corresponds to Chomsky's production rules, and the right box is Fries' list of sentence frames.

At the highest levels of language, schemata represent thematic units, which may be combined to form the plot of a story or the structure of an argument. In extending the techniques of Parry and Lord, C. A. Sowa (1983) developed a three-level classification of the schemata for generating oral poetry:

- *Formulas* operate at the level of short phrases or single lines of verse. They generate the syntactic and metrical patterns in poetry.
- *Type scenes* are stylized settings that extend from a few lines to a few dozen lines. Examples from ancient Greek include calling an assembly, exchanging gifts, battle scenes, or dancing and picking flowers.
- *Themes* are plot structures that govern a complete poem or a major subplot. Examples include the hero's birth and growth to maturity, the marriage of the fertility goddess, and the journey across the water.

Formulas are limited to one language. Type scenes are characteristic of a culture, but they can be translated to other languages. Themes, however, are universal: the same patterns found in ancient epics occur in African folk tales and Hollywood movies. Within a story, one theme controls the plot from beginning to end, while related subthemes govern the episodes and subplots. These structures reflect universal mechanisms for organizing, remembering, and telling stories.

Although Homer could compose the *Iliad* and *Odyssey* a thousand times faster than Vergil composed the *Aeneid*, the intellectual effort they expended was more nearly comparable. Homer may have sung the entire *Odyssey* during a week-long festival, but he must have spent twenty, thirty years or more in mastering the formulas, type scenes, and themes from which he assembled it. The intellectual effort in oral composition may be compared with the performance of a chess player during a difficult match. When two grandmasters spend four hours on a single game, the struggle is physically and mentally exhausting. Yet their efforts during the game are almost insignificant compared to twenty years of study and play when they build up their repertoire of schemata. The years of work by the chess master or the years of rehearsals and performances by the master bard are periods of intense creativity, each insight of which is crystallized in a schema that lies ready for future use. An actual performance by the bard, like a chess game by the grandmaster, draws upon a rich storehouse of creative insights and techniques for applying them.

Homer's high-speed style of creating poetry relied on mechanisms closer to fluent speech than Vergil's painstaking search for elegant variations. Like oral bards, people would have no time to consider meaning if they had to coin a totally new phrase every second. Parry and Lord considered the degree of formulaic structure a criterion for distinguishing oral poetry from written literature. Finnegan (1981), however, cited modern Swahili and Somali literature, where oral forms and patterns are freely borrowed in written styles. She found that one of the best Limba story tellers happened to have a college education, but his stories had the same structure and formulaic style as those told by totally illiterate narrators. None of Finnegan's examples disprove the importance of formulas in oral composition. If anything, they show that formulaic patterns are also used in writing.

Chess, speech, writing, poetry, jazz, and reading music all depend on schemata that span a larger configuration than a single word, musical note, or chess piece. Other intellectual activities, such as computer programming, must also rely on high-level patterns for speed and accuracy. In fact, the methods of structured programming teach programmers to think in larger patterns than single instructions. Yet research in programming is still in its infancy. If a master chess player uses 25,000 schemata, a master programmer would certainly need more than the half-dozen patterns commonly identified with structured programming.

Notopoulos (1959) observed that the formulaic structure of modern Greek epic reflects society in the Greek village, which is "completely traditional and formulaic in all its activities. The peasant is born in a formulaic tradition of attitudes, beliefs, expressions whose roots go back ultimately to classical Greece." Behavioral schemata are no less important in modern societies: Kelly (1955) developed his theory of *personal constructs* for analyzing the patterns that people use in perceiving the world and responding to it. In anthropology, Lévi-Strauss (1963) showed that similar patterns organize every aspect of a culture, including the way people interpret their relationships with each other and with the universe. In AI, Minsky (1975) showed the importance of schemata, which he called *frames*.

2.5 WORKING REGISTERS

William James (1890) distinguished two types of memory: primary or *short-term memory*, which maintains consciousness of the immediate past; and secondary or *long-term memory*, which is "knowledge of a former state of mind after it has already once dropped from consciousness." Although consciousness is a private experience, it is correlated with measurable activity in the cerebral cortex. By mapping the most active areas on a television monitor, Luria (1973) observed "the way in which the point of optimal excitation in fact arises in the cortex of a waking animal, the pattern of its movement over the cortex, and the way in which it loses its mobility, becomes inert, and, finally, is completely extinguished as the animal passes into a state of sleep or, even more obviously, in a dying animal" (p. 44).

The point of optimal excitation focuses activity in certain areas of the cortex, leaving other areas less active. Because of the focusing effect, items not at the center of attention tend to fade away. This effect can be shown experimentally: give subjects a few words to remember, and before they recall the words, have them perform another task, such as counting backwards by threes (e.g. 597, 594, 591...). Without the intervening task, subjects have almost perfect recall after periods of about 20 seconds; but with the task, they cannot recall the words (Peterson & Peterson 1959).

Imagining a scene, performing complex actions, thinking about abstract subjects, and doing mental arithmetic are activities that use different areas of the cortex. Yet a person can do only one complex activity at a time and at most two or three routine activities. In driving a car, for example, a person can carry on a conversation as long as the road is straight and the traffic is light. In that case, the driver's responses are almost automatic, and all of short-term memory can be devoted to the conversation. But at a traffic circle with cars changing lanes and merging from both sides, the driver's conversation quickly stops. When one activity pre-empts the point of optimal excitation, the other activities fade away.

Short-term memory is not dedicated to any particular sensory mode. Instead, it interacts with projection areas in the cerebral cortex for each of the senses. Sperling (1963) did experiments that emphasize the auditory form. He showed subjects a series of words including some that look different, but are pronounced alike, such as *scene* and *seen*. The errors in recall indicate that subjects remember words in an auditory form because they confused words that sound the same. Shepard (1966), however, emphasized the importance of imagery. He asked subjects, "How many windows are in your house?" Almost no one can answer that question immediately. Instead, a person has to generate the number, probably by taking a mental tour of the house, visualizing each room, and counting the windows. Familiar motor activities also have no verbal associations: a person cannot explain how to tie a shoestring without going through the motions, either physically or mentally.

Long-term memories are stored in the cerebral cortex, but other parts of the brain, the hippocampus in particular, play an important role. Milner (1970) observed patients with hippocampal lesions who had normal short-term memory, could recall events of their early lives from long-term memory, yet had total amnesia for events since the lesions. One patient, H.M., could carry on a normal conversation, yet five minutes later, could not remember that the conversation had even existed. After the lesion, he never learned to recognize doctors and nurses he had been seeing daily for years. Milner observed that "forgetting occurred the instant his focus of attention shifted, but in the absence of distraction his capacity for sustained attention was remarkable. Thus, he was able to retain the number 584 for at least 15 minutes, by continuously working out elaborate mnemonic schemes. When asked how he had been able to retain the number for so long, he replied:

> It's easy. You just remember 8. You see 5, 8, and 4 add to 17. You remember 8, subtract it from 17 and it leaves 9. Divide 9 in half and you get 5 and 4 and there you are: 584. Easy.

"A minute or so later, H.M. was unable to recall either the number 584 or any of the associated complex train of thought; in fact, he did not know that he had been given a number to remember because, in the meantime, the examiner had introduced a new topic." Although H.M. could not add new events to long-term memory, his working memory for the tasks measured by IQ tests, was unimpaired by the lesion. His IQ score actually rose from 104 before the lesion to 112 afterwards; the improvement in arithmetic was particularly striking (Scoville & Milner 1957).

Hippocampal lesions do not completely block semantic memory, but they disturb the organization of episodic memory. H.M. and similar patients were able to learn new semantic categories and conditioned responses. They could not, however, organize new facts into episodes classified by time and place. O'Keefe and Nadel (1978) concluded that the primary function of the hippocampus is to form cognitive maps. It organizes spatial relations into a map of the environment and combines separate facts into coherent units or episodes. Hippocampal lesions also disturb spatial relations in both short-term and long-term memory. Although H.M. could use short-term memory for the encoded, symbolic operations measured by IQ tests, he could not store unencoded images for even a few seconds.

The inability of short-term memory to hold unencoded images suggests that it does not contain actual data, but pointers to previously stored memories. Broadbent (1971) maintained that information is recorded in only two forms: transient excitations and long-term records. He compared short-term memory to *address registers* in a computer. The registers themselves do not store data; instead, they point to data held in another storage medium. Records in the cortex are normally held in an inactive, latent state. Short-term memory consists of a limited number of *working registers*, each of which excites or activates some record in long-term storage. The point of optimal excitation in the cortex is a reflection of the underlying working registers. The contents of short-term memory are the activated records in the cortex; the registers that do the activating are supported by the lower brain stem.

If short-term memory is maintained by working registers, a basic question is how many registers are available. Ever since Miller's famous paper, "The Magic Number Seven, Plus or Minus Two," the supposed answer has been about *seven.* Using a variety of evidence, Miller showed that short-term memory can hold about seven *chunks* of information, where a chunk is the amount of information in a schema—a single bit, a decimal digit, a word, or a phrase. The basic property of a chunk is not its size, but its unity as a well-learned, familiar pattern. Even the complete sentence *A stitch in time saves nine* could be stored as a single chunk if it is familiar. Despite the evidence for seven chunks, Broadbent (1975) argued that a better estimate is three working registers rather than seven:

- Although the average span of short-term memory is about seven items, only three or four items can be recalled with a high degree of accuracy.
- Extra items beyond three or four are remembered accurately only if they have associations to other items in the list.
- When people recall items from a familiar category, such as European countries, colors of the rainbow, or the names of the seven dwarfs, they tend to group their responses in bursts of two or three.

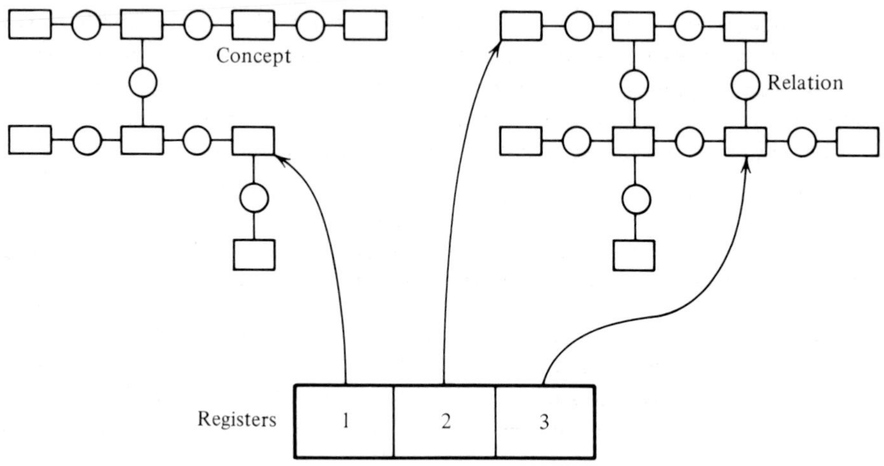

Fig. 2.8 Working registers and schemata

To explain how three registers can lead to an average memory span of seven chunks, Broadbent suggested that the working registers behave like input-output buffers between a processing unit and main memory. When new sensory stimulation comes in, three chunks can be held in the registers. Then the chunks are dispatched to memory as a unit, and the registers can accept new data. When output is generated, the working registers direct attention to the items selected from long-term memory. With three registers, short-term memory can retain three chunks with high reliability. To recall six chunks, the first three chunks in the working registers would be uttered, and the previous group of three, which may be fading rapidly, would be retrieved. The possibility of retaining nine chunks would depend on how fast the chunks fade away when the working registers are directed to other items.

Short-term memory is not just a faster version of long-term memory, but a mechanism based on completely different principles. Using the working registers as memory is about as efficient as using a helicopter to hold up a clothesline. Like the helicopter, the working registers are dynamic and require a continuous flow of energy to remain stationary. When necessary, they can keep a small amount of data active, say a telephone number, just as the helicopter can hover above the ocean while rescuing a shipwrecked sailor. Their function as memory is an artifact of psychological experiments that more easily measure their storage capacity than their dynamic mode of operation.

In normal operation, the working registers are operating units that keep track of active schemata. The size of a chunk depends on the size of a schema, not the size of the register. To join formulas in oral poetry or normal speech, the appropriate schemata are selected and combined. To build a working model that matches sensory input, percepts and schemata are activated and fit together. Figure 2.8 illustrates the way working registers select active schemata. Register 1 points to one schema; Registers 2 and 3 point to different concepts in another schema. With the limited number of registers, some operations are easier to perform than others. Miller and Isard (1964) considered sentences with multiple relative clauses:

```
We cheered the football squad that played the team that brought
the mascot that chased the girls that were in the park.
The girls that the mascot that the team that the football squad
that we cheered played brought chased were in the park.
```

When spoken at a normal rate, the first sentence can be understood, although few people would remember all the isolated relationships. In the second sentence, the clauses are too deeply embedded to be understood as normal speech. Mental grammar rules cannot parse sentences that require too many working registers. Broadbent's suggestion of three registers is consistent with the PARSIFAL program by Marcus (1980): for parsing normal English, Marcus found that three lookahead buffers were sufficient for a deterministic parse if each buffer could hold an arbitrarily large chunk.

2.6 RECOGNITION AND RECALL

Recognition memory is more accurate than unaided recall, and its total capacity is enormous. Shepard (1967) had subjects look through a series of 612 pictures. In a later test, he presented pairs of pictures to the subjects. One member of each pair belonged to the original series, and one member was new. The subjects had to indicate which picture they had seen before. After two hours, the subjects' recognition rate was nearly 100% accurate. After three days, their rate was still 93%; after a week, 92%; and after four months, 57%. Standing (1973) extended Shepard's technique to a series of 10,000 pictures shown over a period of several days. Even for such a long series, the subjects recognized over 90% of them. Since the subjects had little interest in the pictures, they could only recall a small fraction of them. Yet their recognition memory was nearly perfect for short intervals and remarkably good for long intervals.

The simplest hypothesis for explaining the difference between recognition and recall is the *threshold theory*: a weak memory trace is sufficient for recognition, but a stronger trace, exceeding some minimum threshold, is necessary for recall. The *two-process theory*, however, maintains that recognition is a process for checking the familiarity of an image, but recall involves a separate process of retrieval or reconstruction. These two theories raise several complex issues:

- Is there one memory process or two?
- If there are two processes, is recall a simple act of retrieval or a more complex reconstruction?

- Is the memory trace an unprocessed record of a sensory icon, or is it encoded in a conceptual form?
- What mechanisms are used for memory, and what is their relationship to the mechanisms of perception?

The question of one process or two can be resolved by studying the conditions that aid recognition or recall. According to the threshold theory, ease of recognition and ease of recall are directly correlated: anything that improves one must strengthen the memory trace and would also improve the other. Kintsch (1970), however, showed that recall depends on more complex conditions:

- The intention to learn an item improves recall, but has no effect on recognition.
- Items that are difficult to recall may be just as easy to recognize as items that are much easier to recall.
- Structure is important for recall, but irrelevant for recognition.

These three points rule out the threshold theory. Recognition may depend largely on the strength of the trace, but recall depends on the structure of the information and the associations that link it to other things in memory.

Since multiple associations improve recall, some searching must take place. The importance of structure, however, indicates reconstruction. Claparède (1911) showed subjects a series of pictures and asked them to write descriptions of each picture from memory. One description was, "A large basket full of flowers." Upon seeing the picture again, the subject remarked, "I thought it was flowers, but I see it is fruit; I thought the basket was square and lighter in color. Now I remember having seen the apples and pears." Such examples suggest a reconstruction: a simple search would recover information in the way it was stored and would not convert a basket of fruit into a basket of flowers. Since subjects can recognize an image more accurately than they can recall it, the process of recognition must have access to a memory trace in a more accurate, perhaps image-like form. Recall is more of a guessing game: the process of reconstruction must first assemble a trial image and then test it for familiarity. But retrieval must also take place: the pieces must be found before a trial image can be constructed.

What people reconstruct depends on the concepts and schemata that they have for the construction. Piaget (1968) described an experiment where the subjects used two different sets of schemata—one when they first saw the image and another when they recalled it. Children were shown a series of ten sticks, ordered from the longest to the shortest. They were told to have a good look so that they could draw the configuration later. Without seeing the sticks again, the children were asked to draw them a week later and again six months later. After one week, what the children remembered is characteristic of their age level:

- *Level a* (3 to 4 years). Some sticks lined up, but all of the same length.
- *Level b* (4 to 5 years). Some long sticks and some short sticks, but only two sizes.

- *Level c* (4 to 5 years). Three groups of sticks—long, medium, and short.
- *Level d* (5 to 6 years). A series graded from long to short, but with only four or five sticks.
- *Level e* (6 to 7 years). A series like the original with about ten sticks.

After six months, all the children claimed that they remembered the original series of sticks. What is surprising is that none of their memories had deteriorated after six months, and 74% of them had actually *improved*. Most of the improvements were of one or two levels: from *a* to *b*, *b* to *c*, or *c* to *d*. If the memory had been stored as an unprocessed image, it might deteriorate, but it could never improve. If it had been stored in a conceptual encoding, recall would bring back the same concepts that had been stored, but not a better set. But if recall involves reconstruction, the form constructed by the children could improve learned new concepts and schemata.

Some memories, called *eidetic images*, are stored with the accuracy of a photograph (Haber 1979). After looking at a scene for a minute or so, an eidetic subject can recall a vastly greater number of details than an ordinary person. But if the subject is asked to name the things while looking at them, only the named items tend to be remembered. The act of naming forces a conceptual encoding, and the subject loses the unprocessed image. Luria (1968) reported the case of the Russian mnemonist Shereshevskii, who had extremely well-developed imagery and eidetic memory. He could recall vast amounts of information accurately after periods of fifteen years. His memory was so vast that Luria stopped trying to measure its total capacity. Paradoxically, Shereshevskii had such a perfect memory for faces that he had difficulty in recognizing people. If he saw a man laughing, he had an perfect image of the laughing face, but could not associate it with the same man with a sad face. Shereshevskii once lost a job as a newspaper reporter despite his perfect memory. Although he could record events perfectly, he could not abstract significant facts from irrelevant detail. The man relied so heavily on direct associations between images that he never developed the concepts needed for abstract thinking.

Associations between memory units, either images or concepts, are apparent in tip-of-the-tongue phenomena, in the recall of dreams, and in hysterical amnesias. Nemiah (1969) discussed several cases of amnesia that show how memories form complex, interlocking systems. In one case, a man tried to kill his sister-in-law and then shot himself in the head.

> The patient recovered; but for more than 2 years thereafter, systematically repeated testing of his mental functioning revealed a total loss of memory for a period that extended from a month before his homicidal-suicidal act to a date 40 days after the event. Suddenly, 2 years and 3 months later, all the particulars of the impulsive event returned to him in a dream that remained in consciousness when he awoke. Soon he recovered all his lost memory, except, as the case history concludes, "There persisted only a short gap in memory corresponding to the period of post-traumatic confusion."

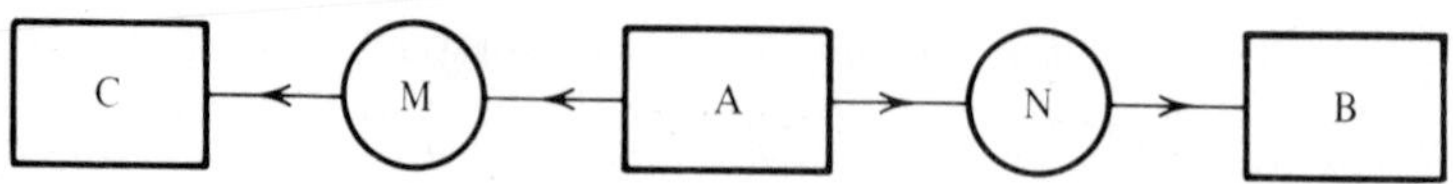

Fig. 2.9 Sample structure in long-term memory

A complete segment of the patient's life was lost, just as if it had been a list structure in computer storage to which a key pointer was destroyed. Whether the segment was lost because of Freudian repression or because of brain damage caused by the bullet, the critical point is that it was lost and subsequently recovered as a complete system of memories. Other examples cited by Nemiah also show that memories lost in amnesias are not isolated facts, but complete systems. The most striking examples are the cases of multiple personality where a patient has alternate systems of memory, each with distinct patterns of behavior. The patient in one state has total amnesia for events that occur in the other states. Memory is organized in episodes and larger contexts of related episodes.

According to Selz's theory of *schematic anticipation*, recall is triggered by a partially completed schema as the memory probe. Suppose that long-term memory contains a concept A linked by relation M to a concept C and linked by relation N to a concept B (Fig. 2.9). When a new copy of A is presented, the associative comparator compares it to all other items in long-term memory. When a match is made, A is *recognized*. To *recall* B or C, a working register must select some schema that anticipates the form of the desired information. Figure 2.10 shows two schemata, each of which matches part of the graph in Fig. 2.9. The question marks serve as *control marks* that direct attention to the unfilled slots. Since the first schema in Fig. 2.10 matches the right side of Fig. 2.9, the control mark would be replaced by the matching concept B. Since the second schema matches the left side of Fig. 2.9, its control mark would be replaced by C.

Selz's theory, although 70 years old, represents a fundamental advance beyond associationism and even beyond the more modern behaviorism, which retained associations but called them stimulus-response chains. According to associationism, the idea A (or stimulus A in behaviorist terms) might lead to idea B (response B) or to idea C (response C). To simulate the effects of learning, some theories increase the probability of a response with repeated associations. Other versions sum up the probabilities so that the combined effect of A and N would have a better chance of leading to B than to C. Selz's theory leaves nothing to chance. It is based on an exact matching of structures rather than a random choice. No matter what the relative probabilities might be, the first schema in Fig. 2.10 would always select B, and the second would always select C.

The associative comparator and the assembler, which were originally proposed as mechanisms of perception, can also serve as mechanisms of memory. In recognizing a sensory icon, the associative comparator compares it with all the records stored in

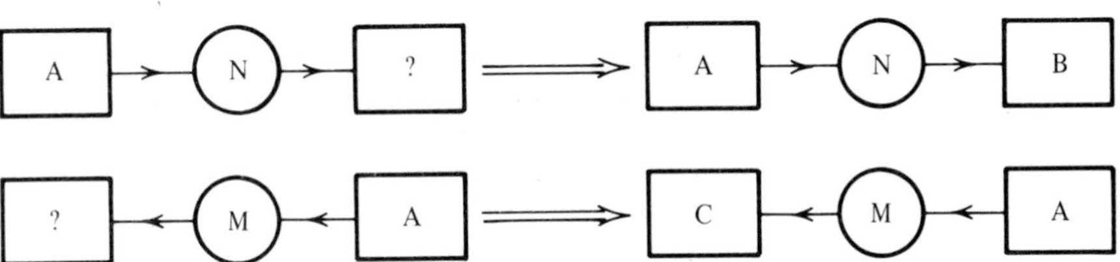

Fig. 2.10 Recall by means of schematic anticipation

long-term memory. For recall, the assembler can join schemata to construct a memory probe. Then the associative comparator can test the probe for recognition and retrieve associated material for recall. As Piaget observed, memory improves in the same measure as perception improves. A better selection of schemata for perception also constitutes a better selection for recall.

2.7 CENTRAL CONTROLLER

In computer systems, a basic part of the CPU is a *sequencer* that controls the low-level, repetitive details of executing instructions: fetching them from main storage, decoding them, computing the address of the data, fetching the data, doing the actual computation, and going on to the next instruction. By themselves, the instructions in computer storage are static data that can do nothing. The sequencer is a simple, repetitive pulse generator. Together, the static data and the simple sequencer are responsible for all the complex behavior of modern computers. Like instructions in a computer, conceptual graphs are static data. To control the linear flow of speech and other behavior, some unit must convert the static data into an ordered sequence of activity. That unit is called the *central controller.*

Lesions of the frontal lobes can cause a sequence of activity to disintegrate into isolated actions. Luria (1966) therefore believed that the frontal lobes must play a major role in regulating activity. Pribram (1973) called them the "executive of the brain," which directs attention to significant stimuli, inhibits distracting stimuli, and maintains the context for organized behavior. Grueninger and Grueninger (1973) suggested that the frontal lobes act like "a finger on the page" that keeps track of the current plan that an animal is following. Without it, the animal cannot return to a sequence that has been temporarily interrupted. The following kinds of evidence point to the frontal lobes as a major control unit:

- Patients with the largest lesions of the frontal lobes "usually lie passively, express no wishes or desires and make no requests; not even a state of hunger can rouse them to take the necessary action" (Luria 1973, p. 198).

- Walter (1973) studied *expectancy waves*, which arise in the frontal lobes and spread across the cerebral cortex when a person is anticipating a stimulus that requires a response. When the person is told that a response is no longer required, the expectancy waves are immediately extinguished.

- Livanov et al. (1973) found that when a person is solving a complex problem, the frontal lobes are highly active and contain many points whose activity is strongly correlated with other points in the cortex. The degree of correlation depends on the complexity of the task. A problem will stimulate a higher degree of correlation in a novice who finds it difficult than in an expert who solves it automatically.

- A dog with its frontal lobes excised can learn and respond to conditioned stimuli, but it is extremely distractible. It always responds to the latest stimulus, and any distraction will divert it from the previous course of action.

- Removal of the frontal lobes increases an animal's responsiveness to novel stimuli, but it significantly decreases orienting reactions, such as the galvanic skin response. The removal causes a decrease in concentration or direction of thought to a specific goal.

- Filippycheva (1952) found that patients who had extensive lesions of the frontal lobes could perform routine actions like putting out a match or smoking a cigarette. But if they were asked to light a match, they could not stop—they would repeatedly strike a match that was already burning. For actions that were not as familiar, the patients had even more difficulty. After lighting a candle, the patient would put it in his mouth as if it were a cigarette or break it as if it were a match. (Cited by Luria 1966, p. 237)

- Lobotomized monkeys have difficulty in completing an organized sequence of actions. But Pribram (1973) found that they could perform almost as well as normal monkeys if the input stimuli were supplemented with appropriate flags, markers, or rhythmic grouping. He concluded that external markers play the role of the frontal lobes in providing a context: the frontal lobes are an internal source of directives for organizing perception and controlling behavior.

Markers organize space, and rhythmic grouping organizes time. Lashley (1951) considered spatial patterns and time sequences as an underlying substratum of all organized activity, of every perception and every coordinated movement. To explain how a spatial pattern could be transformed into a time sequence, Lashley assumed that some mechanism must scan one representation and map it into the other. He cited the problem of playing a melody backwards: "I find that I can do it only by visualizing the music spatially and then reading it backward. I cannot auditorily transform even 'Yankee Doodle' into its inverse without some such process, but it is possible to get a spatial representation of the melody and then to scan the spatial representation" (p. 129).

Music and speech are two kinds of rhythmic activities in which a static pattern must be scanned to produce a time-varying sequence of behavior. In considering the underlying forms of thought from which the sequences of music and speech are produced, James (1890) cited Mozart's description of his usual method of composing:

> First bits and crumbs of the piece come and gradually join together in his mind; then the soul getting warmed to the work, the thing grows more and more, "and I spread it out broader and clearer, and at last it gets almost finished in my head, even when it is a long piece, so that I can see the whole of it at a single glance in my mind, as if it were a beautiful painting or a handsome human being; in which way I do not hear it in my imagination at all as a succession—the way it must come later—but all at once, as it were. It is a rare feast! All the inventing and making goes on in me as in a beautiful strong dream. But the best of all is the *hearing of it all at once*." (p. 255)

James discussed the way people anticipate the form of an argument before they frame it in words. Mozart's ability to "see" an entire piece of music at a single glance is like a writer's ability to see the structure of a story or a mathematician's ability to see the structure of a proof.

To scan a mental image when playing a melody backwards, Lashley had to devote conscious attention to the task. But the process of scanning a conceptual graph in normal speech is outside the range of consciousness. In fact, this point raises a basic question about consciousness: is it merely an *epiphenomenon* that accompanies neural activity, or is it an active process that controls the activity? The most likely hypothesis is that *consciousness* is a feedback mechanism from the association cortex of the brain that can reconstruct and reinterpret the contents of the sensory cortex:

- Consciousness focuses attention by directing the assembler and the associative comparator to the highest priority contents of the cortex.
- The contents of consciousness consist of the interplay of images on the projection areas of the cortex. Those images could arise either from sensory stimulation or from internal processes.
- Since internally generated images have the same nature as sensory icons, consciousness enables the brain to analyze and reinterpret internal images with the same perceptual mechanisms used for sensory input.
- Since concepts are not perceptible images or fragments of images, conceptual processes are outside the range of consciousness. But concrete concepts with associated percepts can be mapped to images that are accessible to consciousness.
- Although conceptual graphs are not consciously accessible, the graphs may be mapped to auditory images called inner speech that is accessible to consciousness.
- Conscious reflection is the use of perceptual mechanisms to reanalyze and reinterpret inner speech.

Only sensory icons and the internally generated images that resemble icons are accessible to consciousness. Since the association areas of the human cortex are much larger than the sensory projection areas, unconscious conceptual processes may be much more extensive than conscious imagery. Even though introspection cannot "see" a conceptual graph, it can "hear" the inner speech into which the graph is mapped. Consciousness therefore supports *higher-order relations* for thinking about thinking. But it requires indirect mappings from concepts to inner speech and back to concepts.

Consciousness directs attention to the highest priority contents, but emotions set the priorities. By themselves, conceptual structures form a static representation of knowledge. Emotions are the driving forces that set goals and determine which structures to process. Arieti's classification of emotions (from Arieti & Bemporad 1978, pp. 114-117) emphasizes the interdependence of emotion and cognition:

- First-order or simple emotions are direct experiences of inner bodily status: tension, appetite, fear, rage, and satisfaction.
- Second-order emotions depend on cognitive processes that evoke images associated with first-order emotions: anxiety, anger, wishing, and security.
- Third-order emotions involve complex conceptual processes that depend heavily on past experiences and future expectations: love, hate, joy, and sadness.

Whereas fear and rage are responses to immediate stimuli, anxiety and anger are imagined fear and imagined rage that may be felt at times and places far removed from the stimuli. Yet second-order emotions are still closely related to first-order ones. Third-order emotions depend on extremely complex and indirect cognitive processes. Trying to relate a person's feelings of love and hate to instances of first-order emotions may take years of psychoanalysis.

Instead of a classification of emotions on based on psychoanalysis, Altman (1978) based a similar hierarchy on neurophysiology. He distinguished three levels of mental processing, supported by different strata in the brain:

- *Pathic level.* The *paleocephalon*, which includes the brain stem and limbic system, is the dominant part of the brain in fishes and lower vertebrates. In human beings, it is the seat of the great driving forces of the first-order emotions.
- *Iconic level.* The *neencephalon* is the cerebral cortex, which becomes prominent in mammals. It supports the percepts and the projection areas for sensory icons that make up the "pictures in the head" of conscious awareness. The ability to imagine fearsome or pleasurable states is a prerequisite for the second-order emotions of anxiety and wishing.
- *Noetic level.* The *anthropocephalon* is the dominant hemisphere of the human brain, which supports speech and abstract symbol manipulation. The use of symbols for analyzing and reflecting upon images is responsible for the most complex forms of thinking and the richness of the third-order emotions.

Classification of phenomena and the neural structures that support them is a necessary step towards understanding them. But it does not yet show how these three levels operate by themselves and interact with each other. That neurophysiology and psychoanalysis should converge on a similar classification is promising. But little is known about the mechanisms that enable pathic forces to set priorities for percepts and schemata at the iconic and noetic levels.

Once a schema is selected, it remains available for directing the thinking process until a state of *closure* is attained. The Gestalt psychologists first applied the principle of closure to perception and later generalized it to thinking: "A problem presents itself as an open Gestalt which *yearns* for solution, and it is the function of thought to find the solution by transforming the open Gestalt into a closed one" (Reiser 1931). An anecdote about the psychologist Kurt Lewin illustrates the effect of closure (Boring 1950, p. 734):

> Lewin and his friends were in a restaurant in Berlin, in the sort of prolonged conversation which always surrounded Lewin. It was a long time since they had ordered and the waiter hovered in the distance. Lewin called him over, asked what he owed, was told instantly and paid, but the conversation went on. Presently Lewin had an insight. He called the waiter back and asked him how much he had been paid. The waiter no longer knew.

One of Lewin's students, Bluma Zeigarnik (1927), pursued this insight with controlled experiments. She had her subjects perform various tasks, such as drawing figures or making models out of paper or clay. She interrupted all the subjects in the middle of the tasks and gave them some distracting task. After the interruption, she allowed some of the subjects to return to the original task and complete it, but the others were dismissed for the day. On the next day, she tested the subjects' ability to recall the details of the interrupted tasks. The result, which has become known as the *Zeigarnik effect*, was that those subjects who had not been allowed to complete their tasks had a better memory of the details than those who went back to the tasks and finished them.

Since Zeigarnik's original experiment, other studies have shown that interruption alone is not the most critical factor (Van Bergen 1968). Closure is more fundamental: the unfilled slots in a schema are flagged with *control marks* that keep the schema active until the slots are filled. In his theory of schematic anticipation, Selz proposed a hierarchy of anticipations and their closures: control marks on a high-level schema may trigger lower-level schemata, each of which may be flagged with control marks that trigger other schemata. In oral composition, for example, a schema for a major theme has slots for various subthemes, which trigger schemata for type scenes, which trigger schemata for formulas, which trigger schemata for words and phrases. When all the schemata for the low-level structures have attained closure, the next higher level is closed, but the highest level schema remains unsatisfied until all its dependent schemata have attained closure. R. Miller (1968) related the hierarchy of closures to the acceptable response times at a computer terminal: a person is willing to wait several minutes for the execution of a major program, a second or for two for a subtask, but no perceptible time whatever for low-level tasks such as typing a single character.

With emotions to set the goals and with the associative comparator and assembler as the major processing units, the chunks, working registers, schemata, expectancy waves, control marks, and closures provide the mechanisms for an intelligent processor. All these components were proposed by psychologists on the basis of traditional psychological evidence. Yet they fit together to form a system that looks remarkably like an AI program:

- The first step in an ordered chain of thought is the selection of a conceptual graph that anticipates the form of the desired goal.
- Certain concepts in the graph are flagged with control marks. Each control mark triggers expectancy waves, which stimulate the associative comparator to find matching schemata.
- When the associative comparator finds a matching schema, the assembler joins it to the working graph. If the resulting graph satisfies the control marks, it attains a state of closure, and the expectancy waves are extinguished.
- The result of joining a schema to the working graph may cause control marks to be propagated to new nodes in the graph. The control marks on the new nodes then trigger further searching.
- The limited number of working registers limits the number of control marks that can be active at the same time. If there are more than three unsatisfied control marks, earlier ones are suspended until the more recent ones are satisfied.
- When control marks for recent subgoals attain closure, earlier control marks are reactivated until the original goal is satisfied.

This outline of how the brain works is far from complete, and many years of experiment and theory will be necessary to fill in the details. On the whole, however, it is highly compatible with current approaches in AI. After the formal theory of conceptual graphs has been presented, Section 4.7 discusses this outline as the basis for an intelligent processing unit.

EXERCISES

Carrying out controlled psychological experiments requires statistical analysis and careful attention to technique. Readers who have the background may choose to develop these exercises into more elaborate experiments. Other readers may treat them as suggestions for informal tests.

2.1 Perform some experiments to determine the effects of encoding information in terms of a discrete set of familiar percepts. Sample tests include the following:

■ Take a walk in the woods and find a large rock, an irregular boulder with a complex pattern of cracks, veins, moss, and lichen. Look at it for a minute or two; then describe it or draw it from memory. Next describe it or draw it while looking at it. How much difference is there in the two descriptions?

■ Write similar descriptions of other naturally occurring patterns, such as the grain in a wood table top, the blades of grass in one square foot of a lawn, or the patterns of foam, ripples, and waves in the ocean surf.

■ Write a description of some man-made object such as an automobile, a piece of furniture, or a building. How much difference is there between descriptions written with or without looking at the object? Are the differences greater or less than the differences for patterns occurring in nature?

2.2 Devise an experiment to test the hypothesis that discrete comparisons are necessary for accurate memory of continuous quantities. One possibility would be to hand subjects some blocks and other small objects and tell them to remember their sizes.

■ Give the control group no other instructions, but tell the test group to compare the objects to the length of their fingers, or some other reference marks.

■ Remove the objects, hand the subjects a ruler, and ask them to note the dimensions of the objects on the ruler.

■ After the subjects report their answers, ask the members of the control group whether they used any conscious strategy for comparing the objects to discrete reference marks.

Are there any significant differences between the control subjects who used no conscious comparisons, the control subjects who did use comparisons, and the test group who were told to make such comparisons? Would a significant difference be conclusive evidence for the hypothesis? Does the amount of time that the subjects spend in manipulating the blocks affect the results? What other factors might be significant? Can you devise a similar experiment to test the memory of sounds and temperatures?

2.3 Listen to (or tape record) informal conversations and note the formulaic phrases used in greetings, showing approval or disapproval, and introducing a new topic. Identify the formulas in some genre of newspaper or television reporting, such as stock market reports, sports stories, or weather reports. Distinguish the patterns that are common in the culture from those that are especially characteristic of individual speakers or writers.

2.4 Repeat Broadbent's experiments in asking people to name items from a familiar category (p. 53). Possible categories include names of cities, football teams, kitchen utensils, or classical composers. Tape record their responses in order to analyze them from different perspectives. How many items occur between pauses? Are there any patterns in the way subjects group items? In listing cities, for example, people might group them geographically or alphabetically. How do subjects differ in the way they group items from the same categories? Is there any correlation with age, experience, or education? Do the results support or conflict with the hypotheses about working registers and schemata?

2.5 This chapter began with the observation that human perception and digital computer processing are very different. Techniques of structured programming and human factors studies are attempts to bridge the communication gap between humans and computers. Review the experiments discussed in this chapter and think of modifications for testing the human factors of computer systems. Bartlett's study of what people remember from stories and pictures might show what features of a program are easiest to remember. What aspects of programming correspond to the formulas, type scenes, and themes of epic poetry? Does there exist a Zeigarnik effect for interrupted tasks on the computer? How might it affect people who switch between editing files and running programs at a terminal? All these factors interact in complicated ways, and initial guesses must be tested by carefully controlled experiments.

2.6 Write a proposal for a computer simulation of the central controller and the other units it interacts with. Assume that some memories are stored as unencoded images and others as conceptual graphs.

- Draw block diagrams showing each of the functional units and their interactions.
- Describe each unit, the kinds of representations it processes, the operations it performs on those representations, and the kinds of signals or data that it passes to the other units.
- How would you propose to map information from the image form to the conceptual form and back again?
- If someone designed an auxiliary processor with a very large associative memory, how could you use it in your system? What kinds of operations would you ask the designer to implement? Would you use it to store images or concepts or both? Would you want a different interface for the conceptual and image information?
- Finally, trace all the steps that occur in responding to the verbal request, *Please shut the door*. Discuss the formation and interpretation of the visual and auditory images, their mapping into a conceptual form, their interaction with a model of the room, the application of schemata for interpreting the sentence in terms of the current model, and the generation of images to control the motor mechanisms. Show what units would be invoked at each step and what operations they would perform.

This exercise could be answered by anything from a term paper to a major research project. First draw a one-page diagram with two or three pages of explanation. Continue elaborating and revising it as you read the remainder of the book.

SUGGESTED READING

For an introduction to cognitive psychology and its relationships to AI and linguistics, see *Human Information Processing* by Lindsay and Norman and *Cognitive Psychology and its Implications* by Anderson. Fodor (1981) discusses the philosophical and psychological arguments for mental representations of knowledge. Of all such representations, conceptual graphs and related systems are the most fully developed. Some psychological works that use versions of them are Norman, Rumelhart, et al. (1975), Anderson (1976), McNeill (1979), Anderson and Bower (1980), and Graesser (1981).

Psychology and Language by Clark and Clark is a comprehensive, but highly readable survey of psycholinguistics. See Klatzy (1980) for a review of experimental studies of memory and *Eyewitness Testimony* by Loftus for a study of the fallibility of memory. *Memory Observed* by Neisser is a collection of readings on memory that ranges from Sigmund Freud's analysis of childhood memories to Albert Lord's study of oral poets. For a general text on visual perception, see Spoehr and Lehmkuhle (1982); for more specialized work, see Kosslyn (1980) and Shepard and Cooper (1982). In *A Generative Theory of Tonal Music*, the composer Lerdahl and the linguist Jackendoff collaborated in analyzing the cognitive principles underlying music composition and perception. The *Readings in Philosophy of Psychology*, edited by Block, address issues of imagery, mental representations, and the relationships between language and thought.

The Essential Piaget, edited by Gruber and Vonèche, has selections from all of Piaget's major works together with explanatory comments. Boden (1981) presents a sympathetic comparison of Piaget's approach with the work in AI; Boden (1979) is a more detailed study of Piaget and the implications of his work for AI and cognitive science. For a debate between Jean Piaget and Noam Chomsky, see the book edited by Piattelli-Palmarini (1980); it covers theories of language and learning with extensive discussion by other psychologists, linguists, and philosophers.

Oral poetry has been studied by philologists and anthropologists, but it has largely been ignored by experimental psychologists. The classic book on the subject is Lord's *Singer of Tales*. More recent works have clarified or corrected the details, but have not altered Lord's overall conception, cf. Nagler (1974), Peabody (1975), C. A. Sowa (1983), and the collection of papers edited by Stolz and Shannon (1976). Propp (1958) analyzed the thematic structures of Russian folktales. Lévi-Strauss is a prolific writer whose work has an important bearing on the subject, but his ideas are difficult to quantify and organize in a formal theory; *Structural Anthropology* is a representative collection of his papers.

Otto Selz's work shows that AI techniques have a psychological motivation that is independent of computer-oriented research. For a recent survey of his work and its implications, see Frijda and de Groot (1981). Selz (1927) is one of the few articles that have been translated into English. For brief English summaries, see Humphrey (1951), de Groot (1965), and Kintsch (1974). From an AI point of view, the most interesting issues are the parallels between Selz's theories and computer techniques. Ironically, the Gestalt psychologists scorned Selz's work as "machine psychology."

Almost all computer languages and interfaces have been designed without controlled psychological experiments to evaluate design choices. Database query languages have been studied in more detail than most systems; see Reisner (1981) for a survey of that work. Shneiderman (1980) summarizes the psychological studies that were made up that time. The results are still tentative, however: a feature that looks poor in one context may turn out to be essential in a slightly changed context. Experience, good taste, sensitivity, comparative studies of systems, controlled psychological experiments, and testing with actual users—both novices and experts—is necessary for designing systems with good human factors.

Detailed issues of neuropsychology are not addressed in this book. For a brief survey, see *The Enlightened Machine* by D. Robinson. For more detailed introductions, see *The Working Brain* by Luria and *The Languages of the Brain* by Pribram. O'Keefe and Nadel (1978) analyze the evidence for cognitive maps in the brain and the mechanisms that support them. Caplan (1980) edited a collection of articles that relate mental processes to neural structures. For attempts to simulate the brain at a physiological level, see the books by Albus (1981), E. Kent (1981), and de Callatay (forthcoming). Hinton and Anderson (1981) edited a collection of papers on holographic and associative models. Those approaches begin with physiological evidence, while the present book starts with linguistics, psychology, and philosophy.

3
Conceptual Graphs

Conceptual graphs form a knowledge representation language based on linguistics, psychology, and philosophy. In the graphs, concept nodes represent entities, attributes, states, and events, and relation nodes show how the concepts are interconnected. This chapter defines the graphs formally, and the next chapter applies them to logic and computation.

3.1 PERCEPTS AND CONCEPTS

Perception is the process of building a *working model* that represents and interprets sensory input. The model has two components: a sensory part formed from a mosaic of *percepts*, each of which matches some aspect of the input; and a more abstract part called a *conceptual graph*, which describes how the percepts fit together to form the mosaic. Perception is based on the following mechanisms:

- Stimulation is recorded for a fraction of a second in a form called a *sensory icon*.
- The *associative comparator* searches long-term memory for percepts that match all or part of an icon.
- The *assembler* puts the percepts together in a working model that forms a close approximation to the input. A record of the assembly is stored as a conceptual graph.
- Conceptual mechanisms process *concrete concepts* that have associated percepts and *abstract concepts* that do not have any associated percepts.

When a person sees a cat, light waves reflected from the cat are received as a sensory icon *s*. The associative comparator matches *s* either to a single cat percept *p* or to a collection of percepts, which are combined by the assembler into a complete image. As the assembler combines percepts, it records the percepts and their intercon-

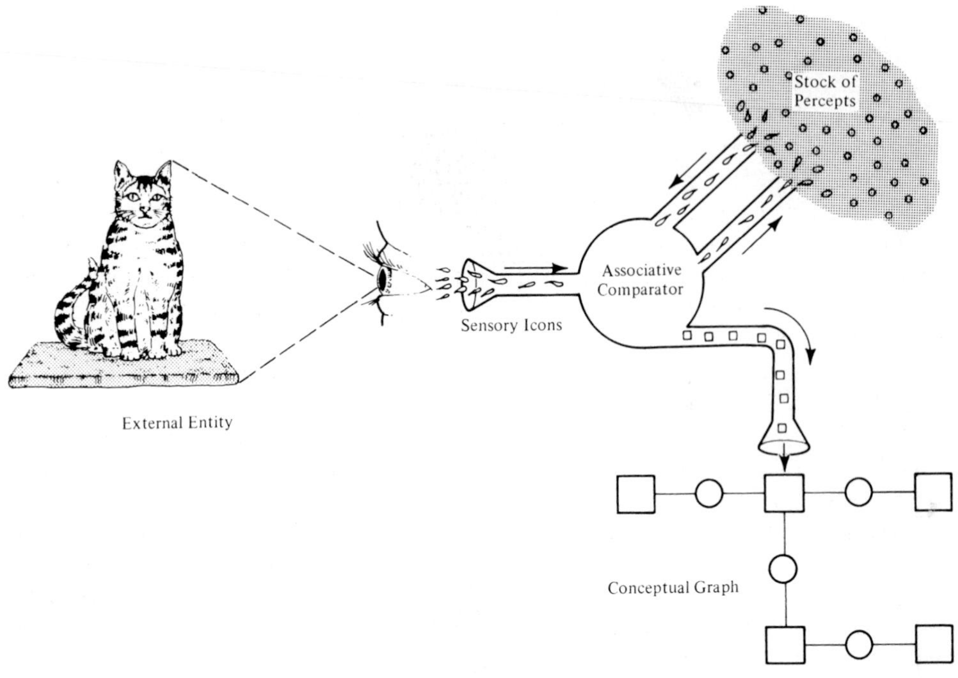

Fig. 3.1 The process of perceiving a cat

nections in a conceptual graph (Fig. 3.1). In diagrams, conceptual graphs are drawn as linked boxes and circles. Those links represent logical associations in the brain, not the actual shapes of the neural excitations.

3.1.1 Assumption. The process of *perception* generates a structure u called a *conceptual graph* in response to some external entity or scene e:

- The entity e gives rise to a *sensory icon* s.
- The *associative comparator* finds one or more *percepts* $p_1,...,p_n$ that match all or part of s.
- The *assembler* combines the percepts $p_1,...,p_n$ to form a *working model* that approximates s.
- If such a working model can be constructed, the entity e is said to be *recognized* by the percepts $p_1,...,p_n$.
- For each percept p_i in the working model, there is a *concept* c_i called the *interpretation* of p_i.
- The concepts $c_1,...,c_n$ are linked by *conceptual relations* to form the conceptual graph u.

Percepts are fragments of images that fit together like the pieces of a jigsaw puzzle. A conceptual graph describes the way percepts are assembled. Conceptual relations specify the *role* that each percept plays: one percept may match a part of an icon to the right or left of another percept; a percept for a color may be combined with a percept of a shape to form a graph that represents a colored shape. For auditory percepts, a graph may specify how percepts for phonemes are assembled to form syllables and words. Such graphs have been used for both language and vision. Winston (1975a) wrote a program based on graphs that learns patterns for various structures. Given graphs for arches and nonarches or pedestals and nonpedestals, his program analyzed the graphs in order to determine the conditions for a structure to be called an arch or a pedestal.

Figure 3.2 (patterned after Winston 1975a, p. 198) shows a conceptual graph that describes a simple arch consisting of two standing bricks and an arbitrary object lying across the bricks. The boxes in the diagram represent concepts and the circles represent conceptual relations. The top concept [ARCH] is linked by the three conceptual relations (PART) to two [BRICK] concepts and a more general concept [PHYSOBJ]. Each [BRICK] is in a state (STAT) of [STAND]. The [PHYSOBJ] is in the state [LIE], supported (SUPP) by each [BRICK]. One [BRICK] has the other [BRICK] to its right (RGHT), and the two bricks do not abut (¬ABUT).

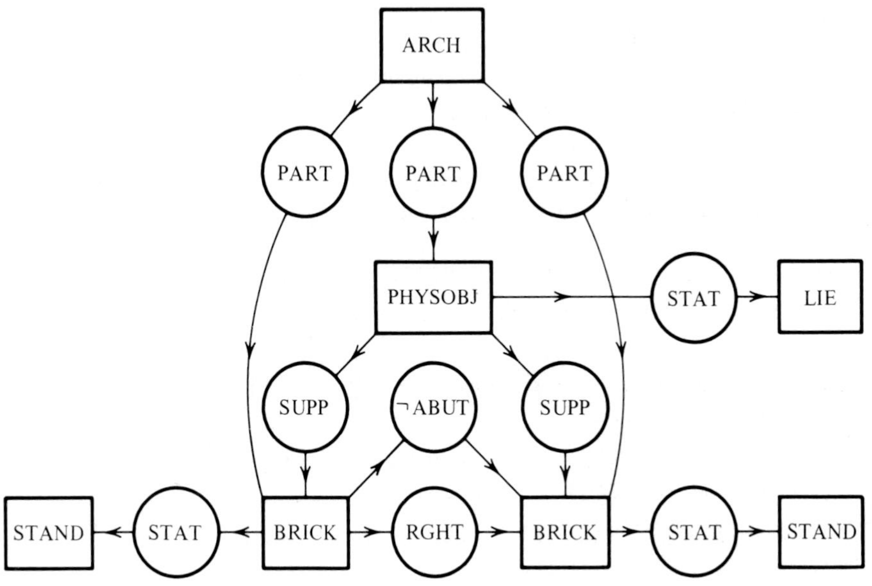

Fig. 3.2 Conceptual graph for an arch

In diagrams, a concept is drawn as a box, a conceptual relation as a circle, and an arc as an arrow that links a box to a circle. In linear text, the boxes may be abbreviated with square brackets, as in [ARCH], and the circles with rounded parentheses, as in (PART). To remember which way to draw the arrows on the arcs, read each subgraph of the form,

$$[\mathrm{CONCEPT}_1]\rightarrow(\mathrm{REL})\rightarrow[\mathrm{CONCEPT}_2]$$

as an English phrase, *the REL of a* $CONCEPT_1$ *is a* $CONCEPT_2$. If the label on the relation is not an English noun, this convention may lead to readings that are not grammatical as in *the RIGHT of a BRICK is a BRICK.* Even when the reading is ungrammatical, it still serves as a memory aid for drawing the arrows. These readings are helpful mnemonics, not linguistic rules for mapping the graphs into English. Section 5.4 presents grammar rules for generating natural language. Depending on context, a graph could be mapped into multiple sentences, a single sentence, a noun phrase, a verb phrase, or just a single word.

Conceptual relations may have any number of arcs, although most of the common ones are dyadic. Some, such as the *past tense marker* (PAST) or the *negation* (NEG), are monadic; others, like *between* (BETW), are triadic; and ones defined by the techniques of Section 3.6 may have an arbitrary number of arcs. Figure 3.3 shows a conceptual graph for the phrase *a space is between a brick and a brick.* For n-adic relations, the nth arc is drawn as an arrow pointing away from the circle, and all the other arcs are drawn as arrows pointing towards the circle. If the relation is monadic or dyadic, this convention is sufficient to distinguish the arcs. If $n \geq 3$, the arrows pointing towards the circle are numbered from 1 to n-1.

Conceptual graphs are finite, connected, bipartite graphs. They are *finite* because any graph in the human brain or computer storage can have only a finite number of concepts and conceptual relations. They are *connected* because two parts that were not connected would simply be called two conceptual graphs. They are *bipartite* because there are two different kinds of nodes—concepts and conceptual relations—and every arc links a node of one kind to a node of the other kind. For a survey of these and other terms from graph theory, see Appendix A.3.

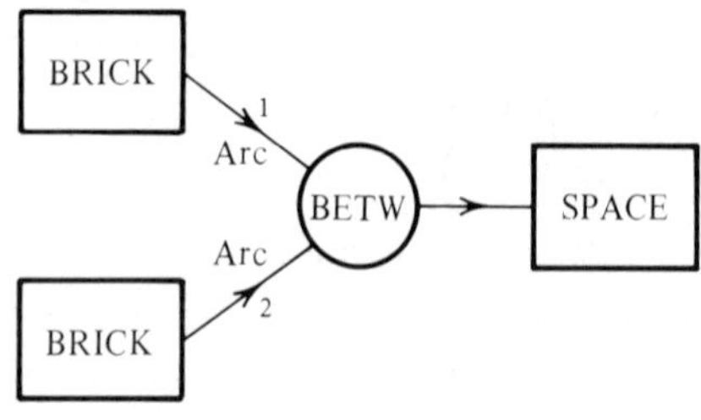

Fig. 3.3 Triadic relation "a space is between a brick and a brick"

3.1.2 Assumption. A *conceptual graph* is a finite, connected, bipartite graph.

- The two kinds of nodes of the bipartite graph are concepts and conceptual relations.
- Every conceptual relation has one or more *arcs*, each of which must be linked to some concept.
- If a relation has *n* arcs, it is said to be *n-adic*, and its arcs are labeled 1, 2, ..., *n*. The term *monadic* is synonymous with 1-adic, *dyadic* with 2-adic, and *triadic* with 3-adic.
- A single concept by itself may form a conceptual graph, but every arc of every conceptual relation must be linked to some concept.

Although diagrams help people to visualize relationships, the theory is independent of the way the graphs are drawn. Only three assumptions, which were analyzed in Section 2.3, are necessary to justify Assumption 3.1.2:

- Concepts are discrete units.
- Combinations of concepts are not diffuse mixtures, but ordered structures.
- Only discrete relationships are recorded in concepts. Continuous forms must be approximated by patterns of discrete units.

The notation of boxes and circles is a convenience, but it is not fundamental. What is fundamental is the mathematical basis, which is general enough to represent any set of relations between discrete things.

For concrete entities like cats and tomatoes, the brain has percepts for recognizing the entity and concepts for thinking about it. People can think about a restaurant as a place for eating food without imagining all the details of red checkered tablecloths and strolling musicians. For abstract types like JUSTICE and HEALTH, only imageless concepts, not percepts, are available. People differ widely in their use of concrete images and abstract concepts, but everybody (except perhaps those with serious brain injuries) is able use both.

3.1.3 Assumption. For every percept *p*, there is a concept *c*, called the *interpretation* of *p*. The percept *p* is called the *image* of *c*. Some concepts have no images.

- If a concept *c* has an image *p*, then *c* is called a *concrete concept*.
- If the concept *c* has no image, then *c* is called an *abstract concept*.
- The image of the interpretation of a percept *p* is identical to *p*.
- Entities recognized by the image of a concrete concept *c* are called *instances* of *c*.

Besides using conceptual graphs for interpreting sensory icons, the brain can also use them for generating or imagining new icons that were never before seen or heard.

A single percept or a structure of percepts can be *activated* to form an *imagined icon* that resembles a sensory icon. A conceptual graph serves as a plan for assembling percepts that form the internal image.

3.1.4 Assumption. Let u be a conceptual graph, whose concepts $c_1,...,c_n$ are all concrete. Then the graph u can serve as a pattern for a neural excitation t called an *imagined icon.* The icon t is identical to a sensory icon s with the following properties:

- The icon s may be matched by percepts $p_1,...,p_n$ where each p_i is the image of the concept c_i in the graph u.
- In matching the percepts $p_1,...,p_n$ to s, the assembler would construct a conceptual graph v identical to u.

The principle of assembling discrete patterns to form a continuous image is illustrated by the kits of plastic overlays used by police departments to form a picture of a crime suspect. The kits have a selection of plastic noses, chins, eyebrows, scars, hairlines, and so forth. The witness picks features from each category and overlays them to form a face. With Gillenson's WHATSISFACE system (1974) for automating the police kits, a witness sits in front of a display screen and answers questions like the following:

```
Is the top of the hairline
   (1) Evenly rounded or flattened
   (2) Parted on the left
   (3) Parted on the right
   (4) Fairly even but fairly pointy
   (5) Bunched up right in the middle
```

As the witness answers questions, selects sample features from a menu, and makes fine adjustments, the system assembles the features and displays a face that comes to resemble the original subject more and more closely. Figure 3.4 shows how well the system works: on the right are two photographs that users of the system were trying to duplicate, and on the left are the two matching faces constructed by the system. By combining discrete patterns, Gillenson's system can form a reasonable approximation to a continuous image. Besides assembling patterns, it also transforms and rotates the image to lengthen, shorten, or adjust the shape of the face and its features. The human brain also performs such transformations in assembling percepts and matching them to icons, but long-term memory quickly loses continuous information about sizes and rotations.

Many pattern recognition and generation systems analyze continuous images in terms of discrete units. By analogy with grammars in linguistics, which define permissible combinations of words, such formalisms are commonly called *picture*

Fig. 3.4 Two faces constructed by assembling patterns

grammars or *shape grammars*. Ledley (1964) wrote a grammar for chromosomes that was based on combinations of curves; he then developed a parsing program that could analyze chromosomes in a photograph and classify them according to the grammar. Even movements of the human body can be described in discrete units. Labanotation (Hutchinson 1970) was originally developed as a language for describing dance movements, but Badler and Smoliar (1979) wrote programs to translate Labanotation into animated images on a computer display. Although these notations are different from conceptual graphs, they, too, illustrate the principle of generating continuous images from discrete plans.

3.2 SEMANTIC NETWORK

Although the concept types CAT and TOMATO map directly to percepts, other types like PRICE, FUNCTION, and JUSTICE have no sensory correlates. Abstract concepts acquire their meaning not through direct associations with percepts, but through a vast network of relationships that ultimately links them to concrete concepts. In philosophy, White (1975) considered the meaning of a concept to be its position in that network:

> To discover the logical relations of a concept is to discover the nature of that concept. For concepts are, in this respect, like points; they have no quality except position. Just as the identity of a point is given by its coordinates, that is, its position relative to other points and ultimately to a set of axes, so the identity of a concept is given by its position relative to other concepts and ultimately to the kind of material to which it is ostensively applicable.... A concept is that which is logically related to others just as a point is that which is spatially related to others.

The collection of all the relationships that concepts have to other concepts, to percepts, to procedures, and to motor mechanisms is called the *semantic network*.

Some concepts in the semantic network are firmly anchored to percepts, but others apply to the ethereal realms of religion, economics, and theoretical physics. Yet concrete concepts are not necessarily more "meaningful" than abstract ones. A physical description of eight hours in a person's life may be an incomprehensible mass of detail, but the detail might be explained by the sentence *Leon had a hectic day at the stock exchange because he is a specialist in XYZ stock and rumors say that another company is trying to buy out XYZ*. Anyone who fails to appreciate the abstraction of this sentence should try defining the types RUMOR, STOCK, and BUY-OUT in purely sensory terms. BUY is a TRANSACTION in which the buyer exchanges MONEY for the OWNERSHIP of some ENTITY. But what are the sensory correlates of OWNERSHIP and MONEY? What distinguishes RUMOR from FACT, FACT from UTTERANCE, or UTTERANCE from SOUND?

A conceptual graph has no meaning in isolation. Only through the semantic network are its concepts and relations linked to context, language, emotion, and perception. Figure 3.5 shows a conceptual graph for *a cat sitting on a mat*. Dotted lines link the nodes of the graph to other parts of the semantic network:

- Concrete concepts are associated with percepts for experiencing the world and motor mechanisms for acting upon it.
- Some concepts are associated with the words and grammar rules of a language.
- A hierarchy of concept types defines the relationships between concepts at different levels of generality.
- Formation rules determine how each type of concept may be linked to conceptual relations.
- Each conceptual graph is linked to some context or episode to which it is relevant.
- Each episode may also have emotional associations, which indirectly confer emotional overtones on the types of concepts involved.

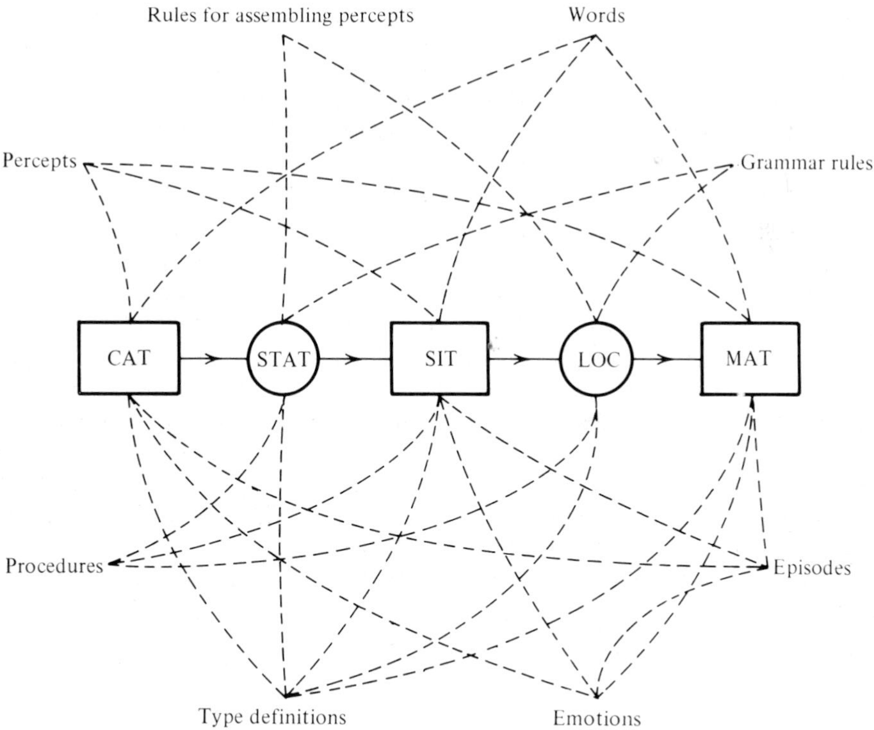

Fig. 3.5 A conceptual graph linked to the semantic network

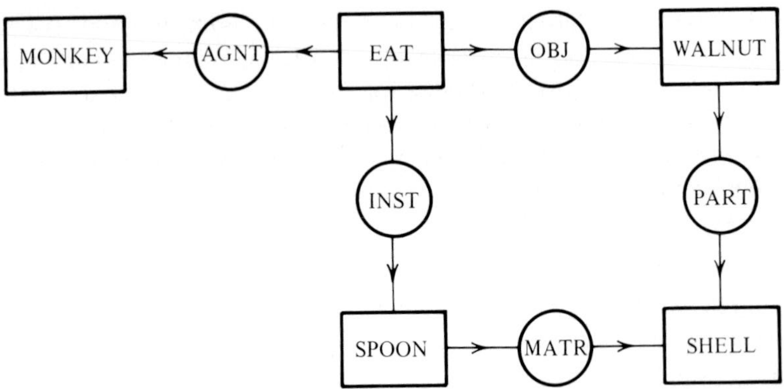

Fig. 3.6 Conceptual graph with a cycle

Some authors use the term *semantic network* in a way that is almost synonymous with *conceptual graph*. In this book, however, they are distinguished. Each conceptual graph asserts a single proposition. The semantic network is much larger. It includes a defining node for each type of concept, subtype links between the defining nodes, and links to perceptual and motor mechanisms. Some aspects of the semantic network, such as the type hierarchy, are treated in great detail. Other aspects, such as emotions, are not discussed in detail—not because they are unimportant, but because no one knows how to treat them formally.

The box and circle notation, called the *display form* for conceptual graphs, cannot be typed easily at a computer terminal. For the cat sitting on a mat in Fig. 3.5, the graph is already linear:

```
[CAT]→(STAT)→[SIT]→(LOC)→[MAT].
```

If any concept or relation is linked to more than two arcs, the graph forms a tree. If there are cycles in the graph, *variables* are needed to show cross references. As an example of a conceptual graph that cannot be represented in either a line or a tree, Fig. 3.6 may be read, *a monkey eating a walnut with a spoon made out of the walnut's shell.* (See Appendix B.3 for the conceptual relations used in these examples.) In the *linear form* for conceptual graphs, some concept or relation must be the *head*. Usually, the result is simplest if the concept with the most arcs linked to it is chosen as head:

```
[EAT]-
   (AGNT)→[MONKEY]
   (OBJ)→[WALNUT:*x]
   (INST)→[SPOON]→(MATR)→[SHELL]←(PART)←[WALNUT:*x].
```

The symbol *x is called a *variable*. It represents an unspecified individual of type WALNUT—which one is not known, but it must be the same one in both occurrences. The hyphen "-" after the concept [EAT] shows that the relations connected to [EAT] are listed on subsequent lines; the period "." terminates the entire graph. Any other concept or relation could have been chosen as head, but the linear form might be more complicated:

```
[SPOON]-
  (INST)←[EAT]-
            (OBJ)→[WALNUT]→(PART)→[SHELL:*y]
            (AGNT)→[MONKEY],
  (MATR)→[SHELL:*y].
```

Both of these linear forms are exactly equivalent to Fig. 3.6 and to each other. The differences between them result from arbitrary choices: which node to pick as the head, which relation to list first in the linear form, and which node to mark with a variable when breaking cycles. In this second form, both [SPOON] and [EAT] are followed by hyphens to show that their relations are listed on subsequent lines. A comma terminates the hyphen after [EAT] so that (MATR) is linked by the previous hyphen on [SPOON]. The hyphen and comma form a *bracketing pair* that is necessary for linearizing a tree. Indentation makes the bracketing more readable. For the detailed syntax of the linear form, see Appendix A.6.

Normally, the entire semantic network is not drawn explicitly because it is too large and unwieldy. Instead, each concept box contains a label that shows the type, and two boxes with the same *type label* represent concepts of the same type. The distinction between type labels and concepts follows the distinction between *types* and *tokens* drawn by Peirce (1906): the word *cat* is a type, and every utterance of *cat* is a new token. Similarly, each occurrence of a concept is a separate token, but the tokens are classified by a set T of basic types.

3.2.1 Assumption. The function *type* maps concepts into a set T, whose elements are called *type labels*. Concepts c and d are of the *same type* if $type(c)=type(d)$.

Some graph notations leave the concept boxes empty, and represent types by special *IS-A links* to a defining node for each type. For many purposes, the two conventions have the same effect, but writing type labels in the boxes instead of IS-A links makes conceptual graphs easier to read. Besides readability, there are theoretical reasons for not drawing IS-A links as circles: conceptual relations show the role that each concept plays; the type hierarchy is a *higher-order relation* not between individual concepts, but between types of individuals. In this book, type labels are written as character strings: RED and PHYSOBJ are type labels for concepts of redness and physical object. A concept of type RED is drawn as a box in a diagram or with square brackets [RED] in the text. For readability, English words in upper case are used for most type labels, but any set of unique identifiers such as numbers or Chinese characters would work just as well.

Whether two concept types are the same depends on their links to the semantic network rather than their external instances. This distinction is important because some types may not have corresponding sets, and some sets may not have types. The set of type UNICORN, for example, is empty. Furthermore, a set of unrelated things like an elephant, a paper clip, and the moon does not correspond to a type. No single percept could recognize all three of them without also recognizing every other rounded object in the world. Instances of the same type have a natural affinity for each other, at least in the eye of some beholder. An arbitrary set, however, may not have such an affinity. For a *natural type* like ROSE or CAT, the instances are related by their nature, not by an arbitrary selection. All the things in the real world that are instances of a type constitute the *denotation* of that type.

3.2.2 Definition. Let t be a type label. The *denotation* of type t, written δt, is the set of all entities that are instances of any concept of type t.

Since no two stimuli are ever identical in all respects, every percept must match a range of sensory icons. A percept that matches a broad range of icons is more general than one that matches only a subrange. The image of type RED is a percept that matches an infinite variety of hues, including those matched by percepts for STRAWBERRY-RED, FIRE-ENGINE-RED, CRIMSON, and SCARLET. Since RED is the label of a more general concept than CRIMSON, the type CRIMSON is called a *subtype* of RED. The denotation of CRIMSON is a subset of the denotation of RED: δCRIMSON is contained in δRED. The symbol ≤ represents subtypes: CRIMSON≤RED, and RED≥CRIMSON. Every type is a subtype of itself: RED≤RED. The symbols < and > exclude the possibility that two labels are equal: CRIMSON<RED, but not RED<RED. But not all types of concepts are comparable: neither RED nor JUSTICE is a subtype of the other. See Appendix A.4 for a definition of partial ordering.

3.2.3 Assumption. The *type hierarchy* is a partial ordering defined over the set of type labels. The symbol ≤ designates the ordering. Let s, t, and u be type labels:

- If $s \le t$, then s is called a *subtype* of t; and t is called a *supertype* of s, written $t \ge s$.
- If $s \le t$ and $s \ne t$, then s is called a *proper subtype* of t, written $s < t$; and t is called a *proper supertype* of s, written $t > s$.
- If s is a subtype of t and a subtype of u ($s \le t$ and $s \le u$), then s is called a *common subtype* of t and u.
- If s is a supertype of t and a supertype of u ($s \ge t$ and $s \ge u$), then s is called a *common supertype* of t and u.

In AI, the type hierarchy supports the inheritance of properties from supertypes to subtypes of concepts. Aristotle first introduced type hierarchies with his theory of categories and syllogisms. He had ten primitive types, a method for defining new types by *genus* and *differentiae*, and the use of syllogisms for analyzing the inheritance of properties. Masterman (1961) introduced the term *semantic net* for the type hierarchy and defined an algorithm that let subtypes inherit the properties or *semantic shells* of supertypes.

The best way to study type hierarchies is to analyze the structure of dictionary definitions, preferably by computer. Amsler (1980) found a rich hierarchy in his analysis of the *Merriam-Webster Pocket Dictionary*. The hierarchy tended to be bushy, with each node having many descendants, but it did not grow very deep. The concept type VEHICLE, for example, had 165 subtypes, but the hierarchy extended for only three levels. At the first level, the immediate subtypes of VEHICLE included AMBULANCE, AUTOMOBILE, BICYCLE, BUCKBOARD, BUS, CARRIAGE, CART, etc. The next level beneath AUTOMOBILE included the subtypes COACH, CONVERTIBLE, COUPE, HOT-ROD, JALOPY, SEDAN, etc. The third level beneath SEDAN included BROUGHAM, LIMOUSINE, and SALOON. Actions, states, and properties can also be grouped in hierarchies. In analyzing verbs, Chodorow (1981) also found bushy, but shallow hierarchies. The concept type COMPLAIN, for example, has subtypes BELLYACHE, BITCH, CRAB, GRIPE, INVEIGH, SQUAWK, and WHIMPER, none of which have any further subtypes.

Corresponding to the type hierarchy for concepts is an *approximation hierarchy* for percepts. A percept for a general type RED makes an approximate match to many different icons. A percept for the subtype CRIMSON matches fewer icons, but it matches them more exactly.

3.2.4 Assumption. The *approximation hierarchy* is a partial ordering of percepts induced by the partial ordering of concept types. If the percept p is the image of a concept of type s and q is the image of a concept of type t where $s \le t$, then define $p \le q$. The following conditions hold:

- Any entity recognized by p is also recognized by q.
- Hence, the denotation of s is a subset of the denotation of t: $\delta s \subseteq \delta t$.
- If an icon i is matched by both percepts p and q, the percept p forms a more exact match to i than the percept q.

The types CAT and DOG have many common supertypes, including ANIMAL, VERTEBRATE, MAMMAL, and CARNIVORE. The *minimal common supertype* of CAT and DOG is CARNIVORE, which is a subtype of all the other supertypes. The concept types FELINE and WILD-ANIMAL have common subtypes

JAGUAR, LION, and TIGER; but none of them is a *maximal common subtype*. The type hierarchy could be refined, however, by adding the type WILD-FELINE, which would be a maximal common subtype of FELINE and WILD-ANIMAL and a minimal common supertype of LION, TIGER, and JAGUAR. When all the intermediate types like WILD-FELINE are introduced, the type hierarchy becomes a *type lattice*. Both Leibniz's Universal Characteristic and Masterman's semantic nets were lattices. See Appendix A.4 for a definition of *lattice*.

3.2.5 Assumption. The type hierarchy forms a lattice, called the *type lattice*:

- Any pair of type labels s and t has a *minimal common supertype*, written $s \cup t$. For any type label u, if $u \geq s$ and $u \geq t$, then $u \geq s \cup t$.
- Any pair of type labels s and t has a *maximal common subtype*, written $s \cap t$. For any type label u, if $u \leq s$ and $u \leq t$, then $u \leq s \cap t$.
- There are two primitive type labels: the *universal type* $\top$ and the *absurd type* $\bot$. For any type label t, $\bot \leq t \leq \top$.

As supertypes of CAT and DOG, the previous discussion did not mention the concept type PET. There is a reason for that omission: the types CAT, DOG, MAMMAL, and ANIMAL are *natural types* that relate to the essence of the entities, but types like PET, PEDESTRIAN, and SPOUSE are *role types* that depend on an accidental relationship to some other entity. Any animal may be a pet if it plays the proper role: a person could have a pet mouse, pet alligator, or pet crab. Even the chimpanzee Washoe had a pet cat. Natural types and role types both occur in the same type lattice. The maximal common subtype of CAT and PET is PET-CAT; the minimal common supertype of PET-CAT and PET-DOG is PET-CARNIVORE.

A lattice must have minimal common supertypes and maximal common subtypes. Yet for most pairs of types, such as CAT and APPLE, SQUARE and CIRCLE, or JUSTICE and DOG, there are no common subtypes. To make the type hierarchy into a lattice, two special type labels must be introduced at its top and bottom: the universal type $\top$ that is a supertype of all other types, and the absurd type $\bot$ that is a subtype of all other types. Everything that exists is an instance of the universal type $\top$. No actual entity could ever be an instance of type $\bot$, since it would have to be a dog, a cat, a circle, a square, an apple, and justice as well as an event, a color, and an emotion, all at the same time.

Many people confuse types and sets. Yet there is a fundamental difference. Statements about types are *analytic*; they must be true by intension. Statements about sets are *synthetic*; they are verified by observing the extensions. To say that the intersection of the set δCAT with the set δDOG is empty simply means that at the moment no individual happens to be both a dog and a cat. A biologist might examine litters of puppies and kittens looking for an exception. But to say that

DOG $\cap$ CAT = $\perp$ means that it is logically impossible for an entity to be both a dog and a cat. Any mutant that might arise could not falsify the statement; it would just force the biologist to invent a new type.

Although the operators $\cup$ and $\cap$ are used for both types and sets, there are important differences in the way they behave on type labels and denotations. For extensions, the union δCAT $\cup$ δDOG is the set of all cats and dogs in the world and nothing else. But for the intensional type labels, CAT $\cup$ DOG is their minimal common supertype CARNIVORE, which also has subtypes BEAR, WEASEL, SKUNK, etc. Since the union of any set S with the empty set leaves S unchanged, the union δCAT $\cup$ δUNICORN is just δCAT. Yet the denotation of UNICORN is empty only in the present world. In some possible world, unicorns might exist. Even in this world, a molecular geneticist may someday find a way of creating one. To allow for such possibilities, CAT $\cup$ UNICORN must be MAMMAL. Even more dramatically, JUSTICE $\cup$ UNICORN is the universal type $\top$, which includes everything. The type lattice represents categories of thought, and the lattice of sets and subsets represents collections of existing things. The two lattices are not isomorphic, and the denotation operator that maps one into the other is neither one-to-one nor onto.

3.2.6 Theorem. Let s and t be any type labels. Then $\delta(s \cup t)$ is a superset of $\delta s \cup \delta t$, and $\delta(s \cap t)$ is a subset of $\delta s \cap \delta t$.

Proof. By definition, both s and t are subtypes of $s \cup t$. Hence by Assumption 3.2.4, any element of δs or of δt must also be an element of $\delta(s \cup t)$. Therefore, $(\delta s \cup \delta t) \subseteq \delta(s \cup t)$. Since $s \cap t$ is a subtype of both s and t, any element of $\delta(s \cap t)$ must be an element of δs and of δt. Therefore, $\delta(s \cap t) \subseteq (\delta s \cap \delta t)$.

Conceptual relations are classified by types in the same way that concepts are classified. A hierarchy is also defined over type labels of conceptual relations. A general relation type LOC for location may have subtypes that specify more details about the location, such as IN, ABOV, or UNDR.

3.2.7 Assumption. The function *type* may be extended to map conceptual relations to type labels.

- The relations r and s are said to be of the *same type* if $type(r) = type(s)$.
- If r and s are of the same type, they must have exactly the same number of arcs.
- For any concept c and conceptual relation r, $type(c) \neq type(r)$.
- The partial ordering of type labels also extends to type labels of conceptual relations, but the type labels of concepts have no common supertype with the type labels of conceptual relations.

3.3 INDIVIDUALS AND NAMES

George Washington and *Grand Central Terminal* are proper names, but *building, lawyer, cat,* and *pedestrian* are common nouns. English and other natural languages distinguish the two kinds of words. A proper name is an arbitrary label that designates a particular person, place, thing, or group. A common noun is a generic term that specifies some attribute of the entities it refers to, but it applies equally well to any entity that has that attribute. Even when a proper name describes some attribute, it remains an arbitrary label: Mont Blanc may be a white mountain, but no other white mountain is named Mont Blanc. In general, common nouns correspond to type labels, and names designate particular individuals. Confusing the two categories of words can easily lead to absurd fallacies:

```
If Clyde is an elephant,            If Clyde is an elephant,
and an elephant is an animal,       and elephant is a species,
then Clyde is an animal.            then Clyde is a species.
```

The statement *Clyde is an elephant* says that a particular individual named Clyde is of type ELEPHANT. The statement *An elephant is an animal* says that any individual of type ELEPHANT is also of type ANIMAL. The first syllogism is therefore valid. But the statement *Elephant is a species* is not directly about individuals. It states that the word *elephant* is the name of a particular species of animal. In that syllogism, the middle term *elephant* is used in two different senses—one of the classic forms of fallacy.

The concepts defined so far are *generic concepts*: they are like variables that represent an unspecified individual of a given type. To distinguish types from individuals, some new features must be added. For database systems, Hall, Owlett, and Todd (1976) introduced unique identifiers or *surrogates* to identify particular individuals. For relational database theory, Codd (1979) adopted surrogates as internal representatives of external entities.

Codd distinguished the *perceived world* from the real world. Surrogates in a database do not directly reflect entities in the real world, but in some system analyst's perception of what is significant and what should be stored. Besides surrogates for specific individuals, a database may also contain *null values*, which are place holders for individuals whose identities are unknown. A database of family relationships, for example, would either have null values for the parents of some people or it would have to contain everybody's genealogy back to Adam and Eve—even then it would have to have null values for the parents of those two.

In conceptual graphs, surrogates are represented by *individual markers*, which are serial numbers like #80972, and null values are represented by asterisks. The concept box is divided into two fields separated by a colon, as in [PERSON:#80972]. The field to the left of the colon contains the type label PERSON. The field to the right of the colon contains the *referent* #80972, which designates a particular person.

If the referent is just an asterisk, as in [PERSON:*], the concept is called a *generic concept*, which may be read *a person* or *some person*. In diagrams, the asterisk is optional. A box with just a type label like [PERSON] is equivalent to [PERSON:*].

3.3.1 Assumption. There is a set I={#1, #2, #3,...} whose elements are called *individual markers*. The function *referent* may be applied to any concept c:

- *referent*(c) is either an individual marker in I or the *generic marker* *.
- When *referent*(c) is in I, then c is said to be an *individual concept*.
- When *referent*(c) is *, then c is said to be a *generic concept*.

An individual marker is a surrogate for some individual in the real world, a perceived world, or a hypothetical world. Any type of concept may have an individual marker: the concept [CAT] or [CAT:*] refers to an unspecified cat, but [CAT:#98077] refers to a particular individual with serial number #98077; the concept [JUMP] refers to an unspecified act of jumping, but [JUMP:#882635] refers to a particular instance of jumping; [HAPPY] refers to some happiness, but [HAPPY:#77289] refers to a particular instance of happiness. Individual concepts can represent *mass nouns* like water or butter and *count nouns* like boy or pencil. The concept [WATER:#2219] would represent a particular mass of water. Having individual markers on mass concepts is necessary to distinguish a new batch of water flowing through a fountain from an old batch recycled.

In a computer simulation, each individual marker is represented by a unique number or symbol. In the human brain, a marker could be represented by an association to the episode or context to which the conceptual graph was originally linked. In that case, a marker is like a special time stamp that specifies the time and place when the concept was recorded. Following is the psychological evidence for such markers:

- All human languages distinguish proper names from common nouns.
- In computer systems, the simplest way of identifying entities is by assigning each a unique marker, such as a time stamp or serial number.
- Macnamara (1982) found that the distinction between proper names and common nouns is among the first ones that children learn, some before the age of 17 months.

Since children learn names so quickly, names must be logically close to the structures that the brain uses for identifying individuals. A name is a perceptible sound or symbol associated with the internal, neural marker. In linguistics, Chomsky (1965) introduced unique indices to specify which noun phrases refer to the same individuals. In psychology, Norman, Rumelhart, et al. (1975) used similar markers for individual concepts.

Individual concepts correspond to constants in logic and programming languages, and generic concepts correspond to variables. In fact, variables like *x or *y in the linear notation are simply the generic marker *, followed by an identifier for indicating cross references. The following two graphs are exactly equivalent:

```
[CAT:*x]→(STAT)→[SIT:*z]→(LOC)→[MAT:*y].
[CAT]→(STAT)→[SIT]→(LOC)→[MAT].
```

Both of these graphs make the same assertion: they say that there exists some cat x, some mat y, and some instance of sitting z by cat x on mat y. If the concept [CAT] had the referent #98077, it would still assert existence, but it would be a definite reference *the cat* instead of an indefinite *a cat*. If the concept [SIT] had an individual marker, the graph could be read *the sitting by a cat on a mat*. Every generic concept is bound by an implicit *existential quantifier*. The next assumption introduces the *formula operator*, represented by the Greek letter ϕ, which translates a conceptual graph into a logical formula.

3.3.2 Assumption. The operator ϕ maps conceptual graphs into formulas in the first-order predicate calculus. If u is any conceptual graph, then ϕu is a formula determined by the following construction:

- If u contains k generic concepts, assign a distinct variable symbol $x_1, x_2, \ldots, x_k$ to each one.
- For each concept c of u, let *identifier*(c) be the variable assigned to c if c is generic or *referent*(c) if c is individual.
- Represent each concept c as a monadic predicate whose name is the same as *type*(c) and whose argument is *identifier*(c).
- Represent each n-adic conceptual relation r of u as an n-adic predicate whose name is the same as *type*(r). For each i from 1 to n, let the ith argument of the predicate be the identifier of the concept linked to the ith arc of r.
- Then ϕu has a *quantifier prefix* $\exists x_1 \exists x_2 \ldots \exists x_k$ and a *body* consisting of the conjunction of all the predicates for the concepts and conceptual relations of u.

Every conceptual graph makes an assertion. The operator ϕ maps that assertion into a logical formula. In the graphs of this chapter, the only logical operators are the conjunction $\wedge$ and the existential quantifier $\exists$. Chapter 4 introduces negation and then defines other operators in terms of $\sim$ and $\wedge$ together with $\exists$. For a review of standard logic, see Appendix A.4. As an example of Assumption 3.3.2, let the graph u be,

```
[CAT:#98077]→(STAT)→[SIT]→(LOC)→[MAT].
```

Since this graph has two generic concepts, assign one variable x to [SIT] and another variable y to [MAT]. Then the three concepts map to the monadic predicates CAT(#98077), SIT(x), and MAT(y). The two conceptual relations map to STAT(#98077,x) and LOC(x,y). Then ϕu is

$$\exists x \exists y(\mathrm{CAT}(\#98077) \land \mathrm{STAT}(\#98077,x) \land \mathrm{SIT}(x) \land \mathrm{LOC}(x,y) \land \mathrm{MAT}(y))$$

When a graph u is mapped into a formula ϕu, the individual concepts of u are mapped to constants, and the generic concepts are mapped to variables. Since a single concept by itself forms a conceptual graph, the operator ϕ maps the concept [PERSON] to the formula $\exists x$PERSON(x). Conceptual graphs are usually more concise than logical formulas because arcs on the graphs show the connections more directly than variable symbols.

An individual marker on a concept must conform to its type label. Any operation that might change the type label must check whether the new label is appropriate for the old individual. If the individual #98077 happened to be a dog, the concept [ANIMAL:#98077] could not be restricted to [CAT:#98077]. The *conformity relation*, denoted by the symbol ::, makes the test: if #98077 is a cat, then CAT::#98077 is true; otherwise, it is false. Note the difference between the single colon and the double colon. In the concept [CAT:#98077], the single colon is just punctuation that separates the type field from the referent field. In the conformity relation CAT::#98077, the double colon is an operator that makes a test.

Suppose that Snoopy is a beagle identified by the marker #2883. Then the relation BEAGLE::#2883 states that the individual #2883 conforms to type BEAGLE and therefore that the concept [BEAGLE:#2883] is well formed. Because of the type hierarchy, the following relationships must also be true: DOG::#2883, MAMMAL::#2883, ANIMAL::#2883, PHYSOBJ::#2883, and ENTITY::#2883. If Snoopy is a beagle and Snoopy is a pet, then Snoopy must also be a pet beagle. BEAGLE::#2883 and PET::#2883 imply PET-BEAGLE::#2883.

3.3.3 Assumption. The *conformity relation* :: relates type labels to individual markers: if t::i is true, then i is said to *conform* to type t. The conformity relation obeys the following conditions:

- The referent of a concept must conform to its type label: if c is a concept, *type*(c)::*referent*(c).
- If an individual marker conforms to type s, it must also conform to all supertypes of s: if $s \leq t$ and s::i, then t::i.
- If an individual marker conforms to types s and t, it must also conform to their maximal common subtype: if s::i and t::i, then $(s \cap t)$::i.
- Every individual marker conforms to the universal type $\top$; no individual marker conforms to the absurd type $\bot$: for all i in I, $\top$::i, but not $\bot$::i.
- The generic marker $*$ conforms to all type labels: for all type labels t, t::$*$.

Once the theory can identify individuals, it has a basis for defining names of individuals. The concept ["Judy"] is a concept of the name *Judy*, as opposed to [PERSON:Judy], which is a concept of the person Judy. The concept ["Judy"] is generic because it is possible to talk about the utterance #423781 of the name *Judy*, which is represented by the concept ["Judy":#423781]. The conceptual relation (NAME) links a concept to a word that names an individual. Only entities can have names. Individuals of other types, such as ACT, cannot be named.

3.3.4 Assumption. NAME is a type label for a dyadic conceptual relation, and ENTITY and WORD are type labels for concepts. Let a and b be any concepts linked to arcs #1 and #2 of a conceptual relation of type NAME: a→(NAME)→b. Then the following conditions must hold:

- *type*(a) is a subtype of ENTITY: *type*(a)≤ENTITY.
- *type*(b) is a proper subtype of WORD: *type*(b)<WORD.

The word *type*(b) is called a *name* of *referent*(a).

The following graph represents a PERSON identified by individual marker #3074, who has a name *Judy*:

```
[PERSON:#3074]→(NAME)→["Judy"].
```

Because names occur so frequently, this graph can be abbreviated by *name contraction* to form just the single concept [PERSON:Judy#3074]. This form corresponds to the English phrase *the person Judy*, which is a contraction of *the person named Judy*. The following graph,

```
[PERSON]→(NAME)→["Judy"],
```

may be contracted to the single concept [PERSON:Judy]. This concept represents the indefinite form *a person named Judy*, but [PERSON:Judy#3074] represents *the person named Judy*. If there is only one person named Judy in the context, the distinction may not matter. If the name *Snoopy* uniquely identifies the individual #2883, the name could also be used in the conformity relation BEAGLE::Snoopy instead of BEAGLE::#2883.

A person may have multiple names or aliases. The following graph shows a person #1196 who has the names Cicero and Tully:

```
["Cicero"]←(NAME)←[PERSON:#1196]→(NAME)→["Tully"].
```

By name contraction, either name could be contracted into the referent field of the concept [PERSON], and the individual marker #1196 could be dropped:

```
[PERSON:Cicero]→(NAME)→["Tully"].
[PERSON:Tully]→(NAME)→["Cicero"].
```

The first graph may be read *Cicero is named Tully*; and the second, *Tully is named Cicero*. The NAME relation applies equally well to names of entities in the real world, other possible worlds, or Platonic realms of ideas. The statement *The present king of France is named Louis XXIV* is mapped to a normal conceptual graph, even though some of the concepts in it may not represent anything in the real world.

Mathematical entities like numbers, sets, and functions can also be represented and named. The English word *four*, the French word *quatre*, the Arabic numeral 4, the Roman numeral IV, and the binary numeral 100 are all names for the same number. The next graph shows the number with two of its names:

```
["IV"]←(NAME)←[NUMBER:#27018]→(NAME)→["4"].
```

The individual marker #27018 distinguishes a concept of a unique number, which has several aliases. This graph would be contracted to [NUMBER:4] in normal computation. The example *Elephant is a species*, which appeared earlier in this section, could be represented by the graph,

```
["elephant"]←(NAME)←[SPECIES]→(MEMB)→[ELEPHANT:{*}].
```

This graph may be read *The word "elephant" is a name of a species whose members are a set of elephants*. The symbol {*}, which is defined in Section 3.7, represents a *generic set* of entities that conform to the type label of the concept.

Measures can be treated in the same way as names: *10 inches* and *25.4 centimeters* are alternative names for the same quantity of linear measure. Like numerals, units of measure belong to a system with rules for converting one name into another. Yet they are still names. *Kilogram* is the name given to the measure of a mass in Sèvres, France; other masses may also have that same measure. In the fully expanded form, conceptual graphs can distinguish a bar, the length of the bar, a measure of that length, and a name for that measure:

```
[BAR]→(CHRC)→[LENGTH]→(MEAS)→[MEASURE]→(NAME)→["25.4 cm"].
```

This graph may be read *a bar with a length with a measure named 25.4 cm*. By name contraction, it may be simplified to

```
[BAR]→(CHRC)→[LENGTH]→(MEAS)→[MEASURE: 25.4 cm].
```

This contracted graph may be read *a bar with a length with a measure of 25.4 cm*. Since units of measure occur so frequently, they may be abbreviated further by *measure contraction*:

```
[BAR]→(CHRC)→[LENGTH: @ 25.4 cm],
```

which may be read *a bar of length 25.4 cm*. The symbol @ shows that the following string is not a name, but a measure. If [LENGTH] originally had an individual marker #7286, then the contracted form would be [LENGTH:#7286@25.4cm].

The contractions for measures are similar to the abbreviations in English and other natural languages. A failure to distinguish the different forms of abbreviation can lead to confusions and paradoxes. Montague (1974), for example, noted a paradox in the sentence *The temperature is ninety but it is rising.* If the copula *is* were interpreted as a sign of equality, this sentence would lead to the absurd conclusion that ninety is rising. Montague resolved the paradox by distinguishing an individual concept from its measure at some instant of time. Although Montague's notation is very different, a similar analysis could be expressed in a conceptual graph:

```
[TEMPERATURE:#55361]→(MEAS)→[MEASURE]→(NAME)→["90°"].
```

This graph says that the instance of temperature designated by #55361 has a measure named 90°. If the temperature #55361 happened to rise, it would have a different measure, which would have a different name. But the measure named 90° would remain the same.

Formally, the referent of a concept is either * for generic concepts or # followed by an integer for individual concepts. The other notations written in the referent field of a concept node are informal abbreviations that can always be converted to the formal notation:

- In the linear form, the * for generic concepts may be followed by a variable name, such as *x or *abc.
- The marker @ shows that the following string is a measure of an entity and not a name or individual marker that designates the entity.
- A character string not preceded by a symbol *, #, or @ represents a name of an individual that must be unique within the current context.
- To represent the definite article, as in *the cat*, the integer following # may be dropped, as in [CAT:#] instead of [CAT:#98077]. This abbreviation is used when there is just a single cat in the context.

More complex referents are introduced in Section 3.7, including sets and nested conceptual graphs.

3.4 CANONICAL GRAPHS

A conceptual graph is a combination of concept nodes and relation nodes where every arc of every conceptual relation is linked to a concept. But not all such combinations make sense. Some of them include absurd combinations like the following:

```
[SLEEP]→(AGNT)→[IDEA]→(COLR)→[GREEN].
```

This is an odd, unusual, or perhaps meaningless graph that may be read *Some act of sleeping has an agent, which is an idea, which has a color, green.* This odd combination could have arisen from Chomsky's famous sentence *Colorless green ideas sleep furiously* (1957). To rule out such sentences, Katz and Fodor (1963) developed a theory of semantics that imposes *selectional constraints* on permissible combinations of words.

To distinguish the meaningful graphs that represent real or possible situations in the external world, certain graphs are declared to be *canonical*. Through experience, each person develops a world view represented in canonical graphs. One source of the graphs is observation: the assembler may combine certain concepts in perception. Since that combination is true of a real situation, it must be canonical. Another source is the derivation of new canonical graphs from other canonical graphs by *formation rules*. The third source is called *insight* or creativity: a person may feel that existing percepts, concepts, and relations do not adequately describe a situation and may invent a radically new configuration that better describes it. Insight leads to new canonical graphs that replace or extend the older ones.

3.4.1 Assumption. Certain conceptual graphs are *canonical*. New graphs may become canonical or be *canonized* by any of the following three processes:

- *Perception*. Any conceptual graph constructed by the assembler in matching a sensory icon is canonical.
- *Formation rules*. New canonical graphs may be derived from other canonical graphs by the rules *copy*, *restrict*, *join*, and *simplify*.
- *Insight*. Arbitrary conceptual graphs may be assumed as canonical.

Before graphs can be derived by formation rules, a starting set must be introduced by insight. A child invents graphs that provide the simplest interpretation of experience. When discrepancies between new experiences and the old graphs become too great, the child invents a newer, more adequate set of graphs. In a knowledge-based system, insight corresponds to the introduction of new graphs by a knowledge engineer. In experimental systems, insight is simulated by learning programs that search for graphs that encode information more efficiently.

The formation rules are a generative grammar for conceptual structures just as Chomsky's production rules are a generative grammar for syntactic structures. All deductions and computations on conceptual graphs involve some combination of them. There are several arguments for this choice of rules:

- *Common practice*. Similar operations have been useful in many AI programs.
- *Modularity*. They allow new graphs to be derived as combinations of standard modules or templates.
- *Selectional constraints*. They enforce constraints that prevent nonsensical combinations from being derived.
- *Theoretical elegance*. They simplify the definitions and proofs of the theory.

By the *copy* rule, an exact copy of a canonical graph is also canonical. The *restrict* rule replaces the type label of a concept with the label of a subtype, as in deriving [GIRL] from [PERSON]. It may also convert a generic concept like

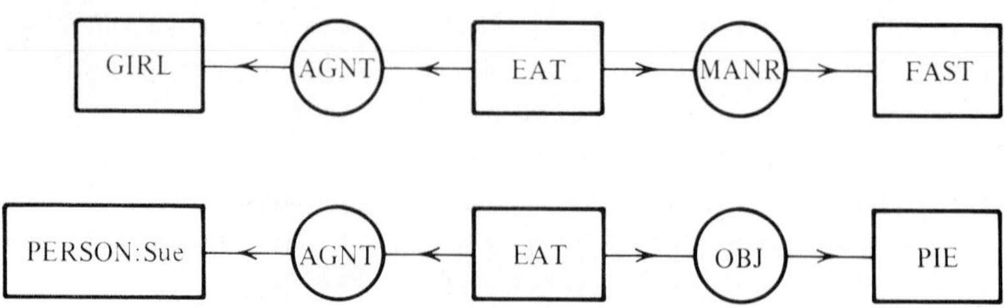

Fig. 3.7 Two canonical graphs

[DOG] to an individual concept [DOG:Snoopy]. For individual concepts, the conformity relation must be checked to make sure that the referent conforms to the new type label. A restriction from [DOG:Snoopy] to [BEAGLE:Snoopy] is permissible, but a restriction to [COLLIE:Snoopy] is not allowed because Snoopy is not a collie.

The join rule merges identical concepts. Two graphs may be joined by overlaying one graph on top of the other so that the two identical concepts merge into a single concept. As a result, all the conceptual relations that had been linked to either concept are linked to the single merged concept. Both the type label and the referent must be the same: [PERSON:Sam] may be joined to [PERSON:Sam] or [CAT] to [CAT]. If one concept is generic and the other is individual, they could be joined after restricting [PERSON] to [PERSON:Sam]. But no restriction could allow [PERSON:Sam] to be joined to [CAT] or [PERSON:Rock].

When two concepts are joined, some relations in the resulting graph may become redundant. One of each pair of duplicates can then be deleted by the rule of *simplification*: when two relations of the same type are linked to the same concepts in the same order, they assert the same information; one of them may therefore be erased. This rule corresponds to the rule of logic that $R(x,y) \wedge R(x,y)$ is equivalent to just $R(x,y)$. But the order of the arcs is significant: the formula $R(x,y) \wedge R(y,x)$ is not equivalent to $R(x,y)$.

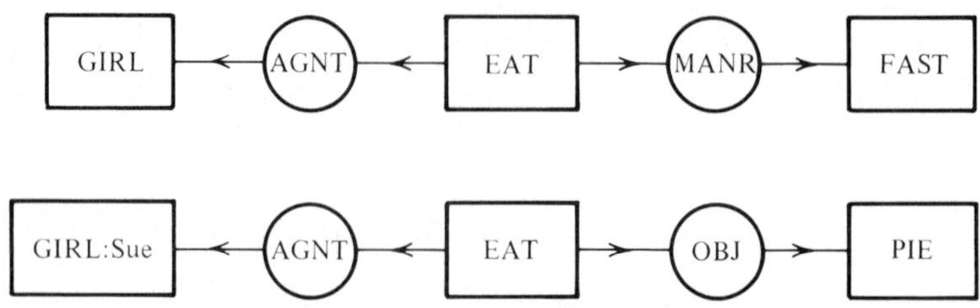

Fig. 3.8 Restriction of the second graph in Fig. 3.7

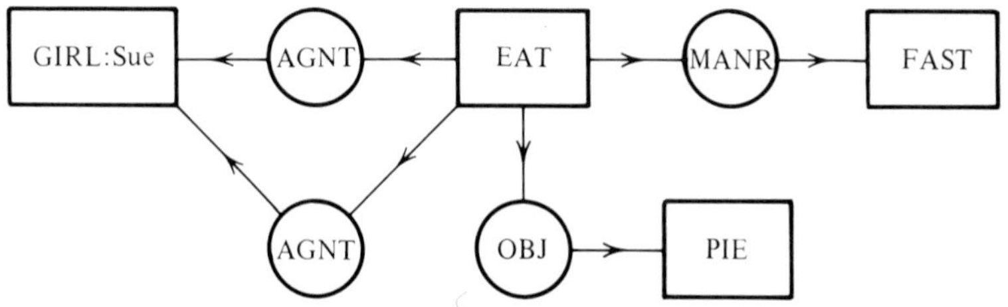

Fig. 3.9 Join of the two graphs in Fig. 3.8

3.4.2 Definition. Two conceptual relations of the same type are *duplicates* if for each *i*, the *i*th arc of one is linked to the same concept as the *i*th arc of the other.

To illustrate the formation rules, Fig. 3.7 shows two canonical graphs. The first one may be read *A girl is eating fast*; and the second, *A person, Sue, is eating pie*. If the concept of type PERSON in the second graph were restricted to type GIRL (by the rule of restriction), then the graphs of Fig. 3.7 would be changed to those in Fig. 3.8. But before doing the restriction, the conformity relation must be checked to ensure that GIRL::Sue is true.

Now the concept [GIRL] in the first graph can also be restricted to [GIRL:Sue]. The two identical pairs of concepts, [GIRL:Sue] and [EAT], can then be joined to each other. The result is Fig. 3.9. In that graph, the two copies of (AGNT) are duplicates. When one of them is deleted by simplification, the graph becomes Fig. 3.10, which may be read *A girl, Sue, is eating pie fast.*

The formation rules are a kind of *graph grammar* for canonical graphs. Besides defining syntax, they also enforce certain semantic constraints. Appendix B.3 shows the number and types of concepts expected for each conceptual relation. The rules can never relax or erase those constraints. If all the graphs in the starting set obey the constraints, then all the derived graphs will also obey them.

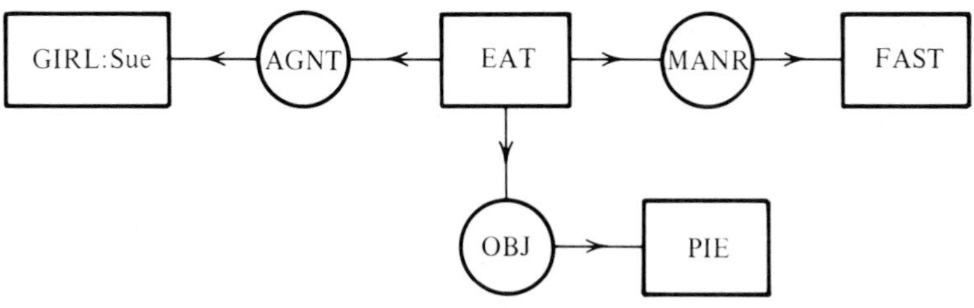

Fig. 3.10 Simplification of Fig. 3.9

3.4.3 Assumption. There are four *canonical formation rules* for deriving a conceptual graph *w* from conceptual graphs *u* and *v* (where *u* and *v* may be the same graph):

- *Copy.* *w* is an exact copy of *u*.
- *Restrict.* For any concept *c* in *u*, *type*(*c*) may be replaced by a subtype; if *c* is generic, its referent may be changed to an individual marker. These changes are permitted only if *referent*(*c*) conforms to *type*(*c*) before and after the change.
- *Join.* If a concept *c* in *u* is identical to a concept *d* in *v*, then let *w* be the graph obtained by deleting *d* and linking to *c* all arcs of conceptual relations that had been linked to *d*.
- *Simplify.* If conceptual relations *r* and *s* in the graph *u* are duplicates, then one of them may be deleted from *u* together with all its arcs.

Although the number of canonical graphs may be infinite, the formation rules can derive all of them from a finite set. Suppose that the following two graphs are in the starting set:

```
[PHYSOBJ]→(ATTR)→[COLOR].
[SLEEP]→(AGNT)→[ANIMAL].
```

By restrict, the type label PHYSOBJ may be restricted to the subtype ANIMAL. Then join can merge the two concepts of type ANIMAL to form the graph,

```
[SLEEP]→(AGNT)→[ANIMAL]→(ATTR)→[COLOR].
```

This graph could be further restricted to form graphs for the sentences *A brown beaver sleeps* or *A purple cow sleeps.* But since IDEA is not a subtype of ANIMAL, there is no way of deriving *A green idea sleeps.* The formation rules enforce selectional constraints by preventing certain combinations from being derived.

Canonical formation rules are not *rules of inference.* If some girl is eating fast and Sue is eating pie, it does not follow that Sue is the one who is eating pie fast. The formation rules enforce selectional constraints, but they make no guarantee of truth or falsity. To see exactly what they do, consider the following levels of meaningfulness, adapted from Sommers (1959) and Odell (1971):

- Gibberish:
  Ozderst vwxo ahlazza.
- English words, but in an ungrammatical sequence:
  A am I number prime.
- Grammatical sequence, but violating selectional constraints:
  I am a prime number.

- Obeying selectional constraints, but violating rules of logic, meaning postulates, or word intensions:
  I am the prime minister of the U.K., and so is Margaret.
- Logically consistent, but possibly false:
  I am the prime minister of the U.K.
- Empirically true:
  I am writing about canonical formation rules in this section.

Syntactic rules can map noncanonical graphs into grammatical, but nonsensical sentences, such as *I am a prime number* or *Colorless green ideas sleep furiously*. Canonical graphs prevent such nonsense from being generated, but they may violate meaning postulates. To say that two people are prime minister at the same time is inconsistent with the meaning postulates for *prime minister*. If a canonical graph is not blocked by inconsistencies, it may be mapped to a logical sentence. To say *I am the prime minister* is logical and meaningful, but false. And if a graph describes an actual situation in the real world, the resulting sentence is empirically true.

The sentence *Colorless green ideas sleep furiously* contains several kinds of anomalies. The combinations *green ideas* and *ideas sleep* violate selectional constraints, and the combination *colorless green* violates rules of logic. The phrase *sleep furiously* does not violate logic or selectional constraints, but it is unexpected, unlikely, and implausible. That combination cannot be ruled out completely since one can imagine a person going to bed a with a dogged determination to spend a night of violent, unconscious tossing and turning. Instead, the *schemata* of Section 4.1 incorporate background knowledge about the world and the usual combinations of entities, attributes, and events in it. Since no schema would contain the combination *sleep furiously*, it would be considered unlikely, but not impossible. Canonical formation rules are a *context-free graph grammar*; they rule out nonsensical sentences with local constraints. Logic, however, requires *context-sensitive rules* that enforce global constraints. Such restrictions are enforced by the rules of inference in Chapter 4.

By means of joins and restrictions, the formation rules let a subtype inherit the properties of its supertype. Schank (1975) presented a list of fifteen primitive graphs from which all his other graphs could be derived by joins and restrictions. Even systems with a linear notation, such as KRL (Bobrow & Winograd 1977), rely on combining operations that have the same effect as joins. For relational databases, a join of two concepts is an intensional operation that parallels Codd's extensional joins (1970). If two database relations are described by conceptual graphs, the join of the two relations on a common domain is described by the join of the two graphs on a common concept.

3.4.4 Definition. Let A be any set of conceptual graphs. A graph w is said to be *canonically derivable* from A if either of the following conditions is true:

- w is a member of A.

- w may be derived by applying a canonical formation rule to graphs u and v that are themselves canonically derivable from A.

Schank's fifteen primitive graphs, from which all his other graphs are derivable, constitute a *canonical basis*. A canonical basis can be as small and simple as Schank's, or it can be a larger, richer set of graphs with more constraints and background information. Various trade-offs are possible. A small, simple basis contains very little knowledge of the world, and more information has to be packed into other structures, such as the schemata defined in Chapter 4.

3.4.5 Assumption. The *canon* contains the information necessary for deriving a set of canonical graphs. It has four components:

- A type hierarchy T,
- A set of individual markers I,
- A conformity relation :: that relates labels in T to markers in I,
- A finite set of conceptual graphs B, called a *canonical basis*, with all type labels in T and all referents either * or markers in I.

The canonical graphs are the *closure* of B under the canonical formation rules. If a new graph is canonized that cannot be canonically derived from B, then it must be added to B.

3.5 GENERALIZATION AND SPECIALIZATION

The canonical formation rules are *specialization rules*. Restriction, for example, specializes the concept [ANIMAL] to [DOG] or [BEAGLE]. Join specializes a graph by adding conditions and attributes from another graph. In the derivation from Fig. 3.7 to Fig. 3.10, the resulting graph has more conditions than either of the graphs from which it was derived, and the generic concept [GIRL] was specialized to the individual [GIRL:Sue]. Copy and simplification do not specialize a graph further, but neither do they generalize it.

This section considers the operation of *generalization*, which proceeds in the reverse order of specialization. Whereas specialization does not preserve truth, generalization does. If the girl Sue is eating pie fast, then it must be true that some girl is eating fast and that the person Sue is eating pie. Unfortunately, generalization does not necessarily preserve selectional constraints. If the girl Sue is eating pie, it follows that some entity is eating some entity, but the graph

```
[ENTITY]←(AGNT)←[EAT]→(OBJ)→[ENTITY]
```

does not include the constraints expected for the concept [EAT]. Even though generalizations are not necessarily canonical, they are important because they form the basis for logic and model theory in Chapter 4.

3.5.1 Definition. If a conceptual graph u is canonically derivable from a conceptual graph v (possibly with the join of other conceptual graphs $w_1,...,w_n$), then u is called a *specialization* of v, written $u \leq v$, and v is called a *generalization* of u.

This definition has important implications: any graph is a generalization of itself; any subgraph is a generalization of the original; replacing a type label with a supertype generalizes a graph; and erasing an individual marker generalizes a graph. In particular, the graph consisting of the single concept [⊤] is a generalization of every other conceptual graph. These properties are proved as the next theorem.

3.5.2 Theorem. Generalization defines a partial ordering of conceptual graphs called the *generalization hierarchy*. For any conceptual graphs u, v, and w, the following properties are true:

- *Reflexive.* $u \leq u$.
- *Transitive.* If $u \leq v$ and $v \leq w$, then $u \leq w$.
- *Antisymmetric.* If $u \leq v$ and $v \leq u$, then $u = v$.
- *Subgraph.* If v is a subgraph of u, then $u \leq v$.
- *Subtypes.* If u is identical to v except that one or more type labels of v are restricted to subtypes in u, then $u \leq v$.
- *Individuals.* If u is identical to v except that one or more generic concepts of v are restricted to individual concepts of the same type, then $u \leq v$.
- *Top.* The graph [⊤] is a generalization of all other conceptual graphs.

Proof. Since u is canonically derivable from itself by the copy rule, $u \leq u$. If u is canonically derivable from v and v is canonically derivable from w, then u must be canonically derivable from w; therefore, $u \leq w$. If u is canonically derivable from v and v is canonically derivable from u, the only way they could have been derived is by copy; therefore, they must be identical. If v is a subgraph of u, then u must be canonically derivable from v by joining the other parts of u that are not included in v; therefore, $u \leq v$. If u is derived from v by restricting type labels to subtypes or generic concepts to individual, then u is canonically derivable from v; therefore, $u \leq v$. Finally, any graph u can be canonically derived from [⊤] (plus some other graph) simply by letting the other graph be u itself; then restrict [⊤] to the type and referent of any concept c in u and join it to c.

If the graph u is a specialization of v, whenever u represents a true situation, v must also represent a true situation. In Section 4.3, that property is shown directly by inferences on conceptual graphs. Another proof would use the operator ϕ that translates conceptual graphs into logical formulas. The next theorem shows that if $u \leq v$, a canonical derivation of u from v corresponds to the reverse of a proof of the formula ϕv from the formula ϕu. The proof depends on the fact that the formation rules add properties to a graph. But if A and B are any properties, then $(A \wedge B) \supset A$. Hence the graph u with more properties implies the simpler graph v.

3.5.3 Theorem. For any conceptual graphs u and v, if $u \leq v$, then $\phi u \supset \phi v$.

Proof. Consider a canonical derivation of u from v with intermediate graphs $v_1, v_2, \ldots, v_n$ where $v = v_1$ and $u = v_n$. To prove that ϕu implies ϕv, show that at each step ϕv_{i+1} implies ϕv_i. Then the sequence of formulas $\phi v_n, \ldots, \phi v_1$ would constitute a proof of ϕv under the hypothesis of ϕu. The rule for deriving the graph v_{i+1} from v_i must be either copy, simplify, restrict, or join:

- If copy, v_{i+1} is identical to v_i. Therefore, ϕv_{i+1} implies ϕv_i.
- If simplify, ϕv_i contains a duplicate predicate that is omitted in ϕv_{i+1}. Since any formula A implies the conjunction $A \wedge A$, ϕv_{i+1} implies ϕv_i.
- If a type label T is restricted to a subtype S, ϕv_i has a predicate $T(x)$ that is replaced by a predicate $S(x)$ in ϕv_{i+1}. By Assumption 3.2.4, $\delta S \subseteq \delta T$. Hence for any x, $S(x)$ implies $T(x)$. If a generic marker is restricted to an individual i, then $S(i)$ implies the generic $\exists x S(x)$. In either case, ϕv_{i+1} implies ϕv_i.
- If join, ϕv_{i+1} is equivalent to a formula of the form $\exists x_1 \ldots \exists x_k (P \wedge Q \wedge x = y)$ where P is the body of ϕv_i, Q is a conjunction of predicates derived from some other graph w that was joined to v_i, and the equation $x = y$ equates the two identifiers of the concepts that were joined. But the conjunction $P \wedge Q \wedge x = y$ implies P. Therefore, ϕv_{i+1} implies ϕv_i.

The canonical formation rules are the opposite of rules of inference. Whereas a rule of inference derives true graphs from true graphs, the canonical formation rules derive false graphs from false graphs. For this reason, they may be called *refutation rules*: one way to refute a graph is to show that it is canonically derivable from a false graph. This property is used in the *open-world models* of Section 4.5: two special sets of graphs T and F are introduced, where all graphs in T are true and all graphs in F are false. If u is a generalization of some graph in T, it must also be true; but if u is a specialization of some graph in F, it must be false.

If u is a specialization of v, there must be a subgraph u' embedded in u that represents the original v to which additional graphs were joined during the canonical derivation. That subgraph u' is called a *projection* of v in u. The Greek letter π is used for a *projection operator*: $u' = \pi v$. Every conceptual relation in πv must be identical to the corresponding relation in v, but some of the concepts in v may have been restricted to subtypes or may have been converted from generic to individual. In the derivation of u from v, some concepts of v may have been joined to each other, and some conceptual relations may have been eliminated as duplicates. Therefore, the projection πv must contain a basic core of v, but its shape and concept types may be different. In fact, v may be a planar, acyclic graph, but πv might be folded back upon itself to form complex cycles.

3.5.4 Theorem. For any conceptual graphs u and v where $u \leq v$, there must exist a mapping π: $v \rightarrow u$, where πv is a subgraph of u called a *projection* of v in u. The *projection operator* π has the following properties:

- For each concept c in v, πc is a concept in πv where $type(\pi c) \leq type(c)$. If c is individual, then $referent(c) = referent(\pi c)$.
- For each conceptual relation r in v, πr is a conceptual relation in πv where $type(\pi r) = type(r)$. If the ith arc of r is linked to a concept c in v, the ith arc of πr must be linked to πc in πv.

The mapping π is not necessarily one-to-one: if x_1 and x_2 are two concepts or conceptual relations where $x_1 \neq x_2$, it may happen that $\pi x_1 = \pi x_2$. The mapping π is not necessarily unique: the graph v may also have another projection $\pi' v$ in u where $\pi' v \neq \pi v$.

Proof. Construct the mapping π as the composition of separate mappings $\pi_1, \ldots, \pi_n$ that correspond to the steps of some canonical derivation of u from v. Consider step i of the derivation:

- If copy, let π_i be the identity mapping.
- If restriction of a concept c, let π_i map c to the newly restricted form, and let it be the identity mapping on the rest of the graph. For π_i, the conclusions of the theorem hold.
- If join, let π_i map both concepts that were joined to the single joined concept, and let it be the identity mapping on the rest of the graph. Since joins do not change referents and they keep relations linked to corresponding concepts, the conclusions must hold.
- If simplify, let π_i map both duplicate relations into the single conceptual relation that remains, and let it be the identity mapping on the rest of the graph. Since duplicate relations, by definition, must be of the same type and be linked to exactly the same concepts in exactly the same order, the conclusions of the theorem must hold.

Let πv be the composition $\pi_n \ldots \pi_1 v$. Since each step π_i preserves the conditions and conclusions of the theorem, the composition π must also preserve them.

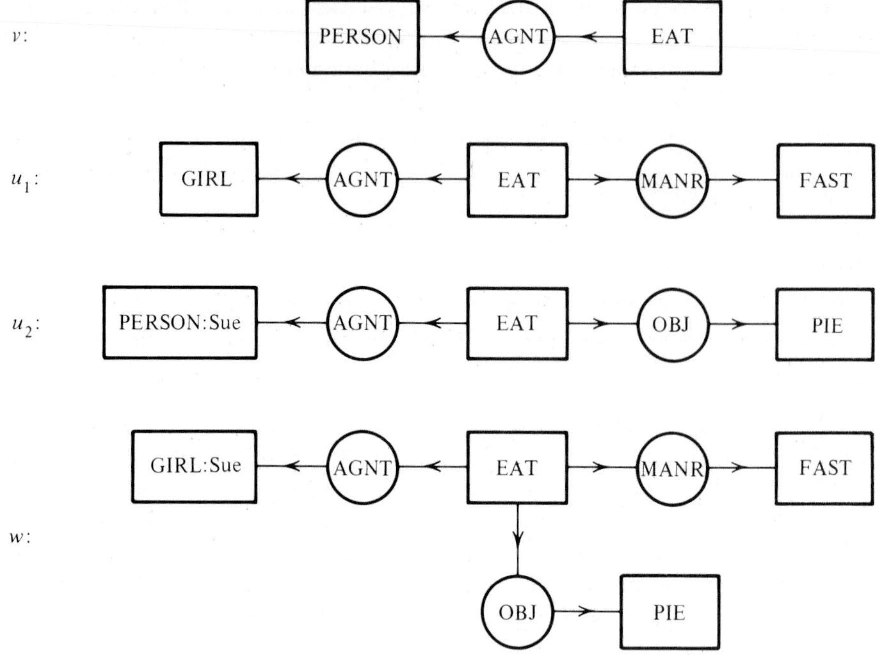

Fig. 3.11 A common generalization and a common specialization

Projections map graphs at higher levels of the generalization hierarchy into ones at lower levels. The hierarchy is not a lattice because two graphs may not have a unique minimal common generalization and a unique maximal common specialization. But any two graphs have at least one *common generalization*, since the graph [⊤] is a common generalization of all. There is no guarantee that they must have a *common specialization*, but many of them do.

3.5.5 Definition. Let u_1, u_2, v, and w be conceptual graphs. If $u_1 \leq v$ and $u_2 \leq v$, then v is called a *common generalization* of u_1 and u_2. If $w \leq u_1$ and $w \leq u_2$, then w is called a *common specialization* of u_1 and u_2.

Whenever two graphs u_1 and u_2 are joined on one or more concepts, the resulting graph w is a common specialization of both. In Fig. 3.11, the two middle graphs were joined to form the lower graph, which is a common specialization. Whenever two graphs are joined in such a way, the parts that were merged must be projections of some common generalization. In this example, they are both projections of the top graph v. Conversely, if two graphs u_1 and u_2 have a common generalization v, then the corresponding projections $\pi_1 v$ in u_1 and $\pi_2 v$ in u_2 are candidates for being merged by a series of joins (possibly with additional restrictions and simplifications). Such a merger might be blocked, however, by incompatible type labels or referents. If there are no incompatibilities, then the two projections are said to be *compatible*.

3.5.6 Definition. Let conceptual graphs u_1 and u_2 have a common generalization v with projections π_1: $v \rightarrow u_1$ and π_2: $v \rightarrow u_2$. The two projections are said to be *compatible* if for each concept c in v, the following conditions are true:

- $type(\pi_1 c) \cap type(\pi_2 c) > \bot$.
- The referents of $\pi_1 c$ and $\pi_2 c$ conform to $type(\pi_1 c) \cap type(\pi_2 c)$.
- If $referent(\pi_1 c)$ is the individual marker i, then $referent(\pi_2 c)$ is either i or $*$.

The common specialization w may be derived by joining the graphs u_1 and u_2 on compatible projections of the more general graph v. A good way to visualize the join is to imagine the graphs u_1 and u_2 drawn on plastic transparencies and then overlaid on each other so that the compatible projections merge (some stretching and twisting may be necessary). Since any graph can be projected into one of its specializations, both u_1 and u_2 can be projected into w. For Fig. 3.11, the subgraph of w that falls in the overlap of u_1 and u_2 is the following projection of v into w:

```
[GIRL:Sue]←(AGNT)←[EAT].
```

The conditions for compatible projections ensure that corresponding concepts can be restricted to identical forms and then be joined. Definition 3.5.6 rules out a restriction to the absurd type $\bot$ since no possible entity could ever conform to type $\bot$. If all the conditions of 3.5.6 are satisfied, the two graphs can be merged by a *join on compatible projections*.

3.5.7 Theorem. If conceptual graphs u_1 and u_2 have a common generalization v with compatible projections π_1: $v \rightarrow u_1$ and π_2: $v \rightarrow u_2$, then there exists a unique conceptual graph w with the following properties:

- w is a common specialization of u_1 and u_2.
- There exist projections π_1': $u_1 \rightarrow w$ and π_2': $u_2 \rightarrow w$ where $\pi_1' \pi_1 v = \pi_2' \pi_2 v$.
- If w' is any other conceptual graph with the above two properties, then $w' < w$.

The graph w is called a *join on compatible projections* of u_1 and u_2. If both u_1 and u_2 are canonical graphs, then so is w.

Proof. The graph w can be constructed from u_1 and u_2 by the following canonical derivation:

- For each concept c_i in v, restrict $\pi_1 c_i$ and $\pi_2 c_i$ to $type(\pi_1 c_i) \cap type(\pi_2 c_i)$.

- For each concept c_i in v, join the newly restricted concepts $\pi_1 c_i$ and $\pi_2 c_i$ to each other.
- Simplify the resulting graph by eliminating duplicate relations.

The definition of compatible projections ensures that these restrictions and joins are permissible. Therefore, w is canonical if u_1 and u_2 are canonical. To show that w is a generalization of any other common specialization of u_1 and u_2 that meets the condition $\pi_1' \pi_1 v = \pi_2' \pi_2 v$, observe that the construction of w does the minimum number of restrictions, joins, and simplifications necessary to meet that condition. Therefore, any other common specialization meeting that condition must be derivable from w by additional applications of the canonical formation rules.

Since two conceptual graphs may have many different common generalizations, they may also have many different pairs of compatible projections. For most computations, large compatible projections are preferred to smaller ones. The next theorem gives the conditions for one pair of compatible projections to be an *extension* of some other pair.

3.5.8 Theorem. Let conceptual graphs u_1 and u_2 have a common generalization v with compatible projections π_1: $v \rightarrow u_1$ and π_2: $v \rightarrow u_2$, and let v' be a proper subgraph of v. Then v' is also a common generalization of u_1 and u_2 with compatible projections π_1: $v' \rightarrow u_1$ and π_2: $v' \rightarrow u_2$. The compatible projections $\pi_1 v$ and $\pi_2 v$ are said to be *extensions* of $\pi_1 v'$ and $\pi_2 v'$.

Proof. Since v' is a subgraph of v, $v \leq v'$. Since $u_1 \leq v$ and $u_2 \leq v$, it follows that $u_1 \leq v'$ and $u_2 \leq v'$. Since $\pi_1 v$ and $\pi_2 v$ are compatible, their subgraphs $\pi_1 v'$ and $\pi_2 v'$ must also be compatible.

If two graphs contain compatible projections of a common generalization v, those projections might be extended by finding a larger common generalization that includes v as a subgraph. Since all conceptual graphs are finite, the process of extension must eventually stop. When it stops, the resulting compatible projections are called *maximally extended.* A join on those projections is then called a *maximal join.* The join is locally maximal, because there may be other compatible projections of two graphs that are also maximally extended.

One algorithm for computing a maximal join is to start by joining two graphs on a single concept. Then extend the join by one conceptual relation at a time by looking for potential candidates along the boundaries of the part that has already been joined. When no more candidates can be found, the join is locally maximal. For unlabeled graphs, finding a globally maximal join is a difficult combinatorial problem. For practical applications, such as comparing organic molecules, analyzing scene descriptions, or joining conceptual graphs, the labels on the nodes reduce the combinations to a manageable number. McGregor (1982) presents efficient algorithms for computing maximal joins.

3.6.9 Definition. Two compatible projections are said to be *maximally extended* if they have no extensions. A join on maximally extended compatible projections is called a *maximal join.*

Maximal joins are important because they join two graphs on maximally connected subparts. They form the basis for *preference semantics* (Wilks 1975), which encourages maximum connectivity in the generated graphs. The mechanisms of type expansion in Section 3.6, schematic join in Section 4.1, heuristic preference rules in Section 4.7, semantic interpretation in Section 5.6, and database inference in Section 6.5 are all based on maximal joins.

3.6 ABSTRACTION AND DEFINITION

Verbs like *think, know*, and *believe* take complete sentences as their objects. They lead to structures of graphs embedded inside the nodes of other graphs. The statement *Norma loves Joe* can be represented in a simple graph, but the statement *I think that Norma loves Joe* leads to the graph,

```
[PROPOSITION: [PERSON:Norma]←(EXPR)←[LOVE]→(OBJ)→[PERSON:Joe]]
```

where the object of [THINK] is a concept with type label PROPOSITION and the graph of *Norma loves Joe* as its referent. One of the most important verbs that takes a sentence as its object is *define.* A definition can equate an entire graph with a name or type label.

Some systems do not support definitions. For MARGIE, Schank (1975) claimed that only eleven primitive types of acts were sufficient to represent a wide range of English. For acts such as BUY, SELL, BEAT, or RACE, the parser for MARGIE translated the complex act into a combination of primitives (Riesbeck 1975). Some systems are not dogmatic about which concepts are primitive, but they have no mechanisms for dynamically defining new types in terms of more primitive ones.

Type definitions provide a way of expanding a concept in primitives or contracting a concept from a graph of primitives. Even though Schank did not have a formal mechanism for definitions, Riesbeck's parser did expansions upon input. For output, Goldman's language generator (1975) contracted large graphs into single verbs like *admit* or *threaten.* Without a formal theory of definitions, the input parser and the output generator used different mechanisms, and Rieger's inference engine (1975) had to do its reasoning upon large graphs expanded in low-level primitives. More recently, Schank and his colleagues have begun to introduce high-level types such as

AUTHORIZE, ORDER, and PETITION (Schank & Carbonell 1979) or KISS, MOAN, and SHOUT (Rieger 1979). Then a single concept like [KISS] can trigger inferences without a search for patterns of passionate lip contact.

Definitions can specify a type in two different ways: by stating necessary and sufficient conditions for the type, or by giving a few examples and saying that everything similar to these belongs to the type. The first method derives from Aristotle's method of definition by *genus* and *differentiae*, and the second is closer to Wittgenstein (1953). AI systems have supported both methods:

- Definitions by genus and differentiae are logically easiest to handle. They have been incorporated in REL (Thompson & Thompson 1975), OWL (Martin 1979), and MCHINE (Ritchie 1980).
- Definitions by examples or prototypes are essential for dealing with natural language and its applications to the real world, but their logical status is unclear. Some systems that support prototypes are KRL (Bobrow & Winograd 1977), KL-ONE (Brachman 1979), and TAXMAN (McCarty & Sridharan 1981).

TAXMAN is designed for legal reasoning in corporate tax law. Since most legal disputes arise when the issues are vague, ill-defined, or otherwise difficult to classify, definitions by necessary and sufficient conditions are not possible. For greater flexibility, TAXMAN uses prototypes that represent the standard cases and *deformations* that adapt the prototypes to changing conditions.

Conceptual graphs support type definitions by genus and differentiae as well as *schemata* and *prototypes*, which specify sets of family resemblances. Both methods are based on *abstractions*, which are canonical graphs with one or more concepts designated as *formal parameters*.

3.6.1 Definition. An *n-adic abstraction*, $\lambda a_1,...,a_n u$, consists of a canonical graph u, called the *body*, together with a list of generic concepts $a_1,...,a_n$ in u, called the *formal parameters*. The *parameter list* following λ distinguishes the formal parameters from the other concepts in u.

An abstraction is like a procedure in a programming language. The Greek letter λ introduces the formal parameters. In the body, each concept used as a parameter contains one of the variable symbols in its referent field:

```
λx,y [SUPPLY]-
        (AGNT)→[SUPPLIER:*x]
        (OBJ)→[PART:*y]→(COLR)→[RED].
```

In this example, λx,y identifies [SUPPLIER:*x] and [PART:*y] as formal parameters. The concepts [SUPPLY] and [RED], which are not parameters, are like local variables in a procedure or function. The body of an abstraction is a conceptual graph that asserts some proposition. When n formal parameters are identified, the abstraction becomes an n-adic predicate, which is true or false only when specific referents are assigned to its parameters. The formula operator ϕ maps abstractions into λ-expressions in standard logic; each such expression defines a new predicate. See Appendix A.2 for a discussion of the lambda calculus.

3.6.2 Assumption. The formula operator ϕ maps n-adic abstractions into n-adic lambda expressions:

- Let $\lambda a_1,...,a_n u$ be an n-adic abstraction.
- Let $x_1,...,x_m$ be variables assigned to the generic concepts of u other than the formal parameters.
- Remove the quantifiers from the formula ϕu to leave the predicates Φ.

Then $\phi\lambda a_1,...,a_n u$ is the lambda expression, $\lambda a_1,...,a_n \exists x_1 ... \exists x_m \Phi$.

For the abstraction relating suppliers and parts in the previous example, the formula operator ϕ would generate the following λ-expression in standard logic:

$$\lambda x,y\exists z\exists w(\text{SUPPLY}(z) \wedge \text{AGNT}(z,x) \wedge \text{SUPPLIER}(x) \wedge \text{OBJ}(z,y) \wedge \text{PART}(y) \wedge \text{COLR}(y,w) \wedge \text{RED}(w)).$$

In some database systems, a lambda expression is used as a query specification. This expression corresponds to the query *List suppliers and parts where the suppliers supply the parts and the parts are colored red.* For that query, the clause that occurs after *where* is mapped to the body of the expression, and the words between *list* and *where* are mapped to the formal parameters. For many queries, the terms marked by question words like *who, which,* or *what* become the formal parameters. To answer the query, the denotation operator δ searches the database for all values of suppliers and parts that make the relationships in the graph true. The denotation of an abstraction is a set of n-tuples (in this case, pairs of SUPPLIER and PART) that may be assigned as the referents of the formal parameters to make the graph true.

The generalization hierarchy of conceptual graphs extends to abstractions. One abstraction is a specialization of another if its body is a specialization of the other's body. There is an additional constraint, however: the projection π from the more general graph to the more specialized one must map corresponding parameters to each other. The hierarchy of abstractions is similar to the hierarchy of procedures in the TAXIS system for database semantics (Mylopoulos et al. 1980).

3.6.3 Assumption. A generalization hierarchy is defined over abstractions. For a pair of n-adic abstractions, $\lambda a_1,...,a_n u \leq \lambda b_1,...,b_n v$ if the following conditions hold:

- For the two bodies, $u \leq v$.
- There exists a projection π of v into u, which for all i maps the parameter b_i of v into the parameter a_i of u.

type KISS(x) is

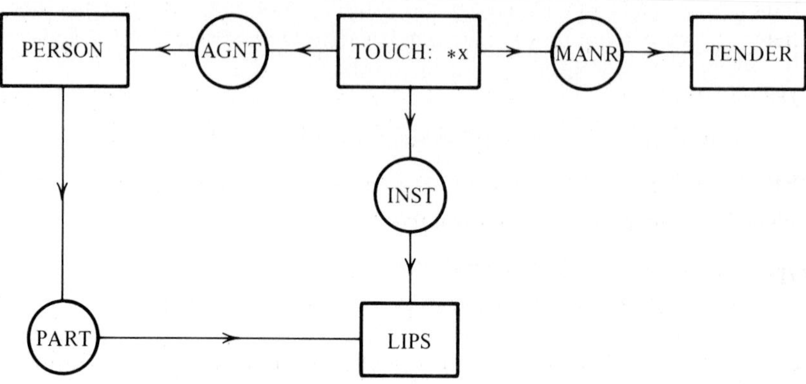

Fig. 3.12 Type definition for KISS

New type labels are defined by an Aristotelian approach. Some type of concept is named as the genus, and a canonical graph, called the differentia, distinguishes the new type from the genus. The differentia is the body of a monadic abstraction, and the genus is the type label of the formal parameter. As an example of type definition, Fig. 3.12 defines KISS with genus TOUCH and with a differentia graph that says that the touching is done by a person's lips in a tender manner. Since the keyword **type** introduces the type label and the parameter list, the symbol λ may be omitted. Type definition is like function definition in LISP: a method for assigning a label to an abstraction. As in LISP, unlabeled abstractions can appear anywhere that a type label might appear, as in the type field of a concept box or relation circle.

3.6.4 Assumption. A *type definition* declares that a type label t is defined by a monadic abstraction $\lambda a\ u$. It is written, **type** $t(a)$ **is** u. The body u is called the *differentia* of t, and $type(a)$ is called the *genus* of t. The abstraction $\lambda a\ u$ may be written in the type field of any concept where the type label t may be written.

Any generic concept in a canonical graph may be chosen as the genus of a type definition. Following are three type definitions based on the same differentia, but with different concepts marked as the genus. The first example defines the label CIRCUS-ELEPHANT as a subtype of ELEPHANT that performs in a circus:

```
type CIRCUS-ELEPHANT(x) is
     [ELEPHANT:*x]←(AGNT)←[PERFORM]→(LOC)→[CIRCUS].
```

Either of the other two concept types in this graph could have been chosen as the genus instead of [ELEPHANT]. If [CIRCUS] had been marked as the formal parameter, it would define a type of CIRCUS that had a performing elephant:

```
type ELEPHANT-CIRCUS(y) is
     [ELEPHANT]←(AGNT)←[PERFORM]→(LOC)→[CIRCUS:*y].
```

If [PERFORM] had been marked as the parameter, it would define a type of performance that an elephant does in a circus:

```
type ELEPHANT-PERFORMANCE(z) is
     [ELEPHANT]←(AGNT)←[PERFORM:*z]→(LOC)→[CIRCUS].
```

This definition implies that an elephant performance must have at least one elephant, but it does not rule out the possibility of multiple elephants. To be more explicit, the notation [ELEPHANT:{*}], introduced in Section 3.7, could be used to represent an arbitrary set of elephants.

An important use for type definition is to describe a *subrange* that limits the possible referents for a concept. The type POSITIVE, for example, could be defined as a number that is greater than zero:

```
type POSITIVE(x) is [NUMBER:*x]→(>)→[NUMBER:0].
```

To avoid the need for defining a special type label for every subrange, the abstraction that defines a type may be used in the type field of a concept without associating it with a particular label. In the following concept, the λ-expression in the type field constrains the referent to be a positive number, in this case, 15:

```
[λx [NUMBER:*x]→(>)→[NUMBER:0]: 15].
```

An even shorter notation is "NUMBER>0" as an abbreviation for the λ-expression. The string ">0" is treated as part of the type field. Since 15 is a positive number, the concept [NUMBER>0:15] is well formed. Similar subranges are 0<NUMBER<25 or SPEED≤55mph. The latter is an abbreviation for the following abstraction:

```
λx [SPEED:*x]→(MEAS)→[MEASURE]→(≤)→[MEASURE:55mph].
```

Once a mechanism is available for defining new types, the definitions can be used to simplify the graphs. Type contraction deletes a complete subgraph and incorporates the equivalent information in the type label of a single concept. If some graph u happens to contain a subgraph u' that corresponds to the body of some type definition $t=\lambda av$, then redundant parts of u' may be deleted. In its place, the concept of u' that corresponds to the parameter a of v has its type label replaced with t. The next definition specifies an algorithm for carrying out the contraction.

3.6.5 Assumption. Let *u* be a canonical graph, and let type *t* be defined as λav. If *u* is a specialization of *v*, π is a projection of *v* into *u*, and $type(\pi a)=type(a)$, then the operation of *type contraction* may be performed on *u* by the following algorithm:

```
replace the type label of πa with t;
leave referent(πa) unchanged;
for b in the concepts and conceptual relations of v where
        b≠a, πb identical to b, and πb not a cutpoint of u loop
    if b is a concept then
        detach πb from u;
    else
        detach πb and all its arcs from u;
    end if;
end loop;
for e in the arcs left in u not linked to a concept loop
    reattach the concept that had been linked to arc e in u;
end loop;
```

If type contraction is performed on a canonical graph, the resulting graph is also canonical. The notation [λa *v*: *i*] represents the contracted form of the concept πa, where the type is λa *v*, and the referent *i* is the original $referent(\pi a)$.

As an example of type contraction, let *u* be the following graph, which may be read *The elephant Clyde, who performs in a circus, is gray*,

```
[GRAY]←(COLR)←[ELEPHANT:Clyde]←(AGNT)←[PERFORM]→(LOC)→[CIRCUS].
```

This graph corresponds to graph *u* in Assumption 3.6.5, and *v* is the differentia for defining CIRCUS-ELEPHANT:

```
[ELEPHANT:*x]←(AGNT)←[PERFORM]→(LOC)→[CIRCUS].
```

The following graph is the projection πv of *v* into *u*:

```
[ELEPHANT:Clyde]←(AGNT)←[PERFORM]→(LOC)→[CIRCUS].
```

The concept [ELEPHANT:Clyde] is πa, which is a projection of the genus concept [ELEPHANT:*x] of *v*. The next stage of type contraction replaces the type label of πa to form the graph,

```
[GRAY]←(COLR)←[CIRCUS-ELEPHANT:Clyde]-
    (AGNT)←[PERFORM]→(LOC)→[CIRCUS].
```

The **for**-loop in Assumption 3.6.5 now begins to detach concepts and conceptual relations from this graph. In the first iteration of the loop, the only candidate for πb is the concept [CIRCUS]. After πb is detached, the relation (LOC) is left with a dangling arc:

```
[GRAY]←(COLR)←[CIRCUS-ELEPHANT:Clyde]-
      (AGNT)←[PERFORM]→(LOC)→
```

When the **for**-loop is repeated, the next candidate for πb is (LOC), which is then detached together with its arcs. Then [PERFORM] is detached, and finally (AGNT) is detached to generate the following graph:

```
[GRAY]←(COLR)←[CIRCUS-ELEPHANT:Clyde].
```

This graph, which may be read *The circus elephant Clyde is gray*, is the final result of type contraction, since no conceptual relations with dangling arcs are left.

Type contraction deletes subgraphs that can be recovered from information in the differentia. If some nodes covered by the differentia are linked to other nodes that are not covered, then they cannot be deleted. Otherwise, the graph would become disconnected. The inverse of type contraction is *type expansion*, which replaces a concept type with its definition. The type label of the genus replaces the defined type label, and the graph for the differentia is joined to the concept.

3.6.6 Definition. Let u be a canonical graph containing a concept a where $type(a)=\lambda b\ v$. Then *minimal type expansion* consists of joining the graphs u and v on the concepts a and b.

A minimal type expansion joins the differentia v to the graph u, but it does not replace the type label of the concept a. The result is canonical because it could be derived simply by restricting b to $type(a)$ and then doing a join. Yet the result of type contraction followed by a minimal type expansion is not identical to the original. It may contain a redundant subgraph, and the type label of the concept a is not restored. A *maximal type expansion*, however, makes more extensive changes to restore the graph to the original as far as possible.

3.6.7 Definition. A *maximal type expansion* starts with a minimal type expansion and takes the following additional steps. Let a, b, u, and v satisfy the same hypotheses as in Definition 3.6.6.

- Extend the join of a and b to a maximal join.
- Replace the type label of concept a with a type label t, where $type(a)\leq t\leq type(b)$, the result of replacing $type(a)$ with t is canonical, and there is no type s where $t<s\leq type(b)$ and the result of replacing $type(a)$ with s would be canonical.

The more conservative, minimal expansion preserves truth: if the original graph is true, the expanded graph must also be true. A maximal expansion merges the new parts with the old parts as far as possible; yet the merger is only plausible, not logically certain. To illustrate type expansion, Fig. 3.13 defines BUY as a type of TRANSACTION. The transaction has two components, each an instance of GIVE.

type BUY(x) is

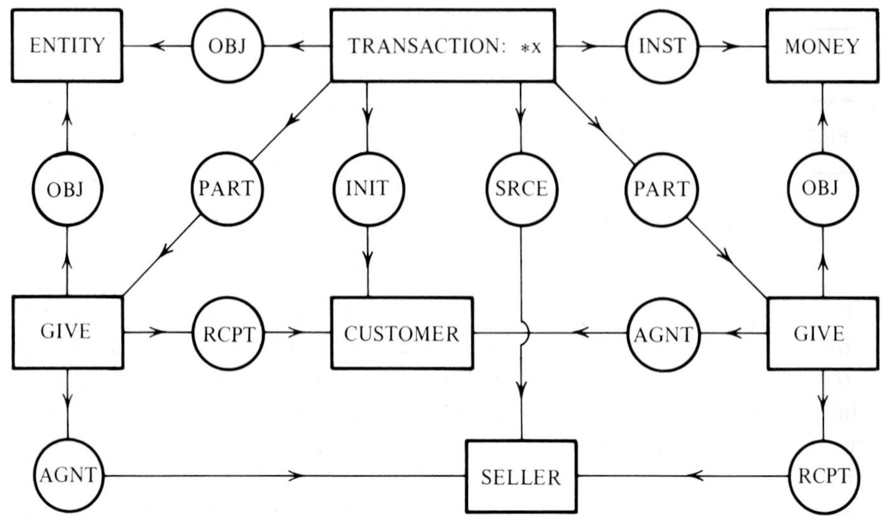

Fig. 3.13 Type definition for BUY

The initiator of the transaction is a CUSTOMER who is the recipient of one act of GIVE and the agent of the other GIVE. The object of the transaction is an ENTITY that is also the object of the first GIVE. The instrument of the transaction is MONEY, which is also the object of the second GIVE. And the source of the transaction is a SELLER who is the agent of one GIVE and the recipient of the other.

Now suppose that the phrase *Joe buying a necktie from Hal for $10* were translated to Fig. 3.14. The concepts [BUY] and [NECKTIE] are generic concepts, [PERSON:Joe] and [PERSON:Hal] are individual concepts, and [MONEY:@$10] is a measure contraction for,

```
[MONEY]→(MEAS)→[MEASURE]→(NAME)→["$10"].
```

The contracted form follows the conventions of Section 3.4 for units of measure. The @ symbol shows that $10 is a measure of money, not the name of some money.

By type expansion, [BUY] in 3.14 would be joined to [TRANSACTION] in 3.13. When the join is extended to a maximal join, the result is Fig. 3.15, in which the generic concepts [CUSTOMER], [SELLER], and [MONEY] have new referents assigned. The concept [NECKTIE] is still generic because no specific necktie was mentioned, but it is more restricted than [ENTITY].

Type expansions should be distinguished from the expansions done by Riesbeck's parser (1975). Instead of generating an intermediate graph like 3.14, Riesbeck translated directly to the primitives. Furthermore, he would generate the same graph

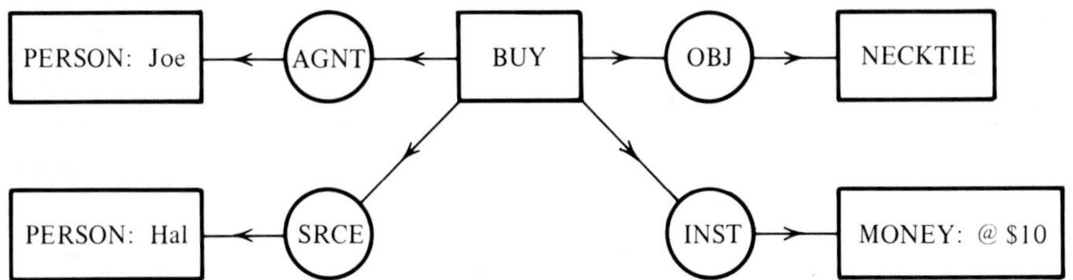

Fig. 3.14 Graph for "Joe buying a necktie from Hal for $10"

for the sentence *Joe bought a necktie from Hal for $10*, its converse *Hal sold Joe a necktie for $10*, and the pair of sentences *Joe gave Hal $10* and *Hal gave Joe a necktie*. Yet generating a single graph for all these sentences loses information about the initiator of the transaction and about the causal relationships. The two acts of giving, for example, might be an exchange of Christmas presents, where notions of buying or selling do not apply. The type definition in Fig. 3.13 explicitly shows that buying is a transaction with two separate acts of giving. Selling would have the same two acts of giving, but with a different initiator. Exchanging Christmas presents would be a different kind of transaction.

In Section 3.2, the type hierarchy was introduced as an *a priori* assumption. If the type labels are specified by type definitions, Assumption 3.6.8 relates the partial

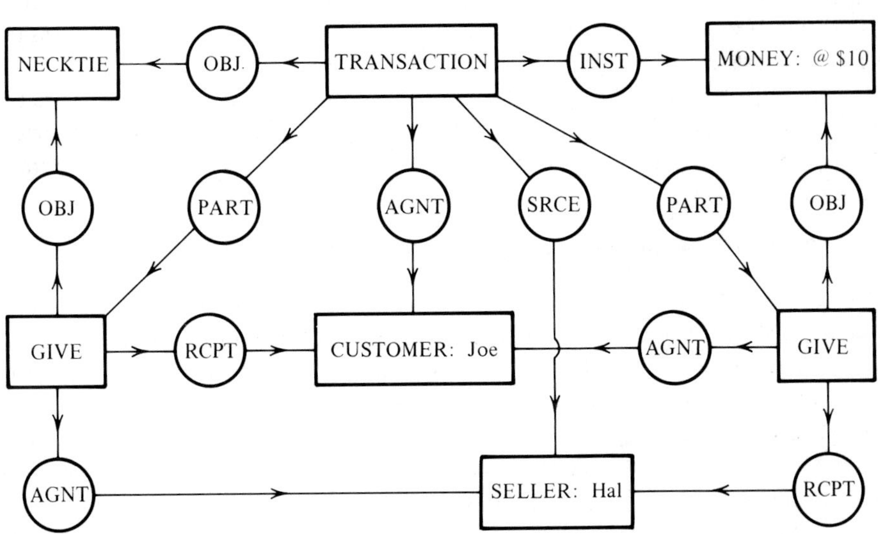

Fig. 3.15 Result of type expansion of Fig. 3.14

ordering to the structure of the definitions. This assumption states the Aristotelian principle that adding more differentiae to a concept restricts it to a lower subtype. Commutativity of type contractions is another common principle: if the type label CIRCUS-ELEPHANT is defined by ELEPHANT which performs in a circus and GRAY-ELEPHANT by ELEPHANT which is gray, then the type label GRAY-CIRCUS-ELEPHANT defined by ELEPHANT which is gray and performs in a circus should be equivalent to CIRCUS-ELEPHANT which is gray and to GRAY-ELEPHANT which performs in a circus.

3.6.8 Assumption. If type t is defined as $\lambda a\ u$, the position of t in the type hierarchy is determined by the following conditions:

- If the graph u consists of the single concept a, then t=$type(a)$.
- If u is larger than than the single concept a, then t<$type(a)$.
- Type contraction is commutative: if the graph u is derivable by joining canonical graphs v and w on the concept a, then $\lambda a\ u = \lambda[\lambda a\ v]w = \lambda[\lambda a\ w]v$.

An Aristotelian type hierarchy is one where the subtypes are determined by explicit type definitions. For Aristotle himself, there were nine or ten primitive types that had no definitions: SUBSTANCE, QUANTITY, QUALITY, RELATION, TIME, POSITION, STATE, ACTIVITY, and PASSIVITY. For the OWL system, the only primitive type is SUMMUM-GENUS, which corresponds to $\top$. All other types are introduced by definitions.

3.6.9 Definition. A type hierarchy T is said to be *Aristotelian* if every type label t that is a proper subtype of another type label is defined by an abstraction $t = \lambda a\ u$.

When all types other than the primitives are introduced by definitions, the partial ordering is completely determined. Furthermore, if one type is a subtype of another, then there must be some graph that states the differentia between the subtype and the supertype. That graph may, in fact, be the join of a large number of graphs if there are many intervening levels in the hierarchy.

3.6.10 Theorem. In an Aristotelian type hierarchy, if a type label s is a proper subtype of t ($s<t$), then there exists a type definition $s=\lambda a\ u$, where $type(a)=t$. The graph u is called the *differentia* between s and t.

Proof. Since $s<t$, there must exist some type definition $s=\lambda a_1 u_1$. Then either $type(a_1)=t$ or else by Assumption 3.6.8 there exists a sequence of type definitions $\lambda a_2 u_2,...,\lambda a_n u_n$ where $type(a_i)=\lambda a_{i+1} u_{i+1}$, for each i from 1 to n-1, and $type(a_n)=t$. Then $s=\lambda[\lambda[...[\lambda a_n u_n]...]u_2]u_1$ and the differentia u is the join of the graphs u_1 through u_n on a_n.

In an Aristotelian type hierarchy, the rule of restricting a type label is redundant. If all subtypes are introduced by type definition, then restriction is equivalent to a join followed by a type contraction. The next theorem proves this fact.

3.6.11 Theorem. If the type hierarchy is Aristotelian, then any graph that is canonically derivable by restricting a type label to a subtype could also be derived by a join followed by a type contraction.

Proof. Let u be a graph derived from a canonical graph v by restricting a concept a in v to a subtype t. By Theorem 3.6.10, there exists a type definition $t=\lambda b\ w$ where $type(b)=type(a)$. Then join concept b of w to a of v. Since a is a cutpoint of the resulting graph, it is possible to do a type contraction by removing the graph w that had just been joined to v and replacing the type label of a with t. The result is u.

An Aristotelian type hierarchy is possible only for the artificially constructed types of a programming language. In the fields of science, accounting, or law, the practitioners strive to develop complete definitions for all concepts. But as long as those fields are growing, that goal can never be achieved. In ordinary language, very few concepts have complete definitions. Some types may be specified by definitions, but most are simply used without definitions. One reason for not defining everything is that present knowledge may be incomplete. A person may know that WOMBAT <MARSUPIAL, but may not have any other information for distinguishing a wombat from a kangaroo or a koala bear. A systems analyst may want to leave the type hierarchy partially undefined as part of a top-down design method. Undefined types are place holders that are filled in as the design progresses. The most compelling reason for not defining all type labels is that such definitions are impossible. Entities in the real world are not arranged in a neat hierarchy with precisely defined boundaries. GAME, for example, is a subtype of ACTIVITY, yet as Wittgenstein (1953) pointed out, different kinds of games bear a family resemblance to one another, but no complete definition by genus and differentiae is possible.

New conceptual relations may also be defined by abstractions. The next definition introduces the monadic relation (PAST) for past tenses:

```
relation PAST(x) is
        [SITUATION: *x]→(PTIM)→[TIME]→(SUCC)→[TIME: Now].
```

According to this graph, (PAST) may be linked to concepts of type SITUATION or its subtypes, such as STATE, EVENT, or ACT. The SITUATION occurs at a point in time, which has a successor, which is a time named Now. The name Now, like all names, must be unique within a context, but different contexts may have different instances of time that are named Now. For a database system, the graph in Fig. 3.16 might represent the sentence *A part number is a characteristic of a set of items, and*

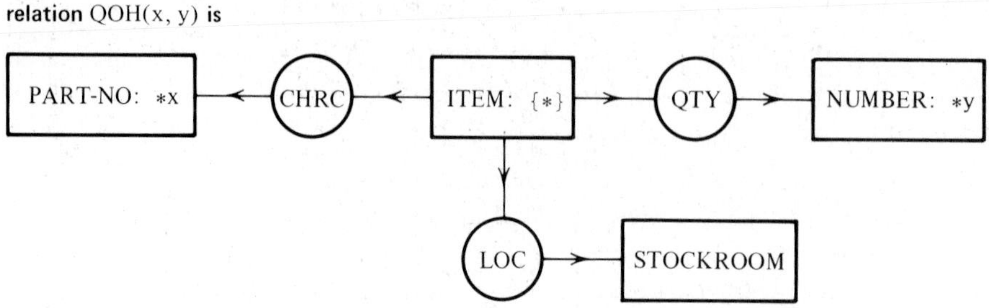

Fig. 3.16 Relational definition for quantity on hand (QOH)

a number is the quantity of such items located in a stock room. The body of the definition is a graph called the *relator* for the new conceptual relation labeled QOH, *quantity on hand.* The two formal parameters of QOH are marked *x and *y. The symbol {*}, which will be treated in Section 3.7, represents a generic set of individuals of type ITEM.

3.6.12 Assumption. A *relational definition*, written **relation** $t(a_1,...,a_n)$ **is** u, declares that the type label t for a conceptual relation is defined by the n-adic abstraction, $\lambda a_1,...,a_n u$. The body u is called the *relator* of t. If r is a conceptual relation of type t, the following conditions must be true:

- r has n arcs.
- If c_i is a concept linked to arc i of r, $type(c_i) \leq type(a_i)$.

In an Aristotelian type hierarchy, all relational definitions could be reduced to a single dyadic relation type, LINK. Even linguistic relations like (AGNT) could be defined in terms of a concept of type AGENT:

relation AGNT(x,y) **is** [ACT:*x]←(LINK)←[AGENT]→(LINK)→[ANIMATE:*y]

where the type labels ANIMATE, AGENT, and ACT are themselves defined in terms of more primitive types. Since the real world is not Aristotelian, however, most types are specified in advance by a built-in set of standard types. The catalog of types listed in Appendix B is a sample starting set.

3.7.13 Assumption. In an Aristotelian type hierarchy T, there is a type label LINK for a dyadic conceptual relation. If t is a type label for a conceptual relation and $t \neq$LINK, then there exists a definition, **relation** $t(a_1,...,a_n)$ **is** u.

Relational contraction and expansion are the counterparts of type contraction and expansion. The relator of Fig. 3.16 may be contracted to

```
[PART-NO]→(QOH)→[NUMBER],
```

which in turn may be expanded back to the full graph form.

3.7.14 Assumption. The operation of *relational contraction* replaces a subgraph v of a conceptual graph w with a single conceptual relation r and the concepts linked to its arcs. Let $b_1,...,b_n$ be n distinct concepts of v, let v have no arcs linked to concepts in w-v, and let u be a copy of v with the concepts $b_1,...,b_n$ replaced by generic concepts $a_1,...,a_n$ where each b_i is a subtype of a_i. Then relational contraction consists of the following steps:

- Delete all of v from w except for $b_1,...,b_n$.
- Let $type(r)=\lambda a_1,...,a_n\ u$.
- For each i, link arc i of r to concept b_i.

If relational contraction is performed on a canonical graph, the resulting graph is canonical.

3.7.15 Definition. The operation of *relational expansion* replaces a conceptual relation and its attached concepts with the relator of a relational definition. Let w be a conceptual graph containing a conceptual relation r where $type(r)=\lambda a_1,...,a_n\ u$. Then relational expansion consists of the following steps:

- Detach r and its arcs from w.
- For each i, if b_i is the concept that was linked to arc i of r, then restrict a_i to $type(b_i)$. This restriction must be possible because of Assumption 3.6.12.
- For each i, join the restricted form of a_i to b_i.

3.7 AGGREGATION AND INDIVIDUATION

Every plural noun represents a set. In philosophy, Nelson Goodman (1951) populated the world with individuals that have other individuals as parts. For database semantics, Smith and Smith (1977) introduced *aggregation* as a method of defining composite entities with other entities as components. Mathematicians define sets that have other things, possibly other sets, as elements. Programming languages define structures that have data elements and other structures as components. The human body has parts like head, hands, and feet. Books have chapters, chapters have sections, sections have paragraphs, paragraphs have sentences, sentences have words, words have letters, and letters have strokes. Clubs have members, gaggles have geese, and even situations, events, and states may have subevents and aspects.

When the referents of concepts are limited to single individuals, as in Assumption 3.3.1, conceptual graphs cannot go beyond first-order logic. Yet many sentences in English cannot be expressed in first-order logic without a special notation for sets. Barwise and Cooper (1981) cited the following sentences, none of which can be translated into a first-order logic without set operations:

```
There are only a finite number of stars.
No one's heart will beat an infinite number of times.
More than half of John's arrows hit the target.
Most people voted for Carter.
```

To represent sets, a concept may contain a set of names or individual markers enclosed in braces: [DOG: {Snoopy,Lassie,Rin-Tin-Tin}]. The referent of this concept is a set of three individuals, all of whom conform to type DOG. When a concept has a set as referent, every element of the set must conform to the type label of the concept. To represent a set of mixed types such as cats, dogs, and lizards, but not palm trees, the type label ANIMAL or VERTEBRATE would be sufficiently general. To represent a completely arbitrary set, a concept could have the type label ⊤, which permits anything as referent.

Concepts with sets as referents are derived from ordinary concepts by *set join* and *set coercion*. As an example, the following two graphs may be joined on the concept [DANCE]:

```
[PERSON: Liz]←(AGNT)←[DANCE].
[PERSON: Kirby]←(AGNT)←[DANCE].
```

The result is a graph that contains two occurrences of the AGNT relation:

```
[PERSON: Liz]←(AGNT)←[DANCE]→(AGNT)→[PERSON: Kirby].
```

The two concepts of type PERSON may not be joined because they are individual concepts with conflicting referents. To make them joinable by set join, the first step is to perform a set coercion, which converts the concept [PERSON:Liz] to the concept [PERSON:{Liz}], which represents *a set of persons consisting of Liz*. After a similar set coercion on Kirby, the above graph becomes,

```
[PERSON: {Liz}]←(AGNT)←[DANCE]→(AGNT)→[PERSON: {Kirby}].
```

A set join of the two concepts of type PERSON forms a set referent that is the union of the sets {Liz} and {Kirby}:

```
[PERSON: {Liz,Kirby}]←(AGNT)←[DANCE].
```

This graph may be read *Liz and Kirby are dancing*. Note that both Liz and Kirby conform to type PERSON. A derivation of set referents by set coercions and set joins guarantees that all elements of the set conform to the type label of the concept.

3.7.1 Assumption. The referent of a concept c may be a set, every element of which must conform to $type(c)$. If c is an individual concept with referent i, the operation of *set coercion* changes the referent of c to the *singleton set* $\{i\}$.

Set coercion introduces sets. The individual referents Liz and Kirby are first coerced to the singleton sets {Liz} and {Kirby}. Then set join combines them to form the set {Liz,Kirby}. Repeated joins can build up arbitrarily large sets.

3.7.2 Assumption. Let a and b be two concepts of the same type whose referents are sets. Then a and b may be joined by the operation of *set join*: first perform a join on the concepts a and b; then change the referent of the resulting concept to the union of $referent(a)$ with $referent(b)$.

Plural noun phrases represent concepts with sets as referents. When the elements are named explicitly, as *Bob and Charlie*, they map to a concept with an ordinary set as referent: [MAN: {Bob,Charlie}]. But the word *men* by itself is a plural word that does not name specific individuals. For such plurals, the symbol {*} represents a *generic set*, whose elements are unspecified. A generic set is related to a set of individuals in the same way as the generic marker * is related to an individual marker. The sentence *Niurka sees two men* would be represented by the graph,

```
[PERSON:Niurka]←(AGNT)←[SEE]→(OBJ)→[MAN:{*}]→(QTY)→[NUMBER:2].
```

The relation (QTY) links a concept whose referent is a set to a number that specifies how many elements are in the set.

3.7.3 Assumption. The symbol {*} represents a *generic set* of zero or more elements, which may occur as the referent of a concept. Set unions with {*} obey the following rules:

- *Empty set.* $\{\} \cup \{*\} = \{*\}$.
- *Generic set.* $\{*\} \cup \{*\} = \{*\}$.
- *Set of individuals.* $\{i_1,...,i_n\} \cup \{*\} = \{i_1,...,i_n,*\}$.

The set $\{i_1,...,i_n,*\}$ is called a *partially specified set*, which consists of the elements $i_1,...,i_n$ plus some unspecified others.

Just as measure contraction and name contraction were used in Section 3.3 to simplify conceptual graphs, the operation of *quantity contraction* may be used to simplify set referents. The symbol @ after a set shows that the following number represents the count of elements or *cardinality* of that set. With this notation, the sentence *Niurka sees two men* may be represented,

```
[PERSON:Niurka]←(AGNT)←[SEE]→(OBJ)→[MAN: {*}@2].
```

With a partially specified set as referent, the phrase *Norma, Frank, and two others* could be represented by the concept [PERSON: {Norma, Frank, *} @ 4].

Like ordinary joins, set joins generate graphs that are more specialized than the originals: they logically imply the graphs they are derived from, but they are not necessarily true if the originals are true. If Liz is dancing and Kirby is dancing, it is not necessarily true that they are dancing together. To handle such sentences in a query system, Dahl (1982) distinguished three different uses for plural noun phrases:

- *Collective.* All elements of a set participate in some relationship together: *Pat and her husband own the estate.*
- *Distributive.* Each element of a set satisfies some relation, but they do so separately: *Betty and Jerry are laughing.*
- *Respective.* Each element of an ordered sequence bears a particular relationship to a corresponding element of another sequence: *Dick, Jerry, Jimmy, and Ron are married to Pat, Betty, Rosalynn, and Nancy, respectively.*

In English, the semantics of the relation implicitly distinguishes the type of plural: two people cannot own the same thing separately, and two people cannot both laugh the same laugh. To be explicit, English uses the word *together* for the collective interpretation, *each* for the distributive, and *respectively* for the respective.

In conceptual graphs, the curly braces indicate a collective interpretation: {Albie,Clara,Ruby}. *Dist* in front of the set indicates a distributive interpretation: Dist{Albie,Clara,Ruby}. And *Resp* in front of a sequence delimited by angle brackets indicates a respective interpretation: Resp⟨Albie,Clara,Ruby⟩. As an example, consider the sentence *Two students read three books*, which could be represented as the graph,

```
[STUDENT: {*}@2]←(AGNT)←[READ]→(OBJ)→[BOOK: {*}@3].
```

This graph does not distinguish whether each student read every book, or one read two of them and the other read one. The following graph represents the sentence, *Two students each read three books.*

```
[STUDENT: Dist{*}@2]←(AGNT)←[READ]→(OBJ)→[BOOK: {*}@3].
```

The prefixes *Dist* and *Resp* indicate how the graphs containing set referents may be factored into graphs without set referents.

Another type of collection is the *disjunctive set*, a set of elements of which one participates in a relationship, but the particular one is not known. As an example, one way to represent the sentence *The elephant Clyde lives in either Africa or Asia* would use two separate propositions linked by an OR relation:

```
[PROPOSITION:
   [ELEPHANT:Clyde]→(STAT)→[LIVE]→(LOC)→[CONTINENT:Africa]]-
(OR)→[PROPOSITION:
   [ELEPHANT:Clyde]→(STAT)→[LIVE]→(LOC)→[CONTINENT:Asia]].
```

This graph, however, is a clumsy way of representing a simple sentence. A set join of the two parts would lead to the concept [CONTINENT:{Africa,Asia}], which would imply that Clyde lives in both places simultaneously. To show that only one of the elements is the actual referent, the elements of a disjunctive set are separated by the vertical bar "|" instead of commas:

```
[ELEPHANT:Clyde]→(STAT)→[LIVE]→(LOC)→[CONTINENT:{Africa|Asia}].
```

Disjunctive, collective, distributive, and respective sets are not four new kinds of sets. Rather, they are four different ways in which the elements of a standard set participate in a relationship.

3.7.4 Assumption. If the referent of a concept is a set, it may be one of four different kinds:

- A *collective set* in which the individuals in the set are separated by commas: $\{i_1,...,i_n\}$,
- A *disjunctive set* in which the individuals in the set are separated by vertical bars: $\{i_1 \mid ... \mid i_n\}$,
- A *distributive set* in which the individuals in the set are separated by commas, but the set itself is preceded by the prefix *Dist*: Dist$\{i_1,...,i_n\}$,
- A *respective set* in which the individuals are listed in a sequence delimited by angle brackets, and the set itself is preceded by the prefix *Resp*: Resp$\langle i_1,...,i_n \rangle$.

A set is a loose association between entities. There is no inherent connection between the elements other than the fact that they occur in the same collection. *Aggregation* is a tighter form of association: a *composite individual* is an aggregate of *components* that are linked by conceptual relations. The basis for an aggregation is some type definition, which sets up a pattern of concept and relation types:

```
type CIRCUS-ELEPHANT(x) is
    [ELEPHANT:*x]←(AGNT)←[PERFORM]→(LOC)→[CIRCUS].
```

A composite individual [CIRCUS-ELEPHANT:Jumbo] is defined by filling in the referent fields of generic concepts in the body of the type definition:

```
individual CIRCUS-ELEPHANT(Jumbo) is
    [ELEPHANT: Jumbo]←(AGNT)←[PERFORM: {*}]-
        (LOC)→[CIRCUS: Barnum & Bailey].
```

This graph defines *Jumbo* as the name of a circus elephant whose ELEPHANT component is Jumbo himself, whose PERFORM component is an unspecified set of performances, and whose CIRCUS component is named Barnum & Bailey. Smith and Smith (1977) introduced aggregation for grouping parts into a whole, and Brachman (1979) used the term *individuation* for specializing generic concepts to individual concepts. Both terms name aspects of the same process: aggregation groups individuals into a composite, and individuation projects a general graph into a composite of individuals.

In database terms, a *basis type* is a descriptor for a class of records, an aggregation is a record of particular data values, individuation is a mapping from the descriptor to the record, and a composite individual is a unique record identifier or *surrogate*. Brodie (1981) defined the entity type HOTEL-RESERVATION as the basis for an aggregation with components PERSON, ROOM, HOTEL, TIME-PERIOD, ARRIVAL-DATE, and DEPARTURE-DATE. In conceptual graphs, Brodie's type definition would take the following form:

```
type HOTEL-RESERVATION(reservation-no) is
   [RESERVATION: *reservation-no]-
      (RCPT)→ [PERSON]
      (OBJ)→  [ROOM]→(LOC)→[HOTEL]
      (DUR)→  [TIME-PERIOD]-
                 (STRT)→ [ARRIVAL-DATE]
                 (UNTL)→ [DEPARTURE-DATE].
```

The type definition explicitly shows the roles that each entity plays: a HOTEL-RESERVATION is a subtype of RESERVATION, it is identified by *reservation-no, and it is linked to a recipient PERSON, an object ROOM located in a HOTEL, and a duration TIME-PERIOD, which starts at an ARRIVAL-DATE and lasts until a DEPARTURE-DATE. A particular reservation identified by the marker #316209 is a composite individual:

```
individual HOTEL-RESERVATION(#316209) is
   [RESERVATION: #316209]-
      (RCPT)→ [PERSON: John Sowa]
      (OBJ)→  [ROOM: 2Q]→(LOC)→[HOTEL: Shelburne]
      (DUR)→  [TIME-PERIOD: @ 4 night]-
                 (STRT)→ [ARRIVAL-DATE: March 14, 1983]
                 (UNTL)→ [DEPARTURE-DATE: March 18, 1983].
```

Note the difference between a type and a composite individual: a type is specified by a differentia graph; a composite individual is specified by an aggregation in which one or more of the generic concepts of the differentia become individual concepts. For hotel reservation #316209, the aggregation contains exactly the same number of concepts and relations as the differentia, but in general, it may contain more. The projection that maps the differentia to the aggregation is called an *individuation*. Not all concepts in an aggregation need to have individual referents: generic concepts correspond to *null values* in the database. If the database contains many composite individuals of the same type, they may be stored in a compact form as *records* or *tuples* that contain only the referents and not the type labels and conceptual relations. The basis type and the record are sufficient to reconstruct the aggregation.

3.7.5 Definition. Let $t = \lambda a\ u$ be a type label; and let v be a canonical graph where $v \leq u$, π is a projection from u into v, and πa is an individual concept in v.

- The graph v is called an *aggregation* of *basis type* t.
- The projection π from the differentia u into the aggregation v is called an *individuation* of t.
- The individual $i = referent(\pi a)$ is called a *composite individual.*
- For any concept c in u, $referent(\pi c)$ is called the c *component* of the composite individual i.

Type definition associates a type label like CIRCUS-ELEPHANT with a graph of generic concepts. Aggregation associates a name like Jumbo or an individual marker like #316209 with a graph of individual concepts. In type expansion, the differentia for a type is joined to a concept. In *aggregate expansion*, the aggregation of a composite individual is joined to a concept. In either kind of expansion, implicit information in a name or type is made explicit.

3.7.6 Definition. Let u be a conceptual graph with a concept a in u where $referent(a)$ is a composite individual with aggregation v and basis type $type(a)$. Then *aggregate expansion* consists of joining the the concept a of u to the concept of v whose referent is the same as $referent(a)$.

A type definition that includes concepts whose type labels are the same as the one being defined is said to be *directly recursive.* If the definition contains type labels that are supertypes of the one being defined, then it is *indirectly recursive.* The following type definition, which is both directly and indirectly recursive, defines a data structure similar to the list structures in the programming language LISP:

```
type LIST(x) is
    [DATA:*x]-
        (HEAD)→ [DATA]
        (TAIL)→ [LIST].
```

This definition says that a LIST is a type of DATA, which is linked via the relation (HEAD) to something of type DATA and via the relation (TAIL) to another LIST. The conceptual relations (HEAD) and (TAIL) have no primitive meaning in the theory of conceptual graphs, but their names were chosen to reflect their use in building list structures. By repeated type expansion of the concept [LIST], the following graph could be derived:

```
[LIST]-
   (HEAD)→ [DATA]
   (TAIL)→ [LIST]-
              (HEAD)→ [DATA]
              (TAIL)→ [LIST]-
                         (HEAD)→ [DATA]
                         (TAIL)→ [LIST].
```

Since LIST<DATA, the three concepts of type DATA could be restricted to LIST and then expanded to form the following graph. Note the placement of commas for closing the subtree linked to the most recent hyphen that is still open.

```
[LIST]-
   (HEAD)→ [LIST]-
              (HEAD)→ [DATA]
              (TAIL)→ [LIST],
   (TAIL)→ [LIST]-
              (HEAD)→ [LIST]-
                         (HEAD)→ [DATA]
                         (TAIL)→ [LIST],
              (TAIL)→ [LIST]-
                         (HEAD)→ [LIST]-
                                    (HEAD)→ [DATA]
                                    (TAIL)→ [LIST],
                         (TAIL)→ [LIST].
```

Such expansions could continue indefinitely. The expansion of type DATA could stop by restricting the type label to some type of data other than LIST. Expansion of type LIST could stop by reaching an individual of type LIST that could not be expanded further.

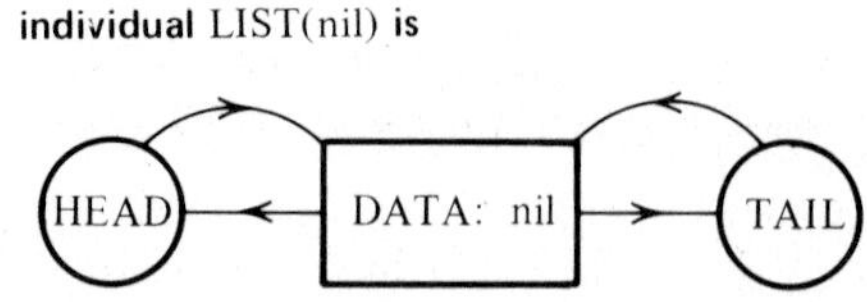

Fig. 3.17 A composite individual of type LIST

To define an individual that would stop the recursion, Fig. 3.17 introduces a composite individual of type LIST that is named *nil*. Because of the cycles in the aggregation, the indefinitely extended tree of type expansions would get mapped back onto itself once it reached a concept of the form [LIST:nil]. The convention that the head and tail of nil are nil itself is implemented in some versions of LISP.

EXERCISES

These exercises test the reader's understanding of the formalism. All readers should do Exercises 3.1, 3.2, and 3.3. Although some of the others require mathematical background, everyone should at least read them because they present interesting points that are not mentioned in the text.

3.1 Classify the anomalies in the following sentences as gibberish, ungrammatical, violations of category restrictions, violations of logic, or empirically false.

- Leon drew a square circle.
- People the the a book.
- All mimsy were the borogoves, and the mome raths outgrabe.
- Sincerity admires John.
- Nelson Rockefeller was elected president of the United States in 1968.

3.2 Translate each of the following conceptual graphs into an English sentence:

```
[PERSON: Clara]←(AGNT)←[WRITE]→(RSLT)→[PROGRAM].

[PERSON: Ivan]←(AGNT)←[THINK]-
   (OBJ)→[PROPOSITION: [PROGRAM:#]→(ATTR)→[GOOD]].

[GIVE]-
   (AGNT)→[PERSON: Ivan]
   (RCPT)→[PERSON: Clara]
   (OBJ)→ [PROMOTION].
```

3.3 Translate the following English sentences into conceptual graphs. Except for proper names, all the words, concepts, and conceptual relations needed for this exercise are listed in Appendix B.

- Dick shipped the hardware from New York to Cleveland via Buffalo.
- Jack is Charlie's philosophy teacher.
- Orders are received by telephone on Fridays.
- The cat is warm in the kitchen.
- Mark thinks that homework is difficult.

Note that some words in the lexicon, such as *the* and *is*, do not have corresponding concepts. Proper names appear in the referent field of a concept, not the type field.

3.4 Map the graphs drawn for the previous exercise into first-order logic according to the formula operator ϕ. Note that the sentence *Mark thinks that homework is difficult* cannot be mapped into a first-order formula by ϕ. Why not?

3.5 Choose three concept types, such as MOVE, HAPPY, and TOOL. Construct a hierarchy of subtypes for those types, using your own analysis as well as a dictionary, thesaurus, or synonym list.

3.6 Construct an example of a type hierarchy where some type labels do not have a unique maximal common subtype. Add new types to the hierarchy to convert it into a lattice.

3.7 Prove that if $s \leq t$, then $s = s \cap t$ and $t = s \cup t$. Since $t \leq t$, $t \cap t = t$ and $t \cup t = t$.

3.8 If two conceptual graphs u and v can be joined, then they must have a common specialization. If no concept of u can be joined to any concept of v, is it still possible for u and v to have a common specialization? When is it possible for two graphs u and v to have no common specializations. Give some examples.

3.9 Let v be a conceptual graph obtained by joining u and w on a compatible projection. If u and w happen to be the same graph, then v must always be smaller than u. But if u and w are different graphs, then v is usually larger than either u or w. In some cases, however, v may be smaller than either u or w. When is that possible? Give an example.

3.10 For a given set of canonical graphs C, there may be two or more different canonical bases from which all graphs in C can be derived. Give an example.

3.11 An earlier version of the theory (Sowa 1976) did not list simplification as a canonical formation rule. Instead, it gave the rule of *detachment*: if u is a canonical graph and r is any conceptual relation of u, then let the resulting graph w be any connected graph that remains when r and its arcs are detached from u.

- Prove that every canonical graph that is derivable by Assumption 3.4.3 is also derivable when the rule of simplification is replaced by the rule of detachment.
- Give some examples of derivations that are possible by detachment, but not by simplification.
- Prove that if every graph in a canonical basis has only a single conceptual relation, then Assumption 3.4.3 generates exactly the same canonical graphs as the rules that use detachment instead of simplification.
- If v was derived from u using the rule of detachment, show that u is not necessarily a generalization of v. (This is the reason why detachment was replaced in the current version of the formation rules.)

3.12 Two canonical graphs can be joined on a compatible projection that is not itself canonical, yet the result is canonical. Explain why the projection need not be canonical to make the result canonical.

3.13 The generalization hierarchy of conceptual graphs is not necessarily a tree or a lattice. In fact, even if the canon is finite, two finite canonical graphs could have an infinite number of common generalizations with no minimal element. Give some examples. (Hint: consider conceptual graphs that contain cycles.)

3.14 Let v be a common generalization of u_1 and u_2 with compatible projections $\pi_1 v$ in u_1 and $\pi_2 v$ in u_2. Prove that if $\pi_1 v$ and $\pi_2 v$ are not maximal compatible projections, then there must exist another graph v' that is also a common generalization of u_1 and u_2, v is a subgraph of v', and v' has exactly one more conceptual relation than v. Then v' is called a *local extension* of the common generalization v.

3.15 The following subranges are abbreviated abstractions. Expand each one into the corresponding λ-expression.

- 0<NUMBER<25
- TEMP>90°F
- MONEY≥$100

3.16 Prove the following statements:

- If v was derived from u by a type contraction, then ϕu is equivalent to ϕv.
- If v was derived from u by a minimal type expansion, then ϕu is equivalent to ϕv.
- If v was derived from u by a maximal type expansion, then ϕv implies ϕu.
- If v was derived from u by a relational contraction or a relational expansion, then ϕu is equivalent to ϕv.

3.17 In an Aristotelian type hierarchy with T as the only primitive concept type and LINK as the only primitive relation type, every other type must be defined in terms of some graph. What techniques can be used keep the differentia graphs distinct? Assume an ample supply of individual markers and give unique definitions for all the basic types.

3.18 Define a concept type LEGAL-CASE, where the definition includes concept types LAWYER, JUDGE, PROSECUTOR, DEFENDANT, and CHARGE. Then define an aggregate of basis type LEGAL-CASE where the components are individual concepts.

3.19 Readers who know LISP should map the list ((5 3) 7 9) into a conceptual graph that uses the type LIST and the individual nil defined in Section 3.7. This mapping illustrates list notation, but sets and aggregates are often more concise.

SUGGESTED READING

The earliest implementations of conceptual graphs were done for machine translation in the 1950s and 1960s; two of the most elaborate systems were Ceccato's *correlational nets* (1961, 1962) and Masterman's *semantic nets* (1961). Schank et al. (1975) developed conceptual dependency graphs to support natural language input, output, and reasoning. Fahlman (1979) proposed a direct hardware implementation for his NETL system. For a survey of various approaches, see the collection of papers edited by Findler (1979). Although many forms of these networks are used in AI, the philosophical and logical questions underlying them have often been ignored; Woods (1975), McDermott (1976), and Israel and Brachman (1981) analyze such issues and criticize the sloppy formulations of many theories in the field.

In this book, conceptual graphs are primarily applied to logic and language, but they could also be applied to spatial representations. Ballard and Brown (1982) is a good text on computer vision that covers general AI techniques as well; it includes about 150 pages of material on knowledge representation, semantic networks, graph matching, inference, and planning. For picture grammars, see Rosenfeld (1979).

For continuing studies on conceptual graphs and related representations, see the proceedings of various conferences on AI, computational linguistics, and cognitive science. Some important journals include *Artificial Intelligence*, *AI Magazine*, the *American Journal of Computational Linguistics*, and *Cognitive Science*. For the latest news, gossip, and reviews, see the SIGART *Newsletter*, published by the ACM Special Interest Group on Artificial Intelligence.

4 Reasoning and Computation

Conceptual graphs are a notation for representing knowledge. But to serve as a basis for thinking, they must be used in computation. This chapter introduces rules of inference for exact deduction, schemata for plausible reasoning, and actors for general computation.

4.1 SCHEMATA AND PROTOTYPES

In normal speech, people never say everything that can be said. Instead, they say just enough for the listener to reconstruct the intended meaning in the given context. According to Merleau-Ponty (1964), "The totality of meaning is never fully rendered: there is an immense mass of implications, even in the most explicit of languages; or rather, nothing is ever completely expressed, nothing exempts the subject who is listening from taking the initiative in giving an interpretation" (p. 29).

Because a human listener uses background knowledge to unravel the immense mass of implications, Bar-Hillel (1960) dismissed the possibility that a computer could ever do high quality machine translation: "What such a suggestion amounts to, if taken seriously, is the requirement that a translation machine should not only be supplied with a dictionary but also with a universal encyclopedia. This is surely utterly chimerical and hardly deserves any further discussion." Yet what seemed impossible with the small, slow, expensive machines of 1960 seems reasonable with the machines of the 1980s. Today, a single disk pack can store the *Encylopaedia Britannica* and transfer any page in a few milliseconds. But storage alone is not enough. Bar-Hillel made the further point that the machine must use the knowledge to make inferences, and "there exists so far no serious proposal for a scheme that would make a machine perform such inferences in the same or similar circumstances under which an intelligent human being would perform them."

Bar-Hillel correctly saw the need for storing and using background knowledge. But instead of looking for ways to represent that knowledge, he dismissed the problem as too difficult to contemplate. In AI, that problem is the central issue. The basic structure for representing background knowledge for human-like inference is called the *schema*. It is a pattern derived from past experience that is used for interpreting, planning, and imagining other experiences. In various implementations, schemata correspond to Ceccato's *constellations* (1961), Minsky's *frames* (1975), and Schank and Abelson's *scripts* (1977). For databases, schemata show the roles played by the entity types and the functional dependencies between them (Sowa 1976). Schemata form the third level of complexity of conceptual graphs:

- Arbitrary conceptual graphs impose no constraints on permissible combinations.
- Canonical graphs enforce *selectional constraints*. They correspond to the case frames in linguistics and the category restrictions in philosophy.
- Schemata incorporate *domain-specific knowledge* about the typical constellations of entities, attributes, and events in the real world.

By enforcing selectional constraints, canonical graphs rule out anomalies like green ideas sleeping, but they allow such unlikely combinations as purple cows:

```
[SLEEP]→(AGNT)→[IDEA]→(COLR)→[GREEN].
[SLEEP]→(AGNT)→[COW]→(COLR)→[PURPLE].
```

By incorporating more knowledge about the world, schemata favor plausible combinations and avoid less likely possibilities. In short, canonical graphs represent everything that is *conceivable*, and schemata represent everything that is *plausible*.

Schemata are similar in structure to type definitions. Yet a concept type may have at most one definition, but arbitrarily many schemata. The difference between them is like Katz's (1972) distinction between a *narrow concept* and a *broad concept*:

> The dictionary sense of *Martian*, the narrow concept of a Martian, is that of a rational creature who is an inhabitant of the planet Mars. But the average person's conception of a Martian, the broad concept of a Martian, might be that of a little green humanoid creature with a plasticlike skin, luminous eyes, bobbing antennae, telepathic powers, and an intelligence vastly superior to ours. (p. 450)

Type definitions present the narrow notion of a concept, and schemata present the broad notion. The Aristotelian and Scholastic distinction between *essence* and *accident* makes a similar point: type definitions are obligatory conditions that state only the essential properties, but schemata are optional defaults that state the commonly associated accidental properties.

Type definitions are based on Aristotle's method of genus and differentiae. They support *decompositional semantics* where a high-level concept type is decomposed into a graph of primitive types. Instead of decomposing a concept, Wittgenstein considered its meaning to be the set of all its possible uses. To clarify that notion, Putnam (1962) introduced the notion of *law cluster*: "Law-cluster concepts are constituted not by a bundle of properties as are the typical general names like MAN and CROW, but by a cluster of laws which, as it were, determine the identity of the con-

schema for BUS(x) is

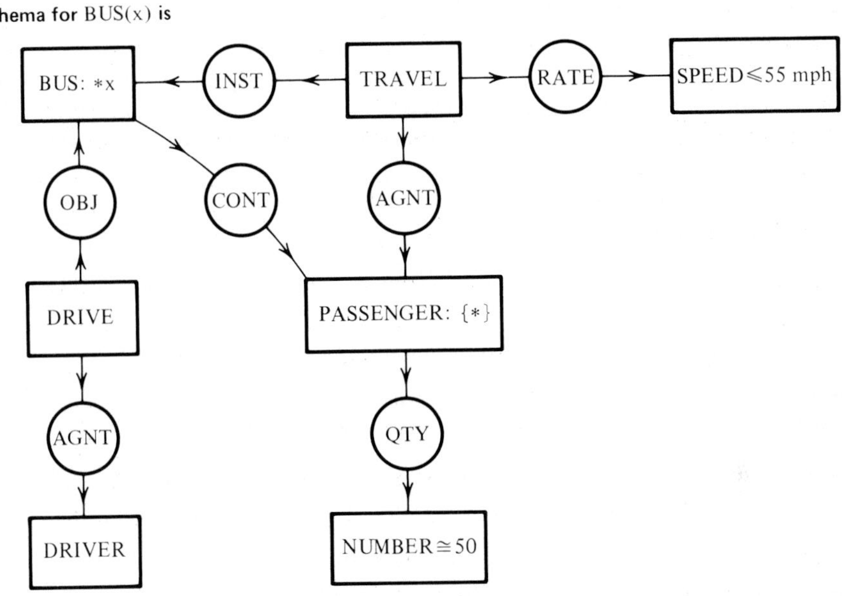

Fig. 4.1 One of the schemata for BUS

cept. The concept ENERGY is an excellent example of a law-cluster concept. It enters into a great many laws. It plays a great many roles, and these laws and inference roles constitute its meaning collectively, not individually."

Putnam's clusters are represented by collections of schemata. Each schema presents a *perspective* on one way a concept type may be used. The collection of all the perspectives for a type is called its *schematic cluster*. Each schema is a monadic abstraction $\lambda a\ u$, as defined in Section 3.6. The formal parameter a is a concept of the type that is being specified, and the body u is a canonical graph that shows a particular use for that type.

4.1.1 Definition. A *schematic cluster* for a type t is a set of monadic abstractions $\{\lambda a_1\ u_1,...,\lambda a_n\ u_n\}$ where each formal parameter a_i is of type t. Each abstraction $\lambda a_i\ u_i$ in the set is called a *schema* for the type t.

Unlike type definitions, which represent necessary conditions, a schema may not be true for every use of the type. Figure 4.1 shows a schema for BUS: the body of the schema says that a bus contains a set of about 50 passengers, it is the instrument of travel by those passengers at a speed less than or equal to 55 miles per hour, and it is the object of driving by some driver. The *generic set* {*} represents an unspecified set of individuals that conform to type PASSENGER, and the *subranges* ≅50 and

≤55mph limit the possible referents for the corresponding concepts. Since BUS is a subtype of ROAD-VEHICLE, common information about buses, trucks, and automobiles need not be stated explicitly in a schema for BUS. Instead, schemata for ROAD-VEHICLE would include information about steering, starting, stopping, passing, speed limits, and so forth. Then all the subtypes of ROAD-VEHICLE would inherit those schemata.

4.1.2 Definition. Any schema for a supertype of a type t is also a schema for t. If $\lambda a\ u$ is a schema in the schematic cluster for t, then it is called an *immediate schema* for t. If a schema occurs in a schematic cluster for a supertype of t, it is called an *indirect schema* for t.

Although the relationships in Fig. 4.1 are commonly true for buses, they may be violated in any particular case. A bus might be remotely controlled, it might have many more than 50 passengers or none at all, and its speed might be greater than 55mph. Other schemata for BUS would show different perspectives: passenger's view, driver's view, bus terminals, and comparisons to other means of travel such as trains, planes, subways, and taxicabs. The concepts and relations of a schema serve both as *conditions* for determining whether the schema is applicable and as *defaults* that may be joined to a graph as long as they are consistent with it. The next definition requires a *schematic join* to be maximal. If it cannot be made maximal, then there must be some conflicting conditions that block the join.

4.1.3 Definition. Let v be a canonical graph containing a concept b, and let $\lambda a\ u$ be a schema for $type(b)$. Then a *schematic join* of $\lambda a\ u$ to v is a maximal join of u to v with the concept b joined to the formal parameter a.

As Selz's theory of schematic anticipation would predict, schemata improve understanding by setting up expectations and preparing slots for future inputs. As soon as the word *bus* appears in a sentence, the listener is prepared for a discussion of the passengers, a driver, traveling, and so forth. None of those concepts are essential, but if they occur, the listener or reader has a mental slot ready for them. To test the effect of schemata on reading speed, Carpenter and Just (1977) studied the difference in eye movements with sentences like the following:

```
It was dark and stormy the night the millionaire ——.
The killer left no clues for the police to trace.
```

When the blank in the first sentence contains *died*, it does not trigger an expectation for *killer*. But when it contains *was murdered*, it leads to a schema with the concept [KILLER]. In the second sentence, when the word *killer* appears, it fits directly in the expected slot. The eye fixation studies did in fact show that readers paused an average of 0.4 sec longer on the word *killer* when it was preceded by *died* than by *was murdered*.

Background information not only enhances understanding, it serves as a guide for organizing new information and for determining how to relate it to previous knowledge. To show how the absence of background information impedes understanding, Bransford and Johnson (1973) asked subjects to read the following passage:

> The procedure is actually quite simple. First you arrange things into different groups depending on their makeup. Of course, one pile may be sufficient depending on how much there is to do. If you have to go somewhere else due to lack of facilities that is the next step, otherwise you are pretty well set. It is important not to overdo any particular endeavor. That is, it is better to do too few things at once than too many. In the short run this may not seem important, but complications from doing too many can easily arise. A mistake can be expensive as well. The manipulation of the appropriate mechanisms should be self-explanatory, and we need not dwell on it here. At first the whole procedure will seem complicated. Soon, however, it will become just another facet of life. It is difficult to foresee any end to the necessity for this task in the immediate future, but then one can never tell.

After reading this paragraph, the subjects who were not told the purpose of the procedure scored poorly on a test of memory and comprehension. But subjects who were told beforehand that the topic was *washing clothes* were able to recall more than twice as much of the material.

To represent background information in a form that a computer could use to analyze stories, Schank and Abelson (1977) developed their theory of *scripts*. A script for a concept type, such as RESTAURANT, is a kind of large schema with conceptual relations that show the sequence of events that normally occur in a restaurant. To illustrate their scripts, Schank and Abelson gave two miniature stories:

```
John was walking on the street.  He thought of cabbages.
He picked up a shoe horn.

John went to a restaurant.  He asked the waitress
for coq au vin.  He paid the check and left.
```

Both stories can be mapped to canonical graphs on a sentence-by-sentence basis. Yet there is no theme or connectivity to the first story. The second one, however, has a logical progression that fits neatly into the slots of the RESTAURANT script.

To use the background knowledge represented in scripts, Cullingford (1977) developed a script applying mechanism (SAM), and Lehnert (1978) developed a question-answering program (QUALM) that worked with SAM. Following is a sample story that was analyzed by SAM (Lehnert p. 20):

> John went to New York by bus. On the bus he talked to an old lady. When he left the bus, he thanked the driver. He took the subway to Leone's. On the subway his pocket was picked. He got off the train and entered Leone's. He had some lasagna. When the check came, he discovered he couldn't pay. The management told him he would have to wash dishes. When he left, he caught a bus to New Haven.

This story has numerous gaps: it says that John had some lasagna, but it does not say how he got it or what he did with it. Nor does it explain why a check came or why he was expected to pay. SAM fills in these gaps by joining conceptual graphs from the RESTAURANT script to conceptual graphs from the story. Then QUALM uses the expanded graphs to answer questions (computer output in upper case):

```
What did John order?
JOHN ORDERED LASAGNA.
Who gave John a menu?
THE WAITRESS GAVE JOHN A MENU.
Did anything unusual happen at the restaurant?
JOHN DISCOVERED THAT HE COULDN'T PAY THE CHECK
   AND SO HE HAD TO WASH DISHES.
Why couldn't John pay the check?
BECAUSE JOHN DID NOT HAVE ANY MONEY.
Why didn't John have any money?
BECAUSE A THIEF PICKED JOHN'S POCKET.
```

For this story, SAM correctly analyzed the input, and QUALM generated appropriate answers. The system refutes Bar-Hillel's contention that a computer could never make the inferences that a person would make in understanding a story. Yet the restaurant story has no literary interest and was written by the same people who developed the system to "understand" it. To show that scripts could handle actual newspaper stories, DeJong (1979) wrote a program called FRUMP, which read stories directly from the UPI wires. Its scripts were indexed by basic keywords. When one of them occurred in a story, FRUMP applied the associated script. For about 10% of the stories, FRUMP correctly analyzed the story. For about 90% of them, it reported that no script was applicable. Occasionally, it would make egregious blunders when it applied the wrong script. For the headline, "Pope's Death Shakes the Western Hemisphere," it reported "There was an earthquake in the western hemisphere. The pope died" (Riesbeck 1982).

For analyzing stories about restaurants, a program could start with a type definition like Fig. 4.2, which defines a restaurant as a business establishment where food is sold for the customers to eat on the premises. In some cases, type definitions alone provide enough background information. For the example *John went to a restaurant*, the concept [RESTAURANT] could be expanded according to Fig. 4.2. The expanded graph would then contain a slot for FOOD that could be restricted to COQ-AU-VIN for the sentence *He asked the waitress for coq au vin*. The concept [WAITRESS], expanded with a type definition such as *woman who serves food in a restaurant*, could then be connected to the other concepts. In the sentence *He paid the check and left*, the word *check* has multiple meanings. The graph for *bill in a restaurant* is the meaning that joins with the other concepts.

Scripts provide more detailed information, but they tend to become too detailed. Even when abbreviated with a shorthand notation for the original graphs and

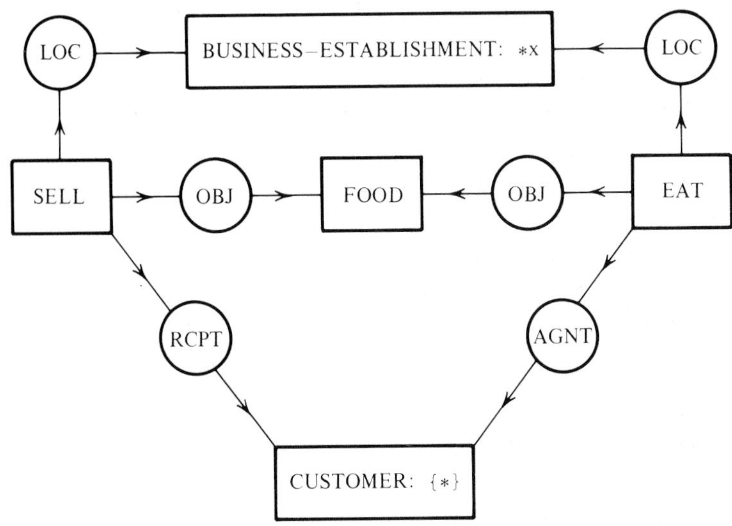

Fig. 4.2 Type definition for RESTAURANT

reduced to a single *track* for coffee shops, the restaurant script covers a page and a half of paper and treats numerous contingencies, such as finding a table, being seated, and getting a menu. Because scripts are such large, complex structures, they are difficult to design and awkward to use. Dyer (1982) noted three desirable properties that they lack:

- *Shared substructures.* Scripts are indivisible units, and parts of one script cannot be transferred to another. Knowledge about meals in the restaurant script, for example, cannot be shared with scripts for picnics or dinners at home.

- *Generality.* Relationships in a script cannot be abstracted to a more general rule that could be applied to other situations. They fail to show the common principle underlying a refusal to pay for burnt food at a restaurant, a refusal to pay for faulty car repairs at a garage, and a demand for a ticket refund when a movie projector breaks down.

- *Intentionality.* Scripts specify what happens, but do not state the intent or purpose. Tipping the waitress is left as an unexplained aspect of dining in a restaurant.

To provide more flexible, modular units, Schank (1981) proposed *memory organization packets* (MOPs), which have "strands that soak up knowledge." Dyer showed how MOPs could remedy some of the problems with scripts: the MOP for the concept type RESTAURANT is a much smaller, simpler graph with strands linking it to

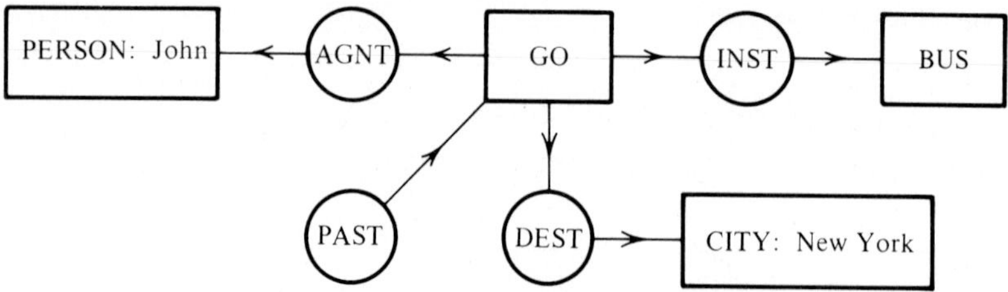

Fig. 4.3 Graph of "John went to New York by bus"

other MOPs for concept types MEAL and SERVICE. The smaller MOPs could be overlaid to form a larger script-like graph, but the modularity of the MOPs allows them to be recombined in different ways to adapt to different situations. With their modularity and combining rules, the MOPs that Dyer used are closer to the schemata described in this chapter than Schank and Abelson's original scripts.

Scripts are like the *sentence frames* that Chomsky (1957) criticized as too specialized: the brain would have to store far too many frames to handle every possible sentence pattern. Instead, he developed generative grammar as a way of creating new sentence frames as needed. The canonical formation rules are the equivalent of a generative grammar. By joining schemata and expanding type definitions, the rules can generate tailor-made scripts for any application.

To illustrate the use of schemata, consider the story about John's trip to Leone's. That story has many concepts that could link to various schemata. The sentence *John went to New York by bus*, would be translated to a graph like Fig. 4.3. The schema for BUS (page 129) could then be joined to Fig. 4.3 on the concept [BUS]. Since a schematic join must be maximal, the join would then merge [GO] with [TRAVEL] since GO is a supertype of TRAVEL. For [PASSENGER:{*}], the referent is a generic set {*}, which represents a set of unspecified individuals of type PASSENGER. By the rules of set coercion and set join (Section 3.7), a join of [PERSON:John] to the PASSENGER concept would result in the referent {John,*}, which may be read *John and others*. The others could include the old lady mentioned in the story. The schema also has a slot for the driver mentioned in the third sentence. The subranges for [NUMBER≅50] and [SPEED≤55mph] give further information that might be useful for understanding other stories.

The concept [TRAVEL] in the BUS schema could serve as a trigger to invoke the TRAVEL schema of Fig. 4.4. Since PASSENGER<PERSON and BUS< VEHICLE, schema 4.4 provides a slot for the destination, New York, and limits the speed to 55 mph. The referent fields of [SPEED], [DISTANCE], and [TIME-PERIOD] contain the symbol @ to show that a *measure* is expected (see Section 3.3). The diamond represents an *actor* named MULTIPLY, which computes the measure of [DISTANCE] when given the measures of [SPEED] and [TIME-PERIOD]. Actors with dotted lines showing inputs and outputs relate the

schema for TRAVEL(x) is

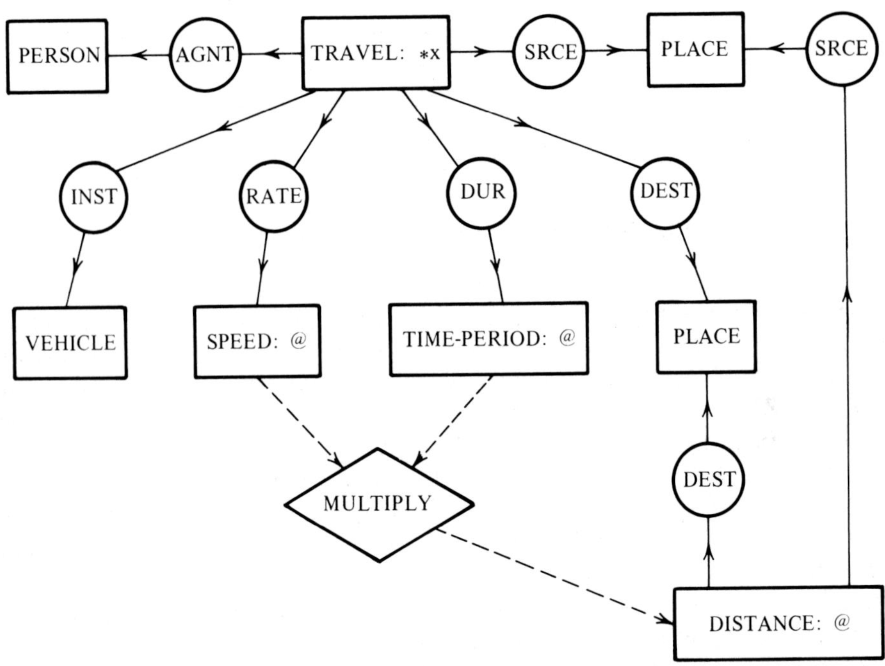

Fig. 4.4 A schema for TRAVEL

schemata to external procedures for computations and database access. They are defined in Section 4.7. If a story never mentions time and speed, the actor would never be invoked, but the schema makes provision for it if necessary.

In these examples, both the type definition for RESTAURANT and the schema for BUS introduce background information. The type definition contains obligatory or essential properties that must hold for the type: a restaurant without a place for customers to eat is not a restaurant but a grocery store or a take-out delicatessen. A bus, however, is still a bus even if it is kept in a museum without being used to carry passengers. As Section 3.6 pointed out, type definitions follow Aristotle. Schemata, however, are Wittgensteinian: a subtype like GAME is differentiated from its supertype ACTIVITY not by a simple definition, but by a cluster of schemata that apply to different kinds of games like chess, football, or solitaire. Type definitions are appropriate for some of the formal concepts of science, law, or accounting. Schemata are necessary for the loosely structured concepts of everyday life. To paraphrase Wittgenstein, the meaning of a concept is the cluster of all the schemata in which it may be used.

Schemata show the typical ways in which a concept may be used, but they do not describe a typical instance of a concept. A *prototype* is a typical instance. Instead of describing a specific individual, it describes a typical or "average" individual. A schema for ELEPHANT might specify a range of characteristics for elephants or a range of behaviors and habitats for elephants. A prototype for ELEPHANT would combine and restrict such schemata to describe a typical elephant. Following is a prototype that gives the typical height, weight, and color of an elephant, as well as attributes of some of its other parts—prehensile nose and floppy ears. The referent {Africa | Asia} is a *disjunctive set* that refers to either Africa or Asia.

```
prototype for ELEPHANT(x) is
   [ELEPHANT: *x]-
      (CHRC)→[HEIGHT: @ 3.3 m]
      (CHRC)→[WEIGHT: @ 5400 kg]
      (COLR)→[DARK-GRAY]
      (PART)→[NOSE]-
                (ATTR)→[PREHENSILE]
                (IDNT)→[TRUNK],
      (PART)→[EAR: {*}]-
                (QTY)→ [NUMBER: 2]
                (ATTR)→[FLOPPY],
      (PART)→[TUSK: {*}]-
                (QTY)→ [NUMBER: 2]
                (MATR)→[IVORY],
      (PART)→[LEG: {*}]→(QTY)→[NUMBER: 4]
      (STAT)→[LIVE]-
                (LOC)→ [CONTINENT: {Africa | Asia}]
                (DUR)→ [TIME: @ 50 years].
```

The concepts and referents in the prototype are standards for comparison. An elephant that is 2 meters tall is a big animal, but compared to the prototype, it is a small elephant. A light gray elephant is still gray, but it might be called a white elephant by contrast. A 15-year-old elephant is young, but the same age is old for a dog and impossibly old for a mouse.

4.2.4 Definition. A *prototype* p for a type t is a monadic abstraction $\lambda a\ u$ with the following properties:

- The formal parameter a is of type t.
- The prototype p is derived by a schematic join of one or more schemata in the schematic cluster for t, with some or all of the concepts in p restricted from generic to individual.

A prototype can be formed from schemata $s_1,...,s_n$ first by maximal joins and then by assigning referents to some of the the generic concepts in the result. The referents assigned to the generic concepts are characteristic *default values*. The following four kinds of structures are all based on monadic abstractions:

- A *type definition* introduces a new type defined in terms of a graph called the *differentia* (see Section 3.6).
- An *aggregation* specializes concepts in the differentia of a *basis type* in order to define a *composite individual* of that type (see Section 3.7).
- A *schema* shows concepts and relations that are commonly associated with a particular concept type. Unlike type definitions, the relationships in a schema are not necessary and sufficient conditions for that type.
- A *prototype* specializes concepts in one or more schemata to show the form of a typical individual. Unlike aggregations, a prototype specifies *defaults* that are true of a typical case, but not necessarily of any particular case.

Mental models are formed by joining schemata and prototypes. In the absence of other information, referents in the prototype may be assumed as defaults. But sometimes those assumptions lead to inconsistencies: if Clyde is an elephant that is only 2 meters tall, the default weight of 5400 kg is probably wrong. Sometimes the joins may result in physically impossible constructions. When the imagination is given free rein, as in myths and fantasies, stories may be told that violate laws of the world. To block the inconsistent or impossible derivations and to encourage the most likely ones, the rest of this chapter develops rules of logic and heuristics.

4.2 FIRST-ORDER LOGIC

Early AI systems for handling language had to face so many problems of syntax and semantics that they ignored logical completeness. During the 1970s, people started to represent all of logic in conceptual graphs. Simmons and Bruce (1971) mapped the graphs into logic, but their notation was not complete. Shapiro (1971) built the first system with a complete graph notation for all the quantifiers and operators in first-order logic. Hendrix (1975) implemented *partitioned nets* as the logical basis for a question-answering system. Schubert (1975) incorporated modal operators and definite and indefinite descriptions into his graphs. Roussopoulos (1976) and Sowa (1976) independently developed graph notations for *branching quantifiers* that go beyond first-order logic.

By the end of the 1970s, graphs were recognized as another notation for logic, but their value was debated by the scruffies and the neats (see Section 1.7). The scruffies dismiss symbolic logic as psychologically unrealistic and linguistically worthless. For them, the important topic is common sense reasoning, and formal systems are misguided or at least irrelevant. The neats, on the other hand, regard the "network hackers" as developing, at best, trivial variants of first-order logic and, at

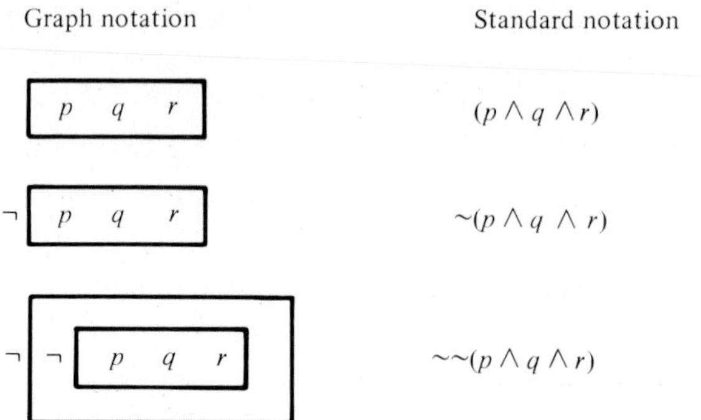

Fig. 4.5 Positive and negative propositions

worst, confused notations with no denotation. Both sides are partly correct. The neats are right in criticizing some of the scruffy programs, but they overlook the importance of a smooth mapping to natural language and the heuristic value of schemata.

The standard notation for symbolic logic was developed by mathematicians like Peano, Russell, and Whitehead, who patterned it after algebra. But one of the pioneers of logic, Charles Sanders Peirce, switched to a graph notation after making major contributions to the linear form. His *existential graphs*, which he called "the logic of the future," form the logical basis for conceptual graphs:

- They have the full power of first-order logic.
- They can represent modal and higher-order logic.
- The rules of inference are simple and elegant.
- The notation is easily adapted to conceptual graphs.

All graph notations represent the conjunction of two graphs by drawing both of them on the same sheet of paper. For the other operators, however, there is no universal convention. Peirce represented negation by a *cut* that partitions the *negative context* from the surrounding *sheet of assertion*. Figure 4.5 shows the graphs *p*, *q*, and *r* asserted in a positive context, a negative context (marked by a ¬ symbol), and a double negation, which has one negative context nested inside another. The AI implementation that most closely resembles Peirce's form is Hendrix's system of partitioned nets.

Since all Boolean operators can be reduced to negation and conjunction, Peirce represented them in terms of nested negative contexts. The disjunction $p \vee q$, for example, could be represented as $\sim(\sim p \wedge \sim q)$. Figure 4.6 shows Peirce's notation and Peano-Russell notation for the Boolean operators. Although nested boxes may look odd to logicians with many years of experience with the linear form, Peirce's

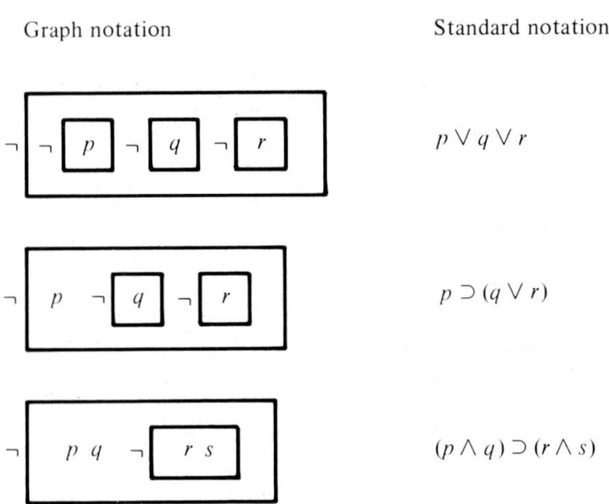

Fig. 4.6 Various Boolean combinations

graphs are very readable: with a little practice, the reader can immediately "see" the various combinations of boxes as disjunctions and implications. For convenience, new relation types OR and IMP may be introduced by relational definitions.

To represent nested graphs, Definition 4.2.1 introduces a *proposition* as a concept whose referent is a set of conceptual graphs that are being asserted. With this definition, propositions assume a form that is similar to Shapiro's SNePS (1979). In those networks, a proposition is a *node* linked to the graphs that are asserted. In conceptual graphs, a proposition is a *box* containing the graphs that are asserted. Although the diagrams look very different, there is a direct mapping between them.

4.2.1 Definition. Let p be a concept of type PROPOSITION whose referent is the set $\{u_1,...,u_n\}$ of conceptual graphs: [PROPOSITION:$\{u_1,...,u_n\}$]. Then each graph u_i in *referent*(p) is said to be *asserted* by the *proposition* p, and u_i is said to occur in the *context* of p.

The monadic relation (NEG) marks a *negative proposition*, which denies the conjunction of the conceptual graphs in its referent. The ¬ symbol of Fig. 4.5 is an informal abbreviation for (NEG). Since complex statements have deeply nested graphs, they may require many repetitions of the type label PROPOSITION. Therefore, PROPOSITION is the default for a box that has no other type label. The notation ¬[u v] is an abbreviation for (NEG)→[PROPOSITION:$\{u,v\}$].

4.2.2 Definition. Let the graphs $\{u_1,...,u_n\}$ be asserted by a proposition p with a relation (NEG) linked to p: (NEG)→[PROPOSITION: $\{u_1,...,u_n\}$]. Then the graph of (NEG) linked to p is called a *negative context*. A negative context containing a single graph that is also a negative context is called a *double negation*.

A major purpose of logic is to define *laws* that are true of the real world. Schemata are defaults that are commonly true, but they may sometimes be wrong. To handle those cases where a schema does not apply, a law must be asserted that blocks the default. Some semantic network, for example, may include the following schema:

schema for `BIRD(x)` **is** `[BIRD:*x]←(AGNT)←[FLY].`

Whenever a canary, eagle, or finch is introduced into a context, this schema may be joined to it. But if an ostrich, kiwi, or penguin is introduced, this schema should not be joined. For each of those concept types, a proposition must be stated that denies the BIRD-FLY schema when applied to that type:

```
¬[ [OSTRICH]←(AGNT)←[FLY]].
```

Since OSTRICH<BIRD, the BIRD-FLY schema would normally be an indirect schema for OSTRICH. This law, however, denies that ostriches fly. If the BIRD-FLY schema were joined to a concept [OSTRICH], this law would raise a contradiction and force the system to erase the join. As a result, the schema and the law have the combined effect, *A typical bird flies, but ostriches don't.*

Peirce assumed that every entity node was existentially quantified: the formula operator ϕ assigns existential quantifiers to each generic concept. The law that ostriches cannot fly would therefore be mapped by ϕ to the following formula in Peano-Russell notation:

$$\sim\exists x \exists y(\text{OSTRICH}(x) \wedge \text{FLY}(y) \wedge \text{AGNT}(y,x)).$$

This formula may be read *It is false that there exist an x and a y where x is an ostrich, y is an instance of flying, and the the agent of y is x.* Since moving a quantifier into or out of a negative context converts ∀ to ∃ and ∃ to ∀, that law is also equivalent to the graph,

$$\forall x \forall y(\sim\text{OSTRICH}(x) \vee \sim\text{FLY}(y) \vee \sim\text{AGNT}(y,x)),$$

which may be read *For all x and y, either x is not an ostrich, or y is not an instance of flying, or the agent of y is not x.* The next assumption extends the operator ϕ to map positive and negative propositions into formulas in first-order logic.

4.2.3 Assumption. If p is a proposition asserting the graphs $u_1,...,u_n$, then ϕp is the formula $(\phi u_1 \wedge ... \wedge \phi u_n)$. If c is a negative context consisting of (NEG) linked to a proposition p, then ϕc is $\sim\phi p$. All generic concepts that occur in p or any context nested in p must be assigned distinct variable symbols by the formula operator ϕ.

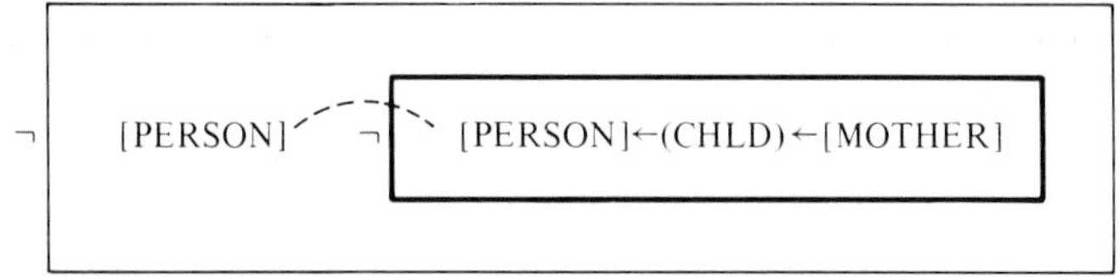

Fig. 4.7 Conceptual graph for "Every person has a mother"

To determine the *scope of quantifiers*, Peirce depended on the nesting of concept nodes in propositions. Deeply nested concepts are within the scope of concepts that are less deeply nested. But there are restrictions: a concept *b* is within the scope of a concept *a* only if the context of *a dominates* the context of *b*. As an example, Fig. 4.7 shows two nested negative contexts. The first concept [PERSON] is enclosed at depth 1. In the innermost context, the two concepts [PERSON] and [MOTHER] are enclosed at depth 2. In this case, the outer context dominates the inner context. The dotted line joining the two concepts [PERSON] is called a *line of identity*, which shows that two nodes represent exactly the same individual. The combination may be read *If there exists a person, then that person is the child of some mother.*

4.2.4 Definition. The *outermost context* is the collection of all conceptual graphs that do not occur in the referent of any concept.

- If a concept or conceptual graph occurs in the outermost context, it is said to be *enclosed* at *depth* 0.
- If x is a negative context that is enclosed at depth n, then any graph or concept that occurs in the context of x is said to be enclosed at depth $n+1$.
- For any integer $n \geq 0$, a graph or concept enclosed at depth $2n$ is said to be *evenly enclosed*, and a graph or concept enclosed at depth $2n+1$ is said to be *oddly enclosed*.
- If a context y occurs in a context x, then x is said to *dominate* y. If y dominates another context z, then x also dominates z. The outermost context dominates all other contexts.

The conceptual graphs in Chapter 3 were bipartite: no arc ever linked a concept to a concept or a relation to a relation. When conceptual graphs were drawn inside the type field or referent field of a concept, the entire graph was limited to one field of a single concept. Lines of identity, however, are separate from the arcs that link boxes and circles. By using overlapping contexts, Hendrix (1975) allowed a concept to occur in more than one context. For many examples, lines of identity and overlapping contexts are equivalent. For complex formulas, Peirce's notation is preferable:

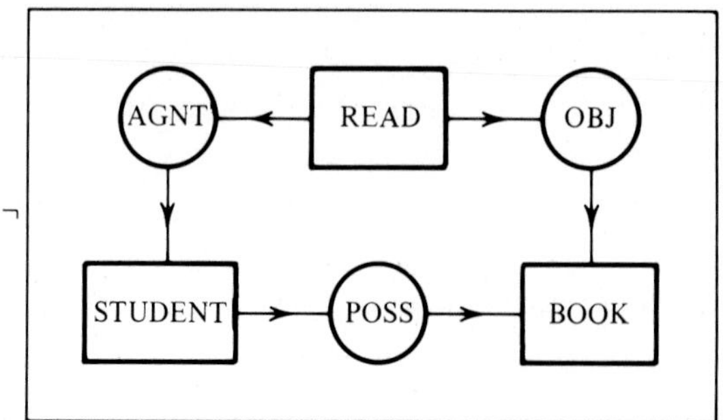

Fig. 4.8 Conceptual graph for "No student read his own book"

Any formula in first-order logic can be expressed with simply nested contexts and lines of identity, but overlapping contexts can lead to context boundaries that cannot be drawn in a plane.

4.2.5 Assumption. A *line of identity* is a connected, undirected graph g whose nodes are concepts and whose arcs are pairs of concepts, called *coreference links*.

- No concept may belong to more than one line of identity.
- A concept a in g is said to *dominate* another concept b if there is a path $\langle a_1,a_2,...,a_n \rangle$ in g where $a=a_1$, $b=a_n$, and for each i, either a_i and a_{i+1} both occur in the same context or the context of a_i dominates the context of a_{i+1}.
- Two concepts a and b are *coreferent* if either a dominates b or b dominates a.
- A concept a is *dominant* if a dominates every concept that dominates a.

A collection of conceptual graphs connected by one or more lines of identity is called a *compound graph*. A conceptual graph without any lines of identity or nested contexts is called a *simple graph*.

Lines of identity show *anaphoric references*: an English pronoun *she* or a noun phrase *the boy* refers to something mentioned earlier, but the referent may not be obvious. Consider the sentence *The teacher scolded the students because no one read his book*. The last clause could mean either no one read his own book or no one read the teacher's book. The interpretation that no one read his own book is shown in Fig. 4.8. Literally, that graph states *It is false that there exists a student who read a book which that student possessed*. In that graph, the student, the instance of reading, and the book are all existentially quantified within the negative context. The negative context denies just the exact configuration inside the box; it does not rule out the possibility that some student may have owned one book and read some other book, but it denies that any student owned and read the same book.

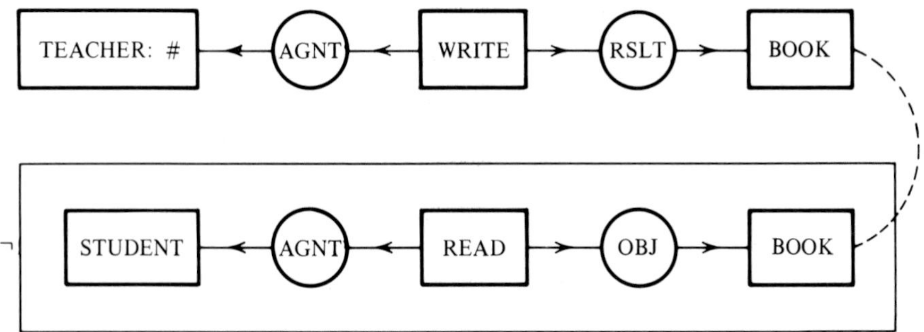

Fig. 4.9 Conceptual graph for "No student read the teacher's book"

The interpretation that no one read the teacher's book is shown in Fig. 4.9. That graph may be read *The teacher wrote a book, and it is false that there exists a student who read that book.* The concepts [STUDENT] and [READ] are quantified within the negative context, but the inner [BOOK] is coreferent with the teacher's [BOOK] outside the negation. The symbol # indicates a reference to a specific teacher; it is an abbreviation for an *individual marker* like #9715.

The operator ϕ that translates conceptual graphs into formulas must also handle lines of identity. One way would be to assign the same identifier (either variable or referent) to all coreferent concepts. In some cases, that solution would work. Problems arise with such sentences as *Rosalie is not Rosann*, represented by the graph,

```
[PERSON:Rosalie]   ¬[ [PERSON:Rosann] ].
```

Replacing the referent Rosann with Rosalie would change the meaning of the sentence. To avoid such problems, the notation is extended to allow multiple referents separated by equal signs. A line of identity is erased only after the identifier of the dominant concept is copied to the referent field of every dominated concept:

```
[PERSON:Rosalie]   ¬[ [PERSON:Rosann=Rosalie] ].
```

When the formula operator ϕ is applied to this graph, it generates the formula,

```
PERSON(Rosalie) ∧ ~(PERSON(Rosann) ∧ Rosann=Rosalie).
```

With this extension, the operator ϕ supports a mapping from conceptual graphs to the first-order predicate calculus with equality. The next assumption states an algorithm for erasing lines of identity and translating the graph u into the formula ϕu.

4.2.6 Assumption. If u is a conceptual graph containing one or more lines of identity, compute the formula ϕu by first transforming the graph u according to the following algorithm:

```
assign a unique variable name to every generic concept of u;
for a in the set of dominant concepts of u loop
   x := identifier(a);
   append "=x" to the referent field
      of every concept dominated by a;
end loop;
erase all coreference links in u;
```

The formula ϕu is the result of applying ϕ to the transformed version of u with the following rule for mapping concepts with multiple referents: if b is a concept of u of the form $[t\colon x_1{=}x_2{=}...{=}x_n]$, then ϕb has the form, $t(x_1) \wedge x_1{=}x_2 \wedge ... \wedge x_1{=}x_n$.

Scope of quantifiers is determined by the levels of nesting of the dominant concepts in a line of identity. The sentence *Every man loves some woman* is ambiguous because there might be a different woman loved by each man or there might be a single woman loved by all the men. Figure 4.10 shows both interpretations. In the upper graph, the concept [WOMAN] is in a context dominated by the concept [MAN]: if there exists a man, then that man loves a woman, but she may (or may not) be a different woman for each man. In the lower graph, the concept [WOMAN] in the inner context is coreferent with the [WOMAN] asserted in the outermost context. That graph may therefore be read, *There exists a woman, and if there exists a man, that man loves that woman.* Although the sentence *Every man loves some woman* is ambiguous, it is more natural to interpret it as the upper graph, since the sentence *Some woman is loved by every man* could be used unambiguously to assert the lower graph of Fig. 4.10.

Conceptual graphs in Peirce's notation usually have fewer symbols than Peano-Russell formulas. To translate Peirce's notation to Peano-Russell notation, the first step is to linearize the graph and assign variables to represent coreference links. For Fig. 4.7, the algorithm of Definition 4.2.6 would lead to,

```
¬[[PERSON:*x] ¬[[PERSON:*y=*x]←(CHLD)←[MOTHER:*z]]].
```

The direct translation of this graph by ϕ leads to an awkward formula with a redundant variable y. By the rules of logic (Appendix A.4), $\sim\exists x$P may be replaced by $\forall x\sim$P, the equality $x{=}y$ allows x to be substituted for y, dropping $x{=}y$ and the quantifier $\exists y$. The duplicate PERSON(x) may also be dropped, and the $\supset$ operator may be inserted. Following are the steps in the translation:

$$\sim\exists x(\mathrm{PERSON}(x) \wedge \sim\exists y\exists z(\mathrm{PERSON}(y) \wedge y{=}x \wedge \mathrm{MOTHER}(z) \wedge \mathrm{CHLD}(y,z)))$$
$$\forall x(\sim\mathrm{PERSON}(x) \vee \exists y\exists z(\mathrm{PERSON}(y) \wedge y{=}x \wedge \mathrm{MOTHER}(z) \wedge \mathrm{CHLD}(y,z)))$$
$$\forall x(\sim\mathrm{PERSON}(x) \vee \exists z(\mathrm{PERSON}(x) \wedge \mathrm{MOTHER}(z) \wedge \mathrm{CHLD}(x,z)))$$
$$\forall x(\mathrm{PERSON}(x) \supset \exists z(\mathrm{MOTHER}(z) \wedge \mathrm{CHLD}(x,z)))$$

The last formula may be read *For all x, if x is a person, then there exists a z where z is a mother and x is a child of z.*

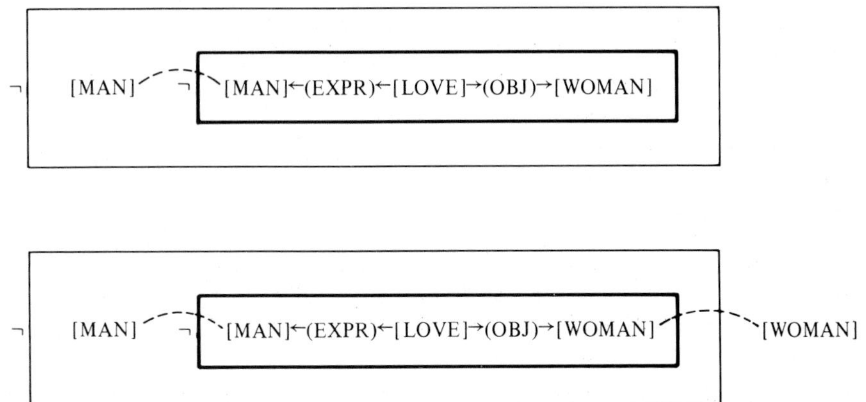

Fig. 4.10 Two interpretations of "Every man loves some woman"

As a further abbreviation, the universal quantifier ∀ may be defined in terms of negation and the existential quantifier: $\forall x\text{P}$ is equivalent to $\sim\exists x\sim\text{P}$. Each generic concept has an implicit existential quantifier. A universal quantifier may be represented with symbol ∀ in the referent field. Then the graph for *Every person has a mother* becomes, [PERSON:∀]←(CHLD)←[MOTHER]. For the first graph in Fig. 4.10, the linear form and its simplification with ∀ are,

```
¬[[MAN:*x] ¬[[MAN:*x]←(EXPR)←[LOVE]→(OBJ)→[WOMAN]]].
[MAN: ∀]←(EXPR)←[LOVE]→(OBJ)→[WOMAN].
```

This latter graph may be read *Every man loves a woman.* The universal quantifier on [MAN:∀] governs both generic concepts [LOVE] and [WOMAN]. Unless a generic concept has a coreference link to a concept in an outer context, it is governed by every universal quantifier in the same context or any dominating context. For the second graph in Fig. 4.10, the linear form and its simplification with ∀ are,

```
[WOMAN:*y] ¬[[MAN:*x]
      ¬[[MAN:*x]←(EXPR)←[LOVE]→(OBJ)→[WOMAN:*y]]].
[WOMAN:*y] [[MAN: ∀]←(EXPR)←[LOVE]→(OBJ)→[WOMAN:*y]].
```

The latter graph may be read *There exists a woman who is loved by every man.* Normally, a context with no attached NEG relation has no effect. But here, it shows that [WOMAN:∗y] is not governed by the quantifier ∀ nested inside the context.

As a general procedure for eliminating universal quantifiers, place ~ before and after each string of ∀ quantifiers, and replace each ∀ with ∃. In Peano-Russell notation, the formula $\exists x\forall y\forall z\exists w\text{P}$ would become $\exists x\sim\exists y\exists z\sim\exists w\text{P}$. This method of replacing universal quantifiers with existential quantifiers generalizes directly to Peirce's notation. The next assumption states the procedure for conceptual graphs.

relation OR(x, y) **is**

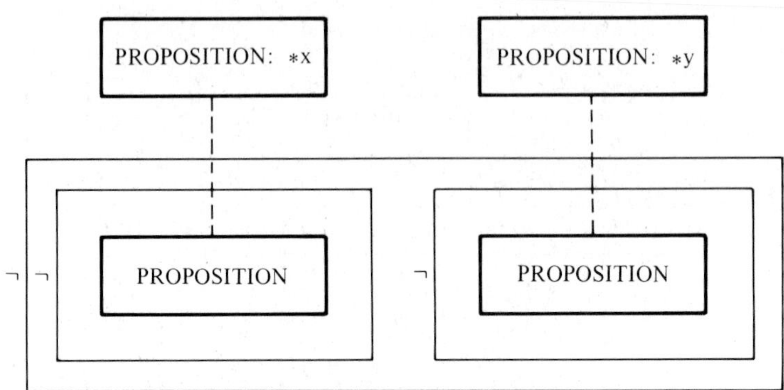

Fig. 4.11 Relational definition for OR

4.2.7 Assumption. The symbol ∀ in the referent field of a generic concept *a* is called a *universal quantifier*, and *a* is said to be *universally quantified*. If a context *c* contains one or more universally quantified concepts, the graphs in *c* may be translated to equivalent graphs without universal quantifiers in the following steps:

- Draw a double negation around all of the graphs in *c*.
- For each universally quantified concept *a* in *c*, erase the quantifier on *a*, insert a copy of *a* between the outer and inner negative contexts that were drawn in the previous step, and draw a coreference link from the copy of *a* to the original concept *a*.
- Repeat the above two steps for any contexts nested inside of *c* that also have universally quantified concepts.

Since English has single words for *or* and *if*, a single conceptual relation for those words would let conceptual graphs express English sentences more directly. Figure 4.11 defines a dyadic relation OR. The two formal parameters must occur in the outer context of the definition because relational expansion, as defined in Section 3.6, does not make any provision for nested contexts. Those parameters, however, are coreferent with concepts nested inside the negative contexts. In the linear notation, lines of identity are shown by copying the parameter symbols *x and *y into the coreferent concepts in the nested contexts. The following definition is exactly equivalent to Fig. 4.11:

relation `OR(x,y)` **is** `[*x] [*y] ¬[¬[[*x]] ¬[[*y]]].`

In this definition, the default type label PROPOSITION has been dropped: [*x] is an abbreviation for [PROPOSITION: *x]. With similar definitions, all Boolean operators could be defined as ordinary conceptual relations. However, the definitions may change the nesting structure that shows scope of quantifiers, as in the definition of implication IMP:

relation IMP(x,y) **is** [*x] [*y] ¬[[*x] ¬[[*y]]].

Lines of identity express *equality*, which is a notion beyond the power of first-order logic. Peirce gave examples like the following, which states that there exist at least two persons:

[PERSON] ¬[[PERSON]] [PERSON].

Since the middle concept is linked by more than one line of identity to concepts that dominate it, the linear notation must represent all the identifiers (referents or variables) of the dominant concepts. The referent field therefore contains a list of identifiers separated by equal signs. The concept's own identifier (if any) must come first, and the identifiers of dominant concepts may follow in any order. Following is the linear form of the above graph and its mapping by ϕ:

[PERSON:*x] [PERSON:*y] ¬[[PERSON:*x=*y]].
$\exists x \exists y$(PERSON(x) ∧ PERSON(y) ∧ $\sim\exists z$(PERSON(z) ∧ $x=z$ ∧ $y=z$)).

This formula may be read *There exist a person x and a person y, and it is false that there exists a person z where x=z and y=z.*

The preceding graph could be generalized to a relational definition stating that two individuals of any type must be distinct. By replacing the type label PERSON with the universal type ⊤, a relation (DFFR) may be defined to state that two concepts have different referents:

relation DFFR(x,y) **is** [⊤:*x] [⊤:*y] ¬[[⊤:*x=*y]].

With the newly defined DFFR relation, the graph stating that there exist at least two persons becomes simply, [PERSON]→(DFFR)→[PERSON]. With the notation $x \neq y$ for DFFR(x,y), this graph is equivalent to the formula,

$\exists x \exists y$(PERSON(x) ∧ PERSON(y) ∧ $x \neq y$).

Any formula in first-order logic can be expressed by nested negative contexts and lines of identity, but as a more compact notation, the symbol ¬ may be used for negating a single type label of a concept or conceptual relation. The conceptual relation (¬PART) represents *not part of* and the concept [¬BOAT] represents something that is not a boat. The ¬ prefix is not a separate mechanism for negation, but an abbreviation that can always be expanded into the basic Peirce form.

4.2.8 Definition. If t is a type label for a concept, the *negated type* $\neg t$ is defined by a type definition of the form, **type** $\neg t$(x) **is** [⊤:∗x] ¬[[t:∗x]].

To perform deductions on a graph that contains a type $\neg t$, the graph is first converted by type expansion. Logical operations can then be performed on the expanded graph. For many examples, *derived rules of inference* are also possible. Instead of replacing the ¬ symbol, inference rules could operate directly on graphs that contain negated labels. Such rules, however, must always be justified by theorems that prove their equivalence to the basic operations on negative contexts.

4.2.9 Definition. Let r be a type label for an n-adic conceptual relation and let t_i be the maximal common subtype of all the concepts that may be linked to arc i of a conceptual relation of type r in any canonical graph. Then the *negated relation* $\neg r$ is defined by a relational definition of the following form:

```
relation ¬r(x1,x2,...,xn) is
    [t1: *x1]  [t2: *x2]  ...  [tn: *xn]
      ¬[ (r)-
            ←[t1: *x1]
            ←[t2: *x2]
              ...
            →[tn: *xn]].
```

Definitions 4.2.8 and 4.2.9 are schematic definitions for an entire class of type labels. For a particular relation such as (¬PART), Definition 4.2.9 could be specialized to,

```
relation ¬PART(x,y) is
    [ENTITY:*x] [ENTITY:*y] ¬[[ENTITY:*x]→(PART)→[ENTITY:*y]].
```

Any particular occurrence of (¬PART) could be eliminated by relational expansion (see Section 3.6). As examples of these abbreviated negations, consider various ways of negating the sentence *The boat Cybele has a motor.* The negation that has the scope of the entire sentence would be

```
¬[[BOAT:Cybele]→(PART)→[MOTOR]].
```

This graph may be read *It is false that the boat Cybele has a motor*, or simply *The boat Cybele doesn't have a motor.* Negating just the type label BOAT produces,

```
[¬BOAT:Cybele]→(PART)→[MOTOR],
```

which may be read *The nonboat Cybele has a motor.* By maximal type expansion, this graph becomes,

```
[ENTITY:Cybele]→(PART)→[MOTOR] ¬[[BOAT:Cybele]].
```

This graph may be read *Cybele has a motor, but Cybele is not a boat.* The next label to be negated is PART:

```
[BOAT:Cybele]→(¬PART)→[MOTOR].
```

This graph could be read *Some motor is not a part of the boat Cybele.* Expanding the relation (¬PART) produces,

```
[BOAT:Cybele] [MOTOR:*x] ¬[[ENTITY:Cybele]→(PART)→[ENTITY:*x]].
```

This graph may be read *Cybele is a boat, and there exists a motor, which is not a part of Cybele.* Note that the graph does not rule out the possibility that Cybele might have some other motor since the concept [MOTOR] is not within the negative context. The last label to be negated is MOTOR:

```
[BOAT:Cybele]→(PART)→[¬MOTOR].
```

This graph may be read *The boat Cybele has a part that is not a motor.* Again, this graph does not rule out the possibility that Cybele might have some other part that is a motor. By type expansion, that graph becomes,

```
[BOAT:Cybele]→(PART)→[ENTITY:*x] ¬[[MOTOR:*x]].
```

4.3 FORMAL DEDUCTION

If conceptual graphs are a variant of first-order logic, one might ask why anyone would use them in preference to Peano-Russell notation, which has a century of development behind it, has been implemented in theorem-proving programs, and is widely known and accepted by philosophers, mathematicians, and computer scientists. That question has several answers:

- First and foremost, conceptual graphs support a more direct mapping to and from natural language. Peano-Russell notation has no standard mapping to English, and textbooks on logic seldom do more than give a few examples and expect the readers to invent their own conventions.
- Second, conceptual graphs have direct extensions to modal logic and other forms that cannot be represented in first-order logic. The box notation is especially convenient for making assertions about contexts. The relations linked to a box can explicitly distinguish modal and intentional contexts.
- Third, all the theoretical developments that went into the linear notation can be transferred directly to the graph notation. In most cases, the graph formalism is simpler, and the proofs are shorter.
- Finally, conceptual graphs can easily coexist with other logical notations. Since they have a direct translation both to natural language and to symbolic logic, they can be used as an intermediate language. The front end of a system would map English into conceptual graphs, and the back end would map the graphs into a programming language.

Standard logic is not widely known, even among computer programmers. For novices, the graph notation is easier to learn and read than the linear notation. In teaching PROLOG, for example, Ennals (1980) taught students to draw semantic nets as an aid to formulating the linear statement. For database design, conceptual graphs are similar to common graphical notations for showing database structure.

To do logic on conceptual graphs, formation rules are not enough. They ensure that canonical graphs obey selectional constraints, but they do not ensure that every graph derived from true graphs is also true. To preserve truth, *rules of inference* carry out only those transformations that follow logically from the previous graphs. Peirce based his rules of inference on simple insertions and erasures of graphs or parts of graphs. As an example, let u, v, and w be any conceptual graphs. Following are four conditions under which graphs may be inserted or erased in the antecedent or consequent of an implication:

- Any graph may be inserted in the antecedent of an implication: if $\neg[u \neg[v]]$, then derive $\neg[u\ w \neg[v]]$.
- Any graph may be erased from the consequent of an implication: if $\neg[u \neg[v\ w]]$, then derive $\neg[u \neg[v]]$.
- A graph may be erased from the antecedent of an implication only if it has been independently asserted: if u and $\neg[u\ v \neg[w]]$, then derive $\neg[v \neg[w]]$.
- A graph may be inserted in the consequent of an implication only if it has been independently asserted: if u and $\neg[v \neg[w]]$, then derive $\neg[v \neg[w\ u]]$.

These operations preserve truth: if all the graphs in a context are true, then all the graphs derived from them will also be true. Peirce generalized these rules to arbitrarily nested contexts; Assumption 4.3.1 adapts them to conceptual graphs. These are Peirce's *Alpha rules* for the propositional calculus; Assumption 4.3.5 generalizes them to the *Beta rules*, which form a complete system for first-order logic.

4.3.1 Assumption. Let the outermost context contain a set S of conceptual graphs. Any graph derived from S by the following *propositional rules of inference* is said to be *provable* from S.

- *Erasure.* Any evenly enclosed graph may be erased.
- *Insertion.* Any graph may be inserted in any oddly enclosed context.
- *Iteration.* A copy of any graph u may be inserted into the same context in which u occurs or into any context dominated by u.
- *Deiteration.* Any graph whose occurrence could be the result of iteration may be erased—i.e. if it is identical to another graph in the same context or in a dominating context.
- *Double negation.* A double negation may be drawn around or removed from any graph or set of graphs in any context.

The empty set of graphs is the only logical axiom; it is written either as {} or as just a blank space. Any graph that is provable from {} by these rules is called a *theorem*.

An empty set of graphs makes no assertion whatever. By convention, it is assumed to be true. The negation of the empty set, called the *empty clause*, must therefore be false; it is written ¬[]. To show that Peirce's rules of inference are at least as strong as standard logic, one could show that the standard axioms are provable from the empty set. Russell and Whitehead (1910) gave the following four axiom schemata, where p, q, and r represent any formulas whatever:

- $(p \vee p) \supset p$.
- $q \supset (p \vee q)$.
- $(p \vee q) \supset (q \vee p)$.
- $(q \supset r) \supset ((p \vee q) \supset (p \vee r))$.

For Peirce's notation, let p, q, and r be arbitrary conceptual graphs. They may be simple graphs, or they may contain negative contexts nested to any depth. To prove that the first axiom is a theorem, start with a blank space, and draw a double negation around it: ¬[¬[ ]]. By the rule of insertion, which permits any graph whatever to be inserted into an oddly enclosed context, insert the graph ¬[p] just inside the outer negative context: ¬[¬[ ] ¬[p]]. By iteration, copy the graph ¬[p] into the inner context: ¬[¬[¬[p]] ¬[p]]. Again by iteration, make another copy of ¬[p] in the inner context: ¬[¬[¬[p] ¬[p]] ¬[p]]. By relational contractions of OR and IMP from Section 4.2, this graph becomes,

```
[[p]→(OR)→[p]]→(IMP)→[p],
```

which represents the formula $(p \vee p) \supset p$. Since the symbol p is an abbreviation for any graph whatever, this method could be used to derive a conceptual graph that is equivalent to any proposition in the form of the first axiom. The other three axioms can be proved by a similar method: first translate each formula to be proved into a conceptual graph, then look at the nesting to determine which double negations to draw and which graphs to insert or delete.

The next step in showing the equivalence to standard logic is to prove that the rules of inference can simulate the rule of *modus ponens*: given p and $p \supset q$, derive q. In terms of conceptual graphs, start with p and ¬[p ¬[q]]. Since the singly enclosed copy of p is dominated by the outer p, the rule of deiteration lets the inner p be erased: ¬[¬[q]]. Since a double negation may be removed from any graph, the graph q by itself can be derived.

Since modus ponens is a useful rule of inference, it can be adopted as a *derived rule of inference* for conceptual graphs. If all graphs in the context linked to arc #1 of (IMP) have been asserted, assert the graphs in the context linked to arc #2. As an example, the following two graphs represent the sentences, *John is tall* and *If John is tall, then John is not short*:

```
[PERSON:John]→(ATTR)→[TALL].
[[PERSON:John]→(ATTR)→[TALL]]-
     (IMP)→[¬[[PERSON:John]→(ATTR)→[SHORT]]].
```

With the rule of modus ponens, the graph for the sentence *John is not short* can be derived in one step:

```
¬[[PERSON:John]→(ATTR)→[SHORT]].
```

Without that rule, (IMP) would first be expanded according to its definition:

```
¬[[PERSON:John]→(ATTR)→[TALL]
     ¬[¬[[PERSON:John]→(ATTR)→[SHORT]]]].
```

Then the same conclusion could be drawn, but with more intermediate steps. Modus ponens does not increase the number of theorems that are provable, but it simplifies some of the proofs. The other rules of inference mentioned in Appendix A.5 also have their counterparts as derived rules of inference for conceptual graphs.

4.3.2 Definition. A set S of conceptual graphs is said to be *consistent* if there is no pair of conceptual graphs p and $\neg[p]$ that are both provable from S. If S is not consistent, it is said to be *inconsistent.*

A deductive system must be strong enough to derive the normal implications of a set of statements, but it must not be so strong that it can derive false statements from true statements. If a theory is inconsistent, then everything is provable, and a proof becomes meaningless. The empty clause ¬[] asserts that the set consisting of no propositions whatever is false. In theorem proving programs, ¬[] is treated as a self-contradictory proposition: whenever it arises during a deduction, it implies that the starting premises are inconsistent.

4.3.3 Theorem. For any set S of conceptual graphs, the following three statements are equivalent:

- S is inconsistent.
- The negation of the empty set ¬[], called the *empty clause*, is provable from S.
- Any conceptual graph whatever is provable from S.

Proof. To prove the equivalence, one can show that the first statement implies the second, the second implies the third, and the third implies the first. Suppose first that S is inconsistent. Then for some conceptual graph p, both p and $\neg[p]$ are provable. By the rule of deiteration, the graph p inside the negative context may be erased. Therefore, the empty clause ¬[] is provable from S. Once ¬[] has been proved, any graph q is provable from it by inserting the graph $\neg[q]$ into the oddly enclosed context by the rule of insertion: ¬[¬[*q*]]. Now erase the double negation to derive *q* by itself. Finally, if any graph is provable from *S*, then some graph *p* and its negation ¬[*p*] must both be provable; hence, *S* is inconsistent.

The next theorem shows that the basic axiom is consistent and that any set of simple graphs containing no negative contexts also consistent. Note the difference between the empty set of graphs {}, the empty context [], and the empty clause ¬[]. The empty set is the basic axiom, which is always true. The empty context is a concept whose referent is the empty set, and it is also true. The empty clause is the negation of the empty set, and it is always false.

4.3.4 Theorem. Any set *S* of simple graphs is consistent. In particular, the empty set {} is consistent.

Proof. Besides graphs that are already in *S*, any graph provable from *S* must have the following form:

- It must consist of an outer negative context *a* that contains at least one nested negative context *b*.
- The context *b* may be empty, or it may contain graphs that are exact copies of graphs in *S*, exact copies of other graphs contained in *a*, or graphs that are provable from *S*.
- Besides *b*, the context *a* may also contain other graphs, which may or may not be in *S* and which may contain any arbitrary combination of nested contexts.

To prove these facts, note that any graph derived from *S* by double negation has this form, and any modification to such a graph by any rule of inference would either have this form or be a graph in *S*. Since the empty clause does not have this form and it is not in *S*, it cannot be provable from *S*. By Theorem 4.3.3, the set *S* must be consistent.

According to this theorem, any set of graphs without negations must be consistent. Since the two statements, *John is tall* and *John is short*, contain no negations, the following two graphs are consistent:

```
[PERSON:John]→(ATTR)→[TALL].
[PERSON:John]→(ATTR)→[SHORT].
```

If nothing else is known about the attributes TALL and SHORT, no inconsistency arises. What causes a problem is the unspoken premise that if John is tall, then John is not short:

```
[[PERSON:John]→(ATTR)→[TALL]]-
    (IMP)→[¬[[PERSON:John]→(ATTR)→[SHORT]]].
```

This graph, in conjunction with the first one, implies the following graph, which contradicts the statement that John is short.

```
¬[[PERSON:John]→(ATTR)→[SHORT]].
```

Although the first two graphs do not contain any negative contexts, the third one does. This example shows that graphs may be consistent by themselves, but when background knowledge is added, a contradiction can arise. This point is important for database systems: the facts in a database are positive assertions that can never lead to inconsistency. In conjunction with *constraints* in a data dictionary, however, inconsistencies can arise.

The propositional rules of inference in Assumption 4.3.1 correspond to Peirce's system Alpha. They treat each graph as a single, indivisible unit and do not allow graphs to be combined or split apart. Furthermore, they do not apply to graphs containing lines of identity. Peirce generalized the Alpha rules to form his Beta rules, which are equivalent to first-order predicate calculus. The next assumption adapts his rules to conceptual graphs; they also make provision for restricting or generalizing type labels and referents—features that were not present in Peirce's original graphs.

4.3.5 Assumption. Let the outermost context contain a set S of conceptual graphs. Any graph derived from S by the following *first-order rules of inference* is said to be *provable* from S.

- *Erasure.* In an evenly enclosed context, any graph may be erased, any coreference link from a dominating concept to an evenly enclosed concept may be erased, any referent may be erased, and any type label may be replaced with a supertype.

- *Insertion.* In an oddly enclosed context, any graph may be inserted, a coreference link may be drawn between any two identical concepts, and restriction may be performed on any concept.

- *Iteration.* A copy of any graph u may be inserted into the same context in which u occurs or into any context dominated by u. A coreference link may be drawn from any concept of u to the corresponding concept in the copy of u. If concepts a and b in some context c are both dominated by a concept d on some line of identity, then a coreference link may be drawn from a to b.

- *Deiteration.* Any graph or coreference link whose occurrence could be the result of iteration may be erased. Duplicate conceptual relations may be erased from any graph.

- *Double negation.* A double negation may be drawn around or removed from any graph in any context.

- *Coreferent join.* Two identical, coreferent concepts in the same context may be joined, and the coreference link between them may then be erased.

■ *Individuals.* If an individual concept a dominates a generic concept b where a and b are coreferent, then *referent*(a) may be copied to b, and the coreference link may be erased.

The empty set of graphs {} is the only logical axiom. Any graph that is provable from {} by these rules is called a *theorem*.

Note that the rules do not depend on the depth of nesting, but on whether a context is even or odd. Any proof that can be performed in the outermost context can be carried out in a context enclosed at any even depth. In oddly enclosed contexts, the rules add properties: they restrict a concept, add graphs, join new parts to a graph, or add coreference links. In evenly enclosed contexts (including the outermost context, which is at level 0), the rules remove properties: they erase graphs, erase coreference links, and replace a concept with a more general one. For iteration and deiteration, the outer copy of a graph determines the truth or falsity of the combination; making or erasing copies has no effect on the overall truth value.

For erasing and extending coreference links, the rules derive from the correspondence between quantifiers and dominant concepts in lines of identity: if a dominant concept is evenly enclosed, it corresponds to an existential quantifier; if oddly enclosed, to a universal. The rule for erasing a coreference link to an evenly enclosed concept permits the derivation from $\forall x(P(x) \supset Q(x))$ to $\forall x(P(x) \supset \exists y Q(y))$. The rule for drawing new coreference links in an oddly enclosed context permits the derivation from $\forall x \forall y(P(x) \wedge Q(y))$ to $\forall x(P(x) \wedge Q(x))$. The rule for extending coreference links from a graph u to a copy of u in a more deeply enclosed context permits the derivation from $\forall x(P(x) \supset \exists y P(y))$ to $\forall x(P(x) \supset P(x))$. To see the relationships, translate each of these formulas into a graph in Peirce's form. Then apply one of the rules of Assumption 4.3.5. Peirce's rules for drawing and erasing coreference links replace the standard rules of *universal instantiation* and *existential generalization.*

To illustrate the first-order rules of inference, suppose that there is a land called Oz, which contains persons named Dorothy, Tinman, and others. The following law defines citizenship in the Lapd of Oz:

> A person is a citizen of Oz if and only if any of the following three conditions is true: (1) he or she was born in Oz; (2) one of his or her parents was a citizen of Oz; or (3) he or she was naturalized in Oz.

Since this law is stated in an *if-and-only-if* form, each clause in it will appear as the antecedent of one implication and as the consequent of some other implication. Figure 4.12 is the translation of that graph into four separate nests of conceptual graphs. Each of the top three states one condition for a person to be a citizen of Oz. If the antecedent of any one of them is true, then the person is a citizen of Oz. Whereas the *if* part of the law is represented as three separate implications, the fourth graph represents the *only-if* part as a single implication that has three alternative consequences, of which only one need be true if the antecedent is true.

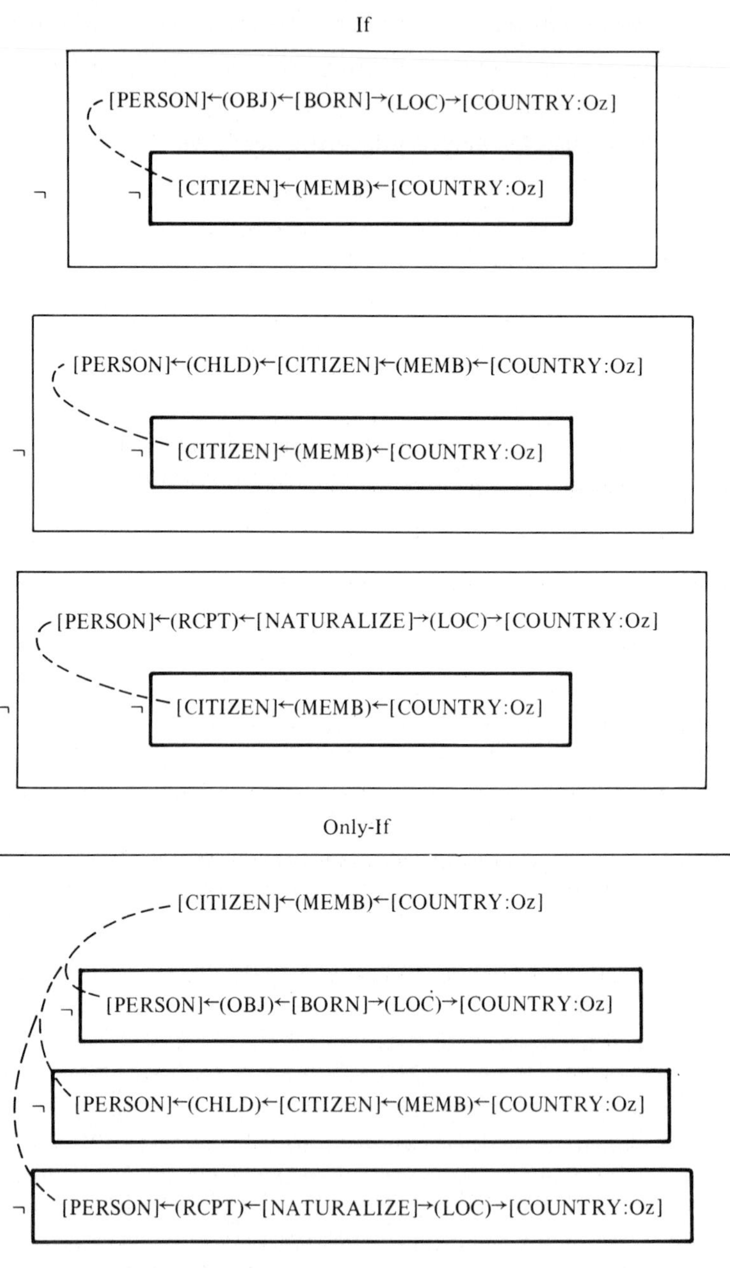

Fig. 4.12 Law defining citizenship in the Land of Oz

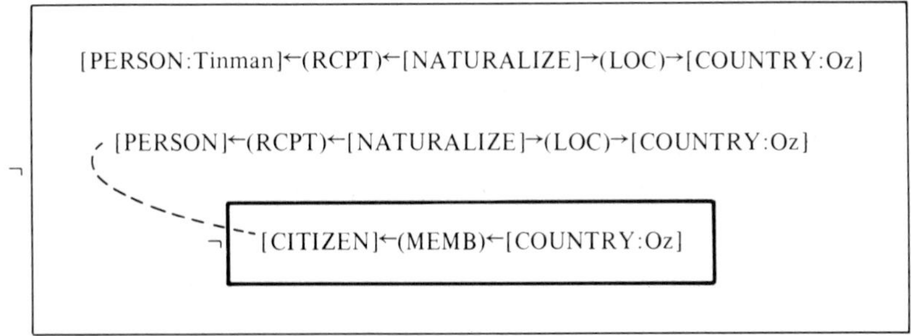

Fig. 4.13 First step in a deduction

Now suppose that the outermost context contains the four graphs of Fig. 4.12 as well as the following graph, which says that the Tinman was naturalized in Oz:

```
[PERSON:Tinman]←(RCPT)←[NATURALIZE]→(LOC)→[COUNTRY:Oz].
```

By iteration, a copy of this graph may be inserted into the third box of Fig. 4.12 to form Fig. 4.13. Then the two oddly enclosed graphs may be joined: first [PERSON] is restricted to [PERSON:Tinman]; then a coreference link is drawn between them; finally, they are joined. Similar joins of [NATURALIZE] to [NATURALIZE] and [COUNTRY:Oz] to [COUNTRY:Oz] may be made. The duplicate copies of (RCPT) and (LOC) may be erased by deiteration. Next, the referent Tinman may be copied to the coreferent concept [CITIZEN] in the innermost context and the coreference link erased. The result is Fig. 4.14.

By deiteration, the oddly enclosed graph in Fig. 4.14 may be erased because it is an exact copy of the graph that says the Tinman was naturalized in Oz. The result is the following graph:

```
¬[¬[[CITIZEN:Tinman]←(MEMB)←[COUNTRY:Oz]]].
```

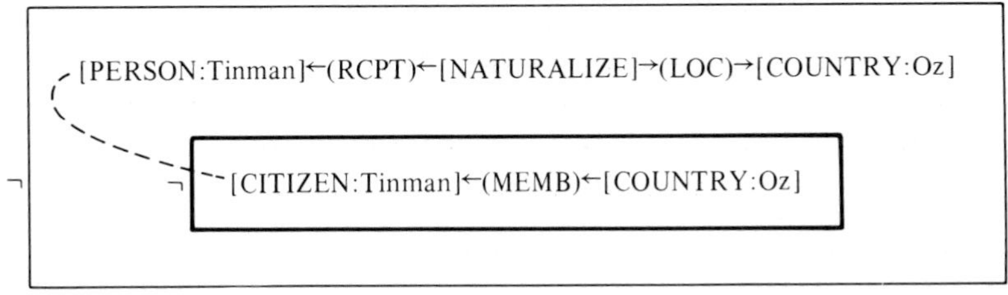

Fig. 4.14 Intermediate step in the deduction

By double negation, the two negative contexts may be erased to derive the conclusion that Tinman is a citizen of Oz:

```
[CITIZEN:Tinman]←(MEMB)←[COUNTRY:Oz].
```

For graphs without coreference links, the Beta rules for first-order logic reduce to the Alpha rules for propositional logic. Whereas the Alpha rules treat graphs as indivisible units that may be copied or erased as a whole, the Beta rules consider the structure of the graphs, especially the lines of identity. Therefore, any proof according to the Alpha rules is also a proof by the Beta rules.

4.3.6 Theorem. If a graph is provable by the propositional rules of Assumption 4.3.1, it is also provable by the first-order rules of Assumption 4.3.5.

Proof. Every rule of 4.3.1 is a special case of a rule of 4.3.5. Therefore, any proof by the propositional rules is also a proof by the first-order rules.

If a graph u is a specialization of v, then Theorem 3.5.3 showed that the formula ϕu in standard logic implies the formula ϕv. Peirce's rules can derive v directly from u. The next theorem proves that fact as well as other derived rules of inference that can shorten deductions with conceptual graphs.

4.3.7 Theorem. The following *derived rules of inference* may be used in proving theorems. Let u and v be any conceptual graphs where $u \le v$ with a projection π: $v \to u$.

- In an oddly enclosed context, v may be replaced with u where each coreference link to a concept c of v is transferred to the corresponding concept πc of u.
- Let p be the graph $\neg[u \neg[v]]$. Then p by itself is a theorem, and p with coreference links $\langle \pi c, c \rangle$ for any or all c in v is also a theorem.
- In an evenly enclosed context, u may be replaced with v where each coreference link to a concept πc of u is transferred to the corresponding concept c of v and the other coreference links attached to u are erased.
- Generalized modus ponens: If the outer context contains the graph u as well as a graph of the form $\neg[v \neg[w]]$, possibly with some coreference links from v to w, then the graph w may be derived with each coreference link attached to a concept c in v reattached to the corresponding concept πc in u.

Proof. To prove these four points, show that any result obtained by one of the derived rules can be obtained by some sequence of rules of Assumption 4.3.5:

- If v occurs in any oddly enclosed context, insert u into the same context by the rule of insertion. Then join each concept c of v to πc of u, using the rules of insertion, restriction of concepts in v, coreferent join, and erasure of duplicate conceptual relations. The resulting graph is identical to u, but with the coreference links transferred from v to u.

- To prove that the graph p is a theorem, draw a double negation around the empty set to form ¬[¬[ ]]. Then insert v into the odd context, and by iteration copy it into the even context: ¬[v ¬[v]]. By the first part of this theorem, which has just been proved, replace v in the outer context with u to derive p: ¬[u ¬[v]]. To prove the version of p with coreference links, before replacing the outer v with u, draw coreference links between corresponding concepts of v in the inner and outer contexts by the rule of iteration.

- To prove the third point, derive a copy of the graph p in the outermost context with coreference links between corresponding concepts of v and u. By iteration, copy p into the evenly enclosed context that contains the graph u. By deiteration, erase the copy of u in the new copy of p and transfer all its coreference links to the corresponding concepts of the original u. Next erase the double negation around v. Finally transfer all coreference links from the original graph u to the coreferent concepts in v, and erase u by the rule of erasure. As a result, the original copy of u in the evenly enclosed context has been replaced by v.

- To prove generalized modus ponens, replace the graph v with u in the oddly enclosed context and transfer all coreference links from v to the new copy of u. By iteration, draw a coreference link from the outermost u to the corresponding concept in the inner u that has a coreference link to w. By deiteration, erase the oddly enclosed copy of u. Finally erase the double negation around the graph w.

With this theorem, proofs become much shorter. The fact that Tinman is a citizen of Oz can be proved in two steps: since the statement that Tinman was naturalized in Oz is a specialization of the oddly enclosed graph in the third box of Fig. 4.12, the evenly enclosed graph may be derived by generalized modus ponens, but with a coreference link from [PERSON:Tinman] to [CITIZEN]. After copying the referent to [CITIZEN:Tinman] and erasing the coreference link, the proof is done. As another example, suppose that a person named Dorothy is a citizen of Oz, she was not born in Oz, and she is not the child of a citizen of Oz. Those statements are represented by the following three graphs:

```
 [CITIZEN:Dorothy]←(MEMB)←[COUNTRY:Oz].
¬[ [PERSON:Dorothy]←(OBJ)←[BORN]→(LOC)→[COUNTRY:Oz]].
¬[ [PERSON:Dorothy]←(CHLD)←[CITIZEN]←(MEMB)←[COUNTRY:Oz]].
```

Since the first graph is a specialization of the oddly enclosed graph in the fourth box of Fig. 4.12, it may replace that graph. By using the rule for copying the individual

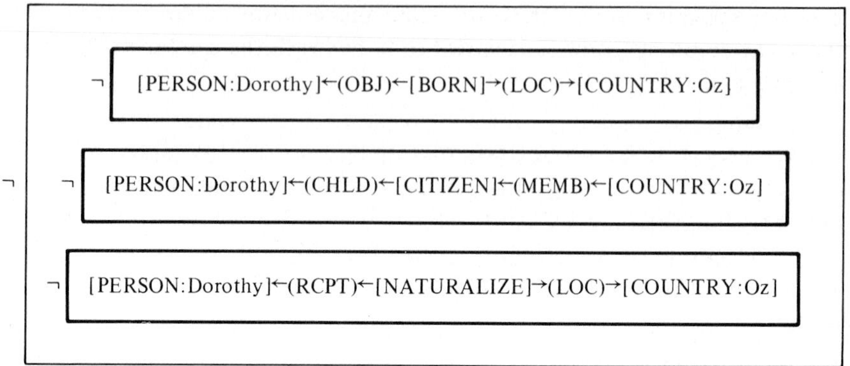

Fig. 4.15 Intermediate step in a deduction about Dorothy's citizenship

referent *Dorothy* and the rule of deiteration to erase the resulting oddly enclosed graph, Fig. 4.15 may be derived. That graph says that Dorothy was either born in Oz, was a child of a citizen of Oz, or was naturalized in Oz.

Deiteration not only applies to simple graphs, but to arbitrarily complex nests of graphs. The two graphs that say that Dorothy was not born in Oz or was not a child of a citizen of Oz each match one of the negative contexts nested in Fig. 4.15. By deiteration, those two contexts may be erased from 4.15 to leave just the graph,

```
¬[¬[[PERSON:Dorothy]←(RCPT)←[NATURALIZE]→(LOC)→[COUNTRY:Oz]]].
```

When the double negation is removed, this graph becomes the following, which says that Dorothy was naturalized in Oz:

```
[PERSON:Dorothy]←(RCPT)←[NATURALIZE]→(LOC)→[COUNTRY:Oz].
```

Peirce's rules of inference allow many of the results of standard logic to be derived in short, simple proofs. One example is the *deduction theorem*, which states that if a graph v is provable from u, then the implication $\neg[u\ \neg[v]]$ is a theorem. The proof follows from the fact that Peirce's rules depend only on the even or odd nesting of contexts, not on the depth of nesting.

4.3.8 Theorem. If the conceptual graph v is provable from the conceptual graph u, then $\neg[u\ \neg[v]]$ is a theorem.

Proof. To derive the graph from {}, draw a double negation around the empty set: $\neg[\ \neg[\ ]\ ]$. By the rule of insertion, insert u into the oddly enclosed context: $\neg[u\ \neg[\ ]]$. By iteration, copy u into the evenly enclosed context: $\neg[u\ \neg[u]]$. Since the rules of 4.3.5 do not depend on the depth of nesting, any derivation of v from u

that can be performed in the outermost context can be repeated inside any evenly nested context: $\neg[u \neg[u\ v]]$. By erasure, erase the evenly enclosed copy of u to derive the graph $\neg[u \neg[v]]$.

The word *theorem* has two meanings: an English statement like 4.3.8 is a theorem about conceptual graphs, but a conceptual graph itself can be a theorem if it is provable from the empty set. In general, the numbered theorems in this book are all *metatheorems* about conceptual graphs. To distinguish the graphs from metalanguage about the graphs, the following conventions are used:

- The metalanguage for talking about conceptual graphs is English augmented with the mathematical symbols of Appendix A. Variables in italics like c and u are *metavariables* that represent concepts and conceptual graphs. A graph that contains such variables, like $\neg[u \neg[v]]$, actually belongs to the metalanguage for describing conceptual graphs.
- When variables are used to specify parameters and coreference links, they are distinguished by asterisks, as in *x and *y. These variables are part of the conceptual graph notation; they are not part of the metalanguage for talking about conceptual graphs.
- In the concept [PROPOSITION:*x], the variable *x refers to another conceptual graph. Such variables were used in Section 4.2 for defining the relations (OR) and (IMP). They are also used in Section 4.5 for stating axioms about conceptual graphs. With such variables, conceptual graphs could be used as their own metalanguage. The paradoxes of self-reference do not arise with those variables, however, since a variable cannot represent the graph in which it occurs—it might represent a copy of that graph, but never the graph itself.

4.4 MODEL THEORY

A notation by itself has no meaning. A serious criticism of semantic networks is that the word *semantics* begs the question: a network is just a different kind of syntactic structure, describable by a *graph grammar* instead of an ordinary *phrase-structure grammar*. This criticism of semantic networks applies equally well to the trees of transformational grammar. Partee (1971) criticized the "near vacuousness" of semantic theories that "give abstract syntax-like structures without simultaneously specifying a logic to operate on them." Linear knowledge representations in AI are even more suspect than semantic networks. At least the discipline of forcing everything into a standard graph form imposes a uniform structure. Some notations provide a collection of features for expressing almost anything together with *procedural attachments* for escaping into LISP whenever the programmer chooses. Such a luxuriance of features can certainly do anything that a Turing machine can do, but it is almost impossible to define formally or even justify informally. McDermott (1978) expressed the disgust of the formalists at such a luxuriant growth with the pithy slogan, "No notation without denotation!"

Symbolic logic is the epitome of a theory with a precisely defined semantics: the truth of a proposition is determined by a *denotation operator* evaluated on a formal model. One way to think about models is to imagine them as relational databases that assert everything that is known to be true. Then the denotation operator δ behaves like a query processor: it treats a formula in first-order logic as a procedure that queries a database. For an existential quantifier $\exists x$, δ searches a set to find some element x with a given property. For a universal quantifier $\forall x$, δ checks whether every x in the set has that property. Woods (1968) used that approach as the basis for a question answering system. The next two questions are typical examples where Woods' system treated quantifiers as database search operators:

```
Does American Airlines have a flight which goes
from Boston to Chicago?

Are all the flights from Boston to Chicago
American Airlines flights?
```

In the first one, *a flight* implies an existential quantifier, which the system handles by searching for an example in the database. In the second sentence, the phrase *all the flights* implies a universal quantifier, which means that the system must check all flights from Boston to Chicago to see whether they are American Airlines flights. Woods' version of *procedural semantics* is a method for evaluating the denotation operator of model theory.

As an example of the denotation operator, consider the question *Did supplier Acme ship parts to Dept. 85?* The answer is *yes* if that fact is in the database and *no* if it isn't. That question could be mapped to the formula,

$$\exists x \exists y \exists z(\mathrm{SUPPLIER(Acme)} \land \mathrm{DEPT(D85)} \land \mathrm{PART}(x) \land \mathrm{DATE}(y) \\ \land \mathrm{SHIPMENT}(z) \land \mathrm{SHIP(Acme,D85,}x,y,z)).$$

The denotation operator δ would search the database to find some part x, date y, and shipment z that would make the predicates in the body of the formula true. If the denotation is **true**, then the answer to the question is *yes*. If the denotation is **false**, then the answer is *no*.

For a *wh*-type of question *What suppliers shipped parts to Dept. 85?*, the answer is a set of suppliers. In symbolic logic, a *yes-no* question corresponds to a proposition where every variable is *bound* by a quantifier. A *wh*-question, however, is mapped to a *lambda expression* with one or more parameters, as in the formula,

$$\lambda w \exists x \exists y \exists z(\mathrm{SUPPLIER}(w) \land \mathrm{DEPT(D85)} \land \mathrm{PART}(x) \land \mathrm{DATE}(y) \\ \land \mathrm{SHIPMENT}(z) \land \mathrm{SHIP}(w,\mathrm{D85},x,y,z)).$$

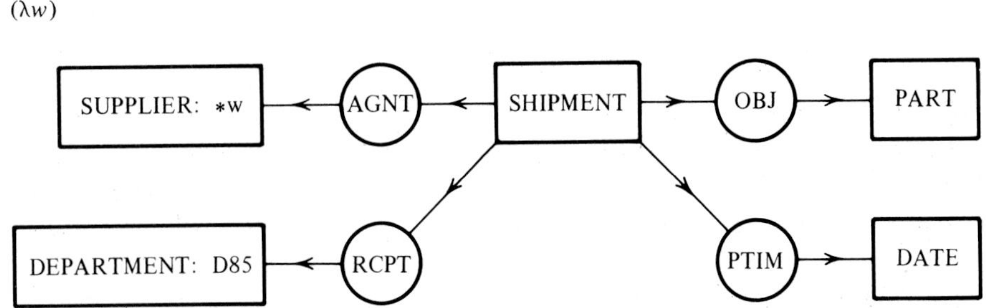

Fig. 4.16 Abstraction for "What suppliers shipped parts to Dept. 85?"

This formula is similar in structure to the previous one, except that the constant *Acme* has been replaced by the formal parameter *w*. The denotation of the lambda expression is not a truth value like **true** or **false**, but rather the set of all instances of SUPPLIERs that could be substituted for *w* to make the body of the expression true.

Lambda calculus combined with symbolic logic makes a powerful database query language. People who know logic find it easy to use, but others find it difficult. To provide the power of lambda calculus in an easy-to-learn system, PHLIQA1 (Bronnenberg et al. 1980) accepts questions in English or Dutch, translates them into lambda expressions, and then evaluates their denotations in the underlying database. Another way to make lambda calculus more palatable is to coat it with *syntactic sugar* in a specially designed query language. In such a language, the operator λ is replaced with a keyword like SELECT, LIST, or PRINT, and the body of the lambda expression is replaced with statements that extract and relate various fields in the database. The query language SQL, for example, would represent the lambda expression for finding suppliers by the query,

```
SELECT SUPPLIER FROM SHIP WHERE DEPT=D85.
```

In SQL, the SELECT clause names the *domain* from which values are selected, the FROM clause names some relation, and the WHERE clause specifies the conditions that determine which *n*-tuples of the relation are selected. The SQL statement is shorter than the formulas in logic because the domains in the SHIP relation that are not referenced may be omitted in SQL. In logic, however, those domains are governed by an explicit existential quantifier. See Date (1981) for an introduction to SQL and other database systems.

In conceptual graphs, a *wh*-question may be represented as an abstraction. The domains specified in the SELECT clause of SQL are the formal parameters of the abstraction. The body of the abstraction determines the database relations to be searched and the conditions to be tested. Figure 4.16 shows a monadic abstraction that corresponds to the *wh*-question asking for the suppliers. A *yes-no* question corresponds to an ordinary conceptual graph with the name *Acme* substituted for the formal parameter *w. The concepts [SHIPMENT], [PART], and [DATE] occur in the graph, but their referents are not of interest in either of these two queries (the type label SHIPMENT is used for the act of shipping instead of SHIP, which refers to the vessel). If the question is *What suppliers shipped what parts to Dept. 85 on what dates?*, then the query graph would be a triadic abstraction with the two additional parameters [PART:*x] and [DATE:*y]. If the query is *What are the shipments of what parts by what suppliers to what departments on what dates?*, then all five concepts would be flagged as formal parameters, and the denotation would be an exhaustive listing of all shipments in the database.

In AI, the databases are usually smaller but more complex than in commercial systems. Instead of dealing with billions of bytes of highly constrained data, they deal with complex structures that are completely contained in main storage. Winograd's SHRDLU (1972), for example, built and transformed *contexts* that contained structures of blocks and pyramids together with a robot arm that could move them around. For the question *Is there a large block behind a pyramid?* SHRDLU evaluated the denotation in terms of the current context. Instead of evaluating denotations, a command is a request to change the model into a new model in which the denotation becomes true. For the command *Pick up a big red block*, SHRDLU transformed the context into one where the robot arm was holding such a block. Although the structure of Winograd's contexts was very different from Woods' database, their procedural approaches were logically equivalent.

After the successful implementation of SHRDLU and LUNAR (Woods, Kaplan, & Webber 1972), a controversy developed in AI over a *procedural approach* to logic versus a *declarative approach*, which is based on inference rules and theorem proving. This controversy is a reflection of Tarski's distinction (1936) between a *model-theoretic* and a *proof-theoretic* definition of *theorem*:

- In proof theory, a theorem is the last line of some proof, where a proof is a sequence of formulas derived from axioms by rules of inference.

- In model theory, a theorem is a formula that is true for all possible models of the axioms. The truth of a formula in a model is evaluated by the denotation operator δ, according to an algorithm similar to Woods' and Winograd's procedures.

For first-order logic, Gödel (1930) proved that these two definitions are equivalent. The set of formulas that are provable from some set of axioms is identical to the set of formulas that are true in all possible models of those axioms. This property is known as *completeness*.

The claim that procedures are more efficient than theorem proving simply means that it is faster to evaluate a denotation in a single finite model than to carry out a general proof for all possible models, whether finite or infinite. Besides efficiency, the proceduralists claimed that actions are easier to express in a programming form than as a series of axioms. The logic programming movement, however, countered by implementing languages like PROLOG, which are essentially high-speed theorem provers. Kowalski (1979) showed how PROLOG could be used in typical AI applications where it competes with LISP in both efficiency and versatility. In arguing for procedural semantics, Woods (1981) claimed that a definition of meaning in terms of procedures eliminates the infinities of possible worlds that arise in model theory. But Hintikka (1973) eliminated the infinities with his *surface models*, which Sowa (1979) adapted to conceptual graphs. In short, proofs and models are two aspects of the same theory. A procedural approach evaluates the denotation of a formula in a particular model, but a theorem prover is needed to show that a formula is true in all possible models. For databases, a procedural approach can answer a particular question, but a theorem prover is needed for general constraints.

In model theory, a model W consists of a set I whose elements are called *individuals* and a collection T of *atomic facts* that are true of the individuals in W. In terms of conceptual graphs, the atomic facts are simple graphs, and the referent of each concept in T is an individual marker in I. The *denotation operator* δ evaluates the truth or falsity of an arbitrary conceptual graph u in terms of the graphs of T:

- For a simple graph u, the denotation δu is either **true** or **false**, depending on whether the particular configuration of concepts and relations in u occurs in some atomic fact.

- For a context c with referent $\{u_1,...,u_n\}$, the denotation δc is **true** if the denotation δu_i is **true** for all i. For a negative context of the form $\neg c$, the denotation $\delta(\neg c)$ is **true** if at least one of the denotations δu_i is **false**.

- For an abstraction $\lambda a\ u$, the denotation $\delta(\lambda a\ u)$ is the set of all individual markers that may be assigned as referents of the concept a in order to cause δu to be **true**.

Procedural semantics focuses on the algorithm for computing denotations, but *denotational semantics* focuses on the result of the computation. If u is any conceptual graph, then the denotation δu is the same as the denotation of the formula ϕu in standard logic.

In a formal definition of δ, the procedure is stated in terms of a projection operator π (see Section 3.5). The graph u makes a true assertion about the model if there exists a projection πu into some atomic fact. For many graphs, the projection π is not unique. The *projective extent* of a graph u in T is the set of all possible ways of projecting u into some graph of T. As an example, the phrase *a cat sitting on a mat* would be translated into the following conceptual graph:

```
[CAT]→(STAT)→[SIT]→(LOC)→[MAT].
```

Since all three concepts in this graph are generic, each one is governed by an implicit existential quantifier: there exists some cat, some mat, and some instance of sitting, where the cat is doing that sitting on that mat. Suppose that the set T of atomic facts includes the following three graphs:

```
[CAT:#297]→(STAT)→[SIT:#3501]→(LOC)→[MAT:#492],
[CAT:#849]→(STAT)→[SIT:#8096]→(LOC)→[MAT:#893],
[CAT:#849]→(STAT)→[SIT:#2271]→(LOC)→[MAT:#492].
```

The graph with all generic concepts could be projected into any one of these three graphs. Each projection would map the three generic concepts into three different individual concepts. If the graph *u* contained one or more individual concepts, the number of possible projections would be more limited. The next graph could be projected into *T* in two ways, since cat #849 had only performed two instances of sitting on a mat:

```
[CAT:#849]→(STAT)→[SIT]→(LOC)→[MAT].
```

The following graph, however, has no projections into *T* because cat #297 had only sat on mat #492 and not on mat #893:

```
[CAT:#297]→(STAT)→[SIT]→(LOC)→[MAT:#893].
```

For the first graph with all generic concepts, the projective extent in *T* consists of three possible mappings. For the graph with cat #849, the projective extent has two possible mappings. For the last graph with cat #297, the projective extent is empty.

4.4.1 Definition. Let *S* and *T* be any sets of simple graphs. Then the *projective extent* of *S* in *T*, written $\Pi(S,T)$, is the set of all possible projections from some graph of *S* into some graph of *T*:

$$\Pi(S,T) = \{\pi \mid u \in S,\ v \in T, \text{ and projection } \pi: u \rightarrow v\}.$$

For a simple graph *u*, the notation $\Pi(\{u\},S)$ or $\Pi(S,\{u\})$ may be abbreviated as $\Pi(u,S)$ or $\Pi(S,u)$.

Projective extents are defined for arbitrary sets of simple graphs. A model, however, is not arbitrary. It is intended to be an accurate record of some actual or hypothetical state of affairs. Reiter (1978) distinguished two kinds of models: a *closed-world model* represents total knowledge about everything in a particular system, and an *open-world model* represents partial knowledge where some things are known to be true, some are known to be false, and others are simply unknown. In a closed world, the denotation of every conceptual graph is either **true** or **false**, and no undefined or inconsistent states are possible. Closed worlds are deductively closed: every possible implication is represented. In an open world, many facts that are deducible might not be represented. Since a finite set of axioms may have an infinite number of implications, a closed world world may require infinite conceptual graphs.

4.4.2 Definition. A *closed world W* is a pair $\langle T,I \rangle$ where *T* is a set of simple graphs, called the *atomic facts* of *W*, and *I* is a set of individual markers, called the *individuals* of *W*.

- For every concept c in every graph in T, *referent*(c) is an individual marker in I.
- No individual marker in I occurs in more than one concept in T.
- T and I may be countably infinite, and some of the graphs in T may also be countably infinite.

Conceptual graphs play a dual role in model theory: they make statements about the world, and they serve as structures that represent the world. In standard logic, models and formulas bear little resemblance to one another: a model represents a possible world, formulas make statements about a world, and the mapping between the two is not obvious. To make the mapping more direct, Hintikka (1969) represented models as collections of simple formulas. Conceptual graphs achieve the same goal by using a common notation for formulas and models. The graphs that model the world and the graphs that describe the world have the same form and may even be identical.

The denotation function δ determines the truth of a conceptual graph by checking possible mappings into a world model. For a simple graph u, the denotation is easy to define. For a closed world $W=\langle T,I\rangle$, δu is **true** if $\Pi(u,T)$ is nonempty, and δu is **false** if $\Pi(u,T)$ is empty. For a compound graph, the denotation is evaluated from the outside in: simple graphs enclosed at depth 0 have no restrictions on their projective extents, but the projections of graphs enclosed at deeper levels are constrained by coreference links from dominating concepts at outer levels. Peirce coined the term *endoporeutic* for this method, but it is easier to say *outside-in evaluation*.

Peirce's way of evaluating denotations is closely related to the *game-theoretical semantics* that has been developed by Hintikka and his colleagues (Saarinen 1979). The *evaluation game* is played between a *proposer* who is trying to show that a graph is true and a *skeptic* who is trying to show that it is false. Given a world model W and a conceptual graph u, the proposer and the skeptic compete to evaluate δu. If the proposer has a winning strategy, δu=**true**; if the skeptic has a winning strategy, δu=**false**. In its basic form, the evaluation game gives the same results as more conventional forms of model theory. It has, however, several desirable properties:

- It readily adapts to Peirce's graph logic.
- It can be generalized to nonstandard versions of model theory by making simple changes in the rules of the game.
- It even generalizes to infinite formulas that cannot be evaluated in standard model theory (Henkin 1959).

This section develops a closed-world game that is exactly equivalent to standard model theory. Then the next section generalizes the game to modal logic and open worlds where the information is incomplete.

The evaluation game is based on the *minimax procedure* of game theory (see Appendix A.3). The next definition introduces three types of moves in the game, each corresponding to one of the three types of constructs in Peirce's graphs: a *project move* assigns referents to generic concepts (existentially quantified variables) and copies them to all coreferent concepts, a *select move* chooses one graph from a conjunction, and a *reduce move* erases a negation and reverses the roles of proposer and skeptic. If a conceptual graph contains other logical operators introduced by definitions, they must be expanded into primitives before the evaluation game is played. Because of coreference links, a concept may acquire multiple referents. The concept [PERSON:Lillian=Lillian] is equivalent to just [PERSON:Lillian], but [PERSON:Lillian=Lester] causes any graph containing it to be false unless Lester happens to be an alias for Lillian.

4.4.3 Definition. An *evaluation game* G on a closed world $W=\langle T,I\rangle$ is a two-person, zero-sum, perfect-information game between two players called *proposer* and *skeptic*. It is defined by the following rules:

- The positions of G are triples $\langle p,t,s\rangle$ where the player on move p is one of {proposer, skeptic}, t is one of three *move types* in the set {project, select, reduce}, and s is any set of conceptual graphs.
- The starting positions of G are all triples $\langle$proposer,project,$s\rangle$ for any set of conceptual graphs s.
- Some graphs in a position may have concepts with two or more distinct referents separated by equal signs. The projective extent in W of any such graph must be empty, since no concept in any atomic fact may have multiple referents.
- From a position $P=\langle p_1,\text{project},\{u_1,\ldots,u_n\}\rangle$, the successors are all positions of the form $\langle p_2,\text{select},\{v_1,\ldots,v_n\}\rangle$ where p_2 is the opponent of p_1 and each v_i is a version of u_i modified by the following algorithm:

```
for each simple graph u_i in P loop
   if Π(u_i,T) is nonempty then
      choose any projection π in Π(u_i,T);
      for each concept c in u_i loop
         copy referent(πc) to the referent field of c.
            and all concepts dominated by c;
         erase any newly added referent on a concept that is
            identical to a referent previously present;
         insert "=" between the referents of concepts that have
            more than one referent;
         erase all coreference links dominated by c;
      end loop;
   end if;
end loop;
```

- From a position $P=\langle p_1$,select,$\{u_1,...,u_n\}\rangle$, the successors are the n positions of the form $\langle p_2$,reduce,$\{u_i\}\rangle$ where p_2 is the opponent of p_1 and i is any integer from 1 to n. If $n=0$, P is an ending position, and p_1 loses.
- From a position $P=\langle p_1$,reduce,$\{u\}\rangle$ where p_2 is the opponent of p_1,

```
if u is a simple graph then
    P is an ending position;
    case value of Π(u,T) is
        when nonempty  =>  p1 wins;
        when empty     =>  p2 wins;
    end case;
else
    u must be a negative context of the form ¬c;
    s := the set of graphs in referent(c);
    the successor to P is ⟨p2,project,s⟩;
end if;
```

To illustrate the evaluation game, start with the simplest case, the empty set. The starting position is ⟨proposer,project,{}⟩. From that position, no iterations of the **for**-loop are taken, and the only successor is ⟨skeptic,select,{}⟩. Since no selections are possible, skeptic loses. Then proposer wins, and the denotation $\delta\{\}$ is **true**.

For a simple graph p, the starting position is ⟨proposer,project,$\{p\}$⟩. Proposer chooses some projection π in $\Pi(p,T)$, if possible, and copies the referents from πp back to p. The next position is ⟨skeptic,select,$\{p\}$⟩. The only choice for skeptic leads to ⟨proposer,reduce,$\{p\}$⟩. Since p is simple, this is an ending position. If $\Pi(p,T)$ is nonempty, proposer wins, and δp is **true**; otherwise, skeptic wins, and δp is **false**.

As a more complicated example, consider the formula $p\wedge(q\supset r)$ with the assumption that p is **true** and q and r are both **false**. Evaluation by *truth tables* (see Appendix A.5) leads to the denotation **true** in standard logic. Since p is **true**, $\Pi(p,T)$ must be nonempty; and since q and r are **false**, $\Pi(q,T)$ and $\Pi(r,T)$ must both be empty. To play the evaluation game, start with the following position, where there are no coreference links between p, q, and r:

⟨proposer, project, $\{p, \neg[q\ \neg[r]]\}$⟩.

The first move is a project move where proposer chooses some projection of p into T. Next, skeptic selects one of the two graphs in the position. Since choosing p leads to a win for proposer (as in the previous example), skeptic should choose the other graph, which leads to,

⟨proposer, reduce, $\{\neg[q\ \neg[r]]\}$⟩.

In this position, the only move for proposer is to remove the outer negative context, leading to the position,

⟨skeptic, project, $\{q, \neg[r]\}$⟩.

Since the projective extent of q in T is empty, the project move does nothing, and the next position is,

⟨proposer, select, {q, ¬[r]}⟩.

If proposer selects q, the next position is,

⟨skeptic, reduce, {q}⟩.

Since q is a simple graph, this is an ending position, and since $\Pi(q,T)$ is empty, skeptic loses. If proposer had chosen the other graph, the position would be,

⟨skeptic, reduce, {¬[r]}⟩.

After the reduction, the next position is,

⟨proposer, project, {r}⟩.

Since the projective extent for r is empty, this position leads to a loss for proposer after the next select and reduce. Some game paths therefore lead to a win for proposer and some to a loss. But since proposer has the choice of moves at the critical point, proposer is the one with a winning strategy, and the denotation is **true**, as in standard logic.

To illustrate the evaluation with coreference links, assume that W has three atomic facts, [PERSON:Joe], [PERSON:Ruby], and [PERSON:Hal], each of which consists of a single concept. Consider the example on page 147 that asserts the existence of at least two different persons:

{[PERSON:*x], [PERSON:*y], ¬[[PERSON:*x=*y]]}.

In the linear notation, the coreference links are indicated by variable symbols *x and *y. At the first move, proposer has three choices for projecting [PERSON:*x] into one of the three graphs of W, and three choices for projecting [PERSON:*y], making 3×3 or 9 possible project moves. One pair of choices leads to the graphs,

{[PERSON:*x=Joe], [PERSON:*y=Hal], ¬[[PERSON:*x=*y=Joe=Hal]]}.

The act of erasing coreference links corresponds to erasing the variable symbols:

{[PERSON:Joe], [PERSON:Hal], ¬[[PERSON:Joe=Hal]]}.

After the project move, skeptic has the option of selecting one of these three graphs. Since choosing either of the first two leads to a loss, skeptic should choose the third graph, leading to the position,

⟨proposer, reduce, {¬[[PERSON:Joe=Hal]]}⟩.

After the reduce move, the position becomes,

⟨skeptic, project, {[PERSON:Joe=Hal]}⟩.

Since [PERSON:Joe=Hal] cannot be projected into W, skeptic loses at the next reduce move. At the first move, if proposer had chosen to project both of the simple graphs into [PERSON:Hal], the result would be,

⟨skeptic, select, {[PERSON:Hal], [PERSON:Hal], ¬[[PERSON:Hal]]}⟩.

If skeptic selects the third graph, the next reduce move by proposer leads to a winning position for skeptic:

⟨skeptic, project, {[PERSON:Hal]}⟩.

Although some game paths lead to a win for skeptic, proposer is the one with a winning strategy, since proposer can force a win with a proper choice of projections at the first move. Therefore, the denotation of the original set of graphs is **true**. If the world W only contained a single person, however, the denotation would be **false**. This result is expected, since the original graph asserts the existence of at least two people.

4.4.4 Theorem. For a finite set s of finite conceptual graphs, all game paths starting from ⟨proposer,project,s⟩ lead to a win for either proposer or skeptic in a finite number of moves. Hence there must be a winning strategy for either proposer or skeptic. If player p has a winning strategy for s, p's opponent has a winning strategy for $\neg[s]$.

Proof. If n is the depth of the most deeply enclosed graph in s, no game path is more than $3(n+1)$ moves in length: a project, select, and reduce move at each level. The fact that a winning strategy exists follows from the fact that the *value* function is defined for all positions in such games (see Appendix A.3). If player p has a winning strategy in the starting position ⟨proposer,project,s⟩, then p's opponent must have a winning strategy in the position ⟨proposer,project,$\neg[s]$⟩, since the first three moves of the game reduce the position to ⟨skeptic,project,s⟩, which is the same state, but with the roles of the players reversed.

4.4.5 Assumption. Let W be a closed world and I the set of individual markers that occur as referents of concepts in W. The *denotation operator* δ for W maps sets of conceptual graphs to **true** or **false** and maps n-adic abstractions to n-tuples of individual markers in I.

- If s is a conceptual graph or a set of conceptual graphs, then δs=**true** if proposer has a winning strategy for the evaluation game on W that starts from the position ⟨proposer,project,s⟩; otherwise, δs=**false**.
- If $\lambda a_1,\ldots,a_n\ u$ is an n-adic abstraction, then $\delta(\lambda a_1,\ldots,a_n\ u)$ is the set of n-tuples, $\{\langle x_1,\ldots,x_n\rangle \mid \delta u=$ **true** when for each i, $x_i \in I$ and $referent(a_i):=x_i\}$.

Soundness means that everything that is provable is true. *Completeness* means that everything that is true is provable. Peirce's rules of inference are both sound and complete: if δs=**true** for some set s and world W, then each graph in s may be derived from the graphs of W by the rules of inference. The theorems provable from {} are the ones that are true in all worlds; therefore, they do not depend on any specific fact in any of them.

4.4.6 Theorem. The first-order rules of inference for conceptual graphs are *sound*. Let s be any set of conceptual graphs, and let G be an evaluation game on a closed world W. Then the following properties are true:

- The rules of Assumption 4.3.5 preserve truth: if δs=**true** and t is any set of conceptual graphs derived from s by any of those rules, then δt=**true**.
- If s is the axiom {}, δs=**true**. Hence, all theorems provable from the axiom have denotation **true** in W.

Proof. The rules of inference increase proposer's chances of winning and decrease skeptic's chances of winning. Therefore, if proposer has a winning strategy for the set s, proposer must also have a winning strategy for t. To verify that fact, consider each of the rules of inference:

- *Erasure.* Erasing an evenly enclosed graph decreases the options for skeptic during a select move. Erasing a coreference link to an evenly enclosed graph decreases proposer's chances of losing by finding some concept with two distinct referents during a reduce move. Erasing a referent or replacing a type label by a supertype increases the possible number of projections of a graph and increases the options for proposer during a project move.
- *Insertion.* Inserting a graph or coreference link into an oddly enclosed context increases skeptic's chances of losing during a reduce move and increases proposer's options during a select move. Restricting a concept decreases the number of possible projections of a graph and reduces the options for skeptic during a project move.
- *Iteration and deiteration.* The chances of winning or losing remain unchanged by iterating or deiterating a graph u: if δu is **true**, copying or erasing u in any context will not change the winning strategy for that context; if δu is **false**, the winning game path will end at the level of u (or before), and will never reach the more deeply enclosed copy of u.
- *Double negation.* The effect of a negation is to reverse the roles of proposer and skeptic. A double reversal leaves the winning strategy unchanged.
- *Coreferent join.* Since each individual marker occurs only once in a closed world W, any two coreferent concepts must be projected into exactly the same concept in W. The options for projecting a pair of graphs with a coreference link between them therefore remain unchanged if the coreferent concepts are joined.
- *Individuals.* Copying the referent from a dominant concept to a coreferent concept and erasing the coreference link between them has no effect on the win or loss, since the same copy would be made anyway during a project move.

A previous example showed that the position ⟨proposer,project,{}⟩ was a win for proposer. Hence, any graph derived from {} by the rules of inference must also lead to a win for proposer.

A *valid graph* has denotation **true** in all possible worlds. A *provable graph* follows from the axiom by the rules of inference. Since the rules of inference and the evaluation game have such different structures, it is remarkable that every valid graph is provable. This property, known as the *completeness* of first-order logic, is not true for all logical systems. In particular, it does not hold for the open-world models defined in the next section.

4.4.7 Theorem. The rules of inference in Assumption 4.3.5 are *complete*: for any closed world W, if δs=**true** for some set of conceptual graphs s, then each graph in s is provable from the graphs of W.

Proof. An indirect proof would show that Peirce's rules of inference can derive any formula provable in standard first-order logic (Exercise 4.19). Since Gödel (1930) showed that first-order logic is complete, Peirce's rules are also complete. A direct proof would show completeness by transforming the game tree that shows δs=**true** into a proof of s from the graphs used in project moves. Since the proof is rather lengthy, it will not be given in this book.

A closed world is the standard assumption in ordinary mathematics, where every statement must be either true or false. It was also Wittgenstein's assumption in the *Tractatus*: the world is everything that is the case—it is the collection of all possible atomic facts. But as Wittgenstein emphasized in the *Philosophical Investigations*, that view is not an accurate description of the real world. The particular set of atomic facts that one chooses to describe the world depends more on the purpose and viewpoint of the analyzer than on the actual state of affairs. Despite its limitations, the notion of a closed world is useful as an ideal of precision and clarity. The next section relaxes the rules of the evaluation game to accommodate a more general set of models.

4.5 TENSES AND MODALITIES

Ordinary language abounds in talk about possibilities, hypothetical events, desired goals, feared outcomes, and plans for the future. Books, movies, and television create a superabundance of possible worlds, fictionalized histories, and imaginary futures. Possible worlds resemble the models in Calvino's *Invisible Cities*:

> In the center of Fedora, that gray stone metropolis, stands a metal building with a crystal globe in every room. Looking into each globe, you see a blue city, the model of a different Fedora. These are the forms the city could have taken if, for one reason or another, it had not become what we see today. In every age someone, looking at Fedora as it was, imagined a way of making it the ideal city, but while he constructed his miniature model, Fedora was already no longer the same as before, and what had been until yesterday a possible future became only a toy in a glass globe. (p. 32)

Episodic memory is a museum for mental models. Like the crystal globes in Fedora, each *context* in long-term memory houses a model that represents a plan for the future, a memory of the past, a wish, a hope, a dream, or a fear. Each of those possible models is represented by a conceptual graph or a collection of conceptual graphs. A canonical basis for conceptual graphs forms an *ontology*, not of all the things that exist in the real world, but of all the things that may be imagined in the mind.

In English, the modes of possibility, necessity, and permission are expressed with *modal auxiliaries* like *can, must*, and *may*. Tenses are expressed with other auxiliary verbs like *will* and *have* or with endings like *-ed* on main verbs. To express the English rules for tense and modality in transformational grammar, Chomsky (1957) proposed the following rule:

```
AUX ⟶ TENSE [MODAL] [have -en] [be -ing].
```

This rule states that the category AUX is defined in terms of a required TENSE, an optional MODAL, an optional form of *have* plus an ending *-en* to be attached to the following verb, and an optional form of *be* plus an ending *-ing* to be attached to the following verb (see Appendix A.6 for a discussion of formal grammar rules). Yet the English practice of hooking tense and modality on the verb, although common in Indo-European languages, is not a universal principle. Chinese omits tenses if the time is obvious from the context. If not, it uses separate words like *now* or *yesterday*, which may or may not modify the verb. The Luiseño language (an Uto-Aztecan language of Southern California) expresses modality by particles associated with the subject (Steele 1981). Japanese puts tense and modality markers at the end of a sentence; verbs that occur in the middle typically omit tense markers. Even English allows nonverbs to have modes and tenses, but usually with a separate modifier, as in the phrases *past president, future earnings*, or *possibly wealthy*.

Although the syntax varies, all natural languages express times and modes in one form or another. But standard symbolic logic, as well Peirce's systems Alpha and Beta, cannot handle modality. In his system Gamma, Peirce added dotted lines and colored areas to distinguish different possible worlds, intentions, and degrees of knowledge. Gamma was, however, a complex system that Peirce never completed. Modern systems of *modal logic* are more modest extensions of standard logic with the symbols $\Box$ for necessity and $\Diamond$ for possibility. The formula $\Box p$ states that p is necessarily true, and the formula $\Diamond p$ states that p is possible. Modal logic includes all of standard logic together with the following rules for the symbols $\Box$ and $\Diamond$:

- Impossible is equivalent to necessarily false: $\sim\Diamond p$ if and only if $\Box\sim p$.
- Anything that is necessarily true is true: $\Box p \supset p$.
- Anything that is true is possible: $p \supset \Diamond p$.
- If it is necessarily true that p implies q, then if p is necessary, q must also be necessary: $\Box(p \supset q) \supset (\Box p \supset \Box q)$.
- Anything that is provable is necessarily true: if p is a theorem, then $\Box p$.

Standard logic extended with these assumptions is called *System T*. More elaborate axioms for modal logic treat *iterated modalities* like $\Diamond\Box\Diamond p$, which says that p is possibly necessarily possible. But such mind-boggling constructions seldom occur in natural languages.

In *case grammar*, Fillmore (1968) followed modal logic in separating the propositional part of a sentence from the modality, in which he included negation and tense as well as the modes of possibility and necessity. For conceptual graphs, the propositional part is stated in the referent of a concept [PROPOSITION], and the monadic conceptual relations (PSBL) or (NECS) indicate the mode. The next graph represents the sentence *It is possible for Julian to fly to Mars*; as before, a concept box without a type label has the default label PROPOSITION.

```
(PSBL)→[[PERSON:Julian]←(AGNT)←[FLY]→(DEST)→[PLANET:Mars]].
```

The extra level of brackets around the nested graph is essential. If (PSBL) were attached directly to [PERSON:Julian], the graph would say *The possible person Julian is flying to Mars.* To map the graph into modal logic, translate the graph by the formula operator ϕ and put the possibility operator $\Diamond$ in front of the formula:

$$\Diamond\exists x(\mathrm{PERSON}(\mathrm{Julian}) \wedge \mathrm{FLY}(x) \wedge \mathrm{PLANET}(\mathrm{Mars}) \\ \wedge \mathrm{AGNT}(x,\mathrm{Julian}) \wedge \mathrm{DEST}(x,\mathrm{Mars})).$$

Modality is an attribute of an entire situation, which may include many graphs: the referent of a proposition could be a set of graphs that specify a fully developed possible world. Grammar rules permit the mode to be combined with the main verb in the sentence *Julian can fly to Mars.* Combining modality with the verb is not a semantic requirement, but a feature of English syntax.

Like modality, tense governs a situation. In the sentence *Julian watched a football game*, the past tense marker governs Julian and the game as much as it does the act of watching:

```
(PAST)→[[PERSON:Julian]←(AGNT)←[WATCH]→(OBJ)→[FOOTBALL-GAME]].
```

The sentence *Julian couldn't fly to Mars* has a proposition modified by three monadic relations: tense (PAST), modality (PSBL), and negation (NEG). Attaching all three of those relations to the same proposition node would be incorrect: literally, it would express the self-contradictory statement *It is possible, past, and false that Julian flew to Mars.* A correct representation must use nested propositions:

```
(PAST)→[ (NEG)→[ (PSBL)→[
      [PERSON:Julian]←(AGNT)←[FLY]→(DEST)→[PLANET:Mars]]]].
```

This graph could be read *It was past that it was false that it was possible for Julian to fly to Mars.* As a further abbreviation, use the negated labels defined in Section 4.2 to combine (NEG) and (PSBL) in the relation (¬PSBL):

```
(PAST)→[ (¬PSBL)→[
      [PERSON:Julian]←(AGNT)←[FLY]→(DEST)→[PLANET:Mars]]].
```

Possibility and necessity are called *alethic modalities* or modes of truth. Natural languages express many other modal forms, which logicians have tried to capture in capture in logic. *Deontic logic* introduces modes for *permission* and *obligation* to support the English modals *may* and *ought*. *Epistemic logic* introduces modes for *knowing* and *believing*, and *temporal logic* introduces modes for *sometimes* and *always* together with their negations *never* and *not always*. Yet there is no limit to the number of modes, and philosophers have proposed an endless variety of them: *per se*, doubtful, thought, clear, generally known, lawful, preferred, certain, probable, improbable, agreed, granted, said by the Ancients, written in Holy Scriptures, *de fide*, heretical, questioning, promising, challenging, protesting, envisaging, favoring, approving (Seuren 1969). If Christians use the mode *written in Holy Scriptures*, Moslems can use the mode *written in the Koran*. A legal system might use the modes hearsay, admitted as evidence, or inadmissible because of illegal wiretaps. All these modes are needed for normal uses of language, and conceptual graphs must be able to represent them.

The unlimited variety of modal forms can be represented by conceptual graphs constructed out of standard concepts and relations. Most such graphs include concept types such as KNOW, THINK, and ASK that take a nested conceptual graph as their object. Following is a graph for the sentence *George asked whether Scott is the author of Waverly*:

```
[PERSON:George]←(AGNT)←[ASK]→(OBJ)→[ [PERSON:Scott=*x]
      [AUTHOR:*x]←(AGNT)←[WRITE]→(OBJ)→[BOOK:Waverly]].
```

Since the name *Scott* does refer to the same person as *the author of Waverly*, the two expressions are sometimes interchangeable: if George saw the author of *Waverly*, then he saw Scott. But George is not asking whether Scott is Scott when asks whether Scott is the author of *Waverly*. Some verbs have entire contexts for their objects. Of those verbs, some behave like *see* in permitting substitutions inside the context. Others behave like *ask* in blocking substitutions.

Verbs that deal with external actions like *see*, *kick*, *carry*, and *take* are called *extensional verbs*. Most of them do not take nested contexts for their objects, but even when they do, the nested context refers to entities and events in the same world as the outer context. Verbs that deal with mental states like *believe*, *hope*, *want*, and *seek* are called *intensional verbs*. Those verbs always have a nested context for their object, and that context may refer to a different possible world from the world that includes the agent of the verb. For a verb like *ask* or *hope* where the inner and outer possible worlds are different, the context is called *opaque*. For a verb like *see* where both possible worlds are the same, the context is called *transparent*.

The rule of iteration in Assumption 4.3.5 can copy a graph into a context with an attached NEG relation. But for contexts that occur as the object of some verb, iteration is not allowed to move graphs across the context boundary. Even for an extensional verb like *see*, iteration into the nested context is not permitted: suppose that John saw Leslie walking home and that Katie also walked home. It does not follow that John saw both Leslie and Katie walking home. Although transparent contexts do not permit an entire graph to be iterated into the context, they do permit coreference links to be iterated into it. If Leslie is Katie's sister and John saw Leslie walking home, then it follows that John saw Katie's sister walking home. Opaque contexts block both kinds of iteration. If John believed that Leslie walked home, it does not follow that John believed that Katie's sister walked home. Only if John also believed that Leslie is Katie's sister could the rules of inference combine the two beliefs. The conclusion that Katie's sister walked home could be deduced within the same context as John's other beliefs.

To handle intensional verbs in natural languages, Montague (1974) applied the formal techniques of model theory to a subset of English. One of his best known examples is the sentence *John seeks a unicorn.* In most theories, that sentence has only one syntactic parsing. Montague, however, maintained that it is ambiguous because there are two interpretations. First, John may be looking for some unicorn, but he doesn't have any specific one in mind. Second, John may have lost his pet unicorn Spike, and he is going in search of Spike. To demonstrate the ambiguity, Montague developed an elaborate grammar that assigns a different parsing to each possible interpretation.

Conceptual graphs handle the same kinds of sentences as Montague grammar, but with a simpler formalism. Instead of assigning the ambiguity to syntax or semantics, the theory maps Montague's sentence into a single conceptual graph:

```
[PERSON:John]←(AGNT)←[SEEK]→(OBJ)→[SITUATION: [UNICORN]].
```

Literally, this graph says that John seeks a situation in which there exists a unicorn. That situation may be part of the same world in which John exists, or it may exist only as a desire in John's mind. The ambiguity occurs not in the syntax nor in the semantics, but in the choice of a possible world in which to evaluate the denotation operator δ. Consider the next two sentences:

```
John saw his pet unicorn jump over the fence.
John hoped that his pet unicorn would jump back.
```

The object of SEE is a conceptual graph that refers to the same world that contains the agent [PERSON:John]. The object of HOPE, however, is a context that refers to a world that exists only in John's mind.

Besides a notation for expressing modality, modal logic includes axioms and rules of inference for transforming modal formulas. Peirce's rules of inference (4.3.5) are sufficient for modal logic as well as first-order logic, but more axioms are needed besides the empty set {}. For the type KNOW, a standard axiom is that if something is known, then it is true:

```
¬[ [KNOW]→(OBJ)→[PROPOSITION: *p] ¬[ [PROPOSITION: *p]]].
```

This graph states that if there exists a proposition *p as the object of KNOW, then that proposition is true. Since the variable *p is of type PROPOSITION, it represents a conceptual graph instead of just a simple individual. Because every generic concept has an implicit existential quantifier, variables like *p support a form of *higher-order logic* with quantifiers that range over conceptual graphs. With such variables, all of the axioms for conceptual graphs can be stated in conceptual graphs. The modal axiom, $\Box p \supset p$, becomes,

```
¬[ (NECS)→[PROPOSITION: *p] ¬[ [PROPOSITION: *p]]].
```

Higher-order variables enable conceptual graphs to be used as a *metalanguage* for talking about conceptual graphs. This approach follows Peirce's system Gamma, in which he stated all the rules of inference for existential graphs (Roberts 1973). Some AI systems that have implemented graph forms of higher-order logic include SNePS (Shapiro 1979) and KL-ONE (Brachman 1979).

The model theory of Section 4.4 provides a semantic basis for only the first-order subset of conceptual graphs. When combined with modal logic, model theory leads to multiplicities of possible worlds and fictitious entities. Combining the modal form *it is possible that...* with standard quantifiers like *there exists...* creates the form *it is possible that there exists....* Such logical forms introduce possible entities and ontological puzzles: a possible entity does not really exist, but it somehow has more status than other nonexistent things. Quine ridiculed the notion of possible entities:

> Take, for instance, the possible fat man in that doorway; and, again, the possible bald man in that doorway. Are they the same possible man, or two possible men? How do we decide? How many possible men are there in that doorway? Are there more possible thin ones than fat ones? How many of them are alike? Or would their being alike make them one? (1961, p. 4)

This objection to possible entities is an understandable reaction to the vague arguments sometimes given for them. Yet an adequate treatment of modal terms is necessary for a large part of ordinary language.

Leibniz introduced the principle that necessary truths hold in all possible worlds. To give a precise treatment of possible worlds, Kripke (1963a,b) combined Leibniz's intuitive notion with Tarski's model theory. Instead of having just one model that represents the real world, Kripke introduced families of models, each representing a different possible world. Besides models of possible worlds, he also introduced an *accessibility relation* between them: a world with a fat man in Quine's doorway would be accessible from a world with an empty doorway or from a different possible world with a thin man in the doorway. There is an infinite number of possible worlds that are accessible from the real world by minor changes. But each world has only a fixed number of entities.

Although Kripke defined a precise model theory for modal logic, he did so at the expense of introducing infinite families of possible worlds, each of which may itself be infinite. Such infinities can be imagined in a mathematical theory or a fictional dialog, but there is no way to represent them in computer storage or the human brain. As a first step in pruning away the infinities, Dunn (1973) proposed an alternative semantics in terms of laws and facts. Each possible world W is characterized by two sets of propositions: laws L and contingent facts T. Every law is also a fact, but not all facts are laws. A proposition is necessarily true if it is provable from the laws, it is empirically true if it happens to be a fact, and it is possible if it is consistent with the laws (but perhaps inconsistent with some fact). Dunn showed that modal semantics in terms of laws and facts is equivalent to Kripke's semantics in terms of possible worlds. For database semantics, the laws are constraints or *meaning postulates* that must be true for all states of the database, and the contingent facts are the collections of data that happen to be stored in it.

A semantic theory based on infinite worlds is acceptable for mathematics and logic, but psychologically, it is unrealistic to assume that people construct infinite models in their heads. In the search for a more realistic semantics, Hintikka (1973) criticized the infinite, closed-world models of standard logic:

> Usually, models are thought of as being given through a specification of a number of properties and relations defined on the domain. If the domain is infinite, this specification (as well as many operations with such entities) may require nontrivial set-theoretical assumptions. The process is thus often nonfinitistic. It is doubtful whether we can realistically expect such structures to be somehow actually involved in our understanding of a sentence or in our contemplation of its meaning, notwithstanding the fact that this meaning is too often thought of as being determined by the class of possible worlds in which the sentence in question is true. It seems to me much likelier that what is involved in one's actual understanding of a sentence S is a mental anticipation of what can happen in one's step-by-step investigation of a world in which S is true.

Instead of infinite models, Hintikka proposed open-ended, finite, *surface models*. Understanding a story would consist of building a surface model containing only those entities that were explicitly mentioned. The model would then be extended in a "step-by-step investigation" of all the implicit entities that must exist to support or interact with the ones that were mentioned. Closed models are limiting cases of surface models that have been extended infinitely far, but at any point in time, only a finite surface model is ever constructed.

In a closed world, there are no gaps in knowledge. If the information, *Mary has a little lamb*, is not present in the database, then one can safely assume that Mary does not have a pet lamb. In mathematics, perfect knowledge is assumed to be possible, and standard model theory assumes a closed world. Some databases, such as an airlines reservation system, are closed worlds: by definition, a reservation that is not listed in the database does not exist. All businesses strive for perfection in their databases, but mistakes are inevitable. Because of a programming error, one insurance company lost a portion of their database. They estimated that the cost to regenerate the missing records from the files on paper would be $3 million. They decided that it was cheaper to pay any claims based on missing policies than to recreate a correct database.

The human brain and most practical databases are open worlds. Some things are known to be true, and others are known to be false. The absence of a proposition does not mean that it is false, but simply that its truth or falsity is unknown. Unlike a closed world where anything that is not known to be true is false, an open world leaves more options available. In the absence of information about Mary's pets, either positive or negative, nothing can be assumed. To accommodate open worlds, the evaluation game of Section 4.4 must support other features:

- Open worlds based on finite, incompletely known states instead of the infinite, completely known states of a closed world,
- Inconsistent states that accommodate the inevitable errors and misinformation in practical systems,
- Modal operations for possibility, necessity, and intensional verbs like *know*, *think*, and *wish*,
- Multiple worlds and contexts for hypothetical and fictional situations.

An *open world* is defined by two sets of graphs: a set T that is known to be true, and a set F that is known to be false. In closed worlds, all concepts are individual, but open worlds allow some concepts to be generic. The set T, for example, might contain the following graph, which says that cat #849 sat on some mat, but it does not identify the particular mat or the particular instance of sitting:

```
[CAT:#849]→(STAT)→[SIT]→(LOC)→[MAT].
```

To rule out the possibility that penguins fly, F could contain the following graph, which would cause any assertion about penguins flying to have denotation **false**:

```
[PENGUIN]→(AGNT)→[FLY].
```

The set F could have implications for Mary's pets without mentioning them explicitly. The sentence *No one who lives in a city keeps a farm animal as a pet* does not mention Mary or lambs, but when combined with information that Mary lives in Boston, it rules out her having a pet lamb. Such general statements are not possible in a closed world where only positive assertions about individuals may be made.

4.5.1 Definition. An *open world* W is a triple $\langle T,F,I \rangle$ where T and F are sets of simple graphs and I is a set of individual markers:

- T is called the *true set*, F is called the *false set*, and the elements of I are called the *individuals* of world W.
- The graphs in T and F may contain either generic concepts or individual concepts with referents in I.
- No individual marker in I occurs in more than one concept in T, but there is no such restriction on the referents of F.

Having both a true set T and a false set F provides more options for evaluating denotations than having just a single set T. For any graph u, if u implies a false graph, then u must be false; but if a true graph implies u, then u must be true. The implications are determined by projections: if there is a projection from a graph u into a graph v, then v must be a specialization of u, and therefore, v implies u (by Theorem 3.5.3 or 4.3.7). For an open world, there are four possibilities to consider:

- $\Pi(u,T)$ and $\Pi(F,u)$ are both empty: there is insufficient information, and δu is **unknown**.
- $\Pi(u,T)$ is nonempty, and $\Pi(F,u)$ is empty: a true graph implies u, and δu must therefore be **true**.
- $\Pi(u,T)$ is empty, and $\Pi(F,u)$ is nonempty: u implies a false graph, and δu must therefore be **false**.
- $\Pi(u,T)$ and $\Pi(F,u)$ are both nonempty: a true graph implies u, and u implies a false graph. The model itself is inconsistent, and δu is **unknown**.

Most logicians would like to forbid inconsistencies, but practical databases are filled with them. Rescher and Brandom (1979) developed a form of model theory that permits incomplete and inconsistent worlds. Their rules of inference are standard, but their model theory allows some propositions to have the denotations **true** and **false** simultaneously, and others to be neither **true** nor **false**. They developed a method for localizing the inconsistencies so that an occasional error in a database would not cause the entire system to collapse.

Standard logic is sometimes called *monotonic logic* because the set of all statements that are provable increases monotonically as new axioms are added. A new axiom can never cause anything that was previously provable to become unprovable. If the new axiom contradicts one of the old ones, an inconsistency arises, and as Theorem 4.3.3 showed, everything becomes provable. When everything is provable, a proof is meaningless, and the whole system of logic collapses. To prevent the collapse, logicians and AI researchers have developed forms of *nonmonotonic logic*. The most elaborate of such logics is *relevance logic* by Anderson and Belnap (1975), which restricts the rules of inference to prevent irrelevant axioms and inconsistencies from affecting a proof. Instead of changing the rules of inference, Rescher and Brandom changed the underlying model theory. As a result, they satisfied the goals of nonmonotonic logic: inconsistencies may occur in the model without causing everything to become provable. In this section, the evaluation game on open worlds follows Rescher and Brandom's approach of changing the model theory instead of changing the rules of inference.

4.5.2 Definition. For an open world $W=\langle T,F,I\rangle$, the evaluation game is played as in Definition 4.4.3, but with a revised definition for the reduce move. Let P be a position $\langle p_1,\text{reduce},\{u\}\rangle$ where p_2 is the opponent of p_1; the reduce move is defined by the following algorithm:

```
if u is a simple graph then
   P is an ending position;
   case value of ⟨Π(u,T), Π(F,u)⟩ is
      when ⟨empty, empty⟩          =>  the game is a draw;
      when ⟨nonempty, empty⟩       =>  p1 wins;
      when ⟨empty, nonempty⟩       =>  p2 wins;
      when ⟨nonempty, nonempty⟩    =>  the game is a draw;
   end case;
else
   u must be a negative context of the form ¬c;
   s := the set of graphs in referent(c);
   the successor to P is ⟨p2,project,s⟩;
end if;
```

According to this definition, there are two ways for the evaluation game to end in a draw: either there is insufficient information when both $\Pi(u,T)$ and $\Pi(F,u)$ are empty, or there is too much information (the model is inconsistent) when both $\Pi(u,T)$ and $\Pi(F,u)$ are nonempty. In either case, the denotation of the graph u is **unknown**.

4.5.3 Assumption. Let $W=\langle T,F,I\rangle$ be an open world. The *denotation operator* δ for W maps sets of conceptual graphs to one of the three *truth values* **true**, **false**, or **unknown** and maps n-adic abstractions to n-tuples of individual markers in I.

- Let s be a conceptual graph or a set of conceptual graphs, and let G be an evaluation game starting from the position ⟨proposer,project,s⟩. Then,

  δs=**true** if proposer has a winning strategy in G,

  δs=**false** if skeptic has a winning strategy in G,

  δs=**unknown** if G is drawn.

- If $\lambda a_1,...,a_n\ u$ is an n-adic abstraction, then $\delta(\lambda a_1,...,a_n\ u)$ is the set of n-tuples,

  $\{\langle x_1,...,x_n\rangle \mid \delta u=$**true** when for each i, $x_i \in I$ and $referent(a_i):=x_i\}$.

Theorem 4.4.6 proved that Peirce's rules of inference are sound: everything that is provable is true. That definition of soundness only holds in a closed world. In an open world, soundness means that nothing provable is false. Since a closed world has only two denotations, **true** and **false**, both definitions of soundness are equivalent. Since an open world also allows the denotation **unknown**, only the weaker version of soundness can be proved. That property makes open worlds a more realistic model of human *belief systems*: people believe the obvious consequences of statements they firmly hold, but they may not be aware of the remote consequences.

4.5.4 Definition. A conceptual graph u is said to be *independent* of a set of simple graphs S if for any simple graph v enclosed at any depth in u, both $\Pi(v,S)$ and $\Pi(S,v)$ are empty.

If a graph u is independent of a set S, the truth or falsity of S can have no effect on the denotation of u. Even if a model becomes inconsistent with S added to both T and F simultaneously, δu will remain unchanged. This property means that inconsistencies in a database are localized: queries that do not depend on the inconsistent data remain unaffected. The next theorem proves that point.

4.5.5 Theorem. Let $W=\langle T,F,I\rangle$ be an open world, and let u be any conceptual graph. If u is independent of a set of simple graphs S, δu remains unchanged whether S is added to the set T or S is added to the set F.

Proof. By the definition of independence, for any simple graph v nested in u, both projective extents $\Pi(v,S)$ and $\Pi(S,v)$ must be empty. Therefore, adding S to either T or F leaves $\Pi(v,T)$ and $\Pi(F,v)$ unchanged and has no effect on the evaluation game. Consequently, either addition must leave δu unchanged.

A person's beliefs grow and change with time. A reasonable person will add newly proved statements to T and refuted statements to F. Yet problems arise when an inconsistency is found. The status of some graphs in T and F must change, but finding the changes that would cause the least disruption to the belief system may take a long period of soul searching. If an open world has no inconsistency, it can evolve into a closed world by the addition of new graphs to T and F. The goal is to reduce the number of graphs for which the denotation is **unknown** because of incomplete information. At the same time, any graph whose denotation is **true** or **false** should not become **unknown** because of a new inconsistency in the model. The limiting case of an open world that has grown infinitely far is a closed world model, but the models actually constructed in the human brain or computer storage never become infinite.

4.5.6 Theorem. Let $W=\langle T,F,I\rangle$ be an open world, and let G be the set of all conceptual graphs whose type labels and individual markers occur in W. Then the following three statements are equivalent:

- No graph in G has denotation **unknown**.
- For any simple graph u in G, one of $\Pi(u,T)$ or $\Pi(F,u)$ is empty, and the other is nonempty.
- There exists a closed world $W'=\langle T',I'\rangle$ for which the denotation of any graph u in G is the same for W and W'.

Proof. To show that three statements are equivalent, prove that the first implies the second, the second implies the third, and the third implies the first. First suppose that no graph in G has denotation **unknown**. Then the second statement must be true; otherwise, δu would be **unknown**, according to Definition 4.5.2. To construct the model W' for the third statement, note that the set F is redundant since the emptiness of $\Pi(F,u)$ can be predicted from $\Pi(u,T)$. To construct the sets T' and I', assign new individual markers that do not occur in I to the generic concepts of graphs in T and add those markers to the set I. The resulting sets are T' and I'. If $\Pi(u,T)$ is nonempty, then $\Pi(u,T')$ is also nonempty: if t is a graph in T where $t \leq u$, then for the modified graph t', $t' \leq t$ and hence $t' \leq u$. If, on the other hand, $\Pi(u,T)$ is empty, then $\Pi(u,T')$ is also empty. Consequently, denotations in W' are the same as in W. To prove the first statement, note that if denotations are the same in W and W', no graph in G can have denotation **unknown**, since W' only permits denotations **true** or **false**.

Open worlds are like Hintikka's surface models. A person who hears a sentence s translates it into a conceptual graph u. Initially, u contains only concepts for the entities, attributes, and events that were explicitly mentioned in s. Hintikka's "step-by-step investigation" is the process of taking u as the nucleus for building a model of a possible world. As the story unfolds, new graphs are joined to the nucleus u. Some graphs come from the story, but background information comes from the schemata and prototypes that represent typical ways that things and events fit together to make up the world. Obligatory constraints come from a set of *laws* that must always be true. The laws state necessary conditions for a possible world, and the schemata and prototypes state defaults and plausible background information. In database terms, T and F are collections of records in storage, and the laws are constraints on permissible values in those records.

4.5.7 Definition. A *world basis* consists of an open world W together with a set L of conceptual graphs call *laws* and a set S of schemata and prototypes. Let u be an arbitrary conceptual graph.

- u is *necessary* if it is provable from L.
- u is *possible* if it is consistent with L (i.e. the empty clause is not provable from L and u).
- u is *plausible* if u is possible and δu becomes **true** when T is replaced with some set of graphs that are canonically derivable from S.

Understanding a story involves the selection of laws and defaults L and S and the construction of a possible world W that is consistent with L and guided by S. The world of Greek mythology is not accessible from the modern world, and different choices of L and S make different events possible and plausible. The statement *Zeus changed himself into a swan and had intercourse with Leda* is true in the world of

Greek mythology, but it is incompatible with our knowledge of the real world. But the statement *Zeus changed himself into an ostrich and had intercourse with Mae West* mixes individuals from the real world and a mythical world in a way that is false for both. Even historically true worlds may be inaccessible from one another: in a story about Christopher Columbus, prototypes in S would specify clothing that today is worn only at a costume party, and the laws in L would imply that travel across the ocean in a few hours is impossible.

If the sets of graphs T, F, I, L, and S are arbitrarily chosen, the world basis may be inconsistent. If a graph u in T is inconsistent with L, then u would not be possible, but its denotation δu would be **true**. Even worse, if the set of laws is itself inconsistent, then every graph would be impossible and necessary at the same time. The next definition defines a world basis to be consistent if it can be extended to a closed world. It may be possible to extend a world basis in many different ways, but at least one extension must exist for it to be consistent.

4.5.8 Definition. Let B be a world basis $\langle W,L,S\rangle$ where the open world W is $\langle T,F,I\rangle$. Then B is said to be *consistent* if there exists a closed world $W'=\langle T',I'\rangle$ with the following properties:

- $T \subseteq T'$, $I \subseteq I'$, and $\Pi(F,T')$ is empty.
- Every graph in L has denotation **true** in W'.
- Every graph in S has denotation **true** in W'.

Then W' is called a *closed-world extension* of W.

Since an open world is not a finished closed world, there may be some graphs that are necessarily true (provable from L) yet whose denotations are **unknown**; those graphs are candidates for addition to T. No graph with denotation **false**, however, could be necessarily true. The next theorem shows that the axioms for System T (p. 174) hold for a consistent world basis. In an open world, a graph that is necessary has a denotation **true** or **unknown**. When the open world evolves into a closed world, then necessary implies **true**, as in standard modal logic.

4.5.9 Theorem. Let $\langle W,L,S\rangle$ be a consistent world basis, and let u and v be any conceptual graphs with the negation relation (NEG) as the only relation that may be linked to a nested context.

- The graph u is not possible if and only if the graph $\neg[u]$ is necessary.
- If u is necessary, then δu is not **false**.
- If δu is **true**, then u is possible.
- If $\neg[u\ \neg[v]]$ is necessary, then the necessity of u implies the necessity of v.
- Every schema and prototype in S is possible.

Proof. If u is not possible, then u and L are inconsistent. Therefore, u and L imply $\neg[u]$. Hence, L by itself must imply $\neg[u]$, and $\neg[u]$ is necessary. Conversely, if $\neg[u]$ is necessary, it is provable from L. Hence, u must not be possible because it would be inconsistent with L. Since the world basis is consistent, let $W'=\langle T',F'\rangle$ be a closed-world extension that satisfies the conditions of Definition 4.5.8. If u is necessary, it must be provable from L. Since δL is **true** in W', soundness (Theorem 4.4.6) implies that δu is also **true** in W', and hence it cannot be **false** in W (see Exercise 4.25). If $\neg[u\ \neg[v]]$ and u are both necessary (provable from L), then v is also provable from L, and hence necessary. Since S and L have denotation **true** in the extension W', they are consistent with each other. Hence, every graph in S is possible.

The same sets L and S may occur in many different world bases. In Kripke's terms, all such worlds are said to be *accessible* from one another. With Dunn's semantics for modal logic (1973), the modes of possibility and necessity are determined by the laws and facts of a world basis without the need for considering infinite collections of infinite worlds. Yet the models described in this section cannot accommodate graphs nested inside the objects of intensional verbs, as in the sentence *It is necessarily possible that Niurka thinks that Clara can fly to Mars.* That sentence can be mapped to a conceptual graph, but computing a denotation for it is more complex. To accommodate such sentences, the models must include nested contexts instead of the simple graphs in the sets T and F. For each context, the models must specify which individuals exist in that context.

A coherent story, either fictional or true, develops a miniature world. Unless the story is treated as myth or fantasy, the laws and defaults for the normal world are assumed. Understanding the story requires the reader or listener to construct the sets T and F of a consistent world basis:

- As the story unfolds, the listener translates each sentence to a conceptual graph and draws coreference links to previous graphs.
- During the translation, schemata are joined to the graphs to resolve ambiguities and incorporate background information.
- Positive assertions from the story are added to the true set T of an open world, and negative assertions go into the false set F.
- Laws of the world behave like demons or triggers that monitor the evolution of the world basis. They block impossible extensions and force necessary graphs to be added to the world.
- The resulting world basis represents the way the story was understood.
- At each stage, the world basis is finite, but a consistent world basis is extendible to a standard closed world. That extension, however, is a limiting case that is never realized in computer storage or in a human brain.

This theory of understanding combines an AI approach to plausible reasoning with Hintikka's surface models and Dunn's semantics for modal logic. This version, which was sketched by Sowa (1979b), is similar to the *situation semantics* of Barwise and Perry (1981). A process of building a partial model, updating it to accommodate new information, and revising it to avoid contradictions has been implemented in the *truth maintenance systems* by Doyle (1979) and McAllester (1979).

4.6 ACTORS IN DATAFLOW GRAPHS

Conceptual graphs represent declarative information. Other graphs in AI are used for doing computation, solving problems, and simulating events and processes. Hewitt's PLASMA system (1977), for example, is a network of *actors* that pass messages to one another. An actor is a process that responds to messages by performing some service and then generating messages that it passes to other actors. The whole system is a society of cooperating actors, each of which passes messages only to a few nearby actors. Networks of actors form *dataflow graphs*, which are as general as conventional procedures (Dennis 1974, 1979). Other networks used in computation are *Petri nets*, which were originally designed to represent parallel computation (Petri 1962, Petersen 1981).

Although graphs for doing computation have been developed by different people for different purposes, they share several common themes:

- *Active elements.* The system is a network of active elements, which may be called *actors, functions*, or *transitions.*
- *Message passing.* Processes consist of signals passing from one actor to another. The signals may be called *messages, data, tokens*, or *control marks.*
- *Modularity.* The internal structure of any actor is irrelevant to the behavior of the system. Replacing an actor with another one that has a different internal structure, but the same message-passing behavior has no effect on the overall system.
- *Definitional mechanisms.* The actors are either unanalyzed primitives implemented directly in hardware or a lower-level programming language or modules which are themselves defined as networks of actors.

The networks are intended for executing or simulating processes. But Rieger (1976) emphasized the possibility of letting the system analyze its own networks to draw inferences about the kinds of events that can occur and about the causal links between them. As a notation for database design, de Antonellis et al. (1979) noted that Petri nets can serve as both a logical schema for describing a database and as an executable form that can compute results. Active networks, therefore, can be used procedurally when they are executed and declaratively when they are treated as a description of functional dependencies.

This section develops a formalism for graphs of actors that are bound to conceptual graphs. The technique is based on a method for answering database queries developed by Sowa (1976). As a conceptual graph is constructed by joining smaller graphs, actor nodes attached to the conceptual graph are also joined to form a dataflow graph. Then *control marks* on the graphs are used to trigger the actors and compute referents for the generic concepts. The dataflow graphs attached to conceptual graphs resemble Petri nets with two kinds of tokens: *assertion marks* are propagated forwards like the tokens on a Petri net, but *request marks* are propagated backwards.

4.6.1 Definition. A *dataflow graph* is a finite, connected, directed, bipartite graph with one set of nodes called *concepts* and the other set of nodes called *actors*.

- If an arc is directed from a concept c to an actor t, then the arc is called an *input arc* of t, and c is called an *input concept* of t.
- If an arc of a dataflow graph is directed from an actor t to a concept c, then the arc is called an *output arc* of t, and c is called an *output concept* of t.

Every actor must be attached to at least one arc (either input or output).

The arcs of a dataflow graph are drawn as dotted lines to distinguish them from the arcs of conceptual graphs. The concepts are still drawn as boxes, but the actors are drawn as diamonds. Figure 4.17 shows three actors <DIVIDE>, <PLUS>, and <SQRT>. The actor <DIVIDE> has input concepts *a of type DIVIDEND and *b of type DIVISOR, and output concepts *d of type QUOTIENT and *e of type REMAINDER. The actor SQRT has [NUMBER:*c] as input and [SQUARE-ROOT:*f] as output, and <PLUS> has *d and *f as input and [SUM:*g] as output. In a conventional programming language, the following statements would generate the same results as the dataflow graph:

```
D := A÷B;
E := REMAINDER(A,B);
F := SQRT(C);
G := D+F;
```

The linear notation for dataflow graphs follows the conventions for conceptual graphs, but the actor nodes are distinguished by angle brackets. The graph in Fig. 4.17 could be written in the following form:

```
<DIVIDE>-
   ←[DIVIDEND:*a]
   ←[DIVISOR:*b]
   →[QUOTIENT:*d]
   →[REMAINDER:*e]-
      →<PLUS>-
         ←[SQUARE-ROOT:*f]←<SQRT>←[NUMBER:*c]
         →[SUM:*g].
```

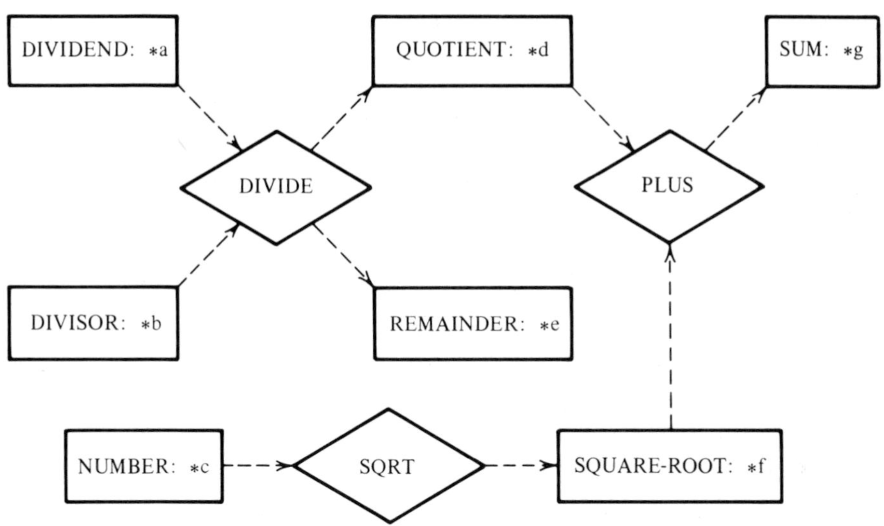

Fig. 4.17 A dataflow graph

The concept types DIVIDEND, DIVISOR, QUOTIENT, REMAINDER, SQUARE-ROOT, and SUM are all subtypes of NUMBER. They are *role types*, which represent a particular way of using the *natural type* NUMBER. In Section 3.2, PET and PEDESTRIAN were cited as role types defined as special uses for the natural types ANIMAL and PERSON. By itself, 7 conforms to the natural type NUMBER, but in a particular context, it may also be the SUM of 3 and 4.

4.6.2 Definition. If all concepts in a dataflow graph *u* are also concepts of a conceptual graph *v*, then *u* is said to be *bound* to *v*. If no concepts of the dataflow graph *u* are concepts of any conceptual graph, then *u* is said to be *free*.

Figure 4.17 is a free dataflow graph since it has no conceptual relations that are also attached to its concepts. Since *a, *b, and *c are only used as inputs to actors, they are called *source concepts*. Since *e and *g are only used as outputs of actors, they are called *sink concepts*. Since concepts *d and *f are used as both input and output concepts, they are called *intermediate concepts*. Bound dataflow graphs are used in Sections 6.4 and 6.5 for database semantics and inferences.

4.6.3 Definition. A concept *c* in a dataflow graph *v* is called:

- A *source concept* of *v* if it is an input concept of one or more actors, but not an output concept of any actor;

- A *sink concept* of v if it is an output concept of exactly one actor, but not an input concept of any actor;
- An *intermediate concept* of v if it is an output concept of exactly one actor and an input concept of one or more actors;
- A *conflicting concept* of v if it is an output concept of two or more actors.

Figure 4.17 is an acyclic dataflow graph since it has no cycles. Since it also has no conflicting concepts, it is a *functional dataflow graph* according to the next definition.

4.6.4 Definition. A *functional dataflow graph* is an acyclic dataflow graph that contains no conflicting concepts.

A functional dataflow graph corresponds to a mathematical expression with functions applied to the outputs of other functions. Each actor corresponds to a function that takes some input and generates some output. Since the graph is acyclic, no actor depends on its own output. Since it has no conflicting concepts, no concept can receive different values from different actors. Each actor may be a primitive implemented in hardware, a program written in a language that is outside the formalism, or a subroutine that is itself defined as a functional dataflow graph.

For database design, each concept in a dataflow graph represents a domain of entities that conform to the type label of that concept. Each actor represents a database relation (Codd 1972), where the input concepts of the actor are the *key* or independent domains, and the output concepts are the domains that are dependent on the keys. A functional dataflow graph represents a join of multiple relations: the source concepts are the keys, sink concepts are dependent on the keys, and intermediate concepts represent *transitive dependencies*. The boxes and diamonds of a dataflow graph resemble Chen's *entity-relationship diagrams* (1976), and the similarity is intended. When a dataflow graph is bound to a conceptual graph, the conceptual relations show the *roles* between entity types, and the actors show the *functional dependencies*. There is a difference, however: Chen represents the entire database with a large diagram that is usually not a functional dataflow graph. Only functional dataflow graphs are needed to describe any particular relation, but many overlapping graphs may be needed to describe a database containing a large number of relations. These correspondences will be explored further in Section 6.4 on database semantics.

Actors may be defined as combinations of other actors in a dataflow graph. Figure 4.18 defines an actor of type FACTORIAL, which has one input and one output. The defining graph for this actor contains six other actors: two actors of type IDENT, which are identity functions whose output is identical to their input; an actor ADD1, which adds 1 to its input; an actor SUB1, which subtracts one from its input; an actor MULTIPLY, which multiplies its two inputs to form the product as output; and finally an actor FACTORIAL of the same type as the actor being

actor FACTORIAL (in n; out x) is

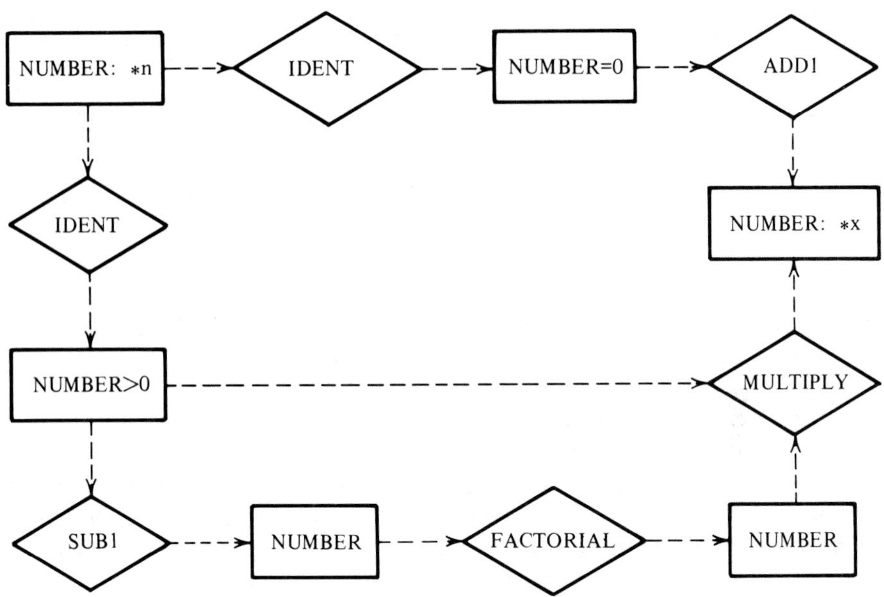

Fig. 4.18 A recursively defined actor

defined. This is an example of a recursive definition where the type that is being defined is used in the defining graph. Four of the concepts in this graph are of type NUMBER, but two of the concepts have subrange types NUMBER>0 and NUMBER=0 (see Section 3.6 for a definition of subranges). Following are λ-expressions for the subranges NUMBER>0 and NUMBER=0:

```
λx [NUMBER:*x]→(>)→[NUMBER:0].
λx [NUMBER:*x]→(=)→[NUMBER:0].
```

These λ-expressions could have been used in the type fields of the concepts instead of the abbreviated subranges. The purpose of the subranges is to block the wrong data from flowing through the graph. Since a positive number conforms to the type NUMBER>0, it can flow through the lower branch. Since the value 0 conforms to the type NUMBER=0, it can flow through the upper branch. A negative number, however, will not be able to flow through the graph at all.

Control marks direct the flow of a computation. Request marks initiate *goal-directed computations* that start at the node where the desired result is to go. Assertion marks trigger *data-directed computations* that start at the original data. Neutral marks have no effect on the computation. In diagrams, control marks are drawn in the referent field after the colon. The concept [WOMAN:?] has a request mark that asks *which woman*, and the concept [WOMAN: Ms. Ahlin!] has an assertion mark that asserts a particular woman named Ms. Ahlin. The neutral mark "°" may be drawn explicitly; but it is typically omitted, since it is merely a place holder that shows the absence of any other mark.

4.6.5 Assumption. The function *mark* maps concepts into the set of *control marks* {?, !, °}:

- "?" is called a *request mark*
- "!" an *assertion mark*
- "°" a *neutral mark*.

For any concept *c*, if *mark*(*c*)= "°" , then *c* is said to be *unmarked*.

Control marks on concepts determine when the actors are executed to compute referents for their output concepts. If all input concepts have referents, then an actor is *ready*. A ready actor will not *fire* unless it is *enabled*. Complications can arise in two cases: either a referent computed by the actor does not conform to the type label of the output concept, or the output concept already has a referent that is different from the one that is computed. In either of those cases, the actor is *blocked*.

4.6.6 Assumption. Associated with each actor *t* is an algorithm private to *t* that computes referents for the output concepts of *t* in terms of the referents of the input concepts of *t*.

- If for each input concept *i* of *t*, *referent*(*i*)≠ "*" , then *t* is said to be *ready*.
- If *t* is ready, then for each output concept *o* of *t*, the algorithm for *t* must compute a referent *r* where *r* conforms to *type*(*o*) and either *referent*(*o*)=*r* or *referent*(*o*)= "*" . If these conditions do not hold, *t* is said to be *blocked*.
- If *t* is ready, not blocked, and either some output concept *o* of *t* has *mark*(*o*)= "?" or some input concept *i* of *t* has *mark*(*i*)= "!" then *t* is said to be *enabled*.

Request marks on output concepts or assertion marks on input concepts enable an actor to fire. An actor may have control marks that would enable it, but it may not be ready because one or more of its input concepts are generic. In that case, the input concepts are marked with request marks. If those inputs are outputs for other actors, then the request marks will either enable them or be propagated back to a previous set of input concepts. In effect, request marks are propagated backwards along the dataflow graph until they reach actors that are ready to fire.

4.6.7 Assumption. If an actor is not ready, but either some output concept *o* has *mark*(*o*)= "?" or some input concept *i* has *mark*(*i*)= "!" then *mark*(*j*) is set to "?" for every input concept *j* for which *referent*(*j*)= "*" .

When an actor is enabled, it may fire. After it fires, all control marks on its inputs are erased (i.e. set to the neutral mark °). Request marks on its outputs are also erased, but assertion marks on its inputs may be copied to its outputs.

4.6.8 Assumption. When an actor *t* is enabled, it may *fire*. After *t* fires, the control marks and referents of its input and output concepts are determined by the following algorithm:

```
for o in set of output concepts of t loop
    r := referent computed by t for o;
    if mark(o)="?" or referent(o)=r then
        mark(o) := "°";
    end if;
    if mark(i)="!" for any input concept i of t and
        mark(o)="°" and referent(o)="*" then
          mark(o) := "!";
    end if;
    referent(o) := r;
end loop;
for i in set of input concepts of t loop
    mark(i) := "°";
end loop;
```

To illustrate the firing rules, the following dataflow graph asserts a value 1 for the input concept of the FACTORIAL actor:

```
[NUMBER: 1!]→<FACTORIAL>→[NUMBER].
```

To evaluate the actor, replace it with a copy of its defining graph, Fig. 4.18, and replace the formal parameter *n with the value and assertion mark (1!). Both IDENT actors are now ready. The upper one, however, is blocked because it would compute the value 1, which does not conform to the type label NUMBER=0. The lower one is enabled. When it fires, it erases the assertion mark on its input and changes its output concept to [NUMBER>0:1!]. This value enables the SUB1 actor, but it does not enable <MULTIPLY> because its other input has no value. After <SUB1> fires, its output concept becomes [NUMBER:0!], which enables the recursive invocation of <FACTORIAL>. The input of <SUB1> loses its assertion mark, but it retains the value 1, which will be used later by <MULTIPLY>. To compute the recursive invocation of <FACTORIAL>, replace it with another copy of the defining graph. With the new input 0!, the upper branch of the graph will be executed to compute 1!, which enables <MULTIPLY>, which computes 1×1 or 1 as the output of <FACTORIAL>.

Assertion marks initiate a computation that starts at the inputs, and request marks trigger a goal-directed computation that starts from the outputs. The following actor is enabled by a request mark:

```
[NUMBER: 1]→<FACTORIAL>→[NUMBER: ?].
```

As in the previous example, the first step if to replace the actor <FACTORIAL> with a copy of its defining graph, Fig. 4.18. The two <IDENT> actors are now ready, but not enabled. The actors <ADD1> and <MULTIPLY> have a request mark on their output, but no values on their inputs. According to Assumption 4.6.7, new request marks are assigned to their input concepts. The upper <IDENT> actor has a request mark on its output concept, [NUMBER=0:?], but it is blocked, since its output 1 does not conform to the type NUMBER=0. The request marks assigned to the inputs of <MULTIPTLY> are then propagated backwards to the input of <FACTORIAL> and the input of <SUB1>. When the left-hand <IDENT> acquires a request mark, it is enabled. When it fires, values propagate forwards to replace the request marks. The actor <FACTORIAL> is invoked once more to compute 1 as the factorial of 0, and <MULTIPLY> generates the answer 1, which replaces the original request mark.

4.6.9 Definition. A dataflow graph is said to be *well-marked* if *referent*(a)= "∗" for every concept a where *mark*(a)= "?" and *referent*(b)≠ "∗" for every concept b where *mark*(b)= "!".

If a concept already has a referent, there is nothing to request; and if it doesn't have a referent, there is nothing to assert. Therefore, only generic concepts (where the referent is ∗) have a request mark, and only individual concepts have an assertion mark. The default is the neutral mark "°" , which is normally omitted from the diagrams.

4.6.10 Theorem. If the initial state of a dataflow graph u is well-marked, then the rules for firing actors and propagating control marks ensure that u remains well-marked.

Proof. After an actor t fires, no request marks remain on any of its input or output concepts, and assertion marks may only occur on output concepts of t for which a referent had just been computed. Assumption 4.6.7 for propagating request marks only adds request marks to generic concepts. Both of these rules therefore preserve the conditions of Assumption 4.6.9 for well-marked dataflow graphs.

The defining graph for <FACTORIAL> is not a functional dataflow graph because [NUMBER:*x] is a conflicting concept. Such conflicts cause a computation to be nondeterministic, since the computed value depends on the actor that fires first. In this case, <FACTORIAL> happens to compute a unique value because the subrange types NUMBER=0 and NUMBER>0 cause one branch or the other to be blocked. When the input value is negative, both branches are blocked, and nothing happens in a forward evaluation of the actor. If the actor were triggered by a request mark on its output, however, it could get into a recursive loop by making repeated, unsatisfiable requests on <FACTORIAL>. Such a loop could be prevented if the actor <MULTIPLY> first requested a value from the concept [NUMBER>0] before requesting a value to be computed by a recursive invocation of <FACTORIAL>. Assumptions 4.6.7 and 4.6.8 do not allow the actors any choice in deciding how the control marks are propagated. Permitting such choices would allow more flexibility, but complicate the theory.

Actors with one output and no input may be used to compute *default values*. The following dataflow graph has a generic concept [NUMBER]:

```
[NUMBER]←<CONSTANT 2>.
```

If the referent is requested, the actor <CONSTANT 2> becomes enabled. When it fires, it generates the integer 2 as its output. For many purposes, this dataflow graph has the same effect as the individual concept [NUMBER:2]. The distinction is that the individual concept has a fixed referent that may never change. The generic concept [NUMBER] is indeterminate and could acquire referents other than 2 either from other actors or by joins with other concepts.

When dataflow graphs are bound to conceptual graphs, the formation rules for joining conceptual graphs can build larger dataflow graphs. This process allows dataflow graphs to be reconfigured dynamically to generate a graph that can perform a desired computation. An advantage of binding the dataflow graphs to conceptual graphs is that new combinations can be assembled from specifications and requests stated in English or other natural languages. For examples, the reader may turn now to Sections 6.4 and 6.5.

4.7 CONCEPTUAL PROCESSOR

A network of actors can simulate processes and compute functions. But a predefined network has a fundamental drawback: it cannot easily adapt to changing conditions. Conventional computer programs, characterized by a fixed flowchart or a fixed program listing, also have that drawback. They execute an *algorithm* that is guaranteed to compute a unique result for every input. People also execute algorithms: children learn algorithms for arithmetic, clerks at the Motor Vehicle Bureau execute an algorithm for registering automobiles, and accountants compute algorithms for earnings, taxes, and depreciation. Routine tasks are ideally suited to well-defined algorithms.

most cases and resort to ingenuity or "common sense" to handle the exceptions. For complex problem solving with changing, unpredictable requirements, almost every case is an exception.

In a dynamically changing network, an actor may not know in advance what other actors to invoke to satisfy a goal. When one actor changes the current data, that change may trigger other actors to perform further operations on the data. These new changes may in turn activate other actors, and so on. This method is called *pattern-directed invocation* because actors do not respond to a specific request, but to changing patterns in the data. Rieger (1978) coined the term *spontaneous computation* to characterize such invocations.

Besides actors for doing work, spontaneous computation requires monitors that check the current state to determine what work should be done. A *demon* is an active unit that looks for a characteristic pattern. When its pattern occurs, the demon takes some action. The result of that action may become part of a pattern that triggers other demons. Mechanisms for pattern-directed control have proliferated in AI (Waterman & Hayes-Roth 1978). Although their notations differ widely, they share three common features:

- The current state of the system is maintained in a structure that may be called a *workspace*, a *context*, a *database*, or a *blackboard*.
- Active elements, called *monitors*, *demons*, or *production rules*, constantly watch the current state to see if their characteristic patterns occur.
- When its pattern occurs, the monitor becomes active and makes some change to the current state.

Various systems use different strategies for deciding when a pattern should be tested and when the corresponding action should be taken. To organize the pattern matching, Hewitt (1972) divided monitors into three classes: those that watch for additions to the state, those that watch for deletions, and those that watch for requests. When a new state triggers two or more monitors simultaneously, some systems activate all of them in parallel; some activate only the one with highest priority; and some have a backtracking scheme that keeps trying each in succession until one of them succeeds.

The most common systems of spontaneous computation are based on *production rules*, which Newell (1973) proposed as a model of human thinking. A production rule has two parts: a *pattern* that matches something in current working storage; and an *action part* that specifies something to be done. The intelligent processor outlined in Section 2.7 could be implemented as a production system with conceptual graphs as the patterns. Now that the graphs have been presented, the outline can be restated as a proposal for a conceptual processor:

- The first step in reasoning or computation is the selection of a conceptual graph that anticipates the form of the desired goal.

- Certain concepts in the graph are flagged with control marks. Each control mark triggers a search for schemata that match all or part of the goal.

- When the associative comparator finds a matching schema, the assembler joins it to the working graph. If the resulting graph satisfies the control marks, it attains a state of closure where all the control marks are erased.

- The result of joining a schema to the working graph may cause control marks to be propagated to new nodes in the graph according to Assumptions 4.6.7 and 4.6.8. When control marks can be neither propagated nor satisfied by the actors currently bound to a conceptual graph, the associative comparator searches for schemata containing other actors.

- The limited number of working registers limits the number of control marks that can be active at the same time. If there are more than three unsatisfied control marks, earlier ones are suspended until the more recent ones are satisfied.

- When control marks for recent subgoals attain closure, earlier control marks are reactivated until the original goal is satisfied.

This outline for a conceptual processor leaves many unspecified details that must be resolved in a computer implementation. The first question is how closely AI systems should attempt to model neural processes. Since no one knows exactly what the neural processes are, any such model must be guided more by programming practice than by neurophysiology. At least at the current state of knowledge, experience with AI systems is more likely to stimulate research in neurophysiology than to be determined by it. Following are the major issues to be resolved:

- *Data structures.* Some production systems match only a simple list. Others permit nested lists of lists. Still others use attribute-value records. All such structures are special cases of conceptual graphs.

- *Pattern matching.* Most production systems use a simple match where working memory contains structures of constants, and only the production rules contain variables. PROLOG and other logic programming systems use the more general *unification algorithm* that allows either or both of the structures to contain variables (Kowalski 1979). For conceptual graphs, maximal joins are the analog of unification.

- *Conflict resolution.* Deciding which pattern match to try first when more than one applies may be time consuming. In most cases, maximizing the number of matching nodes of the graph leads to the best choice. In case of ties, other factors may be considered.

- *Heuristics.* In the search for matching graphs, background knowledge about the application can often speed up the search. Such knowledge is packaged in rules of thumb called *heuristics.*

- *Correctness.* Although production rules are widely used in AI, they frequently lead to *ad hoc* systems whose logical basis is obscure. Proving that a system of production rules is correct is often more difficult than proving that a conventional program is correct. For languages based on logic, such as PROLOG, the proofs can be short and simple.

- *Completeness.* A general theorem prover can take a long time to derive a complex proof. PROLOG improves performance by restricting the axioms to a subset of first-order logic. Yet this restriction results in a loss of completeness: some statements can be proved quickly, but many true statements cannot be proved at all.

Conceptual graphs are general enough to serve as the data structures for a conceptual processor. Three areas for further research are the choice of heuristics for making the process efficient, the logical basis for making it correct, and the optimal trade-offs between completeness and efficiency.

Matching arbitrary graphs is time consuming, but matching two conceptual graphs is fast because the labels on the nodes block unpromising paths (McGregor 1982). Finding the best candidates to match, however, may require extensive searching. In fact, most of the interesting problems in AI require some kind of search. In language analysis, the search is for grammar rules and schemata that correctly interpret a sentence or a story. In game playing programs, the search is for the best move at each turn. In automatic programming, the search is for a sequence of instructions that perform some function. In logic, the search is for a sequence of inferences that prove some theorem. In expert systems, problem solvers, and robot controllers, the search is for operations that transform the current state into a state that meets some desired criteria. Although all searching problems look different on the surface, they can be classified by certain features:

- *Depth.* Every search is characterized by a depth *n*, which is the number of steps from start to finish. If a problem has no solution, *n* may be infinite. If a problem has multiple solutions, *n* may vary for different search paths.

- *Branching factor.* At each step in a search, there may be many possible ways to proceed. The branching factor *k* is the number of options at each step.

- *Direction.* A search may be *data directed* when it goes forward from the original data, it may be *goal directed* when it starts at the goal and goes backward, or it may be *bidirectional* when it does some searching from both ends.

- *Scheduling.* A *breadth-first search* proceeds along all options in parallel, and a *depth-first search* takes one option at each step until it reaches either a goal or a dead end and then backs up to take a previously untried option. A *best-first* search keeps an *agenda* of options to try and uses an *evaluation function* to choose the most promising one at each step.

- *Pruning.* An exhaustive search tests all possibilities, and *pruning* eliminates the unlikely ones. In *forward pruning*, some of the options are rejected before any searching is done. In *backward pruning*, information gained while searching one branch is used to select or reject alternatives on other branches. The *alpha-beta algorithm* is a common form of backward pruning for searching game trees.

- *Termination*. To determine when a goal is reached, there must be some criterion for testing whether the current state is the end. For some searches, the criterion is a binary choice: a statement is true or false; a game is won or lost; a problem is solved or unsolved. For other searches, there is a measure of goodness for each state, and the criterion is either to find the best state or to find one that exceeds a certain threshold.

- *Heuristics*. A systematic guessing strategy can guide or speed up a search. Heuristics may select the best option to try, reduce the branching factor by pruning options, or test the current state against the termination criteria.

The danger that all searching programs have to face is the possibility of a *combinatorial explosion*: the amount of calculation can grow exponentially. For a depth n and a branching factor k, the amount of computation grows as k^n, which for typical values of k can be astronomically large for relatively small n. In chess, k is about 35, the number of possible moves in a typical position. Similarly, a theorem prover might allow 35 options for applying some rule of inference to derive the next step of a proof. If a checkmate or proof requires only one step, the correct option can be found in no more than 35 trials. A chess-playing program that searches only one level deep can respond with no perceptible delay. But if the depth n is 2, then each of the 35 possible moves leads to a new position, each of which has 35 more moves; the number of trials is now k^2 or 1225. The delay in a chess program that searches two levels deep is still short, but noticeable. If n is 4, the number of combinations becomes k^4 or 1.5 million, and the delay is lengthy. At 6 steps, k^6 is over 1.8 billion, and the delay is impractically long. At 8 steps, k^8 is over 2.2 trillion, and the delay is impossibly long, even for an array of supercomputers working in parallel.

Making a computer play a perfect game of chess requires an exhaustive search of possible moves that would take longer than the age of the universe. But the more modest goal of beating 90% of the human players 90% of the time can be met with a $100 microprocessor that takes only two or three minutes per move. *Heuristic programming* is what makes the difference between an attainable level of competence and an impossible perfection. When an exact algorithm would take too long to compute, a heuristic program uses background knowledge to eliminate unpromising paths or to determine an acceptable stopping point. In planning computer system configurations, the expert system R1 (McDermott 1980) typically searches 800 levels deep with a branching factor of 3. Although 3^{800} is astronomical, good heuristics enable R1 to make an optimal or nearly optimal choice at each step. As a result, the computation is nearly linear.

A combinatorial explosion can be controlled by reducing the branching factor k, reducing the depth of search n, or replacing the exponential algorithm with one that is linear (proportional to n) or quadratic (proportional to n^2). The strategies for controlling complexity fall into six categories:

- *Constraints.* Some algorithms eliminate redundant or dead-end trials by enforcing constraints that rule out certain combinations. For interpreting line drawings of three-dimensional scenes, Waltz (1975) took advantage of geometrical constraints to reduce an impossible amount of searching to a largely deterministic algorithm. For games, the alpha-beta algorithm uses the constraint that an exceptionally good line of play for one player will be avoided by the other player and extended searching along that line is fruitless. For an 8-level search, alpha-beta reduces the number of trials from an impossible 2.2 trillion to a feasible 3 million.

- *Shallow search.* For many problems, a perfect solution requires an impossibly deep search, but an acceptable approximation may be found in just a few steps. One approach is to set an arbitrary cutoff, such as 5 levels of searching. If an exact solution is not found within that limit, then the program takes the best one found.

- *Special cases.* Although the general case may be exponential, many useful special cases are linear or quadratic. PROLOG, for example, uses the *Horn clause* subset of logic for highly efficient algorithms (Kowalski 1979). In chess, forcing moves like checks and captures reduce the branching factor and allow a search to proceed to a much greater depth.

- *Generate and test.* Although a proof finder may take exponential time, a proof checker can be linear. If a program uses heuristics to "guess" a solution, a proof checker can quickly test whether the solution is correct.

- *Large knowledge base.* Human experts often solve a problem instantly by classifying it as a minor variation of something they encountered many times before. With a large knowledge base of rules and heuristics, a shallow search may outperform a much deeper search that uses only general rules.

- *Special hardware.* Chess-playing programs might invoke special devices for generating all legal moves in parallel, and theorem provers might use hardware for computing the *unification algorithm* or for testing subtypes and supertypes. Since testing subtypes is fundamental to all versions of conceptual graphs, Fahlman (1979) designed a network machine that would search the type hierarchy in parallel.

Various systems combine these strategies. The chess computer Belle, which has reached the master level in competition with human players, uses the alpha-beta algorithm to prune the options, an arbitrary cutoff to limit the search, special cases for forcing sequences, heuristics for ordering the search and evaluating positions, a knowledge base of opening moves derived from grandmaster practice, and parallel hardware for generating legal moves and computing the value of a position (Condon & Thompson 1982). Special hardware is often the first thing that novices think of when they are trying to speed up a search, but it is usually the *last* resort that should be considered. Special devices are expensive and inflexible, and they improve performance by at best a factor of 10 or 100. Algorithms like alpha-beta can improve performance by a factor of a million without special hardware.

For conceptual graphs, heuristics follow from the graph structure. Domain dependencies reside only in schemata and prototypes. Each schema or prototype is a packet of knowledge about some particular domain. The procedures that handle them are general rules or *metaheuristics* that apply to any domain. The structural properties of conceptual graphs can aid a system in finding and using large amounts of background knowledge:

- *Connectivity.* Standard theorem provers split a formula into a collection of low-level assertions. The inference rules for conceptual graphs, however, keep related facts together. Consequently, they can reduce the amount of searching needed to find all the relevant knowledge.

- *Type hierarchy.* In standard logic, all individual variables are of the same type. In *sorted logic*, variables are classified in different *sorts*, but the structure of the formulas does not lead to convenient heuristics for using the sorts. In conceptual graphs, the type labels on concepts can be used for indexing or classifying graphs, reducing the number of options in joins, and speeding up common inferences such as the inheritance of properties from supertypes to subtypes.

- *Relevance factor.* Unlike theorem provers that deal with a dozen axioms, a knowledge-based system may have thousands of schemata, prototypes, and laws. It may also be connected to a database system with millions of atomic facts. In the human brain, the associative comparator automatically finds the most promising patterns. Information retrieval systems simulate an associative search by indexing thousands of items by keywords and computing a *relevance factor* for choosing the most likely candidates.

- *Preference score.* A relevance factor is not precise enough to select an optimal schema. Wilks (1973) formulated preference rules based on a detailed matching of graphs. When a conceptual graph u can be joined to any of several schemata, the join on the largest compatible projection should be preferred. Relevance factors can reduce the number of choices from thousands to a dozen; then a *preference score*, using compatible projections, can find a more exact match.

The connectivity of conceptual graphs improves efficiency both by reducing the branching factor k and the depth of search n. It reduces k by packaging related items in a single graph, thereby reducing the number of items to consider at each step. It reduces n by shortening proofs: deductions in Peirce's notation usually take fewer steps than in standard logic. To illustrate the way conceptual graphs keep related facts together, consider a graph u and formula ϕu for the sentence *The cat chased a mouse*:

```
[CAT:#98077]←(AGNT)←[CHASE]→(OBJ)→[MOUSE].
```

$\exists x \exists y$(CAT(#98077) ∧ CHASE(x) ∧ MOUSE(y)
∧ AGNT(x,#98077) ∧ OBJ(x,y)).

On the printed page, the conceptual graph is more compact. That space advantage, however, is of minor importance. What is more significant is that the conceptual graph represents each individual with a single node: the graph only requires one node for the cat, one for the mouse, and one for the instance of chasing. The formula repeats the constant #98077 for the cat in two places, the variable x for chasing in four places, and the variable y for the mouse in three places.

Although logic can represent verbs like *chase* with individual variables, it is more common to represent them as relations. But that option is also possible with conceptual graphs. A relation type CHAS may be defined in terms of the concept type CHASE:

relation CHAS(x,y) **is**
[ANIMAL:*x]←(AGNT)←[CHASE]→(OBJ)→[ENTITY:*y].

Then the graph and the formula for the cat chasing a mouse become,

```
[CAT:#98077]→(CHAS)→[MOUSE].
```

$\exists x$(CAT(#98077) ∧ MOUSE(x) ∧ CHAS(#98077,x)).

The formula is simpler than before, but the conceptual graph is even simpler. In *sorted logic*, the monadic predicates for CAT and MOUSE are represented by *sort labels* on the variables and constants. The symbol MOUSE:x represents a variable x of type MOUSE, and CAT:#98077 represents a constant #98077 of type CAT. With such labels, the formula becomes

∃MOUSE:x CHAS(CAT:#98077, MOUSE:x).

Even in sorted logic, duplicate variables still appear. Standard logic emphasizes predicates and scatters variable symbols throughout many different formulas. Conceptual graphs (and Peirce's existential graphs from which they are derived) put primary emphasis on the concept nodes that represent individuals and represent each entity by a single node. There is a duality between predicates and individuals: any proposition stated in one form can be mapped into an equivalent proposition in the other form, but some kinds of statements are easier to express in one form or the other. In particular, natural languages emphasize individuals in a way that maps more directly to conceptual graphs than to standard logic.

One way to speed up the search for schemata is to index them by the concept types they contain. But not all types are good indices for selecting a meaningful schema. The type PERSON, for example, is too general. A more specific subtype like EMPLOYEE, ATHLETE, or KING is much more likely to select an appropriate schema. Schank et al. (1980) associate an *interest value* with each word or concept type. In analyzing a story, they skip the words with low interest and use the high interest words to select appropriate scripts. Schank assigns interest values by hand. A more automatic method may be based on the frequency of occurrence of each concept type: common types have a large number of weak associations; rare types have a much smaller number of strong associations. But some further conditions are necessary: although the universal type ⊤ seldom occurs in schemata, its relevance should be the smallest of all types. Therefore, F(t), the frequency of type t, is defined as the number of schemata or prototypes in which *any subtype* of t occurs. Let S be the set of all schemata and prototypes; then define,

$$\mathrm{F}(t) = count\{s \mid s \in S, \text{ concept } c \in s, \text{ and } type(c) \leq t\}.$$

Then relevance can be defined in terms of frequency: given a graph u and schema s, let C be the set of common type labels in u and s; the relevance of s to u, R(s,u), is the sum of $1/\mathrm{F}(t)$ for all t in C.

Finding relevant schemata is analogous to information retrieval: given a set of documents indexed by keywords and given another set of keywords in a search request, find the most relevant documents for that request. No one has developed a perfect measure of relevance, but retrieval systems have efficient methods for handling thousands of keywords and hundreds of thousands of documents—books, reports, and articles. Those methods could be adapted to retrieving schemata. Given a graph u, the schema s with the highest relevance R(s,u) would be the most promising one to join to u. For studies of relevance measures in information retrieval, see Sparck Jones (1971), Salton (1975), and van Rijsbergen (1979).

Preference semantics encourages joins that increase connectivity. When more than one schema has a high relevance factor, the possible joins may be ranked by a *preference score*. If a graph u and a schema s are joined on a compatible projection, the preference score increases with the size of the projection and decreases with the *semantic distance* between corresponding concept types. The maximum preference score occurs when u is identical to a subgraph of s. Then the compatible projection is identical to u, and the semantic distance between corresponding concept types is zero. For any type labels p and q, the semantic distance between them, *distance*(p,q), may be defined as the number of arcs in the shortest path through the type lattice from p to q that does not pass through the absurd type ⊥.

If CAT and DOG are both immediate subtypes of CARNIVORE, then *distance*(CAT,CARNIVORE)=1 and *distance*(CARNIVORE,DOG)=1; therefore *distance*(CAT,DOG)=2. The shortest path from CAT to DOG passes through their common supertype CARNIVORE. Since the minimal common supertype of CAT and PET is ANIMAL, the path that goes through the ANIMAL node would be much longer than 2. But since CAT and PET have a common subtype PET-CAT, the shortest path would have a distance of only 2. In many cases, the path that defines the semantic distance from s to t passes through either the supertype $s \cup t$ or the subtype $s \cap t$. In some cases, the shortest path may cut across the type lattice with some steps that go up and others that go down. Since CAT ∩ JUSTICE is the absurd type ⊥, the shortest path from CAT to JUSTICE is of length 2. But no path that passes through ⊥ can be used to measure semantic distance. The path from CAT to JUSTICE that avoids ⊥ would go all the way to ⊤ at the top of the type lattice and would be much longer than 2.

When more than one schema is relevant to a goal, some strategy for conflict resolution must be adopted. For answering database queries, Sowa (1976) defined a *preference score* for choosing between schematic joins. Let q be a *query graph* that represents a question to be answered; w, a *working graph* derived by joining other graphs to q; s, a schema; and w' and s', maximal compatible projections of w and s. Then the preference score for s is the sum of the following points:

- One point for each concept in w'.
- An extra point for each concept in w' that originated from the query graph q. Reject s if this value is zero.
- An extra point for each concept in w' that originated in q and has not yet been joined to any other graph in the derivation of w from q.
- One point for each concept c of w' where $mark(c)$=? and the corresponding concept d of s' is the output of some actor; -1 point if the concept d is the input of some actor.
- One point for each concept c of w' where $referent(c) \neq *$ and the corresponding concept d of s' is the input of some actor. Reject s if d is the output of some actor.

This score should be adjusted by the semantic distance: if concepts c and d must be restricted to a common subtype before being joined, their point value may be divided by $distance(type(c),type(d))+1$. The preference rules are heuristics for choosing between alternatives. They encourage joins that have a good chance of satisfying a goal and avoid the less promising ones.

In normal reasoning, people construct mental models rather than formal proofs. They start with a given set of facts and join prototypes and schemata to build a plausible model. The model, however, may not be true. To verify its accuracy, it must be tested for contradictions with laws of the world. As Merleau-Ponty and Bar-Hillel observed (p. 127), the listener understands a story by exploring the immense mass of implications, by joining information from a mental encyclopedia, and by combining the given information with background knowledge. As Hintikka said (p. 179), the process of understanding a story S is "a mental anticipation of what can happen in one's step-by-step investigation of a world in which S is true."

When a law is violated, the possible world becomes inconsistent. A default, however, is optional. If violated, it does not cause an inconsistency. In the story about Leone's (p. 131), only a sequence of unexplained events was stated explicitly: John's pocket was picked, he couldn't pay the check, and the manager told him to wash dishes. Since the causes and effects were not explained, SAM filled in details from a schema that contained expected background information. Other interpretations, however, are logically possible:

> The thief who picked the pocket did not steal John's wallet, but his good luck charm. Losing the charm made John so nervous that he tripped and sprained his wrist. When the check came, John couldn't sign the credit card form. The restaurant manager was a chiropracter who recommended dish-washing therapy for sprained wrists.

This bizarre interpretation is just one of an infinite number of possibilities that are consistent both with the story and with the laws of the world. Ordinary rules of logic cannot distinguish the obvious interpretation from the far-fetched ones. SAM was able to infer the obvious, but only at the risk of making logical errors in other cases.

Exact deduction and plausible, heuristic reasoning are two ends of a continuum: depending on the amount of time and space available, a person can choose any degree of certainty and rigor. Following are the levels of reasoning that are possible:

- Level 0 simply translates an input sentence into a conceptual graph (initial world basis), but performs no inference.
- Level 1 does plausible inferences by joining schemata and prototypes that fill in the missing details.
- Level 2 checks constraints by testing the graphs against the laws. Any join that causes a contradiction must be undone, as in the truth maintenance systems.
- Level 3 joins more schemata to add further background information.
- Level 4 checks further constraints.
- Each succeeding odd level joins more schemata, and each even level checks the laws to enforce constraints.

If the world basis is blocked at level $n+1$ by some law, the system has to backtrack and undo joins at level n. If all possible extensions are blocked by violations of the laws, then that means the original sentence (or story) was inconsistent with the laws. If the world is infinitely extendible, then the original sentence or story was consistent.

Exact deduction may let the world basis grow indefinitely; but for many applications, it is as impractical as letting a chess-playing program search the entire game tree. Plausible inferences with varying degrees of confidence result from stopping the growth at different levels of extension. For story understanding, the initial basis is derived from the input story. For updating a database, the world basis is derived by joining information to a pre-existing database. For question-answering, a query graph is joined to the database; the depth of search permitted determines the limits of complexity of the questions that are answerable. Algorithms for plausible and exact inference can be compared within the same framework; one can then make informed trade-offs of speed vs. consistency in database updates or speed vs. completeness in question answering.

The distinction between optional defaults and obligatory laws is reminiscent of the AND-OR trees that arise in AI searches. A semantic game may be defined for elaborating a world basis in much the same way that a chess-playing program explores the game tree. This game is a *world-building game* that has similarities to the evaluation game of Sections 4.4 and 4.5:

- The starting position of the game is a set of graphs that represent the background information for a story.
- The two players in the game are the proposer or storyteller who is trying to tell a believable story, and the skeptic who is trying to find a contradiction with some law of the world.
- The schemata define possible moves that the storyteller can make in elaborating the world basis.
- Laws of the world are moves that the skeptic makes in forcing the story to be consistent. A disjunction may split the current basis into separate sets of graphs for possible alternative worlds.
- A given story is consistent with the laws of the world if there exists a strategy for extending the basis indefinitely while avoiding contradiction.

By elaborating this analogy, one can adapt the techniques developed for game playing programs to various kinds of reasoning. Proposer wins the game by building a closed world that is consistent with the laws and with the information in the initial story. But like playing a perfect game of chess, the cost of elaborating a complete closed world may be prohibitive, especially since the game may continue infinitely long. Yet computers can beat most people at chess simply by using heuristics to choose plausible moves and terminating their search after only five levels. If the heuristics suggest good moves often enough, the inference mechanisms would usually take the right course of action and avoid the obvious blunders.

EXERCISES

4.1 The schema for BUS given in Fig. 4.1 does not represent all the common background knowledge that people have about buses. Draw some more schemata for BUS.

4.2 The type definition for RESTAURANT in Figure 4.2 states only the necessary conditions for a business establishment to be called a restaurant. Draw schemata for common events in restaurants and for common things that are associated with them. Choose other common concept types, such as FURNITURE, SUPERMARKET, or COOKING, and draw schemata for them.

4.3 Draw the result of maximal joins of the graph in Fig. 4.3 with the schema for BUS (Fig. 4.1) and the schema for TRAVEL (Fig. 4.4).

4.4 Draw schemata for some of the other concept types that occur in the story about Leone's: SUBWAY, POCKET, CHECK, PAY, MANAGEMENT. Include details about fares for rides, money in wallets, etc.

4.5 Map the story about Leone's into conceptual graphs. Show which schemata would be joined to the graphs at each point in the story. What additional laws must be asserted to cover events and situations that do not fit the schemata exactly?

4.6 Give the result of applying the formula operator ϕ to the graph for the sentence, *No student read the teacher's book* (Fig. 4.9). Simplify the resulting formula by eliminating the equality.

4.7 The sentence, *Some peach is not a fuzzy thing*, could be represented by the graph,

```
[PEACH:*x]  ¬[ [ENTITY:*x]→(ATTR)→[FUZZY]].
```

The variable *x represents a coreference link in the linearized notation. Using both the linear form and the full graph form, draw conceptual graphs for the following sentences:

```
Every peach is a fuzzy thing.
No peach is a fuzzy thing.
Some peach is a fuzzy thing.
Some fuzzy thing is not a peach.
Every fuzzy thing is a peach.
No fuzzy thing is a peach.
```

Hint: the statement *Every peach is a fuzzy thing* can be transformed to the statement *If there exists a peach, then it is a fuzzy thing*. By similar transformations, these sentences may be translated to sentences for which the mapping to conceptual graphs is more obvious.

4.8 Draw a conceptual graph that implies there exists exactly one God. Use only the basic Peirce notation with negative contexts and coreference links. Do not use the relation (QTY) or the concept [NUMBER:1].

4.9 Using only the basic Peirce notation and the relation (DFFR), draw a graph stating that there exist at least three persons. Draw another graph stating that there exist exactly three persons. Map both graphs to first-order logic according to the formula operator ϕ.

4.10 Define a type label IFF for the relation *if-and-only-if*. Draw a graph for the sentence *Herman loves Doris if and only if Doris loves Herman*, first by using the relation (IFF) and then by expanding the graph by relational expansion.

4.11 Suppose that the following propositions occur in the outermost context: $(p \vee q)$, $(p \supset r)$, $(q \supset s)$. Translate each one into a graph in Peirce's form, and deduce the graph for $(r \vee s)$.

4.12 Using the rules of inference of Assumption 4.3.1, prove that all four of Whitehead and Russell's axioms for propositional calculus correspond to theorems in Peirce's notation.

4.13 Translate the two sentences *Every sparrow chirps* and *Ivan does not chirp* into conceptual graphs. Show that these two graphs imply the graph for *Ivan is not a sparrow.* To shorten the proof, use the derived rules of Theorem 4.3.7 in addition to the basic rules of Assumption 4.3.5.

4.14 Given the graphs $\neg[u\ v]$ and $\neg[\neg[u]\ w]$, apply Peirce's rules of inference to derive $\neg[v\ w]$. This result is the analog for conceptual graphs of the *resolution principle* for standard logic (Robinson 1965). One proof takes three steps: an insertion, iteration, and deiteration. Another proof takes four steps: an iteration, deiteration, erasure, and removal of a double negation. Find both proofs.

4.15 Translate the laws of citizenship in the land of Oz (Fig. 4.12) into Peano-Russell notation. Carry out the proofs about the Tinman and Dorothy using the rules of standard first-order logic.

4.16 Use relational expansion and other rules of inference to show that the graph,

```
[PERSON:Tully]→(¬DFFR)→[PERSON:Cicero],
```

implies the single concept [PERSON:Tully=Cicero].

4.17 In Section 3.3, a name in the referent field of a concept was permitted as an abbreviation for an individual marker. Since then, however, most of the examples have used names rather than the formally defined markers. If each name is associated with a unique marker, prove that such abbreviations are justified: any proof with names in the referent field can be replaced with an equivalent proof that first expands the name, carries out some equivalent operations, and then replaces each expanded form with a concept having just the name in the referent field. Show that similar operations are justified with measures in the referent field.

4.18 Generalize the proof of Theorem 4.3.4 to show the consistency of the first-order rules of inference of Assumption 4.3.5.

4.19 Show that Peirce's rules of inference are at least as strong as first-order logic by stating and proving the equivalents of each of the first-order rules of inference in Appendix A.5.

4.20 Assumption 3.6.3 defined a generalization hierarchy over abstractions. For any pair of n-adic abstractions a and b where $a \leq b$, prove that the set of n-tuples δa is a subset of δb.

4.21 Play the closed-world game to evaluate the following denotations:

- Evaluate $\neg[u\ \neg[u]\ \neg[v]]$ for any graphs u and v and any closed world W.
- Evaluate the graph in Fig. 4.8 in a world $W=\langle T,I\rangle$ where T is empty.

■ Evaluate the graph in Fig. 4.15 in a world $W=\langle T,I\rangle$ where T contains the graph,

```
[PERSON:Dorothy]←(RCPT)←[NATURALIZE]→(LOC)→[COUNTRY:Oz].
```

4.22 Translate each of the following conceptual graphs into English sentences. First give a literal reading with phrases like *it was not necessary that*; then simplify the sentences with more natural, idiomatic phrases like *he didn't have to.*

```
[PERSON: Erin=*x]←(AGNT)←[WANT]-
   (OBJ)→[SITUATION: [PERSON:*x]←(AGNT)←[FLY]].

(PAST)→[[PERSUADE]-
          (AGNT)→[PERSON: Albie]
          (RCPT)→[PERSON: Kirby=*x]
          (OBJ)→ [PROPOSITION:
             (¬NECS)→[PROPOSITION:
                [PERSON:*x]←(AGNT)←[PAY]→(RCPT)→[WAITER]]].
```

4.23 Express the axioms for modal logic (System T on p. 174) in conceptual graphs.

4.24 Let $W=\langle T,F,I\rangle$ be an open world, and let G be the set of all conceptual graphs whose type labels and individual markers occur in W. If there is no simple graph u in G for which $\delta u=$**unknown**, prove that $\Pi(F,T)$ must be empty.

4.25 Let $B=\langle W,L,S\rangle$ be a consistent world basis with a closed-world extension W'. Prove that if δu in W is not **unknown**, then δu is the same in W and W'.

4.26 Generalize Theorem 4.4.6, which proves soundness in closed worlds, to a proof of soundness in open worlds. For open worlds, soundness means that nothing provable is false instead of the stronger statement that everything provable is true.

4.27 For the input value 2, evaluate the FACTORIAL actor defined in Fig. 4.18, both in the forward direction (triggered by an assertion mark) and in the backward direction (triggered by a request mark). Start with the following two graphs:

```
[NUMBER:2!]→<FACTORIAL>→[NUMBER].
[NUMBER:2]→<FACTORIAL>→[NUMBER:?].
```

Each time <FACTORIAL> fires, it is replaced by a copy of its defining graph, which then completes the computation. Draw the expanded graphs that result from the these two computations.

SUGGESTED READING

For a discussion of schemata and related frames, scripts, and prototypes, see Minsky (1975), Schank and Abelson (1977), Smith and Medin (1981), and Graesser (1981). Lehnert (1978) and Carbonell (1981) describe natural language systems that use scripts. Schank and Riesbeck (1981) present implementation techniques.

For an introduction to Peirce's original form of existential graphs, see Roberts (1973). For a quick survey of logic and its applications to linguistics and philosophy, see Allwood, et al. (1977); they give a brief introduction to model theory on pages 72-88. McCawley (1980) is a more detailed, but still introductory survey of logic and its use in linguistics and knowledge representation. Kempson (1977) uses a minimum of formalism in discussing Tarski's definition of truth and its implications for linguistics. For more detail on logic and models, see a standard textbook such as Lightstone (1978) or Schoenfield (1967). *The Philosophy of Mathematics*, edited by Hintikka, is a collection of classic papers in logic, including Beth's introduction of *semantic tableaux* and Henkin's completeness proofs of first-order and higher-order logic.

For modal logic, the standard textbook is *An Introduction to Modal Logic* by Hughes and Cresswell; its first few chapters are also a good review of standard logic. White (1975b) analyzes the actual use of modal words in ordinary English. Conceptual graphs capture the same insights as Montague grammar, but with a simpler formalism; *Formal Philosophy* is a collection of Montague's basic papers, and *Montague Grammar*, edited by Partee, applies his theory to linguistics. *Truth, Syntax and Modality*, edited by Leblanc, presents alternatives to standard model theory, including Hintikka's game-theoretical semantics, which is developed further in the collection edited by Saarinen (1979). Rescher and Brandom (1979) present a form of logic that can tolerate inconsistent and incomplete knowledge. Relevance logic (Anderson & Belnap 1975) restricts the form of logical arguments to eliminate the paradox that a false proposition implies everything. The journal *Artificial Intelligence* published a double issue (vol. 13, nos. 1 & 2, 1980) on *nonmonotonic logic*, which has close affinities to Rescher and Brandom's logic of inconsistency and Anderson and Belnap's relevance logic.

For six articles on dataflow languages and machines, see the February 1982 issue of *Computer* (vol. 15, no. 2). Peterson (1981) covers Petri nets and the notions of controlling computations by passing tokens from one active element to another. Nilsson (1980) gives a thorough treatment of searching strategies in heuristic programming. Wilensky (1983) presents goal-directed techniques for planning, problem solving, and story understanding.

5
Language

Conceptual graphs are a logical notation with a strong psychological motivation. For determining the relations to represent in the graphs, the primary need is to serve as a semantic basis for natural language. This chapter relates the graphs to language and the problems of generating and interpreting language by people and machines.

5.1 GENESIS OF LANGUAGE

Learning a language is difficult even for an adult—perhaps *especially* for an adult. In a few short years, children acquire a mastery of their native language that an adult starting to learn a foreign language never achieves. After the age of puberty, the brain has matured to a level that is highly efficient for processing the native language. When sentences are spoken in the presence of background noise, adults can understand them much more easily than children. Yet with the gain in efficiency comes a loss of flexibility. The "wild" children who reached puberty without learning a language have never learned to speak one in later life, and an adult will find it difficult or impossible to learn to speak a new language without a foreign accent.

To explain a child's propensity for learning language, Chomsky assumed the existence of a mental organ dedicated solely to language. Yet the term *organ* is controversial because it suggests a physical unit like a liver or kidney. The adult brain does indeed have several areas in the left hemisphere dedicated to language. But a child who suffers an injury to the left hemisphere can still learn language as the right hemisphere takes over the functions of the left. Chomsky (1980), however, doubted that those children are able to master the fine points of syntax. They get by with a mastery of semantics, but they have trouble with passive voice and other complex transformations.

Maturation of the human brain affects other functions in the same way that it affects language. Intellectual activities like music and chess as well as highly skilled physical activities like skiing and gymnastics must be learned at an early age for complete mastery. One man, who had played chess for many years, taught both of his sons to play the game. Although he never rose above the average level at the local club, both sons became chess masters. The intensive drill in the formative years was far more important for the sons than the years of experience by the father. Musicians, skiers, and gymnasts must also begin their practice long before puberty if they aspire to be world-class competitors. As with language, early exposure to these highly complex activities is necessary to bring out the latent capabilities of the brain. But there is no reason for assuming a unique mental organ for chess or skiing.

Since the great apes are the closest relatives to human beings, experiments in teaching them to speak can shed some light on the uniquely human capabilities. The difficulty that apes have with human speech could arise either from a weakness in their conceptual apparatus or from the inability to produce the necessary sounds. Lieberman (1973) found that the chimpanzee vocal tract is not capable of forming all human vowels. With that restriction, chimpanzees can only produce a limited number of syllables. Even if they had the mental capacity for speech, they could not attain human speed and ease of communication.

Chimpanzee infants are also comparatively silent, lacking the innate tendency of the human infant to babble. Since the syllable *ma* is common in babbling, the probability that a human baby will say *mama* is high. If this utterance occurs in the presence of the baby's mother, it is immediately rewarded and tends to occur more often. By contrast, the chimpanzee Viki, who lived in a human family from early infancy, made few natural sounds (Hayes 1951). To teach Viki to say *mama*, the Hayes first trained her to ask for food by saying *ahhh*. Then they pressed her lips together while she was asking for food and caused the sound to become *mama*. Finally, they had to condition her to associate the word with Mrs. Hayes. Without babbling, chimpanzee infants lack the raw material that can be shaped into words by conditioning.

Although chimpanzees cannot talk, they are extremely intelligent. At age three, Viki was six months ahead of human children on nonverbal intelligence tests. In her Tinkertoy creations, Viki could represent objects that were not present in the immediate environment.[1] She formed structures of her own invention that apparently represented dolls: she would kiss them and cover up all but the top with a blanket. Like many children, Viki passed through a fantasy stage that lasted about a month. She played with an imaginary pulltoy, making exactly the same motions she made with some of her real toys. At one point, she acted as though the imaginary string of her imaginary pulltoy had become tangled in the bathroom plumbing. When Mrs. Hayes pretended to untangle the imaginary string, Viki broke into a wide grin and ran about the bathroom with excitement. Just as human children give up their fantasies when an adult begins to share them, Viki gave up her fantasy when Mrs. Hayes invented an imaginary pulltoy of her own.

---

1 Tinkertoy is a trademark of the Questor Educational Products Company.

Since chimpanzees have a great deal of intelligence and imagination, their inability to talk may result from peripheral causes such as a deficiency in their vocal apparatus or the lack of an instinct to babble. Although they cannot speak, they can learn sign language: Gardner and Gardner (1969) taught Washoe a simplified form of the American Sign Language (ASL) used by the deaf, and Premack (1971) taught Sarah to communicate with sequences of plastic markers. Sarah even learned "transformations" for converting *Sarah insert banana pail Sarah insert apple dish* into the sequence *Sarah insert banana pail apple dish.* In recent years, dozens of chimpanzees, gorillas, and orangutans have learned a version of ASL.

Despite impressive results in teaching sign language to the great apes, Terrace et al. (1979) doubted that they have a truly human form of language. Although many of them have a vocabulary of several hundred signs, their syntactic rules for combining the signs are limited. The evidence is not complete, but two points are clear: first, the great apes are highly intelligent animals with a complex conceptual system; second, they lack the human facility for mapping concepts into a linear stream of speech. Further research is needed to determine exactly what aspects of the human linguistic and conceptual systems that the apes have or lack.

Human children learn language at an extremely rapid rate. Studying the stages of learning can show how language works and how it interacts with the conceptual system. The first step in learning a language is building up a stock of words. Learning words and associating them with concepts is a routine process of conditioning that behaviorists have studied exhaustively. The key question of language acquisition is how children learn the appropriate syntactic markers and word order for expressing complex relations.

The simplest strategy for expressing a conceptual graph is to select the most prominent concept in it and to utter the associated word. This strategy is the first one that children adopt. If a child says *Cookie!* the most likely interpretation is that [COOKIE] is prominent in the child's mind. Depending on context, the parent might infer such messages as *Give me a cookie* or *My cookie just fell in a mud puddle.* Following are some one-word utterances by children at the age of about 15 months and the accompanying gestures (from Clark and Clark 1977):

Utterance	**Gesture**
More	Reaching for a cookie
No	Resisting being put to bed
Mama	Whining and reaching for an object
Poo	With hand on bottom after being changed
Bye-bye	Hand waving

Of these early utterances, it is more accurate to say that the word is an integral part of the gesture than to say that the word is accompanied by the gesture. Language evolves out of gestures, just as it does for the chimpanzees and orangutans who are taught sign language. But the human child soon learns syntactic structures that are far more organized than the apes' use of sign language.

The two-word sentence is the next stage in a child's linguistic development. It expresses two prominent concepts, but the listener has to guess the intervening conceptual relation. To say *Pamela has a kitten*, a child might say *Pammy kitty*. As with one-word utterances, limitations in the utterances do not imply limitations in children's conceptual structures, but limitations in their schemata for mapping structures into sentences. Bloom (1968) reported the following series of utterances by a two-year-old girl: "raisin there / buy more grocery store / raisins / buy more grocery store / grocery store / raisin a grocery store." In this case, the child apparently wanted to say *Buy more raisins at the grocery store*, but she could not relate more than two or three concepts in a single sentence. Slobin (1970) mentioned a Samoan child who "could express all the following semantic relations: verb-agent, verb-object, verb-directive, possession, labeling, benefit, and location. Yet he could generally not express more than one such relation in a single utterance." Such evidence shows that the child does have complex conceptual structures, but lacks the linguistic schemata for mapping them to full sentences.

By the end of their third year, children have a mastery of language that includes prepositions, conjunctions, modal auxiliaries, subordinate clauses, and even metalanguage about their language. As an example, one girl, aged two years and ten months, said: "When I was a little girl I could go 'geek-geek' like that. But now I can go 'This is a chair'" (Clark & Clark 1977). In less than two years, children progress from one-word utterances to sentences with a rich syntactic and semantic structure.

Even after children have learned syntax, they still have to integrate it with their informal, common sense background knowledge. Vygotsky (1962) studied children's development of concepts, both from everyday life and from formal instruction in school. He gave them sentence completion tests using both kinds of concepts. The sentences from everyday life included,

```
The boy went to the movies because....
He fell off his bicycle and broke his leg because....
```

Sentences from social science instruction included,

```
A planned economy is possible in the U.S.S.R. because....
```

His findings show a curious phenomenon. At age eight or nine, children correctly use the word *because* in spontaneous conversation. But on the sentence completion tests, they made significantly more errors with everyday concepts than with the ones they learned in school. They might say that the boy fell and broke his leg "because he was taken to the hospital." Yet they use the word correctly in saying that a planned economy is possible in the U.S.S.R. "because there is no private property—all land, factories, and plants belong to the workers and peasants." The children use their newly acquired logical abilities for the concepts they learned in school. For the concepts of everyday life, they tend to use schemata for plausible reasoning without checking for logical consistency.

Word association tests also show the stages in developing the conceptual system. On such tests, children give more highly varied associations than adults; and the younger the child, the more varied the associations. For the word *table*, 200 kindergarten children gave 87 different associations, but 200 college students gave only 28 different associations (Entwisle 1966). Young children tend to respond with a sentence fragment, while older children and adults respond with a word that belongs to the same category as the stimulus. A kindergarten child, for example, might respond to the word *obey* with the response *your mother* and to the word *up* with *stairs*. The older child is more likely to respond to the word *up* with the word *down*. Around the age of seven or eight, children's responses show that they are beginning to rely more heavily on the hierarchy of concept types.

By the age of twelve, children have attained nearly an adult competence with language. Yet there are still some differences in the relative emphasis that children and adults put on syntax and semantics. To determine the differences, Moore (1975) gave adult and child subjects a list of sentences with different kinds of anomalies:

```
Farmers emerge many crops.
Shoes dislike loud noises.
```

The first sentence is syntactically incorrect, but the concepts it expresses belong together semantically. With some additional words, it would form the correct sentence *Farmers cause many crops to emerge*. The second is syntactically correct, but semantically anomalous. No additional words can explain how shoes could dislike anything. Adults judge both sentences as equally unacceptable, but children (age 12) judge the first as much more acceptable than the second. In the presence of background noise, errors of any kind, syntactic or semantic, make sentences more difficult to understand for both children and adults. But children are relatively more sensitive to semantic errors than syntactic ones.

The evidence from language learning shows that language is not a monolithic system, but consists of different functions that are acquired at different stages:

- First, children associate words with the concrete concepts used in perceiving the world and acting upon it.
- Next, they learn syntactic rules for mapping concepts and conceptual relations to well-formed sentences.
- Finally, they master the formal structures of the type hierarchy and the fine points of syntax.

Children use semantics as a guide to learning syntax. Adults, who rely more heavily on the formal structures, use language with greater precision and efficiency. The trade-offs between syntax and semantics are important for both human understanding and computer processing.

5.2 STRATA OF LANGUAGE

Language can be studied on many levels—from the lowest levels of sounds and rhythms to the highest levels of meaning and the relationship between language and the world. Each level forms a complete subsystem with its own elements and rules of combination. And each of the subsystems is rich enough and complex enough to merit study in a fully developed discipline:

- *Prosody*. The rhythm and intonation patterns of language.
- *Phonology*. The sounds or *phonemes* of language.
- *Morphology*. The meaningful elements or *morphemes* that make up the words.
- *Syntax*. The rules for combining words into phrases and sentences.
- *Semantics*. Meaning and its expression.
- *Pragmatics*. The use of language and its effects on the listener.

Traditional grammar books concentrate on morphology and syntax. For highly inflected languages like Latin, they devote most of their attention to morphology. Philosophers have spent most of their efforts on semantics and pragmatics, but usually without a formal notation for recording their insights. Linguists started with phonology and morphology and worked their way through syntax to semantics, although most of them, especially the transformationalists, have devoted far more attention to syntax than to semantics. Workers in AI and computational linguistics have concentrated primarily on syntax and semantics, but those who work on speech have also dealt with phonology. Of all the disciplines, prosody has been the most neglected—except, perhaps, in studies of poetry.

Although rhythm has often been neglected in formal studies, it has a powerful effect. Even before they learn words, babies mimic adult rhythm and intonation patterns in their babbling. In a radio interview, the children's author Maurice Sendak noted that children often read stories aloud in a sing-song tone. To hold their attention, prose has to have a strong rhythm that encourages that tendency. The following passage from Sendak's *In the Night Kitchen* shows the almost hypnotic effect of rhythm. In the story, the hero Mickey had just fallen into a vat of dough while the bakers were making a cake:

```
But right in the middle
of the steaming and the making
and the smelling and the baking
Mickey poked through and said:
I'm not the milk and the milk's not me!
I'm Mickey!
```

Rhythm is not an extra feature that decorates an utterance, but a pattern that provides the slots into which other features are inserted. The left thalamus generates a six-per-second rhythm that apparently serves as a pacemaker for speech rhythms and other communication rhythms. Jaffe (1977) and his colleagues found it to be correlated with the vocalization pause rhythm, the infant face-gaze rhythm, and the syllabic stress rhythm.

The next stratum of language, phonology, has been studied in far greater depth. In the 5th century B.C., Pāṇini and other Indian grammarians did a thorough analysis of Sanskrit phonology that was more precise than any other studies done before the 20th century. Their motivation was partly scientific and partly religious: the popular languages of India were undergoing major sound shifts at that time, and it was important to preserve the exact pronunciation of the sacred language for religious ceremonies. During the first half of the twentieth century, phonology was extensively studied in the United States, especially in the analysis and classification of the American Indian languages. Today, phonology is important in computer processing, both for speech generation and for the much more difficult task of speech recognition. Although concepts are the primary topic of this book, a few observations about phonology are pertinent because they also apply to higher strata of language, especially the conceptual level.

- *Arbitrary standards.* The human vocal cords, lips, and tongue can produce a continuous infinity of possible sounds, but every human language standardizes on only a few dozen phonemes. However, each language, each dialect, and even each individual speaker may select a different set as standard.

- *Structuralism.* Although the standard phonemes are arbitrarily chosen for each language, they form a highly structured, interdependent system. Changes from one dialect to another, from one speaker to another, or from one historical stage to another are not manifested as changes in isolated sounds, but as systematic shifts in the entire set of sounds. If one phoneme is lost in some dialect, the sounds of all the others are shifted to minimize the gap in the vocal repertoire.

- *Family resemblances.* Wittgenstein's observation about family resemblances in word meanings (see Section 1.5) also applies to phonemes. The English phoneme /t/, for example, is realized by a family of different *allophones*: an aspirated sound in *tack*, an unaspirated sound in *stack*, a vocalized flap in *butter*, a glottal stop in some pronunciations of *bottle*, and merely as a cessation of the /n/ sound in *can't go*.

- *Open texture.* In an appropriate context, new sounds that a listener had never heard before may be perceived as familiar phonemes. A puff of white noise in the right context may be heard as a phoneme /p/, /t/, or /k/. Foreign accents, speech by a handicapped person, and computer generated sounds are classified as familiar phonemes, even though none of the sounds conform to the standard dialect. All these examples illustrate what Waismann (1952) called the *open texture* of empirical concepts: no exhaustive classification is possible because new examples can always be found that clearly ought to belong to a class even though they were not anticipated by the taxonomy.

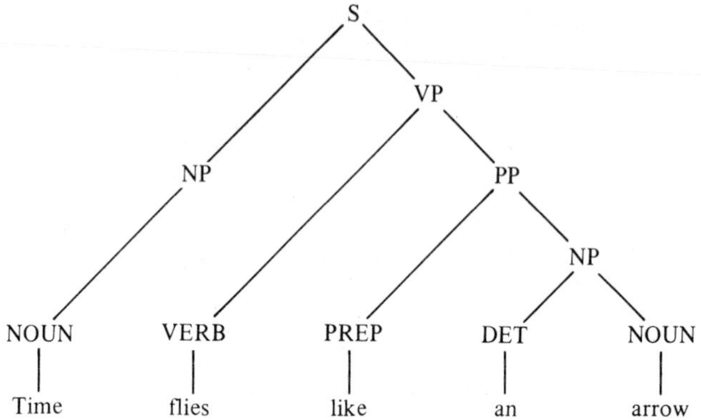

Fig. 5.1 A parse tree for a simple sentence

These four principles of natural language, illustrated at the level of phonology, extend to higher levels as well. They are especially important at the level of semantics, for which Wittgenstein and Waismann originally made their observations. Since they also appear at the level of phonology, they must result from fundamental mechanisms of the brain.

Compared to highly inflected languages like Greek and Latin, English morphology is simple. Most English words are found in the dictionary exactly as written or in a form that follows from stripping off endings like *-s*, *-ed*, or *-ing*. Irregular forms like *children* or *sang* are rare enough to be included in the dictionary as they appear. German morphology is complex because it strings together simple words to form compounds. The word *Lebensversicherungsgesellschaftsangestellter* would not occur in the dictionary, but its components would. *Leben* means life, *Versicherung* means insurance, *Gesellschaft* means company, and *Angestellter* means employee. As one word, it means the same as the English phrase *life insurance company employee.* Subwords like *Angestellter* can be further analyzed into morphemes *An-ge-stell-t-er* with the underlying meaning *one who has been put in a place.* People analyze words into low-level morphemes only when they encounter a new, unfamiliar word. In fluent speech, both people and machines treat common words as indivisible units. In the spoken form, neither English nor German has pauses between subwords; in the written form, the blanks between English words simplify morphological analysis.

Syntax is the stratum that combines words into sentences. *Parsing* is the act of applying grammar rules to determine how the words are combined. A *parse tree* like Fig. 5.1 shows how the grammatical categories are related to the words. In formal grammar theory (Appendix A.6), the symbols at the endpoints of the tree—the words *time*, *flies*, *like*, *an*, and *arrow*—are called *terminal symbols.* The symbols at higher levels in the tree are called *nonterminal symbols.* Each of them is a name for

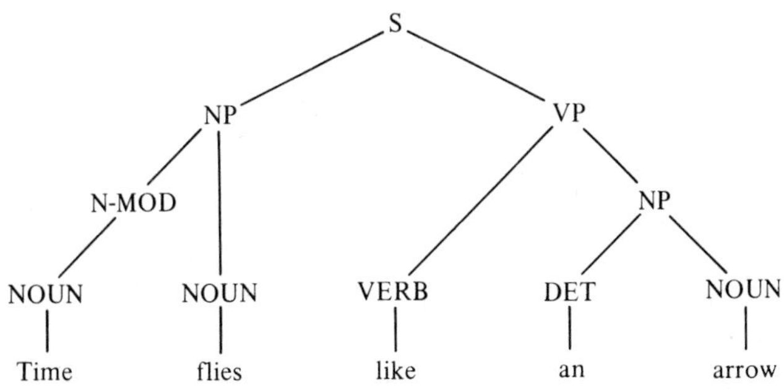

Fig. 5.2 Alternate parse for the same sentence

some grammatical category: S represents a sentence, NP a noun phrase, VP a verb phrase, PP a prepositional phrase, NOUN a noun, VERB a verb, PREP a preposition, and DET a determiner. The following grammar rules determine the parse tree in Fig. 5.1:

```
S ⟶ NP VP.
NP ⟶ [DET] [N-MOD]... NOUN [PP].
N-MOD ⟶ ADJ | NOUN.
VP ⟶ VERB [NP] [PP].
PP ⟶ PREP NP.
```

The first rule defines S as a noun phrase followed by a verb phrase. The second one defines NP as an optional determiner, an optional string of noun modifiers N-MOD, a required noun, and an optional prepositional phrase. The third one defines N-MOD as either an adjective or a noun. The fourth one defines VP as a required verb followed by an optional noun phrase and an optional prepositional phrase. And the last rule defines PP as a preposition followed by a noun phrase. A parsing program applies *phrase structure rules* like these to compute a parse tree.

In the late 1950s, Chomsky had recently published his work on transformational grammar, computers were just becoming widely available, and people were beginning to develop systematic parsing algorithms for analyzing syntax. At that time, the prospects for automated language analysis looked promising. But when computational linguists started to apply their parsers to a large amount of text, they found far more ambiguities than they had ever expected. When the sentence *Time flies like an arrow* is fed to a parser, the computer systematically applies all possible grammar rules to generate parses that a nonlinguist would never expect. Figure 5.2 shows *flies* as a noun, *time* as a noun modifying *flies*, and *like* as a verb. With the same syntax as the sentence *Fruit flies like a banana*, the parse in Fig. 5.2 suggests that a certain kind of flies, the *time flies*, enjoy an arrow.

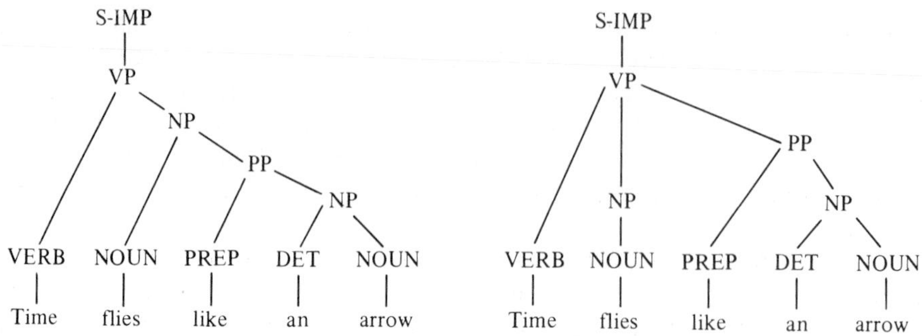

Fig. 5.3 Two additional parses as imperative sentences

Yet the word *time* can also be a verb. A computer would generate two additional parses that interpret the sentence as an imperative. The listener (the subject is an implicit *you*) is asked to use a stopwatch to time the flies. The following grammar rule could be added to the previous ones to define an imperative sentence S-IMP as just a single verb phrase without an explicit subject:

```
S-IMP ⟶ VP.
```

Figure 5.3 shows two possible parsings of the sentence as an imperative. In the first, the prepositional phrase *like an arrow* modifies the noun *flies*. This parse would mean that the listener is asked to time certain flies that resemble an arrow. In the second, the prepositional phrase modifies the verb *time*. This parse could be interpreted in two different ways: *Time the flies in the same way that you would time an arrow* or *Time the flies in the same way that an arrow would time them*. One simple sentence that few English speakers would suspect as ambiguous turns out to have four different parsings, with a total of five different interpretations.

The sentence *Time flies like an arrow* is ambiguous because the first three words could belong to more than one part of speech: *time* and *flies* could be either nouns or verbs, and *like* is either a verb or a preposition. Yet ambiguity of individual words is not the most serious problem, since context is usually sufficient to resolve the part of speech. More serious ambiguities occur with participles and conjunctions where the part of speech is unambiguous, but the syntactic connections are unclear. When Kuno and Oettinger developed their predictive syntactic analyzer, they found such ambiguities in nearly every sentence (Kuno 1965). One of their sentences, *People who apply for marriage licenses wearing shorts or pedal pushers will be denied licenses*, turned out to have 40 different parses. In this sentence, the word *will*, which could be either a noun, a verb, or an auxiliary verb, causes no trouble because in the context it can only be an auxiliary. The words that cause the most trouble are the participle *wearing*, the conjunction *or*, and the participle *denied*.

The phrase *people who apply for marriage licenses* is unambiguous. When the parser reaches the participle *wearing*, however, it has to determine who or what is wearing what. One possibility is that the immediately preceding noun is the agent of *wear*: the marriage licenses are wearing shorts. Another possibility is that the following noun, *shorts*, is the agent: the shorts are wearing marriage licenses. A third possibility is that the subject of the clause *who*, which refers to *people*, is the agent: the people are wearing shorts.

Coordinate conjunctions like *or* present the most difficult parsing problems in English—the only constraint they impose is that the same grammatical category must occur on both sides. In this example, the only possibility that would occur to the human reader is that the NP *shorts* is conjoined with the NP *pedal pushers*. But the NP *marriage licenses wearing shorts* might also be conjoined with the NP *pedal pushers*: the people may apply either for marriage licenses wearing shorts or for pedal pushers. Yet a third possibility is that the NP *people who apply for marriage licenses wearing shorts* is conjoined with the NP *pedal pushers* as a compound subject. Finally, since *pedal* could also be a verb, the VP *apply for marriage licenses wearing shorts* might be conjoined with the VP *pedal pushers*: either those who apply for marriage licenses or those who pedal pushers will be denied licenses.

At the end of the sentence, *denied* causes a problem. One possibility is that *will be denied* is a compound verb—the future passive form of *deny*. Another possibility is that *denied* is used as an adjective modifying *licenses*: those poor unfortunates who apply for marriage licenses under inauspicious circumstances will be reincarnated as denied licenses.

Syntactic ambiguities can be resolved by the next stratum, semantics. As the syntactic component of a parser scans the input string, the semantic component joins canonical graphs to represent the meaning. When the semantic component fails to find a suitable join, it forces the syntactic component to reject the current grammar rule and try a different option. In the previous example, the agent of *wearing* could be determined by semantics. For the word *wear*, the lexicon (Appendix B.1) lists one concept type WEAR for a person wearing clothing, and a type WEAR-OUT for some process that serves as the instrument of wearing out a physical object. Each of the two concepts fits a different canonical graph:

```
[HUMAN]←(AGNT)←[WEAR]→(OBJ)→[CLOTHING].
[TOOL]←(INST)←[WEAR-OUT]→(OBJ)→[PHYSOBJ].
```

In looking for the subject of *wearing*, the syntactic component would find three different options:

```
Marriage licenses are wearing shorts.
Shorts are wearing marriage licenses.
People are wearing shorts.
```

The first two options do not match either canonical graph, but the third one matches the first graph. Therefore, the semantic component signals a preference for that graph, and the syntactic component rejects the other alternatives. Canonical graphs give *semantic preferences* for certain combinations and enforce *selectional constraints* that block other combinations.

The first conceptual parsers were designed for machine translation systems in the early 1960s. Ceccato's *correlational nets* (1962) serve the same purpose as canonical graphs. Using the nets, Ceccato and his colleagues developed a conceptual parser, but their computer was too small and too slow for practical machine translation. Using the semantic primitives of Masterman (1961), Wilks (1972) developed his system of *preference semantics* as the basis for a conceptual parser. Schank and his students and colleagues have emphasized conceptual parsers in their systems (Riesbeck 1975, Schank et al. 1980, Birnbaum & Selfridge 1981, Gershman 1982).

5.3 CASE RELATIONS

English grammar books give three cases for nouns and pronouns: *nominative case* for subjects, *objective case* for objects of verbs and prepositions, and *possessive case* for ownership and other relations between nouns. The only case ending for nouns is the *'s* for possessives, but pronouns show all three cases. Middle English around Chaucer's time also had separate endings for the *dative case*, although the final *-e* that marked the dative was beginning to be lost. In Old English or Anglo-Saxon, four cases were clearly marked, in both the nouns and the accompanying adjectives. Following is the *declension* of *my good man* in Old English:

		Singular			**Plural**	
Nominative:	min	goda	mann	mine	godan	mannas
Genitive:	mines	godan	mannes	minra	godena	manna
Dative:	minum	godan	manne	minum	godum	mannum
Accusative:	minne	godan	mann	mine	godan	mannas

The old nominative case corresponds in name and function to the modern nominative, and the *genitive case* corresponds to the modern possessive. The modern objective case, however, combines the functions of the *accusative case*, which was used for the direct objects of verbs and the objects of some prepositions, and the *dative case*, which was used for indirect objects and objects of other prepositions.

Loss of case distinctions is caused by a simplification of endings to a point where the word forms become the same. As the table shows, the same adjective form *godan* occurs in five out of eight categories. Similarly, the nominative and accusative endings for the noun *mann* are the same in both singular and plural. Further simplifications have led to the complete loss of case endings for adjectives and the loss of all but the possessive ending for nouns. As modern English evolved, the underlying conceptual relations never changed, but the means for expressing them did.

THE WIZARD OF ID by Brant parker and Johnny hart

Fig. 5.4 Confusion of dative and accusative cases

The loss of endings can sometimes contribute to ambiguities. In Fig. 5.4, the waiter intended the word *men* in the dative case as the ones who would have dinner served to them, but the lady interpreted the word in the accusative case as the ones who would be served to her. Yet this cartoon is an anachronism: the setting of the scene is in medieval times when Old English would have distinguished the dative *mannum* from the accusative *mannas*. As in this example, the loss of case endings can cause ambiguities. Sometimes, however, case endings are more ambiguous than prepositions. In Latin, for example, the *ablative case* combined many functions that are expressed by distinct prepositions in English. Languages use different syntactic means for expressing the same underlying relations. A language may express certain relations with great precision and tolerate ambiguity in others.

Case endings are markers for conceptual relations. Fillmore's *case grammar* (1968) had a strong influence on AI because it provided a convenient set of labels for conceptual relations. But he made the point that there is no one-to-one mapping between the surface cases and the underlying relations. As an example, Fillmore cited the following sentences:

```
The door opened.
The janitor opened the door.
The key opened the door.
The janitor opened the door with a key.
```

In all four sentences, the relations between the concept [OPEN] and the concepts [DOOR], [KEY], and [JANITOR] remain constant. Yet the surface cases are very different: each of the first three sentences has a different subject, and the fourth uses the preposition *with*.

Dictionaries traditionally deal with the different options for the verb *open* by saying that it has multiple meanings: in one sense, it is an *intransitive verb* whose subject is the thing that is opening; in another sense, it is a *transitive verb* whose subject is the person who does the opening and whose object is the thing that opens; and in a third sense, it is also a transitive verb, but its subject is the tool or instrument used to do the opening. Fillmore, however, maintained that the concept [OPEN] has only one basic sense, but it has three possible relations attached to it, of which one or two are optional. The janitor is the *agent* who does the opening, the key is the *instrument* of opening, and the door is the *object* of opening. The agent has precedence over all others: if present in the sentence, it must be the subject. If the agent is omitted, the instrument may take the subject position. Finally, if both the agent and instrument are omitted, the object may occur in subject position. For stylistic reasons, the speaker may want to move the object forward while still mentioning the agent. Then the sentence must be transformed to *passive voice* in the sentence *The door was opened by the janitor with a key*. The janitor is no longer the subject of the sentence, but is still the agent of *open*. The surface structures may change, but the underlying conceptual relations do not.

To determine which conceptual relation is expressed by each surface case, a conceptual parser selects a *case frame*, which is a canonical graph that shows the expected configuration of concepts and relations. Figure 5.5 shows a case frame for OPEN. This graph implies that any concept of type OPEN would normally be attached to three conceptual relations of types AGNT, OBJ, and INST. The types ANIMATE, PHYSOBJ, and ¬ANIMATE indicate the most general concept types that may be attached to those relations. (See Definition 4.2.8 for *negated type labels* like ¬ANIMATE.) In parsing a sentence, a conceptual parser treats the generic concepts of a case frame as slots to be specialized by more specific types and referents from the input sentence. For the sentence *The janitor opened the door*, it would generate the following graph:

```
[OPEN]-
   (AGNT)→[JANITOR: #]
   (OBJ)→ [DOOR: #]
   (INST)→[¬ANIMATE].
```

Since the instrument was not mentioned in the sentence, the type ¬ANIMATE was left unchanged. That concept might later be joined to one derived from some other sentence. The marker # shows the definite article in *the janitor* and *the door*; it is an abbreviation for a full individual marker like #5562 or #203.

In a conceptual parser, the analysis is driven by canonical graphs, and many ungrammatical sentences can be parsed by semantic rules. The sentence *My Seymour with a key he opens the door* violates standard rules of syntax, but it can be interpreted by semantics. A conceptual parser begins to select concepts from the sentence before determining the exact places to join them. When it reaches the verb *open*, it selects the case frame for OPEN and checks the available concepts that meet

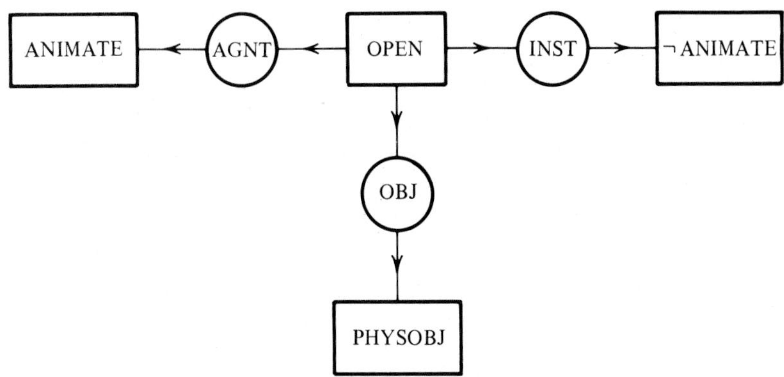

Fig. 5.5 Case frame for OPEN

the constraints. Canonical graphs have strong predictive power that can select the proper interpretation for archaic and dialectical forms, slips of the tongue, and grammar mistakes.

Other languages express the same conceptual relations as English, but with different syntactic means. Japanese, for example, uses *postpositions* that follow the noun instead of *prepositions* that precede the noun. The postposition *ga* indicates the agent (although for some verbs, it may indicate other relations), the postposition *o* indicates the object, and the postposition *de* indicates the instrument. The Japanese sentence (with a one-for-one mapping into English words) would be:

```
seisofu ga kagi de tobira o aketa.
janitor (agnt) key (inst) door (obj) opened.
```

Since postpositions clearly mark the relations, any one of the three nouns may be omitted if it is not of interest, and the word order for the other components need not change:

```
kagi de tobira o aketa.
seisofu ga tobira o aketa.
seisofu ga kagi de aketa.
```

Because of the postpositions, word order in Japanese is much more flexible than in English. Although Japanese does have a passive form, the Japanese speaker has the option of changing the emphasis simply by interchanging the noun phrases together with their postpositions:

```
tobira o seisofu ga kagi de aketa.
door (obj) janitor (agnt) key (inst) opened.
```

Other kinds of postpositions can modify an entire sentence. The particle *ka* at the end of any sentence turns it into a question, and the particle *ne* at the end is like the English *tag* questions, *isn't it?* or *didn't he?*

```
seisofu ga kagi de tobira o aketa ka?
seisofu ga kagi de tobira o aketa ne.
```

The first of these sentences asks the question *Did the janitor open the door with a key?* and the second one says *The janitor opened the door with a key, didn't he?*

Japanese postpositions, English prepositions, and little words like *the*, *a*, *or*, and *it* are called *function words* or *empty words*—as opposed to most nouns, verbs, adjectives, and adverbs, which are called *content words* or *full words*. When a sentence is translated into a conceptual graph, content words appear as concept nodes. Function words, however, tend to disappear. Sometimes they appear in the graph as conceptual relations, but often they merely indicate some twist or turn in the mapping between the linear sentence and the more highly branched graph. Even the English verbs *be* and *have* are function words that rarely map into concept nodes. In the sentence *It is raining*, the only content word is *raining*. The pronoun *it* and the verb *is* are empty words that fill the obligatory subject and verb positions in English. The conceptual graph has only one concept [RAIN], which Latin represents as the single word *pluit*. In the sentence *The book is red*, the content words are *book* and *red*. The determiner *the* marks a reference to something in the current context, and *is* fills the verb position. A Russian sentence would contain only the two content words *Book red*. For either the English or the Russian sentence, the conceptual graph is the same: [BOOK:#]→(ATTR)→[RED].

Some prepositions have content, while others are purely empty. The English preposition *of*, for example, is an empty word that indicates a relation between two nouns. What relation it is can be determined only from a canonical graph or schema that contains the two concepts represented by the nouns: *house of your own*, *house of brick*, *house of cards*, *house of prayer*, *house of ill repute*, *house of Usher*, and so forth. The preposition *above*, by contrast, does have content. It corresponds to the relation (ABOV), which has the following definition:

relation ABOV(x,y) **is**
    [T: *x]→(LOC)→[PLACE]→(ATTR)→[HIGH]→(COMP)→[PLACE: *y].

This definition says that x is located above y if x is at a place that is higher than the place y. The relational definition for ABOV contains several concepts that give content to the preposition *above*.

By determining the appropriate case frame, a conceptual parser can distinguish sentences that have identical surface syntax. The preposition *with*, for example, could indicate either instrument (INST) or accompaniment (ACCM):

```
The janitor opened the door with a key.
The janitor opened the door with a wet noodle.
The janitor opened the door with Albie.
```

In the first sentence, the phrase *with a key* indicates the instrument of [OPEN]. In the second, a wet noodle is an unusual instrument. The reader may wonder how the janitor used it, but would still interpret [NOODLE] as the instrument because it meets the type constraints in the case frame. In the third, however, *with Albie* must be interpreted as accompaniment since Albie is an animate being:

```
[OPEN]-
   (AGNT)→ [JANITOR: #]→(ACCM)→[PERSON: Albie]
   (OBJ)→  [DOOR: #]
   (INST)→ [¬ANIMATE].
```

If a person or computer did not know the word *Albie*, he, she, or it could ask for a definition. The response, however, might be misleading:

```
WHO OR WHAT IS ALBIE?
Albie's one of our key employees.
```

When one noun *key* modifies another noun *employee*, the modifier does not make the employee into a type of key. Instead, it shows that there is some implicit relation between the concepts [KEY] and [EMPLOYEE]. A computer can determine the type of the relation by finding a canonical graph or schema that contains both concept types. If no graph is found, it could either ask the person at the terminal for an explanation or try using a metaphor interpreter. If the dictionary is complete, it might list *key* as an adjective meaning fundamental or indispensable.

The phrase *key employee* cannot be interpreted without a large dictionary or a way of handling metaphor. But similar issues arise with phrases like *John's mathematics teacher*, where no metaphor is intended. The relation between *John* and *teacher* is very different from the relation between *mathematics* and *teacher*. To determine the underlying conceptual relations, the system must check a canonical graph for TEACHER:

```
[TEACHER]←(AGNT)←[TEACH]-
                    (OBJ)→ [SUBJECT-MATTER]
                    (RCPT)→[ANIMATE].
```

The type labels on the concepts constrain [MATHEMATICS] to be the object of the teacher's teaching and [PERSON:John] to be the recipient. The canonical graph for TEACHER is derived from the graph for TEACH, but nouns without associated verbs can still have obligatory canonical graphs. In general, *natural types* like DOG, FLOWER, or PERSON have no obligatory graphs in the canon (although they may have schemata that can also be used for interpreting language). *Role types* like TEACHER, PEDESTRIAN, or PHYSICIAN always have canonical graphs that express obligatory relationships.

Since the word *of* depends on a canonical graph or schema for its proper interpretation, the word that serves as an index to the graph cannot be replaced by a pronoun. Consider the next two sentences:

```
The teacher with a beard is taller than the one with glasses.
The teacher of physics is taller than the one of English.
```

The first sentence sounds normal, but the second one sounds odd. In the first, the phrases *with a beard* and *with glasses* are possible attributes of a human being, but they do not depend on any relations in the canonical graph for TEACHER. In the second, however, the phrases *of physics* and *of English* specialize the SUBJECT-MATTER slot in the graph for TEACHER. When the word *teacher* is replaced by *one*, the reader cannot interpret the word *of* without looking back at the previous occurrence of *teacher*.

Besides nouns and verbs, adjectives and adverbs also map to concept types with obligatory case frames. The canonical graph for WARM includes relations of type EXPR for the ANIMAL that experiences the warmth, INST for the inanimate instrument that is causing the warmth, LOC for the warm place, and PTIM for the point in time of the warmth:

```
[WARM]-
   (EXPR)→ [ANIMAL]
   (INST)→ [¬ANIMATE]
   (LOC)→  [PLACE]
   (PTIM)→ [TIME].
```

Fillmore observed that comparatives and conjunctions may not involve more than one relation type at a time. The following sentences are well formed because they obey that constraint:

```
Rita and Priscilla are warm.               (Both EXPR)
My jacket is warmer than your sweater.     (Both INST)
Texas and Florida are warm.                (Both LOC)
July is warmer than March.                 (Both PTIM)
```

The following sentences are odd because they contain comparatives and conjunctions that mix the relation types:

```
Rita and Florida are warm.                 (EXPR & LOC)
My jacket is warmer than July.             (INST & PTIM)
Texas and your sweater are warm.           (LOC & INST)
Priscilla is warmer than March.            (EXPR & PTIM)
```

If a sentence violates the constraints in a canonical graph, it might still be interpreted by relaxing type constraints. The dog Fido would normally be an animate experiencer of warmth, but the sentence *Fido is warmer than an electric blanket* demotes him to the inanimate role of instrument.

The canonical graphs for TEACHER and WARM explain why certain sentences are well formed while others sound odd. But such examples violate Chomsky's *autonomy principle* that transformations do not take account of semantics in generating sentences. To save the principle, Chomsky added empty nodes to the parse tree to serve as triggers for the syntactic rules. Yet the empty nodes are an embarrassment: they keep semantics out of the transformations at the expense of *ad hoc* nodes that must be justified by an undefined semantic component. Conceptual graphs provide a more complete explanation with a simpler formalism.

The conceptual catalog in Appendix B presents the types of concepts and conceptual relations used in this book together with a sample set of canonical graphs. As an example, Appendix B.2 includes the following graph for the type ARRIVE:

```
[ARRIVE]-
   (AGNT)→ [MOBILE-ENTITY]
   (LOC)→  [PLACE].
```

This graph implies that a concept of type [ARRIVE] is normally linked by a relation of type (AGNT) to a concept of type MOBILE-ENTITY and by a relation of type LOC to a concept of type PLACE. By joins and restrictions, the graphs in the catalog may be combined to form larger canonical graphs. Since ARRIVE<ACT and ACT<EVENT, it follows that ARRIVE<EVENT. In the following graph,

```
[EVENT]→(FREQ)→[TIME: {*}],
```

[EVENT] may be restricted to [ARRIVE] and be joined to the preceding graph. The set of times [TIME:{*}] indicates the frequency (FREQ) of occurrence of the event. The result is the larger canonical graph,

```
[ARRIVE]-
   (AGNT)→ [MOBILE-ENTITY]
   (LOC)→  [PLACE]
   (FREQ)→ [TIME: {*}].
```

Since EVENT<SITUATION, the concept [SITUATION] may also be restricted to [ARRIVE] in the canonical graph,

```
[SITUATION]-
   (LOC)→ [PLACE]
   (DUR)→ [TIME-PERIOD],
```

where [TIME-PERIOD] indicates the duration (DUR) of the situation. The result could be joined to the previous graph to generate the still larger canonical graph,

```
[ARRIVE]-
   (AGNT)→ [MOBILE-ENTITY]
   (LOC)→  [PLACE]
   (FREQ)→ [TIME: {*}]
   (DUR)→  [TIME-PERIOD].
```

Before the join, both graphs contained identical branches for the LOC relation. The duplicate was absorbed in a maximal join, and only the extra branch for (DUR)

remains in the final graph. The canonical basis contains the most general graphs that apply to a given concept type. As this example illustrates, the formation rules allow subtypes to inherit the canonical graphs of the supertype.

Although case relations are an important part of language, linguists have not agreed upon a definitive list of cases. About half a dozen case relations are common to most theories, with some minor variation in terminology, such as *patient* instead of *object*. Differences arise over the treatment of all the locative prepositions in English—whether they should be lumped into a single LOC relation, be assigned a separate relation per preposition, or be expanded into separate concept nodes as if they were ordinary content words. Using a single LOC relation is wrong because it would blur such distinctions as *under* vs. *over* or *in* vs. *on*. With a mechanism for relational definitions, the dispute over assigning relation nodes or concept nodes to prepositions is solvable: map a preposition like *above* into the relation (ABOV) and expand it if desired into the underlying concept nodes. Other differences arise over role types like FATHER and PART—whether they might be more appropriately treated as relation types FATHER-OF or HAS-AS-PART. The definitional mechanisms can resolve that issue also. Since the words *father* and *part* look like ordinary nouns, the parser can map them into concepts. If the semantic routines find it more convenient to deal with them as relations, they can convert them by relational contraction. Having a large number of relation types is convenient, but relational definitions reduce them to a much smaller number of primitives.

5.4 LANGUAGE GENERATION

Generating language involves three stages: determining what to say, how to relate it to the listener, and how to map it into a string of words. The first two stages depend on pragmatics to select some graph to be expressed and to determine which concept should be the subject, which should be the main predicate, and how many modifiers should be attached to each. The third stage scans the graph and maps concepts into words. Determining what to say and how to relate it to the listener involves complex issues that are treated in Section 5.7. This section will concentrate on the third stage of mapping a graph to a sentence. In all of the examples so far, the English readings for conceptual graphs have been informal, intuitive translations from graphs to sentences. This section presents a general theory of how the mapping is done for all languages as well as a notation for stating the grammar rules that define the mapping for a particular language.

The sequence of nodes and arcs that are traversed in mapping a graph to a sentence is called the *utterance path*. If all conceptual graphs were linear chains, the path could start at either end of a chain, visit each node in sequence, and utter the word that corresponds to each concept node. Since conceptual graphs are normally more complex than chains, the path would either have to skip some of the branches, or it would have to take a more circuitous walk that visits some nodes more than once. In a program for generating English, Quillian (1966) chose the simple option of tracing a linear path through the graph and ignoring all side branches. McNeill (1979), however, developed a psychologically motivated theory of the utterance path that permits more complex traversals. Besides grammatical utterances, he also wanted to account for false starts and errors.

The utterance path has a great deal of explanatory power: it unifies observations about language types and imposes strong constraints on transformations. For complex graphs, the utterance path may visit a given concept node more than once. Various languages of the world are characterized by their preference for uttering a word at the first visit to a node, the last visit, or some intermediate visit:

- *Preorder language.* Each word is uttered at the first visit to its concept node. Biblical Hebrew, which puts the verb first and puts nouns before the adjectives, is a preorder language.
- *Postorder language.* Each word is uttered at the last visit to its concept node. An example is Japanese, which puts the verb last, puts nouns after the adjectives, and puts postpositions after the nouns.
- *Inorder language.* Each word is uttered at an intermediate visit to its concept node. English and French, which put verbs in the middle, are approximately inorder languages. English, however, has a postorder tendency to put nouns after the adjectives, and French has a preorder tendency to put nouns in front of the adjectives. French is a closer approximation to an inorder language, since it puts some adjectives in front of the nouns and some after them, as in *un joli chapeau rouge* instead of the English form, *a pretty red hat.*

The terms *preorder, postorder*, and *inorder* are the names of different options for scanning trees and graphs. (For a discussion of graphs and algorithms for traversing them, see Appendix A.3.) Since preorder languages put the verb first, subject next, and object last, they are also called *VSO languages*. Postorder languages are *SOV languages*, and inorder languages are *SVO languages*. Surveys of languages around the world have found that the three patterns, VSO, SOV, and SVO are common, the pattern VOS is rare, and the patterns OSV and OVS do not occur as the default patterns in any known languages (Greenberg 1963, Steele 1978). For emphasis, however, most languages permit optional inversions, such as the English sentence in OSV form, *His new-found friend he took with him to the park*. Such forms, which break the normal pattern of the language, are called *marked forms* as opposed to the normal, unemphatic, *unmarked forms*.

A graph with multiple branches, such as Fig. 5.6, illustrates the options for mapping a conceptual graph to a sentence. The first step is to determine a cyclic walk that starts at the main predicate [DRINK] and visits every node at least once. A sequence of concept nodes visited in such a walk would be [DRINK], [BABY], [BLITHE], [BABY], [BELLY], [FAT], [BELLY], [BABY], [DRINK], [MILK], [FRESH], [MILK], [BOTTLE], [NEW], [BOTTLE], [MILK], [DRINK]. The

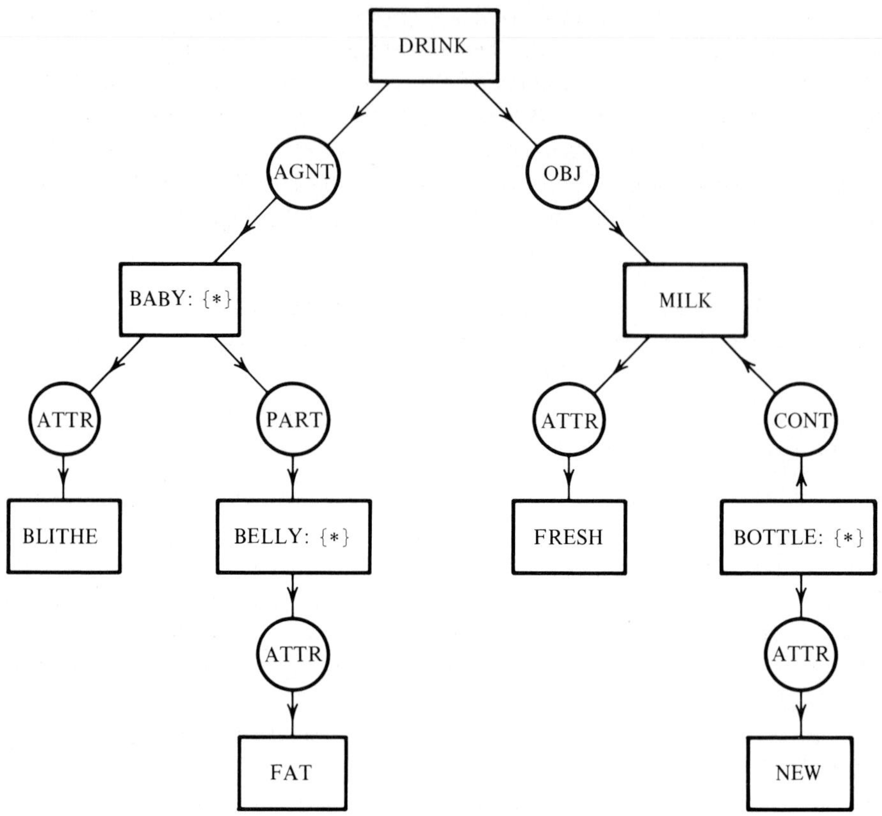

Fig. 5.6 A conceptual graph

concepts at the ends of the branches, [BLITHE], [FAT], [FRESH], and [NEW], are visited only once. For those concepts, the corresponding word must be uttered at the moment the walk visits the node. The other concepts are visited several times, and the words could be uttered at any visit. The following four sentences show the order of uttering words in an inorder language such as English (1), an inorder language such as French (2), a predorder language such as Hebrew (3), and a postorder language such as Japanese (4):

1. Blithe babies with fat bellies drink fresh milk in new bottles.
2. Babies blithe with bellies fat drink milk fresh in bottles new.
3. Drink babies blithe with bellies fat milk fresh in bottles new.
4. Fat bellies with blithe babies new bottles in fresh milk drink.

The *transformations* of transformational grammar result from different options for scanning the graphs. In English, the passive transformation results from following the arc to (OBJ) before the arc to (AGNT). To show that a nonstandard scan is being made, English grammar rules insert function words and inflections: *are* before the main verb, *by* before the agent, and the past participle *drunk* instead of *drink*. When passive rules are applied to Fig. 5.6, the following sentence is generated:

```
Fresh milk in new bottles is drunk by blithe babies
with fat bellies.
```

Any of the eight relations in Fig. 5.6 could have been chosen as the start of an utterance path. If the relation (PART) between [BABY:{*}] and [BELLY:{*}] had been chosen as the main link, the resulting sentence would be,

```
Blithe babies that drink fresh milk in new bottles
have fat bellies.
```

In English sentences generated from conceptual graphs, the verbs *be* and *have* usually correspond to relations rather than concept nodes. Those verbs occur when the main predicate is not an action, but an attribute like *new* or a noun like *belly*. In such cases, a language like Russian does not require a verb and permits forms like *Bottles new* or *At blithe babies fat bellies*. English also uses the verb *do* as a place holder: if the concept [DRINK] is expressed as the subject rather than the verb, some verb form is needed by the grammar rules; since the concept [DRINK] has already been uttered, the rules insert the verb *do* at the point where the utterance path returns to the concept [DRINK]:

```
Drinking fresh milk in new bottles is done by blithe babies
with fat bellies.
```

As these examples illustrate, the same graph can be expressed in many different sentences, depending on the starting point and direction of the utterance path. Yet not all word orders are possible: the utterance path visits each node a limited number of times, and a concept can only be uttered as a word at one of those visits.

These observations can be embodied in a universal algorithm for generating sentences from conceptual graphs: start at the conceptual relation linking the subject to the main predicate, traverse every arc of every conceptual relation, and utter the word corresponding to a concept at one of the visits to its node. If a concept node is visited more than once, grammar rules determine which visit is the one when the word is uttered. The following six rules for translating a conceptual graph into a sentence are adapted from Sowa (1968):

1. The utterance path must visit each concept and relation node at least once. Each concept has an *utterance mark* that indicates whether the concept was uttered as a word. Each conceptual relation has a *traversal mark* that indicates whether the utterance path has traversed the arcs of that relation.

- The conceptual relation that links the subject of the sentence to the main predicate is the starting point of the path. For simple active sentences, it is a relation of type AGNT. For passive sentences, it is a relation of type OBJ or RCPT. In general, it may be a relation of any type.
- From a concept node *c*, the path does not return to the concept from which *c* was reached until all relations linked to *c* have been traversed.
- For relations that have not yet been traversed, syntactic and stylistic rules determine which arc to follow (e.g. in English, the path must visit adverbs of manner before adverbs of time).

2. Since the path may visit a concept several times, syntactic rules determine when that concept is uttered as a word of the sentence. Some concept types may be expressed in some languages as two words (e.g. verb-particle combinations such as *take off* or *carry out*). The separate words may be uttered at either the same or separate visits to the concept node.
3. Adjacent concepts in the graph should be expressed consecutively when possible. When Rule 1 requires the utterance path to take a branch or when Rule 2 skips a concept, the utterance must clarify the order of connections with markers such as intonation, inflection, function words, or conventionalized word order.
4. For graphs nested inside the type or referent field of a concept, the utterance path enters the nested graph when the syntactic rules determine that the containing node is to be expressed. Normally, the entire nested graph is expressed at a single visit to the node, but some syntax rules (such as the *raising rules* of transformational grammar) may permit the utterance path to exit from the nested graph, visit one or more nodes in the outer graph, and then return to finish expressing the nested graph.
5. If the graph has cycles, a concept that is reachable by two or more different paths will only be uttered once with all of its qualifiers. If syntactic rules would also express the concept at a visit reached by a different path, they must instead generate an *anaphoric expression*—either a pronoun or a short noun phrase that has the minimum number of qualifiers needed for a unique reference in the current context.
6. The utterance path is a cyclic walk that visits every node of the graph and returns to the concept that represents the main predicate. If a graph is complicated, rules of inference may break it into multiple simpler graphs before expressing it in a sentence.

These six rules allow considerable variation of word order, but they do not permit arbitrary movement of sentence constituents. If conceptual graphs are assumed to be universal deep structures and if all languages obey the same general rules for mapping graphs to sentences, then all languages must show certain regularities in their surface structures. Following are some of the implications:

- A concept is expressed only when the utterance path visits its node. Therefore, transformations can move a given constituent only to a limited number of positions in a sentence. Unlike transformational grammar, which requires special assumptions to rule out the unnatural transformations, the rules for scanning conceptual graphs have the proper constraints built into them.

- Rules 1 and 6 limit the number of times a node may be visited. In particular, when the path follows a branch of modifiers, all concepts on that branch must be expressed before the walk returns to the main concept.

- Rule 3 prevents the deeply embedded clauses in *The mailman that the dog that the girl that the boy loves owns bit is in the park.* Such a sentence skips every other concept in a chain as the walk passes in one direction; on the way back, it skips the ones expressed in the first direction. Since the single function word *that* is not sufficient to show which concepts were skipped, the deeply embedded clauses violate the rule. A better version would utter adjacent concepts in adjacent content words—either in the active form, *The boy loves the girl that owns the dog that bit the mailman that is in the park*, or in the passive form, *In the park is the mailman that was bitten by the dog that is owned by the girl that is loved by the boy.*

- Rule 4 for nested graphs has the same effect as the *cyclic convention* for applying transformations: all the transformations that apply to embedded clauses are performed before those that apply to higher clauses. But the rule also permits *raising* (Postal 1974), where constituents of a nested graph are expressed at different visits to the containing node. Consider the following graph:

```
[BELIEVE]→(OBJ)→[PROPOSITION: [PERSON:Ivan]←(CONT)←[KITCHEN]].
```

Since the agent of [BELIEVE] is not present in the graph, English inserts the empty word *it* as the subject: *It is believed that Ivan is in the kitchen.* But another rule of English grammar can raise *Ivan* to the subject position of the main clause: *Ivan is believed to be in the kitchen.* To generate this sentence, the utterance path enters the nested graph to utter *Ivan*, exits from it to utter the concept [BELIEVE], and then returns to the nested graph to finish the sentence.

Since the universal rules for translating graphs to sentences allow many options, they must be supplemented with particular rules for any specific language. The specific grammar determines which arc to select when more than one arc attached to the current node remains to be traversed. As they map concepts into content words, the grammar rules also insert function words and word inflections. The most general and flexible notation for stating grammar rules is *augmented phrase structure grammar* (APSG), which Heidorn (1972, 1975) developed for his NLP system (see Section 1.1 for a sample dialog). APSG rules have an underlying skeleton of phrase-structure grammar, but they are *augmented* with conditions to be tested and actions to be performed. Heidorn's NLP supports two types of APSG rules: *encoding rules* map graphs into sentences, and *decoding rules* map sentences into graphs.

APSG rules are extensions to a context-free grammar. The conditions for applying the rules are added on the left of the arrow, and actions are added on the right. As an example, consider the rule that defines a sentence S as a noun phrase NP followed by a verb phrase VP:

```
S ⟶ NP VP.
```

This rule does not show how the noun phrase and verb phrase are derived from a conceptual graph, nor does it show how the person and number from the NP can affect the form of the VP. In an APSG rule, each nonterminal symbol like NP or VP has a record of *attributes* that may be set or tested. The symbol on the left of the arrow represents a goal, such as *generate sentence*. That symbol is followed by *conditions* that must be true before the rule is invoked. On the right of the arrow, each symbol is followed by a list of *actions* for setting attributes or advancing the current concept node to the next node of the utterance path. Following is an example of an APSG rule, but with English comments instead of formal symbols:

```
S (conditions for applying this rule) ⟶
     NP (move the current concept node to the subject;
         get person and number from the current concept)
     VP (move the current concept node to the main ACT;
         copy person and number from the NP record;
         copy mode and tense from the S record).
```

Heidorn's encoding rules have this general form, but with a more succinct, formal notation inside the parentheses. The remainder of this section develops a notation based on Heidorn's APSG, but with symbols and terminology adapted to conceptual graphs. The technique of associating attributes with nonterminal symbols is closely related to Knuth's *attribute grammar* (1968). Kaplan and Bresnan (1982) take a similar approach in *lexical-functional grammar*, which they are developing as an alternative to Chomsky's transformational grammar.

APSG rules are a form of *production rules* that are common in AI systems. The left-hand side of each rule states the conditions for invoking it, and the right-hand side states the actions to be taken, which typically cause other rules to be invoked later. The symbol on the left of the rule (S in the above example) is the goal to be satisfied; the symbols on the right (NP and VP in the example) are subgoals to be achieved. There is a special symbol, called the *start symbol*, which is invoked by some high-level process. That symbol (S in this example) triggers the first production rule. That rule invokes the rules NP and VP, which then trigger other rules. The process continues until the *lexical rules* generate the actual words of a sentence.

The conditions and actions in APSG rules operate on *attribute-value records* associated with each nonterminal symbol. The conceptual graph is the meaning, and the *attributes* determine how it is expressed. The starting S record might have the following attributes:

```
current ○ = relation (AGNT)
tense = PAST
mode = POSSIBLE
```

Conditions on the left of an APSG rule test these attributes and the current node of the conceptual graph. Actions on the right derive further attributes either by copying them from another record or from nodes of the conceptual graph. One of the actions for VP would copy the attributes PAST and POSSIBLE from the S record to the VP record. Later, those attributes would be copied to a record for AUX, which would eventually generate the auxiliary verb *could*. The process that starts the generation creates the original attribute-value record for S. All other attributes are derived while scanning the conceptual graph.

Conditions in APSG rules may test several things: attributes in the current record, the current node of the conceptual graph, concepts and relations linked to the current node, or utterance marks on concepts and traversal marks on conceptual relations. Conditions have the form, ATTRIBUTE OPERATOR TEST; a rule may have zero or more of them. If there are no conditions, the parentheses after the nonterminal symbol are omitted; if there are two or more conditions, they are separated by semicolons. Following are some typical conditions:

```
type(○) = AGNT;
referent(□) not proper name;
number > 1;
tense not present;
□→ATTR not traversed;
```

In the conditions and actions, □ refers to the current concept node of the conceptual graph, and ○ refers to the current conceptual relation. Any of the functions defined in Chapter 3 may be used: *type*(○) retrieves the type label from the current relation, and *referent*(□) retrieves the referent of the current concept. The referent of a concept may be a proper name like Julian, an individual marker like #7189, the generic symbol *, the generic set symbol {*}, or a complete conceptual graph for concept types like PROPOSITION, whose referents may be nested graphs. If the attribute is just a single word like *number* or *tense*, it refers to the record associated with the current nonterminal symbol. The third condition above tests whether the current record has a plural number, and the fourth one tests whether the tense attribute is missing. The symbol □→ATTR refers to the subgraph consisting of the current concept node □ linked by an arc pointing to a conceptual relation of type ATTR.

On the right side of the arrow, three kinds of actions may occur: assignment, move, and mark. Assignment specifies values for the attributes in a record, move specifies the direction of movement along the utterance path, and mark indicates which nodes had already been visited.

■ When an APSG rule is invoked, the records for the symbols on the right of the arrow have no predefined attributes. An assignment causes a new attribute to be created for a record and assigns it a value:

```
voice := ACTIVE;
number := count(referent(□));
tense := tense of VP;
```

The first assignment simply causes the voice attribute of the current record to have the value ACTIVE. The second one counts the number of individuals in the referent of the current concept and assigns it to the number attribute of the current record. The third one copies the tense of a previous VP record to the tense of the current record. Such copies may only be made from a record of a nonterminal symbol in the current rule that occurs *before* the symbol to which the copy is being made.

■ Move causes the symbol □ or ○ to advance to the next node of the utterance path. All records in a rule start with the node □ at the same point. A move action for a given record affects only that record and not any other record in the rule:

```
move AGNT→□;
move OBJ←□;
```

The first move causes the current concept node to become the one linked to the arc pointing *away* from the relation of type AGNT. The second one causes the current concept to be the one linked to the arc pointing *towards* the relation of type AGNT.

■ Mark sets the utterance mark on a concept or the traversal mark on a conceptual relation:

```
mark □→ATTR traversed;
mark □ uttered;
```

The first one sets the traversal mark on the relation of type ATTR that is linked to the current concept node, and the second sets the utterance mark on the current concept node.

The symbol □ is the equivalent of a *cursor* that advances from left to right when a linear language is being parsed. Since conceptual graphs are not linear, □ is not automatically advanced, and the rules must include explicit move actions to advance □ and mark actions to keep it from returning to previously visited nodes.

With this notation for conditions and actions, the APSG rule that defines S may be stated. The condition for invoking the S rule is that the current relation node ○ must be of type AGNT:

```
S (type(○)=AGNT) ⟶
      NP (move AGNT→□; mark AGNT→□ traversed;
          case := NOMINATIVE;
          person := person(referent(□));
          number := count(referent(□)))
      VP (move AGNT←□; voice := ACTIVE;
          tense := tense of S; mode := mode of S;
          person := person of NP; number := number of NP).
```

On the right of the arrow, the actions for the NP record move the current concept node □ to the concept attached to the arc pointing away from the node ○, mark ○ traversed so that no other rule will traverse it again, set the case attribute NOMINATIVE (needed for pronouns, but not for nouns in English), and finally get the person and number attributes from □. The actions for VP move the node □ to the concept attached to the arc pointing towards ○, set the voice attribute ACTIVE, copy the tense and mode attributes from the original S node, and copy the person and number attributes from the record for the preceding NP node.

If sentence generation had started at a relation of type other than AGNT, the preceding rule would not apply. In that case, the system would search for another rule. If the starting relation had been of type OBJ, it would generate a sentence in passive voice:

```
S (type(○)=OBJ) ⟶
      NP (move OBJ→□; mark OBJ→□ traversed;
          case := NOMINATIVE;
          person := person(referent(□));
          number := count(referent(□)))
      VP (move OBJ←□; voice := PASSIVE;
          tense := tense of S; mode := mode of S;
          person := person of NP; number := number of NP).
```

The form of this rule is identical to the previous one, but the voice attribute of the VP record is now set to PASSIVE, and the NP node is generated from the object of the action instead of the agent. Other rules that apply to a VP record in passive voice generate a form of the verb *be* and the preposition *by* for the agent (if it is present in the graph).

Unlike transformational grammar, APSG rules need no global movement operations that transpose subject and object. When sentence generation is started at OBJ instead of AGNT, the rules methodically move from node to node in the conceptual graph and end up with a globally well-formed passive sentence. At no time do the rules ever consider anything but local information in nearby nodes of a conceptual graph or records for the current APSG rule. The following rule expands a VP in passive voice in order to generate a form of the verb *be* followed by the main verb as a past participle:

```
VP (voice=PASSIVE) ⟶
      VERB (type := BE; tense := tense of VP; mode := mode of VP;
            person := person of VP; number := number of VP)
      VP (form := PASTPART).
```

The VERB record has the verb type set to BE; the tense, mode, person, and number are copied from the original VP record on the left. The only attribute for the new VP record on the right of the arrow is the form attribute set to PASTPART. The new VP no longer has any information about tense, mode, person, or number. The type of the main verb is not stated in the record. When the verb type is needed, it is copied from the current □ node of the conceptual graph.

Passive verb phrases can be generated either for main verbs in passive voice or for participial phrases modifying nouns, as in the following sentences:

```
The books were distributed by the teacher.
Niurka ordered books distributed by the teacher.
Niurka ordered books that were distributed by the teacher.
```

In all three sentences, the phrase *distributed by the teacher* has exactly the same form and, for economy, should be generated by exactly the same grammar rules. Following is an APSG rule for noun phrases modified by past participial phrases:

```
NP (□←OBJ not traversed) ⟶
      NP (mark OBJ traversed; case := case of NP)
      VP (move OBJ←□; form := PASTPART).
```

Transformational grammar generates the participial phrase *distributed by the teacher* by deleting *that were* from the relative clause. Yet clauses are more cumbersome constructions than participial phrases. With APSG rules, participial phrases and infinitives are generated directly by the simpler rules, and clauses are generated as special options for greater emphasis.

The AGNT relation is expressed by the preposition *by* in passive verb phrases, but it is not expressed by any special morpheme in a simple active sentence. The following rule generates a prepositional phrase for the agent in passive form:

```
VP (form=PASTPART; AGNT←□ not traversed) ⟶
      VP (form := PASTPART; mark AGNT traversed)
      PP (type := BY; move AGNT→□).
```

The concept [BOOK:{*}], which is uttered as *books*, is the object of both [ORDER] and [DISTRIBUTE] in the following graph:

```
[PERSON:Niurka]→(AGNT)→[ORDER]-
   (OBJ)→[BOOK:{*}]←(OBJ)←[DISTRIBUTE]←(AGNT)←[TEACHER:#].
```

If the utterance path starts at the AGNT relation attached to [ORDER], APSG rules generate the sentence *Niurka ordered books distributed by the teacher.* If the path had started at the AGNT relation linked to [DISTRIBUTE], the same rules would generate the sentence *The teacher distributed books ordered by Niurka.*

Verb phrases may also include adverbs, direct objects, indirect objects, and prepositional phrases. Following is a rule that generates adverbs:

```
VP (□→MANR not traversed) ⟶
      ADV (move MANR→□; mark MANR traversed)
      VP (vform := vform of VP).
```

Since some attributes always occur together, they may be grouped in a collection that can be copied with a single assignment. The name vform represents the attributes tense, mode, person, and number. The next rule generates direct objects:

```
VP (□→OBJ not traversed) ⟶
      VP (vform := vform of VP)
      NP (move OBJ→□; mark OBJ traversed;
         case := OBJECTIVE).
```

After all the conceptual relations for the verb phrase have been processed, the following rule generates the verb itself:

```
VP ⟶ VERB (type := type(□); vform := vform of VP).
```

The rules for each nonterminal symbol are ordered. In determining which rule to execute next, the system performs the first one for which the conditions are true. The simple rule that defines VP as just a VERB should therefore be the last one in the list for VP. Since it has no conditions, it will always succeed, and no subsequent VP rule would ever be performed.

To generate noun phrases, the next rule defines NP as a sequence of determiner, adjective, and noun:

```
NP (referent(□) not proper name; □→ATTR not traversed) ⟶
      DET (referent := referent(□))
      ADJ (move ATTR→□; mark ATTR traversed)
      NOUN (type := type(□); number := count(referent(□))).
```

This applies only when the referent of the current node □ is not a proper name and the node □ is linked to a relation of type ATTR. The action associated with DET extracts information from the referent of □, the action for ADJ moves along the utterance path to the node on the other side of the ATTR relation, and the action for NOUN extracts the type and number of the referent of □.

After the phrase-structure rules have been applied, lower-level, *lexical rules* must be used to generate the actual words of the language. The lexical rules take into account the concept type, the syntactic category, and other attributes of the nonterminal symbol. What they generate is the actual character string (or in the case of spoken language, a string of phonemes):

```
NOUN (type=BABY; number>1) ⟶ "babies".
NOUN (type=BABY; number=1) ⟶ "baby".
VERB (type=DRINK; tense=PAST) ⟶ "drank".
```

The same concept type may be mapped into different word forms for different syntactic categories:

```
NOUN (type=DISTRIBUTE; number=1) ⟶ "distribution".
VERB (type=DISTRIBUTE; number>1; tense=PAST) ⟶ "distributed".
```

In principle, a separate lexical rule may be stated for every word form. In practice, however, a unified morphological stage would look up each concept type in a dictionary and generate the appropriate word for it. The morphological stage can take account of regular rules like *-s* for most plural nouns and apply special rules only for exceptions. It could be a much simpler routine than the APSG processor since it would only have to consider adjacent words in order to generate the article *a* before a consonant or *an* before a vowel.

Generating correct articles in English is difficult because the words *the* and *a* have many different uses. At the first mention of an object, the indefinite article *a* usually introduces it, but subsequent references use the definite article *the*. Often, however, *the* is used to refer to an object that is implicitly introduced into the context: *Do you have a 1982 penny? I want to check the weight.* Although the weight of the coin was not explicitly mentioned, all the usual attributes of an object may be assumed as part of the current context whenever the object itself is introduced. Besides their use in specifying individuals, the articles *the* and *a* are also used in a generic sense:

```
The horse is a noble animal.
A dog is an animal.
```

A complete study of English articles requires a major treatise. As a simplified example, the following three APSG rules generate *the* if the concept is individual, generate *a* if it is generic, and generate the empty string ε if it is a generic set (plural):

```
DET (referent(□) is individual) ⟶ "the".
DET (referent(□)=*) ⟶ "a".
DET (referent(□)={*}) ⟶ ε.
```

The conditions inside the parentheses could be elaborated to make finer distinctions.

Prepositions are usually generated from conceptual relations rather than concept nodes. They are especially sensitive to the direction of the utterance path. Consider the following subgraph of Fig. 5.6:

```
[BABY: {*}]→(PART)→[BELLY: {*}].
```

If the utterance path is moving from [BABY] to [BELLY], the resulting phrase would be *babies with bellies*. But if it is moving from [BELLY] to [BABY], the result would be *bellies of babies*. Unlike lexical rules for nouns and verbs, the rules for generating prepositions depend on the direction of the utterance path. Following is a rule for generating prepositional phrases:

```
PP ⟶
     PREP (type := type of PP; direction := direction of PP)
     NP (case := OBJECTIVE).
```

Since there are no conditions on the left, this rule applies whenever a prepositional phrase is being generated. Since there is no move stated in the action lists, both PREP and NP have the same □ node as PP. The type and direction are copied from the PP record to the PREP record, and the NP record has the case attribute set to OBJECTIVE. In English, the case is needed for pronouns, but it is ignored for nouns. German would set the case attribute DATIVE for some prepositions and ACCUSATIVE for others. The lexical rules for prepositions come in pairs depending on the direction of the utterance path. Following are the rules for the PART and CONT (content) relations:

```
PREP (type=PART; direction="→") ⟶ "of".
PREP (type=PART; direction="←") ⟶ "with".
PREP (type=CONT; direction="→") ⟶ "with".
PREP (type=CONT; direction="←") ⟶ "in".
```

Note that there is no one-to-one mapping between relations and prepositions. Besides the PART and CONT relations, the preposition *with* is also used to express the INST (instrument) and ACCM (accompaniment) relations.

One of Fillmore's principles of case grammar is that the agent, if present, becomes the subject. If the agent is missing, then the next choice for subject is the instrument. When the utterance path starts at a relation (INST), the following APSG rule is invoked:

```
S (type(○)=INST) ⟶
     NP (move INST→□; mark INST traversed;
          person := person(referent(□));
          number := count(referent(□)))
     VP (move INST←□; set voice ACTIVE;
          person := person of NP; number := number of NP).
```

If the earlier rule for S failed, then this one would be tried next. If these conditions also failed, then the system would continue to scan the list of rules for S until it found one whose conditions were satisfied. At the end of the list, there could be a default rule like the following that would print an error message:

```
S ⟶ "Sorry, I don't know how to say what I mean."
```

Since this rule has no conditions, it will always succeed if invoked. But since it offers little help, it is a last resort.

To generate a sentence in Japanese, the following rule generates the SOV word order. It also sets attributes of the noun phrases to generate the postpositions *ga* and *o*, which indicate subject and object in Japanese:

```
S (AGNT←□ not traversed; OBJ←□ not traversed) ⟶
    NP (move AGNT→□; postposition := "ga")
    NP (move OBJ→□; postposition := "o")
    VERB (mark AGNT traversed; mark OBJ traversed).
```

Appropriate changes in the rules could generate the word order for any of the other languages, such as Hebrew or French. Type labels like BIRD and BABY happen to look like English words, but they represent abstract concepts. For generating French, lexical rules like the following could be used:

```
NOUN (type=BIRD; number=1) ⟶ "oiseau".
NOUN (type=BIRD; number>1) ⟶ "oiseaux".
```

The APSG rules described in this section have been adapted from Heidorn's encoding rules in NLP. The primary difference is that this notation is specialized for conceptual graphs, but the NLP rules can process any kind of graphs. The NLP rules also use a more compact notation that is not as immediately readable as the rules given here. All of these rules, however, could be mapped into NLP rules on a one-for-one basis. Using such rules, Heidorn's NLPQ system (1972) was able to map conceptual graphs into the following paragraph:

> The vehicles arrive at the station. The time between arrivals of the vehicles at the station is normally distributed, with a mean of 8 minutes and a standard deviation of 2 minutes. 75 percent of the vehicles are cars, and the rest are trucks. After arriving at the station, if the length of the line at the pump in the station is less than 2, the vehicles will be serviced at the pump in the station. Otherwise, the vehicles will leave the station. The time for the vehicles to be serviced at the pump in the station is exponentially distributed, with a mean of 5 minutes for the cars, and 9 minutes for the trucks. After being serviced at the pump in the station, the vehicles leave the station.

The conceptual graphs that were mapped into this paragraph were generated from the dialog described in Section 1.1.

In generating sentences, APSG rules are invoked in a top-down, goal-directed fashion. The algorithm starts with a single goal—generate sentence, generate paragraph, or even generate story. The initial goal contains a pointer to some node of a conceptual graph: if the goal is to generate a sentence, the pointer would usually select a concept corresponding to the main verb; if the goal is to generate a paragraph or story, the pointer might select a time-ordered sequence of actions, each of which represents a single sentence. The rule invoked for the initial goal makes some tests on the conceptual graph and generates other subgoals—generate noun phrase or generate verb phrase—each of which makes its own tests and generates further subgoals down to such low-level goals as generating a present tense, third-person, singular form of *be*. As each rule invokes other rules as subgoals, the APSG processor makes a cyclic walk of the conceptual graph: the goal of generating a sentence starts at the relation between subject and main predicate, that goal generates a subgoal that follows the AGNT link to the subject, which may in turn generate further subgoals that follow links for adjectives and other modifiers. When each subgoal is finished, the walk returns to the node that invoked it. At the end, the highest-level subgoal returns to the topmost goal, which corresponds to the starting node of the conceptual graph.

Unlike parsing programs, which use many different techniques, most language generators use top-down algorithms. Simmons and Slocum (1972) and Wong (1975) use *augmented transition nets*, which are normally executed in a top-down fashion. Wong took care to generate correct anaphoric expressions: when introducing an event, his program would say, for example, *A boy broke a window*; but when referring back to the boy, it would say *he*, *the boy*, or *the boy who broke the window*, depending on the amount of detail needed to specify the referent uniquely. Goldman's BABEL (1975) is a top-down program for mapping Schank's conceptual dependency graphs into English. One of Goldman's innovations was to make word choices based on *word-sense discrimination nets*. Since Schank's theory now permits high-level concept types like ADMIT and THREATEN, the major discriminations could be made by an earlier inference stage. BABEL, however, had to make all the word choices itself since its input graphs contained only low-level primitives. Although these authors do not use the term *utterance path* and they do not use the APSG notation, their algorithms are similar at an abstract level: they execute rules in a top-down order, the graph serves as a control for selecting rules, and the order of processing nodes may be described as an utterance path.

Although APSG rules have an underlying skeleton of phrase-structure rules, they should be called a mapping grammar, rather than a generative grammar. The mapping from graphs to language meets Chomsky's original goals of relating multiple surface structures to a common deep structure, but with some major advantages:

- *Psychological naturalness.* Graphs are generated by rules of inference and pragmatics, which deal with meaning, rather than rules of syntax that only deal with the forms of expression.

- *Computational efficiency.* Unlike transformational rules that move large constituents during the generation stage, APSG rules obtain the effects of transformations merely by changing the direction of the utterance path. Since the rules generate words one at a time as they are uttered, they reduce the demands on computer storage (or on human short-term memory).

- *Theoretical simplicity.* Constraints on transformations arise from the connectivity of the graphs and the possible ways of scanning them. No special assumptions are needed to block transformations that never occur in natural languages because such transformations violate the universal rules that govern the utterance path.

To give a point-by-point comparison of conceptual graphs with transformational grammar is beyond the scope of this book. But the notion of *traces* (Chomsky 1977) illustrates the difference between the two approaches. A trace is a residue of a noun phrase that has been moved by a transformation. It has no sound itself, but it changes the intonation pattern of the sentence and blocks certain kinds of contractions. The following example shows the trace *t* that is left when *what* is moved to the front of a sentence by the question transformation:

```
Ruby gave what to Clara?
What did Ruby give t to Clara?
```

In terms of Chomsky's approach, a trace is like a "silent pronoun" that is left behind when a noun phrase is moved from one position in a sentence to another. In terms of conceptual graphs, such fictitious pronouns are not needed: the point at which a trace occurs is a point where the utterance path visits a concept whose utterance mark is set on. The blocking of contractions is caused by a break in normal processing when the utterance path stops at a node and bypasses it. The rules for scanning conceptual graphs explain the same kinds of phenomena as transformational grammar, but with a simpler formalism and better motivated assumptions.

5.5 SYNTACTIC ANALYSIS

Ambiguities cause more problems for a parser than for a generator. Since conceptual graphs are unambiguous, the scanner that generates English is a deterministic program whose execution time is linearly proportional to the number of nodes and arcs in the graph. The parser that interprets English, however, requires more information about syntax, semantics, and context to resolve all possible ambiguities. If the parser takes enough information into account, it too can run in time that is linearly proportional to the length of the sentence. The constant of proportionality, however, may be much larger than the constant for the language generator. Boguraev (1979), for example, wrote both a parser that mapped English into a conceptual representation and a generator that mapped the concepts back into English. For a typical ten-word sentence, the parser took about 500 to 800 milliseconds of CPU time to interpret the input, while the generator took only 7 milliseconds to generate its output—a difference of two orders of magnitude.

It seems paradoxical for interpretation to be slower than generation. For people, reading or listening takes less effort than writing or speaking. But the effort that people exert supports more function than Boguraev's program. To generate English, it simply mapped a graph to an English sentence. But people have to think of an idea, work out its consequences, relate it to the context, and finally map it to words and sentences. Of all these steps, the last is the easiest.

The word *parse* comes from the Latin *pars orationis* (part of speech). The basic function of a parser is to determine the function of each word in a sentence—not only its part of speech but also the way it is grouped in phrases with other words. The options for doing the analysis, representing the results, and organizing the algorithms lead to many different approaches, all of which work some of the time and none of which work all of the time. To clarify the issues, the following checklist presents the options that can be taken in designing a parser:

- *Syntactic, semantic, or conceptual.* In a syntactic parser, tests of the input string are based on grammatical categories such as NOUN or VERB. In a semantic parser, the tests are based on concept types such as HUMAN, MOVEMENT, CITY, or SHIP. In a conceptual parser, expectations from the conceptual graph that is being constructed play just as important a role in controlling the analysis as the tests of the current input. In programming terms, a semantic parser differs from a syntactic parser only in the number and kinds of categories it uses; a conceptual parser, however, must adopt a systematic algorithm for dealing with both the input string and the conceptual feedback.

- *Integrated, staged, or coroutined.* An integrated parser uses both syntax and semantics at each point during the processing. A staged parser first uses syntax to generate all possible parses and then uses semantics to filter out the unacceptable ones. Integrated parsers are like *one-pass compilers*, which generate all their output in a single pass over the input. Staged parsers are like *multi-pass compilers*, where each pass translates the result of the previous pass into a notation that is closer to the final form. Like a staged parser, a coroutined parser has separate procedures for morphology, syntax, and semantics, but they operate concurrently so that feedback from the semantic stage can be used to control the processing at the syntactic stage.

- *Top-down, bottom-up, or bidirectional.* A top-down parser is *goal directed*: it starts with the highest goal, *parse sentence*; each goal then invokes the next lower subgoal until the parser reaches the lowest goals like *find noun* or *find verb*. A bottom-up parser is *data directed*: it starts with the input words and combines them into higher level phrases and sentences. Bidirectional parsers combine the two approaches: certain input words trigger rules in a data-directed way, but those rules invoke goals that invoke other subgoals in a top-down way.

- *Backtracking, parallel, or lookahead.* Natural languages are *nondeterministic*. At many points during the parsing, it is not possible to determine uniquely what rule should be tried next. At each *choice point*, a backtracking parser selects a likely rule and continues; if that choice does not work, it backs up to the last choice point and tries some other rule. A parallel parser proceeds in parallel along each possible option; the incorrect parses eventually lead to dead ends, while the correct one continues to be expanded until it covers the entire input sentence. A lookahead parser scans ahead in the input string to gather enough information to narrow down the options to a single, correct choice.

- *Rule-driven or procedural.* A grammar rule is a declarative statement about the way phrases are combined. The following rule, for example, declares that a sentence S consists of a noun phrase NP followed by a verb phrase VP:

```
S ⟶ NP VP.
```

A rule-driven parser applies rules like this to analyze the structure of the input string. A procedural parser consists of programming statements that first search for a noun phrase and then search for a verb phrase. Yet the distinction between rule-driven and procedural is not sharp: the rules in some parsers are actually procedures written in a special notation that happens to look like declarative grammar rules.

- *Interpreted or compiled.* Some rule-driven parsers are *interpreters* that spend time in analyzing the grammar rules each time they are used. Other systems compile the rules into tables or procedures that run more efficiently. Still other systems can run either interpretively or compiled. Woods (1970) and Heidorn (1972) originally wrote interpreters for their rules. Later, they developed compilers that translated the rules into LISP functions, which were then compiled directly into machine language.

- *Rule selection.* Some criteria are necessary for selecting the next rule or procedure to be invoked. A top-down parser has a small option list of subgoals that can be chosen at each stage. In a bottom-up parser, all rules are potentially available at all times, and a *pattern-directed* scheme is required for finding the most appropriate rule. Mückstein (1979) designed a bottom-up parser where the rule selection was controlled by a finite-state machine that produced a top-down effect. The control mechanism serves two purposes: first, it can improve efficiency by selecting the most probable rules to try; second, it enforces constraints that raise the power of the parser from context free to context sensitive.

- *Exception handling.* A parser should produce the single best parse for every sentence. If it cannot, the fault may lie in some inadequacy in the parser, in a limitation of the grammar or semantics used to drive the parser, or in actual errors in the input sentence. If more than one parse is possible, some systems present a menu of options and ask the user which one is correct. If no parse is possible, some systems give up and print a message like "I don't understand," other systems try simple options like spelling correction, and still others try relaxing the constraints to allow the parser to handle ungrammatical sentences.

Multiplying all the options gives hundreds of possible combinations, of which a few dozen have been implemented. The ideal parser would run fast, generate one correct parse for every sentence, and be easy to modify and extend for new vocabulary and domains of discourse. Many parsers are good enough for practical applications, but none of them have attained the ideal.

One of the oldest parsing methods that is still widely used in practical compilers is *recursive descent* (Lucas 1961, Knuth 1971). It is a top-down method that starts from the highest goal, such as *parse sentence*, and invokes other subgoals, many of which call each other recursively, until it reaches low-level goals like *find noun* or *find verb*. It is popular because it is easy to understand, runs fast, and can be implemented without special parser generators or compiler-compilers. Although it is good for most programming languages, it has one fatal flaw for natural languages: it cannot parse any language that has ambiguities or nondeterminism. Despite the flaw, it is worth studying for two reasons: it clearly illustrates the issues between rule-driven and procedural techniques, and all other top-down parsing methods can be viewed as extensions or refinements of it.

The basic idea of recursive descent is simple: every nonterminal symbol maps into a procedure. The grammar rule that defines a sentence as a noun phrase followed by a verb phrase corresponds to a procedure named S, which calls a procedure named NP and then calls another procedure named VP. Additional housekeeping statements must be inserted into each procedure to keep track of the input string, the current word being examined, the result being generated, and the error messages to be returned if the input string is not recognized. The global variable *cursor* is a pointer to the current word being examined; it is advanced by the lower-level procedures that match individual words of input.

```
procedure S(r: parsed result or error message) is
r1: parsed result of NP;
r2: parsed result of VP;
begin;
    save current value of cursor;
    call NP and get r1;
    if r1 shows failure to find noun phrase then
        r := error message;
        reset cursor;
        return;
    end if;
    call VP and get r2;
    if r2 shows failure to find verb phrase then
        r := error message;
        reset cursor;
        return;
    end if;
    r := combination of r1 and r2;
end S;
```

Since every procedure in a recursive descent parser has this basic structure, a top-down parser could simply interpret the original grammar rule as though it were the procedure S. It would automatically save and restore the cursor, check the error messages, and pass the parsed result back to the calling procedure. Additional operators can be added to the notation for testing and setting features like singular or plural, transitive or intransitive, and various semantic conditions.

If there is more than one grammar rule with the same left-hand side, they must all be grouped into a single rule. The following three rules, for example, say that a verb phrase VP consists of a verb followed by either a noun phrase NP, a prepositional phrase PP, or nothing:

```
VP ⟶ VERB NP.
VP ⟶ VERB PP.
VP ⟶ VERB.
```

All three rules could be replaced by a single rule with three options:

```
VP ⟶ VERB {NP | PP | ε}.
```

where the symbol ε represents the empty string. This rule corresponds to a procedure named VP that first calls VERB and then executes a three-option **case**-statement: look for NP; if not found, look for PP; if not found, leave the **case**-statement. In general, option lists in a grammar rule map into **case**-statements, and iterations map into loops. The following rule defines NP as an optional determiner DET, zero or more adjectives ADJ, and a required NOUN:

```
NP ⟶ [DET] [ADJ]... NOUN.
```

This rule would be mapped into a procedure with a **while**-loop for matching a list of adjectives. The loop could also be replaced by a *recursive rule* for a list of adjectives ADJLIST:

```
ADJLIST ⟶ {ADJ ADJLIST | ε}.
```

This rule calls itself recursively, but only after it has matched an ADJ in the input. It can keep calling itself as many times as necessary to match all the adjectives in the input stream. When it runs out of adjectives, it chooses the empty string ε. If no adjectives are present at all, it chooses ε at the first call. As a result, the recursive rule ADJLIST matches the same input as the iteration [ADJ]....

Some kinds of recursion are safe, but *left recursion* creates problems. The following rule, for example, says that an NP may be an NP modified by a prepositional phrase PP, a participial phrase PARTP, a relative clause RELCLAUSE, or nothing:

```
NP ⟶ NP {PP | PARTP | RELCLAUSE | ε}.
```

If this rule were translated into a procedure named NP, its first executable statement would be to call NP, which would call NP, which would call NP, and keep looping until storage was exhausted. This rule is *left recursive* because the leftmost symbol in the definition of NP is NP itself. The rule ADJLIST does not create a problem because the recursive call occurs later in the rule. A recursive rule is safe only if some critical condition changes each time the rule is invoked (e.g. the call to ADJ advances the cursor to the next word of input). To eliminate the left recursion, use the following two rules to define NP:

```
NP ⟶ [DET] [ADJ]... NOUN NPMODS.
NPMODS ⟶ {PP NPMODS | PARTP NPMODS | RELCLAUSE NPMODS | ε}.
```

The NPMODS rule matches a list of zero or more complex modifiers: prepositional phrases, participial phrases, and relative clauses. The two rules NP and NPMODS accept the same input as the previous rules for NP, but NPMODS contains only safe recursions instead of the dangerous left recursion. With iteration, these two rules can be reduced to just a single rule:

```
NP ⟶ [DET] [ADJ]... NOUN [PP | PARTP | RELCLAUSE]...
```

In this example, iteration leads to simpler rules than recursion. But recursion is necessary for embedded constructions, which cannot be handled by simple iteration.

Left recursion can be eliminated by revising the grammar. Nondeterminism is a more serious problem that cannot, in general, be eliminated. In the next two sentences, for example, the first five words are identical:

```
The children left by themselves .
The children left by themselves ate the cookies .
```

Until the parser reaches the sixth word ("ate" or "."), it cannot determine whether the children are the agents or the objects of *left*. In the first sentence, *left* is the main verb; in the second, *ate* is the main verb, and *left* is a participle modifying *children*. A *nondeterminism* occurs when the parser reaches a point where it cannot determine which rule to apply next without looking ahead some unpredictable distance. An *ambiguity* occurs when the nondeterminism cannot be resolved even by searching all the way to the end of the sentence. Every ambiguity is a nondeterminism, but some grammars are nondeterministic without being ambiguous.

One way of handling nondeterminism is *backtracking*: upon encountering a list of options, choose one of them, but set a pointer to the next *choice point*. If the first option leads to a dead end, go back to the most recent choice point and try again. Consider the sentence *The children left by themselves ate the cookies* and its parsing by the following grammar rules. (To simplify the discussion, this NP rule has fewer options than the previous NP rule, but the principle is the same.)

```
S ⟶ NP VP
NP ⟶ DET NOUN {PP | PARTP | ε}.
VP ⟶ VERB NP.
```

In parsing the sentence, the starting goal S invokes the first subgoal NP. Then NP calls DET to match *the* and NOUN to match *children*. Next NP invokes PP, but the word *left* is not a preposition. NP therefore tries the next option PARTP, which matches the phrase *left by themselves*. Having successfully matched that option, NP returns to the S rule, which then invokes the next subgoal VP. Then VP invokes the subgoal VERB, which matches *ate*. The final NP matches *the cookies*, and the sentence is parsed successfully. The only failure was the attempt to match PP to *left*, but the parser immediately recovered with PARTP.

For the sentence *The children left by themselves*, more backtracking is necessary. The parser proceeds as before until it tries to match VERB to ".". When this match fails, the cursor has advanced far beyond the word *left*, which should be matched to VERB. In simple recursive descent, the parser has no way of recovering from a wrong choice made by a rule like NP, which has already finished. With backtracking, however, the parser keeps a record of the environment each time it reaches a list of options. When it finds the failure, it reactivates the NP rule, goes back to the list of options, moves the cursor back to *left*, and takes the empty option ε. Then *left* can be matched when the VERB rule is reinvoked.

A popular top-down backtracking parser is based on *transition nets*, originally developed by Conway (1963) for a COBOL compiler. For handling natural languages, a number of AI researchers extended and refined Conway's method to *augmented transition nets* (ATNs), which perform tests and structure-building operations during the parse. The basic idea is to translate a grammar into a collection of finite state machines or state transition nets that can call one another recursively. Without recursion, the nets are limited to parsing finite-state languages. With recursion but without backtracking, they are exactly equivalent to recursive descent. With backtracking, they are powerful enough to parse any context-free language. With the augmented operators, they are as powerful as a Turing machine. Following are the stages in the evolution of ATNs:

- Conway's original nets supported recursion and backtracking as well as *coroutines* that permit lexical analysis, syntactic analysis, and code generation to run concurrently.

- Thorne et al. (1968) applied a form of recursive transition net to natural language parsing. Instead of backtracking, however, it generated all parses in parallel. The most important contribution was the addition of operators for generating the deep structure of a sentence in a single pass through the input and for testing the partially completed structures to guide the later stages of the parse.

- Although Thorne's parser could handle many linguistic transformations, it was not general enough to handle all of them. Bobrow and Fraser (1969) developed a more general ATN that used arbitrary LISP functions for the structure building and testing operators.

- Bobrow and Fraser's parser was as general as a Turing machine, but it was, in fact, too general. Any operation whatever could be performed in LISP, and they had no guidelines for restricting the operations to a well-structured set. Woods (1970) systematized the ATN formalism by providing a standard set of operators instead of *ad hoc* LISP functions.

■ In Woods' 1970 version of ATNs, the parser first generated all possible parses and then did the semantic interpretation in a later stage. With *cascaded ATNs*, Woods (1980) developed a form that could process syntax and semantics concurrently. The cascades are similar to Conway's original coroutines, but each cascade is itself an ATN. Cascaded ATNs have been used successfully in the RUS parser (R. Bobrow 1978); front-end cascades handle syntax while back-end cascades build the semantic representation.

A practical advantage of ATNs is their graphical notation for grammars, but the notation by itself has no theoretical importance. ATNs actually have two notations: one is the graphical form based on collections of finite-state machines that can call each other recursively, and the other is the executable form that looks like LISP with GOTO statements. Some people have pointed to the graphical form and claimed that ATNs are more readable than phrase structure grammars. Others have pointed to the executable form and argued that grammar rules correspond to a better structured style with recursion, iteration, and option lists, while the ATNs are a tangled mass of GOTOs. The arguments on both sides are exactly equivalent to the arguments for and against flowcharts, structured programming, and GOTOs, since any grammar in one form can be converted to an equivalent grammar in the other form. Which version one chooses is a matter of taste and convenience.

Just as transition nets can be augmented with operations for building and testing structures, ordinary phrase structure grammar can be extended to *augmented phrase structure grammar* (APSG). Heidorn's NLP system (1972) has a bottom-up, parallel parser driven by APSG rules like the following:

```
NP (conditions)  VP (conditions)  ⟶  S (actions).
```

Like the APSG rules for language generation, the left-hand side specifies conditions to be tested, and the right-hand side specifies structure-building actions. The following rule handles nominalized verb phrases like *the dispersal by the wind*:

```
VP(NOM,¬AGNT)  PP('BY')  ⟶  VP1(%VP,AGNT=ENTY(OBJ(PP))).
```

On the left are two phrases found so far: a VP with the NOM attribute (nominalization) and no AGNT attribute, followed by a prepositional phrase PP with *by* as the preposition. On the right is the new structure to be built: another verb phrase of type VP1 containing a copy of the original VP record (indicated by %VP) and with its AGNT attribute set to the entity that is the object of the preposition *by*. In Heidorn's first major application, NLPQ, the rules combine syntax and semantics while parsing. In a grammar checking program (Heidorn et al. 1982), NLP uses almost no semantics in order to process texts on any subject whatever. Besides Heidorn's bottom-up parser, other people have implemented top-down parsers for APSGs that are equivalent to ATNs both in their parsing power and their mode of operation. An example of such a system is DIAGRAM by Robinson (1982). The *metamorphosis grammars* based on PROLOG (Colmerauer 1978) are equivalent to APSGs that are executed in a top-down mode.

Bottom-up parsers start growing their parse trees from low-level constituents (individual words) up to the highest levels like NP, VP, and finally S. In a top-down parser, a high-level goal like S is first given control, and it determines which subgoals to try next. To handle nondeterminism, top-down parsers use backtracking: they pursue one goal as far as possible; if that goal fails, they back up to a previous choice point and try a different goal. Bottom-up parsers, by contrast, often apply all rules in parallel. Kay (1967, 1977) designed a *chart parser* that represents all partial analyses of the input. If more than one rule matches some part of the current chart, the parser does some work for each of them and updates the chart with the new results. When the parser reaches the end of the sentence, each completed path through the chart represents one possible parse; incomplete paths are ignored.

With sufficient lookahead, a bottom-up parser can be completely deterministic. Marcus (1980) implemented PARSIFAL, a bottom-up parser with a buffer that can hold three partially processed phrases. In parsing English, the information needed to make a choice may be arbitrarily many *words* ahead. But Marcus maintained that for normal sentences, the correct choice could be made by looking no farther than three *phrases* ahead. In effect, PARSIFAL adopts a "wait and see" attitude: it scans up to three phrases before deciding how to link them together.

The procedural-declarative controversy affects parsers as well as other AI systems. Procedural parsers were among the first ones to be implemented: the English question-answering program, Baseball, had a procedural parser whose flowcharts took 13 pages for the syntax and another 47 pages for the semantics (Green et al. 1963; Wolf et al. 1963). Winograd's PROGRAMMAR (1972), which served as the parser for SHRDLU, is a more recent example of a procedural parser. It uses recursive descent with a form of backtracking that is under the programmer's control. But such procedural parsers have two fundamental weaknesses:

- *Nonextendibility.* They bind up so many application dependencies with the grammar and semantics that any change requires a major programming effort.

- *Size.* Robinson's DIAGRAM, which supports a richer coverage of English than either Baseball or SHRDLU, takes only 3 pages of APSG rules compared to 13 pages of flowcharts for Baseball. All the rules for noun phrases and their modifiers take 19 lines in DIAGRAM compared to 70 lines of LISP code for just an "excerpt" from the noun phrase parser of PROGRAMMAR.

Even though APSGs and ATNs are rule-driven, their rules may be viewed as miniature programs written in a highly specialized language. In effect, even the rule-driven parsers are procedural. Their procedures, however, are written in a structured way that makes them hardly distinguishable from declarations.

5.6 INTEGRATING SYNTAX AND SEMANTICS

One of the most heated controversies in computational linguistics concerns the roles of syntax and semantics. Purely syntactic parsers, such as Kuno and Oettinger's predictive syntactic analyzer, find an enormous number of ambiguities. Quillian (1966) countered that his program could resolve the ambiguities with a semantic analysis that used almost no syntax. Since then, people have implemented parsers with nearly every possible proportion of syntax and semantics—ranging from syntactic parsers with a highly refined set of categories to conceptual parsers that take into account the subject under discussion, the author's intent, and even the current state of the database. From the debate, some general conclusions may be drawn:

- Without semantics, a program would have no guidelines for choosing the best of the ambiguous parses.
- Without syntax, a program would miss distinctions like the following that have a major impact on meaning (Boguraev 1979):

```
John stopped to help Mary.
John stopped helping Mary.
```

- All parsers use some syntax. A parser for English must be told that subjects come before the verb, objects after the verb, prepositions before their objects, and noun phrases after words like *the* or *a*. Some parsers tolerate occasional irregularities, but none of them can handle an arbitrarily scrambled sentence.

Because of redundancy in language, many sentences can be parsed correctly with only syntax or only semantics. Such redundancy is valuable for children or foreigners who are learning a language. Even for native speakers, redundancy helps to avoid misunderstandings in the presence of noise or grammatical errors. In general, however, both syntax and semantics are important: syntax determines what slots the words fill in the sentence, and semantics determines what slots they fill conceptually.

A syntax-based parser can use the parse tree as the scaffolding on which semantic tests and structure-building operations are hung. That is essentially the approach taken by Katz and Fodor (1963) in associating semantic *projection rules* with their grammar rules. For programming languages, compilers associate a *semantic subroutine* with each grammar rule. Thompson and Thompson (1975) took a similar approach in their Rapidly Extensible Language system (REL), which was one of the first natural language systems widely used by people other than the developers. Its parser is based on Kay's chart method; during the parse, it constructs a graph representing the main verb with links to the noun phrases for each case relation of the verb. Following is a REL parsing rule (written in an APSG form):

```
VP (¬DATIVE) "to" NP (¬POSSESSIVE) ⟶
     VP (set DATIVE link to point to NP).
```

According to this rule, if a VP without a DATIVE attribute is followed by the word *to* and an NP without a POSSESSIVE attribute, then construct a new VP containing all the attributes of the old VP, but with a new DATIVE attribute linked to the representation for the NP. In parsing the sentence *Roy gave a book to Frank*, REL would generate the list,

```
(GAVE (AGENTIVE ROY) (OBJECTIVE BOOK) (DATIVE FRANK)).
```

In conceptual graph notation, that list could be written as,

```
(PAST)→[PROPOSITION: [GIVE]-
                          (AGNT)→[PERSON:Roy]
                          (OBJ)→ [BOOK]
                          (RCPT)→[PERSON:Frank]].
```

One of REL's innovations was the option of letting the user add new definitions dynamically. Some of the definitions are simple abbreviations; others can introduce complex functions and phrases.

By relying on syntax for most of the analysis, REL kept its semantic component simple and easy to extend. Systems with more complex semantics have often been so specialized that they could not be used for another application without being completely rewritten. As an example, SOPHIE (Brown & Burton 1975) is based on a *semantic grammar* for electronic circuit analysis. Instead of using general syntactic rules that relate categories like NP and VP, SOPHIE uses application-oriented rules that relate specific categories like *measurement*, *part*, and *circuit-element*. In parsing the question *What is the voltage of collector Q5?* SOPHIE generates a parse tree that maps directly to the LISP expression,

```
(MEASURE VOLTAGE (COLLECTOR Q5)).
```

The result of executing this expression is the answer to the original question. The semantic grammar allows SOPHIE to accommodate words that are not in its dictionary. In many cases, it can simply ignore those words and still get an acceptable interpretation.

Besides SOPHIE, semantic grammars have been used in several natural language query systems: PLANES for maintenance and flight records for naval aircraft (Waltz 1978); RENDEZVOUS for a database about parts, suppliers, and inventories (Codd 1978); and LADDER for naval logistics data (Hendrix et al. 1978). The parsers for those systems recognize domain-specific terms like PLANE, SUPPLIER, and SHIP. For special applications in a narrow domain of discourse, semantic grammars can be effective. But like Baseball and SHRDLU, they let the grammar and the application dependencies become inextricably entwined. After two years of intensive development, the semantic grammar for LADDER had become so large and unwieldy that even its original designers found it impractical to modify and extend. Slocum (1981) noted that the slightest change could produce "ripple effects which eroded the integrity of the system." In just a few weeks, he revised Robinson's DIAGRAM to handle all the sentences that LADDER could process plus many sentences that were outside the scope of its semantic grammar.

People do use semantics in understanding language, but they do not learn a new grammar for every subject they know. At New York University, the Linguistic String Project (LSP) processes medical texts by combining general syntactic rules with domain-specific *semantic patterns* (Sager 1981, Marsh & Sager 1982). Two such patterns are,

```
BODY-PART  TEST  VERB  RESULT.
{PATIENT | SYMPTOM}  V-RESPOND  MEDICATION.
```

Sentences that fit the first pattern include,

```
Spinal fluid was negative.
Chest X-rays suggest pleural effusion.
```

Sentences that fit the second pattern include,

```
She responded well to penicillin.
Seizures were controlled by valium.
```

On medical reports and diagnoses, a large number (about 49%) of the sentences are incomplete fragments. By matching a fragment to the possible syntactic patterns, the LSP parser can expand it to a complete sentence. The fragments,

```
Stiff neck and fever.
Brain scan negative.
```

were expanded to,

```
Patient had stiff neck and fever.
Brain scan was negative.
```

The LSP semantic patterns serve the same purpose as the semantic grammars in SOPHIE and LADDER. The difference is that LSP does not apply the semantic pattern directly to the input string, but to the result of the syntactic parse. Since the syntax rules transform many complex forms into simple clauses, LSP can handle a large number of sentences with a small number of patterns: all their medical texts were processed with only 6 basic patterns and 41 different subpatterns. Factoring out the semantic patterns from the syntactic rules also makes LSP more flexible: the syntax remains stable, and only the semantic patterns need to be changed for each application. In fact, the semantic patterns may be considered a *canonical basis*.

For a general graph representation, Heidorn's NLP (1972) combines syntactic rules with operators that test conditions in the graphs or perform actions upon them. NLP supports a hierarchy of types and subtypes of concepts and includes a complete set of operators for testing, following, and constructing links in the graphs. With these extensions, NLP rules build complex graphs during the parse whereas ordinary parsers are limited to building trees. The type hierarchy gives NLP the same capabilities as semantic grammars, but as an adjunct to the syntactic rules, not as a replacement for them. As a grammar, NLP rules are declarative. The operators for testing and constructing graphs, however, give the rules procedural power that is as general as a Turing machine. In NLPQ, Heidorn used the procedural features to generate diagnostics like the following:

```
THE FOLLOWING PERCENTAGES DO NOT TOTAL 100:  AFTER UNLOADING
CARGO AT THE THE DOCK FOR 10 MINUTES, 50 PERCENT OF THE TRUCKS
LEAVE THE STATION, AND 33 PERCENT WAIT IN THE DEPOT UNTIL THE
PIER IS AVAILABLE.
```

Like other procedural approaches, such tests in NLPQ are difficult to extend to new applications without a major rewrite. For generality, the EPISTLE system (Heidorn et al. 1982) used only the syntactic capability of NLP to parse texts on any subject whatever.

At Yale University, several parsers have been designed to map English into Schank's conceptual dependency graphs. In a detailed tutorial, Birnbaum and Selfridge (1981) discussed the parser written by Riesbeck (1975) for MARGIE, a later version called ELI, and an extension of ELI called CA:

- These parsers do use syntax. Like most parsers, ELI treats syntax as "knowledge of how to combine word meanings based on their positions in the utterance." Unlike more declarative systems, syntax in ELI is embedded in LISP code.
- Unlike parsers with separate syntactic and semantic stages, ELI uses both types of information concurrently while building a conceptual representation.
- Unlike most parsers, ELI binds syntax and semantics in *word packets* associated with individual words. Each packet contains LISP code stating conditions to be tested and actions to be taken if those conditions are satisfied.

Having a separate rule or procedure for every word wastes storage and misses important generalizations. ELI and CA do permit common code to be factored out of the word packets and put into shared subroutines. Yet like semantic grammars, those parsers combine syntax and semantics in a way that is difficult to extend or modify. Many of the graduate students at Yale found it easier to write new parsers patterned after ELI than to use ELI itself. Schank, Lebowitz, and Birnbaum (1980) pointed out three weaknesses of ELI:

- *Fragility.* When the parser finds an unknown word or phrase, it gives up. It cannot use the known parts to make some sense out of the sentence as a whole.
- *Nonextendibility.* Since the word definitions are LISP programs, the addition of new vocabulary requires a large part of the parsing program to be rewritten.

- *Isolation.* The parsing program is isolated in a separate module from the reasoning programs, and background knowledge and inferences cannot be used in helping to interpret the original input.

To remedy these weaknesses, they designed an integrated partial parser (IPP). To make it less fragile, they let IPP ignore words that it did not recognize. To make it more extendible, they let the word definitions for IPP be more declarative and less procedural than the word packets of ELI. To make it less isolated, they let IPP be driven by the same scripts used in the inference stage.

International terrorism was the first topic that IPP was designed to understand, and the word definitions in its vocabulary were slanted towards that topic. In the context of terrorism, the word *occupied*, for example, would typically refer to a political group occupying a public building and making demands. The following word definition for *occupied* shows the information that IPP uses during the parse:

```
(WORD-DEF OCCUPIED
  INTEREST 5
  TYPE     EB
  SUBCLASS SEB
  TEMPLATE (SCRIPT  $DEMONSTRATE
            ACTOR   NIL
            OBJECT  NIL
            DEMANDS NIL
            METHOD  (SCENE    $OCCUPY
                     ACTOR    NIL
                     LOCATION NIL))
  FILL     (((ACTOR)         (TOP-OF *ACTOR-STACK*))
            ((METHOD ACTOR) (TOP-OF *ACTOR-STACK*)))
  REQS     (FIND-DEMON-OBJECT
            FIND-OCCUPY-LOC
            RECOGNIZE-DEMANDS))
```

This definition contains six major subsections: the *interest value* for OCCUPIED is 5, which indicates moderate significance; its *type* is EB, event builder; its *subclass* is SEB, scene event builder; its *template* is a canonical graph for DEMONSTRATE; its *fill* indicators specify that the actors for DEMONSTRATE and OCCUPY must come from the top of an actor stack; and the three *reqs* request values found elsewhere in a story—the object of DEMONSTRATE, the location of OCCUPY, and the demands to be recognized.

Since it supports a declarative approach, IPP is more easily extendible than ELI. Yet its word definitions are limited to a single domain of discourse. In most contexts, the word *occupied* would not trigger thoughts of international terrorism:

```
This seat is occupied.
Kathy keeps herself occupied.
All the managerial positions are occupied.
Karpov occupied the center with his pawns.
```

Using background knowledge to guide the parser is a desirable goal. Yet binding all knowledge about a word in a single packet is too restrictive. In all its uses, the verb *occupied* has the same syntactic features and the same set of canonical graphs. The schemata for the type OCCUPY are the things that change with every domain of discourse. It should be possible to extend the domain of discourse by adding new schemata without having to revise every word definition.

The method of packaging syntactic and semantic information does not depend on whether it is processed by an integrated, staged, or coroutined parser. ELI, for example, factors some common information out of individual word packets and puts it in separate subroutines, but it uses that information exactly as though it were packaged in a single unit. NLPQ separates the type hierarchy from the syntactic rules, but it uses them concurrently during the parsing. Boguraev's parser (1979) makes a further split between the syntactic rules, the type hierarchy, and the verb frames (which correspond roughly to canonical graphs), but it still uses all three kinds of information concurrently. Schank et al. are correct in saying that the information packaged in scripts should be available while parsing an input sentence, but their conclusion that the scripts should be bound to individual word definitions is premature.

Although the language strata interact closely in the process of understanding, each language level can follow its own rules while operating concurrently with the other levels. The conceptual catalog in Appendix B of this book shows the kinds of information used at different levels; following is the entry for the word *occupy*:

occupy. transitive verb; OCCUPY, OCCUPY-ACT, OCCUPY-ATTN.

This entry says that *occupy* belongs to the syntactic category *transitive verb*; the grammar rules must therefore check for a direct object. It lists three possible word senses, represented by the concept types OCCUPY, OCCUPY-ACT, and OCCUPY-ATTN. Each of those types is represented by a canonical graph in Appendix B.2. The type OCCUPY has a canonical graph for an entity residing in some location:

```
[OCCUPY]-
   (STAT)←[ENTITY]
   (LOC)→ [PLACE].
```

The entity that is in the state of OCCUPY in this graph is passively filling up space. The canonical graph for OCCUPY-ACT would be used for a chess player occupying a position, demonstrators occupying a building, or an army occupying territory:

```
[OCCUPY-ACT]-
   (AGNT)→[ANIMATE]
   (LOC)→ [PLACE]
   (INST)→[ENTITY].
```

The INST relation provides a slot for Karpov's pawns, the demonstrators' bodies, or an army's troops. The canonical graph for OCCUPY-ATTN corresponds to some activity occupying a person's attention:

```
[OCCUPY-ATTN]-
   (AGNT)→[ANIMATE]
   (OBJ)→ [ANIMATE]
   (INST)→[ACTIVITY].
```

This graph would be used for such sentences as *Bob occupied himself by listening to recordings of Luciano Pavarotti.*

Canonical graphs are not definitions. They are simply patterns that show how concepts and relations fit together. Figure 5.7 shows a type definition for OCCUPY-ACT. This definition says that OCCUPY-ACT is a transaction with two parts: one of type TAKE and the other of type OCCUPY. The agent of the entire transaction is also the agent of TAKE, the location of the transaction is the PLACE that is the object of TAKE as well as the location of OCCUPY, and the instrument of the transaction is the ENTITY that is in the state of OCCUPY. Type definitions such as Fig. 5.7 provide only part of the meaning of a concept. Schemata provide the

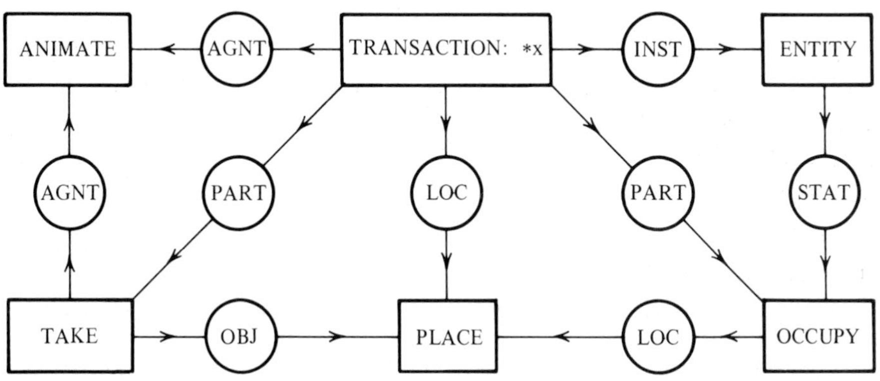

Fig. 5.7 Type definition for OCCUPY-ACT

kind of background knowledge contained in IPP's scripts and scenes. The fill and reqs indicators of the IPP word definition are hints to the parser; the template part corresponds to a canonical graph:

```
[DEMONSTRATE]-
   (AGNT)→[ANIMATE: *x]
   (OBJ)→ [ANIMATE]
   (PURP)→[DEMAND: {*}]
   (METH)→[SCENE: [OCCUPY-ACT]-
                     (AGNT)→[ANIMATE: *x]
                     (LOC)→ [PLACE]].
```

This conceptual graph may be used as the body of a schema for a concept type like DEMONSTRATE, DEMAND, or OCCUPY-ACT. Instead of an interest value in the word definition itself, a *relevance factor* (see Section 4.7) can compute the interest level dynamically: schemata are indexed by the concept types they contain, and the relevance of a type is inversely proportional to the number of schemata in which it occurs. The common words that IPP skips because they have a low interest level would be skipped for the more basic reason that they have too many associations for any one of them to be significant. Emotional involvement, attention, and context can also affect the interest level. Having a fixed interest level in each word definition is not a general or flexible solution.

As an example of the interactions between linguistic strata, the movie *Heartbreak Kid* contains the phrase *Knoll Way Motel*, which is hard to understand, even though it is spoken in a clear voice at normal volume. Although Americans seldom confuse /l/ and /r/, several people initially interpreted the phrase as *Norway Motel*. One of them switched to the interpretation *No Way* because the /r/ didn't sound right. The three possibilities, *Norway*, *No Way*, and *Knoll Way*, are phonologically similar, and the correct interpretation *Knoll Way* is unusual, both syntactically and semantically. Since the setting is Minnesota, which has many residents of Scandinavian descent, background knowledge gives some preference for *Norway*. Although phonology is a low-level, unconscious process, a phoneme that is sufficiently odd may require a conscious decision. Such decisions, however, are exceedingly rare: with a dozen or more phonemes per second, normal speech would be unintelligible if people had to contemplate each one separately.

For optimum speed, each aspect of language should be interpreted at the lowest appropriate level. Phonemes are interpreted at the phonological level, and grammar by syntactic rules. Whatever is ambiguous at one level, however, must be resolved by feedback from a higher level: syntax helps to resolve phonological ambiguities, and conceptual schemata help to resolve syntactic ambiguities. In an extreme case, background knowledge from the highest level may be needed to resolve a phonological

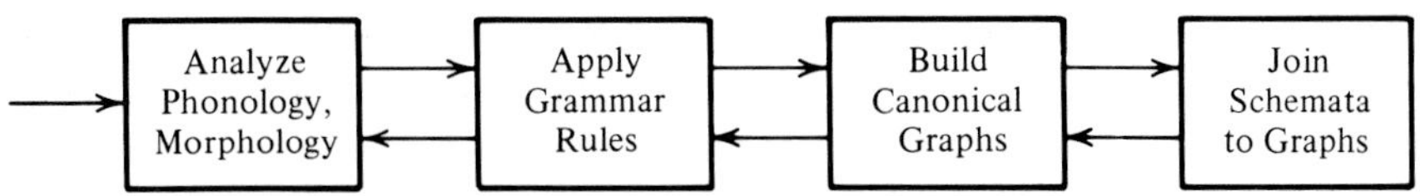

Fig. 5.8 A coroutined language processor

ambiguity at a low level: knowledge about Scandinavian immigrants in Minnesota may influence the choice of /r/ in *Norway* over /l/ in *Knoll Way*. Language is processed in stages with complex interactions:

- Phonology, syntax, and semantics are independent, but interacting strata of language. Each stratum operates by its own rules and principles, but it is intimately connected with the one above and the one below it.

- Feedback from a later semantic level can either encourage or veto interpretations at earlier phonological or syntactic levels.

- A psychologically realistic parser requires immediate feedback between the strata. A staged parser that generates all syntactic parses and then applies a semantic filter is unrealistic.

- With large dictionaries, a parser that packages all the syntactic and semantic information with each word is impractical. Psychologically, it fails to account for the way people learn new words without having to modify their grammar.

- Both from a psychological and a computational point of view, a coroutined parser is promising. It combines the advantage of an integrated parser where all of the strata interact with the modularity of a staged parser where each stratum operates by its own rules on its own kinds of structures.

Figure 5.8 shows the language processor as a series of coroutines, each of which applies the rules appropriate to its level, but all of which run concurrently with continuous feedback between levels.

A subroutine is subordinate to the program that calls it; coroutines, however, run concurrently as equals. REL, NLP, and most compilers give primary control to syntax and interleave calls to semantic subroutines among the syntactic operations. ELI and IPP reverse the roles by giving primary control to the semantics and interleave syntactic tests among the semantic operations. Conway's original transition nets and later Woods' cascaded ATNs run morphology, syntax, and semantics as coroutines. In all these approaches, the amount of computation for each level is comparable, but they differ in which one they choose as primary and which ones they make subordinate or coordinate.

When a subroutine is called, it receives some input arguments, does some computation, returns a result, and when it finishes, discards the intermediate results generated during the computation. Coroutines, however, do not have fixed arguments and results; nor do they run to an end point where they discard all intermediate results. Instead, coroutines pass messages to each other along *streams* or *pipes*. They may reach a temporary stopping point where they wait for further messages, but when they receive a new message, they resume execution where they left off.

5.7 CONTEXT AND BACKGROUND KNOWLEDGE

The meaning of a sentence is only partly determined by the meaning of its words. A large, if not the major part of meaning comes from context, the speaker's intentions, and the listener's expectations. Literal meaning can be dramatically reversed by a gesture, a wink, or an ironic tone of voice. Depending on the tone of voice and the speaker's authority, the sentence *I don't like that* could be a complaint, a warning, or a command. Besides the intention of the speaker, the listener must determine the presuppositions and implications of each sentence, and the *anaphora* or cross references to other entities in the context. Semantics determines the literal meaning. The other factors, which relate language to the world, are called *pragmatics*.

Even when the listener understands the literal meaning exactly, he or she can easily mistake the intentions or the anaphoric references. A famous example of a disastrous mistake was the misinterpretation of the Delphic Oracle by King Croesus of the Lydians: *If Croesus attacks the Persians, he will destroy a mighty empire.* The pronoun *he* refers to Croesus, but the phrase *a mighty empire* is indefinite. Since Croesus had been planning to wage war on the Persians, he interpreted the phrase as a reference to the empire that was uppermost in his mind, the Persian empire. He overlooked the possibility that it might refer to his own empire. His mistake was an incorrect resolution of anaphora. Some authors restrict the word *anaphora* to backward references; they use the word *cataphora* for forward references and *exophora* for references to things outside the text (Halliday & Hasan 1976). Whether Croesus made a mistake in anaphora or exophora depends on his previous conversation with the Delphic priestess.

Croesus had no way of resolving the ambiguous reference in the oracle, but most anaphoric references can be resolved by background knowledge. Consider the sentence *Ivan cut the salami with a knife, and then he put it in his sandwich.* Syntactically, the pronoun *it* could refer either to the salami or to the knife. Physically, either one could be inserted into the sandwich. But reasonably, only the salami is a likely component of a sandwich. Schemata contain the background knowledge that determines what is reasonable. As the syntactic analyzer translates the input sentence into a conceptual graph, the inference mechanisms join schemata to the graph and generate preferences and expectations for likely combinations. The process works just as well for an extended dialog as for the single sentence:

```
A:  Ivan cut the salami.
B:  What did he cut it with?
A:  A knife.
B:  What did he do with it?
A:  He put it in his sandwich.
```

Ivan might have made a mistake and absentmindedly put the knife in his sandwich. If so, the speaker would emphasize the oddity: *Ivan cut the salami with a knife, but it was the knife that he put in his sandwich.*

The question of whether Ivan put the knife or the salami in his sandwich can be answered by checking canonical graphs and schemata. Such tests depend on *semantic memory*, not on the more specific *episodic memory*. In the next two sentences, however, determining the referent of *his* requires knowledge of specific facts:

```
William James cited Mozart's discussion of his composition.
Marvin Minsky cited McCorduck's discussion of his research.
```

The ambiguity in the first sentence is resolved by the fact that Mozart lived a century before William James; hence *his* must refer to Mozart. In the second, the disambiguating fact is that McCorduck is a woman who wrote a history of AI and Minsky was prominently mentioned in it. Linguists have speculated that for any fact in the universe it is possible to construct a grammatical English sentence that is ambiguous to someone who does not know the fact. Bar-Hillel claimed that such ambiguities are a fundamental limitation on a computer's ability to understand language. Yet they are just as much a limitation on a human being's ability. When faced with an unresolvable ambiguity, the computer can do the same thing that people do—ask a question.

Books and articles usually present the facts needed to resolve ambiguities. The most critical facts are stated in the context, usually before, but sometimes immediately after the ambiguity. The sentence *Mary had a little lamb* has only one syntactic parse, but it is *semantically ambiguous*. How the reader interprets it depends on which of the next three sentences follows:

```
Its fleece was white as snow.
But she passed up the mint jelly.
And boy, was she surprised!
```

The verb *have* serves the same function as the preposition *of*: it merely shows that two nouns are related, and the reader or listener must infer the relation from canonical graphs, schemata, context, or background knowledge. In the first interpretation, Mary owned the lamb, but ownership is not the basic meaning of *have*. For a natural language query system, Zoeppritz (1981) treated *have* as a function word with no intrinsic meaning. Her system checked the database relations associated with its subject and object to determine its use in the current context.

Declaratives, questions, imperatives, and exclamations are the four traditional classes of sentences. But these four classes do not exhaust the multiplicity of uses for language. Wittgenstein (1953) emphasized that point: "this multiplicity is not something fixed, given once for all; but new types of language, new language games, as we may say, come into existence, and others become obsolete and get forgotten." Following are Wittgenstein's examples of *language games*:

> Giving orders and obeying them; describing the appearance of an object or giving its measurements; constructing an object from a description (a drawing); reporting an event; speculating about an event; forming and testing a hypothesis; presenting the results of an experiment in tables and diagrams; making up a story and reading it; play acting; singing catches; guessing riddles; making a joke, telling it; solving a problem in practical arithmetic; translating from one language into another; asking, thanking, cursing, greeting, praying.

This list is open ended. People can create new language games for amusement, for business or science, or for intimate conversations between friends. Computational linguistics can support easy-to-use computer systems, but current implementations are limited in the number of different language games they can play. Many systems can play one or two of these games, but none of them can play them all. Nor can any program detect when the other party to a conversation is spontaneously inventing a totally new language game.

In normal conversations, the participants have a common aim: to make themselves understood and to understand the other speaker. The goal of understanding would naturally lead to sentences with all possible qualifiers fully expressed. But at the same time, people don't want to waste their own efforts or let the listeners get bored. Therefore, they omit everything that they believe is common knowledge. Grice (1975) formulated the *cooperative principle*, which speakers are expected to follow: adapt each contribution to the accepted purpose or direction of the conversation. Grice expanded this principle in four basic maxims:

- *Quantity.* Say neither too much nor too little.
- *Quality.* Try to make your contribution one that is true.
- *Relation.* Be relevant.
- *Manner.* Be perspicuous.

These rules are tacit assumptions that underlie normal conversations. They allow people to draw inferences, called *conversational implicatures*, both from what is said and from what is not said. As an example, Grice cited the following exchange:

```
A:  I am out of petrol.
B:  There is a garage round the corner.
```

If B's response is relevant, B must think that the garage is open and has petrol to sell. By the maxim of quantity, B should not say so because B can assume that A can draw the same conclusions. The rules can also resolve ambiguity, as in the sentence *Larry went to the park with the girl.* The phrase *with the girl* could modify either the noun *park* or the verb *went.* But the phrase *with the girl* would only modify *park* if there happened to be more than one park and both the speaker and the listener knew (and knew that each other knew) that only one of them contained the girl in question. If there is only one park in the current context, then *the park* is sufficient to distinguish it, and the girl must be accompanying Larry.

The cooperative principle is an important aid to communication. Yet people are not always cooperative. Sometimes they may be joking, evasive, or even lying. In legal confrontations, they may deliberately follow the opposite maxims of *stonewalling*:

- *Quantity.* Never contribute anything voluntarily.
- *Quality.* Avoid perjury and contempt of court.
- *Relation.* Lead the inquiry astray.
- *Manner.* Be obscure.

Kaplan (1978) noted that computers tend more towards stonewalling than cooperation. His CO-OP system tries to avoid stonewalling by volunteering information that is likely to be relevant to the user's question.

To be cooperative, a system must recognize and respond to the underlying *presuppositions*. The loaded question *Have you stopped beating your wife* presupposes that you have, at some time, been beating her. A *yes* or *no* answer acknowledges that presupposition. Although tricky questions are intended to trap the respondent, loaded questions occur in normal database queries. Webber and Joshi (1982) cited the sentence *Did John take Physics 161 last term?* Although it does not appear to set hidden traps, this question has the following presuppositions that the questioner tacitly assumes to be true:

- There exists a course named Physics 161.
- It was offered last term.
- John was qualified to take it (he was a student, he took the prerequisites, and he had not taken it previously).

The answer *yes* requires no further explanation. But the respondent could be helpful and volunteer related information that the questioner might also want to know: *Yes, John received an A.* If the answer is *no*, the respondent should say which presupposition is violated: *John is not a student* or *He advance-placed Physics 161.* If all the presuppositions are satisfied and the answer is still *no*, the respondent can monitor the database for updates that would change the answer: *Shall I let you know if and when he does?*

Checking presuppositions has been implemented in several natural language query systems; CO-OP was the first to do it. In the next example, Q is a question for CO-OP, the paraphrase P shows that the question was correctly interpreted, and R is a helpful response (Kaplan 1982):

```
Q:  Which projects in oceanography does Nasa Headquarters
    sponsor?

P:  I am assuming that 'Nasa Headquarters' is a SPONSOR NAME.
    I am assuming that 'oceanography' is an AREA OF INTEREST.
    Which projects does Nasa Headquarters sponsor?
    Look for projects that are in oceanography.

R:  I don't know of any projects in oceanography that
    Nasa Headquarters sponsors.  But you may be interested in
    any projects that Nasa Headquarters sponsors...
      (PROJECT/ACCT)      (PROJECT TITLE)
      35071040            NON-EQUILIB. OF ELECTRONS IN SOLAR...
      35071048            OUTER ATMOSPHERES OF DWARF STARS...
```

The terms *Nasa Headquarters* and *oceanography* are not in CO-OP's dictionary, but it uses semantic patterns to determine the expected concept type. Once it finds the concept type, the data dictionary can map the type to the appropriate files and fields. Since the answer set is empty, CO-OP relaxes one of the conditions in the query to find related projects that might interest the user.

The rules of conversational implicature require that both participants form mental models not only of the outside world, but also of the models that they suppose the other speaker is forming. Since no one can have a perfect model of another person, effective communication requires a dialog where each person corrects and extends the other's mental models. During a successful dialog, the participants calibrate their words and their models so that each one knows how a particular word or phrase will affect the other. Carbonell (1981) designed the Mixed-Initiative Conversational System (MICS), which is based on conversational rules similar to Grice's. MICS forms a model of each speaker and searches for a topic of common interest. Following is a dialog between MICS and a person named Dave (computer output in upper case):

```
HELLO, WHAT IS YOUR NAME?
I am Dave.
WHAT'S NEW TODAY, DAVE?
Nothing.  What's your name?
MY NAME IS MICS.
What is your job?
I AM A COMPUTER PROGRAMMER.
That's nice.
WHAT DO YOU DO FOR A LIVING?
I am still a student.
DO YOU LIKE BEING A STUDENT?
For the time being yes.
WHAT WILL YOU DO AFTERWARDS?
I want to be a professor some day.
```

```
WHAT DO YOU DO FOR FUN?
I smoke dope.
YOU MIGHT GET STONED IF YOU SMOKE TOO MUCH.
I know, that's the idea.
YOU MIGHT GET IN TROUBLE IF THE COPS CATCH YOU.
All right, stop moralizing, what do you do for fun?
I LIKE TO PLAY CHESS.
That sounds boring.
NO, IT IS A LOT OF FUN!
My brother Eric plays chess.
HE MUST BE SMART.
I have to go.  Bye MICS.
NICE TALKING TO YOU, DAVE.
```

A short conversation with MICS does not show its full potential. A simple pattern-matching program could look for the pattern *x plays chess* and generate the response *x must be smart.* In response to the input *I want to be a professor some day*, MICS changes the subject without showing that it understood the sentence. Underneath, however, MICS is far more sophisticated: it completely translates the input to conceptual graphs, it combines the graphs with background knowledge embodied in schemata, it forms an internal model of the other speaker, it saves the model for future reference, and it establishes goals and subgoals that direct the flow of conversation. After the previous conversation with Dave, MICS had the following conversation with Pete:

```
HELLO, WHAT IS YOUR NAME?
Pete.
WHAT'S NEW TODAY, PETE?
Professor Stevenson is giving us an exam Friday.
STEVENSON GIVES DIFFICULT EXAMS.
Yeah, do you know that Dave is probably going to flunk?
THAT'S GOING TO MAKE IT HARD FOR DAVE TO BECOME A PROFESSOR.
Too bad, Dave is not too smart anyways.
YES, DAVE LIKES TO SMOKE DOPE.
I've got to go and study.
YOU WILL DO WELL IN THE EXAM.
```

This second conversation shows that MICS really did a complete analysis of the conversation with Dave. It remembers that Dave wants to become a professor and that he smokes dope. More importantly, it combines what it was told with background knowledge: a future professor must do well in school, smoking dope is not smart, and studying enables a student to do well on an exam. Besides combining new information with background knowledge, MICS forms a model of the topic of conversation and the other speaker's knowledge, draws plausible inferences, and introduces new information at appropriate times.

Tone of voice is vital for understanding speech. For recapturing tone of voice from writing, the distribution of words and concepts can sometimes provide subtle clues. In analyzing Milton's *Paradise Lost*, Misek (1972) found that mood swings were typically accompanied by a skewed distribution of syntactic categories. Satan's speeches, for example, show wide variation in the ratio of noun phrases to verb phrases. In the following speech to Abdiel in Heaven (V. 864-866), Satan seems to be elated or haughty, and noun phrases predominate:

```
Our puissance is our own, our own right hand
Shall teach us highest deeds, by proof to try
Who is our equal....
```

In the next speech to Zephon on Earth (IV. 827-829), Satan seems more depressed or scornful, and verb phrases predominate:

```
Know ye not then...
Know ye not me?  ye knew me once no mate
For you, there sitting where ye durst not soar....
```

When Satan seems less distressed, more controlled or calm, the categories are more evenly distributed, as in the following speech to Gabriel on Earth (IV. 886-888):

```
Gabriel, thou hadst in Heav'n th'esteem of wise,
And such I held thee; but this question askt
Puts me in doubt.  Lives there who loves his pain?
```

Similarly skewed distributions have been found in the writings of psychiatric patients as contrasted with the population at large. To analyze such distributions, Misek (1975) developed a network notation called *claim-structure grammar*.

Metaphor is a normal means of adapting existing words to new situations. In the *Poetics*, Aristotle defined metaphor as giving "a thing a name that belongs to something else." He included the transference from subtype to supertype, from supertype to subtype, or from one type to another on the basis of analogy. Ryle (1949) defined metaphor as "the presentation of the facts of one category in the idioms appropriate to another" (p. 8). A metaphor does more than transfer a type label; it transfers an entire schema or cluster of schemata to a new type. As Goodman (1968) said, "A whole set of alternative labels, a whole apparatus of organization, takes over new territory. What occurs is a transfer of schema, a migration of concepts, an alienation of categories. Indeed, a metaphor might be regarded as a calculated category mistake—or rather as a happy and revitalizing, even if bigamous, second marriage." Note how Goodman uses metaphors to describe metaphor: a migration of concepts to new territory, an alienation of categories, or a bigamous second marriage. Since the less familiar type METAPHOR lacks a well-developed schematic cluster, Goodman fills the gap by transferring schemata from the better known types.

In principle, a metaphor could transfer schemata between any two types. In practice, a few dozen analogies account for most of the metaphors in everyday speech (Lakoff & Johnson 1980). Schemata for MONEY, for example, are often transferred to TIME: "spending an hour," "living on borrowed time," or "budgeting time." Schemata for WAR are transferred to ARGUMENT: "Your claims are indefensible," "I demolished his argument," and "He shot down all my arguments." Schemata for ADVERSARY are transferred to INFLATION: "Inflation has attacked the foundation of our economy," "Inflation has robbed me of my savings," and "The dollar has been destroyed by inflation." In classifying these metaphors, Lakoff and Johnson observed that metaphor is not an obscure poetic device, but a fundamental aspect of language that reflects the mechanisms of thought.

Since a metaphor transfers a schema to a new type, sentences containing metaphors typically violate selectional constraints. If a parser fails to construct a canonical graph for a sentence, it should determine whether the failure was caused by a simple mistake or by a use of metaphor. Carbonell (1982) outlined the steps required to recognize metaphors by a computer:

- First try to analyze each sentence literally. If no canonical graph can be formed for a grammatical sentence, consider it as a possible metaphor.
- Check the catalog of common analogies to find a possible transfer of schema for one or more of the concepts in the sentence.
- Determine whether a conceptual graph that represents the sentence can be canonically derived from the transferred schema.
- If a suitable interpretation is found, remember the schema that was transferred, since it is likely to be used again within the same story or conversation.

A standard catalog of metaphors is probably adequate for interpreting everyday speech. Poetry and other imaginative writing have unusual metaphors that may be more difficult to recognize.

A metaphor that does not violate selectional constraints may also be difficult to recognize. Reddy (1969) cited two possible contexts for the sentence *The rock is becoming brittle with age*: first, a group of geologists on a field trip; second, a group of students emerging from the office of an irritable professor emeritus. In the first context, the sentence should be taken in its literal sense; in the second, it is a metaphor even though it violates no selectional constraints. The clue to recognizing it would be the failure to find a literal referent for *the rock*. The analogy of mind as a brittle object is another of Lakoff and Johnson's examples: "Her ego is very fragile," "He broke under cross-examination," "The experience shattered him," and "His mind snapped."

While learning language, children make mistakes. But their mistakes tend to arise from simple misunderstandings, not from the "calculated mistakes" of metaphors. In studying children's speech, Chukovsky (1963) found an extreme literalness and absence of metaphor. He mentioned a four-year-old child who became angry whenever an adult used the term *ladyfinger biscuits* and would protest "They are not made out of fingers, they're made out of dough!" Following is another example from Chukovsky:

```
Betty, why didn't you provide a knife and fork for Mr. White?

Because I thought he didn't need them—daddy said
he ate like a horse.
```

Sometimes an adult may interpret a child's mistakes as metaphors, as in the example "Can't you see? I'm barefoot all over!" Such examples transfer a familiar term to a new case, but Chukovsky did not consider them to be true metaphors.

Besides the local problems in analyzing sentences, story understanding must deal with global connections that cover the entire plot. Two approaches to story analysis include structural studies of themes (see Section 2.4) and cause and effect analysis of relationships between events and the motivations of the characters. These two approaches are complementary: essentially every story has both types of connection, although some genres emphasize one or the other. In the early Greek epic, themes predominate, and events may occur that are thematically correct, but causally unexplained (C. A. Sowa 1983). Homer was a master of his craft, who cast his stories in the traditional forms, but developed a rich network of causal relationships to explain the events and motivations. The BORIS program (Dyer 1982) does an an in-depth analysis of the causal interactions in a story, but it requires a large amount of computation. As a basis for classifying the possible interactions, Lehnert (1982) has been developing a standardized set of *plot units*.

As this section has shown, understanding a conversation or story requires a great deal of background knowledge. Errors can arise, as when Croesus and the Delphic priestess made different assumptions about the anaphoric references. When the process works, it is highly efficient. Problems occur when the participants make different assumptions. The logical positivists tried to "purify" language by making everything explicit. But that attempt was futile: first, it would drain language of its power and flexibility; second, people use the same implicit methods in their thinking, and a language that differs too much from the modes of thought would introduce more errors than it would prevent. A fully explicit language would not help people say something correctly if what it led them to say was not what they meant.

EXERCISES

A person who wants to program a machine to process language must be aware of the pitfalls that mislead people as well as machines. The following exercises include puzzles that can be solved without a formal notation, syntactic problems that use phrase-structure grammars, and semantic problems that use conceptual graphs.

5.1 Using the grammar rules on p. 219, draw a parse tree for each of the following sentences:

```
The quick brown fox jumped over the lazy dog.
The man in the moon eats green cheese.
The direct access storage device control unit cable broke.
```

5.2 Find all the ambiguities in the following sentences. For each interpretation, give another English sentence that states the meaning unambiguously.

```
Nancy missed a sale of books by French authors with red jackets.
Lester left the shower dripping water on the floor.
Beverly saw birds eating worms and squirrels gathering nuts.
Barbie told the man that she loves the truth.
Malcolm noticed that beer can freeze.
```

In the first sentence, consider which word each prepositional phrase modifies; in the next two, consider how the participles and conjunctions are related to the other words; in the last two, consider different uses for the word *that*.

5.3 For the sample grammar rules on p. 219, replace the NP rule with the following three rules. Besides allowing an optional prepositional phrase PP, the first rule also allows an optional participial phrase PARTP or a conjunction CONJ followed by another noun phrase NP. The second rule says that an NP may also be a pronoun or name without any modifiers. The third rule defines PARTP as a PARTICIPLE followed by an optional noun phrase and prepositional phrase.

```
NP ⟶ [DET] [N-MOD]... NOUN [PP | PARTP | CONJ NP].
NP ⟶ PRONOUN | NAME.
PARTP ⟶ PARTICIPLE [NP] [PP].
```

Using this new grammar, draw two parse trees for each of the first three sentences in Exercise 5.1. How many other parses are there for those sentences? Are there any possible interpretations of those sentences that are not represented by this grammar? If so, modify the grammar to accommodate them.

5.4 Extend the grammar rules to handle indirect objects, relative clauses, and noun clauses introduced by *that*. Options of the following form could be added to the grammar:

```
VP ⟶ VERB [NP] [NP].
RELCLAUSE ⟶ RELPRONOUN [NP] VP.
NP ⟶ "that" S.
```

Use this grammar to draw parse trees for the last two sentences in Exercise 5.2.

5.5 The grammar developed for the previous exercise would allow many nonsensical sentences:

```
That wine looks cat glasses convinced the lake whom you gave.
Strength by the sea jumps the old man that justice admires.
Sincerity believes the dog a bone.
```

Draw parse trees for these sentences according to the same grammar used before. Generate three equally nonsensical sentences that are also derivable by that grammar.

5.6 Nonsensical sentences are ruled out by selectional constraints. In each of the nonsensical sentences in the previous exercise, what constraints are violated that would keep the resulting conceptual graphs from being canonical? (You may either state the constraints in English or draw the canonical graphs.) Convert those sentences into normal ones by replacing some of the nouns and verbs with other nouns and verbs that meet the constraints.

5.7 The following sentences are semantically ambiguous, even though there is only one parse tree for each one. Give a paraphrase for each interpretation.

```
Larry used a shovel to hold up the bank.
Sheila called Jane a taxi.
The baby has grown another foot.
```

5.8 In the sentence *The lamb turned on the rotisserie*, the word *on* can be either a preposition with object *rotisserie* or a particle that is treated as part of the verb *turn on*. Draw a parse tree for each of these possibilities. Each syntactic parse has two different semantic interpretations. Give a paraphrase for each of the four possible interpretations.

5.9 For each of the sample sentences in the previous exercises, draw a conceptual graph that represents one of the interpretations.

5.10 Take the phrase-structure grammar developed for exercises 5.2 and 5.3 and expand it with further conditions and actions to form an APSG. Use that grammar to generate an English sentence from Fig. 5.6. List each grammar rule that is used in generating the sentence and the concept that is the current node □ for the application of that rule.

5.11 Parse the following sentences. For each one, determine whether the word *occupy* corresponds to the concept type OCCUPY, OCCUPY-ACT, or OCCUPY-ATTN, choose the appropriate canonical graph for the type, and specialize it to represent the meaning of the sentence.

```
Baird occupied the baby with computer games.
Debbie occupied the office for the afternoon.
The enemy occupied the island with marines.
```

Take the resulting graph that contains a concept of type OCCUPY-ACT and expand it according to the type definition of Fig. 5.7.

5.12 Assume that the meaning of the concept type OCCUPY-ATTN is that x OCCUPY-ATTNs y with some activity if x causes the activity to OCCUPY y's attention. Translate that informal definition into a formal type definition like Fig. 5.7. Take the graph from the Exercise 5.11 that contains a concept of type OCCUPY-ATTN and expand it according to the new type definition.

5.13 The preposition *of* may be used for many different relations between two nouns; Section 5.3 gave some examples in the form *house of*.... Identify the relation in each of the examples, and find some further examples of your own.

5.14 Find three obscure facts in an encyclopedia or other reference book. For each fact, construct an English sentence that would be ambiguous to a person who did not know that fact. (This exercise may be used as a party game or classroom competition: one player states an obscure fact, and the others try to be the first to find an ambiguous sentence that is resolved by that fact.)

5.15 Select a passage from a book or newspaper. For each sentence in it,

- List the concepts expressed and the conceptual relations between those concepts (which may or may not be mentioned explicitly).
- Identify the modalities expressed in the sentences—possibility, necessity, thinking, believing, knowing, hoping, etc.
- Determine which words or phrases are coreferent with other terms in the same sentence or in preceding sentences in the article.
- Analyze the presuppositions that must be true in the normal use of the sentences. Are the presuppositions stated earlier in the article, or are they supposed to be common knowledge?
- Identify every metaphor. Determine what analogy is being used and which schema is being transferred from one type to another. (Just describe each schema with a short sentence; do not draw a complete conceptual graph.)

5.16 Consider Wittgenstein's language games listed on p. 266. Find sample sentences of each type and try to imagine how a computer system might process them. What are the clues that indicate which language game is being played? (It is better to look for actual examples in reading, conversation, radio, and television than to make up artificial ones, because the specially concocted examples are usually oversimplified.)

SUGGESTED READING

For introductory textbooks on linguistics, see Fromkin and Rodman (1978) or Akmajian, Demers, and Harnish (1979). For readers who have long since forgotten what they were taught in grammar school, LaPalombara (1976) gives a systematic survey of traditional grammar before introducing the more modern linguistic material. For the relation of phonology to other aspects of language, Roman Jakobson's *Six Lectures on Sound and Meaning* illuminate every point with a broad range of examples. The most comprehensive grammar of English is by Quirk et al. (1972), who present it in an informal, traditional style. Of the more formal grammars, Harris (1982) is the most detailed, although it too is only semiformalized.

Transformational grammar is an elaborate theory of syntax, but it lags behind AI in semantics and pragmatics. For a survey of transformational grammar, see Culicover (1982). Chomsky (1982) presents his latest theory of *government and binding*. Newmeyer (1980) presents the major issues in transformational grammar and their evolution since the 1950s. *Current Approaches to Syntax*, edited by Moravcsik and Wirth, presents competing approaches. The collection edited by Bresnan (1982) presents *lexical-functional grammar*, which is more compatible with AI and psycholinguistics than Chomsky's approach.

For a broad survey of computational linguistics, see Tennant (1981). Winograd (1983) is a textbook on grammars and parsing that is intended for students of either linguistics or computer science. Schank (1975) presents conceptual dependency theory, and Schank and Riesbeck (1981) include a collection of tutorials on implementation techniques. Sager (1981) presents the grammar and techniques of the Linguistic String Project at New York University; it is a large, well-documented grammar that could be adapted to projects with different theoretical approaches. Robinson's DIAGRAM (1982) is another well-documented grammar that could be used in the syntactic component of a parser. For a variety of approaches, see the collections edited by Schank and Colby (1973), Bobrow and Collins (1975), Charniak and Wilks (1976), Zampolli (1977), Findler (1979), Joshi, Webber, and Sag (1981), and Lehnert and Ringle (1982). Leonard Bolc has edited several collections on computational linguistics, each book containing four or five extended articles of about 70 pages each.

Sidney Lamb (1966) is the linguist who put the greatest emphasis on the study of linguistic strata and their interactions. Clark and Clark (1977) is a good introduction to psycholinguistics with emphasis on children's acquisition of language. Hörmann (1981) presents semantic issues from psychological, linguistic, and philosophical points of view; in contrast to Chomsky's emphasis on syntactic competence, Hörmann treats performance as the central issue in the study of language. The collection of papers edited by Kavanaugh and Cutting (1975) deals with animal communication, sign language, and language evolution. The collection edited by Baker and McCarthy (1981) presents current theoretical positions on language acquisition. For a variety of topics, see *Psycholinguistic Research*, edited by Aaronson and Reiber.

Pragmatics and conversational implicature were developed by philosophers before linguists took up the subject. The classic book is Wittgenstein's *Philosophical Investigations*. Another classic that was influenced by Wittgenstein is Austin's *How to Do Things with Words*. The best study from a linguistic point of view is *Pragmatics* by Gazdar. For discourse analysis and anaphora resolution, see Halliday and Hasan (1976), Webber (1979), and Hirst (1981). Belnap and Steel (1976) discuss questions and answers from a logical point of view; they include an extensive bibliography of the subject. For the use of background knowledge in processing stories and connected discourse, see Clippinger (1977), Lehnert (1978), Carbonell (1981), and the collection edited by Brady and Berwick (1983).

6 Knowledge Engineering

With conventional database systems, the user must know what to ask for and what to do with the results. A knowledge-based system keeps track of the meaning of the data and performs inferences to determine what information is needed even when it has not been explicitly requested. This chapter applies the principles of knowledge representation and language processing to the two major classes of knowledge-based systems: *natural language systems*, which strive to process human languages in as natural and flexible a manner as possible, and *expert systems*, which apply large knowledge bases to solve practical problems.

6.1 EXPERT SYSTEMS

Every program incorporates knowledge about some application, but knowledge-based systems apply knowledge in a more active way than conventional programs. The difference between the two resembles Seneca's distinction between remembering and knowing: "To remember is to preserve something committed to memory; to know, by contrast, is to make each item your own, not to depend on a model and to be constantly looking back at the teacher" *(Letters to Lucilius 33)*. This quotation makes several points that characterize a knowledge-based system:

- Knowledge is more active than rote memory.
- Knowledge does not depend on a fixed model, but can be applied in new ways to novel situations.
- A teacher may be necessary to impart knowledge, but the knower should be able to use it without external guidance.

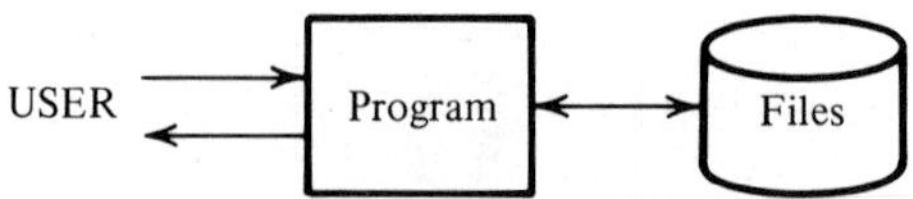

Fig. 6.1 A conventional program

Conventional programs embody Seneca's view of rote memory: they blindly follow a fixed set of instructions and have no way of adapting to changing circumstances. Knowledge-based systems, by contrast, incorporate knowledge that they acquire from human experts, but they apply it in novel ways in different circumstances.

In a conventional program, knowledge is not represented explicitly. Although it affects every instruction written, the knowledge is never separated from the detailed procedures that control the inputs, outputs, and computations (Fig. 6.1). In such programs, knowledge about the application is scattered throughout the code, and changing a single fact may require a change to hundreds of lines of code in dozens of different modules. One retail chain, for example, had nine stores, each represented by a single digit in their inventory and accounting programs. When they added a tenth store, the cost of rewriting all their programs to allow a second digit was over a million dollars.

The problem with conventional programming is that every new fact requires a change to the program. When the post office changes the length of the ZIP code, every program that uses address files has to change. Each change in tax laws, business policies, and report forms requires another patch in the corresponding programs. To simplify change, a database management system (DBMS) removes format descriptors from procedures and puts them in nonprocedural tables. Instead of reading and writing ordinary files, the program calls a DBMS designed for ease of change. Data and device formats are controlled by the DBMS under the guidance of a separate table of descriptors. Whenever formats and devices change, only descriptors are updated; procedures remain the same.

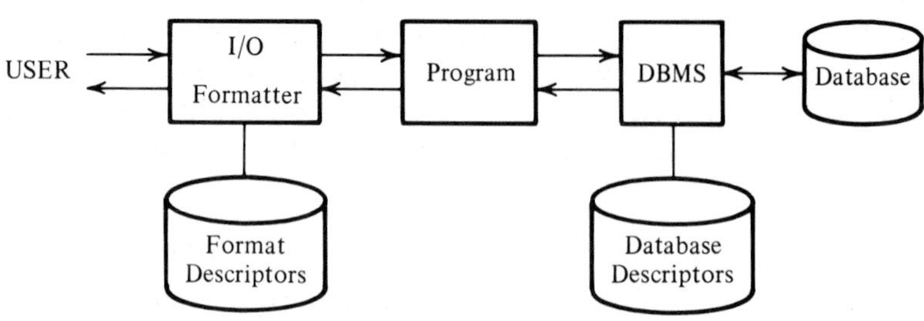

Fig. 6.2 A program with DBMS and I/O formatter

Database systems control the internal formats of permanently stored data. For the external formats on printers and displays, report writers and screen managers take the next step of separating output formats from the procedures. Figure 6.2 shows an application program connected to an I/O formatter and a DBMS, both of which are controlled by separate tables of descriptors. An example of such a system is the IBM Patient Care System (Mishelevich & Van Slyke 1980). Doctors, nurses, and hospital administrators use PCS for keeping track of medical profiles, patients, rooms, and supplies. PCS serves as a central record handler for all the departments, such as emergency room, radiology, pharmacy, and central supply. To control the output, PCS has tables of screen formats and printer formats. For input, it has a screen manager for menu selections and a parser for command strings. For the database, it uses DL/I calls. Although the external I/O and database calls are controlled by rules, PCS is not a knowledge-based system because it still uses conventional programs for computation.

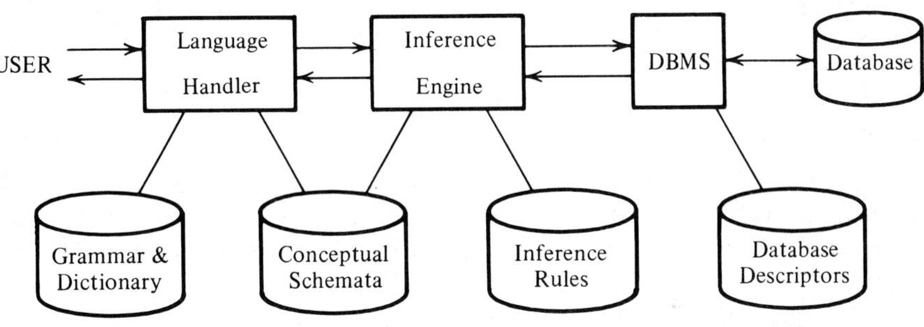

Fig. 6.3 A knowledge-based system

Knowledge-based systems take the ultimate step of separating the computational steps from the control flow and putting them in nonprocedural tables of rules. Figure 6.3 shows the *inference engine* as a small, fixed program that does not change when a new piece of knowledge is added to the system. Every fact is represented only once, and every rule that needs it uses the same representation. The knowledge-based system has three separate rule-driven facilities that serve the user:

- A language handler that analyzes inputs and generates outputs,
- An inference engine that does deductions based on rules of logic rather than procedures,
- A DBMS that stores and retrieves data upon request.

The table of conceptual schemata in Fig. 6.3 may be shared by both the language handler and the inference engine: the same knowledge that provides the semantic basis for natural language can also be used to guide deduction and problem solving.

For a conventional program, the programmer must state exactly how every piece of data is used. In a knowledge-based system, however, rules and facts are invoked associatively when needed. Feigenbaum (1977) coined the term *knowledge engineering* for the process of reducing a large body of knowledge to a precise set of rules and facts. To some extent, knowledge engineering resembles traditional systems analysis. As in any computing project, it must map a vaguely specified problem to a computable form. The difference, however, lies in the ultimate goal of the analysis—nonprocedural rules and facts rather than procedural code. The language handler, inference engine, and DBMS are themselves programs, but they are written only once by a team of system programmers. The application developers are not programmers who write procedural code, but experts in the application areas who prime the tables of rules through a *knowledge acquisition facility*. Such a facility will be discussed in more detail in Section 6.6.

An *expert system* is a knowledge-based system that incorporates enough knowledge to reach expert levels of performance. Early AI systems, such as the General Problem Solver by Newell and Simon (1963), did contain inference engines, but they did not have enough knowledge to solve significant problems. Just as human expertise depends more heavily on experience and background knowledge than on lengthy proofs and deductions, computer expertise depends primarily on the total amount of knowledge that can be brought to bear on a problem. Although an inference engine is an essential component of every expert system, a large amount of domain-specific knowledge is necessary to keep the deductions short.

Since expert systems can be applied to any subject, listing them by subject matter does not bring out the underlying similarities and differences. Instead, they can be grouped in three major categories according to the kinds of problems they address:

- *Classification.* Problems in diagnosing diseases, interpreting geological surveys, and analyzing error reports require a large amount of data to be classified in one or more categories. Since many interacting events can obscure the data, classification systems typically use statistics or *fuzzy logic* to give a range of possibilities rather than a yes/no answer.

- *Design.* These systems search for some combination of structures to satisfy a particular goal. They may design VLSI chips, select components for a computer configuration, or suggest gene-splicing experiments in molecular genetics. Unlike classification systems that apply fuzzy logic to lists of symptoms, design systems use exact reasoning on highly structured data.

- *Decision support.* These systems aid decision making by exploring alternatives, making predictions, and solving problems. They typically serve as intelligent front-ends to a conventional database, but they process the data in more complex ways than a simple query language. They may use statistics in making predictions and summaries or use exact logic for deductions and problem solving.

An important distinction that applies to all three categories of expert systems is the difference between *surface reasoning* and *model-based reasoning.* Surface reasoning classifies symptoms without considering the cause and effect relationships. In diagnosing diseases, for example, surface rules may relate symptoms to the probabilities of various bacteria. Model-based reasoning is more complex: it relates symptoms to a model or simulation of the disease; the suggested therapy is then derived from the model (Weiss et al. 1978). Most classification systems use surface rules, partly because they are easier to define and partly because the available knowledge may be incomplete. Design systems must use model-based reasoning because the very purpose of the system is to build a model. Decision support systems could use either surface reasoning or model-based reasoning.

One of the best known examples of an expert system is MYCIN (Shortliffe 1976). It is a classification system that uses surface rules for diagnosing bacterial infections. Both the experts and the users are doctors: the experts who define the knowledge base are specialists; the users may be general practitioners who need some advice in treating a particular patient. The diagnoses generated by MYCIN were good: a panel of experts judged them as more accurate than ones done by a nonspecialist. In the first stage of a dialog with MYCIN, the system asks a series of questions about the patient, the symptoms, and the tests that were taken (computer output in upper case):

```
WHAT IS THE INFECTION?
Primary bacteremia
PLEASE GIVE THE DATE AND APPROXIMATE TIME WHEN SIGNS OR
SYMPTOMS OF THE PRIMARY BACTEREMIA FIRST APPEARED.
May 5, 1975
FROM WHAT SITE WAS THE SPECIMEN FOR CULTURE-1 TAKEN?
Blood
```

To diagnose the disease, MYCIN applies rules in the knowledge base to the input and, if necessary, asks further questions for background and clarification. For this problem, the solution is a diagnosis of the organism that probably caused the illness and a recommended therapy to cure it. After identifying the possible bacteria, the system generates a prescription like the following (examples from Davis et al., 1977):

```
GIVE:  GENTAMICIN
DOSE:  119 MG (1.7 MG/KG) Q8H IV [OR IM] FOR 10 DAYS
COMMENTS:  MODIFY DOSE IN RENAL FAILURE.
```

To a knowledge engineer, the MYCIN knowledge base is a set of facts together with a set of *production rules* that drive the inference engine. Each production rule has one or more *premises* that are to be matched to the facts and a *conclusion* that is added to the facts if all the premises match. The facts are stored as relations with four fields. The first three fields represent an *attribute*, an *entity*, and a *value* of that attribute; the fourth field is a *certainty factor* (ranging from -1.0 to +1.0) which indicates the strength of the evidence:

```
(SITE CULTURE-1 BLOOD 1.0)
(IDENT ORGANISM-2 KLEBSIELLA .25)
```

For readability, these facts are mapped to the English sentences *The site of culture-1 is blood* and *There is weakly suggestive evidence (.25) that the identity of organism-2 is klebsiella.* The following MYCIN rule shows the premise to be matched and the conclusion to be drawn if the premise matches:

```
If  1) the infection is primary-bacteremia, and
    2) the site of the culture is one of the sterile sites, and
    3) the suspected portal of entry of the organism is the
       gastro-intestinal tract,
Then there is suggestive evidence (.7) that the identity of the
organism is bacteroides.
```

Internally, MYCIN represents the rules in a more compact list structure. For readability, it maps the rules to this English form for the benefit of the users, who understand the subject matter, but not the programming techniques.

A physician would not accept a diagnosis from MYCIN without knowing the reasons for its decisions. MYCIN therefore explains its diagnoses. During the consultation, it keeps a trace of every rule that was applied. When the user asks *How did you decide that organism-1 might be an E. Coli?* MYCIN searches the trace of inference steps and replies that it used rules 21, 84, and 3, which led to a cumulative certainty factor of .74. The user could then ask to see those rules printed out in English. Whenever the computer asks a question, the user can ask why it needs to know that information:

```
HOW MANY OF THE CULTURES WERE POSITIVE FOR THE E. COLI?
Why?
```

MYCIN then explains how that fact is used and what rule requires it. To appreciate the value of such a system, imagine asking a conventional program why it took some action and getting a storage dump in response. Such a dump might be useful to the original programmer, but it would be meaningless to anyone else. The English form of a MYCIN rule is readable by the user as well as the original programmer.

When MYCIN's knowledge base about bacterial infections is taken away, the underlying inference engine EMYCIN (Essential MYCIN) can be applied to many different types of problems. PUFF (Feigenbaum 1977) is EMYCIN with knowledge about lung diseases, SACON (Bennett & Englemore 1979) is EMYCIN with knowledge about structural analysis of aircraft wings, and DART (Bennett & Hollander

1981) is EMYCIN with knowledge about computer networks. In all these applications, the system asks questions to determine the basic problem; then it applies its inference rules to determine the probable cause and the recommended actions. Following is an excerpt from a dialog with DART:

```
WHAT SYMPTOM IS EXHIBITED BY PROBLEM-1?
unable to activate TP network
IS THE NETWORK ACTIVATION PROBLEM OCCURRING IN A SNA NETWORK?
yes
IS THE TERMINAL(S) INVOLVED IN PROBLEM-1 LOCALLY (CHANNEL)
ATTACHED, REMOTELY ATTACHED OR BOTH?
remote
```

In this prototype, the user must type an answer to each question, but in a finished system, most of the information would already be in machine-readable form and would not have to be retyped. After DART has asked all its questions about the access methods, the TP controller, the control program, and the trace information about lines and control units, it applies its rules to determine the cause of the problem—in this case, the most likely source of trouble is LINE01. If the user asks how it reached that conclusion, DART explains its line of reasoning:

> The VTAM IO (RNIO) trace indicates that an ACTLINK was sent to NCP for LINE01 and that a negative response was received. The ACTLINK should have caused NCP to issue an ENABLE to the line, and this, in turn, should have caused the modem to respond with DATA SET READY (DSR). You might want to check the modem interface. If the DSR is active then it is likely that the line is not the source of the failure. A LINE (or PT2) trace could be used to further investigate the problem.

DART illustrates one of the most promising applications of knowledge-based systems—the use of computer systems for explaining and diagnosing their own complexities.

The purpose of a design system is to assemble a structure that meets certain specifications. While it does the assembly, it must observe constraints on the possible ways that the pieces fit together. A typical design system is the R1 computer configurator (McDermott 1982). It starts with a customer's order for a VAX computer system[1] and checks it for consistency. It ensures that required control units, cables, and power supplies are present in the order and prevents mutually exclusive or redundant options from being ordered. After R1 has determined what features are needed, it prints a complete list of components and draws a diagram of the final configuration. Following is one of R1's production rules:

---

1 VAX and UNIBUS are trademarks of the Digital Equipment Corporation.

```
If  1) the most current active context is selecting a box
          and a module to put in it, and
    2) the next module in the optimal sequence is known, and
    3) the number of system units of space that the module
          requires is known, and
    4) at least that much space is available in some box, and
    5) that box does not contain more modules
          than some other box on a different unibus,
Then try to put that module in that box.
```

This rule has been stated in English, but the actual rules in R1 (written in the language OPS4) have a less readable, symbolic form. Unlike EMYCIN, the OPS4 rules are not translated automatically to or from English—partly because OPS4 is more general than EMYCIN and the rules tend to be more complex. Like other design systems, R1 does not use fuzzy logic: a component is either present or absent in the configuration, and certainty factors are always 1.0.

Decision support is one of the most promising applications for expert systems. Whereas a database system answers questions about the past and present, a *decision-support system* (DSS) predicts the effect of a decision on the future. Using a DSS, a manager can test models of possible actions and determine their most likely consequences. Since AI techniques are just beginning to be used for decision support, some of the earlier, non-AI systems provide better examples (Keen & Scott Morton 1978):

- The *Portfolio Management System* is used by banks to analyze stocks and portfolios. It evaluates decisions to buy or sell securities.
- *Brandaid* evaluates decisions by relating possible strategies to sales and profits.
- *Projector* supports corporate short-term planning. It can analyze cash flow, marketing strategy, and mergers or acquisitions.
- The *Geodata Analysis and Display System* constructs and displays maps. It has been used in designing police beats and drawing school boundaries.
- The *Capacity Information System* helps to schedule plants, components, and products for a truck manufacturing company.

These are working systems that have been applied to serious problems. None of them are expert systems, but all of them could benefit from AI techniques for solving problems and organizing a knowledge base. For more general and flexible decision support systems, Vassiliou et al. (1983) are combining an AI system with a relational database.

The scope of applications for expert systems is as wide as the range of human knowledge. Like Wittgenstein's games, expert systems and knowledge-based systems in general have no necessary and sufficient characteristics that clearly distinguish them from application generators and other large, rule-driven systems. The best way to characterize them is by listing examples:

- *Organic chemistry.* DENDRAL determines the structure of organic molecules. It is one of the oldest expert systems. Over a period of nearly two decades, it has evolved into a practical tool for the working chemist (Lindsay et al. 1980).
- *Mineral exploration.* PROSPECTOR interprets geological field data to determine the most likely location for various mineral deposits. Its inference engine is based on a graph processor that was originally designed for a natural language query system (Duda et al. 1979).
- *VLSI design.* EURISKO is a general system for studying and applying heuristics. Its main use is for design systems, although the designs have been in such diverse areas as theorem discovery, game playing, and automatic programming. One of the most promising applications of EURISKO has been the design of three-dimensional VLSI components (Lenat, Sutherland, & Gibbons 1982).
- *Earthquake damage assessment.* SPERIL estimates the degree of damage to a building after an earthquake. Its input includes visual inspections of cracks and deformations, information about the structural materials, and various tests that may be made on the building. Its output is an estimate of the danger of collapse and the need for repairs (Ishizuka et al. 1981).
- *Soybean pathology.* AQ11 is a learning program that derives its own rules for diagnosing soybean diseases. When told the symptoms that accompany various forms of mildew or rot, AQ11 generates appropriate rules that can drive an inference engine (Michalski & Chilausky 1980).
- *Programming by example.* EP and EP-2 also learn from examples. They monitor a user's interaction at a terminal, ask questions about the purpose of various commands, and abstract from the specific operations to a general procedure that can repeat the sequence of commands on other data (Waterman 1978, Faught et al. 1980).

Although these applications are highly diverse, they all have three common features: first, there exist recognized human experts in these fields; second, the knowledge that the experts have is quantifiable; third, the knowledge can be expressed in declarative rules instead of procedures. If a problem is so difficult that no human being knows where to begin, no computer system will be able to solve it either. If the problem requires intuitive judgments about novel situations—like evaluating the market potential of a new invention or movie script—then the intuition cannot be formalized in an expert system. The best applications for an expert system are ones that require a large amount of well-defined, formalizable knowledge.

Expert systems can serve as a filter for distinguishing a critical situation from dozens of routine cases. The R1 configurator handles all the routine orders for VAX systems, but orders with unusual requirements still require the attention of a human expert. One of the advantages of R1 is that special cases that used to cause problems have become routine. Similarly, an expert geologist is better qualified than a computer program to judge the likelihood of oil or mineral deposits at a given site. But the number of sites to be surveyed and the amount of data from each site are so great that a system is needed to select the most promising ones for the geologist to visit. For earthquake damage assessment, the number of experts may be sufficient for periods of calm, but during a major quake, hundreds or thousands of buildings may suffer some damage. With a microprocessor in each building, preliminary estimates of danger could be made immediately.

6.2 NATURAL LANGUAGE SYSTEMS

For most people, natural language is the primary means of thinking, learning, and communicating. No other means is as general or flexible. Menus are good for selecting options, but they are awkward for expressing relationships. Mathematical equations are good for relationships, but they cannot express commands. Programming languages issue commands, but they cannot ask questions. Query languages ask questions, but they cannot give explanations. Only natural languages can serve all the functions of human communication within a common, flexible framework.

As yet, no program can accept the full range of human language and interpret all the nuances and shades of meaning that people normally use. Many programs, however, support a level of communication that is much more natural and convenient than ordinary computer languages. Yet natural language is not a panacea—a few English words or phrases cannot transform a query language into a knowledge-based system. The following sentence, which one manual cited as an "English-like language" for database queries, illustrates the problem:

```
From the skills inventory, get me the name, employee number,
department, and years in service of the engineers with
knowledge of German located in the New York area.
```

A simple syntax analyzer could parse this sentence and replace phrases like *skills inventory* with SKILFILE and *knowledge of* with SKILCODE=. It could also do transformations like replacing *get me* with SELECT and moving the FROM phrase after the SELECT phrase. As a result, it could translate the original sentence into the Structured Query Language (SQL):

```
SELECT NAME, EMPNBR, DEPT, SVCYRS
FROM SKILFILE
WHERE JOBCODE = 'ENG'
      AND SKILCODE = 'GERMAN'
      AND LOC = 'NY'.
```

The SELECT clause in SQL names the attributes or domains to be retrieved. The FROM clause specifies a database file or relation. The WHERE clause or clauses specify conditions on the records or *tuples* to be selected. In this example, the so-called English-like form has no advantage: it takes more keystrokes than the SQL form, and it requires the user to name exactly the same system-dependent files and fields.

To qualify as a knowledge-based system, a program must contribute information that was not already present in the original input. In the previous example, the user still has to name the file to be accessed (calling it skills inventory instead of SKILFILE) as well as the fields to be retrieved. The only advantage of the English sentence is that it allows more natural phrases like *years in service* instead of cryptic abbreviations like SVCYRS. A more helpful system should accept a request like the following:

```
List name, employee no., dept., and service years
for engineers in New York who know German.
```

This query is shorter than either the original English-like example or the SQL translation, and it uses only familiar abbreviations like *no.* and *dept.* But its main advantage is that it omits the file name SKILFILE, which is part of the implementation, not part of the user's view of the world. Yet because the query omits the file name, it cannot be translated to the formal notation by a mere change of syntax. Instead, the system must apply its knowledge of the subject matter and of the database organization to determine what fields and files to access.

Some background knowledge can be added during the parsing stage. The Transformational Question Answering system (TQA) incorporates knowledge about the database organization in the linguistic transformations (Plath 1976; Petrick 1977; Damerau 1981). For a database about city planning, TQA would need little additional knowledge to generate SQL from the following question:

```
What is the total of the parcel areas of the parcels
whose ward block is ward 6 block 72?
```

Unless the users know exactly how the database is organized, they would not ask the question in such an awkward way. They would normally adopt much simpler forms:

```
How large is ward 6 block 72?
What is the area of ward 6 block 72?
```

Since the planners who ask such questions are not database specialists, they do not know how the database is organized. TQA incorporates such knowledge in the transformations. The adjective *large*, when applied to a surface, refers to its area. TQA therefore transforms the question phrase *how large* into the phrase *what is the area of*. Since areas are stored for parcels but not for wards and blocks, TQA derives the area of a ward or block from the total area of the parcels it contains. Either of the two simpler questions would be transformed to exactly the same SQL statement as the more complex question.

To verify that it correctly interpreted the input, a complete system should translate the internal form back into the original language. If there is a misunderstanding, the user can rephrase the question and try again. The Q-TRANS component of TQA translates an SQL statement back into English (Mückstein 1983). For the question *What parcels in the R5 zone on Stevens St. have greater than 5000 sq. ft.?* TQA generated the following SQL statement:

```
SELECT UNIQUE A.JACCN, B.PARAREA
FROM ZONEF A, PARCFL B
WHERE A.JACCN = B.JACCN
      AND B.STN = 'STEVENS ST'
      AND B.PARAREA > 5000
      AND A.ZONE = 'R5'.
```

To ensure that all the stages of translation were performed correctly, Q-TRANS takes the final SQL form as its input rather than some intermediate form. It also uses a dictionary that gives an English term for each field, such as *street name* for STN. For this example, it generated the English sentence,

```
Find the account numbers and parcel areas for lots
that have the street name STEVENS ST, a parcel area
of greater than 5000 sq. ft., and zoning code R5.
```

The primary purpose of Q-TRANS is to serve as a verification aid for TQA. But since it works directly with the SQL form, it could also be used as a training and help facility for users who ask questions directly in SQL.

If a knowledge-based system is not available, menus and prompts can relieve the burden on the user's memory. Abbreviations like EMPNBR or SVCYRS are difficult to recall, but easy to recognize on a menu. Yet some large databases have as many as 3,000 different fields, most of them with odd names like AJDWL for *dwelling unit*. With so many fields, a menu with 10 choices at each level would leave many of them buried deep in a maze of options. To study the human factors of menus vs. keywords, Geller and Lesk (1981) allowed users to choose between two different systems for browsing through a library catalog: a menu system based on Dewey Decimal numbers and a keyword system where the user could type one or more words for the title, author, or subject. The authors let the users choose either system:

> Most users chose the keyword system; of 1952 searches 79% were keyword searches. Twice as many keyword users reported successful searches as menu users. Among known-item searchers, 65% of keyword users found their book while only 30% of the menu users did; and among browsers, 69% of keyword users said they found books in their subject area while only 36% of the menu users

> did. Browsers were somewhat less likely to do keyword searches (76%) than people looking for a particular book (82%), but even this preference drops after experience with the system. Over time, the keyword system became even more popular.

Keywords, of course, are not full natural language, but typing a linear string of words is often preferable to making multiple selections on a menu. One or two menus are good, but when the hierarchy of menus grows too deep, people become lost.

To combine the best features of menus and English, Codd (1978) designed a database query system called RENDEZVOUS. The user can type either a complete question in English, a partially complete question, or just a few words in an ungrammatical sequence. Then RENDEZVOUS presents menus from which the user can make further selections to complete the query. Finally, it translates its internal form back into an English question:

```
THIS IS WHAT THE SYSTEM UNDERSTANDS YOUR QUERY TO BE:
   PRINT THE SERIAL NUMBER, NAME, LOCATION, AND RATING
   OF EVERY SUPPLIER NOT RATED EXCELLENT AND NOT LOCATED
   IN DETROIT WHO, DURING AUGUST 1975, SENT A SHIPMENT
   OF PART NUMBER P37.
IS THE SYSTEM'S UNDERSTANDING
   1 CORRECT AND COMPLETE
   2 NOT YET COMPLETE
   3 NOT CORRECT
```

RENDEZVOUS can formulate a query from nothing but menu selections, but the "maze of menus" leads to a long and tedious interrogation. By combining menus with English, it converges more quickly to a complete and correct statement. Besides its English input, RENDEZVOUS illustrates the possibility of generating English output from menu selections as input. The English output tells the user what the system is doing and helps to catch mistakes and misunderstandings.

At the interface between natural languages and computer languages, some intermediate notation is necessary: it must be expressive enough to capture the English meaning, and it must have a formally defined mapping to logic. Hendrix's *partitioned nets* (1979) are a form of conceptual graphs that have been implemented in several systems. Grosz (1977) used them for supporting English dialogs, and Duda et al. (1979) used them in the PROSPECTOR system for mineral exploration. Their most extensive development was in the LADDER system for database query (Sacerdoti 1977). LADDER accepts questions in English about naval logistics data, translates them to a graph form, performs inferences on the graphs, and accesses databases that may be distributed across several different systems in a computer network. Consider the following question:

```
What ships faster than the Kennedy
are within 500 miles of Naples?
```

To answer this question, LADDER transforms the original conceptual graph into graphs for four separate subquestions: *How fast is the Kennedy? Where is Naples? What ships are within 500 miles of Naples?* and *Which of those ships are faster than the Kennedy?* It then determines what files to access on which system in the network, generates appropriate statements in a database query language, issues them to the system, combines the results into a single answer, and prints the answer for the user.

Besides doing deductions, LADDER also keeps track of the context to determine referents of pronouns and expand elliptical expressions. In the following dialog, the user establishes a context by asking the first question in a full sentence. Once the context is known, LADDER has a basis for interpreting words and phrases that would be meaningless in isolation.

```
What is the length of the Constellation?
(LENGTH 1072 FEET)

of the Nautilus?
TRYING ELLIPSIS:  WHAT IS THE LENGTH OF THE NAUTILUS
(LENGTH 319 FEET)

displacement?
TRYING ELLIPSIS:  WHAT IS THE DISPLACEMENT OF THE NAUTILUS
(STANDARD-DISPLACEMENT 4040 TONS)
```

As this dialog illustrates, questions in English can be much more concise than queries in a database language. The questions need not specify details of files, record formats, or even location of data on any particular computer in the network. Schemata bring in background knowledge, and inference mechanisms work out the implications. LADDER also has features like spelling correction, which do not require a sophisticated knowledge base, but which are useful for good human factors.

A common criticism of natural language systems is that they consume a lot of CPU time. But in LADDER, as in most current systems, the time to parse an English sentence is usually less than the time to access the database. For the question *To what country does each merchant ship in the North Atlantic belong?* the parse time was .386 seconds, and the CPU time to retrieve 79 entries was 5.3 seconds. But the elliptical phrase *the fastest sub* required 1.484 seconds to be expanded into the complete question *To what country does the fastest sub belong?* and the CPU time to retrieve the single entry was only .833 seconds. As these examples show, the English parse time can be negligible (7%) for complex database transactions, but it can be the major part of the processing time (64%) for simple transactions. Systems like LADDER are now being designed for intelligent workstations: the English parsing is done on a small computer, and the translated query is sent to a large database system.

The tutorial system TDUS, which gives directions for assembling an air compressor, uses the same inference engine as LADDER. TDUS converses with a novice who knows how to tighten bolts and assemble parts, but does not know the sequence of steps for assembling the entire machine. Following is a sample dialog between the novice user and TDUS (Robinson 1981):

```
I attached the pump.
OK
Should I install the pulley now?
NO.  THE NEXT STEP IS:
   INSTALL THE AFTERCOOLER ELBOW ON THE PUMP.
      OR
   INSTALL THE BRACE ON THE PUMP.
I'm doing the brace now.
OK
I've done it.
OK
I've installed the pulley.
OK
What should I do now?
INSTALL THE AFTERCOOLER ELBOW ON THE PUMP.
```

During the dialog, TDUS builds a model of the current situation and changes the model after each response from the user. When the user asks for further instructions, TDUS determines the next subgoal to be achieved and prints it in English. This dialog shows how TDUS resolves references to verb phrases. The sentence *I've done it* could mean almost anything in isolation. But in the context, TDUS correctly interprets it as meaning *I have finished installing the brace.*

As a help facility for the UNIX operating system,[2] Wilensky (1983) implemented the problem-solving consultant UC, which allows the user to ask questions in English:

```
User:  I have run out of disk space writing out a file in vi.
UC:    TRY DELETING UNNEEDED FILES.
User:  I still don't have enough space.
UC:    MAIL THE FILE TO YOURSELF.
       THEN ASK THE SYSTEMS MANAGER FOR MORE DISK SPACE.
```

This is the kind of advice that one person would give to another. Unlike typical command systems, UC does not have a predefined program for every option. Instead, it treats the user's problem as a high-level goal. It then formulates a plan to reach that goal, translates each step of the plan into an English sentence, and prints the steps as advice to the user. If the first plan fails (as in the above example), UC tries to find an alternative plan. Natural language is the ideal form of communication

2 UNIX is a trademark of Bell Laboratories.

with a help facility: displaying a menu of commands is not very helpful if the user does not know which one to try. For this problem, the user would be unlikely to select the MAIL command even if it were the first option on a menu.

Tutorial systems like TDUS and UC can help to train people (either programmers or nonprogrammers) to use computers more effectively. A problem that arises with most tutorial and help facilities, however, is that they quickly become out of date: the designers and implementers add new features to the system without bothering to update the help messages. Clancey (1983) implemented the tutorial system GUIDON as an adjunct to MYCIN or other expert systems using EMYCIN. GUIDON alleviates the update problem by using a common knowledge base to drive both the deduction and the tutorial. Although its outputs are in English, GUIDON is not really a natural language system: it assembles fixed phrases in a template instead of generating English from a semantic form as TDUS does. The principle, however, is important: the same knowledge base used for computation should also be used for help and tutorials.

Although most natural language systems emphasize interactive use in commands, queries, and help facilities, the first natural language processors were developed for machine translation in batch mode. The Georgetown Automatic Translation system (GAT), which was completed in 1964, was installed at EURATOM and Oak Ridge for translating physics texts from Russian to English. Over the next decade, GAT translated about 14,000 pages of text, including several books. It was primarily a syntactic processor with little or no semantics; its translations were rough; it often selected the wrong word (*waterfalls* instead of *cascades*); and it omitted the articles *the* and *a*. But the users appreciated the speed and efficiency of the service. Following is some output from GAT (Henisz-Dostert et al. 1979):

> In obtained expression (1.28) there is considered (with error of order SP5 in comparison with unity) influence of viscosity on wave, which moves in ideal liquid with rate S without change of shape of half-wave of cosine curve. Expression (1.29) presents trace, left on free surface after passage of main wave (1.28).

The physicists who used the translations liked the service and were willing to tolerate infelicitous word choices if the system consistently chose the same output for the same input—they even found some of the choices amusing and joked about "nuclear waterfalls." A professional translator who post-edited 5,000 pages of output for NASA said that the work would not have been completed on schedule without the aid of machine translation.

Second generation translation systems were built around an intermediate meaning representation with more semantic features. The Grenoble system (Vauquois 1975) translates Russian into a *pivot language* that is based on Tesnière's dependency grammar. (Since conceptual graphs have also been influenced by Tesnière's graphs, the pivot language bears a strong family resemblance to them.) Finally, the system translates the pivot language into French. Following is a sample translation:

> Le travail de Landau (1) etait un des premiers travaux, consacres a l'etude de l'amortissement d'ondes de choc. En utilisant la solution precise connue d'equations de la dynamique de gaz pour l'onde simple par Riemann, Landau a etudie l'image asymptotique du mouvement, qui apparait pendant la propagation dans le milieu homogene des ondes planes, cylindriques et spheriques sur les grandes distances de la source de leur apparition.

Except for the missing accents (because their printer did not have them), this output is quite good. In theory, the pivot form is an intermediate notation that could be translated into languages other than French. In practice, most translation systems tend to be specialized for a single pair of languages. Making them general enough to handle all languages is not easy.

In Canada, machine translation systems translate weather reports and other routine communications between English and French. For such purposes, the machine output is adequate. For high quality, however, the rough draft from the machine must be edited by a human translator. The major deterrent to the growth of machine translation is the cost of editing: an editor who simply revises the machine output takes almost as much time to read the original and correct the output as an experienced translator would require to do a full translation. The knowledge-based systems of AI show promise of improving the quality of the translations. Yet for handling large volumes of text on a wide range of topics, those systems cannot compete with the simpler approaches, and they still require editing for publishable quality. As translation aids, computers are being used as high-speed dictionaries to ensure that critical words and phrases are translated consistently. They can also provide a usable rough draft. But the goal of fully automated, high-quality machine translation has not yet been achieved.

Natural language systems cannot yet, and perhaps never will be able to handle truly unrestricted language. But for interactive systems, where there is immediate feedback for giving help, detecting errors, and clarifying ambiguities, such systems can be much easier to use than conventional systems. Following are six important features that have been implemented in various AI prototypes. No system has all of them, but each feature has been implemented in at least one system.

- *Flexible dialog.* The user can make a request either by menu selections on a display, by a sequence of simple sentences, or by one complex command—whichever is convenient. The user may switch from one mode to another during the same application, using a full sentence to ask a question or menu selections to answer a question.

- *Mixed initiative.* Both the user and the system may contribute to the conversation and ask questions to clarify or expand an incomplete message. Either party is able to ask a question or state a fact at any time.

- *Inference.* Most sentences can be short and simple because the system is expected to fill in the "obvious" gaps. A complete theorem proving system is not necessary for interpreting English, but a technique for inferring the obvious is essential.

- *Context.* The system remembers the current topic of conversation and uses the context to resolve pronouns, defaults, and incomplete statements.
- *Knowledge base.* Interactions with the user are based on the system's knowledge of the subject. Its range of topics is extendible by adding new knowledge instead of writing detailed procedures for every possible transaction.
- *Metalanguage.* English can be used either to talk about a subject or to talk about what can be said about the subject. It can therefore support prompting and help facilities in the same language used for queries and commands.

These features are characteristic of conversations between people. All six of them are better adapted to natural languages than traditional computer languages. People have proposed computer languages that have pronouns and inferential techniques, but any system that does that much analysis might just as well process natural language. The extra work for the machine is more than compensated by the ease of use for people.

6.3 CONCEPTUAL ANALYSIS

Conceptual analysis is the work of philosophers, lawyers, lexicographers, systems analysts, and database administrators. Philosophers have been doing conceptual analysis ever since Socrates taught Plato how to analyze JUSTICE; lawyers do it whenever they draw fine distinctions in arguing a point of law; lexicographers do it in bulk quantities when they compile dictionaries; and systems analysts and database administrators do it when they translate English specifications into a system design. Conceptual analysis is essential for giving content to the empty boxes and circles of conceptual graphs.

Every discipline that uses conceptual analysis gives it a different name. In the computer field, the most common names are *systems analysis*, *enterprise analysis*, and *knowledge engineering*. Whatever the name, the ultimate goal is a precise, formalizable catalog of concepts, relations, facts, and principles. With conceptual graphs, the goal is to determine the type labels, canonical graphs, schemata, and laws of the world that define some body of knowledge or domain of discourse. In database terms, the domain of discourse is the business enterprise about which data is being stored. The laws define constraints, consistency checks, and implications that must be enforced to keep the database an accurate reflection of the state of the world. The result of the analysis is an *ontology* for a possible world—a catalog of everything that makes up that world, how it's put together, and how it works.

The easiest concepts to analyze are the ones that have already been codified for some technical project: domains in a database, data types in a programming language, or abstract terms in mathematics. The hardest concepts are the ones that are closest to everyday life. For the Canadian census, database designers found thorny problems with basic terms like *building* and *dwelling*. Since the number of possible forms for buildings was so great, they did not even attempt to give a definition. They did require every person to have a dwelling, but the dwelling might not be in a building, since the data included igloos and teepees. When the census takers found one man who lived in a sewer, the database designers had to get a ruling from a high government official that a sewer could be considered a dwelling.

Database design is applied conceptual analysis. If the analysis is incomplete or inaccurate, the resulting database may contain arbitrary restrictions, inconsistent data, or limitations that make future extensions impossible. When two or more programs interact, inconsistent analyses can lead to lost or unusable data. One system could not answer questions about Puerto Rico because the language handler classified it as a country, but the database listed it as a state in the U.S. Kent (1978) cited numerous problems in database design, including an oil company that had two inconsistent definitions of *oil well*:

> In their geological database, a *well* is a single hole drilled in the surface of the earth, whether or not it produces oil. In the production database, a *well* is one or more holes covered by one piece of equipment, which has tapped into a pool of oil. The oil company had trouble integrating these databases to support a new application: the correlation of well productivity with geological characteristics. (p. 6)

Such problems are not unique to computers. They constantly arise in organizing manual filing systems. They even cause problems for supermarkets: the same product may be grouped with breakfast foods in one store, with health foods in another, and with snacks in a third. Advertisers talk about the need for *positioning a product* in the customers' minds. If a product does not belong to a clearly defined category, store managers will not know where to put it, and potential customers will not remember it (Ries & Trout 1981).

Even more troublesome than concrete terms like *dwelling* and *oil well* are comparative terms like *big* and *small* or evaluative terms like *good* and *poor*. A big mouse, for example, is much smaller than a small elephant. Comparative words incorporate standards that must be recognized in conceptual analysis. To answer the following questions, a computer must determine whether *big* refers to height, area, volume, or number of students:

```
How big is the tree?
How big is the farm?
How big is the pot?
How big is the university?
```

The same question in different contexts might require different standards: *How big is the parking lot?* could ask either for area or for number of cars. For evaluative terms, the range of possibilities is even greater. One can compare the sizes of a big mouse and a small elephant, but a good meal and a good musician are not comparable. It is meaningless to ask whether a performance by Jascha Heifetz is better than a dinner at Lutèce. In the phrase *good meal*, the standard for GOOD is implicit in

MEAL. But sometimes the word that sets the standard is elsewhere in the context: in the sentence *Ivan is a poor choice for shortstop, but he's a good choice for catcher*, the same person is both a poor choice and a good choice. In the phrase *a good cup of coffee*, the cup is not treated as a physical object, but as a unit of measure. Since a unit of measure does not normally have a standard for GOOD, it must be the coffee that is good, not the cup. In some cases, however, GOOD applied to a measure might mean a generous portion, as in the phrase *a good pint of beer*.

When a natural concept is expressed in a computable form, its vague boundaries and continuous shadings are replaced by sharp, precise distinctions. Although precision is usually desirable, it can be misleading when a concept defined by family resemblances is replaced with a concept of the same name that is defined by necessary and sufficient conditions. In a knowledge-based system for generating stock market reports, Kukich (1983) had to give a precise meaning to the sentence *The stock market closed mixed*. Informally, *mixed* means that some stocks went up, some went down, and there was no clear trend in either direction. But how many stocks must move and how far must they move for the market to be mixed? Kukich found that newspaper reporters used the term *mixed* in either of the following two conditions:

- The Dow Jones average went up, but the number of declines led the number of advances.
- The Dow Jones average went down, but advances led declines.

Kukich used this definition in her program. Although her definition agrees with informal usage in most cases, it might disagree when the market is moving erratically.

Another problem for conceptual analysis is that the standards for comparative terms may change. To describe the volume of shares traded, stock market analysts use the terms *heavy*, *active*, *moderate*, and *light*. Kukich adjusted the parameters in her program to match newspaper reports as closely as possible. But she noticed that the program, which was written in the fall of 1982, differed from newspaper reports on older data. For June 24, 1982, it called a volume of 57 million shares moderate, but the *Wall Street Journal* on that date called it active. After checking the parameters, she found that the standards had changed. During August, several weeks of record-breaking activity on the stock market had caused the analysts to raise the standards. Just as people change with experience, the schemata and prototypes that reflect standards and default values must grow and change.

Some words describe long-lasting attributes, such as *human* and *cat*, while others apply only to a specific situation, such as *pedestrian* and *customer*. When suitably qualified, nouns can even assume the tenses, aspects, and modalities of verbs: *former thief*, *possible fortune*, *would-be authority*, *once and future king*, *regular customer* (a repetitive state), and *one-shot deal*. The permanent attributes correspond to *natural types* like CAT, RED, and GOLD; the others are *role types* like PET,

WARNING-LIGHT, and MONETARY-STANDARD. A natural type refers to the *essence* of some entity or substance, but a role type refers to *accidental properties* that might have been otherwise: a cat cannot stop being a cat as long as it lives, but it is a pet only when some human being adopts it; red is always red, but some person may or may not use it as the color of a warning light; gold is an unchanging element, but its role as a monetary standard depends on government laws and regulations. This distinction even applies to mathematical concepts: the role types DIVIDEND, DIVISOR, and QUOTIENT are all subtypes of the natural type NUMBER. For the equation 21÷3=7, the numbers 21, 3, and 7 are the referents of concepts [DIVIDEND:21], [DIVISOR:3], and [QUOTIENT:7].

Conceptual analysis clarifies muddled thinking and makes ideas precise. Sloman (1978) commented on a research proposal that looked impressive until its jargon was translated into ordinary English—its purpose was to find out whether people "cooperate more successfully if they get on well together." In presenting a strategy for doing conceptual analysis, Sloman developed a comprehensive checklist of points to consider. The following five points are similar to his checklist, but the terminology is adapted to conceptual graphs:

- *Instances.* Imagine every possible way in which the concept may be used. Look for borderline cases where the concept is almost applicable, but not quite. Use the concept in different linguistic contexts. Do different syntactic and semantic structures have different conceptual connections?

- *Type hierarchy.* Divide the list of instances into subtypes and group them according to different criteria in as many ways as possible. Consider all supertypes of the concept, including the most general category. Search a dictionary or thesaurus for synonyms, antonyms, and related words. Determine what criteria distinguish them and under what conditions each would be used. What new types would have to be added to extend the type hierarchy to a lattice?

- *Canonical graphs.* Is the concept a natural type like CAT, a role type like PEDESTRIAN, a comparative type like BIG, or an evaluative type like GOOD? What other types of concepts must be linked to it in canonical graphs? A natural type like PERSON may not have necessary connections, but a role type like CHILD presupposes a PARENT, and CUSTOMER presupposes a SELLER. Concepts that are naturally expressed as verbs, adjectives, and adverbs always have required links in canonical graphs. Actions and events expressed as nouns like *sale* and *distribution* have the same kinds of links as the corresponding verbs.

- *Definitions.* Most dictionaries are too brief to give a complete analysis, and they do not discuss all related aspects. Check dictionary definitions of the concept, criticize them, and extend or complete them. Is the concept a technical one for which a type definition is possible, or must it be specified by a family of schemata? Look for general primitives that underlie the concept and related ones. BUY, for example, can be defined in terms of a more primitive type GIVE, which can also be used to define SELL, BARTER, EXCHANGE, DONATE, etc.

- *Schemata.* If the concept cannot be defined by necessary and sufficient conditions, list examples of the family of uses that must be specified in schemata. Is some schema central, with the other uses peripheral or metaphorical? List some common metaphors that may be applied to this type (see Section 5.7 for a discussion of metaphor). Does the concept depend on social institutions, customs, or roles? What other concepts belong to the same cultural system, style, or milieu? How is it related to other concepts? Is it a cause, a purpose, an excuse, or a law? What concepts are related as preconditions, postconditions, or effects?

Essential properties of concepts are stated in type definitions, and common properties that are not necessary are stated in schemata. Running, for example, is usually faster than walking. Yet speed is not a defining characteristic because some people can walk faster than others can run. The crucial property is that one foot stays on the ground at all times in walking, but both feet leave the ground periodically in running. A schema for RUN would mention speed, but a type definition would state only the essential properties.

The preceding checklist is organized by structural elements like types and schemata. Sloman supplemented the structural list with tests for exploring the completeness and accuracy of the analysis. These tests lead to common associations that can be codified in types, definitions, and schemata:

- *Teaching.* How would you teach the concept to a child, a foreigner, or a chimpanzee? What examples would you use? What would you mention as something that was *not* an example? What possible confusions might occur? How would you clarify them?

- *Operational tests.* How could you test the truth or falsity of statements about the concept? How could you determine whether another person who uses it intends the same meaning as you?

- *Story telling.* Imagine fictional situations where the concept may be used. Extreme cases in science fiction or mythology may help to reveal the scope and ramifications of the concept.

- *Computer simulation.* For knowledge-based systems, the analysis must enable a computer to converse with people in normal English. Is it missing any aspect that would cause a computer to use the concept incorrectly?

Questions like these are designed to elicit the tacit assumptions that are so obvious that no one thinks of them consciously. The complex cases that people are most aware of are much less fundamental than their unconscious presuppositions.

Since conceptual analysis must deal with so many different aspects, it should be done in stages with deepening precision. The first stage is *brainstorming*: free association with the goal of listing everything related to a concept. Once everything has been put down on paper, the second stage is a more critical analysis of the concept and its relationships. In the initial stage, completeness is more important than neatness and rigor. Instead of drawing all the boxes and circles for conceptual graphs, the analyst should merely draw straight lines from the concept to be analyzed and put ordinary English words and phrases on the lines. Buzan (1974) drew loosely structured diagrams of this sort as an aid for taking notes, solving problems, drafting speeches, and even organizing meetings. An advantage of diagrams over hierarchical outlines is that a hierarchy requires each item to be classified before it can be inserted, but diagrams postpone classification until all the associations have been listed.

Free association is a technique of conceptual analysis that works both for conventional software and for knowledge-based systems. In program design, Archibald (1981) proposed *idea-dependency analysis* for analyzing informal English specifications to define data types for the ADAPT programming language:

- First, the designer lists all the ideas or concept types associated with the problem. In an editing program, for example, the types FILE, LINE, STRING, and INTERPRETER are all associated with EDITOR.
- Second, lines are drawn between the types to show dependencies. For the EDITOR, the type FILE depends on LINE, because a file is an aggregate of lines. Recursive dependencies are possible if a concept type is defined in terms of itself, either directly or indirectly.
- Finally, the informal dependency diagram is mapped into the formalism of the system: procedures and data abstractions in ADAPT or type definitions and schemata in conceptual graphs.

In practice, Archibald found that "users are quickly able to discuss the potential dependencies of ideas; what they do not realize at first is how easily these dependencies can form the foundation of a system description" (p. 156). In an extended example, Power (1981) started with a three-page English specification for a file update program, circled the significant nouns and verbs, drew arrows to show the dependencies, and mapped the dependency diagram into the global program structure. After several iterations, the idea-dependency diagram evolved into a complete program in ADAPT for solving the problem. Circling nouns and verbs is practical for a three-page specification. A complex subject, however, may take hundreds of pages of description. If the specifications are in a machine-readable form, they can be analyzed by a *concordance program*, which lists every occurrence of every word and its surrounding context.

A concordance shows what patterns are associated with a given word. *Co-occurrence relations* show what words are associated with a given pattern. To study co-occurrences, Fries (1952) classified words according to the *sentence frames* in which they occur. The words *eat* and *like*, for example, are both transitive verbs. Therefore, either may occur in the frame,

```
I ate the doughnut.
I liked the doughnut.
```

The following frame, however, sounds natural or normal with the verb *eat*, but it sounds odd with the verb *like*:

```
What I did to the doughnut was eat it.
What I did to the doughnut was like it.
```

Some words that sound equally good in either sentence frame include *mash, bake, dunk, discard,* and *explode.* Besides *like*, some words that fit the first frame, but not the second, include *admire*, *distrust,* and *know.* The difference is between actions and states: verbs in the *eat*-class express actions that can be done to a doughnut; verbs in the *like*-class express states that a person can experience with regard to a doughnut, but they do not affect the doughnut. In another example, Katz (1966) used the frame,

```
The razor blade is good.
The grain of sand is good.
```

The first sentence is complete in itself and needs no further explanation. The second, however, immediately leads the reader to ask, *good for what?* Terms that fit in the same co-occurrence class as *razor blade* include *anesthetic, poker hand,* and *lung.* These words have associated schemata that indicate purposes: a razor blade is supposed to be good for shaving, and a lung for breathing. Words that fit in the same class as *grain of sand* include *molecule, integer, liquid,* and *planet.* These words have no schemata that provide a scale of goodness. A grain of sand may be good for causing an oyster to grow a pearl, and a planet may be good as a target for space exploration, but those are accidental uses that are not a part of the meaning of *sand* or *planet.*

When defining words, translators and lexicographers compare a word with other words that fit the same sentence frames. Often the contexts are redundant, and sometimes they are misleading. Nida (1975) illustrated the technique by considering contexts for the word *tezgüino* , which is used by the Tarahumara Indians of northern Mexico. As examples, he cited the following sentences (p. 167):

```
There is some tezgüino.
A jar of tezgüino is on the table.
```

By comparing other words that fit these frames, one can conclude that *tezgüino* must be a *mass noun* like *water*, *candy*, or *money* instead of a *count noun* like *dog* or *table.* Since it can be put in a jar, it must also be a concrete substance instead of an abstraction like joy. (But one must gather enough examples to make sure that the word is not being used in a metaphorical sense, like the hope contained in Pandora's box.) The next two sentences add further information:

```
You need a lot of tezgüino to get your land cleared.
Everyone likes tezgüino.
```

These two sentences suggest that the word means money, but they are misleading, as the next two sentences indicate:

```
Tezgüino makes you drunk.
We make tezgüino out of corn.
```

These sentences finally suggest that tezgüino is an alcoholic beverage brewed from corn mash. The evidence is not certain, however, because it could also be corn cake soaked in alcohol. Since a lot of it is used by people who clear land, it is more likely to be a kind of beer made from corn. A dozen examples are sufficient to define a concrete word like *tezgüino* , but Plato wrote an entire book to analyze the abstract word *justice*.

Each sentence frame divides a set of words into two co-occurrence classes: those that fit the frame, and those that don't. A second test can subdivide either or both of those classes further. The class of transitive verbs that fit the frame *I —— the doughnut* were subdivided into two subclasses by the frame *What I did to the doughnut was —— it* . With n frames, up to 2^n co-occurrence classes may be distinguished. Each frame tests one *binary feature*, and each co-occurrence class is defined by the presence or absence of each of several binary features. The use of binary features for defining classes of words is an important technique in linguistics that also applies to *enterprise analysis*. The BIAIT technique for analyzing a business is based on seven binary features (Burnstine 1979, Carlson 1979):

- *Bill.* Does the supplier bill the customer, or does the customer pay cash?
- *Future.* Does the supplier deliver the product at some time in the future, or does the customer take the order with him?
- *Profile.* Does the supplier keep a profile of the customer, or is every transaction a surprise?
- *Negotiate.* Is the price negotiated or fixed?
- *Rent.* Is the product rented or purchased?
- *Track.* Does the supplier keep track of the product after it is sold or not?
- *Make to order.* Is the product made to order or provided from stock?

These seven features determine 2^7 or 128 co-occurrence classes of businesses, distinguished by their record keeping needs. The first answer to each question implies more complex record keeping than the second: if the supplier bills the customer, the business must do credit checks, bill preparation, accounts receivable, and debt collection. In anthropology, Lévi-Strauss (1963) used binary features for analyzing kinship systems, social hierarchies, mythic patterns, and other cultural structures. For psychotherapy, Kelly (1955) used binary features for analyzing the *personal constructs* that people use for organizing their thoughts and attitudes about themselves, other people, and the world in general.

The sets of features for BIAIT or Lévi-Strauss's anthropology seem almost obvious once they are presented, but finding the right features and categories may take months or years of analysis. The proper set of categories provides a structural framework that helps to organize the detailed facts and general principles of a system. Without them, nothing seems to fit, and the resulting system is far too complex and unwieldy. As an aid to systems analysis, the Business Systems Planning (BSP) methodology (IBM 1981) suggests a starting set of categories for typical business enterprises, such as an insurance company, a gas company, a hospital, and a university. Although BSP does not use the terminology of conceptual graphs, it requires much of the same information: a hierarchy of types and subtypes of entities, lists of attributes that must be stored for each entity, the actions or processes that use or create data, the systems that perform those processes, and the people and organizations that enter data or request reports.

6.4 DATABASE SEMANTICS

The primary requirement for a database system is not a computer, but a highly structured organization about which one needs to store and process large volumes of data. Business organizations are based on principles of record keeping and accounting that have been developed and perfected since the times of the ancient Sumerians. When computers became available, businesses had well-defined record structures that could immediately be mapped to a computable form. The first steps of database design therefore begin long before a computer is even considered. It starts with an analysis of an enterprise, the tasks to be done, and the records needed to do them. It ends with detailed data structures that are optimized for computer processing. The design takes four stages:

- *Systems and procedures.* Define the forms, procedures, rules, and regulations that make the business work.
- *Systems analysis.* Map information about the business into specifications of input formats, output reports, and internal data that has to be stored and processed.
- *Logical database design.* Analyze the functional dependencies in the data to determine an optimal set of logical relations.
- *Physical database design.* Map the logical relations to files, records, and fields on actual storage devices.

For simple systems on small computers, all four stages may be done by the same person (who may only be dimly aware of separate stages). On large systems, each stage may be handled by a separate group of specialists. Communication then becomes a major problem. The common aspect that unifies all the groups is a knowledge of the meaning of the data and the constraints necessary to keep it a faithful model of the real world. The study of the meaning and constraints on the data is called *database semantics*.

AI systems also represent knowledge about the world, but the systems that they store knowledge about are very different from highly structured business organizations. In typical business systems, much of the complexity has already been codified by a systems analyst, and the databases have many repetitions of a small number of data types: an employee file, for example, might have 2,000 records, each with about 150 fields. Although databases are growing more complex, the number of record types remains much smaller than the number of instances of each type. AI, by contrast, started with problems of everyday life: interpreting ordinary English, analyzing a visual scene, or guiding a robot. For these problems, the total amount of data is usually small enough to reside in main storage. Yet almost every item is unique, and the complexity has never been resolved by a systems analyst.

A typical example of an AI database is CyFr (Schank, Kolodner, & DeJong 1980), which combines FRUMP for reading and summarizing newspaper stories with CYRUS for storing and retrieving information from the stories. In its primary application, CYRUS kept track of newspaper accounts about former secretary of state Cyrus Vance. Whenever a story about Vance appeared on the UPI wires, FRUMP would pass a summary of the story to CYRUS, which would add the information to its database. Then CYRUS could answer questions like the following:

```
How many times has Vance talked to Gromyko recently?
AT LEAST SIX TIMES IN THE LAST 4 MONTHS.
```

CYRUS did not have a general relation for talks between persons. Instead, it searched its collection of graphs for meetings, summit conferences, and negotiations where both Vance and Gromyko were participants. A conventional database is best suited to storing simple properties about a large number of entities. CYRUS, by contrast, stored complex properties about a few individuals. Conventional databases have no direct mapping to and from natural languages, but CYRUS stored its information in conceptual graphs, which map directly to natural language.

The difference between AI and database systems can be measured by the ratio of data descriptors to individual data items. In a database system, one set of descriptors may be sufficient to describe thousands of records. In an AI system such as CyFr, there is so little repetition that each item must have its own descriptor. Most AI systems, in fact, do not distinguish data items from data descriptors. Because of the difference in ratios, the two fields have major differences in emphasis and priorities. Database systems emphasize efficient storage and retrieval: data dictionaries specify how many bytes an employee number requires, but they omit the "obvious" fact that type EMPLOYEE is a subtype of PERSON. Yet to a computer, nothing is obvious unless it is explicitly stated. AI systems, by contrast, have developed highly sophisticated methods for representing the obvious. But they have been impractical for commercial applications because they have high overhead, are usually limited to main storage, and ignore backup and error recovery.

Both AI and database systems have a great deal to contribute to each other. The database field has more practical experience in security, efficiency, and reliability; AI has developed more sophisticated techniques for representing the meaning of data. As AI systems begin to deal with larger amounts of data, they will find more repetition of items with the same descriptors. As database systems move towards less highly structured applications, they will have to put greater emphasis on describing fewer items with more complex relationships. Since anything that can be stored in a database can be expressed in English, the conceptual graphs designed for natural language semantics should be rich enough for defining what is in a database. Sowa (1981) listed seven kinds of knowledge necessary for database semantics:

- *Type hierarchy.* Types of entities in the database are ordered according to levels of generality: ELECTRICAL-ENGINEER, ENGINEER, EMPLOYEE, PERSON, ANIMAL, LIVING-THING, ENTITY.

- *Functional dependencies.* Actors show how the referents of concepts may be found in the database. They show which entity types are *keys* or independent variables and which ones are functionally dependent on the keys. Quantifiers show whether a function is many-to-one, one-to-one, or *n*-to-*m*.

- *Domain roles.* Besides showing that two entity types are functionally dependent, conceptual graphs describe the role that the dependency represents. Instead of merely saying that AGE is functionally dependent on two concepts of type DATE, a conceptual graph can show that one DATE is the point in time of a person's birth and the other DATE is the time at which AGE is being evaluated. Functional dependencies show that two concepts are related, and domain roles show what the relationship means.

- *Definitions.* Aggregations, concept types, relation types, and actors can be defined in terms of other types, relations, and actors. The definition of EMPLOYEE would specify the genus or more general type PERSON and the characteristic differentia *one who works for an organization for pay.*

- *Schemata.* For each concept type, schemata describe the conventional, normally occurring, or default roles that it plays with respect to other concepts. Whereas a type definition for EMPLOYEE presents the primary defining characteristic, a schema would include the background information that an employee has an employee number, earns a salary, reports to a manager, works in a department, and so forth.

- *Procedural attachments.* Actors bound to a schema show how external procedures can compute the referents of concepts. Control marks on concepts determine when an actor is invoked. Actors may describe computed functions, relations stored in the database, or *virtual relations* that are computed as needed.

- *Inferences.* Rules of inference determine implications that follow from the explicitly stored data, detect violations of constraints on the data, and derive new dataflow graphs by joining simpler graphs.

These seven kinds of knowledge constitute the meaning or *intension* of the data. The actual values stored in the database are the *extension.*

Conceptual analysis is the first stage of database design: just as a translator analyzes sentences in order to define a word like *tezgüino* , a systems analyst must analyze an English statement of requirements in order to translate it into files and procedures for a database system. For databases that have a natural language front-end, an analysis of the vocabulary is essential. Even for databases that have a more conventional programming or query interface, a study of word associations by sentence frames and idea-dependency analysis helps to determine the structure of the data, the operations to be performed on the data, and the functional dependencies between entities and attributes. If the database is coupled with a natural language system, the requirements for a smooth mapping from natural language require that the database relations have a direct mapping to the case frames of verbs. In adapting an English query processor to a database of alumni records, Vassiliou (1982) found that the original design did not map easily into English. The original DONATION relation, for example, had the following form:

Name	1983 Amt	1982 Amt	1981 Amt
Archer	$1,000	$0	$125
Bass	$0	$50	$50
Owens	$0	$200	$500

This organization had been chosen because it mapped directly to the reports that were generated from the database. It is awkward, however, because it requires a new column to be added to the relation every year. The following format for DONATION is structurally more flexible, but it does not map as directly to the output reports:

Name	Year	Amount
Archer	1981	$125
Archer	1983	$1,000
Bass	1981	$50
Bass	1982	$50
Owens	1981	$500
Owens	1982	$200

Although the second table does not look like the desired output reports, it more easily maps to a schema for the concept type DONATE and thence to English sentences containing the verb *donate*. In the following schema for DONATE, the concept [PERSON] maps to the name column in the table, [YEAR] maps to the year column, and [MONEY:@] maps to the amount column:

```
schema for DONATE(x) is
   [DONATE: *x]-
      (AGNT)→[PERSON]
      (OBJ)→ [MONEY: @]
      (PTIM)→[YEAR]
      (RCPT)→[SCHOOL: New York University].
```

The recipient, New York University, is not listed in the table since it is a constant implicit in every entry. Note the @ symbol in [MONEY:@]; it indicates a measure of money, not the name of a particular instance of money (see Section 3.3). There is no @ symbol in [YEAR], since 1982 is the name of a year, not its measure. The English question *How much did Archer donate in 1981?* would be translated to the following *query graph*. The question mark on the concept [MONEY:@?] shows where answer the should go:

```
[DONATE]-
   (AGNT)→[PERSON: Archer]
   (OBJ)→ [MONEY: @ ?]
   (PTIM)→[YEAR: 1981].
```

This query graph maps directly to the schema that describes the database relation. The schema then maps to the stored data to select the entries of interest. In this case, the answer selected would be [MONEY:@$125].

In the first donation table, each line represents a set of donations. In the second one, each line represents a single donation. Since the schema for DONATE also represents a single donation, it maps directly to the second table, but not the first. Questions about sets of donations can still be asked. The question *In what years did Owens donate?* would be translated to the following *query graph*:

```
[PERSON:Owens]←(AGNT)←[DONATE]→(PTIM)→[YEAR:{?}].
```

The symbol {?} asks for a set as answer, which is derived by set joins for each of the separate donations (see Section 3.7). The resulting *answer graph* replaces the question mark with the set of values {1981,1982}:

```
[PERSON:Owens]←(AGNT)←[DONATE]→(PTIM)→[YEAR:{1981,1982}].
```

For each field in a database relation, there must be a corresponding concept in the schema. To show how the mapping is done, the schema must be augmented with *actors* that form a dataflow graph (Section 4.6). For the schema for DONATE, the following dataflow graph shows that [PERSON] and [YEAR] are the two input concepts or keys of the actor <DONATION> and the concept [MONEY:@] is the output concept:

```
<DONATION>-
   ←[PERSON]
   ←[YEAR]
   →[MONEY: @].
```

When referents are specified for the concepts [PERSON] and [YEAR], the actors can access the database to find the amount of MONEY. The schema for DONATE with this dataflow graph bound to it forms the intension, and the actual data in the table is the extension.

schema for HIRE(x) **is**

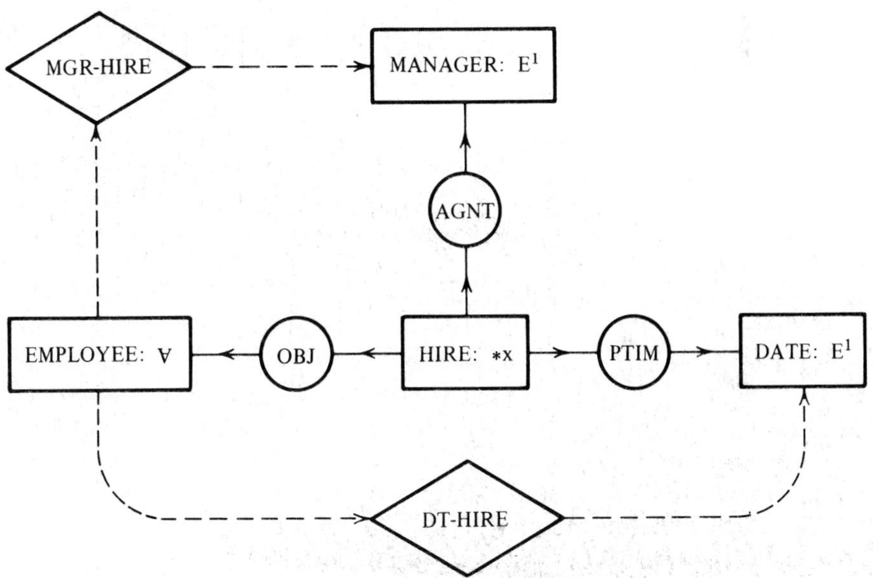

Fig. 6.4 Conceptual schema for the HIRE relation

In a complete schema for a database relation, the conceptual graph is bound to the dataflow graph. Figure 6.4 shows a schema for HIRE with two actors <MGR-HIRE> and <DT-HIRE> bound to it. The conceptual graph part of the schema expresses the *roles* played by the various entities: a manager hires an employee at a certain date. When given the name or individual marker for a particular employee, the actor <MGR-HIRE> is associated with a database relation that

schema for AGE(x) is

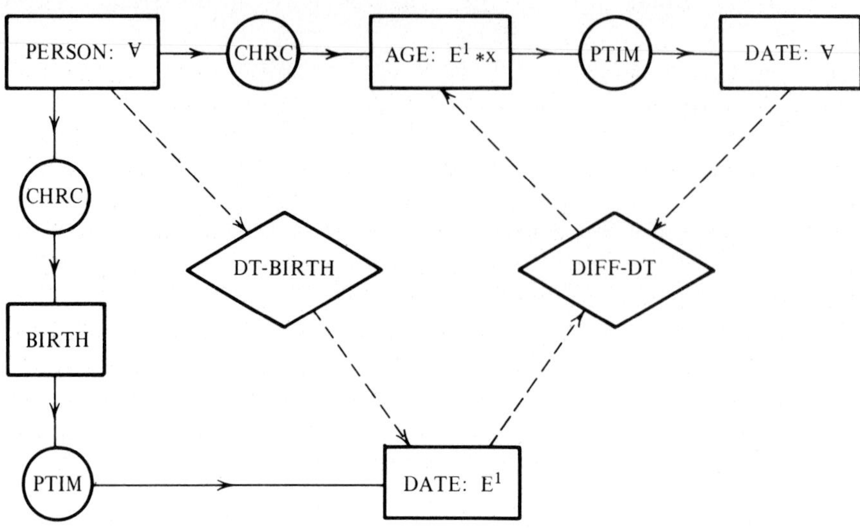

Fig. 6.5 Schema for AGE

determines the hiring manager, and the actor <DT-HIRE> is associated with a database relation that determines the date of hire. The symbol ∀ is a *universal quantifier* and E^1 is a *unique existential quantifier*. The quantifiers show that for each employee there exist a unique manager who hired that employee and a unique date on which that employee was hired.

Actors bound to a schema can represent procedures and virtual relations just as well as relations stored in the database. Figure 6.5 shows a schema for AGE that includes two actors. The actor <DT-BIRTH> computes a person's date of birth. It represents a relation stored in the database whose key is of type PERSON, and whose dependent value is of type DATE. The actor <DIFF-DT> computes the difference of two dates, one of which is the output of the actor <DT-BIRTH>. In principle, <DIFF-DT> could be stored as an enormous table that gave the difference of all possible pairs of dates. In practice, such a table would waste storage since the difference is easily computed on request. Since an actor is characterized solely by its responses to requests, the internal implementation is irrelevant: a stored table, procedural code, or a dataflow graph containing other actors would all have the same effect.

The *keys* of a database relation appear as universally quantified concepts in a schema. In the HIRE schema, [EMPLOYEE:∀] is the key, and [MANAGER:E^1] and [DATE:E^1] are *functionally dependent* on the key. The universal quantifier ∀ shows that every employee is a valid input for the actors <MGR-HIRE> and

<DT-HIRE>. In the AGE schema, [PERSON:∀] and [DATE:∀] are the two keys, and [AGE:E^1] is the unique value that is functionally dependent on the keys. The concept [DATE:E^1] depends on [PERSON:∀]; it lies along a *transitive dependency* since its referent is determined by the referent of PERSON, but it in turn helps to determine the referent of AGE. Because of the transitive dependency, the AGE schema is in *second normal form*, but not *third normal form*. The BIRTH relation in the database, however, may be stored in third normal form if convenient. This example shows how a schema may present a different view of the database from what is stored. To give a full treatment of functional dependencies and normal forms is beyond the scope of this book. For those topics, see a textbook such as Ullman (1982), Date (1981), or Vetter and Maddison (1981).

The generic marker * of an ordinary generic concept represents the existential quantifier ∃ of standard logic, and the generic set {*} is a *set quantifier* (Sowa 1976). If a database relation *r* has more than one *candidate key*, then for each key, there is separate schema *s* that describes a *view* of *r* with that candidate key. Quantifiers on the concepts of *s* have the following significance:

- Each concept of *s* that belongs to the key of *r* contains a universal quantifier in its referent field.
- Each concept of *s* that is functionally dependent on the key contains a unique existential quantifier E^1
- Each concept of *s* that is the target of a *multivalued dependency* contains a generic set referent {*}.

Ordinary generic concepts like [HIRE] in the HIRE schema or [BIRTH] in the AGE schema do not map to anything stored in the database. In principle, they could be stored in it: every instance of birth or hiring might have a unique serial number. But for most applications, those concepts represent entities whose unique identifiers are not of interest to the database designers or users. The actor nodes map to relations in a relational database; they could also be mapped to a network or hierarchical database.

The box and diamond nodes in a dataflow graph resemble the nodes in Chen's *entity-relationship diagrams* (1976). As in Chen's notation, the boxes represent entity types, and the diamonds represent functional relations that may be computed either by a database access or an executable procedure. Because of the similarity, design techniques using entity-relationship diagrams can be adapted to conceptual graphs. There are, however, some important differences:

- Entity-relationship diagrams typically show all the entity types and relationships in the database with a single large graph.
- Conceptual graphs, however, are more modular. Each view of each relation (or network or hierarchy) is described by a separate schema.

- Rules for joining conceptual graphs allow the modular schemata to be reassembled in all combinations that represent meaningful ways of accessing the database.
- Operations on conceptual graphs parallel the operations on database relations. If schema s_1 describes a database relation r_1 and schema s_2 describes relation r_2, the relation formed by joining r_1 and r_2 on a common domain is described by the schema formed by joining s_1 and s_2 on the corresponding concept.

To show the generality and versatility of conceptual graphs, Shasha (1983) translated entity-relationship diagrams and other notations into conceptual graphs.

The term *conceptual schema* derives from the terminology of AI and cognitive psychology, but it also coincides with the ANSI/SPARC terminology for database systems (Tsichritzis & Klug 1978). The ANSI/SPARC framework is based on three schemata, which map directly to the three vertices of the meaning triangle (Fig. 1.4):

- *Concept.* The *conceptual schema* is a catalog of intensions that describe how the users think about the data.
- *Referent.* The *internal schema* describes the catalog of extensions—the stored data about entities and attributes in the real world.
- *Symbol.* The *application schema* defines a mapping to the symbols and statements of programming languages that access the data. (This schema is also called the *external schema*, but that term is misleading because it describes the interface to the programming language, not to the external entities themselves.)

The task of database semantics is to define the meaning of the data in relationship to the real world. It must include everything in the conceptual schema—all the definitions, views, and constraints that reside in the data dictionary.

6.5 DATABASE INFERENCE

When two people are talking, each person uses background information for understanding the other. Sometimes one person has to ask the other for a crucial fact, but conversation is easier and quicker when prompting is not needed. The task of database inference is to determine the background information automatically. As an example, Reisner (1977) cited two ways of asking the same question:

```
How many 727s are dispatched from LaGuardia?
Find the number of 727 planes that are dispatched
  from LaGuardia Airport.
```

The first question is the normal one that people would ask. But since the second one is more explicit, both people and computers find it easier to translate into a formalized query language like SQL:

```
SELECT NUMBER-DISPATCHED
FROM DISPATCH
WHERE AIRPORT = 'LAGUARDIA'
      AND PLANE = 727.
```

The second query is easier to translate because it includes keywords or phrases that show the files and fields that must be accessed. If the keywords are not mentioned, the task is more difficult.

Translating an English question to a formal query requires three kinds of knowledge: syntax, semantics, and domain-specific detail. Linguistic transformations are the most general: a question of the form *How many Xs are Y?* can be mapped to the form *Find the number of Xs that are Y*. To translate *LaGuardia* to *LaGuardia Airport*, however, requires knowledge about the application. To translate *727* into *727 plane*, it must distinguish a number used as a count from a model number or a serial number. In this context, 727 appears as the object of DISPATCH; therefore, the system can determine the possible types by checking a schema for DISPATCH. There could still be an ambiguity: 727 is a plane type, but 7:27 might be a train departure time; the fact that LaGuardia is an airport would be needed to resolve the issue. If all else fails, the system could ask the user for a clarification.

Once the system has determined the type of each term in a query, it may still require further background information. As another example, Reisner cited the query *Find the names of all employees located in Stockton*. If the employee file had the location stored in each record, the SQL statement would be,

```
SELECT NAME
FROM EMP
WHERE LOC = 'STOCKTON'.
```

More likely, all employees in the same department work at the same location, and the location would not have to be repeated in each employee record. The database would be *normalized* by factoring out redundant information. With such a database, the SQL query must refer to the intervening department number, DEPTNO:

```
SELECT NAME
FROM EMP
WHERE DEPTNO =
      SELECT DEPTNO
      FROM DEPT
      WHERE LOC = 'STOCKTON'.
```

This statement selects just those DEPTNOs from the DEPT relation where the location is Stockton. Then it joins the result with the EMP relation, and selects names from that result. In a database without inference, the user must ask a query that explicitly refers to the department: *Find the names of all employees who work in departments located in Stockton.* Since the original query never mentioned the department number, the *hidden join* problem is the task of finding the implicit relations that must be joined to compute the answer.

Finding data types and hidden joins requires an inference method that combines the user's query with background information about the database. That information can be added at three different stages in query processing. Each stage corresponds to one of the components of a knowledge-based system, as described in Section 6.1:

- *Language handler.* Linguistic transformations can insert implicit information. The phrase, *employees located in Stockton*, could be converted to the equivalent phrase, *employees who work in departments located in Stockton.* The latter phrase would then have a more direct mapping to the database.

- *Inference engine.* A separate deductive processor could combine a conceptual graph or other logical form with background information about the database. The language processor would generate a *query graph* that included only the information explicitly mentioned, and the inference engine would combine it with schemata that describe the actual database organization.

- *Database system.* The database administrator could define a *virtual relation* from NAME to LOC that would be computed from the stored relations from NAME to DEPTNO and from DEPTNO to LOC. The language handler would generate SQL queries in terms of the virtual relations, and the database system would map them into the stored relations.

Petrick (1982) noted that the TQA system uses all three stages. Since the first version of TQA had a simpler database system than SQL, it did most of the transformations in the language handler. But with SQL as the query language, more of the work is being done by the database system. The main reason for shifting the work to SQL is to simplify the task of extending and modifying the system. Most database administrators are not trained linguists, but they do understand databases; it is easier for them to define virtual relations in SQL than to add new grammar rules and transformations.

Although virtual relations can simplify the mapping, they do not eliminate the need for an inference engine: some inferences are still needed to determine what virtual relations to access. To answer a question, the language handler first translates it to a query graph q. By joining schemata and doing type expansions, the inference engine expands q to a working graph that incorporates additional background information (Fig. 6.6). Actors bound to the schemata determine which database relations to access and which functions and procedures to execute. The final working graph has a bound dataflow graph that can compute the answer to the original question. With conceptual graphs, the mechanisms for joining graphs and their attached actors support a dynamic way of deriving dataflow graphs. The newly derived graphs can answer questions in forms that were not anticipated by the database administrator.

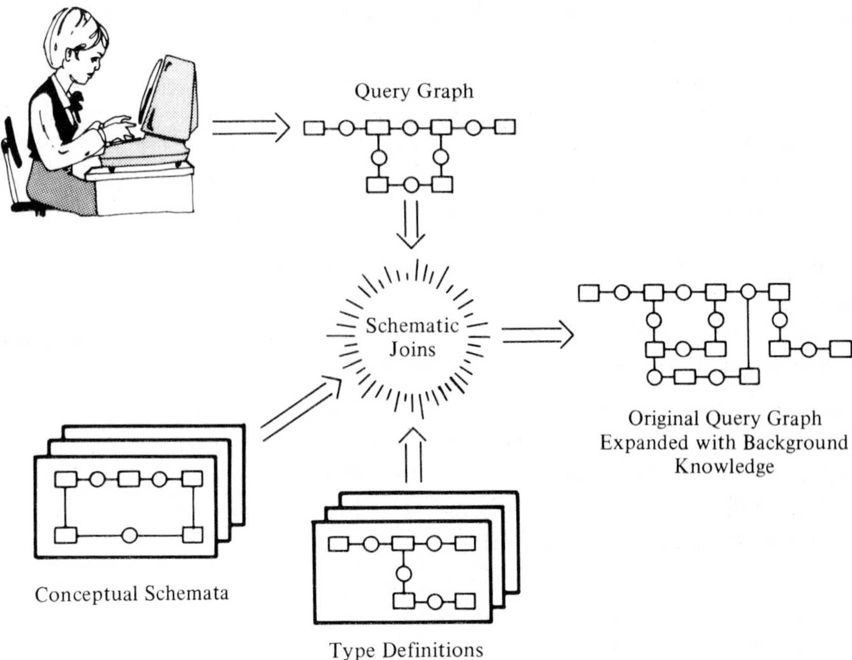

Fig. 6.6 Incorporating background information

In generating the query graph q, the language handler flags every concept whose referent is to be determined with a question mark. To determine referents for the flagged concepts, the inference mechanisms must generate an answer graph w that meets the following criteria:

1. w is a canonical graph.
2. w is true if the database is an accurate model of the world.
3. The answer graph w is a specialization of the query graph q.
4. For every concept in q that had a question mark, the corresponding concept in w has a referent.

Point 1 is satisfied if the system generates w by using the canonical formation rules. Point 2 requires the inference method to be sound. Point 3 implies that w must include all the concepts and relations of the query graph, although some of them may be further restricted: PERSON in the query graph, for example, may be restricted to EMPLOYEE or MANAGER as a result of joining schemata. And point 4 states that w must answer the original question. An incomplete or ambiguous question would not have a unique answer; in that case, the system should issue prompts for further information. It should not require the user to restate the entire question, but only to add the conditions necessary to complete it.

Conceptual graphs may be used with any inference method, but to illustrate the use of actors, this section will present an example from Sowa (1976). If someone asked the question *Who hired Lee?* the language handler would translate it into the following query graph:

```
[PERSON: ?]←(AGNT)←[HIRE]→(OBJ)→[PERSON:Lee].
```

Joining the schema for HIRE (Fig. 6.4) to the query graph produces Fig. 6.7, which completely covers the query graph. But before the join can be made, the conformity relation must be checked to ensure that EMPLOYEE::Lee. If so, the name *Lee* can replace the universal quantifier.

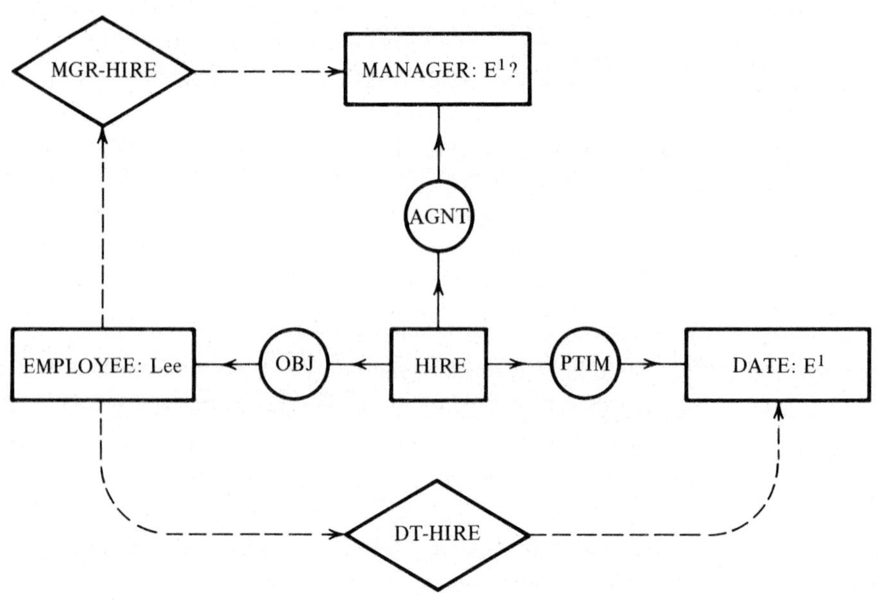

Fig. 6.7 First step towards the answer graph

When the target of an actor is flagged with a question mark and all its sources have referents, then the actor is *enabled* for computing a referent for the target concept. Since [MANAGER:E^1?] is functionally dependent on [EMPLOYEE:Lee], the referent can be computed by the actor <MGR-HIRE>. Then the manager's name would be substituted for the quantifier E^1, and the resulting graph would meet the criteria for an answer. In a more complex case, the target of an actor may be flagged

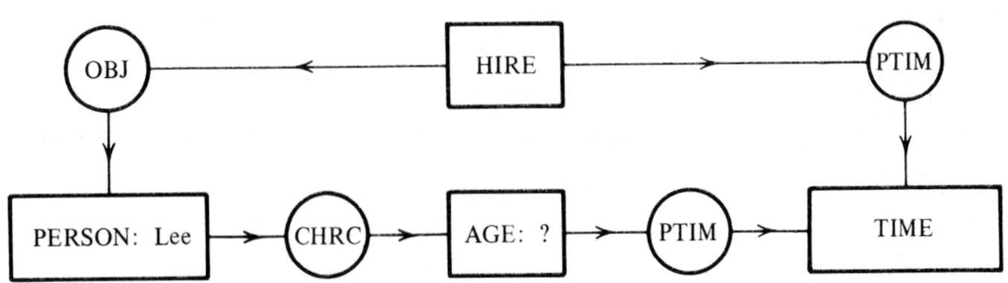

Fig. 6.8 Query graph for "What was Lee's age when hired?"

with a question mark, but one or more sources may not have referents; in that case, question marks are propagated backwards along the dataflow graphs to flag the source concepts whose referents are requested.

Suppose that a person asked *What was Lee's age when hired?* Since laws against age discrimination prohibit age from being considered in hiring, that answer would probably not be stored directly in the database. But for computing retirement benefits, the personnel department may ask that question about someone who was already hired. To answer the question, the system would have to compute several hidden joins: find Lee's date of birth in one relation, find his date of hire in another relation, and then call a procedure to subtract the two dates. If questions of that type are anticipated, the database administrator can define a virtual relation to compute it. A system based on conceptual graphs, however, could accept the question as stated and determine for itself what relations to access.

By the parsing methods of Chapter 5, the language handler would translate the English question into a query graph. In Fig. 6.8, the referent of [AGE:?] is to be determined. The conceptual relation (CHRC) indicates that a person has a characteristic age, and the relation (PTIM) indicates point in time. A phrase of the form *x when y* may be translated into a graph where *x* and *y* occur at the same point in time. Since *hired* is a passive participle, [PERSON:Lee] is the object of [HIRE]. For the question *What was Lee's age when hiring?* [PERSON:Lee] would be the agent of [HIRE].

Since the question mark on AGE cannot be propagated anywhere, the system must find some schema to join to Fig. 6.8. By the rules of Section 4.7, the relevance factor for a common type like PERSON would be low. The types AGE and HIRE are much rarer and hence more likely to select relevant schemata. The preference score for the AGE schema would be exceptionally high because the concept with a question mark [AGE:?] would be joined to a target concept in the schema. Since DATE≤TIME, a maximal common generalization of the query graph and the schema for AGE is the graph,

```
[PERSON]→(CHRC)→[AGE]→(PTIM)→[TIME].
```

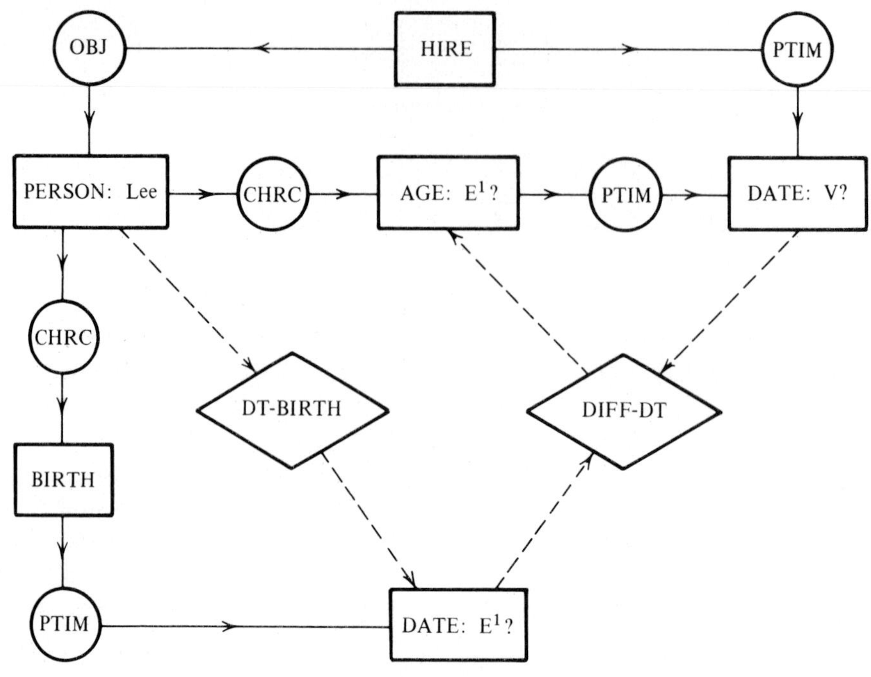

Fig. 6.9 Working graph

In forming the maximal join, the universal quantifier on [PERSON:∀] is replaced with the referent Lee, and the universally quantified concept [DATE:∀] replaces the generic concept [TIME]. The question marks are then propagated from targets to sources of functional dependencies. The result is the working graph in Fig. 6.9, which has actors that determine a person's date of birth and the difference of two dates.

The question mark on [DATE:E^1?] enables the actor <DT-BIRTH> to access Lee's date of birth from the database. That value will satisfy one of the inputs for the actor <DIFF-DT>. The other argument, however, has a question mark that cannot be propagated further. The system must find some other schema in which the concept [DATE:∀?] is functionally dependent on some concept that has a known (or computable) referent. The schema for HIRE (Fig. 6.4) meets these criteria. When it is joined to Fig. 6.9, the system can derive Fig. 6.10.

After the schema for HIRE is joined, the source of the actor <DT-HIRE> has a referent. That actor can then access the database to find Lee's date of hire. When both inputs of the actor <DIFF-DT> have referents, it can compute Lee's age. Note that the HIRE schema contains an actor <MGR-HIRE>, which is not enabled by any control mark. Since it is not needed for the current question, it will not be used.

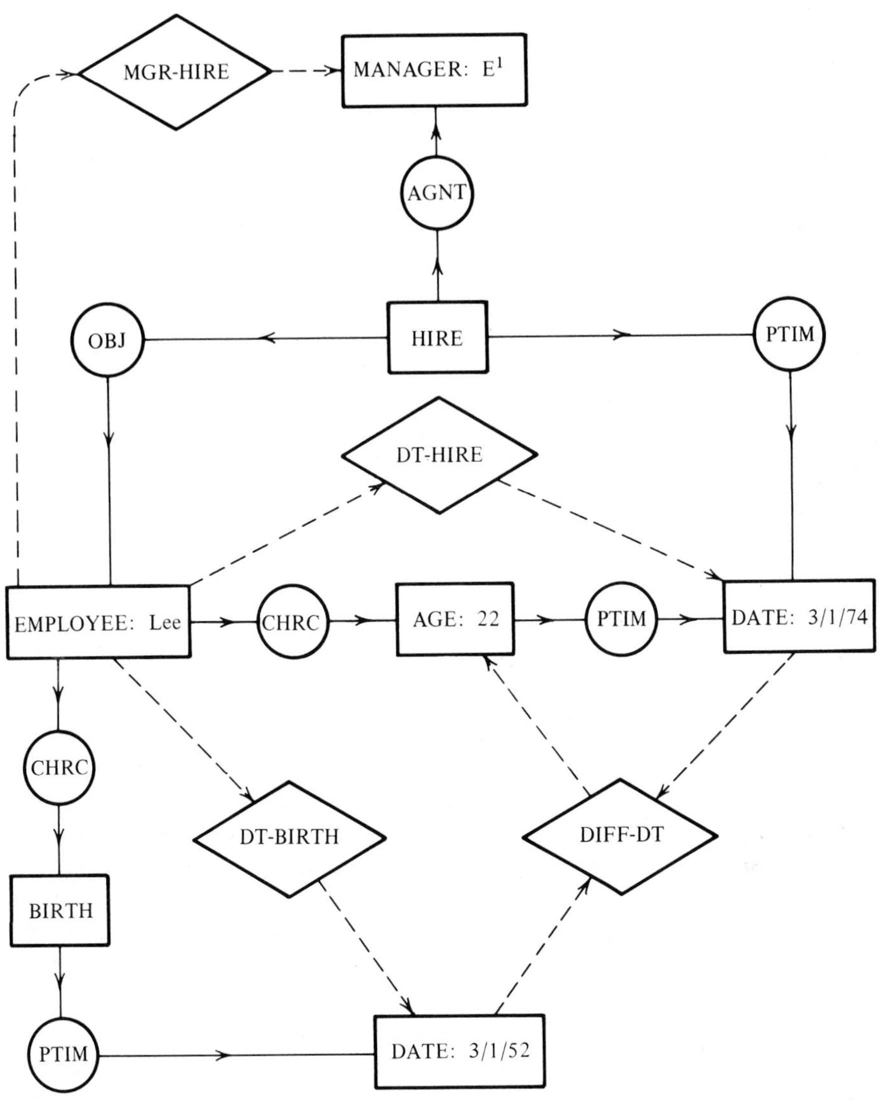

Fig. 6.10 Final working graph

Once the answer has been generated, the graph in Fig. 6.10 is no longer needed. But if the user wanted to know the age when hired for Smith, Jones, and others, then the system could use this dataflow graph as the definition of a new actor <AGE-HIRE>, whose input would be an employee name and whose output would be the employee's age when hired. For optimized execution, it could even compile the dataflow graph that defines <AGE-HIRE> into a procedure in a standard programming language.

Conceptual schemata are data descriptors that describe the intension of the data. The contents of the database itself are the extensions. The steps required to derive Fig. 6.10 are intensional operations that do not require any access to the actual data until the final stage of executing the actors on the dataflow graph. This property is important for a distributed system: each workstation could have its own copy of the data dictionaries that contain the schemata, and a large central system could contain the database itself. All the language analysis and prompting required to interpret the user's question could be handled at the local workstation. Once a working graph like Fig. 6.10 had been derived, the local system would send two simple requests to the central system to determine the results of the actors <DT-BIRTH> and <DT-HIRE>. When it received those results, the local workstation would compute the final answer, *age 22*. Since the final answer is embedded in a complete conceptual graph, the system could translate the graph into a more complete statement:

```
Lee's date of hire is 3/1/74.  Lee's date of birth is 3/1/52.
The difference of those dates is Lee's age when hired, 22 years.
```

Giving a full answer like this helps to catch possible errors and misunderstandings, either in the user's statement of the query or in the computer's interpretation of it.

6.6 KNOWLEDGE ACQUISITION

People acquire knowledge either by learning from experience or by being told new facts by a teacher. Learning is a complex process that will be considered in Section 6.7. This section addresses the simpler, but still difficult problem of designing a *knowledge acquisition facility* that accumulates knowledge by being told. With such a facility, application experts can add knowledge about their domain of expertise. Only after the knowledge has been entered can the inference engine use it to solve problems. Figure 6.11 shows an expert who is priming the knowledge base and an end user who is posing a problem to be solved. Three kinds of experts are needed to write the rules that drive a knowledge-based system:

- Linguists who write the grammars and dictionaries that drive the language handler,
- Knowledge engineers who understand the applications and can describe them in the knowledge representation language,
- Database administrators who define the fields and formats in the database.

Not every application needs a trained linguist: a general grammar could be supplied with the system, and the vocabulary could be extended by adding a new word to the dictionary and saying whether it is a noun or a verb. The database administrator

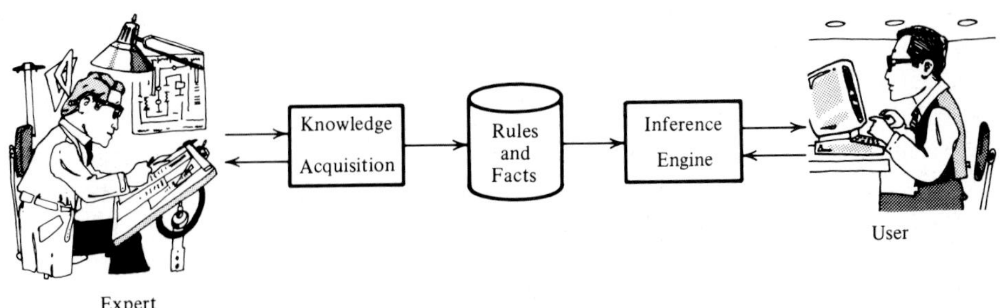

Fig. 6.11 Knowledge acquisition facility for an expert system

would do the same kind of work as on current systems. In fact, exactly the same database might be accessed in batch mode by conventional programs and in interactive mode by a knowledge-based system. The systems analysts, however, must become knowledge engineers. Instead of thinking in procedural terms, they must concentrate on the meaning of the data, the logical interdependencies between facts, and the schemata and inference rules that apply to the data.

Today, the tools for expressing knowledge include languages like PROLOG that are based on symbolic logic and systems like EMYCIN that are driven by production rules. Yet those tools can only be used effectively by people who have undergone a long period of study and apprenticeship. Computers never became practical for widespread use until languages like FORTRAN and COBOL became available. With those languages, an intelligent person can start doing useful work after taking a short course; advanced training, although helpful, is not necessary. Before knowledge-based systems become widely used, knowledge engineering facilities must be developed that are as easy to learn as FORTRAN or COBOL. Those facilities must have the following characteristics:

- Natural forms of expression for the application,
- Absence of machine-dependent details in the knowledge specification,
- Integration with other languages, editors, and facilities that are used on the same system,
- Learnability and usability by today's programmers and systems analysts.

Integration is important. Like database systems, knowledge-based systems must coexist with more conventional programs. Many of the expert systems for medical diagnosis have not been widely used, partly because the effort of logging on a computer and retyping a list of symptoms is a nuisance. If the expert system is part of a record keeping system that the doctors and nurses use every day, it is more likely to be accepted.

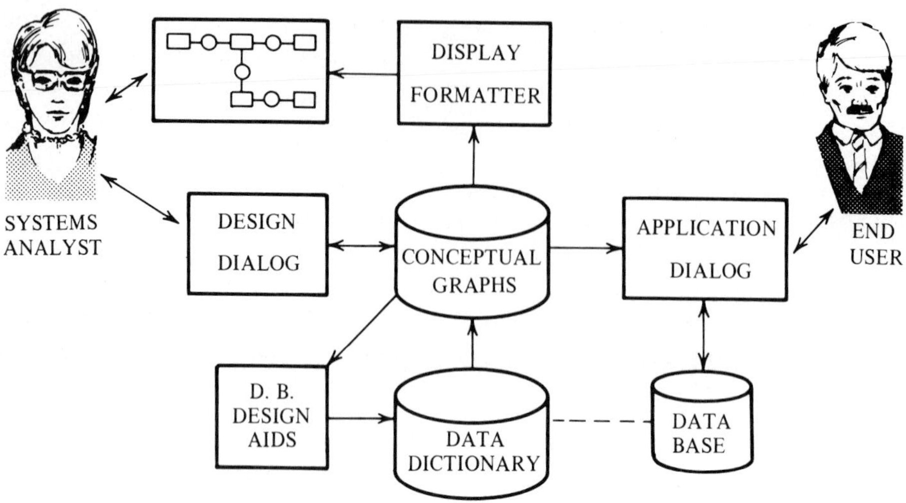

Fig. 6.12 Designing and using a knowledge based system

In an integrated system, the same knowledge base that drives an expert system should also generate the specifications for the conventional programs and databases that interact with it. The knowledge engineers of tomorrow will be today's systems analysts who have taken additional training in defining a knowledge base. Instead of doing low-level file design, the analyst will use interactive tools for translating English specifications into a knowledge representation language. From that language, design aids must generate the following information:

- Rules for driving an expert system,
- Specifications for conventional programs,
- Database definitions for the data dictionary,
- Help and diagnostic aids for programmers and end users.

Figure 6.12 is a more detailed version of Fig. 6.11. The systems analyst on the left is using the knowledge acquisition facility to specify the *target system*. The end user on the right uses the target system to do his job. The dialog with the systems analyst is a *metadialog*, a dialog about the end users' dialog. Following the original specifications, she determines what entities, attributes, and events in the real world are to be represented in the knowledge base, defines the terms by which the end users refer to them, and defines the mapping to the programs and data of the target system. Her metadialog is translated by the system into a knowledge representation, such as conceptual graphs. From those graphs, the system derives the language rules that define the end user's vocabulary and the database rules that map to the stored files and records. Although Fig. 6.12 shows both the systems analyst and the end user working at the same time, the work by the analyst is normally done before the system is implemented, and the work by the end user is done on the finished system. Furthermore, the design work may or may not be done on the same hardware that is used to run the target system.

To the knowledge engineer, the primary interface of an expert system is the language for expressing knowledge. The language level determines the speed of implementing an expert system, the ease of updating and modifying its knowledge base, and the richness of its debugging and explanation facilities. Brachman and Smith (1980) compiled a roster of 83 research projects on knowledge representation with a total of 277 active researchers. The following kinds of languages are being used and developed in those projects:

- *Conventional programming languages.* LISP, Pascal, Ada.
- *Production rule languages.* EMYCIN, OPS5, EXPERT.
- *Logic programming languages.* PROLOG, LOGLISP.
- *Graph languages.* Conceptual graphs, KloneTalk.
- *Formalized English.* ROSIE, LESK, KLAUS.
- *Unrestricted natural languages.* English, Polish, Japanese.

These categories represent major trends, but many combinations and variations are possible. The CENTAUR system (Aikens 1983) combines production rules with prototypes that guide the deduction. PROLOG has been used to implement versions of production rules, prototypes, frames, and graphs. Conceptual graphs have been used as the underlying representation for both logic programming and production rules. And formalized English can be translated or compiled into any of the other notations. The first five language types can be processed automatically, but no system can handle completely unrestricted natural language. Some systems, however, provide aids for helping a knowledge engineer translate natural language into formal rules and facts.

In principle, anything that can be processed by computer can be implemented in a conventional programming language. But in practice, expert systems are so complex that the cost of writing a major application in a conventional language can be prohibitive. Even when it is possible, the result is so tightly bound to one domain that it cannot be applied to another domain without a complete rewrite. For diagnosing lung diseases, PUFF (Feigenbaum 1977) was originally implemented in EMYCIN. But for routine use in the hospital, PUFF was rewritten in BASIC. What was gained by the rewrite was efficiency: instead of taking 4 megabytes of storage, the BASIC version ran in a 64K microprocessor. What was lost was flexibility: the BASIC version of PUFF was a conventional program (Fig. 6.1) that lacked the knowledge engineering tools of EMYCIN for doing updates and extensions.

To evaluate tools for building expert systems, Ennis (1982) implemented a mineral analysis system both in LISP and in higher-level production rules. She found that LISP was adequate for the task, but the resulting program was specific to a single domain and would have to be rewritten for other domains. She also had to spend time in implementing a "user-friendly interface" to allow a mineralogist, who was not a programmer, to add and modify his own rules. A good knowledge acquisition facility would already have that interface.

Many expert systems in the United States are based on production rules that contain a *pattern* and an *action*. In *data-directed* or *forward chaining* execution, each pattern is matched against data in the current working storage. When the pattern matches, the action part is executed to change the data or trigger an external procedure. The OPS4 and OPS5 languages (Forgy 1981), which were used in the R1 configurator, are based on forward chaining. In *goal-directed* or *backward chaining* execution, the action part is treated as a goal to be achieved. When it matches a current goal, the pattern part is invoked as the next subgoal. EMYCIN uses backward chaining. A typical EMYCIN rule looks like the following (van Melle 1981, p. 13):

```
PREMISE: ($AND (SAME CNTXT COMPOSITION (LISTOF METALS))
               (LESSP* (VAL1 CNTXT ERROR) 5)
               (GREATERP* (VAL1 CNTXT ND-STRESS) .5))
               (GREATERP* (VAL1 CNTXT CYCLES) 10000))
ACTION:  (CONCLUDE CNTXT SS-STRESS FATIGUE TALLY 1000)
```

This rule, which is from the SACON system for structural analysis, is not readable to the end users. To make it more readable, EMYCIN associates an English phrase with each parameter: for ND-STRESS, the phrase is *the non-dimensional stress of the substructure*. When it prints out the rule, EMYCIN assembles the stored phrases to form an English statement:

```
If:    1) The material composing the substructure
          is one of the metals,
       2) The analysis error (in percent) that is tolerable
          is less than 5,
       3) The non-dimensional stress of the substructure
          is greater than .5, and
       4) The number of cycles the loading is to be applied
          is greater than 10000
Then:     Fatigue is one of the stress behavior phenomena
          in the substructure.
```

This rule is close to the formalized English forms that some expert systems support. The original MYCIN system allowed rules to be entered in this form, but that option was difficult to support for every possible application. EMYCIN now uses an abbreviated rule language that is easier to read than the internal form, but less readable than formalized English.

One of the most difficult tasks in knowledge engineering is defining a complete, consistent set of rules. In general, proving consistency is impossible: it is a theoretically undecidable issue, like proving that a program will always terminate for any input data. But some inconsistencies, like some program bugs, are easier to detect than others. A program that scans through a set of rules and checks for common errors can be an important development aid. Suwa et al. (1982) wrote a rule-checking program for the ONCOCIN system for cancer therapy consultation. It analyzes EMYCIN rules to check for the following kinds of errors:

- *Conflict*. Two or more rules match the same input data, but produce different results. At least one of them must be wrong.
- *Redundancy*. Two or more rules match the same input, and produce the same result. Although redundancy does not make the system inconsistent, it is often a sign of an incomplete rule or a rule placed in the wrong context.
- *Subsumption*. One rule matches only a subset of the cases matched by a more general rule, and the two rules always generate the same result. In such a case, the general rule *subsumes* the more limited one and makes it redundant.
- *Missing rules*. Certain combinations of input data are possible, but no existing rule matches that combination.

When the rule checker finds these problems, it summarizes them in a *decision table*. The knowledge engineers found the tables convenient for organizing and debugging the ONCOCIN knowledge base. During the design stage, the rule checker found several redundant and conflicting rules; it also suggested several missing rules that had been overlooked by the expert. The ONCOCIN rule checker was able to check all possible cases because of the restricted form of the EMYCIN rules. In more general systems, proving consistency may be impossible.

PROLOG is a *logic programming* language based on first-order logic. No special inference engine is needed since PROLOG itself is an inference engine; the *unification algorithm* in PROLOG provides a more general pattern matcher than the special cases used in systems of production rules. As an example of an expert system implemented in PROLOG, ORBI keeps track of environmental resources for the entire country of Portugal (Pereira et al. 1982). It has aspects of both a classification system for environmental data and a decision-support system for resource planning. ORBI provides the following facilities:

- Graphic input and output of maps via a digitizing tablet and plotter,
- A natural language parser for Portuguese that supports pronouns, ellipses, and other transformations,
- A menu handler for fixed-format input,
- An explanation facility that keeps track of the steps in a deduction and shows them on request,

- Help facilities that explain what is in the database, the kinds of deductions that are possible, and the kinds of vocabulary and syntax that may be used.

ORBI has help and explanation facilities like MYCIN, but its natural language parser is more sophisticated than MYCIN's keyword pattern matcher. Yet ORBI runs on a microprocessor with only 64K bytes of storage. It does, however, require separate overlays for the language processor, the deductive component, and the explanation facility. Advocates of logic programming claim that anything that can be done with production rules can be done more efficiently in PROLOG and with a better structured method (Kowalski 1979; Clocksin & Mellish 1981). For their Fifth Generation Project (Moto-Oka 1982), the Japanese have explicitly chosen PROLOG over LISP as the primary language of AI.

Graph notations were originally designed to represent the semantics of natural language. Since then, they have evolved into complete systems for logic and computation. But the graphs go beyond standard logic with schemata for doing plausible and default reasoning, nested contexts for modalities, and actors for linking to external procedures. The conceptual graphs presented in this book are a synthesis of many existing knowledge representations. Following are some of the major implementations and their chief characteristics:

- Heidorn's *augmented phrase structure grammar* (1972, 1975) is a versatile notation for mapping conceptual graphs to and from natural language. The NLP system, which implements the notation, also supports computational operators on the graphs. For more general deductions, McCord (1983) is designing an inference engine for NLP that is patterned after PROLOG.

- The *conceptual dependency graphs* developed by Schank and his students and colleagues have been used for plausible reasoning that attempts to simulate human thinking rather than formal deduction. The aspects they have explored in most detail are schema-like packages of graphs, called *scripts, scenes, MOPs,* and *TAUs*. The tutorials edited by Schank and Riesbeck (1981) introduce techniques for implementing graph systems and using them in natural language processing.

- The *partitioned nets* of Hendrix (1979) have a logical form that is close to Peirce's notation. They have been used as the logical component of the LADDER query system (Hendrix et al. 1978) and the PROSPECTOR system for mineral exploration (Duda et al. 1979).

- KL-ONE is based on the *structured inheritance networks* designed by Brachman (1979). It makes a clear distinction between individual and generic concepts and emphasizes definitional techniques for constructing a type lattice. The system includes graphics tools for defining and editing the graphs and has been used at several locations for natural language queries and database semantics (Sidner et al. 1981). Fikes (1982) designed KloneTalk, a linear version of KL-ONE that has been used in several knowledge-based systems.

■ Shapiro's SNePS (1979) is a general system for doing logic on graphs. It supports all the primitives of first-order logic in a direct fashion and has extensions to some forms of modal and higher-order logic. The system includes an ATN parser for mapping natural language into the graphs. Tranchell (1982) showed that SNePS is at least as general as KL-ONE by simulating the KL-ONE structures and operations in SNePS. Shapiro (1981) showed how SNePS could be used for expert systems by implementing a MYCIN-like system called COCCI.

To make the knowledge base more readable, some systems represent their rules in a formalized English notation. Such notations are compatible with the preceding ones because they could be compiled into production rules, logic, or graphs. They are designed to meet several requirements:

■ *Readability*. Even without any training in the notation, an expert in the subject matter can read the knowledge definitions.

■ *Precision*. Ambiguity is avoided by severe restrictions on the syntactic forms and range of expression. Syntax checkers enforce the restrictions and ensure that every term is defined before it is used. For top-down designs, the requirements of definition before use may be relaxed by permitting partial specifications that can later be refined.

■ *Learnability*. When used correctly, the syntactic forms of natural languages are valuable guides to logically well-formed expressions. Instead of forcing people to express themselves in a strange notation, formalized English takes advantage of their intuitive understanding of the logic inherent in English grammar. A syntax checker ensures that imprecise and ungrammatical statements are avoided.

Formalized English makes no pretense of being true natural language. Its syntax is unambiguous, it does not rely on the implicit mechanisms of natural language, and its syntax checkers are as rigorous as a compiler for a programming language.

Formalized English is "syntactic sugar" for first-order logic in the same sense that COBOL is syntactic sugar for assembly language. But there are some major differences:

■ When COBOL was defined in 1960, linguistic theory and compiler design were in their infancy. Although COBOL uses English words, it does not take advantage of the rich structure of the English language.

■ COBOL definitions simply give names to files and data fields in computer storage. Formalized English allows the user to introduce new nouns, verbs, and adjectives. Besides introducing words, formalized English associates semantic structures with the words, including a type hierarchy and case frames for the actions.

■ COBOL statements look like English, but their semantics are oriented towards files, records, and other computer features. The semantics of formalized English is based on the real-world entities and events that are being described. Only a professional programmer can read COBOL, but an expert in the subject matter can easily understand rules written in formalized English.

Of all the formalized English notations, the most extensively developed is ROSIE (Fain et al. 1981, 1982).[3] Since ROSIE is designed for implementing expert systems, it has a well-developed format for assertions and inference rules. Although it is general enough for stating conventional algorithms, its notation is somewhat awkward for mathematical expressions. Following is a typical rule in ROSIE:

```
To decide individual is married:
[1] If the individual is married to some person
        or there is a person such that
           that person is married to the individual
        or the individual does have some wife
        or the individual does have some husband
        or the individual does have some spouse
           conclude true.
[2] Conclude false.
End.
```

This rule could be used in a *backward chaining* style of deduction: if ROSIE is trying to prove that a person Allen is married, it would check each of the conditions under [1]; if none of them were true, it would conclude that Allen is not married. ROSIE uses stylistic conventions that are sometimes awkward, but they are still readable. One convention is that the definite article *the* indicates a reference to a previously mentioned entity of the same type. Another convention is the use of *does* to avoid irregular endings on verbs. A third convention is the use of parentheses and hyphens to clarify the parsing, as in the following rule for legal reasoning:

```
If the theory of strict-liability does apply
      to the plaintiff's loss
   and (the use of (the product) by the user is not negligent
        or the product's user is not the victim),
assert the defendant is liable for the plaintiff's loss
   and the liability of the defendant is total.
```

In these examples, the only words that are predefined by ROSIE are the function words like *if*, *the*, *does*, *is*, and *of* together with the words that describe inferences, such as *assert*, *conclude*, and *decide*. All other words, such as *spouse*, *user*, and *victim*, must be defined by some other rule or assertion in the knowledge base. If any definitions are missing, ROSIE's help and debugging aids note the omission. To

3 ROSIE is a trademark of The Rand Corporation.

write rules in ROSIE, a knowledge engineer must learn where to put the commas and parentheses. But the resulting rules are immediately readable by an expert in the subject matter who does not have any training in computers.

Another version of formalized English is the Language for Exactly Stating Knowledge (LESK), which can be compiled into first-order logic augmented with set expressions (Skuce 1982, 1983). The following declaration in LESK introduces an entity type PERSON, with two subtypes MALE PERSON and FEMALE PERSON and two associated entities NAME and BIRTHDATE. The hyphen "-" is an abbreviation for the type that is being defined:

```
every PERSON:
   kinds (by SEX):  MALE -, FEMALE -;
   - has 1 NAME;
   - has 1 BIRTHDATE;
end.
```

The lower case words are predefined LESK terms. The upper case words are introduced by the knowledge engineer. Once PERSON has been defined, the subtype STUDENT can be defined as a PERSON with additional attributes. Every attribute of PERSON is also inherited by STUDENT.

```
every STUDENT:
   kinds:  FULL_TIME -, PART_TIME -;
   kinds:  GRADUATE -, UNDERGRADUATE -;
   - is a PERSON;
   - has 0 or more COURSE_CREDITS;
   - is ENROLLED IN 1 DEGREE PROGRAM;
   - is IN 1 DEPARTMENT;
end.
```

Each *kinds* clause defines mutually exclusive attributes: possible combinations are FULL-TIME UNDERGRADUATE STUDENT or PART-TIME GRADUATE STUDENT, but not FULL-TIME PART-TIME STUDENT. Since the attributes of PERSON are inherited by STUDENT, one can refer to a MALE STUDENT or a FEMALE GRADUATE STUDENT. Actions are declared by stating preconditions and a procedure; this declaration uses variables S and C to show the relationships:

```
to ENROLL a STUDENT S IN a COURSE C:
precond:    S is not ENROLLED IN C;
            S has PASSED all the PREREQUISITES of C;
            S has PAID the FEE of the DEGREE_PROGRAM of S;
procedure:  assert S is ENROLLED in C;
end.
```

Definitions like these serve several purposes. First, they are precise, readable specifications that clarify the understanding between the system users and the system designers. Second, they can serve as input to data dictionaries and database design aids—they specify both the logical structure of the data and the integrity constraints on the database. Third, the definitions can be compiled into executable rules for a knowledge-based system.

LESK builds its vocabulary from the same definitions that introduce new concepts, relations, and actions. Introducing English-like forms in EMYCIN is a burden because the vocabulary is given in sentence frames that are separate from the rule declarations. The LESK compiler, however, updates the dictionary for the language handler as it builds the tables of rules and facts for the knowledge base. As an interactive aid for acquiring new concepts together with the words for expressing them, Haas and Hendrix (1983) designed a knowledge learning and using system (KLAUS). Following is a dialog with NANOKLAUS, a small prototype of a KLAUS (computer output in upper case):

```
What do you know about?
I KNOW ABOUT PHYSICAL OBJECTS, PEOPLE, MEN, WOMEN,
MEASURES, AND THINGS.
A length is a measure.
YOU'RE SAYING THAT ANYTHING THAT IS A LENGTH
IS ALSO A MEASURE.  OK.  NOW I UNDERSTAND LENGTH.
A foot is a unit of length.
FOOTS ARE THE FIRST UNITS OF LENGTH YOU'VE DEFINED.
NOW I UNDERSTAND FOOT.
The plural of foot is feet.
FEET.  GOT IT.  THANKS.
A meter is a unit of length.
HOW IS IT RELATED TO FOOT?
There are 3.3 feet in a meter.
NOW I UNDERSTAND METER.
A physical object has a length.
SO PHYSICAL OBJECTS HAVE LENGTHS.
MUST A PHYSICAL OBJECT HAVE EXACTLY ONE LENGTH?
yes
```

During the dialog, NANOKLAUS builds up its type hierarchy as well as its vocabulary. When it learns a new noun, it repeats it in the plural form; if it makes a mistake, the user corrects it. By asking questions, it determines that there is a functional dependency from physical objects to lengths. After a while, the KLAUS form of dialog can become tedious, but it could be used as an interactive debugging aid for LESK or ROSIE. The LESK notation is more compact for defining a large knowledge base. The KLAUS style of interaction could be used to test and modify the definitions.

6.7 LEARNING

Conceptual analysis enables a systems analyst to define new concepts and schemata for a knowledge-based system. People, however, learn such things from experience. The ideal knowledge acquisition tool would be a computer system that could learn concepts and schemata by itself, either from experience or from reading the same kinds of dictionaries and encyclopedias that people read. The system could be primed with a small, but general vocabulary of about 2,000 words, the concepts and conceptual relations needed for defining those words, and enough syntactic and semantic rules to enable it to read a book to learn more.

Making computers learn the way people do has been the dream of AI from its earliest beginnings. The major obstacle, however, is that nobody knows exactly how people learn. One explanation of learning that has been invented and reinvented in various guises is the *apperceptive mass* or dominant system of ideas. It was originally derived from Leibniz and elaborated by the German psychologist Johann Friederich Herbart (1816). Watson (1963) presented a summary of Herbart's theory:

> There is a unity of consciousness—attention, as one might call it—so that one cannot attend to two ideas at once except in so far as they will unite into a single complex idea. When one idea is at the focus of the consciousness it forces incongruous ideas into the background or out of consciousness altogether. Combined ideas form wholes and a combination of related ideas form an apperceptive mass, into which relevant ideas are welcomed but irrelevant ones are excluded.... If information is to be acquired as easily and as rapidly as possible, it follows that in teaching one should introduce new material by building upon the apperceptive mass of already familiar ideas. Relevant ideas, then, will be most easily assimilated to the apperceptive mass, while irrelevant ideas will tend to be resisted and, consequently, will not be assimilated as readily. (pp. 209-210)

The notion of apperceptive mass dominated German psychology during the nineteenth century and had a strong influence on American educational psychology. But the theory was never expressed in a precise formalism or tested in rigorously controlled experiments. Even William James (1890), who was sympathetic to mentalistic theories, was disenchanted with all the vague speculation about *Vorstellungsmassen* that rise and sink in the threshold of consciousness.

Along with other mentalistic notions, the apperceptive mass went into an eclipse during the behaviorist years. The hallmark of behaviorism was experimental rigor and precise, reproducible results. Learning became synonymous with conditioning: stimulus-response (S-R) chains are built as rats run through mazes and people memorize lists of nonsense syllables. But behaviorism could not explain conceptual processes:

- S-R chains do not have enough structure to support the mechanisms of language, thought, and problem solving.

- Unconscious conditioning changes behavior only after a long series of repetitions. It does not explain how a person can remember and use information that is presented only once.

Although behaviorism cannot explain the most complex facts of language and thought, it does explain a great deal of unconscious, habitual behavior. For the patient H.M. (discussed in Section 2.5), the ability to add new information to episodic memory was completely destroyed by his brain lesion. Yet he could learn conditioned responses and form new semantic categories. Paradoxically, the man could learn, but he could not remember. Conditioning is an unconscious process that builds up semantic memory; then the concepts and schemata in semantic memory form a canonical basis for the conceptual graphs in episodic memory.

With the decline of behaviorism, cognitive psychologists have returned to the accretion of related ideas into a combined whole. Piaget and his colleagues in Geneva observed children and analyzed the schemata they used at various ages. Hebb (1949) maintained that filling up the large association cortex of the human brain would take a long time. Piaget went further in showing that the process of filling the cortex is not as simple as pouring water into a pitcher: learning progresses by stages, not by a constant rate of accretion. At each stage, the brain assimilates new information to its existing structures. When the complexity of the information grows beyond the capacity of the structures at one stage, a minor revolution occurs, and a new schema is created to reorganize the mental structures. The later, more abstract conceptual schemata are built up by generalizing, building upon, and reorganizing patterns derived from sensorimotor schemata in the early years of life.

Piaget distinguished two modes of learning: *assimilation*, when new information is assimilated to the old schemata, and *accommodation*, when the old schemata are modified because the new data does not fit the old categories. Rumelhart and Norman (1978), however, distinguished three different modes:

- *Accretion.* New knowledge can be added to episodic memory without changing semantic memory. The new graphs are canonically derived from existing schemata.
- *Schema tuning.* Minor changes to semantic memory can be made by adding new properties or defaults to schemata or by generalizing them to higher supertypes.
- *Restructuring.* As episodic memory becomes more complex, a major reorganization of semantic memory may be needed. Completely new schemata and concept types can represent the old information more efficiently and support complex deductions in fewer steps.

Piaget's assimilation corresponds to accretion, and accommodation merges tuning and restructuring. Yet restructuring seems so radically different from tuning that it deserves to be called a separate mode of learning. It is responsible for the *plateau effect*: people quickly learn a new skill up to a modest level of proficiency; then they go through a period of stagnation when study and practice fail to show a noticeable improvement; suddenly, they break through to a new plateau where they again progress at a rapid rate—until they reach the next plateau. Restructuring takes place when the apperceptive mass reaches a critical size that is too big to be processed efficiently with the old schemata. When a person attains a new insight, a revolution takes place that repackages the old information in new schemata.

The paradigms that psychologists have proposed for human learning have their counterparts in AI. In a review of machine learning, Carbonell, Michalski, and Mitchell (1983) distinguished three historical periods, each characterized by its own paradigm for learning:

- *Stimulus-response.* In the late 1950s and early 60s, *neural nets* and *self-organizing systems* were designed to start from a neutral state and build up internal connections solely by reinforcement and conditioning. Although these systems have had some influence on modern techniques of pattern recognition, they never achieved any significant amount of learning.
- *Induction of concepts.* A higher form of learning is the induction of new categories from a set of data. It started in the 1960s with clustering and concept learning techniques and is still important today.
- *Knowledge-intensive learning.* Before a system can learn anything new, it must already have a great deal of initial knowledge. The most active research today is on methods for building upon an existing knowledge base. The approach is highly compatible with Piaget's schemata and Rumelhart and Norman's modes of accretion, tuning, and restructuring.

In his program to play checkers, Samuel (1959) viewed tuning as a general paradigm for learning. His evaluation function had coefficients that were refined and perfected in many games. No restructuring was done, however, since the program that used those coefficients could not modify its own categories. One chess playing program that used a similar learning algorithm was swindled by a clever programmer who was a rather weak chess player. Don Taube, the swindler, bet that he could win at least one game out of three with the program. The author of the chess program, knowing how poorly Don played chess, scoffed at him and took the bet. Don, however, made absurd moves for the first two games—giving away a queen for a pawn, advancing a knight and immediately retreating it, and marching his king into the center of the board. By the third game, the program "learned" such totally scrambled coefficients that Don was able to win easily. Unfortunately, the program wrote the scrambled coefficients back to the disk and erased the highly tuned values.

Samuel's learning program did no restructuring. It simply modified the coefficients on a set of functions and categories that Samuel programmed into it. One of the first steps in restructuring is categorization: selecting new concept types, mapping percepts to those types, and assigning the types to the proper level in the type hierarchy. In their study of thinking, Bruner, Goodnow, and Austin (1956) distinguished five major reasons for categorization (p. 12):

- *Reducing complexity.* Grouping many details into a single concept type reduces the complexity of the conceptual graphs.
- *Identifying objects.* Things can be recognized as members of familiar categories instead of unique occurrences. When a sound is recognized as "those porcupines chewing on that old tree stump," it can be distinguished from the sound of prowlers or other dangers.
- *Eliminating redundancy.* Once an object has been identified as TREE, previous experience with trees can be applied to it without having to be relearned.
- *Directing action.* Classifying a person as HONEST or a substance as POISON determines the appropriate and inappropriate actions to be taken.
- *Ordering and relating events.* Events and attributes can be classified as well as objects, and causal relationships between them can be recognized.

Categorization can be done automatically by cluster analysis programs. Michalski and Stepp (1983) developed a clustering program, which they used to classify Spanish folk songs and soybean diseases. When applied to descriptions of examples, the program generates a type hierarchy that gives the simplest and most comprehensive categorization. For the soybean diseases, it "rediscovered" classes that had been known to plant pathologists.

Categorization is the simplest form of restructuring. A more radical alteration of schemata is a leap into the unknown. It requires a person to abandon the comfortable old ways of thought before there is any reassurance that the new schema is any better. To explain how such learning is possible, Peirce proposed the notion of *abduction*, which operates in conjunction with deduction and induction:

- Deduction is logical inference according to rules of strict reasoning or plausible reasoning.
- Induction is gathering and classifying new data according to existing types and schemata.
- Abduction is making a preliminary guess that introduces a new type or schema, followed by deduction for exploring its consequences and by induction for testing it with reality.

Abduction is the wild hunch that may be either a brilliant breakthrough or a dead end. Beforehand, it cannot be justified either logically or empirically. Once it has been made, however, its implications can be derived by deduction and be tested against the facts by induction. In a study of learning, Lewis and Mack (1982) described abduction with a metaphor: a new fact is a grain of sand that irritates the mind, and abduction forms a pearl of wisdom around it.

Abduction has been implemented in several computer learning and problem-solving systems. Pople et al. (1975) implemented abduction in the DIALOG system for medical diagnoses:

- First the user enters a list of symptoms caused by the disease.
- Then the system asks questions to gather background information.
- Next by abduction, the system generates a hypothesis to explain the symptoms.
- Finally by deduction, it explores the consequences to determine if they match the known symptoms.
- If the results match, the system prints its diagnosis. Otherwise, it generates a new hypothesis.

For language learning, Shrier (1977) implemented a grammar discovery program that was based on abduction, and Kučera (1981) surveyed the use of abduction for learning finite-state grammars. In those implementations, abduction consisted of hypothesizing a new grammatical category or state and then keeping it or rejecting it after comparing its implications with the evidence.

Learning new conceptual graphs or schemata can be done by accumulating examples in episodic memory and then searching for recurring patterns. Salveter (1979) wrote MORAN for learning conceptual graphs from descriptions of situations before and after an action. MORAN derives graphs that show the required relations for each action and the expected changes caused by the action. Roger Schank (1981) revived the apperceptive mass with his notion of *memory organization packet* or MOP: "memory is a morass of MOP strands, each connected at the base to the relevant abstractions and generalizations that are the base of the MOP. At the end of each strand are the particular experiences (i.e. individual episodes) or groups of experiences (i.e. scripts)" (p. 135). Each episode is encoded in conceptual graphs, and the system crystallizes new schemata out of the tangled web of nodes and arcs.

Like the apperceptive mass, MOPs serve as a vehicle for accretion and tuning. But a mechanism like abduction must be added for restructuring the mass. The paradox of abduction, however, is that it must be a systematic method for generating wild guesses. No one can predict what the guesses should be, but somehow the system designer must determine in advance what their permissible forms must be. For a particular application, such as learning finite-state grammars, the designer may decide that each new guess will consist of adding a new grammatical category or a new state in the network. That approach does not constrain the possible states or categories that the program may invent, but it limits the kinds of grammars to a very special case. The major problem of abduction is to develop hypothesis generators that are unrestricted enough to come up with interesting discoveries, but limited enough to be executed in a reasonable amount of time. Furthermore, an evaluation function is needed to determine when a discovery is interesting. Some of the early theorem provers "discovered" pages and pages of theorems that were trivial variations of well-known results.

Advanced techniques for restructuring have a great deal in common with expert systems for design. In both cases, the system must assemble structures to meet a goal while obeying certain constraints. To discover new schemata, for example, a system might join canonical graphs in the search for promising patterns; the formation rules enforce constraints that keep the result canonical. In some design systems, the goal is well defined; but in a learning system, the form of the goal may be unknown. Other design systems, however, are more open ended, and closely resemble learning systems. Lenat (1983) implemented EURISKO as a general discovery tool; it has been used in such diverse tasks as discovering theorems in mathematics and designing VLSI components. Some systems analyze and refine their own techniques. The LEX system (Mitchell, Utgoff, & Banerji 1983) learns heuristics for symbolic integration by the following steps:

- Generate a practice problem.
- Use available heuristics to solve the problem.
- Analyze the search towards a solution.
- Propose new heuristics to improve performance on subsequent problems.

Machine learning techniques are promising, but no one has yet built a general learning machine that can go to school like a child and learn from teachers and books. Yet most learning systems are small prototypes. If they were coupled with a general language processor and an inference engine, they might show more impressive results. Building an integrated system that combined all those parts, however, would be a major undertaking. At the present stage of AI, the result would not match the range and generality of human learning, but it might lead to highly flexible and adaptable computer systems.

EXERCISES

These exercises outline the steps of knowledge engineering that are necessary for implementing a knowledge-based system. Doing a thorough job is a major undertaking. To share the work and to enable students to do a more detailed analysis, a class may be divided into working groups of three students each.

6.1 Study the examples of expert systems and natural language systems in Sections 6.1 and 6.2. Consider some application that you are familiar with and propose a knowledge-based system for it. Following are possible applications: a travel advisor that links to various information services and reservation systems; a financial advisor that helps with investments, loans, budgets, and taxes; a computer assistant that helps executives and secretaries keep records, memos, mail, and appointment calendars; a natural language interface for a home computer that controls the furnace, lights, and other appliances either from a standard keyboard or from signals over the telephone; a meal planner that suggests recipes based on food in the refrigerator, family preferences, dietary restrictions, and specials at the local supermarket.

- Describe the current system and the languages and interfaces that are now being used. If this is a new application that has never previously been computerized, describe any similar functions that are now performed without the aid of a computer.

- Who are the people who use the current system (or manual procedures)? What effect will the new system have on them? Will it completely change their way of working, or will it simply make things better? In what way? How much training do the users need for the current system and your proposed knowledge-based system?

- Will the new system have a natural language interface to conventional programs, will it be an expert system with little or no natural language capability, or will it combine aspects of both? If it is an expert system, will it be a classification system, a design system, a decision support system, or some combination of each?

- Write a hypothetical dialog between your system and an intended user. The dialog may include graphical output and menu selections as well as English words and sentences. Your system might not have a conventional terminal. Instead, it might be installed in the basement of a building and be connected to telephones, appliances, and sensors throughout the building.

- What are the components of your system, its dependencies on other software, and the inputs and outputs between it and other computerized and noncomputerized facilities.

- What hardware is needed to support the system? Will it run on currently available equipment, or will it require new hardware? Will it run on a central system that supports multiple terminals, on a self-contained personal computer, or on distributed computers that are connected to a central database? Will it require special devices for voice input and output, handwritten input, telephone connections, special sensors, connections to various appliances, or portable data acquisition devices?

- Assume that the inference engine, the language handler, and other generalized software will be available from an outside source, but that you and your group will have to tailor the package to the application. What level of skills will the systems analysts and other experts need to implement the application? Could a software company or consultant provide a general package of language rules and inference rules that could be customized for the application?

- Evaluate the potential benefits of the proposed system: greater productivity, enhanced usability, faster response time, reduced training time for users, easier maintenance and modification, or performance of some function or service that was not previously possible. For each of the benefits, give an example that compares the old way of doing things to the proposed new way.

Role playing is a good way to generate a sample dialog and get some feeling for how the system would be used. One person plays the role of the expert system, and another plays the role of a user. To make it realistic, the two players should sit at computer terminals and send messages to each other; keep a record of the dialog as a guide to the design.

6.2 Take the sample dialog with your proposed system and circle the key nouns and verbs in it. Apply the techniques of conceptual analysis (Section 6.3) to those terms. By means of idea-dependency analysis, determine the types, subtypes, functional dependencies, part-whole relationships, and other implicit relationships between terms. If you need more material for the analysis, continue the role playing of Exercise 6.1 to generate a longer dialog.

6.3 Assume that your system will allow English-like questions and commands, but that it will not have a full English parser. Instead, identify the keywords and patterns that signal each of the input forms that the system will recognize. How would it distinguish correctly formed patterns from other sentences that happen to use the same keywords?

6.4 If your system will parse English instead of merely searching for keywords, you will have to prepare a dictionary of all the words it will recognize. Make a list of every word used in the sample dialog for Exercise 6.1 and add any other words that seem necessary for the application. List them in the form of the sample lexicon in Appendix B.1.

6.5 Write a grammar for all the command and question forms that your system will process. Start with the grammar rules in Section 5.2, and extend them to handle a larger variety of sentence patterns. What kinds of ambiguities are possible with your grammar? Can you revise the grammar to eliminate the ambiguities? If not, what semantic information can distinguish different interpretations? How would your system generate meaningful diagnostics for sentences that it cannot parse? Give examples of possible errors and the diagnostics that would be generated for them.

6.6 Organize the concept types in a type hierarchy. Extend the set of canonical graphs in Appendix B.2 to include the types required for your system. Use the relations in Appendix B.3 whenever possible, and add new ones if necessary. If the conceptual analysis becomes too complicated, you may need to restrict the range of concepts that the system will handle. Revise the sample dialog of Exercise 6.1 to show where the system fails to recognize input sentences that are outside its scope.

6.7 What database facilities are needed to support your system? Will it be a database on your local system or a shared database on some remote system? Which concept types represent procedures, and which ones map to fields in the database? Draw actors that show the functional dependencies between those fields. Link the actors in dataflow graphs bound to conceptual schemata.

6.8 Study the examples of rules in Section 6.6 and write similar rules to drive your system. Write the rules in an English-like style similar to ROSIE and LESK. Show what sequence of rules would be invoked to handle one of the sentences in the sample dialog. What requests would the rules make to external procedures or a database system?

6.9 If your local computer center provides a suitable language for implementing knowledge-based systems, map the English-like rules in the preceding exercise into an executable form. Do not begin the implementation until you have done all of the preceding exercises. But once you start the implementation, you may find new problems and opportunities that will suggest revisions and extensions to the analysis. If time is short, it is more important to do a thorough analysis with pencil and paper than to do some undirected hacking at the computer.

6.10 If you have used some languages and tools for implementing a knowledge-based system, consider possible ways of extending them and refining them. Could the rule language be made more readable, concise, or expressive? Could the tools be better integrated with other languages and facilities on the same system? Could better help facilities, design aids, graphics packages, and language handlers be provided? How would they simplify the task?

6.11 Reread Section 4.7 about the conceptual processor, Chapter 5 on language, and Section 6.7 on learning. Imagine a system that included the most advanced features of all the examples described. How would those features improve the knowledge acquisition phase? Imagine a dialog with such a system (or simulate it by role playing) where the system asks appropriate questions to aid the conceptual analysis. Study Fig. 6.12 and consider how the knowledge acquisition facility should be linked to other design and programming tools on the system.

SUGGESTED READING

For a survey of knowledge-based systems, see volume 2 of the *Handbook of Artificial Intelligence*, edited by Barr and Feigenbaum, and the collections of papers edited by Michie (1979, 1982). Van Melle (1980) and Hayes-Roth et al. (1983) present more detail on methods of implementing expert systems. Tennant (1981) surveys natural language systems. Lawson (1982) has a collection of papers on current machine translation systems. Feigenbaum and McCorduck (1983) survey the problems and promises of expert systems with emphasis on the Japanese Fifth Generation Project. For more details on the Japanese work, see Moto-Oka (1982) and Kitagawa (1982).

For philosophical work in conceptual analysis, see White (1975a), Chapter 6 of Sloman's *Computer Revolution in Philosophy*, and the readings on conceptual analysis in Klemke (1983). Wittgenstein's *Philosophical Investigations* show his method of using examples to illuminate all points of view about a concept. For the distinction between natural types and role types, see the collection edited by Schwartz (1977), especially the papers by Quine, Putnam, Kripke, and Copi. Conceptual analysis is an important technique of lexicographers and translators. Nida (1975) is a textbook of conceptual analysis for linguists and translators; it presents the techniques of analysis together with 19 pages of exercises for practicing them. The *Longman Lexicon of Contemporary English*, edited by MacArthur, is a good aid to conceptual analysis because it organizes words by semantic categories instead of an alphabetical list.

The standard textbook on database systems is Date (1981); the second volume (1983) includes Codd's extended relational model, RM/T. For more emphasis on theoretical issues, see Ullman (1982) and Maier (1983). For detailed examples of functional dependencies and normal forms, see Vetter and Maddison (1981). For an emphasis on data models and notations for representing them, see Tsichritzis and Lochovsky (1982). For an informal survey of database semantics and its relationship to the real world, see Kent (1978). For database design, see Hubbard (1981). The collection of papers edited by Chen (1981) presents various notations and languages for database semantics.

Work on database semantics derives from a variety of approaches that have been developed over the years. Bachman (1969) developed *data structure diagrams* for representing functional dependencies; they have been widely used as a notation for database design. Codd (1970, 1972) developed the theory of *relational databases* and the use of *normal forms* for logical database design. Griffith (1975, 1982) proposed *information structures* similar to conceptual graphs; they represent domain roles that include the relationships expressed by the boxes and circles of conceptual graphs. Chen (1976) developed the *entity-relationship model* as a refinement of Bachman diagrams; it emphasizes functional dependencies, but does not represent domain roles. Smith and Smith (1977) represent the type hierarchy and aggregations in their system. Hemphill and Rhyne (1978) applied scripts to database semantics with primary emphasis on domain roles and schemata. McSkimin and Minker (1979) developed a version of first-order logic that treats the inference mechanisms, type hierarchy, and functional dependencies. Codd (1979) extended the relational model in RM/T to represent the type hierarchy, functional dependencies, and domain roles. Mylopoulos et al. (1980) developed TAXIS, one of the most complete representations, which includes most of the features present in all the others. De et al. (1982) present the *concept-relationship model*, which combines the entity-relationship model with Smith and Smith's aggregations and AI versions of semantic networks. Sturzda (1983) has been using the IBM Data Dictionary to represent semantic networks and generate English descriptions of a database.

Knowledge engineering bears a strong similarity to systems analysis, and many techniques apply to both. DeMarco (1978) and Gane and Sarson (1979) present systematic tutorials on reducing an informal English description to data definitions, dataflow graphs, and decision tables. *Application Development without Programmers* by Martin surveys current versions of application customizers and other nonprocedural tools for system development. For tools and techniques of software design, see the collections of papers edited by Bergland and Gordon (1981), Cotterman et al. (1981), and Freeman and Wasserman (1980). For software development environments, see the collection edited by Wasserman (1981). For decision support systems, see Keen and Scott Morton (1978), Alter (1980), and Ginzberg et al. (1982). The *IBM Systems Journal* (vol. 21, no. 1, 1982) has five articles on enterprise analysis and related topics on software design and development; the article by Newman (1982) presents a framework for integrating the tools for defining, designing, and implementing systems.

Rich (1983) is an introductory text on AI that goes into some detail on expert systems and natural language systems. For more depth on production rules, searching techniques, and theorem proving, see Nilsson (1980). The logic programming movement, centered on the PROLOG language, is a major alternative to using production rules; see Kowalski (1979) and Clocksin and Mellish (1981) for introductions to PROLOG. For a tutorial on implementing conceptual dependency graphs and scripts, see *Inside Computer Understanding*, edited by Schank and Riesbeck. For a variety of implementations of conceptual graphs and related networks, see the collection edited by Findler (1979).

In a survey of psychological theories of learning, Swenson (1980) presents both the behaviorist techniques of conditioning and reinforcement and the more modern cognitive approaches. Clark and Clark (1977) present psycholinguistic studies of language learning. Wexler and Culicover (1980) develop a formal theory of language acquisition based on transformational grammar. Volume 3 of the *Handbook of Artificial Intelligence*, edited by Cohen and Feigenbaum, has an extensive survey of AI learning techniques. *Machine Learning*, edited by Michalski et al., is a collection of recent papers.

7 Limits of Conceptualization

No theory is fully understood until its limitations are recognized. To avoid the presumption that conceptual mechanisms completely define the human mind, this chapter surveys aspects of the mind that lie beyond (or perhaps beneath) conceptual graphs. These are the continuous aspects of the world that cannot be adequately expressed in discrete concepts and conceptual relations.

7.1 CYBERNETICS

Norbert Wiener (1948) coined the term *cybernetics* for "the entire field of control and communication theory, whether in the machine or in the animal." Wiener's definition is broad enough to include artificial intelligence. But as the fields developed, cybernetics and AI proceeded in different directions. The main difference lies in the problems that they address:

- From its very beginning, cybernetics studied low-level mechanisms such as feedback loops, neural networks, and servomechanisms. It sought a bottom-up view of how such structures could interact to control animal and machine systems.
- Artificial intelligence, however, started with a top-down view of symbols, language, and knowledge and asked what kinds of mechanisms and representations are necessary to simulate human performance.
- Although AI and cybernetics both use networks, the elements in the nets belong to different levels of mental processing. The nets in cybernetics represent individual neurons, but the nets in AI represent high-level concepts and relations, each of which may depend on millions of interacting neurons.

The difference between cybernetics and AI is exactly parallel to the difference between neurophysiology and cognitive psychology. In interdisciplinary studies, AI and cognitive psychology have had a great deal of fruitful interchange. Likewise, neurophysiology and cybernetics have had a strong influence on each other. But despite some attempts to bridge the gap, the two top-down fields have little contact with the two bottom-up fields.

Besides the differences in subject matter, AI and cybernetics inherited different outlooks from their parent disciplines. Cybernetics is descended from analog control systems, but AI is based on digital computer programming. Because of their heritage, they use different formalisms: cybernetics uses continuous mathematics, especially calculus and differential equations; but AI uses discrete mathematics, especially symbolic logic and formal grammars. AI has strong ties to programming language design and natural language processing, but cybernetics has no contact with those fields. Although Wiener's original definition of cybernetics claimed the entire subject matter of AI, his work has had little or no influence on AI.

Among the pioneers of AI, Marvin Minsky is one of the few who has continued to search for low-level neural mechanisms that can support high-level symbolic operations. His widely used textbook on automata theory (1967) contains a major section on neural nets. Yet many teachers who use the book skip that section in their reading assignments. Minsky and Papert (1969) wrote a definitive treatment of *perceptrons*, a class of network machines that can learn to recognize simple patterns. That book was, perhaps, too definitive—after Minsky and Papert showed exactly what the machines could do, people lost interest in them as a field for further research. Minsky's recent work (1981) has been on *K-lines* or *knowledge lines* for passing messages among a society of interacting agents or actors.

Research on K-lines and other kinds of neural networks may someday support symbolic processes as firmly as modern chemistry is supported by physics. But the human brain is vastly more complex than the simple atoms and molecules studied in physics, and many decades of work remain before psychology can be reduced to physiology. In fact, the analogy with chemistry suggests that cognitive science is more likely to guide neurophysiology than to be derived from it: the atomic hypothesis, the theory of valences, and the periodic table were all accepted in chemistry for many years before atoms, electrons, and electronic orbits were discovered in physics. When physics finally caught up with chemistry, the foundations of chemical theory were reinterpreted, but experimental practice remained unchanged.

Attempts to derive psychology from physiology have often been misleading. One source of inspiration for the stimulus-response arc was the view of the brain as a telephone switchboard: each arc would correspond to a nerve fiber linking a point in a sensory region to a point in a motor region. Yet Lashley (1950) showed that even a simple conditioned reflex must involve the concerted action of millions of neurons. Wolfgang Köhler, who had a background in physics, tried to explain Gestalt principles in terms of electrical fields in the brain. Yet the field theory never proved fruitful, although the Gestalt phenomena remain significant. For a long time to come, psychology and neurophysiology will remain independent, but related disciplines. Advances in one field will often clarify problems in the other field, but neither will be wholly derived from the other.

7.2 VAGUENESS AND EXPRESSIVE POWER

Anything that can be stated precisely in any artificial language can be stated equally precisely in English or any other natural language. In fact, most artificial languages may be viewed as extensions or abbreviated forms of natural languages: the equation 2+2=4 is an abbreviation for the sentence *Two plus two equals four.* Other more esoteric notations are defined in terms of simpler notations, which in turn are defined in terms of other notations, until finally one reaches a definition in a natural language. If English did not have a capability for being precise, the languages defined in terms of it could never be precise.

Artificial languages eliminate vagueness by reducing their range of expression. They are defined for a special purpose, have a constrained syntax, and limit the vocabulary to a few hundred symbols. Even more important than the constraints on syntax are the constraints on concepts. With only a small number of concepts, a restricted language can express each one in a single character instead of a full word; if each symbol is limited to a single meaning, ambiguities and metaphors are impossible. Natural languages, by contrast, have the vocabulary and means of expression for talking about anything within the scope of human experience. As the range of experience grows, they can quickly accommodate new definitions and metaphorical extensions. Whatever can only be stated vaguely in English cannot be stated at all in a formal language.

Varying shades of grey instead of black and white dichotomies, family resemblances instead of necessary and sufficient conditions, and issues with more sides to them than there are people to think about them—all these are characteristic of human life. Because natural languages can express anything within human experience, they must accommodate all the variability and vagueness of human emotions and the external world. Odell (1981) summarized the characteristics of natural language in the following ten principles:

- *Context.* "Communication through a natural language is, in large part, a function of context. *Where* and *when* something is said largely determines *what* is said."

- *Emphasis.* "What we mean is also a function of *how* we say it. Where or upon what word or words we place an emphasis (*intonation contour*) as well as how we move various parts of our bodies (*body language*) will frequently affect what we mean."

- *Multiple speech acts.* "The range of things (speech acts) a given sentence can be used to accomplish is limitless."

- *Intentionality.* "What a sentence *means* (a proposition) is often quite different from what we *mean by* it, which is sometimes a statement, sometimes a warning, sometimes a request, and sometimes something else."

- *Nonfunctionality.* "What a given string of words means is not a function of the formal characteristics those strings possess. 'Why not?' can be used to make a request, even though its *form* is that of a question."

- *Family resemblance.* "What most, if not all, general empirical terms *mean* in a natural language, as opposed to what we might *mean by* them on some specific occasion, cannot be specified *formally*, that is, in terms of necessary and sufficient conditions. They are family resemblant in nature."

- *Overlapping and criss-crossing definitions.* "Since most of the general empirical terms of a natural language are family resemblant in nature, it follows that in order to get at their meanings, i.e. the concepts they express, one must specify the set of overlapping and criss-crossing characteristics which determine the similarities and differences relevant to the question of whether or not some imagined or existing case falls under the concept in question."

- *Open texture.* "Even if we legislate sets of necessary and sufficient conditions to govern what they mean, we can't be sure that our legislations will preclude the existence of contexts where we will be uncertain what our words mean, that is, we can still imagine cases where we wouldn't know whether or not a given word applied."

- *Continuity.* "The concept expressed by any given word in a natural language is inextricably tied to the concepts expressed by nearly every other word in the language. While the words themselves are no doubt *discrete*, the concepts they involve, or are tied to, are *continuous* with other concepts."

- *Sincerity.* "A very large number of speech acts which can be implemented in a natural language involve expressing one's emotions. A natural language incorporates the distinction between a genuine and a nongenuine expression of an emotion. Expressing concern and expressing genuine concern are recognizably quite different."

Odell presented these ten characteristics of natural language in arguing against the possibility of processing unrestricted natural language by computer. They also represent ten limitations on the expressive power of artificial languages. No programming language ever designed has been able to deal with any of them. Natural language processors available today cannot satisfy them with the full expressive power that people use, and perhaps they never will. Yet some language processors can approximate some of them. What they do today does not qualify as unrestricted natural language, but it can provide a more natural and flexible environment than the formal programming and query languages.

Critics of natural language emphasize its vagueness and ambiguity. Hill (1972) quoted traffic regulations, cooking recipes, instructions on a shampoo bottle, and the *Book of Common Prayer*. His examples show ambiguities, misleading phrases, and incomplete or inaccurate statements. The examples, however, all show problems with human-to-human communication in English. None of them show that human-to-computer communication would be any more difficult. Hill's final point is that programming languages are more precise and that people ought to learn ALGOL to communicate better with each other. Yet people do not communicate well in ALGOL either: the overwhelming majority of programs written in any programming language are wrong when first submitted to a computer. Mathematics is just as error prone: textbooks by first-rate mathematicians often go through several editions without having all their errors detected and corrected. Artificial languages are designed to be unambiguous, but what they so unambiguously say may bear no resemblance to what the author intended.

Some criticisms arise from the misconception that special symbols and abbreviations are not a part of natural language. One study (Sheppard et al. 1981) concluded that English was harder to understand than a special program design language (PDL). As an example, they compared the PDL form,

```
SET TOTAL = DELIV * PRICE
```

to a supposedly natural form,

```
CALCULATE THE TOTAL PRICE FOR THE ITEM BY MULTIPLYING
THE QUANTITY DELIVERED BY THE PRICE PER ITEM.
```

This sentence is highly unnatural. In an accounting textbook, natural language includes symbols like "=" and "×" :

```
Total price = Quantity delivered × Price per item.
```

What is natural depends on the topic. In chemistry, natural language includes such sentences as *Add 125 ml of conc.* H_2SO_4 *and 125 ml of 85%* H_3PO_4 *and dilute to 1 liter*. In prescribing drugs, a physician might write *penicillamine 250 mg PO QD*. For any subject, natural language is the form of expression that two experts in the field commonly use in speaking or writing to each other. If both persons are mathematicians, their natural language normally includes symbols and formulas. If they are programmers, their natural language may include computer terms and even fragments of programming languages.

Correctness in any language is not possible without a dialog: debugging sessions on a computer, conversations between people, or peer review of scientific literature. The ability to be vague or incomplete lets a person talk about ideas while they are still in a half-formed state. One person can begin a problem-solving session with a tentative, partial statement. Through a dialog, others can analyze, refine, and complete the problem statement. One of the most challenging uses for natural language processing—and potentially the most fruitful—is in working with the user to formulate and complete a newly emerging idea. Several AI prototypes are exploring the use of English as an aid to the analysis and formulation of a problem statement: Heidorn's NLPQ for writing programs (Section 1.1), Codd's RENDEZVOUS for formulating database queries (Section 6.2), and Haas and Hendrix's NANOKLAUS for knowledge acquisition (Section 6.6). With such systems, people do not write programs in English. Instead, they carry on analysis and discussion in English, and the computer itself writes the programs. Even Hill admitted, "The main difficulty in programming lies in deciding *exactly* what is the right thing to do. To put it into a programming language is relatively trivial." Better than any programming language, natural languages are suited to analysis, discussion, design, and planning. Once the analysis is done, the "relatively trivial" task of writing code can be left to the machine.

7.3 CONCEPTUAL RELATIVITY

Concepts are inventions of the human mind used to construct a model of the world. They package reality into discrete units for further processing, they support powerful mechanisms for doing logic, and they are indispensable for precise, extended chains of reasoning. But concepts and percepts cannot form a perfect model of the world—they are abstractions that select features that are important for one purpose, but they ignore details and complexities that may be just as important for some other purpose. Leech (1974) noted that "bony structured" concepts form an imperfect match to a fuzzy world. People make black and white distinctions when the world consists of a continuum of shadings.

For many aspects of the world, a discrete set of concepts is adequate: plants and animals are grouped into species that usually do not interbreed; most substances can quickly be classified as solid, liquid, or gas; the dividing line between a person's body and the rest of the world is fairly sharp. Yet such distinctions break down when pushed to extremes. Many species do interbreed, and the distinctions between variety, subspecies, and species are often arbitrary. Tar, glass, quicksand, and substances under high heat or pressure violate common distinctions between the states of matter. Even the border between the body and the rest of the world is not clear: Are non-living appendages such as hair and fingernails part of the body? If so, then what is the status of fingernail polish, hair dye, and make-up? What about fillings in the teeth or metal reinforcements embedded in a bone? Are tattoos, contact lenses, braces on the teeth, or clothes part of the body? Even the borderline between life and death is vague, to the embarrassment of doctors, lawyers, politicians, and clergymen.

These examples show that concepts are *ad hoc*: they are defined for specific purposes; they may be generalized beyond their original purposes, but they soon come into conflict with other concepts defined for other purposes. This point is not merely a philosophical puzzle; it is a major problem in designing databases and natural language processors. Section 6.3, for example, cited the case of an oil company that could not merge its geological database with its accounting database because the two systems used different definitions of *oil well*. A database system for keeping track of computer production would have a similar problem: the distinctions between minicomputer and mainframe, between microcomputer and minicomputer, between computer and pocket calculator, are all vague. Attempts to draw a firm boundary have become obsolete as big machines become more compact and small machines adopt features from the big ones.

If an oil company can't give a precise definition of oil well, a computer firm can't define computer, and doctors can't define death, can anything be defined precisely? The answer is that the only things that can be represented accurately in concepts are man-made structures that once originated as concepts in some person's mind. The rules of chess, for example, are unambiguous and can be programmed on a digital computer. But a chess piece carved out of wood cannot be described completely because it is partly the product of discrete concepts in the mind of the carver and partly the result of continuous processes in growing the wood and applying the chisel to it. The crucial problem is that the world is a continuum and concepts are discrete. For any specific purpose, a discrete model can form a workable approximation to a continuum, but it is always an approximation that must leave out features that may be essential for other purposes.[1]

Since the world is a continuum and concepts are discrete, a network of concepts can never be a perfect model of the world. At best, it can only be a workable approximation. The psychologist Jaensch (1930) stressed the need for a *principle of tolerance* to accommodate different systems of percepts, concepts, and relations:

> Our investigations show that, like the perceptual world, our world of thought and knowledge is decisively determined by the structure of our consciousness. The kind of structure differs in the various fundamental types. The systems of knowledge of the different sciences are also based to a large extent on the different type of mind-structure operating in them. Different categories correspond to each. Each structure of consciousness separates out different aspects of reality, by reproducing certain categories of reality through the medium of categories of consciousness that are related to them. Those categories of reality, in which corresponding categories of consciousness are not present, remain unapproachable and are apprehended through different structures. The danger of one-sidedness, subjectivity and error in the fundamental questions of knowledge, is chiefly due to the fact that every structure of consciousness claims unlimited validity; but in truth each makes very wide negative abstractions of reality. We can, therefore, only penetrate reality and approach the ideal of "pure experience" by successively taking up the standpoints of different mental structures. (p. 118)

Jaensch emphasized the need for tolerance. A closed, rigid system maintains a sense of security by giving instant answers to all perplexities. But it is a false security that is threatened by any incompatible viewpoint. When the good is defined in absolute terms, anything that differs from the definition is automatically evil.

By drawing distinctions and giving names to the things distinguished, language separates figure from ground. Consider a tree. It has no sharp boundaries between parts; yet words divide the tree into trunk, roots, branches, bark, twigs, leaves, buds, knots, flowers, seeds, fruit, and even finer subparts such as veins in the leaves and

1 Considerations of discrete processes in quantum mechanics are beside the point. The world is a continuum to the finest perceptible resolution: the arguments are the same whether the finite conceptual structures are approximating a continuously infinite universe or one with an incomprehensibly large number of discrete states.

pistils in the flowers. Even the boundary between the tree and the environment may be indistinct: the tree may have started as a sprout from the root of another tree and may still share a root system with its parent and siblings; insects and animals may be living in and on the tree; a vine may be climbing up the trunk, moss may be on the bark, fungus may be growing on a dead branch, and bacteria in root nodules may be supplying nutrients. The arbitrary way that words cut up the world was emphasized by the linguist Benjamin Lee Whorf (1956):

> We dissect nature along lines laid down by our native languages. The categories and types that we isolate from the world of phenomena we do not find there because they stare every observer in the face; on the contrary, the world is presented in a kaleidoscopic flux of impressions which has to be organized by our minds—and this means largely by the linguistic systems in our minds. We cut nature up, organize it into concepts, and ascribe significances as we do, largely because we are parties to an agreement to organize it in this way—an agreement that holds throughout our speech community and is codified in the patterns of our language. (p. 213)

The division of the world into distinct things is a result of language. The philosopher Searle (1978) elaborated on that point:

> I am not saying that language creates reality. Far from it. Rather, I am saying that *what counts* as reality—what counts as a glass of water or a book or a table, what counts as the same glass or a different book or two tables—is a matter of the categories that we impose on the world; and those categories are for the most part linguistic. And furthermore, when we experience the world, we experience it *through* linguistic categories that help to shape the experiences themselves. The world doesn't come to us already sliced up into objects and experiences: what counts as an object is already a function of our system of representation, and how we perceive the world in our experiences is influenced by that system of representation. The mistake is to suppose that the application of language to the world consists of attaching labels to objects that are, so to speak, self identifying. On my view, the world divides the way we divide it, and our main way of dividing things up is in language. Our concept of reality is a matter of our linguistic categories.

The biologist Maturana (1978) summarized the issue in a pithy slogan, "Human beings can talk about things because they generate things by talking about them."

Whorf emphasized the influence of language on thought, but much if not most of the influence results from cultural distinctions that have been codified in language. The concepts of earlier generations, fossilized in language, then shape the perceptions of later generations who learn that language. Polish and Russian illustrate the relative effects of language and culture. Linguistically, the two languages have similar grammars and a large body of cognate words. Culturally, however, Polish has had closer economic, literary, and religious ties to western Europe. In doing conceptual analysis for machine translation, von Glasersfeld et al. (1961) found that the concept types expressed in Polish are more nearly commensurate with the concepts of English or German than with Russian. The Polish word for *write* is *pisać,* which is cognate with the Russian *pisat'*. Yet Russian uses the same verb *pisat'* for writing a letter and painting a picture. Polish, however, borrowed the German word *malen* for *paint* and added a Polish ending to form *malować*. As a result, English, German, and Polish make the same distinction: *write/paint*, *schreiben/malen*, and *pisać/malować*. For many other verbs as well, English, German, and Polish are semantically closer to each other than any of them is to Russian. As a result of cultural contact, the word forms do not change, but the underlying concepts are calibrated so that people (or machines) can translate them more directly.

Although Russian was more isolated from western Europe than Polish, it is still a European language that embodies a European world view. Hungarian and Finnish are not structurally Indo-European, but they are so firmly bound to European culture that their concepts are semantically commensurate with other European languages. Chinese, however, is structurally unlike the European languages, and it was culturally isolated from them for many millennia. Bloom (1981) noted differences of structure in Chinese and English that have a major influence on the modes of thinking in those languages:

- *Morphology*. English and other Indo-European languages can add an ending to a word that converts it into another part of speech: *approve, approval; discuss, discussion; white, whiteness; soft, soften, softness; general, generality, generalize, generalization*. Since Chinese words lack inflections, they behave more like the English words *talk* or *hand*, which can be used as a noun, verb, or adjective without a change of form.

- *Syntax*. Along with the difference in morphology, Chinese lacks the syntactic means for transforming the sentence *Congress approved the measure* into the noun phrase *the approval of the measure by Congress*. As a result, a sentence containing such constructions is difficult to translate into Chinese: *We will put off to next week discussion of the further implications of the new method for calculating the relationship between the rate of economic development and the individual standard of living*. Bloom found that a direct translation of that sentence strikes native Chinese speakers as "Westernized Chinese speech." Furthermore, they found it difficult to understand: 58% of them were unsure about what was to be discussed. A more natural Chinese form would break up the English sentence into three separate sentences with simple, active verbs instead of the more abstract noun phrases.

- *Counterfactual conditionals*. English speakers can easily talk about hypothetical situations that have not happened, but Chinese has no syntactic form for expressing them. Bilingual speakers report that in English they feel comfortable in saying *If the lecture had ended earlier, Bill would have had a chance to prepare for the exam*; but in Chinese they would say *The lecture ended too late, so Bill did not have a chance to prepare for the exam*. Chinese speakers learning English find the most difficulty with sentences containing *would have*. Speakers of other European languages learn the English form without difficulty.

Bloom showed the effects of these differences with both informal anecdotes and controlled psychological experiments. In analyzing a Chinese newspaper over a three-week period, he found only one example of a counterfactual argument, and that was in a translation of a speech by Henry Kissinger. The writings of Mao Tse-Tung, who had studied Western political writings for many years, do contain many such Westernized constructions. Bloom noted, "while Westerners find Mao's writings relatively easier to read than typical Chinese prose, and his logic relatively more accessible, I have been told on repeated occasions by people with extensive experience in mainland China that, for the Chinese, the opposite is very much the case." With its abstract nominalizations and hypothetical expressions, English readily leads to abstract theories, while Chinese tends to be more concrete. For science and philosophy, the two languages have opposite advantages and disadvantages. English leads the speaker (or thinker) to a general principle, but Chinese keeps the speaker closer to the facts and encourages a more thorough search of alternatives.

Different conceptual systems may be internally consistent, but incompatible with one another. In *Either/Or*, Kierkegaard presented the world views of two men: the first man had an esthetic view of the world, and the second an ethical view. Each view contained a comprehensive set of mutually compatible concepts. In terms of them, each man could give a coherent interpretation of his experience. Yet communication between the two broke down because their concepts were incompatible. Even when they used the same words, their concepts were oriented in conflicting directions. Compatible concepts form self-contained systems, and knowing one leads to the discovery of others. Every concept is compatible with its opposite: good and evil, beauty and ugliness, justice and injustice. In the *Book of the Tao*, Lao Tzu said, "When everyone recognizes the good as good, there is beginning of evil. When everyone recognizes the beautiful as beautiful, there is the beginning of ugliness." This seemingly paradoxical statement refers to the interdependence of all the concepts in a compatible set. When smooth, tender skin is classified as beautiful, then coarse, wrinkled skin becomes ugly. In such terms, an elephant may become ugly, even though an elephant, on its own terms, is a very beautiful animal.

Kierkegaard illustrated incompatible conceptual systems through a dialog between two persons. One individual may use incompatible systems to express different aspects of the same situation. An ecological approach to a forest views it as a system of flora and fauna with complex interdependencies. An esthetic approach emphasizes the beauty and variety of the sights, sounds, and smells. A business approach views it as a source of pulp for paper mills. And a religious approach views it as a manifestation of the creativity and harmony of the universe. All these views are true to a certain extent, but none of them is absolutely true. Whenever a concept expresses an aspect of reality, it is partly true, but it is also partly false because the very point of view it espouses forces the exclusion of other, equally valid points of view.

Since concepts are inventions of the mind imposed upon experience, there is no reason to suppose that one set of concepts is more natural or fundamental than another. As Kierkegaard showed in *Either/Or*, two radically different views of life can give equally comprehensive interpretations of experience. There is no form of logic by which one man can refute the other's position because logic can only develop the implications of a compatible set of concepts. It cannot form a bridge between two incompatible conceptual systems. This idea is the starting point for a conceptual theory of relativity. In physics, relativity makes all coordinate systems equally fundamental, although the mathematical equations may be simpler in one system than in another. In philosophy, the analogous principle of conceptual relativity treats all self-consistent conceptual systems as equally fundamental. Some systems may be more comprehensive than others or better attuned to human needs and aspirations. But no single system of concepts can ever capture all of human experience.

Conceptual relativity sets limitations on the generality of conceptual analysis. The concept types and schemata discovered by the analysis hold only for a single culture, language, or domain of discourse. Leibniz's dream of a universal lexicon of concepts that would be fixed for all time is doomed to failure. For a special application or range of applications, it is still possible to have restricted lexicons that are adequate to support knowledge-based systems. A universal expert system, however, would require a method for freely inventing new concepts for any possible domain. Such a system would require learning and discovery techniques that are far beyond present capabilities.

Discrete concepts divide the world into discrete things. The arbitrariness of this division is a common theme of Oriental philosophers. Lao Tzu said, "The Nameless is the origin of heaven and earth, the Named is the mother of all things." The world flows according to the unnamed Tao, but the differentiation of the world into discrete objects is a consequence of the discreteness of the conceptual mechanisms and the words that reflect them. By meditation on paradoxical sayings or *Koans*, Zen Buddhism seeks to undermine a person's conceptual system and promote a direct experience of conceptual relativity. The process cuts through many years of cherished beliefs and automatic ways of thinking and acting. It requires a painful letting go of familiar habits. But the result is a blissful state of Enlightenment where the anxieties based on the old system of concepts melt into insignificance. The most detailed statement of the Buddhist theory of knowledge comes from the *Lankavatara Sutra* (Goddard 1938):

- Appearance knowledge gives names to things. It "belongs to the word mongers who revel in discriminations, assertions, and negations."
- Relative knowledge does more than classifying. "It rises from the mind's ability to arrange, combine, and analyze these relations by its powers of discursive logic and imagination, by reason of which it is able to peer into the meanings and significance of things."

- Perfect knowledge "is the pathway and the entrance into the exalted state of self-realization of Noble Wisdom." Perfect knowledge does not rule out the use of words and concepts, but it goes beyond them to a state of nonattachment to any particular conceptual system.

Concepts are useful fictions that are not absolute. There is a Buddhist saying that words are like a finger pointing to the moon: one who focuses only on the words and the concepts they symbolize will miss the reality they express, just as one who looks only at the finger will not see the moon it points to. Nonattachment to any system does not mean ignorance of all systems; appearance knowledge and relative knowledge are important for everyday life. The enlightened one is free to use concepts, but is not bound to them as absolute. Yet the path to enlightenment requires a painful abandonment of the comfortable old ways of thinking before any assurance is offered that the new way is better.

7.4 CREATIVITY AND INTELLIGENCE

The most obvious way to determine whether a computer is intelligent is to give it an IQ test. Evans (1968) designed a program called ANALOGY to solve geometric analogy problems of the kind that appear on IQ tests. It scored about as well as a typical high-school student. Evans made no claim that his program was as smart as a high-school student, but Good (1965) proposed the following definition:

> Let an ultraintelligent machine be defined as a machine that can far surpass all the intellectual activities of any man however clever. Since the design of machines is one of these intellectual activities, an ultraintelligent machine could design even better machines; there would then unquestionably be an "intelligence explosion," and the intelligence of man would be left far behind. Thus the first ultraintelligent machine is the *last* invention that man need ever make, provided that the machine is docile enough to tell us how to keep it under control.

That statement is merely a definition and, by itself, makes no claim about existence. Good went on, however, to make a further claim:

> It is more probable than not that, within the twentieth century, an ultraintelligent machine will be built and that it will be the last invention that man need make.

Half the time available for Good's prediction has elapsed, and the chance of its coming to pass in the twentieth century is zero. Progress has been made since 1965, many practical applications of AI have been implemented, but deeper analysis of the problems has led to some solutions and to many new problems.

Good's prediction was based on the assumption that intelligence, once simulated, would increase as a direct function of computer speed and storage capacity. IQ scores expressed in simple numbers foster that illusion. Yet IQ scores do not represent the full range of human mental abilities. Besides the issue of cultural influence, there are fundamental questions about the existence of other factors that cannot be measured by IQ tests. Creativity is one such factor that leads to speculation, but seldom to precise theoretical constructs. Most often, psychological testers seem to regard creativity as an annoying residue that spoils the correlation between IQ scores and scholastic achievement.

Getzels and Jackson (1962) carried out a study that clearly shows the importance of mental talents other than IQ. They studied a group of adolescents in a private school where the average IQ was quite high—132. To measure creativity, they administered various tests such as ability to discover multiple associations for words, invent uses for things, find hidden shapes, and make up stories. To get as sharp a distinction as possible between the talents measured by IQ and creativity scores, the experimenters chose not to study those students who scored high on both types of tests or those who scored low on both. Instead, they selected two groups: the high IQ group scored high on the IQ tests, but low on creativity; and the high creatives scored comparatively low on IQ, but high on creativity.

Although one might question what the creativity tests really measure, there is no doubt that they measure a type of mental aptitude quite different from IQ. The average score for the high IQ group was 150, and for the high creative group was 127, five points below the school average. Yet both groups scored significantly better than the school average in scholastic achievement. In fact, the high creatives did slightly better than the high IQ students. The high creatives were not typical overachievers: they did not score higher on tests of motivation, they did not study as much, they were not as well liked by their teachers, and they were sometimes considered lazy. Yet despite their handicap of 23 points in IQ, their poorer study habits, their alleged laziness, and their lower estimation in the eyes of the teachers, they did as well as or better than the high IQ students in scholastic achievement.

Several personality traits correlate strongly with the two kinds of ability. The most prominent trait of the high creatives was a strong sense of humor. They rated it much higher than the high IQ group in traits they considered desirable, and they displayed it in their stories and drawings. The students in the high IQ group were generally better organized, less tolerant of chaos, more predictable, and more conventional—but they wrote boring stories. Wallach and Kogan (1965) explicitly characterized each of the four groups:

- *High creativity, high intelligence.* "These children can experience within themselves both control and freedom, both adultlike and childlike kinds of behavior."
- *High creativity, low intelligence.* "These children are in angry conflict with themselves and with their school environment and are beset by feelings of unworthiness and inadequacy. In a stress-free context, however, they can blossom forth cognitively."
- *Low creativity, high intelligence.* "These children can be described as 'addicted' to school achievement. Academic failure would be perceived by them as catastrophic, so that they must continually strive for academic excellence in order to avoid the possibility of pain."

- *Low creativity, low intelligence.* "Basically bewildered, these children engage in various defensive maneuvers ranging from useful adaptations such as intensive social activity to regression such as passivity or psychosomatic symptoms."

Correlations of mental aptitudes with personality traits do not explain the underlying mechanisms. Bruner (1960) distinguished the processes of creative intuition from the analytic thinking measured by IQ tests:

> Analytic thinking characteristically proceeds a step at a time. Steps are explicit and usually can be adequately reported by the thinker to another individual. Such thinking proceeds with relatively full awareness of the information and operations involved. It may involve careful and deductive reasoning, often using mathematics or logic and an explicit plan of attack. Or it may involve a step-by-step process of induction and experiment.... Intuitive thinking characteristically does not advance in careful, well-planned steps. Indeed, it tends to involve maneuvers based seemingly on an implicit perception of the total problem. The thinker arrives at an answer, which may be right or wrong, with little if any awareness of the process by which he reached it. (pp. 57-58)

When Bruner wrote this passage, the physiological work on left-brain vs. right-brain processes had not yet been done. Analytic thinking has sometimes been characterized as a typically left-brain function, and intuition as a right-brain function. That distinction, however, is too simplistic, and the physiological basis of creativity vs. intelligence or analytic thinking vs. intuition is still unknown.

Creativity and intelligence are apparently unrelated mental aptitudes that are not correlated with each other. Neither one is well defined or well understood in human beings, and the assumption of a single, unified faculty for either one is premature. Instead of just two independent mental aptitudes, Lowen (1982) distinguished sixteen aptitudes. He started with Jung's four categories of feeling, sensation, intuition, and thought, then divided each of those categories according to an extroverted vs. an introverted approach, and finally subdivided each of those categories according to a detailed vs. a global processing style. The resulting sixteen categories are a finer classification of cognitive abilities than a gross dichotomy of analytic vs. intuitive or intelligent vs. creative. Whether or not Lowen's categories prove to be more fruitful than other classifications, they emphasize the complexity of the processes taking place in the brain and the inadequacy of a single factor like IQ as a measure of mental ability.

Because of the different kinds of mental aptitudes, one should not expect to find a computer that uniformly simulates human abilities in all areas. From their earliest beginnings, computers far surpassed people in arithmetic. Today, they surpass all but the masters in chess playing. In pattern recognition, they can read printed material, but they cannot match a child in reading handwriting or recognizing speech. Computers are overwhelmingly superior to people for rote memory, acceptable for certain specialized kinds of learning, but very poor at tasks that require insight and complex analysis. They are good at applying a standard problem-solving method to many different cases, but they are poor at discovering new methods. Current AI simulations behave like people with high IQ, but exceptionally low creativity:

- IQ tests appear to measure speed and accuracy in using a given set of conceptual structures.
- Creativity is the ability to recognize the inadequacy of the old conceptual structures and to invent new ones to replace them.

A conceptual processor that has an encyclopedia of information might achieve an IQ score higher than any human being, yet not have the creativity of a two year old child. Such a machine would not qualify as ultraintelligent according to Good's definition; a better name for it would be Superclerk. Limited precursors of Superclerk are available today, and better ones will be built within the next two decades.

In Lowen's categories, Superclerk would be strongly biased towards verbal, analytic, discursive modes of thought and would have poorly developed intuition. It might not understand a joke, but it would be able to follow directions in English and give helpful explanations. It would not propose new plans on its own initiative, but it would be good at detecting inconsistent and incomplete plans that were given to it. It could read English texts on subjects about which it already had a well-developed set of concepts, but it would be confused by most literary texts and by scientific texts for which its predefined concepts were inadequate. Its novels and poetry would be boring, but it would excel at reading and writing form letters. Because of its uneven simulation of human abilities, Superclerk would not rival human intelligence; but like computers in general, it would make an excellent assistant for routine chores.

7.5 SCIENCE AS A MYTHOLOGY

Constructing a scientific theory means forging a new system of concepts for interpreting the world. Such a construction has a great deal in common with the process of creating a fictional world, as described by the novelist Vladimir Nabokov (1980):

> The material of this world may be real enough (as far as reality goes) but does not exist at all as an accepted entirety: it is chaos, and to this chaos the author says "Go!" allowing the world to flicker and to fuse. It is now recombined in its very atoms, not merely in its visible and superficial parts. The writer is the first man to map it and to name the natural objects it contains. Those berries there are edible. That speckled creature that bolted across my path might be tamed. That lake between those trees will be called Lake Opal or, more artistically, Dishwater Lake. That mist is a mountain—and that mountain must be conquered.

Like the artist, the scientist is confronted with a chaos of data. Out of that chaos, he or she must define the atoms that make up the world, recombine them "not merely in the visible and superficial parts," map the world, and name the natural objects it contains.

In either a work of fiction or a work of science, the task of creation is the same, and as Nabokov continued, "the boundary line between the two is not as clear as is generally believed." One might object that fiction is not true. It just tells stories—popular entertainment that is hardly comparable to precise, experimental science. Yet a work of fiction may contain as much truth as a work of nonfiction; and much of nonfiction may be mistaken, misleading, or wrong-headed. As this chapter has emphasized, the concepts in which supposed truths are expressed are essentially fictions. They may capture some aspect of truth, but there are infinitely many possible truths that they ignore, obscure, or distort.

Truth is only a measure of how well our mental models fit our observations of the world. Since finite, discrete concepts can never form a perfect model of continuous reality, a truly precise, truly objective science is not possible even as an ideal. The truth of any model must be limited to those few aspects of the world that the designer of the model chose to represent. Even for those aspects that the model covers, its truth is limited by the accuracy of the measuring instruments used to test its correspondence with the world: if the only standard of weight is a butcher scale, it is meaningless to say that a particular steak weighs 12.0695 ounces. According to the measuring instruments available five millennia ago, the ancient myths corresponded quite well with reality. Since they covered all aspects of all human concerns, one might even say that they were more true for their society than modern science is for ours.

There is no discontinuity between the thinking processes underlying modern science and the thinking represented in the ancient myths. They both stem from the same impulse—to speculate about phenomena in order to find explanations that make sense out of experience. But to be a science, a mythology must also satisfy some stringent criteria:

- *Predictive.* It must make clearly defined predictions under specific conditions.
- *Empirically testable.* The predictions must be testable by experiments that can be repeated by anyone who has suitable equipment and technique.
- *Cumulative.* The result of one person's theories and experiments must be stated precisely enough that other people can devise further theories and experiments that build upon them.

The scientist is a mythopoet who constructs a system of concepts for interpreting experience and weaves them into a coherent story. But science adds the discipline of prediction, testing, and building upon the results of others. Science is mythology plus discipline.

Without the discipline of scientific technique, speculation becomes mere fantasy. Parapsychology, for example, is speculation supported by an impressive amount of anecdotal evidence. Jahn (1982), the dean of engineering at Princeton, published a sympathetic review of psychic phenomena in the *Proceedings of the IEEE.* Yet no one has found a way of formulating precise, testable, cumulative hypotheses about such phenomena. Perhaps someone may do so in the future, but until then, parapsychology is not a science. By the same criteria, some of the work in AI barely qualifies as a science: people write a program, show some interesting output, and then describe the program in such a vague, qualitative way that no one else can build on their results without duplicating nearly all the work that went into the original program. The difference between AI and parapsychology, however, is that much of AI has been formulated in a precise, testable, cumulative way. All science may indeed be a mythology, but not all mythology qualifies as a science.

The concepts and schemata that direct human thought also determine how scientists carry out their research and interpret their results. Kuhn (1970) called those schemata *paradigms*. He emphasized that there is no such thing as "neutral data." The tracks in a bubble chamber are data only because of complex theories that led to the construction of the chamber, to the design of experiments for producing the tracks, and to the selection of "significant" tracks from commonplace events and background noise. Once a set of conceptual categories has been defined, scientific methodology is purely objective. But the selection of problems to study and the choice of concepts for describing them is a subjective judgment based on a scientist's personal preferences and the currently fashionable trends. The fashionable paradigms determine what questions are asked, what experiments are performed, and what books and articles are published and read. Scientific revolutions occur when one paradigm is replaced by another: associationism by behaviorism, and behaviorism by cognitive psychology.

Even physics, the standard of precision for all experimental science, is a mythology created by human minds guided by the paradigms of the day. Whitehead (1954) expressed the shock that he and other scientists felt when they realized that physics is a fallible human creation:

> I had a good classical education, and when I went up to Cambridge early in the 1880's my mathematical training was continued under good teachers. Now nearly everything was supposed to be known about physics that could be known—except a few spots, such as electromagnetic phenomena, which remained (or so it was thought) to be coordinated with the Newtonian principles. But for the rest, physics was supposed to be nearly a closed subject. Those investigations to coordinate went on through the next dozen years. By the middle of the 1890's there were a few tremors, a slight shiver as of all not being quite secure, but no one sensed what was coming. By 1900 the Newtonian physics was demolished, done for! Still speaking personally, it had a profound effect on me; I have been fooled once, and I'll be damned if I'll be fooled again! Einstein is supposed to have made an epochal discovery. I am respectful and interested, but also skeptical. There is no more reason to suppose that Einstein's relativity is anything final, than Newton's *Principia*. The danger is dogmatic thought; it plays the devil with religion, and science is not immune from it. (p. 277)

Frederick Thompson noted that students at Cal Tech experience a similar shock in their junior year. Bright students with high scores in mathematical aptitude arrive eager to learn all the wonderful truths of science. For the first two years, they really believe it. But in the third year, they study issues in the philosophy of science and discover that it is all a myth. It is a myth with high predictive value, and no other myth has been found to be more accurate. Yet it is not an Eternal Verity, but simply our best guess about how the universe works. When they come to that realization, many of the students go through a profound emotional crisis. Some of them never recover. But the best ones emerge with a deeper understanding of science and a better ability to do original research.

Not only do science and mythology stem from the same urge to speculate and explain, they also serve many of the same functions. According to Campbell (1968), a mythology serves four functions (p. 609):

- *Metaphysical-mystical.* A mythology awakens and maintains "an experience of awe, humility, and respect" in recognition of the ultimate mysteries of life and the universe.
- *Cosmological.* It provides an image of the universe and an explanation of how it operates.
- *Social.* It validates and maintains an established order.
- *Psychological.* It supports "the centering and harmonization of the individual."

In modern western culture, science has largely taken the place of traditional religions in serving these functions. Many millennia ago, orally recited myths represented the best scientific thought of the time. Today, "objective" science is one of our most widely accepted myths.

7.6 MINDS AND MACHINES

The subtitle of this book is *Information Processing in Mind and Machine.* A lot has been said about representing and processing information in machines, a lot has been said about processes in the human brain, but mind itself has never been defined as a formal construct in this theory. Various schools of philosophy have held differing opinions about mind and its relationship to the body:

- *Dualistic.* Mind is a substance separate from the body; it monitors the state of the body and directs its actions.
- *Epiphenomenal.* Only bodies exist, and the mental activity that is accessible to introspection is merely a by-product of neural processes.
- *Mentalistic.* Only minds exist, and bodies are merely illusions or by-products of intercommunicating minds.
- *Conceptual.* The concept of mind belongs to a complete system for talking about people and their ways of knowing, believing, understanding, and intending.

> Neurophysiology provides a totally different system of concepts for describing how the brain works. Although the mind depends on the brain, mental concepts are not definable in neural terms.

The conceptual position, which is the one adopted in this book, derives from the principle of conceptual relativity: a mental description and a physiological description of behavior are internally consistent, but mutually incompatible views, and neither one can be reduced to or be explained in terms of the other. Like Kierkegaard's dichotomy between an esthetic and an ethical view of life, mental terms and neural terms involve concepts and assumptions that are not interdefinable: anger may be correlated with an increase of adrenaline in the blood, but anger is not defined as the level of the adrenaline nor as the concomitant brain states. Just as the beauty of a symphony depends on the sequence of tones and harmonies, the activities of the mind depend on processes in the brain. But it is no more possible to define mind in terms of the brain than it is to define beauty in terms of tones and harmonies.

To illustrate the conceptual position, consider the concept COURAGE. Suppose that someone claims that a computer is courageous because it shows a firmness of purpose and lack of fear in executing any program given to it. But such a claim is silly. Since a computer is not capable of experiencing fear, a lack of fear means nothing. Furthermore, its firmness of purpose is nothing more than mechanical plodding. A horse may show courage in plodding through an icy storm because it is capable of having fear and, by its training, has learned to overcome that fear. Besides the ability to experience fear, courage presupposes honorable intentions, an understanding of the situation, and a reasonable belief that the benefits of the action are worth the risk. If any of these attributes are missing, a dangerous act is not courageous: without honorable intentions, it is despicable; without understanding, it is mistaken; and without a reasonable belief in the benefits, it is foolhardy. Outward signs can show that a person is undertaking a dangerous act without showing fear; but by themselves, they do not prove that the act is courageous. Only a knowledge of the person's mental state can distinguish a courageous act from a despicable, mistaken, or foolhardy act. This discussion illustrates two points: first, the concept of courage presupposes the related concepts of fear, understanding, intentionality, and rational assessment of risks (at least at the level of the higher mammals); second, observable behavior can suggest, but not prove the presence of a mental trait.

Like courage, the concepts of mind, thought, intentions, needs, and understanding belong to a unified, consistent system for interpreting the behavior of people and higher animals. Those terms are interdependent: a speaker cannot apply one of them to a person, animal, or computer system without admitting that the others apply as well. Applying those terms to computer systems raises serious philosophical problems. There are AI programs that simulate emotions, with a *happiness scale* that goes from -10 to +10. But a computer (or person) that simulates an emotion does not experience that emotion. Many AI systems can map an English sentence to a logical formula, derive other formulas from it, and then map those formulas back into English sentences. To say that such a system understands English is equivalent to saying that a theorem-proving program understands symbolic logic. Yet a person can understand an English sentence without realizing all its implications; conversely, a theorem prover can derive the implications of a proposition without being said to understand the proposition.

Even though behavior is governed by the brain, a detailed physiological description would obscure rather than explain normal behavior. Concepts of mind and intentions are a better basis for understanding human behavior than a complete wiring diagram of the brain. As computer systems increase in complexity, the engineers and programmers who design them work on only a small part at a time; complete flowcharts and wiring diagrams of current systems are beyond the capacity of any human being to comprehend as a whole. Large AI systems increase the levels of complexity even further. For such systems, mental analogies may become necessary to make them intelligible to people. Boden (1981) described hypothetical cases where the behavior of a robot could be more easily explained in terms of intentions than in conventional programming terms. In such a case, mental terms may be justified, but they lose their significance if they are casually applied to any AI system that the designer wishes to glorify.

Until one is prepared to say that a computer system has emotions, needs, and intentions, one cannot say that it has understanding. When the qualifier *simulated* can be dropped from the term *emotion*, then it can be dropped from *understanding, thinking*, and *mind* as well. For the AI systems available today, a casual use of terms like *thinking* or *understanding* is a sloppy and misleading practice. Those terms may have a dramatic effect, but they lead to confusion, especially for novices and people who are outside the AI field. McDermott (1976) maintained that they even have a mind-numbing effect on experts within the field.

Wittgenstein (1953) and Ryle (1949) deliberately avoided talk about the neural processes that support language and thought because such processes are irrelevant to understanding the meaning of language. Since Wittgenstein never talked about mental processes, some people have confused his position with a behavioristic denial of such processes. Yet Wittgenstein himself was careful to avoid that confusion. He criticized idle speculation about "the yet uncomprehended process in the yet unexplored medium," but he added, "And now it looks as if we had denied mental processes. And naturally we don't want to deny them." The assumption Wittgenstein denied was that an understanding of neural processes is needed to understand the normal use of language. Children learn the meaning of a word by seeing how adults use it. Philologists determine the meaning of a Latin word by analyzing Latin texts, even though the brains that composed those texts have long since crumbled into dust. Conceptual analysis, either formal or informal, is the basic method of determining meanings, and it requires no peering into the inner workings of brains or machines.

Wittgenstein declined to speculate about mental processes, partly because they were unobservable, but primarily because they cannot, in principle, explain meaning. But some of his followers, such as Malcolm (1977), went much further than the master in dismissing AI, theoretical linguistics, and cognitive psychology as a "mythology of inner guidance systems" (p. 169). Although a study of the human brain cannot explain the meaning of a word, it might uncover the neural mechanisms that process words. In the years since Wittgenstein wrote the *Philosophical Investigations*, new techniques have been found for studying those mechanisms:

- Measuring instruments for observing the electrical and chemical activity in various parts of the brain,
- Reaction-time experiments that can discriminate processes that are almost instantaneous from those that take a few additional milliseconds,
- Formal analyses of language and the mechanisms that generate it or interpret it,
- Detailed hypotheses about language and thought that can be simulated on a digital computer.

What these studies analyze are mechanisms, not meanings. Malcolm is justified in doing conceptual analysis of language without considering "inner guidance systems." But he is wrong in dismissing those systems as unimportant, uninteresting, or even nonexistent. Cognitive psychology may suggest an optimal form for representing and processing meaning, but conceptual analysis is also needed to determine the content that is represented in those forms.

The conceptual position on mind undermines the dualistic distinction between body and mind and thereby removes one prop in the argument for an immortal soul as a substrate for mind. Yet the existence or nonexistence of immortal souls is irrelevant to the question of whether artificial intelligence is possible. If extrasensory perception, telekinesis, and life after death require some sort of psychic ether, then that ether might be just another substrate for representing information and would be computationally indistinguishable from a material substance. If someone should find incontrovertible evidence that conceptual graphs are not represented in the brain but in a psychic ether, that would simply mean that AI would be simulating psychic ether on a computer rather than neural processes. On the other hand, it may turn out that the human brain or some psychic ether relies on continuous processes that are intrinsically different from anything that can be simulated on a digital computer. No one knows for sure, and the only way to see where the limitations might be is to try as hard as possible to see what can be done with the means available.

To return to the question of whether the word *mind* is justified in the title of this book, one can say that the primary justification is that *mind* is a short English word that nicely balances the word *machine*. It tells the reader that this book says something about the way people think and the way computers can simulate thinking. Nowhere, however, does *mind* appear in the formal definitions, assumptions, and theorems. Although this book discusses neural processes that are correlated with activities of the human mind, the word *mind* itself does not refer to any single one of them. An analysis of the concept of mind is an important philosophical issue, but the analysis cannot be reduced to programming or physiological terms.

7.7 PROBLEMS FOR COGNITIVE SCIENCE

Until the nineteenth century, psychology was considered a part of philosophy. The pioneers in the field were philosophers such as Aristotle, Locke, and Kant. Theoretical study of language was also part of philosophy, while the study of word forms was part of philology. When psychology and linguistics became distinct subjects, psychologists developed more precise experimental techniques, and linguists devoted more attention to the details of language. With the improvement in methodology, however, came an increasing specialization. Philosophers, psychologists, and linguists all studied aspects of language, thought, and reasoning, but with little awareness of the results and techniques of the related disciplines. Purity of method became a barrier to collaboration.

With the advent of artificial intelligence, a new methodology, computer simulation of thought processes, became possible. AI is an engineering discipline that uses results from all three fields: knowledge representation from philosophy, grammar rules from linguistics, and mental phenomena from psychology. In response to AI, the new field of cognitive science emerged as a re-integration of philosophy, psychology, and linguistics. What characterizes the field is not a common theory, a common methodology, or an established body of facts. Instead, it has three characteristics:

- Receptiveness to philosophy, psychology, linguistics, and AI,
- Study of behavior, not as an end in itself, but as indirect evidence for the mental processes that produce the behavior,
- Theoretical analysis of phenomena instead of the antitheoretical bias of behaviorism.

These characteristics are so general that they impose few constraints on what cognitive scientists do or how they talk about what they do. On a narrowly defined topic, people working with the same methodology can share insights on issues that are uppermost in everyone's mind. Cognitive science, however, suffers from the problem of many interdisciplinary fields: AI researchers have a lot to say to other AI people; psychologists have a lot to say to other psychologists; but when they try to talk to each other, they continue to use the terminology and research paradigms of their parent disciplines. The difficulty in communication is one more example of conceptual relativity: a given set of phenomena can be described in many different conceptual systems, and the concepts in one system may be incompatible, or at least incommensurate, with those in another.

Cognitive science will not become a clearly defined discipline until it develops its own research paradigms and methodologies. Some of the methodologies may be inherited from the parent disciplines. Others will evolve out of collaboration on serious problems that researchers in all disciplines recognize as important. The following kinds of problems would benefit from a collaboration of two or more disciplines:

▪ *Ecological psychology.* Laboratory experiments in psychology set up artificial tasks like memorizing lists of nonsense syllables. The attempt to study the way people behave outside the laboratory is called *ecological psychology.* Yet the wealth of behavior in natural settings is so complex that it almost defies classification. Is that complexity, as Simon (1969) suggested, the result of a simple organism interacting with a complex environment, or is it the result of an inherent complexity in the human brain? The 3 billion neurons in the brain give an enormous scope for complexity, but is that complexity built up by replicating a few simple forms many times over, or are the underlying forms themselves complex? Are the simplified laboratory experiments fundamentally flawed because they cannot deal with the full complexity of human behavior? If so, how can the complexity contributed by the environment be distinguished from the simplicity or complexity inherent in the brain?

▪ *Strata of mentation.* The human brain is based on a three-level hierarchy: pathic, iconic, and noetic (Section 2.7). Yet except for some isolated attempts, AI simulations are almost exclusively devoted to a noetic approach. What is the relation between emotions and thought? Is the three-level brain a relic of evolutionary history, or is it essential to a human-like intelligence?

▪ *Combining syntax, semantics, and pragmatics.* The most complete grammars for English, such as Quirk et al. (1972), are written as informal descriptions. The most complete formal grammars have been developed by computational linguists, such as Sager (1981), but they are primarily syntactic. Can such grammars be extended with a semantic component based on conceptual graphs, or must they be completely rewritten to accommodate semantics? Pragmatics has been handled by some programs, but often in an *ad hoc* way. Can pragmatic rules be generalized and expressed in a formalism that is compatible with conceptual graphs, APSG rules, and other notations?

▪ *Lexicography.* Natural language processing requires machine-readable dictionaries. Tapes for some of the standard English dictionaries are available, but their formats are designed for people to use, not computer systems. For computational linguistics, a more formal notation, such as conceptual graphs, is necessary. Appendix B suggests the form of such dictionaries. Exactly what information should be contained in them? How should they be constructed? Can they be generated automatically from conventional dictionaries?

▪ *Ontology.* A catalog of concept and relation types is an essential basis for formal lexicography. But since every generic concept has an implicit existential quantifier, a catalog of concept types is also an *ontology*—a catalog of modes of existence. Formulating such a catalog for concrete types is difficult enough, but the more abstract concepts involve complex philosophical issues. Lexicography must be done as a concerted effort of philosophy, logic, linguistics, philology, and AI.

▪ *Conceptual relativity.* A definition of all concepts by necessary and sufficient conditions is impossible. Except for artificially constructed concepts in formal systems, essentially no concepts can be so defined. Because of that limitation, a complete dictionary of English that captures the full meaning of every word (or even the full meaning of just a single word) is impossible. Is it possible, however, to develop a series of specialized dictionaries, each of which would provide a workable approximation to English for a specialized topic? How could a system recognize when the bounds of its dictionary had been exceeded? Could an open-ended family of specialized dictionaries ever grow to approximate the full richness of truly natural language?

- *Humor.* A good sense of humor is one of the characteristics of a creative person, but it is present to some extent in nearly everybody. Humor depends on and promotes insights that lead to new ways of looking at a situation. How is humor related to conceptual relativity? Instead of being a frivolous adjunct to intelligence, could it hold the key to a creative, adaptive form of intelligence? Is there some relationship between humor and metaphor? Between humor and learning? How could one design a program that would invent original, truly funny jokes? What about a program that could appreciate jokes?

- *Historical perspective.* Feigenbaum (1980) deplored "the lack of cumulation of AI methods and techniques. The AI field tends to reward scientifically irresponsible pseudo-innovation. That is, it tends to reward individuals for reinventing and renaming concepts and methods that are well explored." Ideas generated at other research institutions or in related disciplines at the same institution tend to be ignored. People writing on AI often cite an unpublished remark by a colleague who rediscovered a point that Aristotle analyzed 2300 years earlier. The history of philosophy is important, not just as cultural background, but often as the most thorough way of gaining breadth and depth of insight into the full range of issues about mind, meaning, and language.

- *History of linguistics.* AI is not the only field that has neglected its historical roots. Wierzbicka (1980) noted that transformational linguists "behave as if Chomsky's *Syntactic Structures* was the first document of theoretical reflection on language in the entire history of human thought. An abyss has opened between theoretical linguistics as it is currently practiced in many linguistic centers and most linguistic ideas of the past. More than two thousand years of history, in the course of which (particularly in the later Middle Ages and in the seventeenth century) the best minds occupied themselves extensively with language and thought, are blithely or contemptuously dismissed. Aristotle, Boethius, Abelard, Peter of Spain, Roger Bacon, Wilkins, Leibniz, Arnauld, Peirce, Frege, Wittgenstein, Sapir, Jespersen, Bally, etc. are either ignored or solemnly, unwittingly and usually only partially replicated" (pp. 32-33). Studying that history is interesting in its own right, but even more importantly, current theories can be built on more solid ground if they incorporate the centuries of analysis and thinking that have gone before.

- *History of logic.* Standard symbolic logic is based on an extensional approach that has proved useful for foundational studies in mathematics. Yet for over two millennia, logic was dominated by semantic issues in natural language. The medieval Scholastics, in particular, elaborated complex and subtle intensional approaches that have never been analyzed and reinterpreted in modern terms. The various schools of Indian philosophy also elaborated complex logical schemes that have never been reformulated in modern notation. Can those approaches express aspects of meaning that are not captured by standard logic? What light can they shed on foundational issues for conceptual graphs and other AI systems?

- *Fuzzy logic.* Standard logic has only two quantifiers, *for all* and *there exists.* Natural languages, however, express a wide variety of intermediate forms, such as *many, most, almost all, few, very few,* and *practically none.* Zadeh (1982) claimed "almost everything that relates to natural language is a matter of degree." To represent those degrees, he developed *fuzzy logic.* Yet AI has been most successful in dealing with discrete logic. The question remains whether fuzziness occurs in human thought or in the mapping between discrete concepts and the outside world. What is the ultimate source of fuzziness in natural language? Is it in the continuous variability of the real world, the human thinking processes, or both? If a system should permit fuzziness in reasoning, at what stage should it occur?

- *Modes of communication.* Natural languages evolved under two constraints: the linear form of speech and the powers and limitations of the human conceptual system. If a better spoken form were possible, the course of language evolution over the past 30,000 years would have found it. But computer terminals can combine graphics, menus, pushbuttons, and sound in a single interface. Can such systems support a more efficient or accurate form of communication? What is the significance of the gestures and hand waving that usually accompany speech? Could joy sticks or other devices be used as an accompaniment to speech—possibly to emphasize, punctuate, or disambiguate the spoken form?

Each of these problems leads to dozens or hundreds of subtasks, each of which may require many years of research. Not all of them need to be solved in order to support useful applications of AI. But they represent the work that must be done before any system that approaches the versatility of human intelligence can be designed. Whether such systems will ever be possible is still an open question, but no such system will appear within the twentieth century.

EXERCISES

Imagine that you have been invited to contribute an article to a volume of collected papers on conceptual graphs. The articles will be grouped in seven areas—philosophical issues, psychological evidence, formalism, logic and computation, linguistic studies, knowledge engineering, and limits of conceptualization. Choose one of these seven areas, and write a 10 to 20 page article that would be suitable for publication in the volume. Sample topics include the following:

7.1 Map some English sentences into conceptual graphs, and look for constructions that are especially difficult to represent. Develop a systematic way of representing those constructions, and propose it as a general method.

7.2 Follow the guidelines of Section 6.3 for doing a conceptual analysis of some particularly difficult area. Describe your approach, the results of your analysis, and possibilities for simplifying or systematizing the analysis of similar areas.

7.3 Compare conceptual graphs with another formalism you may happen to know, such as transformational grammar, Montague grammar, or entity-relationship diagrams for database design. Map some extended example expressed in that formalism into the conceptual graph notation. Compare the two approaches for perspicuity, expressive power, completeness, naturalness, and ease of use.

7.4 Find some area where conceptual graphs are not expressive enough. Propose some extensions to handle that area, and generalize them into universal principles.

7.5 Explore the formal properties of conceptual graphs or the operations that may be performed on them, and prove some interesting theorems about them.

7.6 Write a computer program to implement some aspect of the theory. Describe the novel features of the program and show some sample output.

7.7 Select some topic in this book that was mentioned in only a brief sentence or paragraph. Develop that topic in depth, citing evidence from the published literature and experiments or analyses that you have done yourself.

7.8 Select some point in the book with which you disagree and develop counterarguments against it. Propose an alternative solution and show how it would either improve the theory or refute some aspect of it.

7.9 Select some psychological, linguistic, or philosophical point that was not mentioned in this book. Relate it to conceptual graphs and show whether it helps to confirm the current theory or requires some extension or modification of it.

7.10 Design a programming language for processing conceptual graphs or the language interface to them. It may, for example, include the canonical formation rules as primitive operations and have a convenient notation for defining new types, schemata, and actions. Implement the language or at least describe how it might be implemented. What kinds of hardware and software would be needed to support it?

SUGGESTED READING

For philosophical treatments of AI, *Minds and Mechanisms* by Boden is one of the best balanced, both from a philosophical and an AI point of view. Haugeland (1981) presents a collection of readings on all points of view about AI. Dreyfus (1979) gleefully and unsympathetically pounces on and debunks rash pronouncements about AI. *The Mind's I*, edited by Hofstadter and Dennet, leans towards mystical visions of minds, both natural and artificial. Weizenbaum (1976) raises ethical questions about the desirability of artificial intelligence. Sloman (1978) and Dennet (1978) are philosophers who have turned their attentions to AI.

The original book on cybernetics is by Wiener (1948). Ashby (1956) is still one of the best introductions to the subject. *The Metaphorical Brain* by Arbib seeks to combine AI with cybernetics and brain theory. *Engineering Intelligent Systems* by Glorioso and Osorio presents a survey of both AI and cybernetics. General systems theory (von Bertalanffy 1968, Klir 1978) is related to cybernetics, but it tries to be so general that it is often rather vague. Fuzzy set theory and fuzzy logic are more closely related to cybernetics than to standard AI approaches. The collection of papers edited by Yager (1982) presents some of the recent developments in fuzzy set theory and its applications.

The classic statement of conceptual relativity is by Whorf (1956). In following Whorf, Bloom (1981) shows some important differences in the structure of the Chinese and English languages and their effects on thought and expression. *About Chinese* by Newnham describes the structure of Chinese and compares its forms to English. The notion of *perspectivism* by Ortega y Gasset is very close to the notion of conceptual relativity; for an introduction to Ortega's philosophy, see his book *The Modern Theme*. The distinction between an esthetic and an ethical viewpoint in Kierkegaard's *Either/Or* is a clear illustration of conceptual relativity. *Psychological Types* by Jung is a classic study of various styles of thinking and understanding; Lowen (1982) presents a finer subdivision of Jung's types.

Oriental philosophy is an important source of insights into conceptual relativity, but it is such a vast field that no short reading list can do justice to it. *Three Pillars of Zen* by Kapleau is good starting point for Zen Buddhism. For a study of Zen koans, see Miura and Sasaki (1965). The two volumes of *Buddhist Logic* by Stcherbatsky are a classic treatment of Buddhist philosophy and its relationships to Western philosophy and logic. The *Source Book in Chinese Philosophy* by Chan is a good collection of original sources; the *Book of the Tao* by Lao Tzu is especially important.

Appendix A Mathematical Background

As Bertrand Russell observed, writing can be either readable or precise, but not at the same time. To achieve a balance, Chapters 3 and 4 alternate informal discussion with formal definitions, assumptions, and theorems. The informal discussions are intended to be readable. The formal sections try to be more precise without being unreadable. This appendix summarizes the mathematical prerequisites needed for the formalism.

A.1 SETS, BAGS, AND SEQUENCES

Elementary or "naive" set theory is the foundation of mathematics. A *set* is an arbitrary collection of elements, which may be real or imaginary, tangible or abstract. Sets in mathematics are usually composed of abstract things like numbers and points, but one can also talk about sets of apples, oranges, people, or canaries. This book talks about sets of type labels, concepts, individual markers, and conceptual graphs. In most cases, the elements are never defined, but are left as abstractions that could be represented in many different ways in the human brain, on a piece of paper, or in computer storage.

Curly braces are used to enclose a set specification. For small, finite sets, the specification of a set can be an exhaustive list of all its elements:

```
{1, 97, 63, 12}.
```

This specifies a set consisting of the four integers 1, 97, 63, and 12. Since the order of listing the elements is immaterial, the following specification is equivalent to the one above:

```
{12, 63, 97, 1}.
```

If the set is very large, like the set of all mammals, a complete listing is impossible. It is hard enough to enumerate all the people in a single city, let alone all the cats, dogs, mice, deer, sheep, and kangaroos in the entire world. For such sets, the specification must state some *rule* or *property* that determines which elements are in the set:

{x | VERTEBRATE(x) & WARM-BLOODED(x) & HAS-HAIR(x) & LACTIFEROUS(x)}

This specification may be read *the set of all x such that x is vertebrate, x is warm blooded, x has hair, and x is lactiferous.* A given set may be specified in more than one way. The following four specifications all determine the same set:

{1, 2, 3}
{x | x is an integer and $0<x<4$}
{x | x is a positive integer, x divides 6, and $x \neq 6$}
{x | $x=1$ or $x=2$ or $x=3$}

A set specification that lists all elements explicitly is called a definition by *extension.* A specification that states a property that must be true of each element is called a definition by *intension.* Only finite sets can be defined by extension. Infinite sets must always be defined by intension or by some operations upon other infinite sets that were previously defined by intension.

In any theory using sets, there are two privileged sets: the *empty set* {}, which contains no elements at all, and the *universal set* $\mathcal{U}$, which contains every element that is being considered. In mathematical discussions, for example, the universal set may be the set of all integers $\mathcal{Z}$ or the set of all real numbers $\mathcal{R}$. In most discussions, the universal set is usually defined at the beginning of the presentation. Thereafter, other sets are built up from $\mathcal{U}$: subsets of $\mathcal{U}$, pairs of elements of $\mathcal{U}$, sets of sets of elements from $\mathcal{U}$, etc.

Of all the operators that deal with sets, the most basic is $\in$, which states whether a particular element is in a set: the notation $x \in S$ means that x is an element of the set S; it may also be read *x is a member of the set S* or simply *x is in S*. All other operators on sets can be defined in terms of $\in$. Let A and B be any two sets. Following are the common operators of set theory; listed for each one is its name, standard symbol, informal English definition, and formal definition in terms of $\in$:

- *Union.* $A \cup B$ is the set that contains all the elements in either A or B or both: $A \cup B = \{x \mid x \in A \text{ or } x \in B\}$.
- *Intersection.* $A \cap B$ is the set that contains all the elements that are in both A and B: $A \cap B = \{x \mid x \in A \text{ and } x \in B\}$.
- *Complement.* $-A$ is the set that contains everything in the universal set that is not in A: $-A = \{x \mid x \in \mathcal{U} \text{ and not } x \in A\}$.
- *Difference.* $A-B$ is the set that contains all the elements that are in A but not in B: $A-B = \{x \mid x \in A \text{ and not } x \in B\}$.
- *Subset.* $A \subseteq B$ means that every element of A is also an element of B: if $x \in A$, then $x \in B$. In particular, every set is a subset of itself: $A \subseteq A$.

- *Proper subset.* A is a proper subset of B if $A \subseteq B$ and there is at least one element of B that is not in A: if $x \in A$, then $x \in B$; and there exists some b where $b \in B$, but not $b \in A$.
- *Superset.* A is a superset of B if B is a subset of A.
- *Empty set.* The empty set has no elements: for every x, it is false that $x \in \{\}$. The empty set is a subset of every set, including itself: for every set A, $\{\} \subseteq A$.

The operators for union, intersection, and complement satisfy several standard identities. Some of the identities listed below are similar to the rules of ordinary arithmetic. Addition and multiplication, for example, obey the rules of commutativity and associativity, and the minus sign obeys the rule of double complementation. Idempotency, absorption, and De Morgan's laws, however, do not hold for ordinary arithmetic. Distributivity holds for multiplication over addition, but addition does not distribute over multiplication.

- *Idempotency.* $A \cap A$ is identical to A, and $A \cup A$ is also identical to A.
- *Commutativity.* $A \cap B$ is identical to $B \cap A$, and $A \cup B$ is identical to $B \cup A$.
- *Associativity.* $A \cap (B \cap C)$ is identical to $(A \cap B) \cap C$, and $A \cup (B \cup C)$ is identical to $(A \cup B) \cup C$.
- *Distributivity.* $A \cap (B \cup C)$ is identical to $(A \cap B) \cup (A \cap C)$, and $A \cup (B \cap C)$ is identical to $(A \cup B) \cap (A \cup C)$.
- *Absorption.* $A \cap (A \cup B)$ is identical to A, and $A \cup (A \cap B)$ is also identical to A.
- *Double complementation.* $--A$ is identical to A.
- *De Morgan's laws.* $-(A \cap B)$ is identical to $-A \cup -B$. and $-(A \cup B)$ is identical to $-A \cap -B$.

For complex sets, the rule for determining which elements are in the set may be too complex to state in a single expression. An example of such a complicated set is the set of all syntactically correct PL/I programs; a rather large compiler is required to test whether a given program belongs to the set. A common technique for specifying such sets is by a *recursive definition*, also called an *inductive definition*:

- First a small starting set of elements is given.
- Then some operations are specified for generating new elements of the set from old elements.
- Finally, the set is defined to be the set containing the starting elements, all others that can be derived from them by repeated application of the generating operations, and no other elements not so derivable.

The set resulting from these operations is said to be the *closure* of the starting set under the given generating operations. As an example of a recursive definition, the set S of all positive integers not divisible by 3 could be specified by intension:

$S = \{x \mid x \text{ is an integer}, x>0, \text{ and } 3 \text{ does not divide } x\}.$

But the property *x is an integer* depends on some prior definition of the set of all integers. The following recursive definition depends only on the act of adding 3:

- Let the set {1, 2} be a subset of *S*.
- If *x* is any element of *S*, then $x+3$ is also an element of *S*.
- No element that cannot be generated from {1, 2} by a finite number of repetitions of the above operation is in *S*.

All elements of *S* may be enumerated by starting with {1, 2}. The first stage of adding 3 generates the new elements 4 and 5, adding 3 to them gives 7 and 8, then 10 and 11, and so on. The set *S* is the closure of the set {1, 2} under the operation of adding 3. A recursive definition is a special kind of definition by intension.

The set of all canonical graphs used as a semantic basis for English is a complex, highly varied set. Since the number of possible English sentences is infinite, the number of canonical graphs must also be infinite. To capture such a great variety within a manageable list of rules, the set is defined recursively:

- A canonical basis is a given starting set of canonical graphs.
- Canonical formation rules generate new canonical graphs from old ones.
- The entire set of canonical graphs is the set containing the canonical basis, all graphs derivable from them by the canonical formation rules, and no other graphs not so derivable.

The set of canonical graphs is the closure of the canonical basis under the canonical formation rules. The formal grammars presented in Section A.6 define languages by similar recursive definitions.

A set has no duplicate elements. Since all duplicates are discarded in computing the union of two sets, the union operator is idempotent: $A \cup A = A$. In some cases, one may want to allow duplicates; therefore, a *bag* is a collection of things with possible duplicates. Since there may be more than one occurrence of a given element *x*, the operator # is a generalization of the element operator $\in$: $x\#A$ is the number of times the element *x* occurs in the bag *A*. Bags are useful for many purposes, such as taking averages: if four men have heights of 178cm, 184cm, 178cm, and 181cm, then the set of those numbers is {178, 181, 184} with the average 181; but the bag of the numbers is {178, 178, 181, 184} with average 180.25.

A *sequence* is an ordered bag. To distinguish ordered sequences from unordered sets and bags, the elements of a sequence are enclosed in angle brackets: $\langle 178, 184, 178, 181 \rangle$; the empty sequence is written $\langle\rangle$. If a sequence has *n* elements, the elements are numbered from 1 to *n* (or alternatively from 0 to n-1). A sequence of two elements is sometimes called an *ordered pair*; a sequence of three elements, a *triple*; a sequence of four, a *quadruple*; a sequence of five, a *quintuple*; and a sequence of *n* elements, an *n-tuple*. Historically, the theory of sets was first defined without considering order. On a piece of paper or in computer storage, however, the elements of a set are always represented in some order. Sequences are therefore easier to represent than bags, and bags are easier to represent than sets: a bag is a sequence with the ordering ignored, and a set is a sequence with both order and duplicates ignored.

New sets may be created by combining elements from the universe $\mathcal{U}$ in various ways. The *cross product* of two sets A and B, written $A \times B$, is the set of all possible ordered pairs with the first element of each pair taken from A and the second element from B. If A is the set {1,2} and B is the set {x,y,z}, then $A \times B$ is the set,

$$\{\langle 1,x\rangle, \langle 1,y\rangle, \langle 1,z\rangle, \langle 2,x\rangle, \langle 2,y\rangle, \langle 2,z\rangle\}.$$

With the notation for defining a set by a property or rule, it is possible to give a general definition for the cross product $A \times B$:

$$\{\langle x,y\rangle \mid x \in A \text{ and } y \in B\}.$$

The cross product can also be extended to three or more sets. The product $A \times B \times C$ is defined as

$$\{\langle x,y,z\rangle \mid x \in A,\ y \in B, \text{ and } z \in C\}.$$

Since René Descartes introduced pairs of numbers for identifying points on a plane, the cross product is also called the *Cartesian product* in his honor.

In this book, most sets are finite. Inside a computer or the human brain, all sets that are explicitly stored must be finite. But mathematical definitions and proofs are generally simpler if there is no upper limit on the size of sets. Therefore, the definitions in this book often permit infinite sets, but with the understanding that any implementation will only choose a finite subset. Whenever infinite sets are considered (such as the collection of all possible conceptual graphs), they are always assumed to be countable: a *countably infinite set* is one whose elements can be put in a one-to-one correspondence with the integers. The set of all real numbers is *uncountable*, but such sets are not used in this book.

The terminology for sets is quite standard, although some authors use the word *class* for set and others make a distinction between classes and sets. Bags are not used as commonly as sets, and the terminology is less standard. Some authors use the word *multiset* for a bag. Sequences are sometimes called *lists* or *vectors*, but some authors draw distinctions between them.

A.2 FUNCTIONS

A *function* is a rule for mapping the elements of one set to elements of another set. The notation $f\colon A \rightarrow B$ means that f is a function that maps any element x in the set A into some element $f(x)$ in the set B. The set A is called the *domain* of f, and B is called the *range* of f. The element x is called the *argument*, and $f(x)$ is called the *result* or the *image* of x under the mapping f.

Suppose $\mathcal{Z}$ is the set of all integers, and $\mathcal{N}$ is the set of non-negative integers (i.e. the positive integers and zero). Then define a function *square*: $\mathcal{Z} \rightarrow \mathcal{N}$ with the mapping rule,

$$square(x) = x^2.$$

The function *square* applies to all elements in its domain $\mathcal{Z}$, but not all elements in its range $\mathcal{N}$ are images of some element of $\mathcal{Z}$: 17, for example, is not the square of any integer. Conversely, some elements in $\mathcal{N}$ are images of two different elements of $\mathcal{Z}$: *square*(3)=9, and *square*(-3)=9.

A function is *onto* if every element of its range is the image of some element of its domain. As an example, define the absolute value function, *abs*: $\mathcal{Z} \rightarrow \mathcal{N}$, with the mapping,

$$abs(x) = \begin{cases} +x & \text{if } x \geq 0 \\ -x & \text{if } x < 0 \end{cases}$$

Every element of $\mathcal{N}$ is the image of at least one element of $\mathcal{Z}$ under the mapping *abs*; therefore *abs* is onto. Note that *abs* is onto only because its range is limited to $\mathcal{N}$. If the range had been $\mathcal{Z}$, it would not be onto because no negative integer is the absolute value of anything in $\mathcal{Z}$.

A function is *one-to-one* if no two elements of its domain are mapped into the same element of its range. The function *abs* is not one-to-one because all the elements of $\mathcal{N}$ except 0 are the images of two different elements of $\mathcal{Z}$: *abs*(-3) and *abs*(3) are both 3. As a more subtle example, consider the function *g*: $\mathcal{Z} \rightarrow \mathcal{N}$ with the mapping,

$$g(x) = 2x^2 + x.$$

Then *g*(0)=0, *g*(1)=3, *g*(-1)=1, *g*(2)=10, *g*(-2)=6, etc. The function *g* is one-to-one since no two elements of $\mathcal{Z}$ are mapped into the same element of $\mathcal{N}$. However, *g* is not onto because many elements of $\mathcal{N}$ are not images of any element of $\mathcal{Z}$. Note that *g* is one-to-one only over the domain $\mathcal{Z}$ of integers. If its domain were extended to the set $\mathcal{R}$ of all real numbers, it would not be one-to-one: *g*(-0.5) and *g*(0), for example, are both 0.

A function that is both one-to-one and onto is called an *isomorphism*. The two sets that form the domain and range of the function are said to be *isomorphic* to each other. Let $\mathcal{E}$ be the set of even integers, and let $\mathcal{O}$ be the set of odd integers. Then define the function *increment*: $\mathcal{E} \rightarrow \mathcal{O}$ with the mapping,

$$increment(x) = x + 1.$$

This function is an isomorphism from the set $\mathcal{E}$ to the set $\mathcal{O}$ because it is both one-to-one and onto. Therefore, the sets $\mathcal{E}$ and $\mathcal{O}$ are isomorphic. Instead of the terms *one-to-one*, *onto*, and *isomorphic*, many authors use the equivalent terms *injective*, *surjective*, and *bijective*.

For many applications, isomorphic structures are considered equivalent. In computer systems, for example, holes on a punched card can represent the same data as magnetized spots on tape or currents flowing in transistors. Differences in the hardware are critical for the engineer, but irrelevant to the programmer. When programmers copy data from cards to tape, they blithely talk about "loading cards onto tape" as if the actual paper were moved. One mythical programmer even wrote a suggestion for reducing the shipping costs in recycling old cards: load the cards onto tape and punch them out at the recycling works.

If f is an isomorphism from A to B, then there exists an *inverse function*, $f^{-1}: B \rightarrow A$. The inverse of the function *increment* is the function *decrement*: $\mathcal{O} \rightarrow \mathcal{E}$ with the mapping,

$$decrement(x) = x - 1.$$

The *composition* of two functions is the application of one function to the result of the other. Suppose that $f: A \rightarrow B$ and $g: B \rightarrow C$ are two functions. Then their composition $g(f(x))$ is a function from A to C. The composition of a function with its inverse produces the *identity function*, which maps any element onto itself. For any x in $\mathcal{E}$, *decrement*(*increment*(x)) is the original element x.

Functions may have more than one argument. A function of two arguments whose first argument comes from a set A, second argument from a set B, and result from set C is specified $f: A \times B \rightarrow C$. A function with one argument is called *monadic*, with two arguments *dyadic*, with three arguments *triadic*, and with n arguments *n-adic*. Those terms are derived from Greek. Some authors prefer the Latin terms *unary, binary, ternary*, and *n-ary*.

Instead of defining a function $f:A \rightarrow B$ as a rule for for mapping A to B, it may also be treated as a set of ordered pairs:

$$\{\langle a_1, b_1 \rangle, \langle a_2, b_2 \rangle, \langle a_3, b_3 \rangle, \ldots\}.$$

where the first element of each pair is an element x of A, and the second is the image $f(x)$ in the set B. Such a list of ordered pairs is called the *extension* of the function f. A definition by extension is only possible when the domain A is finite. In all other cases, the function must be defined by a rule, which is called the *intension* of f. (One could, of course, define the extension of a function as an infinite set, but the set itself would have to be defined by some rule or intension.)

Defining a function by a rule is more natural or intuitive than defining it as a set of ordered pairs. But a problem can occur when two or more different rules or intensions lead to the same sets of ordered pairs or extensions. Are two functions considered the same if they have the same sets of ordered pairs, but different mapping rules? To distinguish the intension and extension of functions and to formalize the rules for defining them, Alonzo Church (1941) developed a system called the *lambda calculus*, which uses the Greek letter λ to indicate the parameters of a function. Instead of defining the mapping g with the notation,

$$g(x) = 2x^2 + 3x - 2,$$

Church introduced the notation,

$$g = \lambda x(2x^2 + 3x - 2).$$

The symbol x that appears after λ is called the *formal parameter*, and the expression that follows is called the *body*. Whenever a term like $g(5)$ is used, it may be *expanded* by replacing it with the body of the definition and substituting the argument 5 for every occurrence of x.

An important advantage of the lambda notation is that it defines a mapping independently of the act of naming it. As a result, an unnamed lambda expression can be used anywhere that a function name could be used. This feature is especially useful for applications that create new functions dynamically and then immediately pass them as arguments to another function. In processing database queries, for example, some systems translate an English question into a lambda expression and then pass the expression to a query processor. A requirement that these temporary functions have names would be unnecessary and inefficient.

Church's rules for the lambda calculus are formal statements of the common rules for defining and using functions. His major contribution was to state the rules precisely and analyze their consequences systematically. With such rules, he was able to answer the question of when two functions are equal: they are equal by extension if they have the same sets of ordered pairs; they are equal by intension if their definitions are reducible to the same canonical form by the rules of *lambda conversion*. An important result of the lambda calculus is the Church-Rosser theorem: when more than one function in an expression is expandable, the order of expansion is irrelevant because the same canonical form would be obtained with any sequence of expansions. In Section 3.6, the lambda calculus has been adapted to graphs for defining new types of concepts and relations.

Since a function is a rule for mapping one set into another, the term *mapping* is sometimes used as a synonym for *function*. Another synonym for *function* is the term *operator*. Addition, subtraction, multiplication, and division are dyadic functions defined over the real numbers, but they are more commonly called operators. A commonly observed distinction is that functions have ordinary alphabetic names, but operators are designated by special symbols like $+$ or $\div$. The formal discussions in this book observe the following conventions:

- If the domain of a function is a set of simple things like numbers and type labels, it will be called a *function*.
- If its domain and range are sets of complex structures like conceptual graphs, it will be called a *mapping*.
- If its name is being spelled in full for readability, it will be written as an English word in italics, like *type*(x) and *referent*(x).

- If it often occurs in complex expressions, it will be designated by a single Greek letter and be called an *operator*, like a projection operator π or the formula operator ϕ.

A major reason for the functional notation is to keep the formalism independent of diagrams and implementation details. If c is any concept, *type*(c) is its type label, and its representation as a character string or a neural fiber is irrelevant. Diagrams are intended for readability and intuitive appeal. The formalism must also be readable, but its primary requirements are precision and freedom from implementation details.

A.3 GRAPHS

In diagrams, a graph is normally drawn as a network of nodes connected by arcs. Such diagrams introduce arbitrary conventions that are irrelevant to the mathematical definitions and theorems: Are the arcs drawn curved or straight? Short or long? Are the nodes drawn as dots, circles, or other shapes? Is there any significance in having node a above, below, to the right, or to the left of node b? To avoid such questions, a graph is defined formally without any reference to a diagram. Diagrams are then introduced as informal illustrations. Diagrams are essential for developing an intuitive understanding, but the definitions and proofs are independent of them.

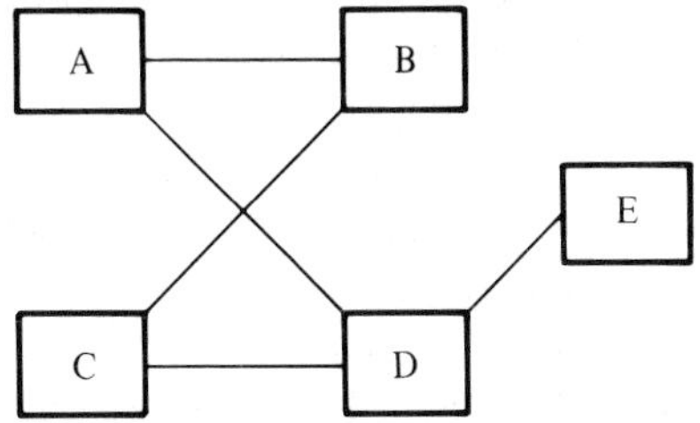

Fig. A.1 Sample graph

Formally, a *graph* G consists of a nonempty set N, whose elements are called *nodes*, and a set A, whose elements are called *arcs*. Every arc in A is a pair of nodes from the set N. Figure A.1 shows an example of a graph. The set of nodes is {A, B, C, D, E}, and the set of arcs is {⟨A,B⟩, ⟨A,D⟩, ⟨B,C⟩, ⟨C,D⟩, ⟨D,E⟩}. Notice that node D happens to be an endpoint of three different arcs. That is a property that can be seen instantly from the diagram, but it takes careful checking to verify it from the set of pairs. For people, diagrams are the most convenient way of dealing with graphs; but for computers, a set of pairs is easier to represent.

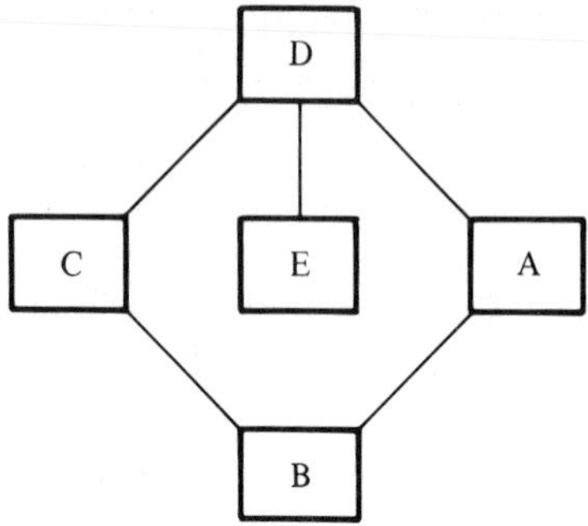

Fig. A.2 Alternate way of drawing the graph in Fig. A.1

Figure A.2 is another way of drawing the same graph shown in Fig. A.1. The two diagrams look very different, but their abstract representations as sets of nodes and arcs are the same. Even when graphs are defined in a purely abstract way, questions may arise about the order of the two nodes of an arc. If the order is irrelevant, the notation {A,B} shows that the arc is an unordered set of two nodes. A graph whose arcs are unordered pairs is said to be *undirected.* If the order is significant, ⟨A,B⟩ and ⟨B,A⟩ represent distinct arcs, and the graph is said to be *directed.* Figure A.3 shows a directed graph. Its four arcs are {⟨A,C⟩, ⟨C,A⟩, ⟨A,D⟩, ⟨B,C⟩}. By convention, an arrowhead on each arc points to the second node of each ordered pair.

Although graphs are defined abstractly, mathematicians normally imagine them as diagrams. The common conventions for drawing graphs are reflected in descriptive terms like *endpoint*, *loop*, *path*, and *cycle.* Let e be the arc $\langle a,b\rangle$. Then the nodes a and b are said to be *endpoints* of e, and e is said to *connect* a and b. If e is an arc of a directed graph, then the first endpoint a is called the *source* of e, and the second endpoint b is called the *target* of e. The word *target* is easy to remember since that is the direction the arrow points. A *loop* is an arc e whose endpoints are the same node: $e=\langle a,a\rangle$.

Chapter 5 of this book discusses ways of traversing a conceptual graph while mapping it into a sentence in some language. A *walk* through a graph is a sequence of nodes $\langle a_0, a_1, ..., a_n\rangle$ for which any two adjacent nodes a_i and a_{i+1} are the endpoints of some arc. Any arc whose endpoints are adjacent nodes of a walk is said to be *traversed* by the walk. A walk that contains n+1 nodes must traverse n arcs and is therefore said to be of length n. A *path* is a walk in which all nodes are distinct. A walk with only one node $\langle a_0\rangle$ is a path of length 0. If the first and last nodes of a walk are the same, but all other nodes are distinct, then the walk is called a *cycle.* Every loop is a cycle of length 1, but cycles may traverse more than one arc.

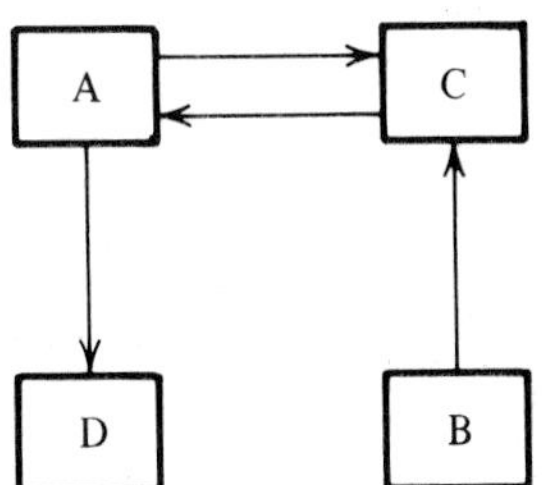

Fig. A.3 Directed graph

For the graph in Fig. A.2, the walk ⟨E, D, A, B⟩ is a path because all nodes are distinct. The path is of length 3, which is equal to the number of arcs traversed by a point that moves along the path. The walk ⟨D, C, B, A, D⟩ is a cycle because it starts and ends at the same node.

If G is a directed graph, then a walk, path, or cycle through G may or may not follow the same direction as the arrows. A walk, path, or cycle through G is said to be *directed* if adjacent nodes occur in the same order in which they occur in some arc of G: if a_i and a_{i+1} are adjacent nodes on the walk, then the ordered pair $\langle a_i, a_{i+1} \rangle$ must be an arc of G. An arc of a directed graph is like a one-way street, and a directed walk obeys all the one-way signs (arrowheads). An undirected walk through a directed graph is possible, simply by ignoring the ordering.

A graph is *connected* if there is a possible path (directed or undirected) between any two nodes. If it is not connected, then it breaks down into disjoint *components*, each of which is connected, but none of which has a path linking it to any other component. A *cutpoint* of a graph is a node, which when removed, causes the graph (or the component in which it is located) to separate into two or more disconnected components.

Certain special cases of graphs are important enough to be given special names: an *acyclic* graph is one that has no cycles, and a *tree* is an acyclic connected graph for which the path between any two nodes is unique. The most commonly used trees are *rooted trees*:

- The arcs of a rooted tree are directed.
- If $\langle a,b \rangle$ is an arc of the tree, the node a is called the *parent* of b, and b is a *child* of a.
- There is a privileged node called the *root*, which has no parent.
- Every node except the root has exactly one parent.
- A node that has no child is called a *leaf*.

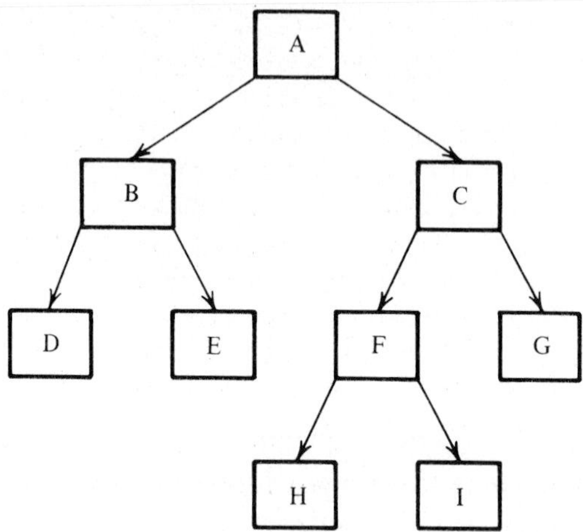

Fig. A.4 Binary tree

The terminology of trees is extended to related graphs: a *forest* is a collection of disconnected trees; a *chain* is a tree with no branches—all the nodes lie along a single path; and a *seed* has only one node and no arcs.

A *binary tree* is a rooted tree where every node that is not a leaf has exactly two children (Fig. A.4). In a binary tree, the two children of each node are usually designated as the *left child* and the *right child.* In computer applications, each node of a tree or other graph may contain some data to be processed. For the tree in Fig. A.4, imagine a walk that starts at the root, visits every node at least once, and finally returns to the root; assume that the left child is always visited before the right child. Such a walk will visit the leaves of the tree only once, but it will visit every other node three times: ⟨A, B, D, B, E, B, A, C, F, H, F, I, F, C, G, C, A⟩. There are therefore three options for processing the data at each node:

- *Preorder.* Process the data at the first visit to the node. For Fig. A.4, the nodes would be processed in the order A, B, D, E, C, F, H, I, G.
- *Postorder.* Process the data at the last visit to each node. For Fig. A.4, the nodes would be processed in the order D, E, B, H, I, F, G, C, A.
- *Inorder.* Process the data at the middle visit to each node. For Fig. A.4, the nodes would be processed in the order D, B, E, A, H, F, I, C, G.

Chapter 5 shows how various options in walking through a conceptual graph result in different word orders for different languages. Classical Hebrew is a preorder language that puts the verb first, Japanese is a postorder language that puts the verb last, and English and French are inorder languages that put the verb in the middle.

In AI, trees and graphs are used to represent games. Chess, checkers, and tic-tac-toe may be considered graphs where the nodes are *positions* and the arcs are *moves*. A complete play of the game, called a *game path*, is a directed walk from some starting position to an ending position that determines a win, loss, or draw. The games that are considered in this book are called *two-person zero-sum perfect-information games*. They are called two-person games to distinguish them from games like poker with many players; they are zero-sum games because anything that one player loses the other player wins (as opposed to *negative-sum* games where the house takes a cut or *positive-sum* games where new values are created); and they are perfect-information games because each player can see the complete position at all times (as opposed to poker or bridge where some of the most significant information is hidden). Following are some basic definitions:

- A *game G* is a directed graph with a set of nodes *P* called *positions* and a set of arcs *M* called *moves*.
- If $\langle P_1,P_2\rangle$ is a move in *M*, then position P_2 is called a *successor* of P_1.
- Each position is an *n*-tuple $\langle p_1,...,p_n\rangle$ that describes the current state of the game. The first element p_1 is called the *player on move* and the remaining elements $p_2,...,p_n$ depend on the type of game.
- For a *two-person game*, the player on move is either of two elements $\{A,B\}$. Each player is called an *opponent* of the other player.
- There is a nonempty subset *S* of *P* called the *starting positions* of the game.
- There is a nonempty subset *E* of *P* called the *ending positions* of the game. *E* consists of all positions that have no successors.
- A *game path* is a directed walk from a starting position to an ending position.
- There is a function *payoff* that maps ending positions into numbers. For any ending position *P*, if *payoff*(*P*) is positive, then *A* has a *win* and *B* has a *loss*; if it is negative, then *B* has a *win* and *A* has a *loss*; and if it is zero, then *A* and *B* both have a *draw*.

This definition is used in Section 4.4 as a basis for *game-theoretical semantics*. It is not general enough to handle all possible games, but it is general enough for typical board games. It allows the possibility of games with more than one starting position, as in a game of chess where one player is given a handicap. For many games, the payoff is +1 for a win, and -1 for a loss. Other games have a numerical *score* that varies widely.

The play of the game consists of moves from position to position. For a position $\langle p_1,...,p_n\rangle$, player p_1 is the one who chooses the next move, and the format of the state information $p_2,...,p_n$ depends on the particular game. In chess, for example, the current state describes the location of all the pieces on the board, but it also includes control information about the possibility of castling or *en passant* pawn captures. In choosing moves, *A*'s strategy is to maximize the payoff, and *B*'s strategy is to minimize the payoff. Since the payoff function is only defined for ending positions, the *value* of nonending positions may be computed on the assumption that each player makes an optimal choice at each move. Let P be any position in the game G; the function *value* is defined recursively:

- If P is an ending position, $value(P)= payoff(P)$.
- If P is a nonending position with player A on move, let $Q_1,...,Q_n$ be the successors to position P. Then $value(P)$ is the maximum of $value(Q_1),...,value(Q_n)$.
- If P is a nonending position with player B on move, let $Q_1,...,Q_n$ be the successors to position P. Then $value(P)$ is the minimum of $value(Q_1),...,value(Q_n)$.
- If $value(P)$ is positive, then A is said to have a *winning strategy* in position P. If it is negative, then B is said to a have a winning strategy in P.

The *value* function computes the expected payoff if both players make the best moves at each turn. If some game paths are infinite, $value(P)$ may be undefined for some positions P; if all game paths are finite, $value(P)$ is defined for all P. Books on AI that cover game playing programs discuss ways of evaluating this function efficiently or approximating it if an exact evaluation would take too much time. The *value* function is also called the *backed-up value* because it computes the value of a nonending position P in terms of the ending positions that are reachable from P.

The terminology for graphs in this section is fairly standard, but many of the ideas have been developed independently by different people, who have introduced different terms. Some authors use the terms *vertex* and *edge* instead of *node* and *arc*. Others distinguish degrees of connectivity in a directed graph: it is *strongly connected* if there is a directed path between any two nodes, and it is *weakly connected* if there is only an undirected path between some pair of nodes. Some authors use the term *digraph* as an abbreviation for *directed graph*, but that use is etymologically illiterate, since *digraph* should mean *double graph*. Occasionally, people introduce fancy terms like *arborescence* for rooted tree, but the simpler terminology is more descriptive.

A.4 RELATIONS

A *relation* is a function of one or more arguments whose range is the set of *truth values*, {**true**,**false**}. An example of a dyadic or binary relation is the function *less than* represented by the operator symbol <. Its domain is the set of integers $\mathcal{Z}$:

$<: \mathcal{Z}\times\mathcal{Z} \rightarrow \{\mathbf{true},\mathbf{false}\}$.

When applied to the integers 5 and 12, 5<12 gives the result **true**, but 12<5 gives the result **false**. Relations are often written as infix operators with special symbols, $x<y$ or $x \in S$; they may sometimes be represented by single letters, R(x,y) or S(x,y,z); or they may be represented by arbitrarily long alphanumeric strings, MOTHER(x,y) or BETWEEN(x,y,z). Traditional mathematics only uses single letters or symbols, but programming languages and database systems allow arbitrarily long identifiers.

Since longer names are more readable, this book uses relation names like MOTHER instead of cryptic symbols like *M*. The term *predicate* is a synonym for relation. Some authors say that relations must have two or more arguments and call a predicate with one argument a *property*. In this book, however, the terms *predicate* and *relation* are used interchangeably.

As with other functions, relations may be defined either by intension or by extension. An intensional definition is a rule for computing a value **true** or **false** for each possible input. An extensional definition is a set of all combinations of arguments for which the relation is **true**; for all other combinations, the relation is **false**. In a database, a *stored relation* is one whose values are listed by extension, and a *virtual relation* is computed by some rule. In theory, implementation issues are irrelevant. In practice, the question of how a relation is implemented is of vital importance: the relation $x<y$ is trivial to compute but would require an infinite amount of space to store.

Graphs and binary relations are equivalent ways of describing the same mathematical structures. Historically, graphs are more closely associated with geometric properties that can be seen from diagrams, and relations are associated with more abstract mathematics and logic. But every binary relation can be represented as a graph, and every graph defines a binary relation. Let *G* be a graph, and let the symbol ⊙ represent the equivalent binary relation. If *x* and *y* are nodes in the graph *G*, define $x{\odot}y$=**true** if the pair $\langle x,y \rangle$ is an arc of *G*, and $x{\odot}y$=**false** if $\langle x,y \rangle$ is not an arc of *G*. If the graph is undirected, then ⊙ is *symmetric* because it obeys the constraint $x{\odot}y=y{\odot}x$. Following are some common properties of relations:

Name	Constraint	Example
Reflexive	for all x, $x{\odot}x$	x is as old as y
Irreflexive	for all x, not($x{\odot}x$)	x is the mother of y
Symmetric	$x{\odot}y$ implies $y{\odot}x$	x is the spouse of y
Asymmetric	$x{\odot}y$ implies not($y{\odot}x$)	x is the husband of y
Antisymmetric	$x{\odot}y$ & $y{\odot}x$ implies $x=y$	x was present at y's birth
Transitive	$x{\odot}y$ & $y{\odot}z$ implies $x{\odot}z$	x is an ancestor of y

Certain combinations of these properties are also common. A *partial ordering*, represented by the symbol ≤, is a binary relation that is reflexive, antisymmetric, and transitive. The subset relation ⊆ is the most common partial ordering over sets. It is antisymmetric because $x \subseteq y$ and $y \subseteq x$ imply that $x=y$. A *linear ordering* is a partial ordering where $x \le y$ or $y \le x$ for every pair *x* and *y*. For real numbers, ≤ represents the linear ordering *less than or equal to*. The subset relation is only a partial ordering because there are many sets for which neither $x \subseteq y$ nor $y \subseteq x$ is true. The most important partial ordering in this book is the type hierarchy of concepts.

A mathematical *structure* is a set together with one or more relations and operators defined over the set. A *lattice* is a structure consisting of a set *L*, a partial ordering ≤, and two binary operators ∩ and ∪. If *a* and *b* are elements of *L*, $a \cap b$ is called the *greatest lower bound* or *infimum* of a and b; $a \cup b$ is called the *least upper bound* or *supremum* of a and b. (Alternate terms are *meet* and *join*, but they conflict with the *joins* of conceptual graphs.) These operators satisfy the following axioms:

- For any a and b in L, $a \cap b \leq a$, $a \cap b \leq b$, and if c is any element of L for which $c \leq a$ and $c \leq b$, then $c \leq a \cap b$.
- For any a and b in L, $a \leq a \cup b$, $b \leq a \cup b$, and if c is any element of L for which $a \leq c$ and $b \leq c$, then $a \cup b \leq c$.

The symbols $\cap$ and $\cup$ are the same as the symbols for intersection and union of sets. This similarity is not an accident because the set of all subsets of a universal set $\mathcal{U}$ forms a lattice with the subset relation $\subseteq$ as the partial ordering. A *bounded lattice* is one with a top $\top$ and a bottom $\bot$, where for any element a in the lattice, $\bot \leq a \leq \top$. All finite lattices are bounded, and so are many infinite ones. In a lattice of subsets, the universal set $\mathcal{U}$ itself is $\top$, and the empty set $\{\}$ is $\bot$.

Since the $\cup$ and $\cap$ operators on lattices are so similar to the unions and intersections of sets, they have many of the same properties. Following are the identities defined for the set operators that also hold for lattice operators:

- *Idempotency.* $A \cap A$ is identical to A, and $A \cup A$ is also identical to A.
- *Commutativity.* $A \cap B$ is identical to $B \cap A$, and $A \cup B$ is identical to $B \cup A$.
- *Associativity.* $A \cap (B \cap C)$ is identical to $(A \cap B) \cap C$, and $A \cup (B \cup C)$ is identical to $(A \cup B) \cup C$.
- *Absorption.* $A \cap (A \cup B)$ is identical to A, and $A \cup (A \cap B)$ is also identical to A.

These identities hold for all lattices. A *distributive lattice* is one for which the distributive law also holds. A *complemented lattice* is one for which a complement operator and De Morgan's laws apply. The lattice of all subsets of some set is an example of a *distributive complemented lattice*, for which all the identities hold.

Graphs of mathematical lattices look like the lattices that one would expect a wisteria vine to climb on. Figure A.5 shows the graphs for three kinds of partial orderings: a tree, a lattice, and a general acyclic graph. To simplify the drawings, a common convention for acyclic graphs is to omit the arrows on the arcs, but to assume that an arc connecting nodes a and b is directed from the higher one to the lower one.

The term *hierarchy* is often used indiscriminately for any partial ordering. Fahlman (1979) used *hierarchy* to mean a tree, and *tangled hierarchy* to mean a general acyclic graph. In Assumption 3.2.3, the type hierarchy is a general partial ordering, which is equivalent to an acyclic graph. The type lattice defined in Assumption 3.2.6 is a type hierarchy that also has the $\cap$ and $\cup$ operators. In that case, $a \cap b$ is called the *maximal common subtype* of a and b, and $a \cup b$ is the *minimal common supertype* of a and b. In general, every tree is an acyclic graph, and every

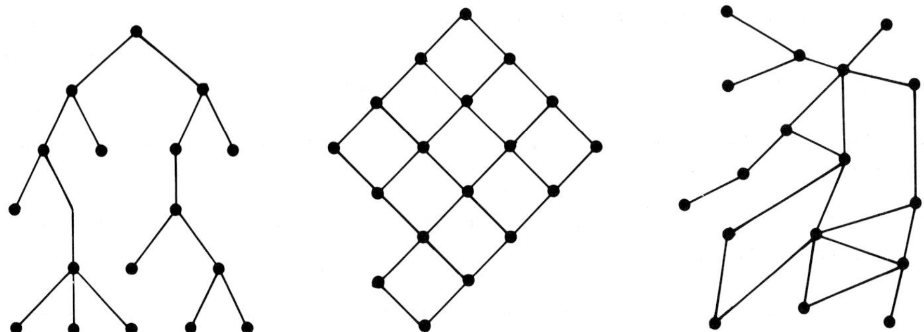

Fig. A.5 A tree, a lattice, and an acyclic graph

lattice is also an acyclic graph; but most lattices are not trees, and most trees are not lattices. In fact, the only graphs that are both trees and lattices are the simple chains (which are linearly ordered).

Many people represent type hierarchies in forms that are equivalent to lattices. Leibniz's Universal Characteristic, for example, is a lattice:

- Each primitive type is represented as a single prime number.
- Composite types are products of primes.
- Type a is a subtype of b if a is divisible by b.
- $a \cup b$ is the greatest common divisor of a and b.
- $a \cap b$ is the smallest integer divisible by both a and b.
- The top $\top$ is 1.
- The bottom $\bot$ is the product of the first n primes, where n is the total number of primitive concept types.

A representation of concept types as conjunctions of features or semantic markers is isomorphic to a representation as a product of primes. If n is the number of primitives, either form could be mapped into bit strings of length n:

- Each prime number or semantic feature is represented as a bit string with a single 1 and all other bits 0.
- A composite type that is the product of two or more primes has a 1 in the position that corresponds to each of its primes.
- Type a is a subtype of b if each position that has a 1 bit in b has a 1 bit in a.
- $a \cup b$ is the logical AND of the bit strings for a and b.
- $a \cap b$ is the logical OR of the bit strings for a and b.
- The top $\top$ is the string with all bits 0.

- The bottom ⊥ is the string with all bits 1.

Note the inverse relationship between the number of features for a concept type and the number of entities to which it applies. The type DOG applies to fewer entities in the real world than its supertype ANIMAL, but more features are required to describe it. This inverse relationship between the number of properties required to define a concept and the number of entities to which it applies was first noted by Aristotle. It is called the *duality of intension and extension.*

Representing the elements of a type lattice as a set of features or a product of primes is a special case, because not all lattices can be factored into primitives. To define a more general type lattice, Section 3.6 of this book uses a version of the lambda calculus applied to graphs instead of simple conjunctions of features or semantic markers. A lattice itself is a special case of a partial ordering, because the operators ∩ and ∪ cannot be defined for all partial orderings.

If a binary relation is reflexive, symmetric, and transitive, it is called an *equivalence relation.* The archetype of an equivalence relation is equality: it is reflexive, because $x=x$; it is symmetric, because $x=y$ implies $y=x$; and it is transitive, because $x=y$ and $y=z$ imply $x=z$. But there are many other equivalence relations. For example, *born under the same sign of the zodiac* is an equivalence relation over the set of all people.

Whenever an equivalence relation is defined over a set, it divides the set into *equivalence classes.* The zodiac relation divides the set of all human beings into 12 equivalence classes that have the traditional labels Aries, Taurus, ..., Pisces. In Assumption 3.2.1, the relation *same type* is an equivalence relation defined over the set of concepts. For that relation, there is one equivalence class for every concept type label.

A.5 SYMBOLIC LOGIC

Symbolic logic has two main branches: *propositional calculus* and *predicate calculus.* Propositional calculus deals with statements or *propositions* and the connections between them. The symbol m, for example, could represent the proposition, *Lillian is the mother of Leslie.* Predicate calculus, however, would represent that proposition by a predicate MOTHER applied to the two individuals: MOTHER(Lillian,Leslie). Whereas propositional calculus represents a complete statement by a single symbol, predicate calculus analyzes the statement into finer components. Besides symbols for propositions, propositional calculus also includes symbols for operators like *and, or, not,* and *if-then.* Let p be the proposition *The sun is shining,* and let q be the proposition *It is raining.* The most commonly used operators in the propositional calculus correspond to the English words *and, or, not, if-then,* and *if-and-only-if:*

- *Conjunction* (and). $p \wedge q$ represents the proposition *The sun is shining, and it is raining.*
- *Disjunction* (or). $p \vee q$ represents *The sun is shining, or it is raining.*
- *Negation* (not). $\sim p$ represents *The sun is not shining.*
- *Material implication* (if-then). $p \supset q$ represents *If the sun is shining, then it is raining.*
- *Biconditional* (if-and-only-if). $p \equiv q$ represents *The sun is shining if and only if it is raining.*

The operators $\wedge$, $\vee$, $\sim$, $\supset$, and $\equiv$ are usually called *Boolean operators.*

The propositions represented in symbolic logic may be true or false. The rules of propositional calculus compute the truth value of a *compound proposition* from the truth or falsity of the elementary propositions contained within it. Figure A.6 shows the truth values of compound propositions as functions of the truth values of their components (the letter T is an abbreviation for **true**, and F is an abbreviation for **false**). Such tables, which resemble the addition and multiplication tables of arithmetic, are known as *truth tables.*

p q	$p \wedge q$	$p \vee q$	$\sim p$	$p \supset q$	$p \equiv q$
T T	T	T	F	T	T
T F	F	T	F	F	F
F T	F	T	T	T	F
F F	F	F	T	T	T

Fig. A.6 A truth table

Boolean operators are called *truth functions* because they take truth values as input and generate truth values as output. There are 16 possible truth functions of two arguments, but the five listed in Fig. A.6 are the most commonly used. Another operator that is sometimes used is *exclusive or*, which is equivalent to p or q, but not both. Two operators commonly used in computer circuit design are *nand* and *nor* with the symbols $\barwedge$ and $\veebar$: $(p \barwedge q)$ is equivalent to $\sim(p \wedge q)$, and $(p \veebar q)$ is equivalent to $\sim(p \vee q)$.

If one or two Boolean operators are taken as primitives, the others can be defined in terms of them. One common choice of primitives is the pair $\sim$ and $\wedge$. Then the other operators in Fig. A.6 are defined as follows:

$p \vee q$	is equivalent to	$\sim(\sim p \wedge \sim q)$
$p \supset q$	is equivalent to	$\sim(p \wedge \sim q)$
$p \equiv q$	is equivalent to	$\sim(p \wedge \sim q) \wedge \sim(\sim p \wedge q)$

In fact, only one primitive operator, either $\barwedge$ or $\veebar$, is necessary since both ~ and ∧ can be defined in terms of either one of them:

$\sim p$	is equivalent to	$(p \barwedge p)$
$\sim p$	is equivalent to	$(p \veebar p)$
$p \wedge q$	is equivalent to	$(p \barwedge q) \barwedge (p \barwedge q)$
$p \wedge q$	is equivalent to	$(p \veebar p) \veebar (q \veebar q)$

Peirce's *existential graphs*, which are developed in Chapter 4 as the logical basis for conceptual graphs, take negation and conjunction as the two primitives. Peirce was also the first person to discover that all the other Boolean operators could be defined in terms of $\barwedge$ or $\veebar$.

In propositional calculus, the proposition *All peaches are fuzzy* may be represented by a single symbol p. In predicate calculus, however, the fine structure of the proposition is analyzed in detail. Then p would be represented by an entire *formula*,

$$\forall x(\text{PEACH}(x) \supset \text{FUZZY}(x)).$$

The symbol ∀ is called the *universal quantifier*, and the symbols PEACH and FUZZY are predicates like the ones described in Section A.4. The combination $\forall x$ is commonly read *for all x*, the combination PEACH(x) may be read *x is a peach*, and the combination FUZZY(x) may be read *x is fuzzy*. The entire formula, therefore, may be read *For all x, if x is a peach, then x is fuzzy*. Since predicates (or relations) are functions that yield truth values as results and since the Boolean operators are functions that take truth values as their inputs, predicates can be combined with the same operators used in the propositional calculus.

Predicate calculus has one additional symbol, the *existential quantifier* represented as ∃; the combination $\exists x$ may be read *there exists an x such that*. The following formula uses an existential quantifier:

$$\sim\exists x(\text{PEACH}(x) \wedge \sim\text{FUZZY}(x)).$$

This may be read *It is false that there exists an x such that x is a peach and x is not fuzzy*. Formulas with more than one quantifier are possible. The English statement *For any integer x, there is a prime number greater than x* is represented as,

$$\forall x \exists y(\text{INTEGER}(x) \supset (\text{PRIME}(y) \wedge x<y)).$$

Literally, this formula may be read *For all x, there exists a y such that if x is an integer, then y is prime and x is less than y*.

The two types of quantifiers, Boolean operators, variables, predicates, and the rules for putting them together in formulas make up the entire notation of *first-order predicate calculus*, which is also known as *first-order logic*. It is called *first order* because the range of quantifiers is restricted to simple, unanalyzable individuals. Higher-order logic also allows function symbols and predicate symbols to be governed by the quantifiers. An example of a higher-order formula is the *axiom of induction*:

$$\forall P((P(0) \wedge \forall n(P(n) \supset P(n+1)) \supset \forall n P(n)).$$

This formula may be read, *For all predicates P, if P is true for 0, and for all n, P(n) implies P(n+1), then P is true for all n.* This is the only axiom for arithmetic that requires more expressive power than first-order logic.

Any of the functions, operators, relations, and predicates of Sections A.1 through A.4 can also be used in the formulas of first-order logic. Following are the *formation rules* that define the syntax of formulas:

- A *term* is either a *constant* like 2, a *variable* like x, or an n-adic function symbol applied to n arguments, each of which is itself a term.
- An *atom* is either a single letter like p that represents a proposition or an n-adic predicate symbol applied to n arguments, each of which is a term.
- A *formula* is either an atom, a formula preceded by ~, any two formulas A and B together with any dyadic Boolean operator ⊙ in the combination ($A \odot B$), or any formula A and any variable x in either of the combinations $\exists xA$ or $\forall xA$.

More detailed treatments of logic go into greater detail about the syntactic form of variables, constants, and functions. In this book, those details will be avoided by preceding the formulas with a declaration like *let x be a variable* or *let c be a constant.* These formation rules lead to many levels of nested parentheses. In the main body of the book, the extra parentheses are dropped whenever they are not necessary to prevent ambiguity.

The formation rules of first-order logic are an example of a recursive definition as described in Section A.1. By applying them repeatedly, any possible formula can be derived. Suppose that f is a monadic function and + is a dyadic operator; then $f(x)$ and 2+2 are terms. (By the conventions of Section A.2, functions written with single characters are called operators, but they form terms just like other functions.) If P is a dyadic predicate and Q is a monadic predicate, then P(f(x),2+2) and Q(7) are atoms. Since all atoms are formulas, these two formulas can be combined by the Boolean operator ⊃ to form a new formula:

$$(P(f(x),2+2) \supset Q(7)).$$

Since any formula may be preceded by ~ to form another formula, the following formula may be derived:

$$\sim(P(f(x),2+2) \supset Q(7)).$$

Putting the quantifier ($\forall y$) in front of it produces,

$$(\forall y)\sim(P(f(x),2+2) \supset Q(7)).$$

Adding another quantifier $\exists x$ produces,

$$\exists x \forall y \sim(P(f(x),2+2) \supset Q(7)).$$

And preceding this formula with ~ produces,

$\sim\exists x \forall y \sim$(P($f(x)$,2+2) ⊃ Q(7)).

In this formula, the occurrence of x in $f(x)$ is *bound* by the quantifier $\exists x$, but the quantifier $\forall y$ has no effect on the formula.

The order of quantifiers in symbolic logic makes a crucial difference, as it does in English. Consider the sentence *Every man in department C99 married a woman who came from Boston*, which may be represented by the formula,

$\forall x \exists y$((MAN(x) ∧ DEPT(x,C99)) ⊃
(WOMAN(y) ∧ HOMETOWN(y,Boston) ∧ MARRIED(x,y))).

This formula says that for every x there exists a y such that if x is a man and x works in department C99, then y is a woman, the home town of y is Boston, and x married y. Since the dyadic predicate MARRIED is symmetric, MARRIED(Ike,Mamie) is equivalent to MARRIED(Mamie,Ike). Interchanging the arguments of that predicate makes no difference, but interchanging the two quantifiers leads to the formula,

$\exists y \forall x$((MAN(x) ∧ DEPT(x,C99)) ⊃
(WOMAN(y) ∧ HOMETOWN(y,Boston) ∧ MARRIED(x,y))).

This formula says that there exists a y such that for every x, if x is a man and x works in department C99, then y is a woman, the home town of y is Boston, and x married y. In ordinary English, that would be the same as saying, *A woman who came from Boston married every man in department C99*. If there is more than one man in department C99, this sentence has implications that are very different from the preceding one.

Formation rules define the syntax of first-order logic. They do not, however, say anything about the meaning of the formulas or about their truth or falsity. To derive true formulas from other true formulas, additional rules are needed. These rules, called *rules of inference*, determine whether one formula is implied by another. The following two formulas are equivalent—each one implies the other:

$\forall x$(PEACH(x) ⊃ FUZZY(x))
$\sim\exists x$(PEACH(x) ∧ ~FUZZY(x))

If the first one were represented by the single variable p and the second by q, there would be no way to prove that $p \equiv q$. In the predicate calculus, however, they can be shown to be equivalent. First of all, the following two equivalences are assumed:

$\exists x A$	is identical to	$\sim\forall x \sim A$
$\forall x A$	is identical to	$\sim\exists x \sim A$

where A is any formula whatever. By using the equivalence for $\forall$, the first of the PEACH formulas can be transformed to

$\sim\exists x \sim$(PEACH(x) ⊃ FUZZY(x)).

But now the symbol ⊃ can be reduced to ∧ and ~ by the definitions given for the Boolean operators other than ∧ and ~:

~∃x~~(PEACH(x) ∧ ~FUZZY(x)).

Whenever a double negation (a sequence of two consecutive ~ symbols) occurs, both can be deleted. Then the formula becomes

~∃x(PEACH(x) ∧ ~FUZZY(x)),

which is identical to the second PEACH formula.

In a *sound theory*, the rules of inference preserve truth. If all formulas in the starting set are true, only true formulas can be inferred from them. Following are some rules of inference for the propositional calculus. The symbols p, q, and r represent any formulas whatever.

- *Modus ponens*. From p and $p \supset q$, derive q.
- *Modus tollens*. From $\sim q$ and $p \supset q$, derive $\sim p$.
- *Hypothetical syllogism*. From $p \supset q$ and $q \supset r$, derive $p \supset r$.
- *Disjunctive syllogism*. From $p \vee q$ and $\sim p$, derive q.
- *Conjunction*. From p and q, derive $p \wedge q$.
- *Addition*. From p, derive $p \vee q$. This rule allows any formula whatever to be added to a disjunction.
- *Subtraction*. From $p \wedge q$, derive p. This rule simplifies formulas by throwing away unneeded conjuncts.

Not all of these rules are primitive. In developing a theory of logic, logicians try to minimize the number of primitive rules. Then they show that other rules, called *derived rules of inference*, can be defined in terms of them. Chapter 4 presents a small number of primitive rules for conceptual graphs and derives a larger set of rules from them. In particular, all the rules in this appendix have equivalents in conceptual graph notation.

Following are some common identities. Either of the formulas in an identity can be substituted for any occurrence of the other, either alone or as part of some larger formula:

- *Idempotency*. $p \wedge p$ is identical to p, and $p \vee p$ is also identical to p.
- *Commutativity*. $p \wedge q$ is identical to $q \wedge p$, and $p \vee q$ is identical to $q \vee p$.
- *Associativity*. $p \wedge (q \wedge r)$ is identical to $(p \wedge q) \wedge r$, and $p \vee (q \vee r)$ is identical to $(p \vee q) \vee r$.
- *Distributivity*. $p \wedge (q \vee r)$ is identical to $(p \wedge q) \vee (p \wedge r)$, and $p \vee (q \wedge r)$ is identical to $(p \vee q) \wedge (p \vee r)$.
- *Absorption*. $p \wedge (p \vee q)$ is identical to p, and $p \vee (p \wedge q)$ is identical to p.

- *Double negation.* p is identical to $\sim\sim p$.
- *De Morgan's laws.* $\sim(p \wedge q)$ is identical to $\sim p \vee \sim q$, and $\sim(p \vee q)$ is identical to $\sim p \wedge \sim q$.

These identities happen to have exactly the same form as the ones for union and intersection of sets. This similarity is not an accident because, like sets and subsets, propositions form a distributive, complemented lattice: the partial order $p \leq q$ is defined as material implication $p \supset q$; $p \cup q$ is defined as $p \vee q$; $p \cap q$ is defined as $p \wedge q$; the complement $-p$ is defined as $\sim p$; the top $\top$ is the truth value **true**; and the bottom $\bot$ is the truth value **false**. (See the discussion of lattices in Section A.4.)

For first-order predicate calculus, the rules of inference include the rules of propositional calculus together with rules for handling quantifiers. Before those rules can be stated, however, a distinction must be drawn between *free occurrences* and *bound occurrences* of a variable:

- If A is an atom, then all occurrences of a variable x in A are said to be free.
- If a formula C was derived from formulas A and B by combining them with Boolean operators, then all occurrences of variables that are free in A and B are also free in C.
- If a formula C was derived from a formula A by preceding A with either $\forall x$ or $\exists x$, then all free occurrences of x in A are said to be *bound* in C. All free occurrences of other variables in A remain free in C.

The most complicated rules in logic are the ones that deal with variables. They must determine which occurrences are free and bound and which symbols can be replaced by other symbols without causing unwanted side effects. Peirce's graph logic (developed in Chapter 4) makes proofs shorter and simpler because variable symbols are completely eliminated.

Once the definitions of free and bound occurrences have been stated, rules of inference that deal with quantifiers can be given. Let $\Phi(x)$ be a formula containing a free occurrence of a variable x. Then $\Phi(t)$ is the result of substituting a term t for every free occurrence of x in Φ. Following are the additional rules of inference:

- *Universal instantiation.* From $\forall x \Phi(x)$, derive $\Phi(c)$, where c is any constant.
- *Existential generalization.* From $\Phi(c)$, where c is any constant, derive $\exists x \Phi(x)$, provided that every occurrence of x in $\Phi(x)$ must be free.
- *Dropping quantifiers.* If the variable x does not occur free in Φ, then from $\exists x \Phi$ derive Φ, and from $\forall x \Phi$ derive Φ.
- *Adding quantifiers.* From Φ derive $\forall x \Phi$ or derive $\exists x \Phi$, where x is any variable whatever.
- *Substituting equals for equals.* From $\Phi(t)$ and $t=u$, derive $\Phi(u)$, provided that all free occurrences of variables in u remain free in $\Phi(u)$.

The standard notation for logic, which has been presented in this section, is based on the symbols used by Giuseppe Peano (1889) and extended by Whitehead and Russell in the *Principia Mathematica*. Many equivalent notations have been developed over the years, and in almost all of them, the formation rules and the rules of inference are simpler than in the *Principia*. Frege's *Begriffsschrift* (1879), which was the first complete form of the predicate calculus, used a graphical notation. It never became popular, partly because it took too much space on the printed page. Many Polish logicians adopted Jan Lukasiewicz's prefix notation, which has been called *Polish notation*; but for complex formulas, most people find it more difficult to read than an infix notation. Another Polish logician, Lesniewski, developed an elegant infix notation with highly symmetric rules of inference (Luschei 1962). But of all the alternatives to Peano-Russell notation, one of the simplest and most elegant is Charles Sanders Peirce's notation for *existential graphs* (1897).

Peirce's notation is developed in Chapter 4 as the logical basis for conceptual graphs. Many important topics that have not been presented in this section are discussed in some detail in Chapter 4: proofs, modal logic, philosophical implications, and the use of logic for analyzing and representing sentences in natural language.

A.6 FORMAL GRAMMARS

Systems of *production rules* were first developed by Thue (1914) for transforming strings of characters. They were used as a basis for computation by Post (1943) and Markov (1954) and were adapted by Chomsky (1957) to the formal description of grammars. About the same time that Chomsky was developing formal grammars for English, John Backus, who was the manager of the first FORTRAN project, independently developed a similar notation for defining programming languages. The main difference between the two forms is that Backus limited his notation to the *context-free grammars*, while Chomsky also defined the more general *context-sensitive* and *general-rewrite* grammars.

A grammar has two main categories of symbols: *terminal symbols* like *the*, *dog*, or *jump*, which appear in the sentences of the language itself; and *nonterminal* symbols like N, NP, and S, which represent the grammatical categories noun, noun phrase, and sentence. The production rules state how the nonterminal symbols are transformed in generating sentences of the language. Terminal symbols are called *terminal* because no production rules apply to them: when a derivation generates a string consisting only of terminal symbols, it must terminate. Nonterminal symbols, however, keep getting replaced during the derivation. A formal grammar G has four components:

- A set of symbols T, called the *terminal symbols*,
- A set of symbols N, called the *nonterminal symbols*, with the restriction that T and N have no symbols in common: $T \cap N = \{\}$.

- A special nonterminal symbol S, called the *start symbol*,
- A set of *production rules* P, of the form:

  $$A \longrightarrow B$$

  where A is a sequence of symbols having at least one nonterminal, and B is the result of replacing some nonterminal symbol in A with a sequence of symbols (possibly empty) from T and N.

The start symbol corresponds to the highest level category that is recognized by the grammar, such as *sentence*. The production rules generate sentences by starting with the start symbol and systematically replacing nonterminal symbols until a string consisting only of terminals is derived. Grammars of this form are called *phrase structure grammars* because they determine the structure of a sentence as a hierarchy of phrases.

Some convention must be adopted for distinguishing terminals from nonterminals. Some people write terminal symbols in lower case letters and nonterminals in upper case; other people adopt the opposite convention. To be explicit, this book will enclose terminal symbols in double quotes: "the" or "[". To illustrate the formalism, the following grammar defines a small fragment of English:

```
Terminal symbols T:  {"the", "a", "cat", "dog", "saw", "chased"}
Nonterminal symbols N:  {S, NP, VP, DET, N, V}
Start symbol S:  S
```

The set T defines a 6-word vocabulary, and the set N defines the basic grammatical categories. The starting symbol S represents a complete sentence. The symbol NP represents a noun phrase, VP a verb phrase, DET a determiner, N a noun, and V a verb. The following 9 production rules determine the grammatical combinations for this language:

```
S    ⟶  NP VP
NP   ⟶  DET N
VP   ⟶  V NP
DET  ⟶  "the"
DET  ⟶  "a"
N    ⟶  "cat"
N    ⟶  "dog"
V    ⟶  "saw"
V    ⟶  "chased"
```

This grammar may be used to generate sentences by starting with the symbol S and successively replacing nonterminal symbols on the left-hand side of some rule with the string of symbols on the right:

```
S
NP VP
DET N VP
a N VP
a dog VP
a dog V NP
a dog chased NP
a dog chased DET N
a dog chased the N
a dog chased the dog
```

Since the last line contains only terminal symbols, the derivation stops. When more than one rule applies, any one may be used. The symbol V, for example, could have been replaced by *saw* instead of *chased.* The same grammar could be used to *parse* a sentence by applying the rules in reverse. The parsing would start with a sentence like *a dog chased the dog* and reduce it to the start symbol S.

The production rules for the above grammar belong to the category of context-free rules. Other classes of grammars are ranked according to the complexity of their production rules. The following four categories of complexity were originally defined by Chomsky:

- A *finite-state* or *regular grammar* only has production rules of the following two forms:

  $$A \longrightarrow x\ B$$
  $$C \longrightarrow y$$

  where A, B, and C are single nonterminal symbols, and x and y represent single terminal symbols.

- A *context-free grammar* only has production rules of the following form:

  $$A \longrightarrow B\ C\ \ldots\ D$$

  where A is a single nonterminal symbol, and B C ... D is any sequence of one or more symbols, either terminal or nonterminal.

- A *context-sensitive grammar* has production rules of the following form:

  $$a\ A\ z \longrightarrow a\ B\ C\ \ldots\ D\ z$$

  where A is a single nonterminal symbol, a and z are strings of zero or more symbols (terminal or nonterminal), and $B\ C$ ... D is a string of one or more terminal or nonterminal symbols.

- A *general-rewrite grammar* permits all the forms of a context-sensitive grammar plus the possibility that some nonterminal symbols may be replaced by the empty string.

Each one of these classes of grammars is more general than the one before and requires more complex *parsing algorithms* for analyzing sentences in the language. Every finite-state grammar is also context free, every context-free grammar is also context sensitive, and every context-sensitive grammar is also a general-rewrite grammar. But the converses do not hold. Since Chomsky's original work, intermediate levels of complexity have been defined for which parsing algorithms of greater or lesser efficiency can be written.

Once a grammar is defined, all valid forms in the language can be derived by using the following replacement rules:

- Write the start symbol as the first line of a derivation.
- To derive a new line, find some production rule whose left-hand side matches a substring of symbols in the current line. Then copy the current line, replacing the matching substring with the symbols on the right-hand side of the production rule.
- If more than one production rule has a matching left-hand side, then any one of them may be applied.
- Stop when the current line contains only terminal symbols.

The presence of nonterminal symbols is a necessary condition for the derivation to continue. When only terminal symbols are left, the derivation must terminate. The last line in a derivation is called a *sentence* of the language defined by the given grammar.

For convenience, production rules may be written in an *extended notation*, which uses some additional symbols. The new symbols do not increase the number of sentences that can be derived, but they reduce the total number of grammar rules that need to be written and make the grammar easier to read.

- The vertical bar "|" separates alternatives.
- Square brackets "[" and "]" indicate an option.
- Curly braces "{" and "}" indicate grouping.
- Three dots "..." indicate 1 or more repetitions of the preceding symbol or group of symbols.
- Brackets followed by three dots "[ ]..." indicate 0 or more repetitions.

The techniques for defining grammars are standard, but notations vary. Some authors use braces "{" and "}" to mean zero or more repetitions, and others use a trailing "*" to mean zero or more repetitions and a trailing "" to mean one or more repetitions.Some authors put terminal symbols in quotes like "the" or "dog"; others put nonterminal symbols in angle brackets like ⟨N⟩ or ⟨V⟩. All these variations, however, are minor notational differences; the principles are well established.

Some examples may help to show how the extended notation simplifies the rules. By using the vertical bar, the following two production rules,

```
N ⟶ "cat"
N ⟶ "dog"
```

can be combined in a single rule:

```
N ⟶ "cat" | "dog"
```

If the grammar permits a noun phrase to contain an optional adjective, it might use the following two rules to define NP:

```
NP ⟶ DET N
NP ⟶ DET ADJ N
```

Then both rules can be combined by using square brackets:

```
NP ⟶ DET [ADJ] N
```

If an optional list of adjectives is permitted, then the rule could be extended further:

```
NP ⟶ DET [ADJ]... N
```

This single rule in the extended notation is equivalent to the following four rules in the standard notation:

```
NP ⟶ DET N
NP ⟶ DET ADJLIST N
ADJLIST ⟶ ADJ
ADJLIST ⟶ ADJ ADJLIST
```

This last production rule is *recursive* because the nonterminal symbol ADJLIST on the left-hand side of the rule is replaced by a string that includes the same symbol ADJLIST. To generate an unlimited number of possible sentences, a grammar must have at least one rule that is directly or indirectly recursive. Since the grammar on page 392 has no recursive rules, it can only generate a finite number of different sentences (in this case 32).

Both to illustrate the formalism and to define the linear notation for conceptual graphs, a formal grammar will be given. The nonterminal symbol CGRAPH represents a conceptual graph consisting of either a CONCEPT followed by an optional relational link RLINK, or a RELATION followed by a required concept link CONLINK. It is terminated by either a period or a semicolon:

```
CGRAPH ⟶ {CONCEPT [RLINK] | RELATION CONLINK} {"." | ";"}
```

An RLINK is either an ARC, a RELATION, and an optional CONLINK or a hyphen, an RLIST, and a comma:

```
RLINK ⟶ ARC RELATION [CONLINK] | "-" RLIST ","
```

A CONLINK is either an ARC, a CONCEPT, and an optional RLINK or a hyphen, a CONLIST, and a comma:

```
CONLINK ⟶ ARC CONCEPT [RLINK] | "-" CONLIST ","
```

An RLIST consists of one or more repetitions of the following: a NEWLINE, a RELATION, and an optional CONLINK:

```
RLIST ⟶ {NEWLINE RELATION [CONLINK]}...
```

A CONLIST consists of one or more repetitions of the following: a NEWLINE, an ARC, a CONCEPT, and an optional RLINK:

```
CONLIST ⟶ {NEWLINE ARC CONCEPT [RLINK]}...
```

A CONCEPT consists of a left bracket, a TYPEFIELD, an optional colon and REFFIELD, and finally a right bracket:

```
CONCEPT ⟶ "[" TYPEFIELD [":" REFFIELD] "]"
```

Note that the quotes distinguish the brackets that occur in the language being defined from the brackets used in the defining language (the *metalanguage*). A RELATION consists of a left parenthesis, a TYPELABEL, and a right parenthesis:

```
RELATION ⟶ "(" TYPELABEL ")"
```

An ARC consists of an optional NUMBER followed by either a left arrow or a right arrow:

```
ARC ⟶ [NUMBER] {"←" | "→"}
```

A NUMBER is a string of one or more DIGITs:

```
NUMBER ⟶ DIGIT...
```

A DIGIT is any of the ten decimal digits:

```
DIGIT ⟶ "0" | "1" | ... | "9"
```

The details of TYPEFIELD and REFFIELD are presented in Sections 3.3, 3.6, 3.7, and 4.2. Following are examples of concepts with various referents and their readings in English phrases:

Kind of Referent	Notation	English Reading
Generic	[CAT]	a cat
Individual	[CAT: #3829]	the cat
Named individual	[CAT: Morris]	Morris
Measure	[LENGTH: @ 5 ft.]	a length of 5 ft.
Generic set	[CAT: {*}]	cats
Set and quantity	[CAT: {*} @ 5]	five cats
Set of individuals	[CAT: {Morris,Felix}]	Morris and Felix
Partially specified	[CAT: {Morris,*}]	Morris and others

These English readings are simplified examples of the way a concept node can be mapped into an English word or phrase; the actual choice of articles, pronouns, names, and modifiers depends on the entire context, including the speaker's implicit knowledge about the listener's expectations. The above table did not show a nested context as referent, since it would not fit in the available space. As an example, the next graph represents the sentence *Sam thinks that Jocko loves Mimi*:

```
[PERSON:Sam]←(AGNT)←[THINK]→(OBJ)→[PROPOSITION:
     [MONKEY:Jocko]←(EXPR)←[LOVE]→(OBJ)→[MONKEY:Mimi]].
```

The TYPEFIELD is commonly a simple type label, represented by a character string in upper case letters. But Section 3.6 allows the type field to include lambda expressions and subranges, which are abbreviations for certain kinds of lambda expressions.

The grammar for the linear form of conceptual graphs defines only the context-free conditions. Other restrictions are difficult or impossible to state in a purely context-free way, since they depend on the presence or absence of something else in another part of the string. Although there exist notations for defining context-sensitive constraints, they are rather complex. Instead, the constraints are easier to state in English:

- A string of one of more commas immediately preceding the final period or semicolon must be deleted.
- Each n-adic relation type must have exactly n arcs adjacent to it, with one arc of each number from 1 to n. The numbers are optional for monadic and dyadic relations, but if $n>2$, the numbers $1,...,n\text{-}1$ are required. The highest numbered arc must point away from the relation adjacent to it, and all the others must point towards that relation.

The rules for numbering the arcs were given in Section 3.1. When a relation has more than one concept attached to it, context-free rules cannot enforce the condition that each arc must have a different number. Context-free rules cannot check the relation type to see whether it is monadic, dyadic, or n-adic. for some higher n. This context-sensitive rule states the necessary constraints.

A.7 ALGORITHMS

An *algorithm* is a specification for a sequence of operations that perform some computation. Some authors add the further requirement that an algorithm must terminate after a finite number of steps. The specification must always be given in some notation, either a programming language or a set of instructions for an abstract automaton. The ideal language would be as readable as English, as precise as symbolic logic, as widely implemented as FORTRAN, and as powerful for list processing as LISP. Unfortunately, no such language exists. A convenient compromise is to use a notation that is sometimes called *structured English* or *pseudocode*. All the control structures are written in a format similar to a standard programming language, but the operations are described in a clear, precise English. In this book, the control structures are taken from the language Ada, which is a modern language with a good, readable notation.[1] The Ada keywords are printed in bold face type. The English descriptions use words like *concept* or *conceptual relation* that have a technical meaning in the theory.

The most common Ada statement is *assignment*. The symbol := shows that the value on the right-hand side is assigned to the variable on the left. Sample assignment statements are

```
x := a + b;
y := y + 1;
z := the concept attached to arc 1 of r;
```

As in Ada, a semicolon ends each statement. Note that the first two statements, which use only ordinary arithmetic, are valid Ada statements; the third statement, however, uses special terms from the theory of conceptual graphs that have no equivalent Ada notation.

The most basic control structure is the **if**-statement. It has the following form:

```
if condition to be tested then
   what to do if condition is true;
else
   what to do if condition is false;
end if;
```

The **else**-clause is optional and may be omitted; in that case, no action is taken if the condition is false. Following is a sample of structured English that uses an **if**-statement:

```
c := the concept attached to arc 1 of (AGNT);
if t is a subtype of type(c) then
   restrict c to type t;
else
   join_flag := false;
end if;
```

The **case**-statement selects one of an arbitrary number of options, depending on the value of some variable or expression. It has the following form:

1 Ada is a trademark of the U.S. Department of Defense.

```
case expression or variable to be tested is
   when choice-1  =>  what to do if test value equals choice-1;
   when choice-2  =>  what to do if test value equals choice-2;
      . . .
   when others   =>  what to do if all other tests fail;
end case;
```

Most of the algorithms given in this book do some form of looping to repeat some operation on all nodes of a graph or all elements of a set. One form of loop in Ada starts with the keyword **loop** and ends with the phrase **end loop**. Following is a sample loop that prints prime numbers. Since there is no stopping test, it will loop forever.

```
n := 1;
loop
    if n is a prime number then
       print n;
    end if;
    n := n + 1;
end loop;
```

Note that the condition "*n* is a prime number" is not a simple test. Evaluating that condition would itself involve complex computations, but those are hidden beneath the simple English phrase. Since the algorithms in this book illustrate specific points, they deliberately hide irrelevant details beneath English prose. If the details are important, the accompanying text cites further discussion elsewhere in this book or in some other publication.

Infinite loops are generally undesirable, and the program should make some provision for quitting. The next loop is a revised version of the previous one with an **exit** statement for leaving the loop when the printer runs out of paper.

```
n := 1;
loop
   exit when there is no more paper left in the printer;
   if n is a prime number then
      print n;
   end if;
   n := n + 1;
end loop;
```

An **exit** statement may occur anywhere in a loop. A **while** clause in front of a loop states a condition for continuing the iteration. The next loop uses a **while** clause that has exactly the same effect as the previous loop:

```
n := 1;
while there is more paper left in the printer loop
   if n is a prime number then
      print n;
   end if;
   n := n + 1;
end loop;
```

Instead of exhausting all paper in the printer, it may be preferable to print only a small subset of the prime numbers. The following loop uses the **for** condition to initialize *n* to 1 and continue incrementing *n* by 1 up to 100. After it has completed the iteration for *n*=100, it exits from the loop:

```
for n in 1..100 loop
   if n is a prime number then
      print n;
   end if;
end loop;
```

The **in** clause specifies the range of values that the loop control variable *n* may assume. Since the **for** loop automatically assigns values to *n*, there is no need for the initial statement "*n*:=1" and the incrementing statement "*n*:=*n*+1" . In Ada, only simple ranges such as 1..100 may occur in the **in** clause of a **for** loop. This book, however, uses arbitrary sets in the **in** clause:

```
for c in the set of concepts in the graph u loop
```

This specification will cause the loop to be repeated once for each concept node in *u*, each time assigning a different concept to the variable *c*. The order of selecting elements from the set is unspecified.

The last Ada control structure used in this book is the *procedure*. It defines a sequence of statements that may be *called* from some statement in another procedure. Procedures start with the keyword **procedure** followed by the name of the procedure, a list of *formal parameters* enclosed in parentheses, the keyword **is**, a list of local variables if any, the keyword **begin**, a list of statements, and finally the keyword **end** followed by the name of the procedure itself. Following is a procedure named Primes that has two parameters, *m* and *plist*:

```
procedure Primes (m: maximum number to test for being prime;
                  plist: list of primes up to m) is
begin;
   plist := empty list;
   for n in 1..m loop
      if n is a prime number then
         plist := plist concatenated with n;
      end if;
   end loop;
end Primes;
```

This procedure takes an integer *m* as input and computes a list of all the prime numbers less than or equal to *m*. Following each of the formal parameters is a short phrase that describes the type and purpose of that parameter.

Besides control structures, Ada also provides a way of declaring data structures. In a declaration, a colon separates the name of a variable from the name of its type:

```
x: INTEGER;
c: CONCEPT;
```

These two declarations specify that *x* is an INTEGER and *c* is a CONCEPT. The type INTEGER is standard in Ada, but the type CONCEPT is defined by the following type declaration:

```
type CONCEPT is
   record
      LABEL: access TYPE_DEF;
      REFERENT: access INDIVIDUAL;
      RLIST: access RLINK;
   end record;
```

This declaration states that every concept is a record in storage that has three parts: LABEL, REFERENT, and RLIST. The first part, LABEL, is an access pointer to something of type TYPE_DEF, where the keyword **access** in Ada indicates a location in computer storage. (Since the term *pointer* is more widely used than *access*, this book uses the compromise *access pointer*.) REFERENT is an access pointer to something of type INDIVIDUAL, and RLIST is an access pointer to something of type RLINK. The types TYPE_DEF, INDIVIDUAL, and RLINK would themselves be defined in other type definitions. A possible definition of RLINK is the following:

```
type RLINK is
   record
      NEXT: access RLINK;
      REL: access RELATION;
   end record;
```

This declaration states that RLINK contains two access pointers. The first one points to the continuation of the list, and the second one points to a single relation in the list. At the end of the list, the NEXT pointer would contain the special value **null**.

In conceptual graphs, a concept node may be attached to an arbitrary number of relations. Therefore, each concept record points to a list of zero or more relations. Each relation, however, is always attached to a fixed number of concepts: an *n*-adic relation is attached to exactly *n* of them. The following declaration specifies the type RELATION with a *discriminant* variable N_ADIC, which states the number of arcs linked to that relation. The variable CONLINK in the relation is an array of access pointers to concept nodes; the number of pointers in the array is equal to N_ADIC.

```
type RELATION (N_ADIC: INTEGER) is
   record
      LABEL: access TYPE_DEF;
      CONLINK: array(1..N_ADIC) of access CONCEPT;
   end record;
```

Although these type declarations are stated in terms of Ada, similar declarations are possible in PASCAL, PL/I, and other languages that support pointers. In LISP, the structures would be even simpler because the pointers are hidden from the user. In languages like FORTRAN that do not support pointers, the implementation would be more awkward and inefficient, but it would still be possible by indexing into vectors and arrays. The data structures specified by these declarations have several desirable properties:

- From any concept node, all the attached relations are accessible by following a chain of access pointers.
- From any relation node, the access pointer for the *i*-th arc is directly accessible as CONLINK(I).
- Since the type fields and referent fields are represented by access pointers, there is no limit on the size of the type definition or referent.

These sample type declarations illustrate a possible way of implementing conceptual graphs. In any particular language or system, there may be other representations that are more convenient or efficient. Other fields might be added for convenience. In Section 5.4, the algorithm for mapping a conceptual graph into English assumed the presence of utterance marks on concepts and traversal marks on conceptual relations. Those marks could be stored either in additional fields of the records or in a separate table of concepts and conceptual relations. The advantage of a separate table is that the conceptual graphs would remain unchanged and could be used by other algorithms without erasing the marks.

SUGGESTED READING

The material covered in this appendix would be taught in an undergraduate course on discrete mathematics for computer science. Most courses and textbooks, however, only cover about five or six of the seven subjects presented in this appendix. Some texts that cover sets, functions, relations, propositional calculus, and one or two other topics include Stanat and McAllister (1977), Arbib et al. (1981), Lipschutz (1982), and Kandel et al. (1983).

Since this book is about graphs, some feeling for graph theory is important for understanding the theorems and proofs in chapters 3 and 4. An excellent introduction that assumes no mathematics beyond high school algebra is *Graphs and Their Uses*, by Ore. The book by Roberts (1978) is only slightly more advanced and is also available in paperback. More detailed mathematical treatments include Harary (1969) and Wilson (1972). Biggs, Lloyd, and Wilson (1976) present graph theory as it was developed historically from 1736 to 1936. Knuth (1973) is a standard textbook of algorithms for processing lists, trees, and general graphs; the terms *preorder*, *inorder*, and *postorder* are consistent with Knuth's second edition, but his first edition used different terms.

The classic book on game theory is by von Neumann and Morgenstern (1953), but it, like most of its successors, does not develop game graphs in detail. The AI texts on searching game trees and graphs are more relevant to game-theoretical semantics. See, for example, Slagle (1971), Nilsson (1980), or Banerji (1980).

A short, readable introduction to logic with applications to linguistics is *Logic in Linguistics* by Allwood, Andersson, and Dahl. A more comprehensive survey is *Everything that Linguists Have Always Wanted to Know about Logic* by McCawley. For an introduction to the philosophical implications of logic, see *From a Logical Point of View* by Quine. A standard textbook that has gone through many editions is *Symbolic Logic* by Copi. For modal logic, the standard text is *An Introduction to Modal Logic* by Hughes and Cresswell.

Goldschlager and Lister (1982) is a clear, simple introduction to algorithms and other topics of computer science; it presents the basic concepts of recursion, stepwise refinement, Turing machines, computability, formal grammars, compilers, and operating systems. The report by Rosser (1982) gives a history of the lambda calculus and a survey of applications to computer programming. *What Can Be Automated?* edited by Arden (1980) is a collection of 50-page articles that survey all of computer science; the most relevant parts for this book are the chapters on formal grammars, artificial intelligence, natural language processing, and database management systems. Winograd (1983) is a comprehensive textbook of grammars and parsers for natural language. For the Ada programming language, many textbooks are available; Barnes (1982) is a comprehensive survey written by one of the designers of the language.

Appendix B Conceptual Catalog

Theories of knowledge must distinguish form and content. The theory of conceptual graphs is primarily formal; conceptual analysis determines the content. This appendix shows how the form can be applied to some of the words and concepts used in this book. For any particular application, these lists can serve as a starter set that the reader may extend or modify as appropriate.

B.1 LEXICON

A *lexicon* or *dictionary* relates the words of a language to their grammatical categories and their underlying concepts. In this lexicon, each entry has the following format:

```
WORD "." {CATEGORY ";" {TYPE | "no concept"} "."}...
```

The WORD is in bold face letters, CATEGORY gives the grammatical category of the word, and TYPE gives the type label of the associated concept. Some words, such as prepositions and conjunctions, correspond to conceptual relations rather than concepts. Others, such as proper names, indicate a specific referent rather than a type. Most pronouns are *indexical terms* that indicate cross references to other concepts in the current context. They inherit the type labels from those other concepts. The pronoun *she*, for example, indicates FEMALE, but does not indicate the species; if *she* referred to an entity of type HORSE, the corresponding concept would have the type FEMALE ∩ HORSE or MARE.

a. indefinite article; no concept.

are. 3rd person plural of *be*; no concept.

book. count noun; BOOK.

by. preposition; no concept.

cake. count noun; CAKE. mass noun; CAKE-STUFF.

cat. count noun; CAT.

Dick. proper name; [PERSON:Dick].

difficult. adjective; DIFFICULT.

Friday. count noun; FRIDAY.

from. preposition; no concept.

give. transitive verb with indirect object; GIVE.

hardware. mass noun; HARDWARE.

he. pronoun, nominative case, indexical term; MALE.

her. pronoun, objective case, indexical term; FEMALE. pronoun, possessive case, indexical term; FEMALE.

homework. mass noun; HOMEWORK.

I. pronoun, nominative case, indexical term; PERSON.

in. preposition; no concept.

is. verb, present tense, 3rd person singular of *be*; no concept.

jack. count noun; JACK.

Jack. proper name; [PERSON:Jack].

kitchen. count noun; KITCHEN.

money. mass noun; MONEY.

number. count noun; NUMBER. transitive verb; COUNT.

occupy. transitive verb; OCCUPY, OCCUPY-ACT, OCCUPY-ATTN.

on. preposition; no concept.

order. count noun; ORDER. transitive verb; ORDER.

perform. transitive verb; PERFORM.

philosophy. mass noun; PHILOSOPHY.

receive. transitive verb; RECEIVE.

reservation. count noun; RESERVATION.

she. pronoun, nominative case, indexical term; FEMALE.

ship. count noun; SHIP. transitive verb; SHIPMENT.

shipment. count noun; SHIPMENT.

sit. intransitive verb; SIT.

stuff. mass noun; STUFF.

teacher. count noun; TEACHER.

telephone. count noun; TELEPHONE. transitive verb; PHONE.

temperature. abstract noun; TEMPERATURE.

that. indexical pronoun; ENTITY. indexical adjective; no concept. subordinate conjunction; no concept.

the. definite article; no concept.

think. transitive verb; THINK.

to. preposition; no concept.

via. preposition; no concept.

warm. adjective; WARM.

wear. transitive verb; WEAR, WEAR-OUT.

B.2 CONCEPTS

This section lists type labels used in the examples of this book. For each type, one or more type labels are shown as supertypes. Many concept types, especially those that represent actions, attributes, and role types are always attached to certain types of relations. For those types, a canonical graph is listed that shows the expected context. The canonical graphs define *selectional constraints* on possible combinations of concepts.

These graphs are not definitions, but a *canonical basis* from which other canonical graphs may be derived. For most concepts, an explicit type definition is not possible. The *semantic network* constitutes an implicit definition of all concept and relation types (see Section 3.2). The English sentence that follows each type is an informal comment; it may help the reader to relate the type to the semantic network in his or her own head.

ACT < EVENT. An act is an event with an animate agent.

```
[ACT]→(AGNT)→[ANIMATE].
```

AGE < CHARACTERISTIC. Age is characteristic of an entity at a point in time.

```
[AGE]-
   (CHRC)→ [ENTITY]
   (PTIM)→ [TIME].
```

ANGEL < ANIMATE, MOBILE-ENTITY, ¬PHYSOBJ. An angel is an animate being, but not an animal.

ANIMAL < ANIMATE, MOBILE-ENTITY, PHYSOBJ, ¬MACHINE. Animals are physical objects, unlike angels; and they are not machines, unlike robots.

ANIMATE < ENTITY. Animate beings are the agents of actions; they include nonanimals, such as angels and robots.

ARRIVE < ACT. A mobile entity arrives at a place.

```
[ARRIVE]-
   (AGNT)→ [MOBILE-ENTITY]
   (LOC)→  [PLACE].
```

ATTRIBUTE < T. An attribute is a quality of an entity.

```
[ATTRIBUTE]←(ATTR)←[ENTITY].
```

BELIEVE < STATE. To believe is to experience a particular state with regard to a proposition.

```
[BELIEVE]-
   (EXPR)→ [ANIMATE]
   (OBJ)→  [PROPOSITION].
```

BIG < MAGNITUDE. Comparatives like BIG require a standard, which may be different for each type that is being compared.

```
[BIG]-
   (SIZE)← [PHYSOBJ]
   (COMP)→ [PHYSOBJ].
```

CAKE < FOOD, PHYSOBJ. As a count noun, *cake* refers to a cake.

CAKE-STUFF < FOOD, STUFF. As a mass noun, *cake* refers to the stuff of which a cake is made.

```
[CAKE-STUFF]←(MATR)←[CAKE].
```

CAT < ANIMAL. A cat is an animal; as a natural type, it has no necessary canonical graph.

CHARACTERISTIC < ATTRIBUTE. A characteristic is an essential attribute, such as age, as opposed to an accidental attribute, such as fuzzy.

CHILD < PERSON. A child is a person that is linked to some other person by the relation (CHLD).

```
[CHILD]←(CHLD)←[PERSON].
```

CITY < PLACE, SOCIETY. A city may be viewed as either a place or a society.

COMMAND < MESSAGE. A command is a message given to a person who is being ordered to do something.

```
[COMMAND]←(OBJ)←[ORDER]→(RCPT)→[PERSON].
```

COLOR < ATTRIBUTE. A color is an attribute of a physical object.

```
[COLOR]←(ATTR)←[PHYSOBJ].
```

COMMUNICATE < GIVE. To communicate is to give information; the instrument is a means of communication, such as mail, telephone, speech, or gesture.

```
[COMMUNICATE]-
   (AGNT)→ [ANIMATE]
   (RCPT)→ [ANIMATE]
   (INST)→ [ENTITY]
   (OBJ)→  [INFORMATION].
```

CONTAIN < STATE. An entity *x* contains an entity *y* if *y* is located in the interior *z* of *x*.

```
[CONTAIN]-
   (LOC)→[ENTITY:*x]→(PART)→[INTERIOR:*z]
   (OBJ)→[ENTITY:*y]→(LOC)→[INTERIOR:*z].
```

CUT < ACT. An animate being cuts a physical object with another physical object that has attribute sharp.

```
[CUT]-
   (AGNT)→ [ANIMATE]
   (INST)→ [PHYSOBJ]→(ATTR)→[SHARP]
   (OBJ)→  [PHYSOBJ].
```

DIFFICULT < MANNER. An act has manner difficult only for an animate being that can experience the difficulty.

```
[DIFFICULT]-
   (EXPR)→ [ANIMATE]
   (MANR)← [ACT].
```

ENTITY < T. Entities include physical objects as well as abstractions.

EVENT < T. Events include acts by animate agents as well as happenings like explosions, where an agent may not be present.

GIVE < ACT. An act of giving presupposes a giver, a recipient, and a gift.

```
[GIVE]-
   (AGNT)→ [ANIMATE]
   (RCPT)→ [ANIMATE]
   (OBJ)→  [ENTITY].
```

HARDWARE < STUFF. Hardware is stuff, as opposed to nails and screws, which are counted as separate entities.

HOMEWORK < WORK. Homework is a kind of work.

INFORMATION < T. Information includes anything that can be communicated.

INTERIOR < ENTITY. An interior is a role played by part of a physical object.

```
[INTERIOR]←(PART)←[ENTITY].
```

JACK < TOOL. A jack is a type of tool, as opposed to a person named Jack.

KITCHEN < ROOM. A kitchen is a type of room.

KNOW < STATE. To know is to experience a particular state with regard to a proposition.

```
[KNOW]-
   (EXPR)→ [ANIMATE]
   (STAT)→ [PROPOSITION].
```

LAY < ACT. An animate agent lays a physical object in a place; the object is then in a state of lying.

```
[LAY]-
   (AGNT)→ [ANIMATE]
   (STAT)→ [PHYSOBJ]
   (LOC)→  [PLACE].
```

LOVE < STATE. Love is a state experienced by an animate being towards some entity.

```
[LOVE]-
   (EXPR)→ [ANIMATE]
   (OBJ)→  [ENTITY].
```

MAKE < ACT. To make is to use some material to achieve a result.

```
[MAKE]-
   (AGNT)→ [ANIMATE]
   (MATR)→ [SUBSTANCE].
   (RSLT)→ [PHYSOBJ].
```

MEASURE < T. Measure has no supertypes other than T.

MESSAGE < INFORMATION. A message is information in the role of being communicated.

```
[MESSAGE]←(OBJ)←[COMMUNICATE].
```

MOBILE-ENTITY < ENTITY. Mobile entities are entities that can move around.

ORDER < COMMUNICATE. An order is a kind of communication; see the entry for COMMAND.

PARENT < PERSON. A parent is linked to another person by the relation (CHLD), but in the opposite direction from the type CHILD.

```
[PARENT]→(CHLD)→[PERSON].
```

PERSON < ANIMAL. A person is a kind of animal.

PET < ANIMAL. A pet is an animal that plays the role of pet.

```
[PET]←(POSS)←[PERSON].
```

PHYSOBJ < ENTITY. A physical object is a type of entity.

PLACE < STATIONARY-ENTITY. A place is role played by a stationary entity.

```
[PLACE]←(LOC)←[T].
```

PROPOSITION < INFORMATION. A proposition is a type of symbolic information, as opposed to images.

RECEIVE < ACT. For the verb *receive*, the subject is the recipient.

```
[RECEIVE]-
   (RCPT)→ [ANIMATE]
   (INST)→ [ENTITY]
   (OBJ)→  [ENTITY]
   (SRCE)→ [PLACE].
```

ROBOT < ANIMATE, MACHINE, MOBILE-ENTITY. A robot is an animate machine that can move around.

SHIP < MOBILE-ENTITY. A ship sails the seas.

SHIPMENT < TRANSPORT. A shipment is an act of shipping.

```
[SHIPMENT]-
   (AGNT)→ [ANIMATE]
   (INST)→ [CONVEYANCE]
   (SRCE)→ [PLACE]
   (DEST)→ [PLACE]
   (PATH)→ [PLACE: {*}]
   (OBJ)→  [PHYSOBJ].
```

SET < ACT. An animate agent sets an entity, which is then in a state of sitting.

```
[SET]-
   (AGNT)→ [ANIMATE]
   (STAT)→ [PHYSOBJ]
   (LOC)→  [PLACE].
```

STATE < T. States have duration, as opposed to events, which are in flux.

```
[STATE]-
   (DUR)→ [TIME-PERIOD]
   (LOC)→ [PLACE].
```

TEACH < ACT. An animate being teaches some subject matter to another animate being.

```
[TEACH]-
   (AGNT)→ [ANIMATE]
   (RCPT)→ [ANIMATE]
   (OBJ)→  [SUBJECT-MATTER].
```

TEACHER < PERSON. A teacher is a person in the role of teaching.

```
[TEACHER]-
   (AGNT)← [TEACH]-
              (RCPT)→ [ANIMATE]
              (OBJ)→  [SUBJECT-MATTER].
```

TELEPHONE < PHYSOBJ. A telephone is a means of communication.

```
[TELEPHONE]←(INST)←[COMMUNICATE].
```

THINK < ACT. Thinking is an act that animate beings perform on propositions.

```
[THINK]-
   (AGNT)→ [ANIMATE]
   (OBJ)→  [PROPOSITION].
```

THOUGHT < PROPOSITION. A thought is the object of thinking.

```
[THOUGHT]←(OBJ)←[THINK].
```

TOOL < ENTITY. A tool is an entity that plays the role of instrument for some act.

```
[TOOL]←(INST)←[ACT].
```

UNICORN < MAMMAL, MYTHICAL-CREATURE. A unicorn is a mythical creature that would be a mammal if it existed.

USE < ACT. The object of the verb *use* is the instrument of some unspecified act.

```
[USE]-
   (AGNT)→ [ANIMATE]
   (INST)→ [ENTITY].
```

WARM < STATE. Warmth is a state experienced by some animate being by means of some warm, inanimate instrument.

```
[WARM]-
   (EXPR)→ [ANIMAL]
   (INST)→ [¬ANIMATE].
```

WORK < ACT. Work is a kind of act.

WEAR < ACT. People wear clothes.

```
[HUMAN]←(AGNT)←[WEAR]→(OBJ)→[CLOTHING].
```

WEAR-OUT < PROCESS. Something wears out a physical object.

```
[TOOL]←(INST)←[WEAR-OUT]→(OBJ)→[PHYSOBJ].
```

⊤ > all other types.

⊥ < all other types.

B.3 CONCEPTUAL RELATIONS

Some conceptual relations used in examples of this book are listed here. As in Section B.2, these entries are not definitions, but constraints on the use of the relations in conceptual graphs. For each entry, the leading word is the name of the relation, such as *agent*. Following the name is a four-letter (or shorter) type label, such as (AGNT). After that are the *maximal types* of concepts that may be linked to each arc of the relation, as "links [ACT] to [ANIMATE]." Next comes an informal comment about the use of the relation: "the animate concept represents the actor of the action." Finally, there is an example that shows how the relation may be used.

To remember the direction of the arrows, read the relation name and the concepts attached to it as an English phrase *the RELATION of a* $CONCEPT_1$ *is a* $CONCEPT_2$. With this convention, the graph,

```
[BITE]→(AGNT)→[PERSON: Eve],
```

may be read *the agent of a BITE is a PERSON, Eve.* An equivalent convention is to read *a BITE has an agent which is a PERSON, Eve.* When scanning the graph in the opposite direction from the arrows, another convention is to read the arrow pointing away from the circle as *is a* and the one pointing towards the circle as *of.* With this convention, the above graph would be read *PERSON, Eve, is an agent of BITE.*

accompaniment. (ACCM) links [ENTITY:*x] to [ENTITY:*y], where *y is accompanying *x. Example: *Ronnie left with Nancy.*

```
[LEAVE]→(AGNT)→[PERSON:Ronnie]→(ACCM)→[PERSON:Nancy].
```

agent. (AGNT) links [ACT] to [ANIMATE], where the ANIMATE concept represents the actor of the action. Example: *Eve bit an apple.*

```
[PERSON:Eve]←(AGNT)←[BITE]→(OBJ)→[APPLE].
```

argument. (ARG) links [FUNCTION] to [DATA], which is input to the function. If the function takes more than one input, the arguments may be distinguished as ARG1, ARG2, ARG3, ... This relation is used primarily for representing mathematical expressions, not for natural language. Example: *SQRT(16)=4.*

```
[NUMBER: 16]←(ARG)←[SQRT]→(RSLT)→[NUMBER: 4].
```

attribute. (ATTR) links [ENTITY:*x] to [ENTITY:*y] where *x has an attribute *y. Example: *The rose is red.*

```
[ROSE: #]→(ATTR)→[RED].
```

cause. (CAUS) links [STATE:*x] to [STATE:*y], where *x has a cause *y. Example: *If you are wet, it is raining.*

```
[STATE: [PERSON:You]←(EXPR)←[WET]]→(CAUS)→[STATE: [RAIN]].
```

characteristic. (CHRC) links [ENTITY:*x] to [ENTITY:*y] where *x has a characteristic *y. Example: *Eubie was 100 years old.*

```
(PAST)→[PROPOSITION: [PERSON:Eubie]→(CHRC)→[AGE:@100yrs]].
```

child. (CHLD) links a [PERSON] to another [PERSON], who is a child of the former. Example: *Lillian is Katie's mother.*

```
[MOTHER: Lillian]→(CHLD)→[PERSON: Katie].
```

content. (CONT) links [ENTITY:*x] to [ENTITY:*y], where *x has content *y. It may be defined in terms of the relations LOC and PART. Example: *A baby is in a pen.*

```
[PLAYPEN]→(CONT)→[BABY].
```

destination. (DEST) links an [ACT] to an [ENTITY], towards which the action is directed. Example: *Bob went to Danbury.*

```
[PERSON: Bob]←(AGNT)←[GO]→(DEST)→[CITY: Danbury].
```

duration. (DUR) links a [STATE] to a [TIME-PERIOD], during which the state persists. Example: *The truck was serviced for 5 hours.*

```
[TRUCK: #]←(OBJ)←[SERVICE]→(DUR)→[TIME-PERIOD: @5hrs].
```

experiencer. (EXPR) links a [STATE] to an [ANIMATE], who is experiencing that state. Example: *Clara is cold.*

```
[PERSON: Clara]←(EXPR)←[COLD].
```

frequency. (FREQ) links an [EVENT] to a set of [TIME], at which it occurs. Example: *Packages are sent on Mondays.*

```
[PACKAGE: {*}]←(OBJ)←[SEND]→(FREQ)→[MONDAY: {*}].
```

initiator. (INIT) links an [ACT] to an [ANIMATE] who is responsible for initiating it, but who does not perform it directly. Example: *Tony boiled the potatoes.*

```
[PERSON: Tony]←(INIT)←[BOIL]→(OBJ)→[POTATO: {*}].
```

instrument. (INST) links an [ENTITY] to an [ACT] in which the entity is causally involved. Example: *The key opened the door.*

```
[KEY: #]←(INST)←[OPEN]→(OBJ)→[DOOR: #].
```

link. (LINK) links [⊤] to [⊤]. It is used primarily as a primitive in terms of which all other relations can be defined. The relation type AGNT may be defined in terms of a concept type AGENT:

```
relation AGNT(x,y) is
   [ACT:*x]→(LINK)→[AGENT]→(LINK)→[ANIMATE:*y].
```

location. (LOC) links a [⊤] to a [PLACE]. Example: *Vehicles arrive at a station.*

```
[VEHICLE: {*}]←(AGNT)←[ARRIVE]→(LOC)→[STATION].
```

manner. (MANR) links an [ACT] to an [ATTRIBUTE]. Example: *The ambulance arrived quickly.*

```
[AMBULANCE:#]←(AGNT)←[ARRIVE]→(MANR)→[QUICK].
```

material. (MATR) links an [ACT] to a [SUBSTANCE] used in the process. Example: *The gun was carved out of soap.*

```
[GUN]←(RSLT)←[CARVE]→(MATR)→[SOAP].
```

measure. (MEAS) links a [DIMENSION] to a [MEASURE] of that dimension. Example: *The ski is 167cm long.*

```
[SKI]→(CHRC)→[LENGTH]→(MEAS)→[MEASURE: 167cm].
```

By measure contraction (Section 3.3), the MEAS relation can be contracted to form the concept [LENGTH:@167cm].

method. (METH) links an [ACT:*x] to a [SITUATION:*y] that shows how the act *x is accomplished. Example: *Larry caught the crook with a mighty leap.*

```
[ACT: [PERSON: Larry=*x]←(AGNT)←[CATCH]→(OBJ)→[CROOK]]-
   (METH)→[ACT: [PERSON: *x]←(AGNT)←[LEAP]→(MANR)→[MIGHTY]].
```

name. (NAME) links an [ENTITY] to a [WORD], which is a name of the entity. Example: *Cicero is named Tully.*

```
[PERSON: Cicero]→(NAME)→["Tully"].
```

Example: *"4" and "IV" are names for the same number.*

```
["4"]←(NAME)←[NUMBER]→(NAME)→["IV"].
```

necessary. (NECS) is a monadic relation that links to a [PROPOSITION], which is necessarily true. Example: *It is necessarily true that a woman is female.*

```
(NECS)→[PROPOSITION: [WOMAN]→(ATTR)→[FEMALE]].
```

negation. (NEG) is a monadic relation that links to a [PROPOSITION], which is asserted to be false. Example: *Kirby did not eat an apple.*

```
(NEG)→[PROPOSITION: [PERSON:Kirby]←(AGNT)←[EAT]→(OBJ)→[APPLE]].
```

object. (OBJ) links an [ACT] to an [ENTITY], which is acted upon. Example: *The cat swallowed the canary.*

```
[CAT: #]←(AGNT)←[SWALLOW]→(OBJ)→[CANARY: #].
```

part. (PART) links an [ENTITY:*x] to an [ENTITY:*y] where *y is part of *x. Example: *A finger is a part of a hand.*

```
[HAND]→(PART)→[FINGER].
```

past. (PAST) is a monadic relation that links to a [PROPOSITION], that was true at some time preceding the present. Example: *Judy left.*

```
(PAST)→[PROPOSITION: [PERSON:Judy]←(AGNT)←[LEAVE]].
```

Note: most of the sample sentences in this book are stated in the past tense, but the relation (PAST) is often omitted when it is not important to the discussion. In effect, one could assume that all of the sentences were asserted in one large context to which the relation (PAST) is linked.

path. (PATH) links an [ACT] to a set of [PLACE]'s along which the action occurs. Example: *The pizza was shipped via Albany and Buffalo.*

```
[PIZZA: #]←(OBJ)←[SHIPMENT]→(PATH)→[CITY: {Albany, Buffalo}].
```

point-in-time. (PTIM) links [⊤] to a [TIME] at which it occurs. Example: *At 5:25 PM, Erin left.*

```
[TIME: 5:25pm]←(PTIM)←[PROPOSITION: [PERSON:Erin]←(AGNT)←[LEAVE]].
```

possession. (POSS) links an [ANIMATE] to an [ENTITY], which is possessed by the animate being. Example: *Niurka's watch stopped.*

```
[PERSON: Niurka]→(POSS)→[WRISTWATCH]←(OBJ)←[STOP].
```

possible. (PSBL) is a monadic relation that links to a [PROPOSITION], which is possibly true. Example: *The baby can talk.*

```
(PSBL)→[PROPOSITION: [BABY: #]←(AGNT)←[TALK]].
```

quantity. (QTY) links a set of [ENTITY: {*}] to a [NUMBER] that indicates the number of entities in that set. Example: *There are 50 passengers on the bus.*

```
[BUS: #]←(LOC)←[PASSENGER: {*}]→(QTY)→[NUMBER: 50].
```

By quantity contraction (Section 3.7), the QTY relation can be contracted to form the concept [PASSENGER:{*}@50].

recipient. (RCPT) links an [ACT] to an [ANIMATE], which receives the object or result of the action. Example: *Diamonds were given to Ruby.*

```
[DIAMOND: {*}]←(OBJ)←[GIVE]→(RCPT)→[PERSON: Ruby].
```

result. (RSLT) links an [ACT] to an [ENTITY] that is generated by the act. Example: *Erich built a house.*

```
[PERSON: Erich]←(AGNT)←[BUILD]→(RSLT)→[HOUSE].
```

source. (SRCE) links an [ACT] to an [ENTITY] from which it originates. Example: *The pail was carried from the shed.*

```
[PAIL: #]←(OBJ)←[CARRY]→(SRCE)→[SHED].
```

support. (SUPP) links an [ENTITY:*x] to another [ENTITY:*y] where *x has support *y. Example: *The frost is on the pumpkin.*

```
[FROST]→(SUPP)→[PUMPKIN].
```

successor. (SUCC) links a [⊤] to another [⊤], which follows the first one. Example: *After Billy ate the pretzel, he drank some beer.*

```
[EVENT:
   [PERSON: Billy=*x]←(AGNT)←[EAT]→(OBJ)→[PRETZEL: #]]-
(SUCC)→[EVENT:
   [PERSON: *x]←(AGNT)←[DRINK]→(OBJ)→[BEER]].
```

until. (UNTL) links a STATE to a TIME at which the state ceases to exist. Example: *The ticket is valid until 1 AM.*

```
[STATE: [TICKET]→(ATTR)→[VALID]]→(UNTL)→[TIME: 1 AM].
```

B.4 GRAMMATICAL CATEGORIES

Modern linguistic theory has made the old grammatical categories more precise. It has not replaced them, but refined them. This section surveys the traditional grammatical terms. Readers may find this survey helpful background for the more theoretical material in Chapters 3, 4, and 5.

A *noun* is a name for a thing, although some of the "things" may be rather abstract, such as joy or whiteness. Nouns can be divided into mutually exclusive categories in several ways: *proper noun* vs. *common noun*, *mass noun* vs. *count noun*, or *concrete noun* vs. *abstract noun*. Following are the major subcategories of nouns:

■ *Proper nouns* or *names* designate individual people or things. Examples include *Judy, Pittsburgh, Mont Blanc, Jumbo, The Empire State Building, The Roman Catholic Church, The Declaration of Independence,* and *The New York Yankees.* When referring to the subject matter, *physics* is a common noun; but when used as the name of a particular course at a university, *Physics 201* is a proper noun.

■ *Common nouns* include all nouns other than proper names. Examples include *elephant, air, safety, science, idea,* and *extension.* All the nouns in the following categories are common nouns.

■ *Mass nouns* refer to substances like water or butter that come in continuous quantities rather than discrete units. Mass nouns include concrete ones like *bread, steel,* and *meat* as well as abstractions like *gratitude* and *mercy.* Mass nouns cannot occur in the plural, and they cannot be preceded with *a* or *an* in the singular.

■ *Count nouns* refer to discrete things that can be counted. Examples include *angel, corporation,* and *hole.* A count noun can be used in the plural, and *a* or *an* precedes it in the singular. Some nouns are used as either mass nouns or count nouns: *a cake* refers to the entire object as baked, but *cake* as a mass noun refers to the substance of which the cake is composed.

■ *Concrete nouns* refer to physical objects and substances. They include count nouns like *person, house,* and *electron* as well as mass nouns like *oil* and *water.* Nouns like *unicorn* and *ambrosia* are concrete, even though they refer to mythical things.

■ *Abstract nouns* refer to states and actions that have no physical embodiment. Examples include *stress, virtue,* and *hospitality.* They include count nouns like *idea* and mass nouns like *gratitude.*

■ *Nominalizations* are abstract nouns derived from verbs and adjectives: *assistance* from *assist*; *distribution* from *distribute*; *warmth* from *warm*; *happiness* from *happy*; and *generality* from *general.* Many simple verbs can be used as nouns without any ending: *help, move, talk, punch,* and *race.* Nominalized verbs are mass nouns when they refer to the process, but they are count nouns when they refer to specific instances: *Talk is cheap, Michael won a race yesterday,* and *Generalization leads to generalities.*

Verbs typically refer to actions and states. That statement is not a definition, since verbs like *saddle, hammer,* and *hand* are derived from nouns; and nouns like *sale, departure,* and *belief* refer to actions and states. Tense endings are characteristic of English verbs, but Chinese verbs have no endings. A precise definition of verb requires a formal grammar (Section A.6). Following are some informal examples that illustrate the major categories:

■ *Main verbs* can occur as the only verb in a sentence. They may refer to actions like *jump, sing,* or *distribute* and states like *love, believe,* or *admire.*

■ *Auxiliary verbs* are used with main verbs to form a *compound verb* like *may have been walking.* The *modal auxiliaries* like *can, may,* and *must* are always used with a main verb in combinations like *may go, can be seen,* or *must have been mistaken.* The special verbs *be, have,* and *do* can be used alone or as auxiliary verbs in combinations like *is written, have completed,* and *does apply.*

■ *Intransitive verbs* do not take a direct object, as in the sentences *I walked, She is living,* and *The cat paused.*

■ *Transitive verbs* are main verbs that take a direct object: *I bought the book, We drank the wine,* and *They sold the house.*

■ *Bitransitive verbs* are main verbs that take a direct object plus an indirect object: *John gave Mary an aspirin* and *Avdo told Milman a story.*

■ Some transitive verbs take an extra noun phrase or adjective, called a *complement,* after the direct object: *She painted the kitchen yellow, She named her cat Thothmes III,* and *They considered her smart.*

Adjectives modify nouns, although the kind of modification varies widely. A *cashmere sweater* is a kind of sweater, a *former president* is no longer a president, and a *teddy bear* never was a real bear. Following are various kinds of adjectives:

■ *Attributive adjectives* occur in front of a noun and state some attribute of that noun: *the happy elephant, a former neighbor, a tall building,* and *the expensive wristwatch.* This is the normal position for adjectives.

■ *Predicative adjectives* are used after linking verbs like *be, seem, look,* and *feel*: *The elephant is happy, The building seems tall,* and *The wristwatch looks expensive.* Most adjectives can be used in either attributive position or predicative position, but some can only be used attributively. The following sentences, for example, are incorrect: *The neighbor is former, The student is medical,* and *The physicist is nuclear.*

■ *Determiners* come at the beginning of a noun phrase. They include the articles *a, an,* and *the*; quantifiers such as *each, every,* and *some*; possessive pronouns such as *my, your,* and *its*; and demonstratives such as *this, that,* and *these.* What distinguishes a determiner is that it occurs in the same position as an article, and at most one can occur before a head noun: *the book, my little book,* and *each little blue book* are all correct; but *a my book* and *each the book* are incorrect.

■ *Participles* are verb forms that are used, like adjectives, to modify nouns. *Present participles* end in *-ing,* and *past participles* end in *-ed,* except for irregular forms like *torn* or *broken.* By itself, a participle can precede a noun, like any other adjective: *a broken window, a walking skeleton, an enchanted forest,* and *a practicing witch.* When the participle is combined with other verbal modifiers, it normally follows the noun: *a window broken by a skeleton walking out of a forest enchanted by a witch practicing without a license.*

Adverbs modify verbs, adjectives, other adverbs, and entire sentences as a whole. Some are formed by adding *-ly* to adjectives. But some *-ly* words, such as *curly* and *friendly*, are adjectives; and many adverbs, such as *fast*, *well*, and *often*, do not end in *-ly*. Following are some categories of adverbs:

- *Adverbs of manner* are the most common ones. They specify the manner in which some action is performed and are commonly formed from adjectives with *-ly*: *gracefully, happily, smoothly,* and *enticingly.*
- *Sentential adverbs* modify an entire sentence. They include adverbs like *possibly* and *certainly* that express modal information. Sentential adverbs are commonly placed at the beginning of a sentence: *Surprisingly, the house remained standing.*
- *Conjunctive adverbs* behave like conjunctions in linking one sentence to another, but they do not bind the sentences as tightly as conjunctions. Some examples include *however, nevertheless, therefore, thus, so,* and *otherwise.*
- *Degree adverbs* intensify or weaken the meaning of the word they modify: *very, rather, somewhat, almost, scarcely, barely, hardly,* and *quite.*
- *Negative adverbs* negate a verb or sentence. The primary one is *not*, but there are others, such as *never* and *nowhere.* Adjectives are typically negated with a prefix *un-*, *non-*, *in-* (and its variants *im-*, *il-*, and *ir-*), or *a-* and *an-* (which are used only with words of Greek origin).

Pronouns occur in the same positions as noun phrases. If a noun phrase, *the clever little boy*, occurred in a sentence, the pronoun *he* could be used in its place. Following are categories of pronouns:

- *Personal pronouns* refer to persons or things. They include the common pronouns *I, me, we, us, you, he, him, she, her, it, they,* and *them.*
- *Demonstrative pronouns* point out particular persons or things: *this, that, these,* and *those.*
- *Interrogative pronouns* are used to ask questions. They include *who* and *what* in such sentences as *Who is knocking at my door?* or *What do you mean?*
- *Relative pronouns* include the words *who, whom, which,* and *that*, which are used in a relative clause for linking to other noun phrases in the same sentence. In the sentence *The man who installs telephones is knocking at your door*, the word *who* refers back to the previous noun phrase *the man.*

Prepositions, as their name indicates, occur before nouns. In Japanese, the equivalent function is performed by *postpositions*, which occur after nouns. The following sentence has six noun phrases related to the main verb: *At lunch time, Ruby bought her son a present from the street vendor for five dollars.* Three of the relationships are shown by word order: the subject, *Ruby*; the indirect object, *her son*; and the direct object, *a present.* The other three relationships are marked by the prepositions *at, from,* and *for.*

Conjunctions join two phrases in a sentence. They are often confused with prepositions, which also join phrases, but the kind of joining is different. Following are categories of conjunctions:

- *Coordinate conjunctions*, which include *and, or, but,* and *nor*, join two phrases of the same grammatical category to form a larger phrase of the same category: noun phrases, *the owl and the pussycat*; verb phrases, *eat, drink, and be merry*; adjectives, *a brilliant but erratic student*; adverbs, *raining lightly but steadily*; and sentences, *The kittens went to sleep, or they continued to play.*

- *Subordinate conjunctions* join two sentences. But one of them, the *subordinate clause*, is treated as a modifier of the other, called the *main clause*. Some examples are *although, because, whenever, since, after,* and *while.*

- The word *that* converts a sentence into a *clause* that is used as a noun phrase. The clause is most commonly used as a direct object of such verbs as *say, tell, believe,* and *persuade*, but it can also be used as a subject: *I convinced him that the snack bar was inadequate*, and *That the traffic was unbearable surprised no one.*

- *Correlatives* are pairs of words used as conjunctions: *either—or, neither—nor, both—and,* and *not only—but also.*

Interjections are little words interjected into a sentence or used by themselves in an exclamation: *ah, aha, oh, ouch, hey, wow, heck, golly, yecch,*and many obscenities and profanities.

All these categories of words combine to form larger units called *phrases*, which are defined by a formal grammar (Section A.6). The largest phrase is called a sentence, of which there are several kinds:

- *Declarative* sentences make statements. They normally include a noun phrase called the *subject* and a verb phrase called the *predicate*: *The lecture was soporific, Everyone in the audience fell asleep,* and *The speaker didn't notice because he was asleep too.*

- *Interrogative* sentences ask questions. They are distinguished from declarative sentences in three ways: an introductory question word, *How many books were sold?* an auxiliary verb preceding the subject, *Do you want to buy one?* or a rising tone of voice (which cannot be shown in print), *You have one?*

- *Imperative* sentences make requests or commands. They normally lack a subject, which is understood to be the person addressed: *Go home, Eat your lunch,* and *Come back when you're ready to work.*

- *Exclamations* are sentence fragments that express a strong feeling: *Oh what a beautiful morning! How wonderful!* and *Dreadful!*

- *Sentence fragments* of various kinds are used when the listener can infer the missing elements from the context: *Did you play golf? No, tennis,* and *Why are the housing prices so low? Dioxin in the lawn.*

SUGGESTED READING

The types and relations in this appendix are presented as examples. They may be used as a starting point for further development, but they should not be considered a definitive compendium of all language categories. Before adopting these lists or any other list, the reader should study conceptual analysis. A good textbook for such techniques is Nida's *Componential Analysis of Meaning*. Chafe (1970) analyzes many of the categories and relations that must be represented in a semantic theory.

For types and categories of words, the *Longman Dictionary of Contemporary English* has a more finely subdivided set of syntactic categories than most dictionaries and uses a restricted vocabulary of only 2,000 words for its definitions. Its categories are keyed to the grammar by Quirk et al. (1972), which is the most comprehensive grammar available for English. A companion volume to the dictionary is the *Longman Lexicon of Contemporary English*, edited by MacArthur; it contains 15,000 words organized by types and semantic relations instead of an alphabetical list. Amsler (1980) did a computer analysis of the type hierarchy implicit in the definitions of the *Merriam-Webster Pocket Dictionary*.

The conceptual relations listed in Appendix B.3 have been adapted from many sources. Ceccato (1962) used 56 relations for his work on machine translation. Fillmore's article on case grammar (1968) is a basic reference that most people cite. J. M. Anderson (1977) and Cook (1979) expanded case grammar to full book-length treatments. Dik (1978) avoids the word *case* because it is too closely bound to surface structure; his version of *functional grammar*, however, has many similarities to case grammar. Bruce (1975) analyzed a dozen versions of case systems that have been implemented in AI programs. Wilkins' *Notional Syllabus* is a catalog of relations, mostly outside the case grammar framework. Evens et al. (1980) compiled lists of case relations and other kinds of relations that have been proposed by linguists, psychologists, and anthropologists. Wierzbicka (1980) presents a philosophical and psychological analysis of semantic categories and relations.

Bibliography

Aaronson, Doris, & Robert W. Rieber, eds. (1979) *Psycholinguistic Research*, Lawrence Erlbaum Associates, Hillsdale, NJ.

Abrial, J. R. (1974) "Data semantics," in Klimbie & Koffeman (1974) 1-60.

Aikens, Janice S. (1983) "Prototypical knowledge for expert systems," *Artificial Intelligence* **20:2**, 163-210.

Akmajian, Adrian, Richard A. Demers, & Robert M. Harnish (1979) *Linguistics: An Introduction to Language and Communication*, MIT Press, Cambridge, MA.

Albus, James S. (1981) *Brains, Behavior, and Robotics*, Byte Books, Peterborough, NH.

Allwood, Jens, Lars-Gunnar Andersson, Östen Dahl (1977) *Logic in Linguistics*, Cambridge University Press, Cambridge.

Alston, William P. (1964) *The Philosophy of Language*, Prentice-Hall, Englewood Cliffs, NJ.

Alter, Steven L. (1980) *Decision Support Systems*, Addison-Wesley, Reading, MA.

Altman, Joseph (1978) "Three levels of mentation and the hierarchic organization of the human brain," in Miller & Lenneberg (1978) 87-109.

Amsler, Robert A. (1980) *The Structure of the Merriam-Webster Pocket Dictionary*, Technical Report TR-164, University of Texas, Austin.

Anderson, Alan Ross, & Nuel D. Belnap, Jr. (1975) *Entailment: The Logic of Relevance and Necessity*, Princeton University Press, Princeton.

Anderson, John M. (1977) *On Case Grammar*, Croom Helm, London.

Anderson, John R. (1976) *Language, Memory, and Thought*, Wiley, New York.

—— (1980) *Cognitive Psychology and its Implications*, Freeman, San Francisco.

Anderson, John R., & Gordon H. Bower (1980) *Human Associative Memory: A Brief Edition*, Lawrence Erlbaum Associates, Hillsdale, NJ.

Arbib, Michael A. (1972) *The Metaphorical Brain*, Wiley, New York.

Arbib, Michael A., A. J. Kfoury, & Robert N. Moll (1981) *A Basis for Theoretical Computer Science*, Springer-Verlag, New York.

d'Arcais, G. B. Flores, & W. J. M. Levelt, eds. (1970) *Advances in Psycholinguistics*, North-Holland, Amsterdam.

Archibald, Jerry L. (1981) "The external structure: experience with an automated module interconnection language," *J. of Systems and Software* **2**, 147-157.

Arden, Bruce W. (1980) *What Can Be Automated?* MIT Press, Cambridge, MA.

Arieti, Silvano, & Jules Bemporad (1978) *Severe and Mild Depression*, Basic Books, New York.

Aristotle, *The Categories, On Interpretation, Prior Analytics, Posterior Analytics, Topica,*Loeb Classical Library, Harvard University Press, Cambridge, MA.

Ashby, W. Ross (1956) *An Introduction to Cybernetics*, Methuen, London.

Austin, J. L. (1962) *How to Do Things with Words*, Oxford University Press, Oxford.

Bach, Emmon, & Robert T. Harms, eds. (1968) *Universals in Linguistic Theory*, Holt, Rinehart and Winston, New York.

Bachman, Charles W. (1969) "Data structure diagrams," *Data Base* **1:2**, 4-10.

Baddeley, Alan D. (1976) *The Psychology of Memory*, Basic Books, New York.

Badler, Norman I., & Stephen W. Smoliar (1979) "Digital representations of human movement," *Computing Surveys* **11:1**, 19-38.

Baker, C. L, & John J. McCarthy, eds. (1981) *The Logical Problem of Language Acquisition*, MIT Press, Cambridge, MA.

Ballard, Dana H., & Christopher M. Brown (1982) *Computer Vision*, Prentice-Hall, Englewood Cliffs, NJ.

Banerji, Ranan B. (1980) *Artificial Intelligence: A Theoretical Approach*, North-Holland, New York.

Bar-Hillel, Yehoshua (1960) "The present status of automatic translation of languages," in F. L. Alt, ed., *Advances in Computers* **1**, Academic Press, New York, 91-163.

Barnes, J. G. P. (1982) *Programming in Ada*, Addison-Wesley, Reading, MA.

Barr, Avron, & Edward A. Feigenbaum, eds. (1981-1982) *The Handbook of Artificial Intelligence*, vols. 1 & 2, William Kaufmann, Inc., Los Altos, CA. (See Cohen & Feigenbaum (1982) for vol. 3.)

Bartlett, Frederic C. (1932) *Remembering*, Cambridge University Press, Cambridge.

Barwise, Jon (1981) "Some computational aspects of situation semantics," *Proc. 19th Annual Meeting of the ACL*, 109-111.

Barwise, Jon, & Robin Cooper (1981) "Generalized quantifiers and natural language," *Linguistics and Philosophy* **4**, 159-219.

Barwise, Jon, & John Perry (1981) "Situations and attitudes," *J. of Philosophy* **4**, 159-219.

Bäuerle, R., U. Egli, & A. von Stechow, eds. (1979) *Semantics from Different Points of View*, Springer-Verlag, Berlin.

Beardslee, David C., & Michael Wertheimer, eds. (1958) *Readings in Perception*, Van Nostrand, New York.

Belnap, Nuel D., Jr., & Thomas B. Steel, Jr. (1976) *The Logic of Questions and Answers*, Yale University Press, New Haven.

Bennett, James S., & Robert S. Englemore (1979) "SACON: a knowledge-based consultant for structural analysis," *Proc. IJCAI-79*, 47-49.

Bennett, James S., & Clifford R. Hollander (1981) "DART: an expert system for computer fault diagnosis," *Proc. IJCAI-81*, 843-845.

Bergland, Glenn D., & Ronald D. Gordon, eds. (1981) *Software Design Strategies*, IEEE Computer Society, Los Angeles.

Bever, Thomas G. (1970) "The influence of speech performance on linguistic structure," d'Arcais & Levelt (1970) 4-30.

Bierwisch, Manfred, & Karl Erich Heidolph, eds. (1970) *Progress in Linguistics*, Mouton, The Hague.

Biggs, Norman L., E. Keith Lloyd, & Robin J. Wilson (1976) *Graph Theory 1736-1936*, Clarendon Press, Oxford.

Birnbaum, Lawrence, & Mallory Selfridge (1981) "Conceptual analysis of natural language," in Schank & Riesbeck (1981) 318-372.

Block, Ned, ed. (1980, 1981) *Readings in Philosophy of Psychology*, two vols., Harvard University Press, Cambridge, MA.

Bloom, Alfred (1981) *The Linguistic Shaping of Thought*, Lawrence Erlbaum Associates, Hillsdale, NJ.

Bobrow, Daniel G., & J. Bruce Fraser (1969) "An augmented state transition network analysis procedure," *Proc. IJCAI-69*, 557-567.

Bobrow, Daniel G., & Allan Collins, eds. (1975) *Representation and Understanding: Studies in Cognitive Science*, Academic Press, New York.

Bobrow, Daniel G., & Terry Winograd (1977) "An overview of KRL, a knowledge representation language," *Cognitive Science*, vol 1, 3-46.

Bobrow, R. J. (1978) "The RUS system," in B. L. Webber & R. J. Bobrow, *Research in Natural Language Understanding*, BBN Report 3878, Cambridge, MA.

Bocheński, Innocenty M. (1970) *A History of Formal Logic*, 2nd edition, Chelsea Publishing Co., New York.

Boden, Margaret A. (1977) *Artificial Intelligence and Natural Man*, Basic Books, New York.

—— (1979) *Jean Piaget*, Viking Press, New York.

—— (1981) *Minds and Mechanisms*, Cornell University Press, Ithaca, NY.

Boguraev, Branimir Konstantinov (1979) *Automatic Resolution of Linguistic Ambiguities*, Technical Report 11, University of Cambridge Computer Laboratory.

Bolc, Leonard, ed. (1978) *Speech Communication with Computers*, Macmillan, London.

——, ed. (1980a) *Natural Language Question Answering Systems*, Carl Hanser Verlag, Munich.

——, ed. (1980b) *Natural Language Based Computer Systems*, Carl Hanser Verlag, Munich.

——, ed. (1980c) *Representation and Processing of Natural Language*, Carl Hanser Verlag, Munich.

Boole, George (1854) *An Investigation of the Laws of Thought*, Dover, New York.

Boring, Edwin G. (1950) *A History of Experimental Psychology*, 2nd edition, Appleton Century Crofts, New York.

—— (1953) "The role of theory in experimental psychology," *American J. of Psychology* **66**, 169-184.

Brachman, Ronald J. (1979) "On the epistemological status of semantic networks," in Findler (1979) 3-50.

Brachman, Ronald J., & Brian C. Smith, eds. (1980) *SIGART Newsletter*, no. 70, Feb. 1980.

Brady, Michael, & Robert C. Berwick, eds. (1983) *Computational Models of Discourse*, MIT Press, Cambridge, MA.

Bransford, J. D., & J. J. Franks (1971) "The abstraction of linguistic ideas," *Cognitive Psychology* **2**, 331-350.

Bransford, J. D., & M. K. Johnson (1972) "Contextual prerequisites for understanding," *J. of Verbal Learning and Verbal Behavior* **61**, 717-726.

Bransford, J. D., & M. K. Johnson (1973) "Considerations of some problems of comprehension," in Chase (1973) 383-438.

Bresnan, Joan W., ed. (1982) *The Mental Representation of Grammatical Relations*, MIT Press, Cambridge, MA.

Broadbent, Donald Eric (1971) *Decision and Stress*, Academic Press, New York.

—— (1975) "The magic number seven after fifteen years," in A. Kennedy & A. Wilkes, eds., *Studies in Long Term Memory*, Wiley, London.

—— (1981) "From the percept to the cognitive structure," in Long & Baddeley (1981) 1-24.

Brodie, Michael L. (1981) "On modelling behavioral semantics of databases," *Proc. VLDB*, IEEE Computer Society Press, 32-42.

Bronnenberg, W. J. H. J., H. C. Bunt, S. P. J. Landsbergen, R. J. H. Scha, W. J. Schoenmakers, & E. P. C. van Utteren (1980) "The question-answering system PHLIQA1," in Bolc (1980a) 215-305.

Brown, John Seely, & Richard R. Burton (1975) "Multiple representations of knowledge for tutorial reasoning,"in Bobrow & Collins (1975) 311-349.

Bruce, Betram (1975) "Case systems for natural language," *Artificial Intelligence* **6**, 327-360.

Bruner, Jerome S. (1960) *The Process of Education*, Harvard University Press, Cambridge, MA.

Bruner, Jerome S., Jacqueline J. Goodnow, & George A. Austin (1956) *A Study of Thinking*, Wiley & Sons, New York.

Burnstine, D. C. (1979) *The Theory behind BIAIT—Business Information Analysis and Integration Technique*, BIAIT International, Petersburg, NY.

Bundy, Alan (1982) "What is the well-dressed AI educator wearing now?" *AI Magazine* **3:1**, 13-14.

Bundy, A., R. M. Burstall, S. Weir, & R. M. Young (1978) *Artificial Intelligence: An Introductory Course*, North-Holland, New York.

Buzan, Tony (1974) *Use Both Sides of Your Brain*, E. P. Dutton, New York.

Callatay, Armand M. (1982) *A Flow Processor Architecture for a Brain Model*, Report IEC-0035, IBM, La Hulpe, Belgium. Revised version forthcoming.

Calvino, Italo (1974) *Invisible Cities*, Harcourt Brace Jovanovitch, New York.

Campbell, Joseph (1968) *The Masks of God: Creative Mythology*, Viking Press, New York.

Caplan, David, ed. (1980) *Biological Studies of Mental Processes*, MIT Press, Cambridge, MA.

Carbonell, Jaime G. (1981) *Subjective Understanding: Computer Models of Belief Systems*, UMI Research Press, Ann Arbor, MI.

—— (1982) "Metaphor: an inescapable phenomenon in natural-language comprehension," in Lehnert & Ringle (1982) 415-434.

Carbonell, Jaime G., Ryszard S. Michalski, & Tom M. Mitchell (1983) "An overview of machine learning," in Michalski et al. (1983) 3-23.

Carlson, W. M. (1979) "The new horizon in business information analysis," *Data Base* **10:4**, 3-9.

Carnap, Rudolf (1956) *Meaning and Necessity*, University of Chicago Press, Chicago.

Carpenter, Patricia A., & Marcel Adam Just (1977) "Sentence comprehension: A psycholinguistic processing model of verification,"in Just & Carpenter (1977) 109-139.

Ceccato, Silvio (1961) *Linguistic Analysis and Programming for Mechanical Translation*, Gordon and Breach, New York.

—— (1962) "Automatic translation of languages," presented at the NATO Summer School, Venice. Reprinted in *Information Storage and Retrieval* **2:3**, 105-158, 1964.

Chafe, Wallace L. (1970) *Meaning and the Structure of Language*, University of Chicago Press, Chicago.

Chan, Wing-Tsit (1963) *A Source Book in Chinese Philosophy*, Princeton University Press, Princeton.

Charniak, Eugene, & Yorick Wilks, eds. (1976) *Computational Semantics*, North-Holland, Amsterdam.

Charniak, Eugene, Christopher K. Riesbeck, & Drew V. McDermott (1980) *Artificial Intelligence Programming*, Lawrence Erlbaum Associates, Hillsdale, NJ.

Chase, William G., ed. (1973) *Visual Information Processing*, Academic Press, New York.

Chase, William G., & Herbert A. Simon (1973) "The mind's eye in chess," in Chase (1973) 215-281.

Chen, Peter Pin-Shan (1976) "The entity-relationship model—toward a unified view of data," *ACM Transactions on Database Systems* **1:1**, 9-36.

——, ed. (1981) *Entity-Relationship Approach to Information Modeling and Analysis*, ER Institute, Saugus, CA.

Cherry, E. Colin (1962) "Why we have two ears," *Advancement of Science*, Sept. 1962, 218-221.

Chodorow, Martin S. (1981) "Growing taxonomic word trees from dictionaries," workshop presentation. Report forthcoming, IBM Research Center, Yorktown Heights, NY.

Chomsky, Noam (1957) *Syntactic Structures*, Mouton, The Hague.

—— (1965) *Aspects of the Theory of Syntax*, MIT Press, Cambridge, MA.

—— (1977) "Conditions on rules of grammar," in R. W. Cole, ed., *Current Issues in Linguistic Theory*, Indiana University Press, Bloomington, 3-50.

—— (1979) *Language and Responsibility*, Pantheon Books, New York.

—— (1980) *Rules and Representations*, Columbia University Press, New York.

—— (1982) *Some Concepts and Consequences of the Theory of Government and Binding*, MIT Press, Cambridge, MA.

Chukovsky, Kornei (1963) *From Two to Five*, University of California Press, Berkeley.

Church, Alonzo (1941) *The Calculi of Lambda Conversion*, Princeton University Press, Princeton, NJ.

Clancey, William J. (1983) "The epistemology of a rule-based expert system," *Artificial Intelligence* **20**.

Claparède, E. (1911) "Recognition et moiïté," translated in D. Rapaport, ed., *Organization and Pathology of Thought*, Columbia University Press, New York, 58-75.

Clark, Herbert H., & Eve V. Clark (1977) *Psychology and Language*, Harcourt Brace Jovanovich, New York.

Clark, K. L., & S.-A. Tärnlund, eds. (1982) *Logic Programming*, Academic Press, New York.

Claus, Volker, Hartmut Ehrig, & Grzegorz Rozenberg, eds. (1979) *Graph Grammars and Their Application to Computer Science and Biology*, Springer-Verlag, Berlin.

Clippinger, John Henry, Jr. (1977) *Meaning and Discourse*, Johns Hopkins University Press, Baltimore.

Clocksin, W., & C. Mellish (1981) *Programming in PROLOG*, Springer-Verlag, New York.

Codd, E. F. (1970) "A relational model of data for large shared data banks," *Comm. ACM* **13:6**, 377-387.

—— (1972) "Further normalization of the data base relational model," in R. Rustin, ed., *Data Base Systems*, Prentice-Hall, Englewood Cliffs, NJ, 33-64.

—— (1974) "Seven steps to rendezvous with the casual user," in Klimbie & Koffeman (1974) 179-200.

—— (1978) "How about recently?" in Shneiderman (1978) 3-28.

—— (1979) "Extending the database relational model to capture more meaning," *ACM Transactions on Database Systems* **4:4**, 397-434.

Cohen, Paul R., & Edward A. Feigenbaum, eds. (1982) *The Handbook of Artificial Intelligence* **3**, William Kaufmann, Inc., Los Altos, CA.

Cohors-Fresenborg, E., & H. J. Strüber (1980) "The learning of algorithmic concepts by action. A study with deaf-mutes," *Revue de Phonétique Appliquée*, Nos. 55-56.

Cole, Peter, ed. (1978) *Syntax and Semantics 9: Pragmatics*, Academic Press, New York.

Cole, Peter, & Jerry L. Morgan, eds. (1975) *Syntax and Semantics 3: Speech Acts*, Academic Press, New York.

Collins, Allan M., & M. Ross Quillian (1969) "Retrieval time from semantic memory," *J. of Verbal Learning and Verbal Behavior* **8**, 240-247.

—— (1972) "How to make a language user," in Tulving & Donaldson (1972) 309-351.

Colmerauer, Alain (1978) "Metamorphosis grammars," in Bolc (1978) 133-189.

Condon, J. H., & K. Thompson (1982) "Belle chess hardware," in M .R. B. Clarke, ed., *Advances in Computer Chess* **3**, Pergamon Press, Elmsford, NY, 45-54.

Conway, Melvin E. (1963) "Design of a separable transition-diagram compiler," *Comm. ACM* **6**, 396-408.

Cook, Walter A. (1979) *Case Grammar: Development of the Matrix Model*, Georgetown University Press, Washington, DC.

Coope, Christopher, Peter Geach, Timothy Potts, & Roger White (1970) *A Wittgenstein Workbook*, University of California Press, Berkeley.

Copi, Irving M. (1979) *Symbolic Logic*, 5th edition, Macmillan, New York.

Cotterman, William W., J. Daniel Cougar, Norman L. Enger, & Frederick Harold, eds. (1981) *Systems Analysis and Design*, North-Holland, New York.

Craik, Kenneth J. W. (1943) *The Nature of Explanation*, Cambridge University Press, Cambridge.

Culicover, Peter W. (1982) *Syntax*, 2nd edition, Academic Press, New York.

Cullingford, Richard E. (1977) "Controlling inference in story understanding," *Proc. IJCAI-77*, 17.

Dahl, Veronica (1982) "On database systems development through logic," *ACM Transactions on Database Systems* **7**, 102-123.

Damerau, Fred J. (1981) "Operating statistics for the transformational question answering system," *American J. of Computational Linguistics* **7:1**, 30-42.

Date, C. J. (1981) *An Introduction to Database Systems*, 3rd edition, Addison-Wesley Publishing Co., Reading, MA.

—— (1983) *An Introduction to Database Systems* **2**, Addison-Wesley Publishing Co., Reading, MA.

Davis, Randall, Bruce Buchanan, & Edward Shortliffe (1977) "Production rules as a representation for a knowledge-based consultation program," *Artificial Intelligence* **8**, 15-45.

Davis, Randall, & Douglas B. Lenat (1982) *Knowledge-Based Systems in Artificial Intelligence*, McGraw-Hill, New York.

De, Prabuddha, Arun Sen, & Ehud Gudes (1982) "A new model for data base abstraction," *Information Systems* **7**, 1-12.

de Antonellis, V., F. de Cindio, G. Degli Antoni, & G. Mauri (1979) "Use of bipartite graphs as a notation for data bases," *Information Systems* **4**, 137-141.

de Groot, Adriaan D. (1965) *Thought and Choice in Chess*, Mouton, The Hague.

—— (1966) "Perception and memory versus thought: some old ideas and recent findings" in B. Kleinmuntz, ed., *Problem Solving*, Wiley, New York.

DeMarco, Tom (1978) *Structured Analysis and System Specification*, Yourdon Inc., New York.

Dennet, Daniel C. (1978) *Brainstorms*, Bradford Books, Montgomery, VT.

Dennis, Jack B. (1974) "First version of a data flow procedure language," in B. Robinet, ed., *Programming Symposium*, Springer-Verlag, New York, 362-376.

—— (1979) "The varieties of data flow computers," *Proc. First International Conference on Distributed Computing Systems*, IEEE Computer Society, 430-439.

De Valois, Karen K., & Russell L. De Valois (1980) "Spatial vision," *Annual Review of Psychology* **31**, 309-341.

Dik, Simon C. (1978) *Functional Grammar*, North-Holland, New York.

Doyle, Jon (1979) "A truth maintenance system," *Artificial Intelligence* **12**, 231-272.

Dreyfus, Hubert L. (1979) *What Computers Can't Do*, 2nd edition, Harper & Row, New York.

Dreyfus, Hubert L., ed. (1982) *Husserl, Intentionality, and Cognitive Science*, MIT Press, Cambridge, MA.

Duda, Richard, John Gaschnig, & Peter Hart (1979) "Model design in the PROSPECTOR consultant system for mineral exploration,"in Michie (1979) 153-167.

Dunn, J. Michael (1973) "A truth value semantics for modal logic," in Leblanc (1973) 87-100.

Dyer, Michael George (1982) *In-Depth Understanding*, Report #219, Dept. of Computer Science, Yale University.

Ennals, J. R. (1980) *Logic as a Computer Language for Children*, Dept. of Computing, Imperial College, London.

Ennis, Susan P. (1982) "Expert systems: a user's perspective of some current tools," *Proc. of AAAI-82*, 319-321.

Entwisle, Doris R. (1966) *Word Associations of Young Children*, The Johns Hopkins Press, Baltimore.

Evans, Thomas G. (1968) "A program for the solution of geometric-analogy intelligence test questions," in Minsky (1968) 271-353.

Evens, Martha W., Bonnie E. Litowitz, Judith A. Markowitz, Raoul N. Smith, & Oswald Werner (1980) *Lexical-Semantic Relations*, Linguistic Research Inc., Carbondale, IL.

Fahlman, Scott E. (1979) *NETL: A System for Representing and Using Real-World Knowledge*, MIT Press, Cambridge, MA.

Fain, J., D. Gorlin, F. Hayes-Roth, S. Rosenschein, H. Sowizral, & D. Waterman (1981) *The ROSIE Language Reference Manual*, The Rand Corporation, N-1647-ARPA.

Fain, J., F. Hayes-Roth, H. Sowizral, & D. Waterman (1982) *Programming in ROSIE*, The Rand Corporation, N-1646-ARPA.

Faught, W. S., D. A. Waterman, P. Klahr, S. J. Rosenschein, D. M. Gorlin, & S. J. Tepper (1980) *EP-2: An Exemplary Programming System*, Report R-2411-ARPA, Rand Corporation, Santa Monica, CA.

Feigenbaum, Edward A. (1977) "The art of artificial intelligence," *Proc. IJCAI-77*, 1014-1029.

—— (1980) *Knowledge Engineering: the Applied Side of Artificial Intelligence*, Report STAN-CS-80-812, Dept. of Computer Science, Stanford University.

Feigenbaum, Edward A., & Julian Feldman, eds. (1963) *Computers and Thought*, McGraw-Hill, New York.

Feigenbaum, Edward A., & Pamela McCorduck (1983) *The Fifth Generation*, Addison-Wesley, Reading, MA.

Fikes, Richard E. (1982) "A representation system user interface for knowledge base designers," *AI Magazine* **3:4**, 28-33.

Filippycheva, N. A. (1952) *Inertia of the Higher Cortical Processes in Local Lesions of the Cerebral Hemispheres*, USSR Acad. Med. Sci., Moscow. Quoted by Luria (1966).

Fillmore, Charles J. (1968) "The case for case" in Bach & Harms (1968) 1-88.

Findler, Nicholas V., ed. (1979) *Associative Networks: Representation and Use of Knowledge by Computers*, Academic Press, New York.

Finnegan, Ruth (1981) "Literacy and literature," in Lloyd & Gay (1981) 234-255.

Flew, Anthony, ed. (1979) *A Dictionary of Philosophy*, St. Martin's Press, New York.

Fodor, Janet Dean (1977) *Semantics: Theories of Meaning in Generative Grammar*, Harper & Row, New York.

Fodor, Jerry A. (1981) *Representations: Philosophical Essays on the Foundations of Cognitive Science*, MIT Press, Cambridge, MA.

Fodor, Jerry A., & Jerrold J. Katz, eds. (1964) *The Structure of Language*, Prentice-Hall, Englewood Cliffs, NJ.

Forgy, Charles L. (1981) *OPS5 User's Manual*, Dept. of Computer Science, Carnegie-Mellon University.

Freeman, Peter, & Anthony I. Wasserman, eds. (1980) *Software Design Techniques*, IEEE Computer Society, Long Beach, CA.

Frege, Gottlob (1879) *Begriffsschrift*, translated in van Heijenoort (1967) 1-82.

Frijda, N. H., & A. D. de Groot (1981) *Otto Selz: His Contribution to Psychology*, Mouton, The Hague.

Fries, Charles Carpenter (1952) *The Structure of English*, Harcourt, Brace & World, New York.

Fromkin, Victoria, & Robert Rodman (1978) *An Introduction to Language*, 2nd edition, Holt, Rinehart, and Winston, New York.

Gallaire, Hervé, & Jack Minker, eds. (1978) *Logic and Data Bases*, Plenum Press, New York.

Gane, Chris, & Trish Sarson (1979) *Structured Systems Analysis*, Prentice-Hall, Englewood Cliffs, NJ.

Gardner, R. Allen, & Beatrice T. Gardner (1969) "Teaching sign language to a chimpanzee," *Science* **165**, 664-672.

Gazdar, Gerald (1979) *Pragmatics*, Academic Press, New York.

Geller, V. J., & M. E. Lesk (1981) "How users search: a comparison of menu and attribute retrieval systems on a library catalog,"Technical Report, Bell Laboratories, Murray Hill.

Gershman, Anatole V. (1982) "A framework for conceptual analyzers," in Lehnert & Ringle (1982) 177-197.

Getzels, Jacob W., & Philip W. Jackson (1962) *Creativity and Intelligence*, Wiley, New York.

Gillenson, Mark L. (1974) *The Interactive Generation of Facial Images on a CRT Using a Heuristic Strategy*, Ph.D. Dissertation, Department of Computer and Information Science, Ohio State University.

Ginzberg, Michael J., Walter Reitman, & Edward A. Stohr (1982) *Decision Support Systems*, North-Holland, New York.

Glorioso, Robert M., & Fernando C. Colón Osorio (1980) *Engineering Intelligent Systems*, Digital Press, Bedford, MA.

Gödel, Kurt (1930) "The completeness of the axioms of the functional calculus of logic," in van Heijenoort (1967) 582-591.

—— (1931) "On formally undecidable propositions of *Principia Mathematica* and related systems," in van Heijenoort (1967) 592-617.

Goddard, Dwight, ed. (1938) *A Buddhist Bible*, Beacon Press, Boston.

Goldman, Neil M. (1975) "Conceptual generation," in Schank (1975) 289-371.

Goldschlager, Les, & Andrew Lister (1982) *Computer Science*, Prentice-Hall International, Englewood Cliffs, NJ.

Good, Irving John (1965) "Speculations concerning the first ultraintelligent machine" in F. L. Alt & M. Rubinoff, eds., *Advances in Computers* **6**, Academic Press, New York, 31-88.

Goodman, Nelson (1951) *The Structure of Appearance*, Harvard University Press, Cambridge, MA.

—— (1968) *Languages of Art*, Bobbs-Merrill, Indianapolis.

Graesser, Arthur C. (1981) *Prose Comprehension Beyond the Word*, Springer-Verlag, New York.

Green, Bert F., Jr., Alice K. Wolf, Carol Chomsky, & Kenneth Laughery (1963) "Baseball: an automatic question answerer," in Feigenbaum & Feldman (1963) 207-216.

Greenberg, Joseph H. (1963) "Some universals of grammar with particular reference to the order of meaningful elements,"in J. H. Greenberg, ed. *Universals of Language*, MIT Press, Cambridge, MA, 58-90.

——, ed. (1978) *Universals of Human Language*, 4 vols., Stanford University Press, Stanford, CA.

Grice, H. Paul (1975) "Logic and conversation," in Cole & Morgan (1975) 41-58.

Griffith, Robert L. (1975) *Information Structures*, Technical Report TR03.013, IBM, Santa Teresa Laboratory.

—— (1982) "Three principles of representation for semantic networks," *ACM Transactions on Database Systems* **7**, 417-442.

Grosz, Barbara J. (1977) "The representation and use of focus in a system for understanding dialog," *Proc. IJCAI-77*, 67-76.

Gruber, Howard E., & J. Jacques Vonèche, eds. (1977) *The Essential Piaget*, Basic Books, New York.

Grueninger, Walter, & Jane Grueninger (1973) "The primate frontal cortex and allassostasis," in Pribram & Luria (1973) 253-290.

Haas, Norman, & Gary G. Hendrix (1983) "Learning by Being Told," in Michalski et al. (1983) 405-427.

Haber, Ralph Norman (1979) "Twenty years of haunting eidetic imagery: Where's the ghost?" *The Behavioral and Brain Sciences* **2**, 583-629.

—— (1983) "The impending demise of the icon," *The Behavioral and Brain Sciences* **6:1**, 1-54.

Hadamard, Jacques (1945) *The Psychology of Invention in the Mathematical Field*, Princeton University Press, Princeton.

Hall, Patrick, John Owlett, and Stephen Todd (1976) "Relations and entities," in G. M. Nijssen, ed., *Modelling in Data Base Management Systems*, North-Holland, New York.

Halliday, M. A. K., & Ruqaiya Hasan (1976) *Cohesion in English*, Longman, London.

Harary, Frank (1969) *Graph Theory*, Addison-Wesley, Reading, MA.

Harris, Zellig (1981) *Papers on Syntax*, edited by H. Hiz, Reidel, Boston.

—— (1982) *A Grammar of English on Mathematical Principles*, Wiley, New York.

Haugeland, John, ed. (1981) *Mind Design*, MIT Press, Cambridge, MA.

Hayes, Cathy (1951) *The Ape in Our House*, Harper & Brothers, New York.

Hayes, J. E., Donald Michie, & Y-H Pao, ed. (1982) *Machine Intelligence* **10**, Wiley, New York.

Hayes-Roth, Frederick, Donald Waterman, & Douglas Lenat, eds. (1983) *Building Expert Systems*, Addison-Wesley, Reading, MA.

Hebb, Donald O. (1949) *Organization of Behavior*, Wiley & Sons, New York.

—— (1968) "Concerning imagery," *Psychological Review* **75**, 466-477.

Heidorn, George E. (1972) *Natural Language Inputs to a Simulation Programming System*, Report NPS-55HD72101A, Naval Postgraduate School, Monterey.

—— (1974) "English as a very high level language for simulation programming," *Proc. Symposium on Very High Level Languages, SIGPLAN Notices*,**9**, April 1974, 91-100.

—— (1975) "Augmented phrase structure grammar," in Schank & Nash-Webber (1975) 1-5.

Heidorn, G. E., K. Jensen, L. A. Miller, R. J. Byrd, & M. S. Chodorow (1982) "The EPISTLE text-critiquing system," *IBM Systems J.* **21**, 305-326.

Hemphill, Linda G., & James R. Rhyne (1978) *A Model for Information Representation in Natural Language Query Systems*, Report RJ-2304, IBM San Jose.

Hendrix, Gary G. (1975) "Expanding the utility of semantic networks through partitioning," in *Proc. IJCAI-75*, 115-121.

—— (1979) "Encoding knowledge in partitioned networks," in Findler (1979) 51-92.

Hendrix, Gary G., Earl D. Sacerdoti, Daniel Sagalowicz, & Jonathan Slocum (1978) "Developing a natural language interface to complex data," *ACM Transactions on Database Systems* **3**, 105-147.

Henisz-Dostert, Bozena, R. Ross Macdonald, & Michael Zarechnak (1979) *Machine Translation*, Mouton, The Hague.

Henkin, Leon (1959) "Some remarks on infinitely long formulas," *Infinitistic Methods*, Proc. Symp. Foundations of Math., Warsaw, 167-183.

Herbart, Johann Friederich (1816) *A Text-Book in Psychology*, 2nd edition, translated by Margaret K. Smith, Appleton, New York, 1891.

Hewitt, Carl (1972) "Description and theoretical analysis (using schemata) of PLANNER," Report TR-258, MIT AI Laboratory.

Hewitt, Carl (1977) "Viewing control structures as patterns of passing messages," *Artificial Intelligence* **8**, 323-364.

Hilgard, Ernest R. (1980) "Consciousness in contemporary psychology," *Annual Review of Psychology* **31**, 1-26.

Hill, I. D. (1972) "Wouldn't it be nice if we could write computer programs in ordinary English—or would it?" *Computer Bulletin* **16**, 306-312.

Hintikka, Jaakko (1969) *Models for Modalities*, Reidel, Dordrecht.

——, ed. (1969) *The Philosophy of Mathematics*, Oxford University Press, Oxford.

—— (1973) "Surface semantics: definition and its motivation," in Leblanc (1973) 128-147.

Hinton, Geoffrey E., & James A. Anderson, eds. (1981) *Parallel Models of Associative Memory*, Lawrence Erlbaum Associates, Hillsdale, NJ.

Hirst, Graeme (1981) *Anaphora in Natural Language Understanding*, Springer-Verlag, New York.

Hörmann, Hans (1981) *To Mean—to Understand* , Springer-Verlag, New York.

Hoffman, Robert R. (1980) "Metaphor in science," in R. P. Honeck & R. R. Hoffman, eds., *Cognition and Figurative Language*, Lawrence Erlbaum Associates, Hillsdale, NJ, 393-423.

Hofstadter, Douglas R. (1979) *Gödel, Escher, Bach: An Eternal Golden Braid* , Basic Books, New York.

Hofstadter, Douglas R., & Daniel C. Dennet (1981) *The Mind's I*, Basic Books, New York.

Horn, G. (1960) "Electrical activity of the cerebral cortex of the unanesthetized cat during attentive behavior," *Brain* **83**, 57-76.

Hubbard, George U. (1981) *Computer-Assisted Data Base Design*, Van Nostrand Reinhold, New York.

Hughes, G. E., & M. J. Cresswell (1968) *An Introduction to Modal Logic*, Methuen and Co., London.

Hull, Clark L. (1951) *Essentials of Behavior*, Yale University Press, New Haven.

Humphrey, George (1951) *Thinking*, Wiley, New York.

Hutchinson, A. (1970) *Labanotation*, Theatre Arts Books, New York.

IBM Corporation (1981) *Business Systems Planning—Information Systems Planning Guide*, Manual GE20-0527.

Ishizuka, Mitsuru, K. S. Fu, & James T. P. Yao (1981) "Inexact inference for rule-based damage assessment of existing structures," *Proc. IJCAI-81*, 837-842.

Israel, David J., & Ronald J. Brachman (1981) "Distinctions and confusions: a catalogue raisonée," *Proc. IJCAI-81*, 452-459.

Jackendoff, Ray S. (1972) *Semantic Interpretation in Generative Grammar*, MIT Press, Cambridge, MA.

Jackson, Philip C. (1974) *Introduction to Artificial Intelligence*, Petrocelli Books, New York.

Jaensch, E. R. (1930) *Eidetic Imagery*, Kegan Paul, Trench, Trubner & Co., London.

Jaffe, Joseph (1977) "The biological significance of communication rhythms," in Rosenberg (1977) 51-63.

Jaffe, Joseph, Samuel W. Anderson, & Daniel N. Stern (1979) "Conversational rhythms," in Aaronson & Reiber (1979) 393-431.

Jahn, Robert G. (1982) "The persistent paradox of psychic phenomena: an engineering perspective," *Proc. of the IEEE* **70**, 136-170.

Jakobson, Roman (1978) *Six Lectures on Sound and Meaning*, MIT Press, Cambridge, MA.

James, William (1890) *The Principles of Psychology*, 2 vols., Dover, New York.

Jensen, Karen, & George E. Heidorn (1983) "The fitted parse: 100% parsing capability in a syntactic grammar of English," *Proc. Conference on Applied Natural Language Processing*, Santa Monica, 93-98.

John, E. Roy (1964) "Electrophysiological studies of memory mechanisms," in D. P. Kimble, ed., *The Organization of Recall*, New York Academy of Sciences, New York, 294-321.

Johnson-Laird, P. N., & P. C. Wason, eds. (1977) *Thinking: Readings in Cognitive Science*, Cambridge University Press, Cambridge.

Joshi, Aravind K., Bonnie L. Webber, & Ivan A. Sag, eds. (1981) *Elements of Discourse Understanding*, Cambridge University Press, Cambridge.

Jung, Carl Gustav (1921) *Psychological Types*, Princeton University Press, Princeton, NJ.

Just, Marcel Adam, & Patricia A. Carpenter, eds. (1977) *Cognitive Processes in Comprehension*, Lawrence Erlbaum Associates, Hillsdale, NJ.

Kandel, Abe, Joe Mott, & Ted Baker (1983) *Discrete Mathematics and its Applications for Computer Scientists*, Reston Publishing Co., Reston, VA.

Kant, Immanuel (1781) *Critique of Pure Reason*, translated by F. Max Müller, Anchor Books, Garden City, NY.

Kaplan, Ronald M., & Joan W. Bresnan (1982) "Lexical-functional grammar: a formal syntax for grammatical representation,"in Bresnan (1982).

Kaplan, S. Jerrold (1978) "Indirect responses to loaded questions," *Proc. of TINLAP-2*, ACM, 202-209.

—— (1982) "Cooperative responses from a portable natural language query system," *Artificial Intelligence* **19**, 165-187.

Kapleau, Philip, ed. (1965) *The Three Pillars of Zen*, Beacon Press, Boston.

Katz, Jerrold J. (1966) *The Philosophy of Language*, Harper & Row, New York.

—— (1972) *Semantic Theory*, Harper & Row, New York.

Katz, Jerrold J., & Jerry A. Fodor (1963) "The structure of a semantic theory," *Language* **39**, 170-210. Reprinted in Fodor & Katz (1964) 479-518.

Kavanaugh, James F., & James E. Cutting (1975) *The Role of Speech in Language*, MIT Press, Cambridge, MA.

Kay, Martin (1967) *Experiments with a Powerful Parser*, Report RM-5452-PR, Rand Corporation, Santa Monica, CA.

—— (1977) "Morphological and syntactic analysis," in Zampolli (1977) 131-234.

Keele, Steven W. (1973) *Attention and Human Performance*, Goodyear Publishing Co., Pacific Palisades, California.

Keen, Peter G. W., & Michael S. Scott Morton (1978) *Decision Support Systems*, Addison-Wesley, Reading, MA.

Keenan, Edward L. (1972) "On semantically based grammar," *Linguistic Inquiry* **3**, 413-462.

Kelly, George A. (1955) *Psychology of Personal Constructs*, W. W. Norton, New York.

Kempson, Ruth M. (1977) *Semantic Theory*, Cambridge University Press, Cambridge.

Kent, Ernest W. (1981) *The Brains of Men and Machines*, BYTE/McGraw Hill, Peterborough, NH.

Kent, William (1978) *Data and Reality*, North-Holland, New York.

Kierkegaard, Soren (1843) *Either/Or*, two vols., Anchor Books, Garden City, NY.

Kintsch, Walter (1970) "Models for free recall and recognition" in D. A. Norman, ed., *Models of Human Memory*, Academic Press, New York, 331-373.

—— (1974) *The Representation of Meaning in Memory*, Lawrence Erlbaum Associates, Hillsdale, NJ.

Kitagawa, T. (1982) *Computer Science and Technologies*, North-Holland, New York.

Klatzky, Roberta L. (1980) *Human Memory*, Freeman, San Francisco.

Klemke, E. D., ed. (1983) *Contemporary Analytic and Linguistic Philosophies*, Prometheus Books, Buffalo.

Klimbie, J. W., & K. L. Koffeman, eds. (1974) *Data Base Management*, North-Holland, Amsterdam.

Klir, George J., ed. (1978) *Applied General Systems Research*, Plenum Press, New York.

Kneale, William, & Martha Kneale (1962) *The Development of Logic*, Clarendon Press, Oxford.

Knuth, Donald E. (1968) "Semantics of context-free languages," *Mathematical Systems Theory* **2**, 127-145. Reprinted in Pao & Ernst (1982) 92-112.

—— (1971) "Top-down syntax analysis," *Acta Informatica* **1**, 79-110.

—— (1973) *The Art of Computer Programming, Vol. 1, Fundamental Algorithms*, 2nd edition, Addison-Wesley, Reading, MA.

Konorski, Jerzy (1967) *Integrative Activity of the Brain*, University of Chicago Press, Chicago.

Kosslyn, Stephen Michael (1980) *Image and Mind*, Harvard University Press, Cambridge, MA.

Kowalski, Robert (1979) *Logic for Problem Solving*, North-Holland, New York.

Kripke, Saul A. (1963a) "Semantical considerations on modal logic," *Acta Philosophica Fennica*, Fasc. XVI, 1963, 83-94.

—— (1963b) "Semantical analysis of modal logic I," *Zeitschrift für mathematische Logik und Grundlagen der Mathematik* **9**, 67-96.

Kučera, Henry (1981) "The learning of grammar," *Perspectives in Computing* **1:2**, 28-35.

Kuhn, Thomas S. (1970) *The Structure of Scientific Revolutions*, University of Chicago Press, Chicago, 2nd edition.

Kukich, Karen (1983) Lecture at workshop. Doctoral dissertation forthcoming, Information Science Department, University of Pittsburgh.

Külpe, Oswald (1912) "Über die moderne Psychologie des Denkens." Translated in J. M. Mandler & G. Mandler, eds., *Thinking: From Association to Gestalt*, Wiley, New York, 208-216.

Kuno, Susumu (1965) "The predictive analyzer and a path elimination technique," *Comm. ACM* **8**, 453-462.

Lakoff, George, & Mark Johnson (1980) *Metaphors We Live by*, University of Chicago Press, Chicago.

Lamb, Sidney M. (1966) *Outline of Stratificational Grammar*, Georgetown University Press, Washington, DC.

Lao Tzu, *Tao-Te Ching*, in Wing-Tsit Chan, ed., *A Source Book in Chinese Philosophy*, Princeton University Press, Princeton, NJ.

LaPalombara, Lyda E. (1976) *An Introduction to Grammar*, Winthrop Publishers, Cambridge, MA.

Lashley, Karl S. (1942) "The problem of cerebral organization in vision," *Biological Symposia* **7**, 301-322.

—— (1950) "In search of the engram" in *Physiological Mechanisms in Animal Behavior*, Society of Experimental Biology Symposium No. 4, Cambridge, 454-482.

—— (1951) "The problem of serial order in behavior," in L. A. Jefress, ed., *Cerebral Mechanisms in Behavior*, Wiley, New York, 112-146.

Lawson, Veronica, ed. (1982) *Practical Experience of Machine Translation*, North-Holland, New York.

Leblanc, Hughes, ed. (1973) *Truth, Syntax and Modality*, North-Holland, Amsterdam.

Ledley, R. S. (1964) "High-Speed Automatic Analysis of Biomedical Pictures," *Science* **146**, 216-223.

Leech, Geoffrey (1974) *Linguistics*, Penguin Books, Baltimore.

Lehnert, Wendy G. (1978) *The Process of Question Answering*, Lawrence Erlbaum Associates, Hillsdale, NJ.

—— (1982) "Plot units: a narrative summation strategy," in Lehnert & Ringle (1982) 375-412.

Lehnert, Wendy G., and Martin H. Ringle, eds. (1982) *Strategies for Natural Language Processing*, Lawrence Erlbaum Associates, Hillsdale, NJ.

Leiber, Justin (1975) *Noam Chomsky: A Philosophic Overview*, St. Martin's Press, New York.

Leibniz, Gottfried Wilhelm (1679) "Elementa characteristica universalis," in L. Couturat, ed., *Opuscules et Fragments inédits de Leibniz*, Ancienne Librairie Germer Bailliere, Paris, 1903, 42-92.

Lenat, Douglas B. (1983) "The role of heuristics in learning by discovery," in Michalski et al. (1983) 243-306.

Lenat, Douglas B., W. R. Sutherland, & J. Gibbons (1982) "Heuristic search for new microcircuit structures," *AI Magazine* **3:3**, 17-33.

Lenihan, John (1975) *Human Engineering*, George Braziller, New York.

Lerdahl, Fred, & Ray Jackendoff (1983) *A Generative Theory of Tonal Music*, MIT Press, Cambridge, MA.

Lévi-Strauss, Claude (1963) *Structural Anthropology*, Anchor Books, Doubleday & Co., Garden City, NY.

Lewis, Clarence Irving (1912) "Implication and the algebra of logic," reprinted in J. D. Goheen & J. L. Mothershead, Jr., eds., *Collected Papers of Clarence Irving Lewis*, Stanford University Press, Stanford.

Lewis, Clayton, & Robert Mack (1982) "The role of abduction in learning to use a computer system," Report RC 9433, IBM Research, Yorktown Heights.

Lieberman, Philip (1973) "On the evolution of human language" in S. R. Anderson & P. Kiparsky, eds., *A Festschrift for Morris Halle*, Holt, Rinehart, & Winston, New York, 107-127.

Lightstone, A. H. (1978) *Mathematical Logic: An Introduction to Model Theory*, Plenum Press, New York.

Lindsay, Peter H., & Donald A. Norman (1977) *Human Information Processing*, 2nd edition, Academic Press, New York.

Lindsay, Robert K., Bruce G. Buchanan, Edward A. Feigenbaum, & Joshua Lederberg (1980) *Applications of Artificial Intelligence for Organic Chemistry*, McGraw-Hill, New York.

Lipschutz, Seymour (1982) *Essential Computer Mathematics*, Schaum's Outline Series, McGraw-Hill, NY.

Livanov, M. N., N. A. Gavrilova, & A. S. Aslanov (1973) "Correlation of biopotentials in the frontal parts of the human brain,"in Pribram & Luria (1973) 91-107.

Lloyd, Barbara, & John Gay, eds. (1981) *Universals of Human Thought: Some African Evidence*, Cambridge University Press, Cambridge.

Loftus, Elizabeth (1980) *Eyewitness Testimony*, Harvard University Press, Cambridge, MA.

Long, John, & Alan Baddeley, eds. (1981) *Attention and Performance* **9**, Lawrence Erlbaum Associates, Hillsdale, NJ.

Longman Group Ltd. (1978) *Longman Dictionary of Contemporary English*, Longman, London.

Lord, Albert B. (1960) *The Singer of Tales*, Harvard University Press, Cambridge, MA.

Lowen, Walter (1982) *Dichotomies of the Mind*, Wiley, New York.

Lubar, Joel F., ed. (1972) *A First Reader in Physiological Psychology*, Harper & Row, New York.

Lucas, Peter (1961) "Die Strukturanalyse von Formelübersetzern," *Elektronische Rechenanlagen* **3**, 159-167. English version, "The structure of formula translators," *ALGOL Bulletin*, Supplement no. 16, Sept. 1961.

Luria, Alexandr Romanovich (1966) *Higher Cortical Functions in Man*, Basic Books, New York.

—— (1968) *The Mind of a Mnemonist*, Basic Books, New York.

—— (1973) *The Working Brain*, Basic Books, New York.

—— (1976) *Cognitive Development*, Harvard University Press, Cambridge, MA.

Luschei, Eugene C. (1962) *The Logical Systems of Lesniewski*, North-Holland, Amsterdam.

Lyons, John (1977) *Semantics*, 2 vols., Cambridge University Press, New York.

MacArthur, Tom (1981) *Longman Lexicon of Contemporary English*, Longman, London.

Macnamara, John (1982) *Names for Things*, MIT Press, Cambridge, MA.

Magee, Bryan (1978) *Men of Ideas*, Oxford University Press, New York.

Magoun, Horace W., Louise Darling, & J. Prost (1960) "The evolution of man's brain," reprinted in Lubar (1972) 35-47.

Maier, David (1983) *The Theory of Relational Databases*, Computer Science Press, Rockville, MD.

Malcolm, Norman (1977) *Thought and knowledge*, Cornell University Press, Ithaca.

Marcus, Mitchell P. (1980) *A Theory of Syntactic Recognition for Natural Language*, MIT Press, Cambridge, MA.

Markov, A. A. (1954) *Theory of Algorithms*, Academy of Sciences of the USSR, Moscow.

Marsh, Elaine, & Naomi Sager (1982) "Analysis and processing of compact text," *COLING 82*, North-Holland, New York, 201-206.

Martin, James (1982) *Application Development without Programmers*, Prentice-Hall, Englewood Cliffs, NJ.

Martin, William A. (1979) "Descriptions and the specialization of concepts," in Winston & Brown (1979) 375-419.

Masterman, Margaret (1961) "Semantic message detection for machine translation, using an interlingua," *Proc. 1961 International Conf. on Machine Translation*, 438-475.

Maturana, Humberto R. (1978) "Biology of language," in Miller & Lenneberg (1978) 27-63.

McAllester, D. A. (1979) *The use of equality in deduction and knowledge representation*, MS Thesis, MIT.

McCarthy, John (1968) "Programs with common sense," in Minsky (1968) 403-418.

McCarty, L. Thorne, & N. S. Sridharan (1981) "The representation of an evolving system of legal concepts: II. prototypes and deformations," *Proc. IJCAI-81*, 246-253.

McCawley, James D. (1981) *Everything that Linguists Have Always Wanted to Know about Logic*, Chicago University Press, Chicago.

McCord, Michael C. (1983) Lecture at Workshop. Report forthcoming, IBM Research, Yorktown Heights, NY.

McCorduck, Pamela (1979) *Machines Who Think*, Freeman, San Francisco.

McDermott, Drew V. (1976) "Artificial intelligence meets natural stupidity," *SIGART Newsletter*, no. 57, April 1976. Reprinted in Haugeland (1981) 143-160.

—— (1978) "Tarskian semantics, or no notation without denotation!" *Cognitive Science* **2**, 277-282.

McDermott, John (1982) "R1: a rule-based configurer of computer systems," *Artificial Intelligence* **19**, 39-88.

McGregor, James J. (1982) "Backtrack search algorithms and the maximal common subgraph problem," *Software—Practice and Experience* **12**, 23-34.

McNeill, David (1970) *The Acquisition of Language*, Harper & Row, New York.

—— (1979) *The Conceptual Basis of Language*, Lawrence Erlbaum Associates, Hillsdale, NJ.

McSkimin, James R., & Jack Minker (1979) "A predicate calculus based semantic network for deductive searching," in Findler (1979) 205-238.

Mealy, George H. (1967) "Another look at data," *Proc. 1967 FJCC*, 525-534.

Merleau-Ponty, Maurice (1964) *Consciousness and the Acquisition of Language*, Northwestern University Press, Evanston.

Michalski, Ryszard S., & R. L. Chilausky (1980) "Knowledge acquisition by encoding expert rules versus computer induction from examples," *International J. of Man-Machine Studies* **12**, 63-87.

Michalski, Ryszard S., & Robert E. Stepp (1983) "Learning from observation: conceptual clustering," in Michalski, Carbonell, & Mitchell (1983) 331-363.

Michalski, Ryszard S., Jaime G. Carbonell, & Tom M. Mitchell, eds. (1983) *Machine Learning*, Tioga Publishing Co., Palo Alto, CA.

Michie, Donald, ed. (1979) *Expert Systems in the Micro-electronic Age*, Edinburgh University Press, Edinburgh.

——, ed. (1982) *Introductory Readings in Expert Systems*, Gordon and Breach, New York.

Mill, James (1829) *Analysis of the Phenomena of the Human Mind*, 2nd edition, Longmans, London, 1878.

Mill, John Stuart (1865) *A System of Logic*, Longmans, London.

Miller, George A. (1956) "The magic number seven, plus or minus two," *Psychological Review* **63**, 81-97.

—— (1981) *Language and Speech*, Freeman, San Francisco.

Miller, George A., & Stephen Isard (1963) "Some perceptual consequences of linguistic rules," *J. of Verbal Learning and Verbal Behavior* **2:3**, 217-228.

Miller, George A., & Elizabeth Lenneberg, eds. (1978) *Psychology and Biology of Language and Thought*, Academic Press, New York.

Miller, Robert B. (1968) "Response time in man-computer conversational transactions," *Proc. 1968 FJCC*, 267-277.

Milner, Brenda (1970) "Memory and the medial temporal regions of the brain" in K. H. Pribram & D. E. Broadbent, eds., *Biology of Memory*, Academic Press, New York, 29-50.

Minsky, Marvin (1967) *Computation: Finite and Infinite Machines*, Prentice-Hall, Englewood Cliffs, NJ.

——, ed. (1968) *Semantic Information Processing*, MIT Press, Cambridge, MA.

—— (1975) "A framework for representing knowledge," in Winston (1975b) 211-280. Reprinted in Haugeland (1981) 95-128.

—— (1981) "K-lines: a theory of memory," in Norman (1981) 87-103.

Minsky, Marvin, & Seymour Papert (1969) *Perceptrons*, MIT Press, Cambridge, MA.

Misek, Linda D. (1972) *Computing a Context: Style, Structure, and the Self-Image of Satan in Paradise Lost*, PhD dissertation, Dept. of English, Case Western Reserve University.

—— (1975) "Claim structure grammar," Paper presented at the Annual Meeting of the Association for Computational Linguistics, San Francisco.

Mishelevich, David J., & Don Van Slyke (1980) "The IBM Patient Care System," *Data Base* **11:3**, 64-75.

Mitchell, Tom M., Paul E. Utgoff, & Ranan B. Banerji (1983) "Learning by experimentation: acquiring and refining problem-solving heuristics," in Michalski et al. (1983) 163-190.

Miura, Isshu, & Ruth Fuller Sasaki (1965) *The Zen Koan*, Harcourt, Brace, & World, New York.

Montague, Richard (1974) *Formal Philosophy*, Yale University Press, New Haven.

Moore, Timothy E. (1975) "Linguistic intuitions of twelve year olds," *Language and Speech* **18**, 213-218.

Moravcsik, Edith A., & Jessica R. Wirth, eds. (1980) *Current Approaches to Syntax*, Academic Press, New York.

Moto-Oka, T., ed. (1982) *Fifth Generation Computer Systems*, North-Holland, New York.

Mückstein, Eva-Maria M. (1979) "A natural language parser with statistical applications," Report RC-7516, IBM, Yorktown Heights, NY.

Mückstein, Eva-Maria M. (1983) "Q-TRANS: query translation into English," Report RC-9841, IBM, Yorktown Heights, NY.

Müller, Georg Elias (1913) "Zur Analyse der Gedächtnistätigkeit und des Vorstellungsverlaufes," *Zeitschrift für Psychologie* , Ergänzungsband **8**.

Mylopoulos, John, Philip A. Bernstein, & Harry K. T. Wong (1980) "A language facility for designing interactive database-intensive applications," *Transactions on Database Systems* **5**, 185-207.

Nabokov, Vladimir (1980) *Lectures on Literature*, edited by Fredson Bowers, Harcourt Brace Jovanovich, New York.

Nagler, Michael N. (1974) *Spontaneity and Tradition*, University of California Press, Berkeley.

Neisser, Ulrich (1967) *Cognitive Psychology*, Appleton Century Crofts, New York.

——, ed. (1982) *Memory Observed*, Freeman, San Francisco.

Nemiah, John C. (1969) "Hysterical amnesia," in G. A. Talland & N. C. Waugh, eds., *The Pathology of Memory*, Academic Press, New York.

Newell, Allen (1973) "Production systems: models of control structures," in Chase (1973) 463-526.

Newell, Allen, & Herbert A. Simon (1963) "GPS, a program that simulates human thought," in Feigenbaum & Feldman (1963) 279-293.

—— (1972) *Human Problem Solving*, Prentice-Hall, Englewood Cliffs, NJ.

Newman, Paula S. (1982) "Towards an integrated development environment," *IBM Systems Journal* **21**, 81-107.

Newmeyer, Frederick J. (1980) *Linguistic Theory in America*, Academic Press, New York.

Newnham, Richard (1971) *About Chinese*, Penguin Books, London.

Nida, Eugene A. (1975) *Componential Analysis of Meaning*, Mouton, The Hague.

Nilsson, Nils J. (1980) *Principles of Artificial Intelligence*, Tioga Publishing Co., Palo Alto, CA.

Norman, Donald A., ed. (1981) *Perspectives on Cognitive Science*, Lawrence Erlbaum Associates, Hillsdale, NJ.

Norman, Donald A., David E. Rumelhart, & the LNR Research Group (1975) *Explorations in Cognition*, Freeman, San Francisco.

Notopoulos, James A. (1959) *Modern Greek Heroic Oral Poetry*, Album FE 4468, Ethnic Folkways Library, New York.

Odell, S. Jack (1971) "Nonsense," *Metaphilosophy* **2**, 44-49.

—— (1981) *Are Natural Language Interfaces Possible?* Report TR 73-024, IBM Systems Research Institute, New York.

Ogden, C. K., & I. A. Richards (1923) *The Meaning of Meaning*, Harcourt, Brace, and World, New York, 8th edition 1946.

O'Keefe, John, & Lynn Nadel (1978) *The Hippocampus as a Cognitive Map*, Clarendon Press, Oxford.

Ore, Oystein (1962) *Theory of Graphs*, American Mathematical Society, Providence.

Ortega y Gasset, José (1923) *The Modern Theme*, translated by James Cleugh, Harper & Row, New York.

Pao, Yoh-Han, & George W. Ernst, eds. (1982) *Context-Directed Pattern Recognition and Machine Intelligence Techniques for Information Processing*, IEEE Computer Society Press, Los Angeles.

Parry, Milman (1930) "Studies in the epic technique of oral verse-making I: Homer and Homeric style," *Harvard Studies in Classical Philology*, vol. 41.

Partee, Barbara Hall (1971) "Linguistic metatheory," reprinted in G. Harman, ed., *On Noam Chomsky: Critical Essays*, Anchor Books, Garden City, NY, 301-315.

——, ed. (1976) *Montague Grammar*, Academic Press, New York.

—— (1979) "Semantics—mathematics or psychology?" in Bäuerle et al. (1979) 1-14.

Peabody, Berkley (1975) *The Winged Word*, State University of New York Press, Albany.

Pedersen, Gert Schmeltz (1978) *Conceptual Graphs I*, Technical Report 78/9, DIKU, Copenhagen University.

Peirce, Charles Sanders (1897-1906) Manuscripts on existential graphs. Some reprinted in Peirce (1960) vol. 4, 320-410, and others summarized by Roberts (1973).

—— (1906) "Prolegomena to an apology for pragmatism," *The Monist* **16**, 492-546.

—— (1960) *Collected Papers of Charles Sanders Peirce*, edited by Arthur W. Burks, 8 vols., Harvard University Press, Cambridge, MA.

Pereira, Luis Moniz, Paul Sabatier, Eugénio de Oliveira (1982) "ORBI, an expert system for environmental resource evaluation through natural language," Report FCT/DI-3/82, Departamento de Informatica, Universidade Nova de Lisboa.

Perky, Cheves West (1910) "An experimental study of imagination," *American J. of Psychology* **21**, 422-452. Abridged version in Beardslee & Wertheimer (1958) 545-551.

Peterson, James L. (1981) *Petri Net Theory and the Modeling of Systems*, Prentice-Hall, Englewood Cliffs, NJ.

Petri, Carl Adam (1962) *Kommunikation mit Automaten*, Ph.D. dissertation, University of Bonn.

—— (1977) "Modeling as a communication discipline," in Berliner & Gelenbe, eds., *Measuring, Modeling, and Evaluating Computer Systems*, North-Holland, New York.

Petrick, Stanley R. (1977) "Semantic interpretation in the REQUEST system," *Proc. International Conference on Computational Linguistics*, Pisa, 585-610.

—— (1982) "Theoretical/technical issues in natural language access to databases," *Proc. 20th Annual Meeting of the ACL*, 51-56.

Piaget, Jean (1968) *On the Development of Memory and Identity*, Clark University Press, Barre, MA.

—— (1970) *Genetic Epistemology*, Columbia University Press, New York.

Piatelli-Palmarini, Massimo, ed. (1980) *Language and Learning*, Harvard University Press, Cambridge, MA.

Pike, Kenneth A. (1967) *A Unified Theory of Human Behavior*, 2nd edition, Mouton, The Hague.

Plath, Warren J. (1976) "REQUEST: a natural language question-answering system," *IBM J. of Research and Development* **20:4**, 326-335.

Pople, Harry E., Jack D. Myers, Randolph A. Miller (1975) "DIALOG: a model of diagnostic logic for internal medicine," *Proc. IJCAI-75*, 848-855.

Post, Emil L. (1943) "Formal reductions of the general combinatorial decision problem," *American J. of Mathematics* **65**, 197-268.

Postal, Paul M. (1974) *On Raising*, MIT Press, Cambridge, MA.

Power, Leigh R. (1981) "The UPDATE command class problem," Software Technology Memo 28, IBM, Yorktown Heights, NY.

Premack, David (1971) "Language in chimpanzee?" *Science* **172**, 808-822.

—— (1983) "The codes of man and beasts," *Behavioral and Brain Sciences* **6:1**, 125-167.

Pribram, Karl H. (1971) *Languages of the Brain*, Prentice-Hall, Englewood Cliffs, NJ.

—— (1973) "The primate frontal cortex—executive of the brain," in Pribram & Luria (1973) 293-314.

Pribram, Karl H., & A. R. Luria, eds. (1973)*Psychophysiology of the Frontal Lobes*, Academic Press, New York.

Pritchard, Roy M. (1961) "Stabilized images on the retina," *Scientific American* **204:6**, June 1961, 72-78.

Pritchard, Roy M., W. Heron, & D. O. Hebb (1960) "Visual perception approached by the method of stabilized images," *Canadian J. of Psychology* **14:2**, 67-77.

Propp, Vladimir (1968) *Morphology of the Folktale*, University of Texas Press, Austin.

Putnam, Hilary (1962) "The analytic and the synthetic," reprinted in H. Putnam, *Mind, Language, and Reality,* Cambridge University Press, Cambridge, 33-69.

Pylyshyn, Zenon W. (1973) "What the mind's eye tells the mind's brain: a critique of mental imagery," *Psychological Bulletin* **80**, 1-24.

Quillian, M. Ross (1966) *Semantic Memory*, Report AD-641671, Clearinghouse for Federal Scientific and Technical Information. Abridged version in Minsky (1968) 227-270.

Quine, Willard Van Orman (1960) *Word and Object*, MIT Press, Cambridge, MA.

—— (1961) *From a Logical Point of View*, Harvard University Press, Cambridge, MA.

—— (1969) *Ontological relativity and other essays*, Columbia University Press, New York.

Quirk, Randolph, Sidney Greenbaum, Geoffrey Leech, & Jan Svartik (1972) *A Grammar of Contemporary English*, Longman, London.

Raphael, Bertram (1976) *The Thinking Computer*, Freeman, San Francisco.

Rawson, Freeman (1980) *Representing Type Hierarchies*, Report TR 73-006, IBM Systems Research Institute, New York.

Reddy, Michael J. (1969) "A semantic approach to metaphor," *Papers from the Fifth Regional Meeting*, Chicago Linguistic Society, Dept. of Linguistics, University of Chicago.

Reiser, O. L. (1931) "The logic of Gestalt psychology," *Psychological Review* **38**, 359-368.

Reisner, Phyllis (1977) "Use of psychological experimentation as an aid to development of a query language," *IEEE Transactions on Software Engineering* **SE-3**, 218-229.

—— (1981) "Human factors studies of database query languages," *Computing Surveys* **13:1**, 13-31.

Reiter, Raymond (1978) "On closed world data bases," in Gallaire & Minker (1978) 55-76.

Rescher, Nicholas, & Robert Brandom (1979) *The Logic of Inconsistency*, Rowman and Littlefield, Totowa, NJ.

Rich, Elaine (1983) *Artificial Intelligence*, McGraw-Hill, New York.

Rieger, Chuck (1975) "Conceptual memory and inference," in Schank (1975) 157-288.

—— (1976) "An organization of knowledge for problem solving and language comprehension," *Artificial Intelligence* **7**, 89-127.

—— (1978) "Spontaneous computation and its role in AI modeling," in Waterman & Hayes-Roth (1978) 69-97.

Ries, Al, & Jack Trout (1981) *Positioning: The Battle for your Mind*, Warner Books, New York.

Riesbeck, Christopher K. (1975) "Conceptual analysis," in Schank (1975) 83-156.

—— (1982) "Realistic language comprehension," in Lehnert & Ringle (1982) 37-54.

Ringle, Martin H., ed. (1979) *Philosophical Perspectives in Artificial Intelligence*, Humanities Press, Atlantic Highlands, NJ.

Ritchie, Graeme D. (1980) *Computational Grammar*, Barnes & Noble Books, Totowa, NJ.

Roberts, Fred S. (1978) *Graph Theory and its Applications to Problems of Society*, Society for Industrial and Applied Mathematics, Philadelphia.

Roberts, Don D. (1973) *The Existential Graphs of Charles S. Peirce*, Mouton, The Hague.

Robinson, Ann E. (1981) "Determining verb phrase referents in dialogs," *American J. of Computational Linguistics* **7**, 1-16.

Robinson, Daniel N. (1973) *The Enlightened Machine*, Columbia University Press, New York.

Robinson, J. A. (1965) "A machine-oriented logic based on the resolution principle," *J. of the ACM* **12**, 23-41.

Robinson, J. A., & E. E. Sibert (1982) "LOGLISP," in Clark & Tärnlund (1982) 299-313.

Robinson, Jane J. (1982) "DIAGRAM: a grammar for dialogues," *Comm. ACM* **25**, 27-47.

Rosch, Eleanor, & Barbara B. Lloyd, eds. (1978) *Cognition and Categorization*, Lawrence Erlbaum Associates, Hillsdale, NJ.

Rosenfeld, Azriel (1979) *Picture Languages*, Academic Press, New York.

Rosser, J. Barkely (1982) "Highlights of the history of the lambda calculus," Report MRC-TSR-2441, Wisconsin University.

Roussopoulos, Nicholas D. (1976) *A Semantic Network Model of Data Bases*, PhD Thesis, University of Toronto, Dept. of Computer Science.

Rumelhart, David E., & Donald A. Norman (1978) "Accretion, tuning, and restructuring: three modes of learning." in J. W. Cotton & R. L. Klatzky, eds., *Semantic Factors in Cognition*, Lawrence Erlbaum Associates, Hillsdale, NJ, 37-54.

Ryle, Gilbert (1949) *The Concept of Mind*, Barnes and Noble Books, New York.

Saarinen, Esa, ed. (1979) *Game-Theoretical Semantics*, Reidel, Dordrecht.

Sager, Naomi (1981) *Natural Language Information Processing*, Addison-Wesley, Reading, MA.

Salton, Gerard (1975) *Dynamic Information and Library Processing*, Prentice-Hall, Englewood Cliffs, NJ.

Salveter, Sharon C. (1979) "Inferring conceptual graphs," *Cognitive Science* **3**, 141-166.

Samuel, Arthur L. (1959) "Some studies in machine learning using the game of checkers," *IBM J. of Research and Development* **3**, 211-229. Reprinted in Feigenbaum & Feldman (1963) 71-105.

Saussure, Ferdinand de (1916) *Cours de Linguistique Generale*, translated by W. Baskin, Philosophical Library, New York, 1959.

Schank, Roger C., ed. (1975) *Conceptual Information Processing*, North-Holland, Amsterdam.

—— (1981) "Language and memory," in Norman (1981) 105-146.

—— (1982) *Dynamic Memory*, Cambridge University Press, New York.

Schank, Roger C., & Lawrence G. Tesler (1969) "A conceptual parser for natural language," *Proc. IJCAI-69*, 569-578.

Schank, Roger C., & Kenneth Mark Colby, eds. (1973) *Computer Models of Thought and Language*, Freeman, San Francisco.

Schank, Roger C., & Bonnie L. Nash-Webber, eds. (1975) *Theoretical Issues in Natural Language Processing*, Association for Computational Linguistics.

Schank, Roger C., & Robert P. Abelson (1977) *Scripts, Plans, Goals and Understanding*, Lawrence Erlbaum Associates, New York.

Schank, Roger C., & Jaime G. Carbonell, Jr. (1979) "Re: the Gettysburg Address," in Findler (1979) 327-362.

Schank, Roger C., Janet Kolodner, & Gerald DeJong (1980) *Conceptual Information Retrieval*, Report #190, Department of Computer Science, Yale University.

Schank, Roger C., Michael Lebowitz, & Lawrence Birnbaum (1980) "An integrated understander," *American J. of Computational Linguistics* **6**, 13-30.

Schank, Roger C., & Christopher K. Riesbeck, eds. (1981) *Inside Computer Understanding: Five Programs Plus Miniatures*, Lawrence Erlbaum Associates, Hillsdale, NJ.

Schneider, Gerald E. (1969) "Two visual systems," *Science* **163**, 895-902.

Schoenfield, Joseph R. (1967) *Mathematical Logic*, Addison-Wesley, Reading, MA.

Schubert, Lenhart K. (1975) "Extending the expressive power of semantic networks," *Proc. IJCAI-75*, 158-164.

Schwartz, Stephen P., ed. (1977) *Naming, Necessity, and Natural Kinds*, Cornell University Press, Ithaca.

Scoville, William B., & Brenda Milner (1957) "Loss of recent memory after bilateral hippocampal lesions," *J. of Neurology, Neurosurgery, and Psychiatry* **20**. Reprinted in Lubar (1972) 141-154.

Scruton, Roger (1981) *From Descartes to Wittgenstein*, Harper & Row, New York.

Searle, John (1969) *Speech Acts*, Cambridge University Press, New York.

—— (1978) "The Philosophy of Language," in Magee (1978) 153-172.

Segal, Sydney Joelson (1972) "Assimilation of a stimulus in the construction of an image: the Perky effect revisited,"in P. W. Sheehan, ed., *The Function and Nature of Imagery*, Academic Press, New York, 203-230.

Segall, Marshall H., Donald T. Campbell, & Melville J. Herskovits (1966) *The Influence of Culture on Visual Perception*, Bobbs-Merrill, Indianapolis.

Selz, Otto (1913) *Über die Gesetze des geordneten Denkverlaufs* , Spemann, Stuttgart.

—— (1922) *Zur Psychologie des produktiven Denkens und des Irrtums*, Friedrich Cohen, Bonn.

—— (1924) *Die Gesetze der produktiven und reproduktiven Geistestätigkeit,* abridged edition, Friedrich Cohen, Bonn.

—— (1927) "The Revision of the Fundamental Conceptions of Intellectual Processes" in J. M. Mandler & G. Mandler, eds., *Thinking: from Association to Gestalt*, Wiley, New York, 225-234.

Sendak, Maurice (1970) *In the Night Kitchen*, Harper & Row, New York.

Seneca, Lucius Annaeus, *Epistolae.*

Seuren, Pieter A. M. (1969) *Operators and Nucleus*, Cambridge University Press, Cambridge.

——, ed. (1974) *Semantic Syntax*, Oxford University Press, Oxford.

Sgall, Petr (1964) "Zum Verhältnis von Grammatik und Semantik im generativen System" in G. E. Meier, ed., *Zeichen und System der Sprache* **3**, Berlin, 225-239.

Shapiro, Stuart C. (1971) "A net structure for semantic information storage, deduction and retrieval," *Proc. IJCAI-71*, 512-523.

—— (1979) "The SNePS semantic network processing system," in Findler (1979) 179-203.

—— (1981) *COCCI: a deductive semantic network program for solving microbiology unknowns*, Technical Report 173, Dept. of Computer Science, SUNY at Buffalo.

Shasha, Dennis E. (1983) "Knowledge-based system design using conceptual graphs," Report TR 73-023, IBM Systems Research Institute, New York.

Shepard, Roger N. (1966) "Learning and recall as organization and search," *J. of Verbal Learning and Verbal Behavior* **5**, 201-204.

—— (1967) "Recognition memory for words, sentences, and pictures," *J. of Verbal Learning and Verbal Behavior* **6**, 156-163.

Shepard, Roger N., & Jacqueline Metzler (1971) "Mental rotation of three-dimensional objects," *Science* **171**, 701-703.

Shepard, Roger N., & Lynn A. Cooper (1982) *Mental Images and their Transformations*, MIT Press, Cambridge, MA.

Sheppard, Sylvia B., Elizabeth Kruesi, & Bill Curtis (1981) "The effects of symbology and spatial arrangement on the comprehension of software specifications," *Proc. Fifth International Conference on Software Engineering*, 207-214.

Shneiderman, Ben, ed. (1978) *Databases: Improving Usability and Responsiveness*, Academic Press, New York.

—— (1980) *Software Psychology*, Winthrop Publishers, Cambridge, MA.

Shortliffe, Edward Hance (1976) *Computer-Based Medical Consultations: MYCIN*, Elsevier, New York.

Shrier, S. (1977) "Abduction algorithms for grammar discovery," Technical Report, Division of Applied Mathematics, Brown University, Providence, RI.

Sidner, C. L., M. Bates, R. J. Bobrow, J. Schmolze, R. J. Brachman, P. R. Cohen, D. J. Israel, B. L. Webber, & W. A. Woods (1981) *Research in Knowledge Representation and Natural Language Understanding*, Report 4785, Bolt Beranek and Newman Inc., Cambridge, MA.

Simmons, Robert F., & Bertram C. Bruce (1971) "Some relations between predicate calculus and semantic net representations of discourse," *Proc. IJCAI-71*, 524-530.

Simmons, Robert F., & Jonathan Slocum (1972) "Generating English discourse from semantic networks," *Comm. ACM* **15**, 891-905.

Simon, Herbert A. (1969) *The Sciences of the Artificial*, MIT Press, Cambridge, MA.

—— (1974) "How big is a chunk?" *Science* **183**, 482-488.

Skuce, Douglas R. (1982) "LESK: a language synthesizing natural language, computer language, and logic," *COLING 82 Abstracts*, 262-265.

—— (1983) "A logic-based knowledge acquisition language and its representation in PROLOG," Technical Report, Dept. of Computer Science, University of Ottawa.

Slagle, James R. (1971) *Artificial Intelligence: The Heuristic Programming Approach*, McGraw-Hill, New York.

Slobin, Dan I. (1970) "Universals of grammatical development in children," in d'Arcais & Levelt (1970) 174-186.

Slocum, Jonathan (1981) "A practical comparison of parsing strategies," *Proc. 19th Annual Meeting of the ACL*, 1-6.

Sloman, Aaron (1978) *The Computer Revolution in Philosophy*, Humanities Press, Atlantic Highlands, NJ.

Smith, Edward E., & Douglas L. Medin (1981) *Categories and Concepts*, Harvard University Press, Cambridge, MA.

Smith, Frank, & George A. Miller, eds. (1966) *The Genesis of Language*, MIT Press, Cambridge, MA.

Smith, John M., & Diane C. P. Smith (1977) "Database abstractions: aggregation and generalization," *ACM Transactions on Database Systems* **2:2**, 105-133.

—— (1980) "A data base approach to software specifications," in W. E. Riddle & R. E. Fairley, eds., *Software Development Tools*, Springer-Verlag, New York, 176-200.

Sommers, Fred (1959) "The ordinary language tree," *Mind*, 160-185.

—— (1963) "Types and ontology," *Philosophical Review*, 327-363.

Sowa, Cora Angier (1983) *Traditional Themes and the Homeric Hymns*, Bolchazy-Carducci Publishers, Chicago.

Sowa, Cora Angier, & John F. Sowa (1974) "Thought clusters in early Greek oral poetry," *Computers and the Humanities* **8**, 131-146.

Sowa, John F. (1968) *Conceptual Structures: A Model for Language*, unpublished manuscript.

—— (1976) "Conceptual graphs for a data base interface," *IBM J. of Research and Development* **20:4**, 336-357.

—— (1979a) "Definitional mechanisms for conceptual graphs," in Claus, Ehrig, & Rozenberg (1979) 426-439.

—— (1979b) "Semantics of conceptual graphs," *Proc. 17th Annual Meeting of the ACL*, 39-44.

—— (1981) "A conceptual schema for knowledge-based systems," *Proc. Workshop on Data Abstraction, Databases, and Conceptual Modeling, SIGMOD Record* **11:2**, 193-195.

—— (1983) "Generating language from conceptual graphs," *Computers and Mathematics with Applications* **8**.

Sparck Jones, Karen (1971) *Automatic Keyword Classification for Information Retrieval*, Butterworths, London.

Sperling, George (1963) "A model for visual memory tasks," *Human Factors* **5**, 19-31.

Spoehr, Kathryn T., & Stephen W. Lehmkuhle (1982) *Visual Information Processing*, Freeman, San Francisco.

Spong, Paul, Manfred Haider, & Donald B. Lindsley (1965) "Selective Attention and Cortical Evoked Responses to Visual and Auditory Stimuli," *Science* **148**, 395-397.

Stanat, Donald F., & David McAllister (1977) *Discrete Mathematics in Computer Science*, Prentice-Hall, Englewood Cliffs, NJ.

Standing, L. (1973) "Learning 10,000 pictures," *Quarterly J. of Experimental Psychology* **25**, 207-222.

Stcherbatsky, F. Th. (1930) *Buddhist Logic*, 2 vols., Dover, New York.

Steele, Susan (1978) "Word order variation: a typological study," in Greenberg (1978) 585-623.

—— (1981) *An Enclyclopedia of AUX*, MIT Press, Cambridge, MA.

Steinberg, Danny D., & Leon A. Jakobovits, eds. (1971) *Semantics*, Cambridge University Press, Cambridge.

Stolz, Benjamin A., & Richard S. Shannon, eds. (1976) *Oral Literature and the Formula*, Center for the Coordination of Ancient and Modern Studies, University of Michigan, Ann Arbor.

Sturzda, Paltin (1983) "From database to knowledge base: artificial intelligence with an IBM data dictionary," *Proc. International Conf. on Computer Capacity Management*, New Orleans.

Suwa, Motoi, A. Carlisle Scott, & Edward H. Shortliffe (1982) "An approach to verifying completeness and consistency in a rule-based expert system," *AI Magazine* **3:4**, 16-21.

Tarski, Alfred (1936) "On the concept of logical consequence," reprinted in Tarski, *Logic, Semantics, Metamathematics*, Clarendon, Oxford, 409-420.

Tennant, Harry (1981) *Natural Language Processing*, Petrocelli Books, New York.

Tesnière, Lucien (1959) *Eléments de Syntaxe Structurale*, 2nd edition, Librairie C. Klincksieck, Paris, 1965.

Thompson, Frederick B., & Bozena Henisz Thompson (1975) "Practical natural language processing: the REL system as prototype," in M. Rubinoff & M. C. Yovits, eds., *Advances in Computers 13*, Academic Press, New York, 109-168.

Thorne, J. P., P. Bratley, & H. Dewar (1968) "The syntactic analysis of English by machine," in D. Michie, ed., *Machine Intelligence* **3**, American Elsevier, New York, 281-299.

Thue, Axel (1914) "Probleme über Veränderungen von Zeichenreihen nach gegebenen Regeln," *Skrifter utgit av Videnskapsselskapet i Kristiania* **1:10**.

Tolman, Edward Chase (1932) *Purposive Behavior in Animals and Men*, Appleton-Century-Crofts, New York, second printing 1967.

Torrey, J. (1969) "The learning of grammatical patterns," *J. of Verbal Learning and Verbal Behavior* **8**, 360-368.

Tranchell, Lynn M. (1982) "A SNePS implementation of KL-ONE," Technical Report 198, Dept. of Computer Science, SUNY at Buffalo.

Tsichritzis, Dionysios C., & Anthony Klug, eds. (1978) "The ANSI/X3/SPARC DBMS framework," *Information Systems* **3**, 173-191.

Tsichritzis, Dionysios C., & Frederick H. Lochovsky (1982) *Data Models*, Prentice-Hall, Englewood Cliffs, NJ.

Tulving, Endel (1972) "Episodic and semantic memory," in Tulving & Donaldson (1972).

Tulving, Endel, & Wayne Donaldson, eds. (1972) *Organization of Memory*, Academic Press, New York.

Ullman, Jeffrey D. (1982) *Principles of Database Systems*, 2nd edition, Computer Science Press, Potomac, MD.

van Bergen, Annie (1968) *Task Interruption*, North-Holland, Amsterdam.

van Heijenoort, Jean (1967) *From Frege to Gödel* , Harvard University Press, Cambridge, MA.

van Melle, William J. (1981) *System Aids in Constructing Consultation Programs*, UMI Research Press, Ann Arbor, MI.

van Rijsbergen, C. J. (1979) *Information Retrieval*, Butterworths, London.

Vassiliou, Yannis (1982) "Application development for a natural language retrieval system," Workshop presentation.

Vassiliou, Yannis, James Clifford, & Matthias Jarke (1983) "How does an expert system get its data?" Report GBA #83-26 (CR), New York University, Graduate School of Business Administration.

Vauquois, Bernard (1975) *La Traduction automatique à Grenoble* , Dunod, Paris.

Vetter, M., & R. N. Maddison (1981) *Database Design Methodology*, Prentice-Hall International, Englewood Cliffs, NJ.

von Bertalanffy, Ludwig (1968) *General Systems Theory*, George Brazziller, New York.

von Glasersfeld, E., Sergei Perschke, & Elsa Samet (1961) "Human translation and translation by machine," *Proc. 1961 International Conf. on Machine Translation*, 507-530.

von Neumann, John, & Oskar Morgenstern (1947) *Theory of Games and Economic Behavior*, Princeton University Press, Princeton.

Vygotsky, Lev Semenovich (1934) *Thought and Language*, MIT Press, Cambridge, MA, 1962.

Waismann, Friedrich (1952) "Verifiability," in A. Flew, ed. *Logic and language*, first series, Basil Blackwell, Oxford.

Wallach, Michael A., & Nathan Kogan (1965) *Modes of Thinking in Young Children*, Holt, Rinehart & Winston, New York.

Walter, W. Grey (1973) "Human frontal-lobe function in sensory-motor association," in Pribram & Luria (1973) 109-122.

Waltz, David L. (1975) "Understanding line drawings of scenes with shadows," in Winston (1975b) 19-91.

—— (1978) "An English language question answering system for a large relational database," *Comm. ACM* **21:7**, 526-539.

—— (1981) "Toward a detailed model of processing for language describing the physical world," *Proc. IJCAI-81*, 1-6.

Wasserman, Anthony I., ed. (1981) *Software Development Environments*, IEEE Computer Society, Los Alamitos, CA.

Waterman, D. A. (1978) "Exemplary programming in RITA," in Waterman & Hayes-Roth (1978) 261-279.

Waterman, D. A., & Frederick Hayes-Roth, eds. (1978) *Pattern-Directed Inference Systems*, Academic Press, New York.

Watkins, Calvert (1969) "Indo-European and the Indo-Europeans," *American Heritage Dictionary of the English Language*, American Heritage, Boston, 1496-1502.

Watson, Robert I. (1963) *The Great Psychologists from Aristotle to Freud*, J. B. Lippincott Co., New York.

Webber, Bonnie Lynn (1979) *A Formal Approach to Discourse Anaphora*, Garland Publishing, New York.

Webber, Bonnie, & Aravind Joshi (1982) "Taking the initiative in natural language data base interactions: justifying why,"Report MS-CIS-82-1, University of Pennsylvania.

Webber, Bonnie Lynn, & Nils J. Nilsson (1982) *Readings in Artificial Intelligence*, Tioga Publishing Co., Palo Alto, CA.

Weiss, Sholom M., Casimir A. Kulikowski, Saul Amarel, & Aran Safir (1978) "A model-based method for computer-aided medical decision making," *Artificial Intelligence* **11**, 145-172.

Weisstein, Naomi (1973) "Beyond the yellow-Volkswagen detector and the grandmother cell," in R. L. Solso, ed., *Contemporary Issues in Cognitive Psychology*, V. H. Winston & Sons, Washington, DC, 17-51.

Weizenbaum, Joseph (1966) "ELIZA—a computer program for the study of natural language communication between man and machines," *Comm. ACM* **9**, 36-45.

—— (1976) *Computer Power and Human Reason*, Freeman, San Francisco.

Wexler, Kenneth, and Peter W. Culicover (1980) *Formal Principles of Language Acquisition*, MIT Press, Cambridge, MA.

Whewell, William (1858) *History of Scientific Ideas*, 2 vols., J. W. Parker, London.

White, Alan R. (1975a) "Conceptual analysis," in C. J. Bontempo & S. J. Odell, eds., *The Owl of Minerva*, McGraw-Hill, New York, 103-117.

—— (1975b) *Modal Thinking*, Cornell University Press, Ithaca.

White, George M. (1978) "Automatic speech recognition of large vocabularies," in Bolc (1978) 43-53.

Whitehead, Alfred North (1954) *Dialogues of Alfred North Whitehead*, as recorded by Lucien Price, Mentor Books, New York.

Whitehead, Alfred North, & Bertrand Russell (1910) *Principia Mathematica*, 2nd edition, Cambridge University Press, Cambridge, 1925.

Whorf, Benjamin Lee (1956) *Language, Thought, and Reality*, MIT Press, Cambridge, MA.

Wiener, Norbert (1948) *Cybernetics*, Wiley, New York.

Wierzbicka, Anna (1980) *Lingua Mentalis: the Semantics of Natural Language*, Academic Press, New York.

Wilensky, Robert (1983) *Planning and Understanding*, Addison-Wesley, Reading, MA.

Wilkins, D. A. (1976) *Notional Syllabuses*, Oxford University Press, Oxford.

Wilks, Yorick Alexander (1972) *Grammar, Meaning, and the Machine Analysis of Language*, Routledge & Kegan Paul, London.

—— (1975) "An intelligent analyzer and understander of English," *Comm. ACM* **18:5**, 264-274.

Willwoll, Alexander (1926) *Begriffsbildung*, S. Hirzel, Leipzig.

Wilson, Robin J. (1972) *Introduction to Graph Theory*, Longman, London.

Winograd, Terry (1972) *Understanding Natural Language*, Academic Press, New York.

—— (1975) "Frame representations and the declarative/procedural controversy," in Bobrow & Collins (1975) 185-210.

—— (1983) *Language as a Cognitive Process. Volume I: Syntax*, Addison-Wesley, Reading, MA.

Winston, Patrick Henry, (1975a) "Learning structural descriptions from examples," in Winston (1975b) 157-209.

——, ed. (1975b) *The Psychology of Computer Vision*, McGraw-Hill, New York.

—— (1977) *Artificial Intelligence*, Addison-Wesley, Reading, MA.

Winston, Patrick Henry, & Richard Henry Brown, eds. (1979) *Artificial intelligence: an MIT perspective*, MIT Press, Cambridge, MA.

Wittgenstein, Ludwig (1921) *Tractatus Logico-Philosophicus*, Routledge & Kegan Paul, London, 1961.

—— (1953) *Philosophical Investigations*, Basil Blackwell, Oxford.

Wolf, A. K., C. S. Chomsky, & B. E. Green, Jr. (1963) *The Baseball Program: An Automatic Question-Answerer*, Report ESD-TDR-63-598, Lincoln Laboratories, MIT.

Wolf, Thomas (1976) "A cognitive model of musical sight-reading," *J. of Psycholinguistic Research* **5**, 143-171.

Wong, Harry K. T. (1975) *Generating English Sentences from Semantic Structures*, Technical Report 84, Dept. of Computer Science, University of Toronto.

Woods, William A. (1968) "Procedural semantics for a question-answering machine," *AFIPS Conference Proc.*, 1968 FJCC, 457-471.

—— (1970) "Transition network grammars for natural language analysis," *Comm. ACM* **10**, 591-606.

—— (1975) "What's in a link: foundations for semantic networks," in Bobrow & Collins (1975) 35-82.

—— (1980) "Cascaded ATN grammars," *American J. of Computational Linguistics* **6**, 1-12.

—— (1981) "Procedural semantics as a theory of meaning," in Joshi et al. (1981) 300-334.

Woods, William A., R. M. Kaplan, & B. L. Nash-Webber (1972) *The LUNAR Sciences Natural Language System*, Final Report, NTIS N72-28984.

Yager, Ronald R., ed. (1982) *Fuzzy Set and Possibility Theory*, Pergamon Press, New York.

Zadeh, Lofti A. (1974) "Fuzzy logic and its application to approximate reasoning," *Information Processing 74*, North-Holland, Amsterdam, 591-594.

—— (1982) "Test-score semantics for natural languages," *COLING 82*, North-Holland, New York, 425-430.

Zampolli, Antonio, ed. (1977) *Linguistic Structures Processing*, North-Holland, New York.

Zeigarnik, Bluma (1927) "Über das Behalten von erledigten und unerledigten Handlungen," *Psychologische Forschung* **9**, 1-85. Excerpt translated in W. D. Ellis, ed., *A Source Book of Gestalt Psychology*, Routledge & Kegan Paul, London.

Zoeppritz, Magdalena (1981) "The meaning of *of* and *have* in the USL system," *American J. of Computational Linguistics* **7**, 109-119.

Author Index

Subject Index